# MARXISM AND AESTHETICS

AIMS Bibliographical Series
No. 4

# MARXISM
## AND
# AESTHETICS

*A SELECTIVE ANNOTATED BIBLIOGRAPHY*

BOOKS AND ARTICLES
IN THE
ENGLISH LANGUAGE

COMPILED BY
## LEE BAXANDALL

HUMANITIES PRESS INC.
NEW YORK 1968

# ACKNOWLEDGEMENTS

Gratefully the compiler acknowledges the criticisms, suggestions and additions offered by Willi Beitz, Sidney Finkelstein, Franklin Folsom, Michael B. Folsom, James Gilbert, Walter Goldwater, Louis Harap, Leo Hurwitz, Arnold Kettle, Will Lee, Gaylord C. LeRoy, Jack Lindsay, Herbert Marshall, George Moberg, A. L. Morton, Paul Romaine, Stuart Samuels, Edith Segal and Maynard Solomon during the preparation of the bibliography. Use of the facilities of the Library of Congress, New York Public Library, British Museum, Library of the Museum of Modern Art and the Tamiment Institute in New York, AIA Gallery of London, the libraries of Yale, Columbia and Harvard universities and the University of Wisconsin is also deeply appreciated. Encouragement and assistance offered by the American Institute for Marxist Studies and its Director, Dr. Herbert Aptheker, and its Chairman, Prof. Robert S. Cohen, were fundamental to the completion of this work. A special gratitude is due Louise Thompson of the AIMS staff, who devoted extreme care and many hours to preparation of the manuscript. For errors of fact, as well as for the choice of the criteria for selection and evaluation, the compiler alone is responsible.

# TABLE OF CONTENTS

# INTRODUCTION

This volume presents a perspective on Marxist writings on the arts and literature which are available in English.

Since the late 19th Century outstanding historians, critics and philosophers of the arts and literature have been nurtured by the historio-philosophical method of analysis, the morality and aesthetics that stem from Marx. A number of artists of world stature also have derived much of their outlook from this source, as this bibliography confirms. Yet the question still is asked frequently, at least in America: Can there truly be a *Marxist* aesthetics?

The persistence of this doubt can be attributed to several causes. Basic texts have not been translated into English in a lamentable number of cases; or have been translated only recently (the first collection of writings by Marx and Engels on art was published only in 1947). Where a translation exists, it may be faulty. Almost certainly no scholarly annotation and apparatus will have been provided. Many of the translations and the texts originally written in English that do exist are often not drawn upon because they are not known; the present bibliography is, indeed, the first with comprehensive aims and an anticipated broad circulation. Moreover, knowledge of Marxist aesthetics and a respect for it have been minimized by antipathy toward Communism and Cold War prejudices. Yet another factor has been the rather limited success by many American Marxists, in contrast to the work of the better of their European counterparts, in applying creative aesthetic thought. As a consequence, in America the Marxian contribution to aesthetics and criticism largely remains unappreciated, a circumstance that the compiler judges to be a misfortune for American aesthetics and criticism in general on the strength of even those texts available in English. The vitality of Marx's outlook in the area of aesthetics will, it is hoped, become apparent to the curious and motivated reader who employs the materials organized for reference in the present work. Beyond the disputes and the flaws of bias and haste which have occured within the international gamut of Marxist aesthetics and criticism is located an essential perspective on the creative arts and culture. Modern thought proves less than comprehensive and humanistic where it has not assimilated and extended the perspective of Karl Marx.

## Criteria for Inclusion in the Bibliography

Decisions as to whether some writings "really" were Marxist had no place in the compilation of this volume. When in doubt the compiler opted to include rather than exclude. The appropriate writings are here when an author has deemed himself Marxist at some point in or throughout his career and where authors employ an analysis which, internal evidence indicates, depends in a fundamental way upon Marxist thought.

The reader may decide for himself the relation to Marxism of controversial figures such as Andre Breton, Leon Trotsky or Jean-Paul Sartre—as he will surely do in respect to figures such as Andrei Zhdanov, Earl Browder and Leopold Averbach.

Some of the still-active writers included have abandoned political Marxism and have emerged at times as opponents of the politics of Communism. Harold Rosenberg and Meyer Schapiro are examples. These men, however, retain much of the perspective they gained as Marxists. Consequently their recent writings are included along with their earlier, unlike others, such as Granville Hicks, Philip Rahv and Andre Breton who abandoned the Marxist tools of analysis yet have similiar political careers.

While one might endlessly catalogue the reiterations by various critics of received world Communist positions, the bibliography would thereupon have been expanded to unmanageable length and to no discernable theoretical purpose. Therefore the most central and motive of such views have been included, whereas their restatement in book reviews and editorials which add little or nothing to the original formulation has been foregone.

Every book and pamphlet treating of aesthetics from a Marxist viewpoint is nonetheless included, whether originally in English or translated. Articles and essays which have been selected meet one or both of these criteria, in the compiler's judgment: a) The article or essay provides an *intrinsic contribution to the theory and understanding* of Marxist aesthetics in general or of a particular writer, artist, movement or genre; b) The article or essay possesses *historical prominence* in the Marxist aesthetic debates or development of cultural organizations.

A scholar or literary historian is unlikely to find his particular subject exhaustively compiled in these pages. The Hemingway expert, for example, will not find listed all or even most of the many mentions and reviews concerning Hemingway in the left press—although he will find references to the major interpretations of Hemingway relevant to this volume. The main effort has been to afford a guide to the chief Marxist theoretical contributions, practical studies and controversies; however, many items may be found here, which even the perseverant scholar or historian on a single limited topic might miss.

While no specific checklist for further research has been included, virtually every left cultural periodical in English has been cited, at least once, and the reader who is concerned with the more ephemeral materials, such as book reviews, will wish to examine these periodicals.

With the exception of the early and prime sources of Marxist aesthetics— Marx, Engels, Plekhanov, Mehring, Lenin, Lukacs—for whom the earliest appearance in English of their essays was sought, no attempt has been made to include every English-language edition of a work. The exceptions were included owing to the impact or absence of influence that these writings may have had on aesthetic studies in the English-speaking nations. In most cases the conveniently available edition is listed, with the paperback edition where available.

Works of major authors which do not concern aesthetics directly—for example, Marx's *German Ideology*—have not been listed although such works may provide a part of the groundwork of Marxist philosophy. It is assumed that Marxist aesthetics cannot be comprehended outside the context of the Marxian historio-philosophical perspective. That perspective has often been described, however, and its basic texts republished and listed, while the texts of Marxist aesthetics have not found this attention. Space limitations, and the reader's own desire and prior need to understand the fundamentals of Marxism, are thus involved in this principle of selection. On the other hand, Marxists who primarily are aestheticians, artists or critics are occasionally represented here by texts which also indicate their philosophical or political orientations.

Articles from liberal-left journals of the 1930s such as the *Nation* and the *New Republic* may seem underrepresented. The focus of the bibliography, however, is upon theoretically important Marxist materials and such materials as were important in debates among Marxists. Owing to the essentially popular-front nature of the participation of these periodicals in Marxist discussion, consultation of these journals reveals only sporadic presentation of a distinct Marxist viewpoint, even when the same authors may have been outspoken in writing for other journals definitely outside the liberal orbit. For historians, of course, such articles in the popular-front periodicals are well worth examination.

A certain number of small-circulation, mimeographed and printed publications could not be located. While these typically would provide little of theoretical interest, nonetheless the historian of Marxism and culture will wish to seek them out, often by going directly to participants in the events and problems under study.

The compiler sought to locate the Marxist cultural journals of India, Canada, Australia, Africa, the West Indies. He met with small success and with little cooperation from the appropriate persons in those nations; and the bibliography is quite inadequate in these areas.

Background materials have been noted where the compiler found it advisable. They will be discovered at the end of an author's listing.

It must be emphasized that a true picture of the scope and accomplishment of Marxist aesthetics cannot be derived solely on the basis of texts presently in English. Together with Prof. Stefan Morawski of the University of Warsaw, the compiler presently is co-editing a compendium of basic texts from 1839 to 1945, many now unavailable in English. The volume will provide extensive historical and critical commentary, and is soon to be published. The reader may find it helpful in gaining overall perspective on the Marxist philosophy of art. An anthology of post-1960 texts, edited by Gaylord C. LeRoy and Ursula Beitz, is also projected.

## Principles of Organization

Organization is primarily by the author's nationality or language-grouping. Where confusion concerning a writer's location in the volume may occur, special indications are given. Thus in the section for Germany George Lukacs, who writes in German, is described as being located in the Hungary section. Please note: Austrian are included with German authors. Scottish and Irish authors are listed under Great Britain. American Negro authors, owing to affinity of problems and outlook, are grouped under African and Afro-American.

Writings which chiefly owe their interest to a role in semi-official or Party debates or cultural undertakings are generally listed in separate national sections entitled *Chronological*. Chronological sections have been supplied for China, the USSR, and the USA.

To facilitate reference within the USSR and USA listings, writings have been further subdivided according to categories. The subdivisions are Architecture, Art and Sculpture, Cinema, Dance, Literature and General, Music, and Theatre. An author may be listed in more than one of the categories.

*International congresses* of artists and writers generally are listed in the USSR Chronological section. The only exceptions are the gatherings of Afro-Asian intellectuals and authors which are listed in the China Chronological section; and the gatherings of African and Afro-American authors which are listed in the section for these writers.

Additionally, special sections are included for the purpose of making the bibliography more useful. Several *appendices* contain critiques of Marxist aesthetic theory and practice. These follow the national sections for China, Cuba, France, Germany, Great Britain, the USSR and the USA. (Where numerous Marxist and non-Marxist critiques pertain to a particular author they generally follow that author's listings; e.g., Gorky, Lukacs, Caudwell.) In addition, appendices for African and Afro-American, India, and several other categories may contain relevant Marxist material. Included also is a special section on views of their role in society by artists and writers who are non-Marxist; as is an extended section of materials that represent socially-involved but non-Marxist approaches, some of which anticipate Marxism, some of which are eclectic or anarchist, and some of which are academic-sociological. Finally a section of supplementary and previously-compiled bibliographies is included.

The materials are also referred to in Topic Indexes.

## Topic Indexes

A *General Topic Index* is provided. It is subdivided according to artistic categories, in the same way as are the major national groupings of authors.

In the General Topic Index are the topics, such as the proletarian novel, taste, creative method, formalism, realism, etc., which pertain to no single nation. *Ancient Greek* topics also are listed here.

These topic listings fall very short of being comprehensive, and must be taken only as suggestive of authors whose writings on particular topics should not be overlooked.

Certain authors, among them Arnold Hauser, have treated of so many topics that their works should be consulted in almost every case. This has not been indicated through what would have been a repetitious topic-listing of such authors. The reader will by experience develop a familiarity with the more comprehensive authors.

For the major national groupings, *national Topic Indexes* also have been provided. Here will be found the topic listings of particular relevance to a country, and foremost, listings of writers and artists of these nations whose works have been analyzed by Marxists, together with discussion of the Marxist cultural initiatives within those countries.

The reader interested in Marxist and related writings on Shelley will turn to the Topic Index for Great Britain. For the writers and artists of these countries the reader must *also* turn, however, to the Literature, History or comparable national topic headings; no effort has been made to indicate in the topic listings the total contents of most cultural histories or studies, and the reader should consult these wherever they are relevant.

In the case of the USSR and the USA, the National Topic Indexes have been subdivided by artistic genre.

*In the various Topic Indexes, the authors' names—when they are not from the nation in question—will be followed by roman numerals in parentheses. The roman numerals refer to the national listings where the authors' writings on the topic appear.*

*These section numbers are catalogued, together with the pages to consult, in the Table of Contents. They appear also, in sequence through the volume, at the top of the appropriate pages.*

Following is an instance of how the Topic Indexes are planned to be employed. Not given elsewhere in the volume, this example also indicates authors for the reader who wishes to go at once to the major writings on the Marxist philosophy of art available in English:

```
AESTHETICS, MARXIST.  Cesaire, Senghor
    (I); Breton, Lafargue, Sartre (XIX);
    Brecht, Fischer, Marx and Engels,
    Mehring (XXI); Caudwell, Morris
    (XXIII); Hauser, Lukacs (XXVII);
    Gramsci, Labriola  (XXX); Morawski
    (XXXVI); Bogdanov, Bukharin, Gorky,
    Lenin, Lifshitz, Lunacharsky, Ple-
    khanov, Trotsky (XLVI); Baxandall,
    Dunham, Finkelstein, Harap (LVI).
```

The various concerns of Marxist aesthetics interweave and overlap and this circumstance is implicit in the organization of the General Topic Index. Under the topic of Marxist Aesthetics one understands concerns such as the definitions of art and aesthetics, aesthetic emotion, social class and art, ideology and art, progress in art, form and content, the function of style and subject-matter, the questions of freedom and artistic truth. These topics are taken up more particularly under related headings in the General Topic Index, and are dealt with also in studies listed for individual writers and artists. The student of general aesthetic problems should encounter no difficulties in locating the materials relevant to his study, if he makes thoughtful use of the references in the example above and of the authors cited in topic listings elsewhere.

## *Annotation*

Annotation of the listings is descriptive rather than judgmental and, owing to space limitations, it is brief.

No relation between the length of an annotation and the importance of an item is intended or is to be assumed.

Indeed, works of first rank are often but briefly described owing to their ready availability and the impossibility of adequate summary, while slighter materials may be annotated more fully due to probable difficulty of reader access.

On occasion, the compiler has provided the title for an essay which lacked a title or which had a title that did not clearly suggest the relevant content. In each case this editorial substitution is indicated by the omission of quotation marks around the title.

Publishers are cited where the compiler believes the work to be still in print.

Where no place of publication is cited, place of publication is New York.

Where the compiler has known a text to be abridged he has so indicated: abdgd.

Where the place and date of original publication has been known it has been provided.

If a text is known to the compiler to be the text of a speech, that fact has been indicated.

Frequently cited organizations are abbreviated: CP for Communist Party, CC for Central Committee, Politburo for Political Bureau.

With the exception of May, June and July, the month of publication is abbreviated: Jan, Feb, Mch, Apr, Aug, Sept, Oct, Nov, Dec. Where installment publication has occurred, an initial full reference is given and thereafter the year and perhaps month of appearance is omitted if no confusion seems possible.

The spelling of authors' names not originally in English, generally follows the practice of the publications consulted. All diacritical marks—accents, umlauts, etc.—are, however, omitted.

## *Location of Materials*

If not otherwise indicated, materials were consulted at the New York Public Library. Abbreviations of library names and of journal titles are given in a list immediately following this Introduction.

For the files of journals maintained at the various libraries of the United States and Canada, the reader may consult these reference works, available in most libraries: the *Union List of Serials* and its *Supplements* for 1941-43 and 1944-49, and *New Serial Titles*.

As a final recourse in locating a book or journal, inquiries may be mailed to the Reference Librarian, National Union Catalog, the Library of Congress, Washington, D.C.

Some periodicals could not be located. The coverage here of publications from Canada, India and Australia is scanty. The compiler welcomes information about sources together with correction of errors of selection and descriptive evaluation. It is hoped that supplements to this work may be published from time to time.

*     *     *

Hopefully also an increase of monographic study of the history and problems of Marxist aesthetics may be rendered more feasible through the existence of a bibliography indicating, if only topographically and in one language, what is available. The limitations and fallibility of an initial bibliography of this sort must be apparent—undertaken as it was without secretarial or research assistance, in the absence of scholarly historical delineation of most of the outlines of Marxist aesthetics, with the judgment and knowledge of a single compiler brought to bear. Researching, organizing and annotating the bibliography has itself been an education. The compiler wishes his work could have come more close to a definitive survey. That aim will require, however, greater bibliographical facilities on the one hand, so that all the articles that deal with Marxism and aesthetics in all the primarily non-Marxist as well as Marxist journals may be catalogued; and, in another sense, the aim of a definitive listing requires an increased production of aesthetic analyses by Marxists, of a quantity and quality greater than now is generally available in English. The compiler looks forward to the day when on both of these grounds the present bibliography will be rendered obsolete.

One final note: Relevant post-1966 materials are included only in part, due to the circumstance that basic research on the volume was concluded early in 1967.

AAC    American Artists Congress. Proceedings I, 1936

ACA    American Contemporary Art (New York)

AF     Art Front (New York)

AL     Acta Litteraria (Budapest) [DLC]

AmD    American Dialog (New York)

AO     Archiv Orientalni (Prague)

ARSU   American Review on the Soviet Union (New York)

ASP    Anvil and Student Partisan (New York)

AWC    The American Writers Congress, ed. Henry Hart, 1935.

BCH    Britain's Cultural Heritage, Arena Publication, London, 1951.

BJA    British Journal of Aesthetics (London)

[BM]   The British Museum, London W.C. 1. Microfilms and photocopies may be ordered from the Photographic Service.

Brno   Brno, Czechoslovakia. Universita. Filosoficka Faculta. Brno Studies In English.

Bul-   Bulletin of the League of Ameri-
letin  can Writers (New York) [LAW]

[cc]   Collection of the compiler.

CDSP   Current Digest of the Soviet Press (New York)

ChL    Chinese Literature (Peking)

ChQ    The China Quarterly (New York)

CI     The Communist International (Moscow)

CL     Czechoslovak Life (Prague)

C&L    Culture and Life (Moscow)

Comm   The Communist (New York; became Political Affairs)

CQ     California Quarterly (Los Angeles)

CR     Communist Review (London)

CS     The Class Struggle (New York)

Dec    Decision (New York)

Dia    Dialectics (New York)

Dis    Dissent (New York)

[DLC]  Collection of the Library of Congress, Washington.

DO     Dance Observer (New York)

DW     Daily Worker; also Worker (Chicago; New York)

DW(L)  Daily Worker (London). Collection of the Colindale Branch of the British Museum; not available in the United States.

DWSup  Weekly Supplement of Daily Worker (New York). (Has many names; may not be separately titled or paginated.)

EE     East Europe (New York)

EH     Eastern Horizon (Hong Kong)

En     Encounter (London)

[ES]   Collection of Edith Segal.

ESR    Essays On Socialist Realism and the British Cultural Tradition, Arena Publication, London, n.d. (early 50s).

ESS    Encyclopedia Of the Social Sciences, 1933.

FI     Fourth International (New York)

FKSup  Filologiai Kozlony, Annual Supplement (Budapest)

FLP    For a Lasting Peace, For a People's Democracy

FW     Fighting Words, ed. Donald Ogden Stewart, 1940.

| | | | |
|---|---|---|---|
| HSE | Hungarian Studies in English | LR | Left Review (London) |
| IC(1) | 1st International Congress of Negro Writers and Artists, Paris, 1956. Presence Africaine, Special Issue, 1956. In English. [cc] | LWR | Literature of the World Revolution (Moscow; continues as International Literature) |
| IC(2) | 2nd Congress of Negro Writers and Artists, Rome, 1959. Presence Africaine, Special Issue, 1959. In English. [cc] | Main | Mainstream (New York) |
| | | MaQ(L) | Marxist Quarterly (London) |
| | | MaQ(NY) | Marxist Quarterly (New York) |
| IL | International Literature (Moscow) | MaQ(T) | Marxist Quarterly (Toronto) |
| IndL | Indian Literature (Bombay) | MassR | Massachussetts Review (Amherst) |
| ISCUS | ISCUS (Bombay) | MF | Music Front (New York) |
| ISM | International Socialist Miscellany (New Delhi) | M&L | Music and Life (London) |
| ISR | International Socialist Review (Chicago) | M&M | Masses and Mainstream (New York; later simply Mainstream; not to be confused with the Mainstream listed above) |
| ITh | International Theatre (Moscow) [Tamiment] | [MMA] | Museum of Modern Art Library, New York. |
| IWT | International Workers Theatre (Moscow) [ES] | MN | Moscow News (Moscow) |
| | | modulo | modulo (Brazil) [MMA] |
| JAAC | Journal of Aesthetics and Art Criticism (Cleveland) | ModM | Modern Music (New York) |
| JC | Jewish Currents (New York) | MQ(B) | Modern Quarterly; also Modern Monthly (Baltimore) |
| JHI | Journal of the History of Ideas (New York) | MQ(L) | Modern Quarterly (London) |
| JL | Jewish Life (New York) | MQM | Modern Quarterly Miscellany #1 (London), 1947. |
| J | Jugoslavia (Belgrade) | MR | Monthly Review (New York) |
| KN | Kwartalnik Neofilologiczny (Warsaw) | MRSup | Monthly Review, Cultural Supplement (New York) |
| | | M&S | Music and Society (London) mimeo. |
| LA | Living Age (New York) | MT | Marxism Today (London) |
| [LAW] | Papers of the League of American Writers; Collection of the Library of the University of California (Berkeley). | MV | Music Vanguard (New York) |
| Le | Leftward (Boston) [Yale] | NB | New Bulgaria (Sofia) [DLC] |
| Lib | The Liberator (New York) | NCEO | New Central European Observer (London) |
| LM | Labour Monthly (London) | ND | New Dance (New York) [ES] |

| | | | |
|---|---|---|---|
| NDC | Proceedings of the 1st National Dance Congress and Festival, 1936. [ES] | PR | Partisan Review (New York) |
| | | PolR | Polish Reports (Warsaw) |
| NF | New Foundations (New York) | PSL | Problems of Soviet Literature, ed. H.G. Scott, 1934. |
| NFr | New Freeman (New York) | | |
| NG | National Guardian (New York) | PW | Pacific Weekly (San Francisco) |
| NHQ | New Hungarian Quarterly (Budapest) | Real | Reality; A Journal of Artists' Opinions (New York) |
| NI | The New International (New York) | | |
| NLR | New Left Review (London) | Rev | Revolution (Paris) |
| NM | New Masses (New York) | RR | Rumanian Review (Bucharest) |
| NO | New Orient (Prague) [DLC] | [SC] | Schomburg Collection, New York Public Library. |
| NP | New Politics (New York) | | |
| NR | The New Review (New York) | SCR | Soviet Culture Review (Moscow) |
| NRep | New Republic (Washington) | SCW | Shakespeare In a Changing World, ed. Arnold Kettle, International: 1964. |
| NS | New Statesman (London) | | |
| NT | New Times (Moscow) | SH | Soviet Highlights (New York) |
| NTh | New Theatre (New York) | SL | Soviet Literature (Moscow) |
| NUT | New University Thought (Chicago; Detroit) | SOL | Studies On the Left (Madison, Wisc; New York) |
| NV | New Verse (London) | SR | Soviet Review (Moscow) |
| NWM | New World Monthly (New York) | SS | Soviet Studies (New York) |
| | | S&S | Science and Society (New York) |
| NWR | New World Review (New York) | SSL | Soviet Studies In Literature (White Plains, N.Y.) |
| OH | Communist Party of Great Britain. Historians' Group. Our History. mimeo. (London) | SSU | Shakespeare In the Soviet Union, Progress: Moscow, 1966. Compiled by Roman Samarin and Alexander Nikolyukin. |
| OT | Our Time (London) | | |
| | | SUR | Soviet Union Review (Moscow) |
| PA | Political Affairs (New York) | Survey | Survey; also Soviet Survey (London) |
| PC | Problems of Communism (Washington) | | |
| PekR | Peking Review (Peking) | SW | Sunday Worker (London) |
| PhPr | Philologica Pragensia (Prague) | [Tamiment] | Tamiment Institute Library, New York. |
| Plebs | The Plebs (London) | | |
| PP | Polish Perspectives (Warsaw) | TDR | Tulane Drama Review (New Orleans) |
| P&P | Poetry and the People (London) [Yale] | TU | Papers of New York Theatre Union, Theatre Collection, "cage" file, New York Public Library. |

| | | | |
|---|---|---|---|
| TW | Theatre Workshop (New York) | WCW | The Writer in A Changing World, ed Henry Hart, 1937. |
| UF | University Forward (London) [Yale] | WD | The Workers' Dreadnaught (London) |
| ULR | Universities and Left Review (London) | WDLB | Workers Dance League Bulletin (New York) [ES] |
| Un | Unison (New York) | WM | The Workers' Monthly (New York; became The Communist) |
| Unity | Unity For a People's Culture (Bombay) | WMR | World Marxist Review (Toronto) |
| | | WT | Workers Theatre (New York) [Tamiment] |
| V.O.K.S. | V.O.K.S; also V.O.K.S. Bulletin (Moscow) | | |
| | | YFS | Yale French Studies (New Haven) |
| VOO | Voices Of October, ed. Joseph Freeman et al, 1930. | ZAA | Zeitschrift fur Anglistik und Amerikanistik (Berlin) |

# MARXISM AND AESTHETICS

# G E N E R A L   T O P I C   I N D E X

(SEE ALSO: Arnold Hauser (XXVII), on all topics to 1920s.)

## Architecture

CITY PLANNING. Niemeyer (VI); Stojanovic (LXI); Mumford (LXII).

GENERAL AESTHETICS. Caudwell (XXIII).

MODERN. Niemeyer (VI); Teige,Weiss (XV); Campbell (XXIII); Major,Revai (XXVII); Gratkowski (XXXVI); 1936 (XLI); Danin, Kucherenko, Nekrasov, Vlasov (XLII); Trotsky (XLVI); Flynt (LVI); Egbert (LIX); Stojanovic (LXI); Corbusier, Gropius (LXIII).

THEATRE. Meyerhold (XLVIII).

## Art and Sculpture

ABSTRACTIONIST AND SURREALIST. Castro (XIII); Calas, Cassou, Leger, Lurcat, Nadeau (XIX); Fischer, Raphael (XXI); Bernal, Klingender, Kolpinsky, Lindsay, Lloyd, Read, Surrealist, O. Thomson, Watkinson (XXIII); Guttuso (XXX); Siqueiros (XXXIII); Wallis, Morawski (XXXVI); Picasso (XL); Neizvestny (XLIII); Lifshitz, Trotsky (XLVI); Baskin, Humboldt, Meltzoff, Schapiro, Summers, Weigand (LIII); Barr, Dondero (LIX); Supek (LXI); Harrell (LXII); 'Cahiers', 'Lettres', Maddox, Moore, Orozco (LXIII).

ANIMALS IN ART. Klingender (XXIII).

ART HISTORY, METHOD. Antal, Lukacs (XXVII); Levine (LXII).

ARTIST AGAINST SOCIETY. Severini (XXXI); Seltman, Taylor (LXII); Artaud, Rivers, Shahn (LXIII).

BAROQUE. Fischer (XXI).

CARTOONING, REVOLUTIONARY. Calverton, Debs, Ellis, Gropper, Minor (LIII); Eastman (LIX).

CONSTRUCTIVISM. Zadkine (XIX); Berger (XXIII); Nekrasov (XLII); also USSR Topics, Architecture.

CRITICISM, PROBLEMS. Berger (XXIII); Summers (LIII).

CUBISM. Garaudy (XIX); Berger, Bernal (XXIII); Einstein (XXI); Rivera (XXXIII); Sternberg (XLIII); Plekhanov (XLVI); Brown, Clark, Fraina, Schapiro (LIII).

DADA. Aragon (XIX).

DECORATIVE (OR APPLIED) ART. Leger (XIX); Fischer (XXI); Caudwell, Klingender, Morris, Read, Watkinson (XXIII); Ilyin (XLIII); Plekhanov (XLVI); Finkelstein (LIII); Veblen (LXII).

EGYPTIAN. Fischer, Raphael (XXI).

EXPRESSIONISM. Robeson (I); Portinari (VI); Berger (XXIII); Weigand (LIII); Lowenfels (LVI).

FAUVISM. Berger (XXIII); Brown (LIII).

FIGURE IN ART. Gide (XIX); Siqueiros (XXXIII); Zimenko (XLIII); Baskin, Evergood, Levine, Summers (LIII).

FOLK ART. Portinari (VI); Toure (I); Rodman (II); Cassou (XIX); Fischer (XXI); Hauser (XXVII); Rivera (XXXIII); Solonkhin (XLIII); Finkelstein (LIII); Boas, Grosse (LXII).

FREUD. Schapiro (LIII); Abell, Wittkower (LXII).

FUTURISM. Fraina (LIII); Also USSR Topics, Art and Sculpture.

GOTHIC. Fischer (XXI).

IMPRESSIONISM. Fischer (XXI); Berger (XXIII); Plekhanov (XLVI).

INDUSTRIAL. Klingender (XXIII); Flynt (LVI); Veblen (LXII).

MANNERISM. Sartre (XIX); Blunt (XXIII); Antal, Hauser (XXVII); Haskell (LXII).

MECHANICAL REPRODUCTION. Benjamin (XXI); Smith (LXII).

MEDIEVAL. Fischer (XXI); Klingender (XXIII); Evans, Taylor (LXII).

MURAL. Leger (XIX); Guerrero, O'Higgins, Rivera, Ruiz, Siqueiros, Syndicate

ALIENATION AND CULTURE. Dover (I); Dumazedier, Garaudy (XIX); Fischer, Marx and Engels, Weiss (XXI); Read (XXIII); Lukacs (XXVII); Plekhanov, Trotsky (XLVI); Baxandall, Finkelstein, Langford, Marcuse, Rosenberg (LVI); Bell (LIX); Supek (LXI); Crafts, Dewey, Mead, Mills, Myers, Plessner, Rader, Wittkower (LXII).

ALLEGORY. Auerbach (LXII).

ARISTOPHANES. Willets (XXIII); Gassner (LVIII); Auerbach, Ehrenburg (LXII).

ARISTOTLE. Brecht (XXI); Caudwell, Thomson (XXIII); Plekhanov (XLVI); Minar, Rudich (LVI); Auerbach (LXII).

ART FOR ART'S SAKE. Lukacs (XXVII); Plekhanov, Tratsky (XLVI); Bowra, Guerard (LXII).

AUDIENCE, PROBLEMS OF COMMUNICATION. Leger (XIX); Craig (XXIII); Benjamin, Brecht (XXI); Lukacs (XXVII); Burgum (LVI); Bowra, Sontag (LXII).

AUTOBIOGRAPHY. Pascal (XXIII); Gorky (XLVI).

AVANT-GARDE VALUES, AND EDUCATIONAL NEEDS OF THE MASSES. Toure (I) Teige, Weiss (XV); Fischer (XXI); Central Committee, Katona, Lukacs (XXVII); Morawski (XXXVI); Aizerman, Lunacharsky, Plekhanov, Trotsky (XLVI); Corbusier (LXIII).

BIBLE. Gassner (LVIII); Auerbach (LXII).

BOHEMIANISM. Grana (XX); Trotsky (XLVI); Bodenheim, Gold (LVI); Dell, Wittkower (LXII).

BYZANTINE STUDIES. Browning, Lindsay (XXIII).

CATHARSIS, SOCIAL FUNCTION. Senghor (I); Brecht (XXI); Thomson (XXIII); Lukacs (XXVII); Plekhanov (XLVI); Burke, Rahv, Samson (LVI).

CHARACTERIZATION IN FICTION. Marx and Engels, Seghers (XXI); Fox, Kettle (XXIII); Lukacs (XXVII); Horodinca (XXXVIII); Ehrenburg, Gorky, Pitlyar (XLVI); Eng-Liedmeier (XLIX); Brand, Roe (LVI).

CHILDREN'S WRITING. Reich (XXI); Gorky (XLVI); Lapsley, Raymond, Ward (LVI).

CLASSICISM AS ARTISTIC CATEGORY. Fischer, Marx and Engels (XXI); Blunt (XXIII); Antal, Lukacs (XXVII); Lunacharsky, Plekhanov (XLVI); Auerbach, Valentiner (LXII).

COGNITION THEORY. Senghor (I); Pavlov (VII); "Discussion," Chu Kwang-Tsien, "On the Question" (XI); Fischer, Marx and Engels (XXI); Lukacs (XXVII); Labriola (XXX); Plekhanov, Trotsky, Vygotsky (XLVI); LeRoy, Rudich (LVI); Dewey, Gotshalk, Mannheim, Sontag (LXII); Robbe-Grillet, Snowday (LXIII).

CONDITIONED REFLEXES AND AESTHETICS. Sindelar (XV); Meilakh (XLVI); Kryshanovsky (LXII).

CREATIVE PROCESS. Senghor (I); Adamov, Sartre (XIX); Fischer, Marx and Engels, Seghers (XXI); Berger, Caudwell (XXIII); Lukacs (XXVII); Eisenstein (LXIV); Gorky, Meilakh, Plekhanov, Trotsky (XLVI); Fizer (XLIX); Baxandall, Burke, Dunham (LVI); Supek (LXI); Wittkower (LXII).

CRITICISM, SCHOLARLY PRINCIPLES OF, AND MARXISM. Mehring (XXI); Lunacharsky, Timofeev (XLVI); Erlich (XLIX); Clecak, Hicks, Schlauch (LVI).

DARWIN AND AESTHETICS. Plekhanov (XLVI); Kryzhanovsky (XLVII).

DECADENCE AS ARTISTIC CATEGORY. Fischer, Marx and Engels (XXI); Lukacs, Szenczi (XXVII); Lindsay (XXIII); Plekhanov, Trotsky (XLVI); Calmer, Goldstein, Heifetz, Lawson (LVI); Summers (LVII); Supek (LXI); Auerbach (LXII).

DECADENCE OF CAPITALIST CULTURE. Fanon, Toure (I); Fischer, Marx and Engels (XXI); Breton (XIX); USA Threat (XXIII); Lukacs (XXVII); Bukharin, Gorky, Kuznetsov, Lenin, Plekhanov, Radek, Trotsky (XLVI); Harap, Harrington, Jerome, Lawson (LVI); Harrison, Heap, Lambert, Trilling (LXII); Genet (LXIII).

DETECTIVE STORY. Malraux (XIX); Vishnevskaya (XLVI).

DOCUMENTARY WRITING. Malraux (XIX); Weiss (XXI); Peliyevsky, Tretyakov (XLVI); Harris (LVI).

EGYPT, ANCIENT. Raphael (XXI); Lindsay (XXIII).

EPIC. Prusek (XV); Brecht (XXI); Lukacs (XXVII); Dneprov (XLVI); Auerbach, Routh (LXII).

EURIPIDES. Thomson (XXIII); Gassner (LVIII); Auerbach (LXII).

EXPERIENCE AND THEORETICAL CORRECTNESS IN MARXIST WRITING. Becher (XXI); Mitchell (XXIII); Lukacs (XXVII); Gorky, Trotsky (XLVI); Fearing, Gregory (LVI); Bowra (LXII).

FANTASY IN REALISTIC WRITING. Alexis, Cesaire, Senghor (I); Prusek (XV); Brecht (XXI); Lukacs (XXVII); Dneprov, Dubrovin, Obretenov (XLVI); Baxandall, Burgum, LeRoy (LVI); Lind (LXIII).

FASCISM, LITERARY STRATEGY AGSINST. Dimitrov (VII); Brecht, Seghers (XXI); Rickword, Strachey (XXIII); Gorky (XLVI); Hoellerer (LXII); also US Topics, Fascism.

FIGURAL INTERPRETATION. Auerbach (LXII).

FORM AND CONTENT. Fischer, Marx and Engels (XXI); Caudwell, Fox, Klingender, West (XXIII); Angarov, Burov, Dneprov, Trotsky (XLVI); Baxandall, Dunham, Finkelstein, Phillips (LVI); Auerbach (LXII).

FORM, SOCIAL DETERMINANTS. Senghor (I); Fischer, Marx and Engels, Mehring (XXI); Lindsay (XXIII); Lukacs (XXVII); Lunacharsky, Plekhanov, Sholokhov, Trotsky (XLVI); Harap (LVI); Adam, Auerbach, Gotshalk, Grosse, Guerard, Kroeber, Mukerjee, Simons, Sorokin, Taine, Tomars, Wilson, Woodcock (LXII).

FORMALISM (OR MODERNISM), AGAINST. Lukacs, Revai (XXVII); 1936-64 (XLI); Lifshitz, Trotsky (XLVI); LeRoy (LVI).

FREUD, CONTRIBUTIONS. Reich (XXI); Caudwell (XXIII); Hauser (XXVII); Trotsky (XLVI); Burgum, Calverton, Marcuse, Slochower, Wilson (LVI).

FREUD, FALLACIES. Caudwell (XXIII); Dneprov, Friche, Stolyarov (XLVI); Schapiro (LIII); Trilling (LXII).

GOVERNMENT AND BUSINESS PATRONAGE UNDER CAPITALISM. Kondrashov (XLVI); Adams, Alsberg, Baumol, Dowd, Eells, Fox, Priestley, Read, Rockefeller, Rush, Schechner, Toffler, White, Wieruszowski, Wollheim (LXII); also US Topics, Literature and General, WPA.

GREECE, ANCIENT, LITERATURE. Prusek (XV); Bonnard, Lafargue (XIX); Bloch, Marx and Engels (XXI); Lindsay, Thomson, Willetts (XXIII); Lukacs (XXVII); Plekhanov (XLVI); Brown, Winspear (LVI); Auerbach, Bowra, Ehrenburg, Finley, Routh (LXII).

IMAGE. Fischer (XXI); Eisenstein (XLIV); Bogdanov, Kozhinov, Palievsky, Ryurikov (XLVI); Auerbach (LXII).

INDIVIDUALITY AND COMMUNIST WRITING. Becher, Brecht, Fischer, Heym, Weiss (XXI); 'Viewpoint' (XXIII); Lukacs (XXVII); Gorky, Trotsky, Zimenko (XLVI).

INDUSTRIALISM, RESULTS. Senghor (I); Dumazedier, Leger (XIX); Benjamin, Marx and Engels (XXI); Klingender, Levy, Read (XXIII); Lukacs (XXVII); Trotsky (XLVI); Fraina, Harap, Marcuse (LVI); Capouya, Francastel, Jacobs, Larrabee, Mead, Mumford, Smith, Weber (LXII).

LINGUISTICS. Neustupny, Simko (XV); Fischer, Richter (XXI); Caudwell, Fraser, Richmond, Thomson (XXIII); Schaff (XXXVI); Skolimowski (XXXVII); Desheriyev, Ryurikov, Stalin, Trotsky, Vygotsky (XLVI); Schlauch (LVI); Auerbach, Cohen, Jones, Levi-Strauss (LXII).

MASS CULTURE, PROBLEMS, UNDER SOCIALISM. Fanon, Senghor, Toure (I); Weiss, Zazunek (XV); Situationniste Internationale (XIX); Fischer (XXI); Berger, Morris, Morton (XXIII); Jardanyi, Lukacs, Sas, Veres (XXVII); Fuentes (XXXIII); Cieslik, Hernas, Kloskowski, Wiatr, Zolkiewski (XXXVI); Picasso (XL); Gorky, Lunacharsky, Trotsky, USSR Speaks (XLVI); Hoggart, Lowenthal, Mead (LXII); Pound (LXIII).

MASS CULTURE UNDER CAPITALISM. Marx and Engels (XXI); Woddis (XXIII); Lukacs (XXVII); Gorky, Plekhanov (XLVI); Baxandall, Greenberg, Rosenberg (LVI); Adorno, Arnold, Lowenthal, Toffler, Tomars, Veblen (LXII).

MECHANISTIC MARXIST AESTHETICS, AGAINST. Karvas (XV); Fischer (XXI); Lukacs (XXVII); Gramsci, Labriola (XXX); Trotsky (XLVI); Calmer, Clecak, Dunham, Phillips (LVI).

MYTH AND SOCIETY. Dover (I); Fischer, Reich (XXI); Caudwell (XXIII); Lukacs (XXVII); Gorky, Lunacharsky, Plekhanov, Trotsky (XLVI); Burke (LVI); Duncan,

Nedoshivin, Plekhanov, Trotsky, Zis (XLVI); Baxandall, Humboldt, Finkelstein, LeRoy, Rudich (LVI); Auerbach, Darrow, Gotshalk, Levin, Mannheim, Mukerjee, 'World Theatre' (LXII); Robbe-Grillet (LXIII).

RELATIVISM IN AESTHETIC JUDGMENT. Fischer (XXI); Klingender (XXIII); Lukacs (XXVII); 1936-39 (XLI); Lunacharsky, Plekhanov, Rosenthal (XLVI); Supek (LXI); also USSR Topics, Literature and General, Leninist Aesthetics.

ROMANTICISM, BOURGEOIS, AS ARTISTIC CATEGORY. Mao Tun (XI); Fischer, Marx and Engels (XXI); Hobsbawm, Lindsay, Mitchell (XXIII); Antal, Lukacs (XXVII); Gorky, Lunacharsky, Plekhanov, Trotsky (XLVI); LeRoy, Taggard (LVI); Auerbach (LXII).

SATIRE. Lafargue (XIX); Brecht, Kautsky (XXI); Eventov (XLIV); Yershov (IL).

SCIENCE AND FICTION. Brandis, Granin, Kitaigorodsky, Urban (XLVI); Yershov XLIX).

SENSIBILITY, ROLE OF WRITER'S. Fischer (XXI); A. Mitchell, Morton (XXIII); Lukacs (XXVII); Gorky, Plekhanov, Trotsky (XLVI); Burke, Calverton, Fearing, Funaroff, Gregory, Phillips, Rudich, Taggard (LVI); Eliot (LIX); Capouya, Orwell (LXII).

SEX EXPRESSION IN LITERATURE. Adamov (XIX); Reich (XXI); Arundel (XXIII); Friche (XLVI); Calverton, Marcuse (LVI); Dell (LXII).

SINCERITY AS ARTISTIC CATEGORY. Mao Tun (XI): Kopeczi, Lukacs (XXVII); Gorky, Paliyevsky, Pomerantsev, Volkov (XLVI); Appell, Brand, Gold (LVI); Capouya (LXII).

SOCIALIST REALISM. Agosti (IV); Teitelboim (IX); 1949-1967 (X); Brecht, Fischer, Kantorowicz (XXI); Breton, Garaudy (XIX); Camus (XX); Aaronovitch, Fox, Hartley, Heinemann, Lindsay, O'Casey (XXIII); Central Committee, Kopeczy, Lukacs (XXVII); 1932 ff (XLI); Almazov, Bogdanov, Dubrovin, Eventov, Gladkov, Gorky, Lunacharsky, Sinyavsky, Soviet Writers, Zhdanov (XLVI); LeRoy (LVI); Ermolaev, Harper, Mathewson, Vickery, Zekulin (XLIX); Nguyen Khai (LX).

SOPHOCLES. Lukacs (XXVII); Gassner (LVIII).

SURREALISM, LITERARY. Adamov, Aragon, Breton, Calas, Nadeau, Nouge, Sartre, Tzara (XIX); Etiemble, Short (XX); Fischer (XXI); Caudwell (XXIII); Ehrenburg, Fried, Kulikova (XLVI).

SYMBOLIC COMMUNICATION, AS ART. Burke (LVI); Duncan (LXII).

SYMBOLISM. Senghor (I); Brecht, Fischer (XXI); Lindsay (XXIII); Lukacs (XXVII); Plekhanov, Trotsky (XLVI); Glass (LVI).

TASTE, CLASS DETERMINANTS. Marx and Engels, Mehring (XXI); Caudwell, Nuttall (XXIII); Antal, Lukacs (XXVII); Morawski (XXXVI); Plekhanov, Trotsky (XLVI); Baxandall (LVI); Ebisch, Gordon, Kellett, Reitlinger (LXII).

TASTE SAMPLING. Sas (XXVII); Adamic (LIX); Albrecht, Barnett, Duncan, Mueller, Mulligan, Schuessler (LXII).

TEACHING LITERATURE. Hicks (LVI).

TIME IN LITERATURE. Lindsay (XXIII); Hauser, Lukacs (XXVII).

TRADITION, EFFECT. Malraux (XIX); Marx and Engels (XXI); Kettle (XXIII); Lukacs (XXVII); Bogdanov, Lenin, Lunacharsky (XLVI); Harap (LVI).

TRANSLATION. Brecht (XXI); Kalashnikova (XLVI).

TYPICAL, THE. Lafargue (XIX); Brecht, Fischer, Marx and Engels (XXI); Lukacs (XXVII); 'Kommunist', Kozhinov (XLVI); Auerbach (LXII).

UNIVERSAL VS. CLASS ATTRIBUTES OF ART. Fanon, Senghor (I); 1964 (X); Brecht, Fischer, Marx and Engels (XXI); Lukacs (XXVII); Siqueiros (XXXIII); Chukhrai (XLIV); Burov, Gei, Humanism, Novichenko, Plekhanov, Trotsky (XLIV); Rosenberg (LVI); Gotshalk, Mitchells (LXII).

UTOPIA AS A LITERARY GENRE. Bloch (XXI); Kardos (XXVII); Burgum (LVI); Morton, (XXIII).

## Music

CRITICISM. Sartre (XIX); Sands (LVII).

DISSONANCE AND CONSONANCE. Cabrero (XXXIII); Cazden (LVII); Dunwell, Weber (LXII).

EXPRESSIONISM. Danilevich (XLVII).

FILM MUSIC. Eisler (XXI).

FOLK MUSIC. Pin Chih (XI); Carpentier (XIII); Sartre (XIX); Dallas, Lloyd, MacColl (XXIII); Jardanyi, Kodaly (XXVII); Khachaturian, Shostakovich, Tchemodanoff (XLVII); Harap (LVI); Cazden, Finkelstein, Guthrie, Seeger (LVII); Greenway, Harrison, Lengyel (LXII); Bartok, Ochs (LXIII).

FORM AND REALITY. Sartre (XIX); Bloch (XXI); Bush, Caudwell, Mellers, Russell (XXIII); Ujfalussy (XXVII); Morawski (XXXVI); Plekhanov (XLVI); Danilevich, Nestiev (XLVII); Cazden, Dale (LVII); Adorno, Kryzhanovsky, Lambert, McAllister, Weber (LXII); Bartok (LXIII).

HISTORY. Mellers (XXIII); Finkelstein, Seeger, Siegmeister (LXII); Sachs, Weber (LXII).

HUMOR. Cazden (LVII).

INNOVATION. Sartre (XIX); Eisler (XXI); Nono (XXX); Revueltas (XXXIII); Balan (XXXVIII); Khachaturian, Shostakovich (XLVII); Taubman (IL); Blitzstein LVII); Leibowitz, Wagner (LXIII).

JAZZ, HISTORY. Brown, Spellman (I); Lang, Lloyd, Morton, Newton (XXIII); Finkelstein (LVII); Lengyel (LXII).

JAZZ, PROGRESSIVE OR BOURGEOIS? Cruse, James (I); Jones (II); 'Rude Bravo' (XV); Breton, Sartre (XIX); Beckett, Borneman, Caudwell, Lang, Logue, Newton (XXIII); Alchwang, Gerasimova, Kabelevsky, Konen, Sokolsky (XLVII); Young (XLIX); Finkelstein, Fraina, Hutchinson, Kofsky, Robbins, Smith (LVII); Adorno, Peterson (LXII); Colman (LXIII).

LINGUISTIC FACTORS. Sartre (XIX); Cazden, Seeger (LVII).

MUSICOLOGY, PROBLEMS. Ujfalussy (XXVII); Cazden, Seeger (LVII); Kryzhanovsky, Weber (LXII).

OPERA. Seeger (XXI).

PROLETARIAN MUSIC. Chiang, 1964 (X); Li Huan-Chih (XI); Chenneviere (XIX); Bloch, Eisler, Marx and Engels (XXI); Bond, Short (XXIII); 1929 (XLI); Gachev, Lebedinsky, Ramm, Tsytovich (XLVII); Flynt (LVI); Adohmyan, Feder, Julian, Morgenstern, Sands, Seeger,

Schapiro (LVII).

RADIO MUSIC. Adorno (LXII).

ROCK AND ROLL MUSIC. Beckett (XXIII); Bardacke, Goldman, Kofsky (LVII).

SERIAL MUSIC. Sartre (XIX); Nono (XXX); Cazden (LVII); Lambert (LXII); Leibowitz (LXIII).

SOCIAL DETERMINANTS. Rolland, Sartre (XIX); Eisler (XXI); Bush, Lloyd, Mellers, Sear (XXIII); Bukharin (XLVI); Lebedinsky, Tchemodanoff (XLVII); Julian, Siegmeister (LVII); Adorno, Dunwell, Kryzhanovsky, Lengyel, Mueller, Nash, Schuessler, Weber (LXII); Leinsdorf (LXIII).

TASTE, SOCIAL LAG IN. Sartre (XIX); Shostakovich (XLVII); copland (LVII).

THEATRE MUSIC. Mellers (XXIII); Blitzstein (LVII).

## Theatre

AGITPROP. Foster, Hughes, Jackson (I); Brecht, Toller, Wolf (XXI); Jones (XXIII); Vandurski (XXXVI); Bykov, Tikhanovich (XLVIII); Gold, Valdez (LVIII); Flanagan (LIX).

AUDIENCE AND CLASS. Brecht (XXI); Lukacs (XXVII); Mulligan (LXII).

AVANT-GARDE. Adamov, Dort, Sartre (XIX); Brecht, Piscator, Weiss (XXI); Auden, O'Casey (XXIII); Lukacs (XXVII); Ivascu (XXXVIII); Baxandall (LVIII); Meyerhold (XLVIII); Beck, Davis, Genet (LXIII).

CLASSICS, REVISING. Planchon (XIX); Brecht (XXI); Boyadzhiev, Meyerhold, Radlov (XLVIII); Beck (LXIII).

CRITICAL REALIST. Sartre (XIX); Brecht, Wolf (XXI); Jackson (XXIII); Lukacs (XXVII); Kott (XXXVI); Codignola (XXX); Blake (LVIII); Goldman (LXII); Beck (LXIII).

DESIGNING THE STAGE. Brecht, Piscator (XXI); Meyerhold (XLVIII); Gorelik (LVIII).

EPIC. Sartre (XIX); Brecht, Piscator (XXI); Lukacs (XXVII); Gorelik (LVIII).

EXPRESSIONIST. Brecht, Kerr, Toller (XXI); Lawson (LVIII).

GREECE, ANCIENT. Marx and Engels (XXI);
Thomson (XXIII); Lukacs (XXVII); Law-
son, Weisinger (LVI); Gassner, Odets
(LVIII); Auerbach (LXII).

HAPPENINGS. Baxandall (LVIII); Dewey,
Kaprow, Snowday (LXIII).

INTERNATIONAL UNION OF REVOLUTIONARY
THEATRE. Diament, International
(XLVIII); Blake (IL).

MASKS. Sartre (XIX); Brecht (XXI); Levi-
Strauss (LXII).

MEDIEVAL. Lukacs (XXVII); Gvosdev
(XLVIII); Auerbach, Kernodle (LXII).

MODERN HISTORY. Capon (XXIII); Lukacs
(XXVII); Gvosdev (XLVIII); Gassner,
Gorelik (LVIII); Suvin (LXI); Auerbach,
Goldman, Lowenthal, Williams (LXII).

NATURALISM. Baxandall (LVI); Gorelik
(LVIII).

ORIGINS. Thomson (XXIII); Devecseri
(XXVII); Gassner (LVIII).

POPULAR THEATRE. Burian (XV); Planchon,
Vilar (XIX); Brecht, Toller (XXI);
Littlewood, O'Casey (XXIII); Rolland-
Holst (XXVI); Gupta (XXVIII); Martin
(XXIX); Grassi (XXX); Leon (XL);
Meyerhold (XLVIII); Blankfort, Davis
(LVIII); Blau, Kernodle, Tynan (LXII);
Lorca, O'Neal (LXIII).

PRODUCTION METHODS. Planchon, Vilar
(XIX); Brecht, Piscator (XXI);
Anikst, Meyerhold (XLVIII); Lawson
(LVIII); Beck (LXIII).

PUPPETRY. Bunin (LVIII).

SOCIALIST REALIST. Kahler (XXI); Lukacs
(XXVII ); Lovinescu (XXXVIII); Luna-
charsky, Meyerhold,Novitsky (XLVIII);
Allen (LVIII); Macleod (XLIX); Duberman
(LXII).

THEORY. Dort, Sartre (XIX); Benjamin,
Brecht, Marx and Engels (XXI); Auden
(XXIII); Eisenstein (LXIV); Gorky
(XLVI); Weisinger (LVI); Allen, Baxan-
dall, Blankfort, Lawson (LVIII); Suvin
(LXI); Durrenmatt, Miller (LXIII).

WRITING OF DRAMA. Piscator (XXI); Lukacs
(XXVII); Gorky (XLVI); Egri, Lawson
(LVIII).

# LISTINGS BY NATIONS

## AFRICAN AND AFRO-AMERICAN

### Topic Index

AESTHETICS. Senghor.

ASIAN-AFRICAN WRITERS' CONGRESSES. See
(X).

BALDWIN, J. Mayfield, Smith. Finkelstein (LVI); Howe (LXII).

CHESNUTT, C. See (II).

CLASS AND BLACK WRITERS. Bland, Brown,
Cesaire, Coombs, Dover, Fanon, Frazier,
Gordon, Mphahlele, Toure, Wright.
Glenson, Melone (II). Holmes (LVI).

COMMUNISM, ATTITUDES TO. Cesaire, Clay,
Gordon, Hughes, Robeson, Senghor,
Wright.

DANCE. Writers Program (II).

ECONOMIC DETERMINANTS. Dover, Fanon,
Senghor. Calverton (II).

GUINEA. Toure.

HAITI. Alexis, Efron, Roumain. Garrett, Rodman (II).

JAZZ. See General Topic Index, Music.

MARTINIQUE. Cesaire.

McKAY, C. Cooper (II).

MINI, V. Anon.

NEGRITUDE. Fanon, Senghor. Gerard,
LeMelle, Tzara (II).

NETO, A.  Merwin.

PAINTING.  Douglas, Dover, Harlem Art-
    ists Guild.  D'Usseau, Minor, Rodman,
    Writers Program (II).

POETRY.  Cesaire, Fanon, Hughes, Senghor.
    Jones (II); Sartre (XIX).

PORTUGUESE.  Margarido.

'PRIMITIVE' ARTS AND COSMOPOLITAN INFLU-
    ENCES.  Brown, Toure, Wright.  Cre-
    monius (II); Kofsky (LVII).

RACISM, WHITE, IN CULTURE.  Alfa, Ce-
    saire, Clay, Cruse, Fanon, Farnum,
    Gordon, Senghor, Wright.  Jones (II);
    Sartre (XIX); Finkelstein, Flynt
    (LVI); Kofsky (LVII).

SENEGAL.  Senghor.

SOUTH AFRICA.  Mphahlele.

SURREALISM.  Sartre (XIX).

THEATRE.  Foster, Hansberry, Hughes,
    Jackson, 'New Theatre'. L. Jones,
    Robeson, Writers Program (II); Duber-
    man(LXII);Beck, Davis, O'Neal (LXIII).

THEMATIC MATTER.  Brown, Brown, Clay,
    Dover, Ellison, Hughes, Motley, Wil-
    kerson.  Aptheker, Chesnutt (II);
    Sartre (XIX); Galvin (XXIII); Holmes
    (LVI); Killens (LXIII).

WEST INDIES.  Drayton, James.

WRIGHT, R.  See below.

### I.  Authors

ALEXIS, Jacques Stephen, "Of the Marvel-
    ous Realism Of the Haitians," IC(1),
    249-275.  Basis and development of
    Haitian culture.  Haiti's realism,
    comprised of fantastic elements that
    relate it to other Negro cultures and
    separate it from Western culture.  Re-
    latedness of this Marvelous Realism to
    Socialist Realist canons, 'humanist in
    content, national in form.'  Problems
    of the Creole tongue.

ALFA, Abdou, "The Politics Of Culture,"
    Rev, July 1963, 120-125.  Influence of
    Congress for Cultural Freedom and other
    "Western auspices" on African writers
    and artists.  "The expression of the
    culture of Africa cannot be African if
    it is controlled and directed either

at home or abroad by cultural neo-
colonialism."

[2nd] ALL-SOUTHERN NEGRO YOUTH CONGRESS.
    PROCEEDINGS.  [not located.]

ANONYMOUS, "South African Freedom Songs:
    A Tribute to the Patriot Vuyisile Mini",
    African Communist (London), #20 (1965),
    15-19.  Songs that assist intertribal
    unity.

BLAND, Edward, "Social Forces Shaping
    the Negro Novel," Negro Quarterly,
    I iii, 241-248.

BROWN, Lloyd L., "Which Way for Negro
    Writers," M&M, Mch 1951, 53-63; Apr,
    50-59.  Analysis of special literature
    issue of 'Phylon' indicts trend away
    from protest toward escape into non-
    Negro subjects. - Blyden Jackson an-
    swers Brown: Phylon, XII (1951), 378-
    388.

BROWN, Sterling A., "The Problems Of the
    Negro Writer," [Second] National Negro
    Congress, October 15-17, 1937, Official
    Proceedings, Washington, D. C., n.d.,
    n.p. abdgd.  Social realism as only
    style for "recording a world of injus-
    tice and exploitation, a world that
    must be changed."  The resistance to
    this style of the conventional stereo-
    types about Negroes - and the new,
    idealized Negro of the black bourgeoi-
    sie. - Comment by Alain Locke, who
    agrees "social realism is right and
    even inescapable for these times" and
    relates needs of American Negroes to
    "the cultural minorities art program
    being consistently and brilliantly de-
    veloped in the Soviet Federation."

_____, "Negro Folk Expression," Phylon,
    XI (1950), 318-327; XIII (1952), 286-
    292; XIV (1953), 45-61.

_____, "A Century of Negro Portraiture In
    American Literature," MassR, Winter
    1966, 73-96.

_____, SEE ALSO: Eugene Clay, "Sterling
    Brown: American Peoples' Poet,"
    IL, 1934 #2, 117-122.

CESAIRE, Aime, "Culture and Colonization,"
    IC(1), 193-207.  Analyzes stages of
    breakup of native cultures by colonial-
    ism.  Suggests means by which the cul-
    tures will be reintegrated at a new level.

_____, Letter to Maurice Thorez, Presence

Africaine: Paris, 1957. 16pp. [cc]
Dated Oct 24, 1956. Resigns from Party
of "French Stalinism that's more die-
hard and enduring than Stalin himself."
Charges Communism "as it is put into
practice" with chauvinism and ignorance
of the complex problems of colored
peoples. "Our paths towards the future...aren't ready-traced on any map;
they remain to be discovered....What I
want is that Marxism and Communism be
harnessed into the service of colored
peoples, and not colored peoples into
the service of Marxism and Communism."

_____, "The Man Of Culture and His Re-
sponsibilities," IC(2), 125-132. "There
is never any failure of national sentiment. There is merely inadequacy on
the part of the man of culture....It
has been said that writers are the engineers of the soul. In the circumstances in which we find ourselves, we
are the propagators of the soul."
Warns that after national liberation
colonial culture may persist among
local bourgeoisie, as in Latin America.
"That is why true decolonization will
be revolutionary or nothing."

_____, SEE ALSO: Janheinz Jahn, "Aime
Cesaire," Black Orpheus, Jan
1958, 32-36. Excellent introduction.

CLAY, Eugene, "The Negro In Recent American Literature," AWC, 145-153. Definition of revolutionary content in
work of Hughes, Wright, et al.

_____, "The Negro and American Litera-
ture," IL, 1935 #6, 77-89.

[1st] CONFERENCE OF NEGRO WRITERS, The
American Negro Writer and His Roots,
American Society of African Culture:
1960. illus. [SC] Papers by Saunders
Redding, Samuel W. Allen, John H.
Clarke, Julian Mayfield, Arthur P.
Davis, Langston Hughes, William Branch,
Arna Bontemps, Loften Mitchell, Sarah
E. Wright, John Killens.

COOMBS, H. A., "We Need a Negro People's
Theatre," WT, July-Aug 1933, 6-7. Survey of beginnings and possibilities.
Calls for folk-plays about Negroes
with a major theme being the "disap-
pointed and stunted lives" of the
black bourgeoisie.

CRUSE, Harold, "Rebellion Or Revolution?"
Liberator, Dec 1963, 14-17; Jan 1964,

14-16. The 'Aesthetic of Negritude'
in America.

DAVIS, Ossie, "The Arts As Fulcrum In
Civil Rights," N. Y. Times, Feb 1,
1965. 16. abdgd.

_____, "The Significance of Lorraine
Hansberry," Freedomways (New York),
Summer 1965, 397-402. "Raisin In the
Sun' offered "universal" rather than
historio-racially defined characters,
an error.

DOUGLAS, Aaron, "The Negro In American
Culture," AAC. The vicissitudes of
Negroes in American culture; reasons
for the slight showing of Negroes in
painting.

DOVER, Cedric, "Notes On Colored Writing,"
Phylon, VIII (1947), 213-224. Social
situation of Negro writer.

_____, "Culture and Creativity," IC(1),
285-306. Myth as backbone of culture.
Advantages of backward societies taking social-revolutionary leaps, compared to ideologically-fragmented
Western society, in the matter of maintaining continuity of myths and common
culture. Problems of Negroes with a
minority culture: in USA, India, etc.
Inadequacy of a narrow Marxist view of
proletariat as driving force; potency
of the Chinese example in politics and
culture.

_____, American Negro Art, New York Gra-
phic Society: 1960. illus. Outstanding survey defines social soil on which
Negro art must subsist: a mulatto culture, uprooted, petty-bourgeois, uncon-
ducive to taste or aesthetic productivity.

DRAYTON, Arthur D., "West Indian Fiction
and West Indian Society," Kenyon Review, XXV (1963), 129-141. Author
teaches English literature at Ibadan,
Nigeria. Describes aptness of social
realism in West Indies.

DU BOIS, W. E. B., "The Social Origins Of
American Negro Art," MQ(B), III i
(1925), 53-56.
EFRON, Edith, "The 'New Movement' In
Haiti," Caribbean Quarterly, Jan 1955,
14-31. Struggle of artists and writers
- e. g, Jacques Roumain, author of
'Masters of the Dew' - to assert Haitian popular culture against snobbism
of a Frenchified mulatto elite.

ELLISON, Ralph, "Recent Negro Fiction,"
  NM, Aug 5, 1941, 22-26.

FANON, Frantz, "Racism and Culture,"
  IC(1), 122-131. Also in Streets,
  May-June 1965, 5-12. Profound analysis
  of "racism on the cultural level" Dis-
  cerns stages through which a colonized
  people passes and its options for
  achieving a universalized culture.

_____, "The Reciprocal Basis Of National
  Cultures and the Struggles For Liberation," IC(2), 89-97. Reprinted in The
  Damned (see below). Close account of
  how national political struggle revit-
  alizes arts which in turn revitalize
  the people. Insists that only through
  national armed struggle can the colonized mentality be changed to "excep-
  tional cultural fertility."

_____, "This Is the Voice Of Algeria,"
  in his Studies In a Dying Colonialism,
  Monthly Review: 1965, 69-97. The role
  of radio in a revolutionary situation.

_____, The Damned, Presence Africaine:
  Paris, 1963; also published as The
  Wretched of the Earth, Grove: 1965.
  Preface by Jean-Paul Sartre. First
  publ. 1955. See esp. "National Culture," 167-189. Fanon is most vehement opponent of 'Negritude' enthus-
  iasts, regards it as backward-looking
  and insists national struggles are
  required, not racial research. Accuses
  Senghor of aiding French in combatting
  the Algerian Revolution all the while
  he spoke of African unity. "The desire to attach oneself to tradition
  or bring abandoned traditions to life
  again does not only mean going against
  the current of history but also oppos-
  ing one's own people." Demands poetry
  that is pedagogical, clear, forward-
  looking so "the understanding of the
  poem is not merely an intellectual
  advance, but a political advance."

FARNAM, George T, "Shakespeare and the
  Blacks," Freedomways (New York) Fall
  1964, 479-486. Shakespeare's humanism
  stops short of the black race. Othello
  ends as a "raving savage." - Comment
  by Nancy Lubka, ibid, Summer 1965,
  424-426.

FOSTER, Joe, "The 'Negro People's Theatre'," DW, May 28, 1935, 5. illus.
  Foundation. Rehearsal approach to
  'Waiting for Lefty' by a company led
  by Rose McClendon and Chick McKinney,

characterized as United Front in orientation. - This production reviewed by
Leon Alexander, DW, June 5, 1935, 5. -
Further plans: DW, June 28, 1935, 5. -
Success with agitprop drama before
worker audiences, and vitalizing effect
of proletarian contact on the group's
thinking: Joe Foster, "A Negro People's
Theatre Is Born," DW, Aug 16, 1935, 5.

FRAZIER, E. Franklin, The Negro In the
  United States, Macmillan: 1949. "Negro
  Press and Literature," 492-519.

GORDON, Eugene, "A Literary Criticism,"
  Le, I i (Nov 1932), 25-27. Deference
  to USSR prestige: "The authority of
  the International Union of Revolutionary Writers....is itself the authority
  of Marx plus Lenin."

_____, "The Role Of the Proletarian Crit-
  ic," Le, Feb 1933, 17-19. Asserts primary task of proletarian critics is to
  examine content; affirms exhaustion of
  bourgeois literary forms.

_____, "Negro Novelists and the Negro
  Masses," NM, July 1933, 16-20. Hazards
  for black writers: inherited ignorance
  and "the poison of bourgeois propaganda."

_____, "Social and Political Problems Of
  the Negro Writer," AWC, 141-145. The
  Negro writer's temptation to go with
  the black bourgeoisie.

GUILLEN, Nicolas. See (XIII).

HANSBERRY, Lorraine, On a Negro Theatre.
  M&M, Dec 1951, 59-60. Formulates dream
  of a realistic Negro drama.

_____, "Arthur Miller's 'The Crucible',"
  June 1953, 18-19. Critical of Miller's
  perspective.

_____, SEE ALSO: Joanne Grant, "Lorraine
      Hansberry," NG, Jan 23, 1965,
      12. Over-view of her career. -
      Julian Mayfield, Letter, Libera-
      tor, Apr 1965, 28. - O. Davis
      (above). - Lucille Banta, "Lor-
      raine Hansberry," AmD, May-June
      1965, 25-27.

HARLEM ARTISTS' GUILD. See Gwendolyn
  Bennett, AF, May 1937, 20.

HUGHES, Langston, "Moscow and Me," IL,
  1933 #3, 61-66. Warm response to USSR
  while travelling there. "But then the
  papers of the other lands are always

calling the Muscovites red. I guess
its the red that makes the difference.
I'll be glad when Chicago gets that
way, and Birmingham."

_____, "Negroes In Moscow," IL, 1933 #4,
78-81.

_____, "To Negro Writers," AWC, 139-141.
Suggests themes which should concern
socially aware Negro writers.

_____, "Trouble With the Angels," NTh,
July 1935, 6-7. 'Green Pastures',
great triumph of Negro theatre in the
30s, torn apart.

_____, Speech to 2nd International Wri-
ters Congress, Paris. DW, Sept 23,
1937, 7. The Negro and the struggle
against fascism.

_____, "Writers and the World," Bulletin,
V i (Fall 1938), 1, 10. Speech to Extraordinary Session of International
Association of Writers in Defense of
Culture, Paris, July 23, 1938. "Words
big with the building of life rather
than its destruction, filled with
faith in life rather than doubt and
distress, such words entering into the
minds of men, last much longer than
today's dinner in the belly or next
year's overcoat on the back. And such
words, even when forgotten, may still
be reflected in terms of motives and
actions, and so go out from the reader
to many people who have never seen the
original words themselves."

_____, Speech to 3rd Congress of American
Writers. DW, June 5, 1939, 9. Also
in FW, 58-63. abdgd.

_____, "My Adventures as a Social Poet,"
Phylon, VIII (1947), 205-212. Account
of threats, detainments, censorship,
his motives for social engagement.

_____, "Some Practical Observations,"
Phylon, XI (1950), 307-311. Directions for Negro literary effort.

_____, I Wonder As I Wander, 1956: Ameri-
can Century paperback, 1964. Autobiography of the 30s.

_____, SEE ALSO: Lydia Filatova, "Langs-
ton Hughes: American Writer,"
IL, 1933 #1, 99-107.

Edith Hale, "Harlem Suitcase
Theatre," DW, Nov 23, 1938, 9.

illus. Agitprop theatre headed by Hughes. - Also DW, Apr
20, 1938, 7, for Hughes' comments.

INTERNATIONAL CONFERENCES OF NEGRO WRIT-
ERS AND ARTISTS. The Sorbonne, Paris,
1956; Rome, 1959. See IC(1), IC(2).

JACKSON, James E, Jr, "South's First Negro People's Theatre, " DW, May 26,
1938, 7. Thomas Richardson, formerly
of Theatre of Action, headed amateur
group performing labor plays in his
native Richmond, Virginia.

JAMES, Cyril Lionel Robert, Mariners,
Renegades and Castaways: The Story Of
Herman Melville and the World We Live
In, 1953.

_____, "The Mighty Sparrow," in his:
Party Politics In the West Indies,
Port of Spain: 1962, 164-175. A
great calypso artist, and relation of
calypso to West Indian nationalism.

_____, Wilson Harris: A Philosophical
Approach, Univ. of West Indies: Trini-
dad, 1966. Analysis of the Guyanese
novelist. (This and above works available from: Facing Reality, 14131 Wood-
ward Ave., Detroit, Mich.)

_____, Lectures On Shakespeare. mimeo.
Available from the British Broadcast-
ing Company, London. Recorded Oct 31,
Nov 15 and Nov 26, 1963; broadcast on
Caribbean Service.

_____, Beyond a Boundary, Hutchinson:
London, 1963. Cricket in England and
the West Indies, its role in nation-
building. Sport as a popular art; art
as a form of sport. Critique of fine
arts in this light. Berenson.

_____, "Guyana Takes the Lead," and "Gath-
ering Of the Clan," Sunday Mirror
(Port of Spain), June 12 and 19, 1966.
Unsigned. A conference of writers and
artists held in Guyana on the occasion
of independence.

_____, "A New View of West Indian Histo-
ry," available from Extra-Mural Dept,
Univ. of the West Indies, Mona, Jamai-
ca. mimeo. Delivered June 3, 1965.
Considerable material on West Indian
writers.

_____, Modern Politics, PNM: Port of
Spain, 1961. Final chapter includes

survey of modern poetry, drama, painting and cinema.

_____, Unpublished papers, including
draft of a book 'Shakespeare and Lenin',
and correspondence ranging over the
whole of Western art, e.g., Greek drama, Shakespeare, Michelangelo, Renaissance, Chaplin, Eisenstein, Griffith.
Collections of Mrs. Constance Pearl-
stien, 23 E. 10th St., N.Y.C., and of
Martin Glaberman, 14832 Parkside,
Detroit, Mich.

_____, SEE ALSO: Martin Glaberman "C.L.R.
        James - The Man and His Work,"
        New World (Georgetown, British
        Guiana), Jan 7, 1966, 21-24.

LAWRENCE, Jacob, Interview.  In: Selden
Rodman, Conversations with Artists,
1957, 204-207.

_____, SEE ALSO; Elizabeth McCausland,
        "Jacob Lawrence," Magazine of
        Art, Nov 1945, 251-254.

MARGARIDO, Alfredo, "The Social and Economic Background Of Portuguese Negro
Poetry," Diogenes, Spring 1962, 50-74.

MAYFIELD, Julian, "And Then Came Baldwin,"
Freedomways, Spring 1963, 143-155.
Baldwin's place in the tradition of
Negro protest set in social perspective.

MERWIN, U.S, "To Name the Wrong," Black
Orpheus (Ibadan), #15 (1964), 34-37.
The Angolan guerilla leader and poet
Agostinho Neto.

MOTLEY, Willard, "The Education Of a Wri-
er," The New Idea (Madison, Wisc.),
Winter 1960, 11-20, 26, 28. [cc]  His
work method, development, views on
society and creativity.

_____, SEE ALSO: Obituary, N.Y. Times,
Mch 5, 1965, 30. illus.

MPHAHLELE, M.E, "Negro Culture In a Mul-
ti-Racial Society In Africa," IC(2),
221-227.  Details of South African cultural advance and difficulties. Growth
of proletarian Negro culture.

NEW THEATRE, Special Negro Theatre Issue.
NTh, July 1935.  Articles by Langston
Hughes, Paul Robeson, Eugene Gordon,
Lawrence Gellert, et al.

RICHARDSON, Ben, "New Horizons For the
Negro Artist," ACA, Winter 1946, 8-10.
Negro painters in history.

ROBESON, Paul, Interview with Philip
Bolsover.  DW, Nov 4, 1937, 7.  The
decision to act as working-class par-
tisan. - See also: Speech for Aid to
Spain, Albert Hall, London: DWSup,
Nov 14, 1937, 11

_____, On Joining London's Unity Theatre.
DW(L), Oct 18, 1937, 4.  Interview explains his desire for identification
with the working class. - See also
Reynold's News (London), Oct 10, 1937.

_____,"Primitives," NS, Aug 8, 1936,
190-192.  The superiority of "concrete
symbols" of African art over European
abstractionist art.

_____, On Robert Gwathmey.  DW, Feb 4,
1946, 11.  illus. Aesthetic and social
analysis of a Virginian's painting.

_____, SEE: Special Robeson Issue, Free-
domways (New York), Summer 1965.  ill.
Includes speech by Robeson on his return to US.

[ROUMAIN, Jacques.]  See: Madeleine Simon, "Jacques Roumain: Poet In Chains,"
DW, Feb 28, 1936, 7.  Good survey of
his career, prepared with aid of Roumain. Also: DW, Nov 10, 1939, 7. illus.

SENGHOR, Leopold Sedar, "The Spirit Of
Civilization, Or the Laws Of African
Negro Culture," IC(1), 51-64.  General
characteristics of Negro as distinct
from European culture. - Challenged by
Richard Wright as inapplicable to American Negro's situation, 66-68, 220. -
By Jacques Alexis for failing to consider specific African peoples' process
of liberation from colonialism, 68-70,
74-76. - Senghor's replies, 70-71, 73-
74. - Comment by Damz, 82-83. - Senghor importantly adds to his analysis,
218-219.

_____, "Constructive Elements Of a Civi-
lization Of African Negro Inspiration,"
IC(2), 262-294.  African climate, family and tribal structure, religion, work,
as they "determine, to a great extent"
the characteristics of African art.
"With regard to art, we have nothing to
learn from Europe" and it would be a
mistake simply to import Socialist
Realism: "we are on our own ground. The
lessons of Negro-African art should all
be retained."  Rejects charges that
Negritude excludes a role for Reason:
'the Negro elan, the active abandon of
the African Negro towards the object,
is animated by reason.  As Marx wrote

to Arnold Ruge, 'Reason has always existed, but not under the rational
form.'...Under the rational, technical
structures of society, what shines
through, in analysis, are the human,
thus psychological relations: the relations of consciousness, where imagination, the daughter of desire, plays
an essential role.  The most rational-
ized society, the Soviet, does not escape this rule."

_____, "African-Negro Aesthetics,"
Diogenes, Winter 1956, 23-38.  Brilliant exposition.

_____, "On Negrohood: Psychology Of the
African Negro," Diogenes, Spring 1962,
1-15. Complementary to foregoing essay.

_____, On African Socialism: A Report to
Constitutive Congress of the Party of
African Federalism, American Society
of African Culture: 1959.  "We shall
start from Marx and Engels" in defining relevance of Socialism to Africa,
but "we shall retain only the method
and the ideas" while working out
their application under new conditions.

_____, "West Africa in Evolution," For-
eign Affairs, Jan 1961, 240-246.  "In
spite of destroying our traditional
institutions and our works of art,
France has left us with a positive asset: a cultural, political, social and
economic infra-structure.  And with
ideas....Luckily, although African Negro values are emaciated they are not
uprooted....Senegal ought to be a research laboratory, a vast workshop,
where new creations take form."

_____, SEE ALSO: Biography by Joseph
        Wershba, N.Y. Post, Oct 31,
        1961, 44.

        Samuel W. Allen, "Negritude and
        Its Relevance to the American
        Negro Writer," The American
        Negro Writer and His Roots,
        American Society of African
        Culture: 1960, 8-20.

SMITH, William Garner, "Why Some American
Negroes Prefer Life Abroad," NG, Mch 7,
1960, 7.

SPELLMAN, A.B., Four Lives in the Bebop
Business, Pantheon: 1966.  C. Taylor,
O. Colman, H. Nichols, J. McLean;
jazz and commerce.

TOURE, Sekou, "The Political Leader Considered As the Representative Of a
Culture," IC(2), 112-124.  Combatting
Western "depersonalization of Africa"
through defense of peasant and village
culture.  "The voice of the African
peoples has no features, no name, no
individual ring.  But in the circles
which have been contaminated by the
spirit of the colonizers, who has not
observed the progress of personal ego-
ism?  Who has not heard the defense of
the theory of art for art's sake, the
theory of poetry for poetry's sake, the
theory of every man for himself? Whereas our anonymous artists are the wonder
of the world."

WARD, Theodore, "Five Negro Novelists:
Revolt and Retreat," Main, Winter 1947,
100-110. Attaway, Offord, Himes, Petry,
Yerby.

WILKERSON, Doxey, "Negro Culture: Heritage and Weapon," M&M, Aug 1949, 3-24.

WRIGHT, Richard, "Blueprint for Negro
Writing," New Challenge, Fall 1937,
53-64.  [SC]  "Negro writing has been
addressed in the main to a small white
audience rather than a Negro one." Proposes use of the masses' folklore.
"The Negroes' most powerful images of
hope and despair still remain in the
fluid state of daily speech," while
"it is through a Marxist conception of
reality and society that the maximum
degree of freedom in thought and feeling can be gained for the Negro writer"
- if he uses Marxism in a broad, concrete perspective.

_____, "Negro Writers Launch Literary
Quarterly," DW, June 8, 1937, 7. "New
Challenge' and the organization of
left Negro writers.

_____, Interview with Alfred Davis. DW,
Feb 25, 1938, 7.  "I owe my literary
development to the Communist Party and
its influence....It gave me my first
full-bodied vision of Negro life in
America."

_____, How "Bigger" Was Born, 1940; sec-
tions prepublished in SatR, June 1,
1940, 3-4, 17-20.  Genesis of his
'Native Son'.

_____, Interview with Marcia Minor.  DW,
Dec 13, 1938, 7.  illus.  His writing
method.

_____, "What We Think Of Their War,"
Speech to 4th American Writers Congress, June, 1941. [LAW]  Also in NM,
June 17, 1941, 8-12.  "The Negro's experience with past wars, his attitude
toward the present one, his attitude
of chronic distrust, constitute the
most incisive and graphic refutation
of every idealistic statement made by
the war leaders as to the alleged democratic goal and aim of this war."  Numerous examples of American treatment
of Negroes which hardly commend a war
against Hitler to them on  basis of bad
treatment of Jews.  Powerful indictment.

_____, Backing the Hitler-Stalin Pact.
DW, Feb 11, 1940, 7.

_____, Account of Relations with the
Communist Party.  In: The God That
Failed, ed. Richard Crossman, 1949,
115-162.

_____, SEE ALSO: Critique of 'Native Son'
    by Ben Davis, Jr.  DW, Apr 14,
    1940,4,6. Finds "distortions."
    - Answer by Michael Gold, DW,
    Apr 17, 1940, 7.  Says Davis
    looks for "agitational tracts"
    while Wright uses psychology of
    a Dostoevsky. - Letters from
    Herbert Neuton, Herbert Apthe-
    ker, DW, Apr 26, 1940, 7. -
    Gold, DW, Apr 29, 1940, 7. -
    Davis, DWSup, June 23, 1940, 4,
    6: basically concedes but as-
    similates Wright to Gorky rath-
    er than Dostoevsky. - Gold, DW,
    Sept 29, 1940, 5: questions re-
    marks by Wright in a talk about
    'Native Son'.

    Michael Gold, The Communist Ca-
      reer of Richard Wright. DW,
      Mch 31, 1940.

    See also Sartre (XIX); Slochower
      (LVI); Madden (LIX).

## II.  Appendix

APTHEKER, Herbert, "The Negro's Contribution to American Culture," Speech to
4th American Writers Congress. [LAW]
Cites the many Negro slave revolts and
paucity of fiction recounting them.
"It is an immediate and important task
for all progressive intellectuals, be
their medium what it may, to concen-
trate upon and to revivify the epic
story of the American Negro."

_____, "The Superiority Of the Negro,"

AmD, Oct-Nov 1965, 33-35. Examples
from  Negro literature of "the general
moral superiority of the oppressed....
the salvation of America depends upon
the victory of the Negro movement."

CALVERTON, Victor F, "The Growth of Negro
Literature," in his: Anthology of American Negro Literature, 1929, 1-17; reprinted in: Nancy Cunard, ed, Negro
Anthology, London, 1934, 101-105. abdgd.
Economic foundations of American Negro
originality and expression.

CHESNUTT, Helen M, Charles Waddell Chesnutt: Pioneer of the Color Line, Chapel
Hill, 1952.  Biography of pioneer American Negro realist writer by his daughter. - For a definition of Chesnutt's
role see Russell Ames (LVI).

COOPER, Wayne F, Claude McKay.  Dissertation-in-progress, New York Univ.

CREMONINI, Leonardo, "Will Handicrafts
Survive?"  Rev, Oct 1963, 136-142. The
modes probed whereby African artisan
products might survive industrialization.

D'USSEAU, Arnaud, "The Negro As an Artist," ACA, Winter 1946, 8-10.  Negro
painters in history.  Negro painters
should include the more general social
struggle.

GARRETT, Naomi Mills, The Renaissance of
Haitian Poetry, Ph. D. dissertation,
Columbia Univ: 1954; publ. by Presence
Africaine, Paris, 1964.

GERARD, Albert, "Historical Origins and
Literary Destiny of Negritude," Diogenes, Winter 1964, 14-38.

GLENSON, Judith, "Sembene Ousmane - A
Proletarian Novelist," African Forum,
Fall 1965, 106-108.

JONES, Edward Allen, "Contemporary French
Negro Poets," Phylon, XII (1951), 20-
28.  Chiefly Senghor and Cesaire; fine
survey.

JONES, LeRoi, and Archie Shepp, Art and
Politics: A Debate with Larry Rivers
and Jonas Mekas.  Report in Village
Voice, Mch 4, 1965, 5-6, 16-17.  Also:
N.Y. Times, Feb 10, 1965.  Black na-
tionalist perspectives on the arts.

_____, "The Revolutionary Theatre," Liber-
ator, July 1965, 4-6.  "It looks at the
sky with the victims' eyes, and moves

the victims to look at the strength in their minds and their bodies....it is a political theatre, a weapon to help in the slaughter of these dimwitted fat-bellied white guys who somehow believe that the rest of the world is here for them to slobber on."

_____, Home; Social Essays, 1966

LeMELLE, W. J, "A Return to Senghor's Theme on African Socialism," Phylon, XXVI (1965), 330-343.

MELONE, Thomas, "New Voices of African Poetry in French," African Forum, Spring 1966, 65-76.  Poets of class solidarity are replacing poets of negritude.

MINOR, Marcia, Jacob Lawrence's Works and Development.  DW, Aug 17, 1938, 7. illus.

RODMAN, Selden, Renaissance in Haiti: Popular Painters in the Black Republic, 1948. illus. Sudden emergence of re-markable folk art.

SOVIET STUDIES AND TRANSLATIONS OF AFRI-CAN WRITING.  Summarized in SL, 1966 #2, 176-180. - See also SL, 1967 #1, 170-176.

TZARA, Tristan, "Negritude?  Dangerous Mystification," Rev, June, 1963, 140-143.  The founder of Dada and longtime student of African art says "Negro art is dead.  Long live African art!"

WRITERS' PROGRAM, WORKS PROGRESS ADMIN-ISTRATION, left many manuscripts un-published on such topics as American Negro writing, dance, art, theatre, etc.  Now in Schomburg Collection [SC].

## ARGENTINA

### III.  Authors

AGOSTI, Hector P, "A Defense of Realism," in: George J. Becker, ed, Documents of Modern Literary Realism, Princeton Univ: Princeton, N.J., 1963, 489-505. Dated 1944.  Contrasts Marxian dynamic, interpretive realism with bourgeois passive realism.

## ASIA MINOR

### IV. Authors

BECKA, J, "New Papers on Rudaki by Tad-

zhik and Other Soviet Scholars," AO, XXVIII (1960), 494-501.  State of scholarship on the founder of Persian poetry.

ESFANDIARY, F.M, "Iran: Goodby To the Nightingale," Nation, Apr 18, 1966, 468-470.  Novelist defends a modern, popular literature.

KARPAT, Kemal A, "The Turkish  Left," Journal of Contemporary History, I ii (1966), 169-186.  The central role of literature in Turkish Marxism. -

See also: Sabiha Sertel, "Reminiscences Of Nazim Hikmet," NO, 1967 #2, 42-46. illus. Important account of his early career.

SHAKI, Mansour, "Development of Realism in Persian Art," NO, Oct 1961, 139-142. Detailed discussion. - See also Machal-ski (XV).

## AUSTRALIA

### V.  Authors

CULTURE, DEMOCRACY AND AUSTRALIA.  Marx House Publication #1, Sydney, 1943. 32 pp. [Harvard]  A note terms this pamph-let the first Australian effort of the sort.  Zetkin on Lenin, Olesha, 'Prav-da', A. Tolstoy on Shostakovich formal-ism debate; also a brief excerpt from speech by J.B. Miles, head of Austral-ian CP, to 13th National Congress of CP, urging  on "agitpropers."

GOULD, L.H, Art, Science and Communism, Sidney, 1946.  31 pp.

HARDY, Frank, "An Introduction to Austral-ian Democratic Literature," ZAA, II iv (1954), 429-437). - See also: Petrikov-skaya (XLVI).

LINDSAY, Jack.  See (XXIII).

MANIFOLD, John S, "The Australian Scene," M&M, Apr 1954, 50-54.  Survey of left writers.

MORTIER, Paul, Art: Its Origin and Social Function.  [not located.]

## BRAZIL

### VI.  Authors

FREYRE, Gilberto, "The Modern Literature of Brazil; Its Relation to Brazillian Social Problems" in his: New World In

The Tropics; The Culture of Modern
Brazil, Knopf: 1959, 209-229.

JULIAO, Francisco, "A Means Of Propaganda: Poetry," Rev, I xii (1964), 102-107.
Organizer of the Peasant Leagues describes the revolutionary role of popular poetic broadsides and singers.

NIEMEYER, Oscar, "Testimony," modulo #9
(Feb 1958), 3-6. Critique of his earlier work - when, he confesses, he in-
dulged in frivolous extremes of originality because he held a deprecating
attitude toward his profession, believing it lacked the "social ballast"
that social equality might provide and
depended rather on wealthy patrons.
Statement also of values incorporated
in his designs for Brasilia.

_____, "Man and the Modern City," modulo
#11 (Dec 1958), 3-6. Paper presented
at International Architectural Students'
Conference, Leningrad. Reflections on
the plastic beauty of man's greatest
monuments and the oppression and injustice of societies that built them. One
now sees only the beauty and not the
cost. The road lies open to a classless society and a new urban architecture.

_____, "Prefabricated Housing in Brasil-
ia," modulo #27 (Mch 1962), 27-38.
illus. Theory of a new urbanism to
replace architecture of alienation
with a healthy communal living which
is also technologically practical.

_____, "Form and Function in Architec-
ture," modulo #21 ( Dec 1960), 3-7.
"I am in favor of an almost unlimited
plastic freedom."

_____, SEE ALSO: Jorge Amado, "Master of
Humanism and Peace," modulo #34
(Aug 1963), 8-9. illus. On the
award of a Lenin Prize to Niemeyer. "Oscar Niemeyer is un-
questionably the best symbol of
an architecture aware of its
social role, its true function."

Stamo Papadaki, The Work of Oscar Niemeyer, 1950. illus.

Robert Van Steen, "Oscar Niemeyer and Brazilia," Show,
Nov 1962, 70-73. illus.

[PORTINARI, Candido] Portinari, His Life
and Art, Chicago, 1940. illus. Intro-

duction by Rockwell Kent. Brief biography and many reproductions.

_____, SEE ALSO; Flavio de Aquino, "Can-
dido Portinari, the Painter,"
modulo #27 (Mch 1962), 20-22.
illus. Portinari was "one of the
great expressionists of our
time." - Also: Jose Roberto
Teixeira Leite, "Candido Portinari," ibid, 23-26. illus. "He
has been the spokesman of the
humble masses of Brazil."

_____, SEE ALSO: Samuel Putnam, "Brazil-
ian Culture Under Vargas," S&S,
Winter 1942, 34-57. And: Samuel
Putnam, Marvelous Journey; A
Survey of Four Centuries of
Brazilian Writing, 1948.

BULGARIA

VII. Authors

DIMITROV, Georgi, Speech to Soviet Writers Association. LR, June 1935, 343-
346. The just-released defendant of
the Reichstag Trial calls for a literature of anti-Fascism. Key document
of international United Front in culture.

_____, "Socialism and Culture," NCEO, II
(1949), 223-224. Extract from February
1949 speech in Sofia.

_____, The Guidance of the Arts. La Bul-
garie, III iii-iv (May 1950). English
translation of text introducing catalog of XXI General Art Exhibition.

KARASLAVOV, Georgi, "Writers Get Closer
To the People," NB, Apr 1959, 23.
General Secretary of Union of Bulgarian
Writers.

PAVLOV, Todor, "The Firm Foundations of
the Marxist Theory of Cognition and
Aesthetics," C&L, 1959 #7, 36-39.
Strict defense of Lenin's theory of
reflection in aesthetics.

ROUSSAKIEV, Simeon, "Lyuben Karavelov, A
Great Revolutionary and a Realist Writer," NB, May 1959, 3. The nation's
"founder of realism."

ZHIVKOV, Todor, Against Bourgeois Ideology in Artistic Endeavor. EE, June
1963, 24-28. From 'Rabotnichesko
Delo', Apr 24, 1963.

CANADA

## VIII.　Authors

CECIL-SMITH, E, "The Workers' Theatre In Canada," Canadian Forum, Nov 1933, 68-70.

FAIRLEY, Margaret, "Socialist Poet of Upper Canada," NF, IV i (Spring 1955), 34-38. ⌊Harvard⌋ Thomas Macqueen.

H. F, Letter to Michael Gold. DW, Feb 15, 1935, 5. Ontario writer tells lack of progressive journals in Canada while finding scant interest in Canadian literature among US leftists.

CHILE

## IX. Authors

NERUDA, Pablo, "Toward an Impure Poetry," in: Selected Poems of Pablo Neruda, ed. Ben Belitt, Grove Press: 1961, 39-40

_____, "Poetry and Obscurity," M&M, July 1953, 20-26. Speech to Continental Congress of Culture, Santiago, Chile, April 26-May 2, 1953. Describes reasons for choosing a simple clear style in preference to his earlier hermeticism.

_____, "The Job In the Cultural Field," DW, Nov 1, 1949, 12; another translation in M&M, Nov 1949, 16-23. Speech to Continental Congress for World Peace, Mexico City. Demands positive note in writing. Denounces Sartre and Eliot: "they are the active germs of destruction"and when Fadaev said they wrote like hyenas, "he offended the animal kingdom."

_____, "Latin America Today," M&M, Oct 1962, 20-25. Speech to a Congress of the Chilean CP.

_____, SEE ALSO: Angel Flores, Biographical Essay. The Inter-American, May 1943, 34, 37. illus.

　V. Kuteishchikova, Neruda's Reception in the USSR. C&L, 1964 #7, 45. illus.

　Alastair Reid, "A Visit to Neruda," En, Sept 1965, 67-70.

　Ilya Ehrenburg, "A Portrait of Neruda," M&M, Mch 1950, 22-38

　Luis Enrique Delano, "Pablo Neruda: Poet in Arms," Main, I iv (Fall 1947), 424-439. Full and important discussion by an old friend.

　Jean Marcenac, "Peace and Poetry: A Talk with Pablo Neruda," M&M, May 1951, 30-41.

　Samuel Putnam, in: NM, July 31, 1945, 25-26.

　Maurice Halperin, Interview. Books Abroad, Apr 1941, 164-168.

TEITELBOIM, V, "Literature and Socialism," WMR, Mch 1960, 45-50. Problems of an emerging socialist realism in Latin America.

CHINA

## Topic Index

(XXIII); Boorman, Fokkema, Goldman, Hughes, Hsia, MacFarquhar, Matthews, Read, Walzer (XII).

REVOLUTIONARY CULTURE, PRE-1942. Emi Siao, Fang, Hsiao Wen, Lu Hsun, May Fourth, Ting Ling, Yao Hsin-nung (XI); Smedley (XII).

SONGS, REVOLUTIONARY. Li Huan-chih (XI).

SOVIET CRITICISM. 1964-66 (XLI).

'THE DREAM OF THE RED CHAMBER'. Ho Chi-fang, Hsu Min, Mao Tun (XI); Prusek (XV).

'THE SCHOLARS'. Kral (XV).

TRADITION AND INNOVATION. Lu Hsun, Mao Tun (XI); Prusek (XV).

TU FU. Feng Chih (XI).

YU TA-FU. Dolezalova-Vlckova (XV).

## X.  Chronological

(Most materials available in English re-present positions of the Party or debates of Party policy, and so are organized here by date of appearance.)

MAO TSE-TUNG: THE YENAN FORUMS (1942) AND AFTER. Mao Tse-Tung On Art and Liter-ature, Peking, 1960. The Yenan Talks, still the guideline; Myth and Reality; The May Fourth Movement; New-Democratic Culture; On Letting a Hundred Flowers Blossom; On Literary Style; Campaign for Education and Culture; Letter About Poetry. - See Goodman (XII).

_____, Five Documents on Literature and Art. PekR, June 2, 1967, 5-8. Not included above. Revising the old operas (1944); the need for positive heroes in films and for vigilance in Marxist criticism (1951); on a Marxist attitude toward classics like 'The Dream Of the Red Chamber' (1954); on the need for a change in the cultural bureaucracy (1963, 1964).

1st ALL-CHINA CONFERENCE OF WRITERS AND ARTISTS (1950). The People's New Literature, Peking, 1950. Speeches by Chou En-Lai, Kuo Mo-jo, Mao Tun, Chou Yang.

CHOU YANG, "The Practice of Mao Tse-Tung's Thought in Chinese Art and Literature," ChL, Autumn 1951, 5-18. Lecture de-livered at Central Institute of Liter-ature. Published as keynote article in ChL's initial issue. Important as ear-ly affirmation and application of Yenan Forum principles.

_____, "The Reform and Development of Chinese Opera," ChL, 1953 #2, 23-37. Concluding speech of 1st National Fes-tival of Classical and Folk Drama, Peking, Nov 14, 1952.

MAO TUN, "Remould Our Thought To Serve the Masses," ChL, Spring, 1953, 13-25.

HU CHIAO-MU, "On the Ideological Remould-ing of Writers and Artists," ChL, Spring 1953, 5-12.

MAO TUN, "New Realities and New Tasks," ChL, 1954 #1, 1-23. Report to 2nd Con-ference of Chinese Writers.

TING LING, "Life and Creative Writing," ChL, 1954 #3, 152-158. Describes writ-er's imperative to escape bourgeois isolation and "settle down among the masses" if he is to escape stagnation.

2nd COUNCIL MEETING OF THE UNION OF CHI-NESE WRITERS (1956). ChL, 1956 #3, 203-205. illus. Report.

CHOU YANG, "Building a Socialist Litera-ture," ChL, 1956 #4, 198-222. Speech to 2nd Council Meeting. Review of successfully-concluded battle against "the Hu Feng clique" which spoke of "wounds of spiritual servitude" among the people and demanded "sincerity" in writing. Chou also warns against "a very injurious and fairly wide-spread fault in our literary creation - an inclination to create stereotyped plots and characters." All the same "writers should know and respect govern-ment and Party policy....Literature which departs from policy abandons its stand of serving the current political struggles."

MAO TUN, "The Key Problems in Art and Literature," ChL, 1956 #4, 223-228. Speech to 2nd Council Meeting. Notes growing disinterest of populace in the new literature, theatre, etc. The Hun-dred Flowers campaign, he says, will rectify this. "We must make room for various schools to exist in the world of art and literature, and give them the chance to stand the test of free discussion and mutual competition.... While we encourage and give publicity to the creative method of socialist realism, at the same time, we feel strongly that each writer should be entirely free to choose his own creative method, the one that suits him best."

LU TING-YI, <u>Let a Hundred Flowers Blossom, A Hundred Schools of Thought Contend</u>, Peking, 1957. Speech delivered by Director of Propaganda Section of Party CC on May 26, 1956. Launched the diversification policy in aesthetics.

CHEN CHI-TUNG, Chen Ya-Ting, Ma Han-Ping and Lu Leh, "Our Views on Contemporary Literature and Art," <u>ChL</u>, 1957 #3, 195-197. From 'People's Daily', Jan 7, 1957. Views results of Hundred Flowers campaign with alarm.

CHEN LIAO, "Some Comments On the Views of Chen Chi-Tung and Others," <u>ChL</u>, 1957 #3, 198-201. From 'People's Daily', Mch 1, 1957. Declares the backsliding assertions false.

MAO TUN, "Oppose Doctrinaire and Petty-Bourgeois Thinking," <u>ChL</u>, 1957 #3, 184-187. From 'People's Daily', Mch 18, 1957. Calls position of Chen Chi-Tung doctrinaire.

CHANG TIEN-YI, "Writing About Contradictions," <u>ChL</u>, 1957 #3, 210-213. From 'People's Daily', Mch 19, 1957. Implicitly accepting that a socialist society is permeated with contradictions, the author tries to clarify problems of viewpoint that confront writers.

CHOU YANG, "Answers to 'Wen Wei Pao' Correspondents' Questions," <u>ChL</u>, 1957 #3, 188-194. From 'People's Daily', Apr 9, 1957. Central policy clarification. "We know truth can only grow out of the struggle against error.... We should not try to prevent people from seeing the seamy side of things, but help them to see it in its true light."

'WEN TI PAO' EDITORIAL, <u>ChL</u>, 1957 #3, 202-209. From 'Literary Gazette', Apr 14, 1957. Attack on opponents of the Hundred Flowers.

CHU KUANG-CHIEN, "My Understanding," <u>ChL</u>, 1957 #4, 171-174. Author is elderly professor of literature at Peking University, a former follower of Croce's

aesthetics. Relates how Yenan Forum Talks "were nothing short of a club, a club that hit hard and accurately"knocking props out from under "my whole subjective idealist and bohemian literary theories."

CHOU YANG, "The October Revolution and the Task of Building a Socialist Culture," <u>ChL</u>, 1958 #1, 123-129. Instances of "rightist" and "bourgeois" viewpoints unintentionally released in the Hundred Flowers campaign.

SHAO CHUAN-LIN, "The Struggle Between Two Trends in Literature," <u>ChL</u>, 1958 #1, 130-141. The famed writers Ting Ling, Chen Chi-hsia, and Feng Hsueh-feng named as an "anti-Party clique," chief propagators of "bourgeois individualism." The immediate task is to "smash the anti-Party cliques within the Party, strengthen the Party spirit of our writers...and set the relationship between the Party and literature in a proper perspective." Details of a "carefully laid plot;" in <u>ChL</u>, 1958 #3, 153-161, description of a special issue of 'Literary Gazette' issued to document "treasonous" viewpoint held by named authors during bleak Yenan days in 1942.

YAO WEN-YUAN, "Revisionist Ideas in Literature," <u>ChL</u>, 1958 #2, 108-116. Further polemic against "bourgeois intellectuals."

CHOU YANG, "A Great Debate On the Literary Front," <u>ChL</u>, 1958 #3, 107-135; also published as <u>A Great Debate On the Literary Front</u>, Peking, 1958. Revised, expanded text of speech to Communist Section of Chines Writers Union, Sept 16, 1957. Once more systematically attacks Ting Ling, Feng Hsueh-feng, Chen Chi-hsia and all who have a"longing for the past " and refuse to "subordinate individual interests to group interest" and "be loyal to the people's cause under any circumstances."

"WRITERS AND ARTISTS FORGE AHEAD", <u>ChL</u>, 1958 #4, 139-140. Report on new Great Leap Forward campaign in culture. Writers and others tightening production schedules and planning shorter, more up-to-date works while many go to the country to learn the conditions of labor.

KUO MO-JO, "Romanticism and Realism," <u>PekR</u>, July 15, 1958, 7-11. abdgd. From 'Hongqi', July 1, 1958. Mao's life and

literary style as supreme example of
realism and romanticism forged into
unity.

1st AFRO-ASIAN WRITERS CONFERENCE (TASH-
KENT, 1958).  See: Ralph Parker, "The
Afro-Asian Writers Conference," NWR,
Jan 1959, 16-21.  Report with excerpts
of speeches. - See also:

CHOU YANG, "Free Culture From Colonialism," PekR, Oct 21, 1958, 15-16. abdgd.
Speech to Afro-Asian Writers Conference.  Analyzes technique of cultural
colonialism, condemns "irresponsible"
Asians and Africans such as the "shame-
less" Lin Yu-tang, prolific populariz-
er of Chinese culture to the West.

SHAO CHUAN-LIN, "Chinese Literature in
1958," ChL, 1959 #1, 7-15.  Report on
first year of Great Leap Forward in
culture, in the countryside in particular.

MAO TUN, "Rambling Notes On Literature,"
ChL, 1959 #1, 206-229; #2, 183-195;
#3, 147-166; #4, 118-136.  In purpose
a reconsideration of Hundred Flowers
episode.  In effect an historical inquiry into role of realism and ideology in literature.  The first install-
ments view struggle between realism
and "anti-realism" in Chinese past and
link latter with the exploiting classes.  Third installment considers emergence of modernism from classicism in
French literature.  Fourth discusses
the real and ideal in literature.

LIN MO-HAN, "Raise Higher the Banner of
Mao-Tse-tung's Thought on Literature
and Art," ChL, Apr 1960, 106-119; May,
93-109.  Also published as Raise Higher the Banner of Mao Tse-tung's Thought
On Art and Literature, Peking, 1961.
The Vice-Minister of Culture offers a
theory of progress from Marx to Lenin
to Mao within aesthetics: there were
no genuinely proletarian writers in
Marx and Engel's day, so their demands
upon writers had to remain quite limited while "in Lenin's day" a Party program for demanding proletarian literature "could be done."  Mao "creatively
expands" the demand since "Lenin did
not have time" to provide "the thorough solution of these problems."  Yenan
Forum Talks are "a complete scientific
treatise on Marxist literary and art
principles."

LIN FENG, "Carry Out the Cultural Revolution in a Big Way, Help the Workers and

Peasants Become Well Educated and the
Intellectuals Become Labouring People,"
PekR, June 21, 1960, 14-18; June 28,
19-22.  Speech by member of CC to National Conference of Outstanding Groups
and Individuals In Socialist Construction In the Fields of Education, Culture, Health, Physical Culture and
Journalism.

3rd CONGRESS OF CHINESE LITERATURE AND
ART WORKERS (Peking, 1960).  Report in
ChL, Oct 1960, 65-71.  See also:

LU TING-YI, "Greetings to Writers' and
Artists' Congress," PekR, July 26,1960,
6-8.  Also: ChL, Oct 1960, 3-11.  Con-
veys views of CC to the Congress.

CHOU YANG, "The Path of Socialist Literature and Art In Our Country," ChL, Oct
1960, 12-64.  Also in PekR, Sept 20,
1960, 6-15; Sept 27, 15-24.  Report to
3rd Congress of Chinese  Literature and
and Art  Workers, July 22, 1960.  "A
summing up of our experiences" including
results of sending intelligentsia into
the fields and factories.  Current view
of Hundred Flowers campaign especially
as it affected diversification of styles
and themes.  The function of Revolutionary Romanticism.

MAO TUN, "Reflect the Age of the Socialist Leap Forward, Promote the Leap Forward of the Socialist Age," ChL, Nov
1960, 3-32; Dec, 12-40.  First part
surveys literary accomplishments in
light of Party demands.  Second part
discusses Romanticism as a Maoist aesthetic requirement and as a current in
Chinese literary history; problems of
portraying heroic characters without
sacrifice of sincerity.

2nd ASIAN-AFRICAN WRITERS CONFERENCE
(CAIRO, FEBRUARY 12-15, 1962).  Report
in ChL, May 1962, 84-92.  See also:

MAO TUN, "For the Glorious Future of
Afro-Asian Literature in a Tempestuous
Age!" ChL, May 1962, 78-84.  Speech to
2nd Asian-African Writers Conference.
Problems of doing away with cultural
colonialism.

'HONGQI' EDITORIAL, "The Intellectuals'
Way Forward," PekR, May 25, 1962, 5-9.
On 20th anniversary of Mao's Yenan
Forum Talks his policy is praised and
reaffirmed - with particular reference
to "modern revisionists" who equate
"petty-bourgeois self-expression" with
Marxism-Leninism.

LI SHU-CHIH, "Revisionism In Art and Literature," PekR, Feb 8, 1963, 11-15. A 'Hongqi' article that attacks praise lavished by "modern revisionists" on "writing honestly." This emphasis on sincerity is bourgeois since it is treated outside a class struggle context. "Revolutionary writers should realize that real honesty for them means to extoll the new people with wholehearted enthusiasm and describe their struggles....They should never lose their bearings because of difficulties arising in their creative work due to the fact that they did not have a rich enough experience of life or for the time being lack literary skill."

3rd NATIONAL COMMITTEE OF ALL-CHINA FEDERATION OF LITERARY AND ART CRITICS, PekR, May 31, 1963, 7-9. Report of proceedings, summaries of speeches, resolutions. See also ChL, Aug 1963, 3-10. Summary of Chou En-lai's speech and of unanimous resolution condemning "degeneration in the ranks of world socialist literature and art."

CHIN LI, "Revolutionary Art and Literature: Their Educative Role," PekR, July 5, 1963, 23-25. Against revisionist approaches.

FANG CHI, Meeting of Executive Committee of Afro-Asian Writers Conference, Bali, July 16-20, 1963. PekR, Aug 30, 1963, 24-26. Sino-Soviet split reverberations.

CHANG KUANG-NIEN, "An Example of Modern Revisionism In Art," PekR, Dec 13, 1963, 6-13. Critique of films and statements of Grigori Chukhrai, director of 'Clear Skies' and other Soviet films. "His main philosophical concept and the philosophical foundation of the 'Soviet new wave' he advocates is abstract humanism with extreme individualism at its core....a thoroughly idealistic and bourgeois theory of human nature."

CHIANG CHING, "On the Revolution In Peking Opera," PekR, May 12, 1967, 13-15. First publication of speech given at Forum Of Theatrical Workers, July 1964. - Visit of Mao to reformed Peking operas, PekR, June 23 and June 30, 1967. illus.

LU TING-YI, "For More and Finer Peking Operas On Contemporary Themes," PekR, June 12, 1964, 7-9. Vice-Premier's remarks against "ghost operas and other harmful operas" which "helped feudal superstitions to raise their ugly heads" constituting "an unbridled attack against socialism by the bourgeoisie and the feudal forces....Peking opera needs a new revolutionary flower ....new historical plays."

'HONGQI' EDITORIAL, "A Great Revolution On the Cultural Front," PekR, July 3, 1964, 5-8. Against Krushchev revisionism, praise of drive for "revolutionary Peking operas on contemporary themes."- See also, Yuan Shih-hai, "Peking Opera Festival," ibid, July 24, 1964, 21-24, for the view of an opera performer.

PENG CHEN, "Peking Opera To Serve Socialism," PekR, Aug 7, 1964, 6-11. Member of the Politburo in keynote address to 1964 Festival of Peking Opera on Contemporary Themes, Peking, July 1. - See also: "Festival Discussions," ibid, 30-31.

KO CHING-SHIH, "A Flourishing Theatre To Serve the Socialist Economic Base," PekR, Aug 28, 1964, 14-23; Sept 11, 1964, 20-26. Member of Politburo in speech to East China Modern Drama Festival, on theatre reform.

LU TING-YI, "Cultural Revolution of China's National Minorities," PekR, Dec 4, 1964, 22-24. - See also ibid, Dec 18, 1964, 30-31, for report on Tibetan and Sinkiang arts.

'WENYI BAO' EDITORIAL, "'Writing About Middle Characters' - A Bourgeois Literary Notion," PekR, Dec 18, 1964, 16-21; Dec 25, 1964, 18-22. Interprets Engels on tendency. Defense of "heroic literary images of workers, peasants and soldiers" as serving social construction better than can depiction of transitional or average human types.

3rd ASIAN-AFRICAN WRITERS CONFERENCE (JAKARTA). Advance remarks on plans and nature of conference, SL, 1964 #8, 175-177. - For the actual conference, see: 1967 (XLI).

'JIEFANGJUN BAO' EDITORIAL, "Hold High the Great Red Banner of Mao Tse-Tung's Thinking; Actively Participate In the Great Socialist Cultural Revolution," PekR, Apr 29, 1966, 5-10. The Army, under leadership of Lin Piao, as chief means to "transform our literary and art criticism into daggers and hand-

grenades....we still have a fairly
large number of bourgeois intellectuals...their methods of fighting us
have become increasingly insidious,
indirect and underhand....we find only
a small number of good or basically
sound works truly praising our revolutionary heroes, serving the workers,
peasants and soldiers, and serving
socialism".

HSIANG HUNG and Wei Ning, Some Questions
Concerning Modern Revisionist Litera-
ture In the Soviet Union, Foreign Lan-
guages Press: Peking, 1966. Includes
"Selected Statements by Sholokhov, The
Renegade Author," compiled by Chang
Chun, and "The True Features Of the
Renegade Sholokhov," by Tsai Hui. The
Soviet literary establishment seen as
capitulating to American capitalism.

LU HSUN AND THE CULTURAL REVOLUTION.
PekR, Nov 4, 1966, 6-23; reprinted in
ChL, 1967 #1, 4-48. Speeches at a
commemorative meeting of Oct 31, 1966,
attended by Chou En-lai, which claim
Lu Hsun's authority for the Cultural
Revolution. Speakers include Yao Wen-
yuan, Kuo Mo-jo, Chen Po-ta, two Red
Guards, and Lu Hsun's wife. - For a
Russian counter-estimate of Lu Hsun's
meaning, see CDSP, Oct 19, 1966, 23.

CHIN CHING-MAI, "Break With 'Self' and
Foster Devotion To the Public, Write
For the Revolution," ChL, 1967 #2,
92-112. The author of 'The Song of
Ouyang Hai', a novel highly esteemed
by the Cultural Revolution, describes
his method.

YAO WEN-YUAN, "On the Counter-revolutionary Double-Dealer Chou Yang,"
ChL, 1967 #3, 24-71. Exposure of the
former cultural chief's opposition to
Mao's instructions during sixteen
years. - For the eradication of Chou's
influence upon the All-Union Artists'
Union, see Chao Hui, "An Art Program
Serving the Restauration of Capitalism," ChL, 1967 #4, 122-136.

ON THE REACTIONARY NATURE OF WESTERN AND
RUSSIAN LITERATURE. Survey, Apr 1967,
64-66. A collection of views in the
Chinese press, compiled by 'Literaturnaya Gazeta'. Shakespeare, Balzac,
Stendhal, Hugo, Beethoven, classical
ballet, Pushkin, Tolstoy, Gogol, Belinsky.

MAO TSE-TUNG'S THOUGHT VICTORIOUS IN THE
THEATRE. ChL, 1967 #3, 1-23. Details

of how Chiang Ching defeated the reactionary policies of Chou Yang and made
genuinely Maoist ballet, theatre, opera
and symphonic music possible. - See
also ChL, 1967 #4, 97-110, for sculpture.

25th ANNIVERSARY OF MAO'S 'TALKS AT THE
YENAN FORUM ON LITERATURE AND ART'.
PekR, May 26, 1967, 18-41. Speeches
by Chen Po-ta and Chi Pen-yu and a Declaration from a mass rally on May 23,
and laudatory newspaper editorials.
For Mao's thought, the eradication of
bourgeois cultural vestiges, and literary and art criticism "by the masses
of workers, peasants and soldiers" as
against an elite.

SEMINAR OF AFRO-ASIAN WRITERS' BUREAU,
Peking, May 31-June 5, 1967. PekR,
June 9, 1967, 16-24; June 16, 1967,
6-7, 18-25. Declarations supporting
Mao's thought and the Cultural Revolu-
tion, after six days of studying the
Yenan Talks; speeches by Kuo Mo-jo,
Chi Pen-yu.

ACCLAIM FOR NEWLY PUBLISHED MAO TEXTS.
PekR, June 2, 1967, 17-21. These are
the Five Documents (see Mao, above).
Editorials praise them as showing Mao's
long-term struggle for the correct
cultural attitude, at last being won
by the Cultural Revolution of the
masses.

MAO TSE-TUNG, ed, "Summary Of the Forum
On the Work In Literature and Art In
the Armed Forces With Which Comrade
Lin Piao Entrusted Comrade Chiang
Ching," PekR, June 2, 1967, 10-16, 21-
27, 33. A basic document in launching
the Cultural Revolution against recal-
citrant bureaucrats, it represents the
views of Lin Piao and of Mao's wife
Chiang Ching as developed at a Shanghai
armed forces forum, Feb 2-20, 1966.
Three times revised by Mao himself.
Several editorials give the background.

THE COUNTER-REVOLUTIONARY POSITION OF LIU
SHAU-CHI IN THE ARTS, PekR, June 30,
1967, 33-36. Activities of the "top
person taking the road to capitalism"
and author of 'How To Be a Good Commu-
ist'.

## XI.   Authors

A. H, "Revolution and Poetry in China,"
DWSup, Oct 23, 1926.

'ARCHIV ORIENTALNI' (Prague), for specialized Orientalist articles and book reviews, chiefly in English.

CHANG AN-CHIH, "Perspective In Chinese Painting," ChL, 1964 #5, 105-113. illus. Sensitive discussion of old and new uses of Chinese painting technique by an artist and teacher of traditional painting at the Central Academy of Fine Arts.

CHU KWANG-TSIEN, "The Problem of 'Formal Beauty' In Recent Discussions In China," EH, May 1964, 12-16. Report on major positions taken and some of the analysis.

"DISCUSSION ON AESTHETICS," ChL, 1957 #3, 214-216. Report and summary of significant academic debate whether beauty is real or imagined.

EMI SIAO, "Chinese Revolutionary Literature," IL, 1934 #5, 121-133.

Y FANG, "The Recent Chinese Theatre," ITh, #3 (1933), 16-19. Activity among revolutionary groups.

FENG CHIH, "Tu Fu: A Short Biography," M&M, Aug 1962, 7-22.

FENG YUAN-CHUN, A Short History of Classical Chinese Literature, Peking, 1958.

HO CHI-FANG, "On 'The Dream of the Red Chamber'," ChL, Jan 1963, 65-86. Abridgement of monograph by famous poet and critic who heads Institute of Literary Research at Academy of Sciences.

HSIAO WEN, "Drama For a Great Cause," ChL, 1965 #11, 103-109. Anti-Japanese Resistance theatre.

HSU MIN, "'The Dream of the Red Chamber' and Its Author," PekR, Oct 25, 1963, 25-28.

LI HUAN-CHIH, "Revolutionary Songs In China," ChL, 1965 #9, 97-105. Historical account, with examples.

LU HSUN, Essays. In his Selected Works, Peking, 1957-60, vols. II, III, IV. The major pre-Revolution Marxist cultural figure.

_____, A Brief History of Chinese Fiction, Peking, 1959.

_____, "The Historical Development of Chinese Fiction," ChL, 1958 #5, 103-117;

#6, 135-153. Lectures delivered at a Sian summer school in 1924. As his 'Brief History of Chinese Fiction' dates from just before, the lectures may be regarded as a synopsis and, on some points, an expansion.

_____, SEE ALSO: Chu Chiu-Pai, "Writing For a Great Cause; Preface To the Selected Essays of Lu Hsun," ChL, 1959 #5, 40-68. Dated April 8, 1933. Author was a pioneer of the May Fourth movement and a prominent early Communist (once Secretary of the CC). His intent is to point out "the value of these essays and Lu Hsun's important position in the history of the battle of ideas."

Feng Hsueh-feng, "Lu Hsun: His Life and Thought," ChL, Spring 1952, 139-160.

_____, "The Trail Blazed by Lu Hsun," ChL, 1956 #4, 33-42. illus. Creative method and development.

Prusek, J.  See (XV).

Reminiscences by the literary scholar Tang Tao, Lu Hsun's wife Hsu Kuang-ping, Prof. Li Chi-yeh, Lu Hsun's student and later editor Sun Fu-yuan. ChL, Sept 1961, 96-123. illus.

Huang Sung-K'ang, Lu Hsun and the New Culture Movement of Modern China, Amsterdam, 1957. Perceptive, indispensable volume.

Charles Humboldt, "The Art of Lu Hsun," M&M, July 1957, 10-30.

Harriet C. Mills, "Lu Hsun and the Communist Party," ChQ, Oct-Dec 1960, 17-27. "As with his European counterparts Lu Hsun's sympathy grew out of desperation and remained more emotional than intellectual....intellectually he had not become a Marxist."

Pearl Hsia Chen, The Social Thought of Lusin, 1881-1936, unpublished Ph.D. dissertation, Univ. of Chicago, 1953. biblio.

KUO HAN-CHENG, "On the Adaptation of China's Classical Drama," ChL, Dec 1962, 100-108. Author is head of Research Institute, Academy of Chinese Traditional Drama. Thorough discussion.

MAO TSE-TUNG. See (X).

MAO TUN, "What We Know of Tsao Hsueh-chin," ChL, 1964 #5, 85-104. Commemorative essay on 200th anniversary of death of author of 'Dream of the Red Chamber'.

_____, See also (X).

_____, SEE: Vincent Y. C. Shih, "Mao Tun: The Critic," ChQ #19 (1964), 84-98; #20 (1964), 128-162. - See also Galik (XV).

MAY FOURTH CULTURAL MOVEMENT, ChL, 1959 #5, 153-163. Retrospective articles by Mao Tun, Cheng Po-chi, Hsu Kuang-ping. - See also: Huang Sung-K'ang, Lu Hsun and the New Culture Movement of Modern China, Amsterdam, 1957.

MEI LAN-FANG, "My Life On the Stage," ChL, Nov 1961, 3-35; also in EH, Sept 1961, 11-29. illus. The great opera star.

_____, SEE ALSO: Yen Yung, in PekR, Aug 17, 1962, 17-20. Mei Lan-Fang's life and views recounted in detail.

"ON NATURE POETRY," ChL, Nov 1962, 101-106. A controversy whether nature poetry has a class character.

"ON THE QUESTION OF BEAUTY," ChL, Aug 1960, 112-120; Oct 1961, 92-99. Report of ongoing debate in literary, art and philosophical circles.

PIN CHIH, "Peasant Poets and Their Songs," ChL, 1965 #10, 101-107.

TING LING, Account of Her Kidnapping. IL, 1933 #3, 158-159. illus.

TSUNG PAI-HUA, "Abstraction and Reality in Chinese Art," ChL, Dec 1961, 82-86; also in EH, Feb 1962, 46-48. The peculiarly Chinese features of this problem.

YAO HSIN-NUNG, "The Eve of a United Cultural Front In China," Life and Letters To-Day, Winter 1937, 26-28.

## XII. Appendix

BONOSKY, Phillip, Dragon Pink On Old White, Marzani & Munsell: 1963.

BOORMAN, Howard L, "The Literary World of Mao Tse-Tung," ChQ, Jan-Mch 1963, 15-38. On cultural controls.

BRAGA, Anthony, "'Ayiguli' - A New Operatic Heroine," EH, July 1966, 23-24. illus. Close account of a revolutionized Peking opera.

CHEN, Jerome, "Introduction to Mao's Poems," in his: Mao and the Chinese Revolution, Oxford: 1965, 315-319. Followed by translations of 37 poems. - For a Soviet view: Survey, Apr 1967, 188-190.

DEL VAYO, Julio Alvarez, China Triumphs, Monthly Review: 1964.

FOKKEMA, D. W., Literary Doctrine in China and Soviet Influence, 1956-1960, Mouton: The Hague, 1965

_____, "Chinese Criticism Of Humanism: Campaigns Against the Intellectuals, 1964-1965," ChQ, #26 (1966), 68-81.

GOLDMAN, Merle, Literary Dissent In Communist China, Harvard Univ: Cambridge, 1967. Relations of Party and particular writers in the 1940s and 1950s.

GOODMAN, Merle, "Writers' Criticism Of the Party in 1942," ChQ, Jan-Mch 1964, 205-228. Account of articles by revolutionary writers around the time of Mao's Yenan talks, and the Party reaction. Ting Ling, Lo Feng, Wan Shih-wei, Hsiao Chun, Ai Ching.

HSIA, C. T, A History Of Modern Chinese Fiction, 1917-1957, Yale: New Haven, 1961. - Critical review-essay by Z. Slupski, AO, XXXII (1964), 139-152.

HSIA, T. A., "Twenty Years After the Yenan Forum," ChQ, Jan-Mch 1963, 226-253. The propagation of Mao's views.

HUGHES, Richard, "Chinese Opera Walks the Party Line," N.Y. Times Magazine, Mch 21, 1965, 62-69. illus. Cites Party theory and results.

MA Szu-tsung, Interview with Douglas Robinson. N.Y. Times, Apr 13, 1967, 1, 4. illus. Violinist and President of

Central Academy of Music in Peking
describes his reasons for fleeing China during Red Guard upheaval.

_____, "Terror At the Hands Of the Red
Guard," Life, June 2, 1967, 22-29,
63-65. illus. Describes his many
former privileges and humiliation by
his own students.

MACFARQUHAR, Roderick, The Hundred Flowers Campaign and the Chinese Intellectuals, 1960.

MATTHEWS, Denis and Anna, "A New Chinese
Renaissance?" Arts and Sciences In
China, I i (Jan-Mch 1963), 20-24. How
aesthetic dictums are applied.

READ, Herbert, Art In China: A Report.
The Second Coming (New York), Jan 1965,
69-72. Various post-Revolution trends;
conflict facing traditionalist painters
as discussed by them. "The writers and
painters I met in China are fully conscious of the problems to which the revolution has given birth, and although
some of their solutions are too doctrinaire and even too naive, there is
a prevailing spirit of humility and
sincerity which holds great promise
for the future."

SMEDLEY, Agnes, "The Chinese Theatre In
the Trenches," DW, Oct 28, 1937, 9.

SNOW, Edgar, The Other Side of the River;
Red China Today, Random House: 1962.

TANNENBAUM, Gerald, "The New Ballet in
China," EH, Oct 1965, 7-19. illus.
Study of the introduction of Western
ballet with national communist content.
- Other articles on related topics,
also in EH.

_____, "Culture For China's Hinterlands,"
EH, Aug 1966, 6-11. First hand account
of the exemplary Ulanmuchi, a travelling
cultural unit.

_____, "Another Triumph In Chinese Bal-
let: 'The White-Haired Girl'," EH,
Dec 1966, 21-29. illus. Close, vivid
account. - See also PekR, May 20, 1966,
25-27.

WALZER, Michael, "When The Hundred Flowers
Withered," Dis, Autumn 1958, 360-374.

YOUNG LUN-CHANG, Literary Reflections Of
Social Change In China, 1914-1949,
Ph.D. Dissertation, Univ. of Nebraska,
1964.

# CUBA

## XIII.  Authors

1st NATIONAL WRITERS AND ARTISTS CONGRESS,
Havana, August 18-22, 1961.  Republic
of Cuba.  Ministry of Foreign Affairs.
Cultural Bulletin, I iv (1961). 32 pp.
[cc]  Includes: Organizing document.
Talk by Fidel Castro at a preparatory
meeting, in which he urges the "opportunity" for intellectuals and artists
to "do their share" in "merciless war
against lack of culture" which "is the
work of this generation."  Declares the
revolution will trust and count upon
"honest writers and artists who are not
revolutionaries." abdgd.  Carlos Rafael
Rodriguez in another preparatory talk
says "the revolution forces all of us
to commit ourselves" to "communicating
with the masses."  Remarks by Nazim
Hikmet, Vincentina Antuna, Rene Depestre, Roberto Fernandez Retamar.  The
Congress: speeches by Vincentina Antuna, Nicolas Guillen, Oswaldo Dorticos
(abdgd), Alejo Carpentier, Jose Portuondo.  Statutes.  Final resolution.
Officers.

_____, SEE ALSO: Republic of Cuba.  Min-
istry of Foreign Relations, The Revolution and Cultural Problems in Cuba,
Havana: 1962.  Contains the addresses
by Castro, Guillen, Dorticos.

CARPENTIER, Alejo, "Variations On a Cuban
Theme," Americas, Feb 1950, 20-23, 38-
39.  illus.  Cuban efforts to evolve a
national music style in the decades
after Spain's withdrawal.

_____, Interview.  In: Luis Harss and
Barbara Dohmann, Into the Mainstream,
Harper & Row: 1967, 37-67.

CASA DE LAS AMERICAS, COMMITTEE OF WRITERS,
"Declaration," NG, May 13, 1967, 6.
Call for a tri-continental meeting of
anti-imperialist writers.  Cites US
efforts to co-opt and silence Latin
American authors.  Declares "the most
unrestricted creative freedom is the
true capital of the revolution."
Signed by E. Carballo, J. Cortazar, R.
Dalton, R. Depestre, E. Desnoes, R. F.
Retamar, A. Fornet, M. Galich, L. Otero,
G. Pogolotti, A. Rama, M. V. Llosa, D.
Vinas, J. Zalamea.

CASTRO, Fidel, "To the Intellectuals,"
quoted in: Jose A. Portuondo, "The
Cuban Revolution and the Intellectual,"

NT, Sept 2, 1964, 20-23. "What rights do writers and artists have, whether revolutionary or non-revolutionary? All rights if for the revolution, none if against the revolution....Does that mean that we intend to tell people what to write? No. Let each write what he likes. If what he writes is no good, that is his affair....And let each choose the form that suits him, let each express freely the idea he wants to." - See also, above.

_____, On Krushchev's Speech On Art and Literature of March 23, 1963. I. F. Stone's Weekly, Apr 15, 1963, 2. From 'Le Monde', Mch 23, 1963. "When Krushchev criticizes abstract painting, the satellites here ask me to forbid abstract painting. But I tell them our adversaries are capitalism and imperialism, not the abstract painters."

_____, Interview With Lee Lockwood. Lee Lockwood, Castro's Cuba, Cuba's Fidel, Macmillan: 1967, 126-128, 180. The work of revolution as an art; the arts of Cuba as shaping the free, happy and thinking man, in the broadest sense.

DORTICOS, Oswaldo, Remarks to Marc Schleifer. MR, Apr 1964, 655-656. The Cuban president discusses regime's attitudes toward artistic freedom and abstract art. - See also, 1st National Writers and Artists Congress.

GUEVARA, Alfredo, "The Cuban Cinema," NT, July 26, 1961, 16-17. Background and operation of the new cinema.

GUEVARA, Che, "Socialism and Man In Cuba," Progressive Labor, Dec 1965, 83-95. The importance of art to creating a new man; the absence of such revolutionary art in Cuba; capitalism's making of a "free" debased art; the faults of Socialist Realism and the advance of present art over 19th Century realism; the need for artistic liberty to permit an emergence of revolutionary creativity in art and life.

GUILLEN, Nicolas, "Our America," NF, IV i (Spring 1955), 17-18. View of peace and imperialism.

_____, Speech to 1st National Writers and Artists Congress. See above.

_____, Speech to 2nd National Writers and Artists Congress, Havana, August 1963. MQ(T), Spring 1964, 67-70. The famed

poet discusses artistic freedom and potential sources of revolutionary creation in contact with working people.

_____, SEE ALSO: Michael Gold, Travelling Cuba with Guillen. DW, May 22, 1939, 7. Popular enthusiam for Guillen vividly recounted.

    Angel Augier, "The Cuban Poetry of Nicolas Guillen," Phylon, XII (1951), 29-36. Leading Cuban literary critic reviews the poet's career, its racial and class repercussions.

MARINELLO, Juan, "Picasso - A Timeless Artist," ACA, May 1944, 4-7; reprinted in NM, June 13, 1944, 23-28. An appreciation.

_____, "Militant Art of Jose Marti," V.O.K.S., 1953 #79, 127-130. illus. Marti's role in Latin American life and literature.

_____, SEE ALSO: Joseph Freeman, "Cuba's Famous Exile," DWSup, May 9, 1937, 4; May 16, 9. His career and views gathered from an interview.

PORTUONDO, Jose A, "A New Art For Cuba," Pa'lante (New York), I i (1962), 48-52. Speech to 1st Congress of Cuban Artists and Writers.

_____, "The Cuban Revolution and the Intellectual," NT, Sept 2, 1964, 20-23. From 'Cuba Socialista', June, 1964. Elaborates Castro's "To the Intellectuals." Describes loyalty of most writers and artists to the revolution.

RODRIGUEZ, J. M. On Cuban Revolutionary Poetry. IL, 1934 #6, 135-138.

## XIV.  Appendix

ANONYMOUS, "Pillaging of Cuban Art Collections," Art Journal, XXII (1962-63), 106. Purportedly a disclosure smuggled from Cuba; the island's most valuable art heirlooms are said to be in transit to Eastern Europe while artists and writers are subjugated.

BROOK, Peter, "The Cuban Enterprise," Sight and Sound, Spring 1961, 78-79. illus. ICAIC's cinema activities.

COHEN, J.M, "Culture In Cuba," NLR, #34 (1965), 78-81.

GAMEZ, Tana de, "A Cuban Literary Letter," Minority Of One, June 1965, 15-18. illus.

_____, "The Position Of the Artist In Cuba Today," Art News, Sept 1964, 36-39, 61. illus.

_____, "Alicia Alonso and the National Ballet of Cuba," Dance Magazine, July 1964, 30-35. illus. Really on general cultural developments under the Revolution.

HOFMANN, Paul, "Literary Letter From Cuba," N.Y. Times Book Review, Mch 7, 1965. - Answer by Tana de Gamez, ibid, Apr 18, 1965, 18.

KREBS, Sharon, "Art In Cuba; A Talk With Jose Delarra," Weapon, #1 (1965), 68-69. The outlook of artists of middle-class roots.

MILLS, C. Wright, "Culture In Cuba," in his Listen Yankee, Ballantine paperback: 1960, 133-150. Education and the arts as discussed by the revolutionaries.

SARTRE, Jean-Paul, see (XIX).

SUTHERLAND, Elizabeth, First Congress of Cuban Writers and Artists. Nation, Nov 4, 1961, 358-361. Eyewitness report.

## CZECHOSLOVAKIA

### Topic Index

AESTHETICS. Sindelar. Bradac (XVI).

ARCHITECTURE. Teige, Weiss.

CINEMA. Liehm, Weiss.

JAZZ. 'Rude Bravo'.

KAFKA, F. Baum, Fuchs, Goldstucker. Garaudy, Sartre (XIX); Fischer, Mayer (XXI); Pascal, Spender (XXIII); Hauser, Lukacs (XXVII); Suchkov (XLVI); Soviet (XLIX); Baxandall, Burgum, Finkelstein, LeRoy (LVI); Auerbach, Goodman, Woodcock (LXII).

NOVEL, POST-STALIN. Hajek.

TEACHING OF LITERATURE. Milner (XVI); Matthiessen (LXII).

TELEVISION. Lederer.

THEATRE. Burian.

### XV. Authors

BAUM, Oskar, Franz Kafka. In: Angel Flores, ed, The Kafka Problem, 1946, 25-31. A writer, long intimate with Kafka, offers reasons for believing "Kafka's world of ideas is not founded on a world-view of inescapable despair, as many assume," nor does it ignore the misery of the poor.

BURIAN, Emil F, Interview with Robert Muller. Theatre Newsletter, Oct 16, 1948, 5. The concept of a people's theatre and the plays he has staged.

_____, "My Aims In the Theatre," New Theatre (London), July 1947, 5. illus.

_____, SEE ALSO: E. Novak, "E. F. Burian and the D34 Theatre," ITh, 1934 #2, 34-36.

  Peter Noble, "Burian: Portrait Of a Fighter," New Theatre (London), Nov 1946, 19-21. illus.

  Jiri Weiss, Account of Burian's Production of 'Romeo and Juliet'. Theatre Today, I ii (1946), 5-7.

CAPEK, Abe, "The Development of Thomas Wolfe In the Light of His Letters," ZAA, X (1962), 162-178. "Wolfe was among the outstanding few whose artistic integrity and social criticism grew stronger and stronger, to the very end."

DOLEZALOVA-VLCKOVA, Anna, "Remarks On the Life and Work Of Yu Ta-Fu Up To 1930," Asian and African Studies (Bratislava), I (1965), 53-79.

FUCHS, Rudolf, "Social Awareness In Kafka," in: Angel Flores, ed, The Kafka Problem, 1946, 247-250. From 'Internationale Literatur'. Fuchs was Kafka's friend and a well-known poet.

GALIK, Marian, "A Comment On Two Studies [By Yeh Tzu-ming and F. V. Sorokin] Written On the Works Of Mao Tun," Asian and African Studies (Bratislava), I (1965), 81-101.

_____, "A Comment On Two Collections Of Mao Tun's Works," <u>AO</u>, XXXIII (1965), 614-638. An overview of Mao Tun's production, and the omissions in the Chinese and Japanese collections.

GOLDSTUCKER, Eduard, "The Problem of Franz Kafka," <u>EE</u>, Apr 1963, 29-30. abdgd. From 'Literaturni Noviny', Feb 16, 1963. Valid and invalid approaches to Kafka, by leading Czech authority.

_____, "Franz Kafka," <u>CL</u>, Sept 1963, 21-24. illus. Kafka's life and views.

_____, Symposium In Prague On the Question Of Decadence. <u>Streets</u>, May-June 1965, 46-55. With J.P. Sartre, Milan Kundera, Ernst Fischer.

HAJEK, Jiri, Speech to Conference of European Writers, Leningrad, Summer 1963. <u>NLR</u> #29 (Jan-Feb 1965), 19-22. Problems of the post-Stalin Socialist novel.

HRDLICKOVA, Vena, "The Professional Training of Chinese Storytellers and the Storytellers' Guilds," <u>AO</u>, XXXIII (1965), 225-248.

KALVODOVA, D, "The Origin and Character Of the Szechwan Theatre," <u>AO</u>, XXXIV (1966), 505-523.

KARVAS, Peter, Criticism of Mechanistic Views of Art In Society. <u>WMR</u>, Jan 1965, 93-98.

KOCMANOVA, Jessie, "Art and Revolution In the Poetry Of Hugh MacDiarmid," <u>PhPr</u>, V (1962), 218-225.

_____, "Two Uses Of the Dream-Form As a Means Of Confronting the Present With the National Past: William Morris and Svatopluk Cech," <u>Brno</u>, II, c. 68 (1960), 113-148.

_____, <u>The Poetic Maturing Of William</u> Morris, pub. as <u>Brno</u>, V (1964).

KRAL, Oldrich, "Several Artistic Methods In the Classic Chinese Novel 'Ju-lin wai-shih'," <u>AO</u>, XXXII (1964), 16-43. Structural analysis of the 18th century novel, in particular Wu Ching-tu's 'Scholars'. Comparisons with European techniques.

KUNDERA, Milan, Symposium In Prague On the Question of Decadence. <u>Streets</u>,

May-June 1965, 46-55. With J.P. Sartre, Ernst Fischer, Eduard Goldstucker.

LEDERER, Jiri, "Television Lights and Shadows," <u>Survey</u>, Apr 1966, 30-35. History of Czech television.

LIEHM, A.J, "Success On the Screen," <u>Survey</u>, Apr 1966, 12-20. History of Czech cinema and its current organization.

MACHALSKI, Franciszek, "New Poetry In Iran," <u>NO</u>, 1965 #2, 33-36.

NEUSTUPNY, J.V, A Sociological Linguistics. <u>AO</u>, XXXIII (1965), 83-92.

NOVAK, Miroslav, "A True Report of an Ego's World," <u>NO</u>, IV i (Feb 1965), 1-4. Modern Japanese literature.

NOVOMESKY, Laco, "On Artistic Freedom," <u>Tri-Quarterly</u>, Spring 1967, 189-197. An older Slovak socialist politician and poet, jailed for a time, propounds the arguments for artistic liberty.

POKORNY, Jaroslav, <u>Shakespeare In Czechoslovakia</u>, Prague, 1955.

PRAGUE NEWS LETTER. Source of continuing reportage on cultural events.

PRUSEK, Jaroslav, "Researches Into the Beginnings of the Chinese Popular Novel," <u>AO</u>, XI (1939), 91-132; XXIII (1955), 620-662. Surveys research by Lu Hsun. Offers own results to date.

_____, "The Importance of Tradition In Chinese Literature," <u>AO</u>, XXVI (1958), 212-223. Historical preponderance of traditional literary forms over individual innovations. Importance of this for recent Chinese literature. Realism in medieval Chinese folk literature.

_____, "The Realistic and Lyric Elements In the Chinese Medieval Story," <u>AO</u>, XXXII (1964), 4-15.

_____, "New Studies of the Chinese Colloquial Short Story," <u>AO</u>, XXV (1957), 452-499. Review of recent literature.

_____, "Subjectivism and Individualism In Modern Chinese Literature," <u>AO</u>, XXV (1957), 261-286. Results in Manchu and revolutionary-epoch literature of the breakdown of the feudal order.

_____, "History and Epics, In China and In the West," <u>NO</u>, Feb 1962, 1-8; also in <u>Diogenes</u>, Summer 1963, 20-43. Ancient Greek writing had the pacing of events, the exception, the special, the individual at its core; Chinese writing had the norm, the principle, the rule as its basis and only sought adequate stylistic expression.

_____, "The Realistic and Lyric Elements In the Chinese Medieval Short Story," <u>AO</u>, XXXII (1964), 4-15. Lecture given at Univ. of California at Berkeley, Apr 5, 1963. Draws on theories of V. Dneprov (XLVI) concerning historical causes for the mixing of genres, to analyze origins and nature of Chinese <u>hua-pen</u>, popular tales of the 12th-13th centuries.

_____, "A Confrontation Of Traditional Oriental Literature With Modern European Literature In the Context Of the Chinese Literary Revolution," <u>AO</u>, XXXII (1964), 365-375; also in <u>Acta Of the Ninth Congress Of the International Federation For Modern Languages and Literature</u>, New York Univ: 1965, 165-176. 20th century Chinese literary innovation.

_____, "Reality and Art In Chinese Literature," <u>AO</u>, XXXII (1964), 605-618. Speech given at Berlin Sinological Conference. The tendency to unsynthetic fact-recording in traditional, upper-class Chinese literature ('The Scholars') is continued in writing since the revolution. Favors the now-neglected trend of fantastic imagination in popular tales and the personal synthesizing emotion of "Dream Of the Red Chamber', employed in 1930s by Lu Hsun.

_____, ed, <u>Studies In Modern Chinese Literature</u>, Akademie-Verlag: Berlin, 1964. Especially the editor's introduction, pp. 1-43.

_____, SEE ALSO: Jaroslav Prusek: Bibliography, 1931-1956, <u>AO</u>, XXIV (1956), 347-355; Bibliography, 1956-1965, <u>AO</u>, XXXIV (1966), 574-586. - Also, A. Palat, "J. Prusek, Sexagenarian," <u>AO</u>, XXXIV (1966), 481-493. Biography.

'RUDE BRAVO' EDITORIAL, On Jazz. <u>EE</u>, Feb 1963, 25-27.

SIMKO, Jan, "Problems Of Contemporary Linguistics," <u>KN</u>, VIII (1961), 53-59.

_____, "'King Lear' and 'Timon Of Athens'," <u>PhPr</u>, VIII (1965), 320-342.

SINDELAR, Dusan, "Contemporary Czech Aesthetics," <u>JAAC</u>, XVIII (Sept 1959), 116-126. Author is lecturer at Charles University, Prague. Describes Pavlovian theory of Mirko Novak based on conditioned reflexes. Also the work of J. Volek, J. Mukarovsky, D. Sindelar, K. Chvatik, Nejedly.

STEPANIK, Karel, "Fact and Fiction In the Novels Of Daniel Defoe," <u>PhPr</u>, III (1960), 227-240.

_____, "The Reflections of Social Reality in Keats's Poems and Letters," Masarykova Universita, Brno; Filosoficka Fakulta. Spisy. Cislo 55. <u>Brno Studies In English</u> (Prague), vol. I (1959), 69-102. Locates Keats with the progressive or revolutionary Romantics, finding him close in this respect to Byron and Shelley.

_____, "The Idea Of Progress in Keats's 'Hyperion'," <u>PhPr</u>, VI (1963), 35-48.

STOLL, Ladislav, On the Thirties and the New Generation. <u>EE</u>, Aug 1964, 7-9. The ex-Minister of Education and Culture defends the proletarian poetry and literary theory of the 1930s against attack by younger writers.

_____, <u>Face To Face With Reality</u>, Prague: 1948. 62 pp. Address to Congress of National Culture, April 11, 1948, on committed art and its creative problems.

STRIBRNY, Zdenek, "Henry V and History," in <u>SCW</u>, 84-101.

_____, "Shakespeare's History Plays," <u>MT</u>, Nov 1959, 328-334. Summary of book published in Czech on the subject.

_____, "Some Affinities Between Shakespeare's Age and Ours," <u>PhPr</u>, V (1962), 1-3.

TEIGE, Karel, Modern Architecture in Czechoslovakia. <u>Czechoslovakia</u> (Prague), Special Issue, 1947. [MMA]

WEISS, Jiri, "Art In New-Born Socialism," <u>NCEO</u>, II (1949), 199. Plea for under standing of USSR neo-classical architecture. Weiss calls it the result of socio-psychological exigencies, and transitional. "We have denied people trash. We have to make good for that....

we are trying to do so in good faith...
Our task in the new democracies is to
give civilization and culture a new
basis" even if aesthetic advances must
be deferred.

_____, "Czechoslovak Films in 1949,"
NCEO, II (1950), 19. Outspoken comment on problems of Socialist cinema.
The practice of creating positive heroes Weiss compares to the wartime
priorities he knew in Great Britain.

_____, "Five Years of Our Nationalized
Films," NCEO, IV (1951), 270.

ZAZUNEK, Jiri, "Culture and the Masses,"
WMR, July 1965, 35-44. Complex discussion of the social basis for mass
culture today. Suggests that since so
much "high" culture moves through "mass"
channels, the chief distinction is not
"mass" or "high" culture but "active"
or "passive" consumption. Mass art
should "foster" the "active elements
in the life of society" and not adapt
itself to "institutionalized demand"
or "underestimate the public" as an
"active co-author". Points out the
variety of taste and capabilities to
be coped with. Rejects "accessibility
for all" criterion of socialist art as
meaning the lowest "common denominator".

ZBAVITCH, Dusan, "Rabindranath Tagore,"
AO, XXIV (1956), 581-590; XXV (1957),
405-425; XXVI (1958), 101-113, 366-384;
XXVII(1959),60-75, 251-271. Tagore in
the national and popular struggles of
his period. Distortions of his work
in the West.

ZBAVITEL, Dusan, Bengali Folk Ballads
From Mymensingh and the Problem of
Their Authenticity, Univ. of Calcutta:
1963. A neglected popular tradition.

## XVI. Appendix

BRADAC, Olga, "Aesthetic Trends In Russia
and Czechoslovakia," JAAC, IX ii (Dec

1950), 97-105. Czech aesthetics after
1945. Bradac, Secretary of the Philosophical Society, left Czechoslovakia
in 1949.

KARNET, George, "The Literature Of De-
stalinization," EE, Dec 1964, 3-6.

MILNER, Ian, "English Studies At Charles
University," CL, Oct 1963, 14-16, 32.

POPKIN, Henry, "Theatre In Eastern Europe," TDR, Spring, 1967, 23-51. illus.

REES, Garonwy, "A Visa For Kafka," En,
Sept 1964, 27-34. On the revival of
interest in Kafka.


DENMARK

### Topic Index

JACOBSEN. Lukacs (XXVII).

### XVII. Authors

NEXO, Martin Anderson, On the USSR. IL,
1934 #4, 76-77.

_____, Autobiographical Sketches. IL,
1935 #5, 105-106. illus. Also in M&M,
July 1954, 49-52.

_____, SEE ALSO: Ella Reeve Bloor, "Mar-
tin Anderson Nexo," Lib, Mch
1923, 24.

Sergei Tretyakov, "Comrade Martin," IL, 1934 #6, 117-122.

Harry Slochower: See (LVI).


ECUADOR

### XVIII. Authors

SALVADOR. Umberto, "Contemporary Poetry
of Ecuador," IL, 1939 #10, 79-80.


FRANCE

(SEE ALSO; Arnold Hauser (XXVII), on
all topics to 1920s.)

### Topic Index

ANTOINE. Gassner, Gorelik (LVIII).

ARAGON. See (XIX).

ART, SOCIAL, HISTORY. Cassou. Herbert
(XX); Evans (LXII).

AUGIER. Gassner (LVIII).

BALZAC. Malraux. Marx and Engels (XXI);
Fox (XXIII); Bonhomme (XXIV); Kopeczi,
Lukacs (XXVII); Grib (XLVI); Finkelstein,

Harrington, Humboldt (LVI); Auerbach, Brandes, Levin (LXII).

BARBUSSE. Aragon. Kurella (XXI); Auerbach, Gorky, Lenin (XLVI). See Barbusse (XX).

BAUDELAIRE. Fischer (XXI); Plekhanov (XLVI); Auerbach, Turnell (LXII). See Baudelaire (LXIII).

BEAUMARCHAIS. Gassner (LVIII).

BECQUE. Gassner (LVIII).

BELLOC, H. Slochower (LVI).

BOILEAU. Auerbach (LXII).

BOSSUET. Goldmann. Auerbach (LXII).

BRAQUE. Einstein (XXI); Berger (XXIII); 'Cahiers', 'Lettres' (LXIII).

BRETON. See (XIX).

BRIFFAULT. Sloan (XXIII).

BUTOR, M. Fraser (XXIII).

CAMUS. Sartre. Fischer (XXI); Finkelstein, Goldman, Harrington (LVI).

CELINE. Radek, Trotsky (XLVI); Slochower (LVI); Howe (LXII).

CEZANNE. Berger, Long (XXIII); Summers (LIII).

CHANSON. Auerbach (LXII).

CHARDIN. Meltzoff (LIII).

CHATEAUBRIAND. Marx and Engels (XXI).

CHRETIEN DE TROYES. Auerbach (LXII).

CINEMA, HISTORY. Sadoul.

CLAIR, R. Sadoul. Potamkin (LIV).

CLAUDEL. Slochower (LVI).

COMMUNE, AND CULTURE. Farmer (XX); Blunt, Jellinak (XXIII).

CORNEILLE. Plekhanov (XLVI): Boyadzhiev (XLVIII); Gassner (LVIII); Auerbach (LXII).

CORBUSIER. See (LXIII).

COROT. Berger (XXIII).

COUPERIN. Mellers (XXIII).

COURBET. Fischer (XXI); Berger (XXIII); Larkin, Schapiro (LIII); Boas (LXII).

COURTLY ROMANCES. Auerbach (LXII).

DALOU. Blunt, Klingender (XXIII).

DAUMIER. Berger (XXIII); Larkin (LIII).

DAVID, J.-L. Billiet. Lindsay (XXIII); Antal (XXVII); Plekhanov (XLVI); Brown (LIII); Dowd, Valentiner (LXII).

DELACROIX. Fischer (XXI); Berger, Lindsay (XXIII); Antal (XXVII).

DIDEROT. Marx and Engels (XXI); Plekhanov (XLVI); Kemp (LVI); Auerbach (LXII).

DUBUFFET. Berger (XXIII); 'Lettres' (LXIII).

DUFY. Berger (XXIII).

DU GARD. Lukacs (XXVII).

DUMAS. Plekhanov (XLVI); Gassner (LVIII)

ELUARD. See (XIX).

EXISTENTIALISM. Sartre. Lindsay (XXIII); Frid (XLVI); Glass, Finkelstein, Harap, Heifetz, Lawson, Oglesby, Rudich (LVI).

FABLIAUX. Auerbach (LXII).

FLAUBERT. Sartre. Fischer (XXI); Fox (XXIII); Lukacs (XXVII); Eisenstein (XLIV); Plekhanov (XLVI); Wilson (LVI); Auerbach, Levin (LXII).

FRANCE, A. Lunacharsky (XLVI).

FRENCH REVOLUTION, AND LITERATURE. Auerbach (LXII).

FRENCH REVOLUTION, AND MUSIC. Hobsbawm (XXIII); Hughes (LIII).

FRENCH REVOLUTION, AND PAINTING. Billiet (XIX); Hobsbawm, Klingender, Lindsay (XXIII); Antal (XXVII); Brown (LIII); Dowd (LXII).

FROISSART. Auerbach (LXII).

FROMENTIN. Schapiro (LIII).

GAUTIER. Plekhanov (LXVI).

GAUGUIN. Berger (XXIII); Slochower (LVI).

GENET. Sartre. Heifetz (LVI). See
(LXIII).

GERICAULT. Fischer (XXI); Antal (XXVII).

GIDE. Sartre. Lukacs (XXVII); Slochower
(LVI); Auerbach (LXII). See (XIX).

GIRAUDOUT. Sartre.

GIRODET. Antal (XXVII).

GODARD, J. Russell (XXIII).

GONCOURTS. Fox (XXIII); Lukacs (XXVII);
Plekhanov (XLVI); Auerbach (LXII).

GORZ, A. Sartre.

GREGORY OF TOURS. Auerbach (LXII).

GREUZE. Antal (XXVII); Plekhanov (XLVI).

GRUBER. 'Lettres' (LXIII).

HUGO. Rolland. Evans, Herbert (XX);
Lukacs (XXVII); Plekhanov (XLVI);
Mufson (LVI); Gassner (LVIII); Auerbach
(LXII).

HUYSMANS. Lukacs (XXVII); Plekhanov
(XLVI).

LA BRUYERE. Auerbach (LXII).

LAMARTINE. Plekhanov (XLVI).

LAPIQUE. 'Cahiers' (LXIII).

LA SALE. Auerbach (LXII).

LA TOUR. Berger (XXIII).

LAURENS. "Lettres' (LXIII).

LE BRUN. Plekhanov (XLVI).

LECONTE DE LISLE. Plekhanov (XLVI);
Wilson (LIV).

LE NAINS. Meltzoff (LIII).

LITERARY THEORY, RENAISSANCE. Hall
(LXII).

LITERATURE, RADICAL HISTORY. Garaudy,
Morgan, Nizan. Caute, Evans, Sanborn
(XX).

LUCE, M. Herbert (XX).

LUMIERE. Gorky (XLVI).

MALAQUAIS. Trotsky (XLVI).

MALLARME. Aragon, Sartre. Aubery (XX);
Fischer (XXI); Bowra (LXII).

MALRAUX. See (XIX).

MARTINET. Trotsky (XLVI).

MASSON. 'Cahiers' (LXIII).

MATISSE. Berger (XXIII); 1947 (XLI);
Romm (XLIII); 'Cahiers', 'Lettres'
(LXIII).

MAUPASSANT. Lukacs (XXVII).

MAURIAC. Garaudy, Sartre.

MEDIEVAL MORALITY PLAYS. Gassner (LVIII);
Auerbach (LXII).

MERIMEE. Lukacs (XXVII).

MERLEAU-PONTY. Sartre.

MEUNIER. Herbert (XX); Bogdanov (XLVI);
Spargo (LIII).

MILLET. Fischer (XXI); Berger (XXIII);
Abbott (LVI).

MOLIERE. Lafargue. Kott (XXXVI); Ple-
khanov (XLVI); Boyadzhiev (XLVIII);
Gassner (LVIII); Auerbach, Turnell
(LXII).

MONTAIGNE. Auerbach (LXII).

MONTHERLANT. Lukacs (XXVII).

MUSSET. Plekhanov (XLVI).

NEGRO WRITERS AND FRANCE. Cesaire, Senghor, Smith (I).

NIZAN. Sartre.

NOVEL, 'NOUVELLE VAGUE'. Sartre. Horodinca (XXXVIII). See Robbe-Grillet
(LXIII).

PAINTING, CLASSICIST. Antal (XXVII);
Plekhanov (XLVI).

PAINTING, ROMANTIC. Antal (XXVII);
Plekhanov (XLVI); White (LXII).

PASCAL. Goldmann. Auerbach (LXII).

PISSARRO. Herbert (XX); Rose (XXIII);
Nicolson (LXII). See Pissarro (LXIII).

POPULAR FRONT. Aragon, Gide, Malraux.
Caute (XX).

POTTIER, E.  Gatov (XLVII).

POUSSIN. Berger (XXIII); Plekhanov(XLVI).

PROVENCAL POETRY. Marx and Engels (XXI);
   Lindsay (XXIII); Auerbach (LXII).

PROUDHON. Raphael (XXI);Woodcock (LXII).

PROUST.  Fischer (XXI); Lindsay (XXIII);
   Lukacs (XXVII); Lunacharsky, Tolmachev
   (XLVI); Burgum, Harrington, Slochower,
   Wilson (LVI); Auerbach, Levin (LXII).

RABELAIS.  Fox (XXIII); Lawson (LVI);
   Auerbach (LXII).

RACINE.  Goldmann.  Fischer (XXI); Lukacs
   (XXVII); Boyadzhiev (XLVIII); Plekhanov
   (XLVI); Gassner (LVIII); Auerbach,
   Barthes (LXII).

RENOIR, A.  Berger (XXIII); Lunacharsky
   (XLVI).

RENOIR, J.  See (LXIII).

RESNAIS.  Chukhrai (XLIV).

RIMBAUD.  St. Aubyn (XX); Fischer (XXI);
   Wilson (LVI).

ROBBE-GRILLET.  Fischer (XXI); Kopeczi
   (XXVII).  See (LXIII).

ROLLAND.  Balashova, Machan (XX); Ilberg
   (XXI); Lukacs (XXVII); Gorky, Radek
   (XLVI).

 ROUSSEAU.  Auerbach (LXII).

SADE.  Beauvoir, Calas. Fraina, Hodges
   (LVI).

SAINT-BEUVE.  Plekhanov (XLVI).

SAND, G.  Evans (XX); Plekhanov (XLVI).

SARDOU.  Gassner (LVIII).

SARTRE, J.-P.  See (XIX).

SCRIBE.  Gassner (LVIII).

SERRAULT, N.  Sartre.

SEURAT.  Herbert (XX).

SIGNAC.  Herbert (XX).

STEINLEN.  Herbert (XX).
STENDHAL.  Fischer (XXI); Haldane (XXIII);
   Lukacs (XXVII); Ehrenburg, Gorky (XLVI);

Auerbach, Howe,Levin, Merrill (LXII).

SUE, E.  Marx and Engels (XXI).

SYMBOLISM.  Aubery, Herbert (XX); Bowra
   (LXII).

TAINE.  Plekhanov (XLVI); Morawski (XXVI);
   Lukacs (XXVII); Auerbach, Kahn (LXII).

THEATRE, IN PARIS COMMUNE. Danilin (XLVIII).

THEATRE, RECENT.  Tynan (LXII).

THEATRE, WORKERS'.  Moussinac.  Herbert,
   Machan (XX).

TZARA.  See (II), (XIX).

VALERY.  Larnac.  Wilson (LVI).

VAN GOGH.  Herbert (XX); Fischer (XXI);
   Berger (XXIII); Gold, Levine, Rosenberg
   (LIII); Artaud, Van Gogh (LXIII).

VERCORS.  Garaudy.

VERLAINE.  Gorky (XLVI).

VIGNY.  Evans (XX); Lukacs (XXVII);
   Plekhanov (XLVI).

VILLON.  'Lettres' (LXIII).

VOLTAIRE.  Lukacs (XXVII); Plekhanov
   (XLVI); Auerbach (LXII).

WATTEAU.  Berger (XXIII).

ZOLA.  Aragon, Lafargue, Longuet.
   Herbert (XX);  Fischer (XXI); Fox
   (XXIII); Lukacs (XXVII); Krushchev,
   Plekhanov (XLVI); Gassner (LVIII);
   Auerbach, Levin (LXII).  See Zola
   (LXIII).

## XIX.  Authors

ADAMOV, Arthur, Interview with Carl Wild-
   man.  Observer (London), July 1, 1962.
   "I have put the accent on the curable
   ill, the social one, rather than the
   incurable one....when one has said that
   life is absurd, that means that one is
   not struggling and that it's all complacent  fun for readers of 'Le Figaro'...
   I haven't changed whether as a Marxist
   or non-Marxist.  The only thing is to
   know how to use your neuroses."

_____, Interview with Roger Hudson.
   Prompt (London), #2 (Spring 1963), 16-
   19.  ilus.  "I don't think all theatre

must be political but I think all
theatre must seriously observe <u>real</u>
processes whether they be dreams, or
the class struggle, or the national
struggles of colonial peoples against
colonialism." Reflections on his
development.

ARAGON, Louis, "From Dada To Red Front,"
<u>NM</u>, May 14, 1935, 23-24. Revised
translation in <u>AWC</u>, 33-38. Written
contribution to 1st American Writers
Congress. Account of his conversion
experience. Enthusiastic on Socialist
Realism. Considerable mention of US
writers he knows.

_____, "Mors et Vita, or the Lesson Of
Henri Barbusse," <u>Life and Letters To-
day</u>, Dec 1935, 57-60.

_____, "The Return To Reality," <u>IL</u>, 1936
#1, 100-106. Advocating Narrative
Realism, he passionately attacks Surrealists.

_____, "Painting and Reality," <u>transition</u>
#25 (1936), 93-103, 119-122. From a
discussion at Maison de la Culture,
Paris, May 1936. Also in <u>AF</u>, Jan 1937,
7-11. - Answer by Salvador Dali, and
comment by Clarence Weinstock [C. Hum-
boldt] and Samuel Putnam, <u>AF</u>, Mch 1937,
7-12.

_____, "French Writers and the People's
Front," <u>LR</u>, May 1936, 378-380.

_____, Interview with Herbert Rosen. <u>DW</u>,
June 1, 1939, 7.

_____, Speech to 3rd Congress of American
Writers. <u>Bulletin</u>, VI i (1939), 3-4,
8. abdgd. Full text in ms. [LAW] Activities of International Writers'
Association in defense of authors in
exile.

_____, "The Example of Maxim Gorki," <u>OT</u>,
Aug 1946, 7-8. Estimate of his greatness. Influence on Aragon's thought.

_____, "Mallarme: Obscurity In Poetry,"
<u>Anvil: Life and the Arts</u>, ed. Jack
Lindsay, London, 1947, 54-64. In effect an indignant protest against exegesis of poetry which in Aragon's
view ignores its real values.

_____, "Emile Zola," <u>NM</u>, Dec 3, 1946, 3-7.

_____, "A Fresh Look At Socialist Real-
ism," <u>M&M</u>, Oct 1959, 1-22. Pegging

discussion on his novel 'Holy Week'
Aragon argues Socialist Realism is a
"conception" come to by individual
writers, not an orthodoxy and not a
"style."

_____, "Writers and Critics," <u>M&M</u>, Jan
1963, 23-29. Speech delivered at
Charles University, Prague on Aragon's
60th birthday. Attacks dogmatism
which prejudges literature. Calls for
positive heroes, defends Realism.

_____, SEE ALSO: Frida Stewart, "Aragon:
    Development of a Communist Poet,"
    <u>MQ(L)</u>, Summer 1946, 41-56.

    Michael Gold, "Aragon: Poet-Or-
        ganizer," <u>M&M</u>, May 1950, 11-
        24. Intimate portrait.

    J. Fried, "Surrealism - and
        Louis Aragon," <u>IL</u>, 1934 #4,
        125-129.

    <u>Aragon Poet of the French Re-
        sistance</u>, ed. Hannah Josephson
        and Malcolm Cowley, 1945. Se-
        lection of wartime poems and
        writings. Essays by Waldo
        Frank, Peter Rhodes, Cowley.

    Samuel Putnam, <u>Paris Was Our
        Mistress</u>, 1947, 178-189.

    D.S. Mirsky, "Aragon Arrives,"
        <u>Living Age</u>, Mch 1935, 66-70.
        From 'Literaturnaia Gazeta'.
        Review of 'Les Cloches de
        Bale'.

    Malcolm Cowley, Remembrances of
        Aragon. <u>NRep</u>, Oct 7, 1936, 258.

    Francoise Gilot and Carlton Lake,
        <u>Life With Picasso</u>, McGraw-Hill:
        1964. Picasso's relations
        with Aragon.

    See Garaudy (XIX); Caute, Savage
        (XX); Pascal, Spender (XXIII).

BEAUVOIR, Simone de, "Must We Burn Sade?"
in her <u>Marquis de Sade</u>: <u>Selections</u>,
Evergreen paperback: 1954, 11-82. His
despotic eroticism as one form declining nobility's absolutism can take.

BILLIET, Joseph, "The French Revolution
and the Fine Arts," in <u>Essays On the
French Revolution</u>, London, 1945, 197-208.

BLOCH, Jean-Richard, "Literary Creation

and Human Society," LR, Aug 1935, 464-
468.  Speech to 1st International Congress of Writers, Paris.

_____, SEE ALSO: Samuel Sillen, Jean-
        Richard Bloch.  DW, Mch 26,
        1947, 11.

BONNARD, Andre, Greek Civilization From
the Iliad To the Parthenon, Macmillan:
1957.

_____, Greek Civilization From Euripides
To Alexandria, Macmillan: 1961.  These
studies are a lively, humane, popular
treatment of highlights and development of Greek civilization.

BRETON, Andre, "Surrealism: Yesterday,
To-Day and To-Morrow," This Quarter,
Sept 1932, 7-44.  For the English
reader, Breton traces development of
Surrealism from idealism to historical
materialism.  Lengthy extracts from
'Second Manifesto of Surrealism' and
from "Misere de la Poesie', Breton's
critique of Aragon's 'Front Rouge'.

_____, "Legitimate Defense," in: Maurice
Nadeau, The History Of Surrealism,
Macmillan: 1965, 242-256.  Surrealism
as a dialectical materialist outlook
which cannot, however, be channelled
as the CP or any other "external"
control may wish.  From 1926.

_____, "The Poverty Of Poetry: The Aragon
Affair Before Public Opinion," in:
Maurice Nadeau, The History Of Sur-
realism, Macmillan: 1965, 296-303.
Aragon's turn toward a CP position as
mistaken.

_____, Paul Eluard, Rene Char, Rene Cre-
vel, et al, "Murderous Humanitarian-
ism," in: Nancy Cunard, ed, Negro
Anthology, London, 1934, 574-575.
Jazz as commercialized exoticism of a
Western civilization that must soon
go under.

_____, What Is Surrealism?  Criterion
Miscellany, London, 1936.  Especially
prepared for 1st International Surrealist Exhibition, London, June 1936.
Final chapter in: Eugen Weber, ed,
Paths To the Present, Dodd, Mead paperback: 1960, 254-280.  Fine statement
of Surrealist Marxism.  "Surrealism
and Painting" praises Picasso's fine
audacity.  "The Communicating Vessels:
The Phantom Object" begins by distin-
guishing healthy artistic fantasy from
the sickly mysticism decried by Engels.

_____, "Limits Not Frontiers of Surreal-
ism," Surrealism, ed. Herbert Read,
London, 1936, 95-116.  Especially written for volume that follows up 1st
International Surrealist Exhibition.
Vehement in affirming materialism,
dialectical method, Marxism.  Calls for
a workers' militia in Paris and revolution in the streets; supports the Spanish Republicans; rejects Socialist
Realism as contradicting Engels' in-
junction not to let the ideology show.

_____, Bulletin International du Surreal-
isme, #4, Sept 1936.  In English.  Heat-
ed defense of Surrealism having genuinely Marxist-revolutionary character.

_____, Preface to The International Sur-
realist Exhibition [Catalog], London,
1936, 6-8.  [MMA]  Surrealism is to
painting as Marxism is to philosophy,
a rational and demystifying approach.

_____, and Diego Rivera, "Manifesto: To-
wards a Free Revolutionary Art," PR,
Fall 1938, 49-53. - Also in Labour Review, VII iii (Autumn 1962), 114-116,
and in Workers International News
(London), Apr 1939.  Attack on "the
official art of Stalinism" and call
for "complete freedom of art" for revolutionary artists in a revolutionary
State.  Announces formation of International rallying point. - For Trotsky's enthusiastic welcome to this project, see his letter to Andre Breton,
PR, Winter 1939, 126-127.

_____, "The Situation of Surrealism Be-
tween The Two Wars," YFS, I ii (Fall-
Winter 1948), 67-78.  No discussion of
politics or Marxism.

_____, "The Second Ark," transition 48,
#2 (1948), 64-67.  Breton's disillusion
with Stalinist Communism.  "Art will
never take orders, whatever happens."
Rejects charges that his art is bourgeois and decadent.  Obliquely attacks
Sartre's 'engagement'.

_____, SEE ALSO: Ilya Ehrenburg, "The Sur-
        realists," PR, Oct-Nov 1935, 11-16.
        Masterfully malicious appraisal.
        Also: Short (XX).

CALAS, Nicolas, "On Revolutionary Sadism,"
PR, Jan-Feb 1940, 41-49.  Excerpts from
'Foyers d'Incendie'.

_____, Confound the Wise, 1942.  Surreal-
ist interplay of Freud and Marx over

history and art.

_____, "Towards a Third Surrealist Manifesto," New Directions 1940, 408-421.

CASANOVA, Laurent, "Communism, Thought and Art," CR, Oct 1947, 312-317. Speech to 11th Congress of French CP on political responsibilities of artists and writers.

CASSOU, Jean, 19th Century French Writing. DW, Oct 27, 1939, 7. "The return to nature...implies the existence of a revolutionary spirit."

_____, "Cervantes," IL, 1937 #9, 33-50. Also in Angel Flores and M.J. Bernardete, eds, Cervantes Across the Centuries, 1947, 3-31, a poorer translation, abdgd.

_____, "The Climate of Thought," in Gateway To the Twentieth Century: Art and Culture In a Changing World, ed. Cassou et al, McGraw-Hill: 1962, 5-115. Masterful essay on society that conditioned crisis of modern painting.

_____, "2,000 Years Of Mexican Art," UNESCO Courier, June 1952, 3-4. Emphasizes popular character of Mexican art.

CHENNEVIERE, R.D, "The Rise Of the Musical Proletariat," Musical Quarterly, Oct 1920, 500-509.

CORNU, A, "Marxism and Literary Decadence," MQ(L), Spring 1947, 155-162. Rilke as a prime example of a mystified class outlook.

DORT, Bernard, "A Comprehensive Realism," World Theatre, Mch-Apr 1965, 108-118. Draws on Meyerhold to define a realism employing fantasy and abstraction.

DUCLOS, Jacques, The Party and the Writer. DW, Feb 27, 1939, 7; Feb 28, 7; Mch 1, 7.

DUMAZEDIER, Joffre, "The Masses, Culture and Leisure," Diogenes, Winter 1963, 33-42. Author is director of Groupe Sociologique du Loisir et de la Culture Populaire, Paris.

ELUARD, Paul, "Poetry Must Have As Its Aim Truth in Action," CQ, III ii (1954), 19. A clever answer to those shocked by social relevance in poetry. - See also: Frank J. Carmody, "Eluard's

Rupture With Surrealism," PMLA, Summer 1961, 436-446.

FOUGERON, Andre, Realism and Art. transition 49, #5 (1949), 123.

FREVILLE, Jean, "What Is the Marxist Approach to Literature?" Dia, #1 (1937), 1-10.

GARAUDY, Roger, "Jean Paul Sartre - False Prophet," DW, Mch 8, 1946, 11.

_____, et al, "Communism and Art - A Controversy," report by F.D. Klingender, CR, Jan 1947, 18-21. Important 1946 debate among French Communists whether there can be a Party line in aesthetics. Garaudy and Pierre Herve say no, Louis Aragon argues yes. Many extracts.

_____, "French Culture and Marxism," NM, Mch 5, 1946, 5-9, 18. Speech to 10th National Congress of the French CP. Outlines plans for cultural rebirth in France.

_____, Literature Of the Graveyard, 1948. Sartre, Mauriac, Malraux, Koestler.

_____, "New Currents In French Writing," M&M, Oct 1954, 46-55. Discusses productive relation of several writers, e.g. Vercors, Vailland, Sartre, to the CP and deleterious rejection of Communism by others: Mauriac, Malraux.

_____, Stalin, Picasso and Kafka. EE, Dec 1963, 23-25. abdgd. Speech to Kafka Conference, Liblice, May 1963.

_____, D'un Realisme sans Rivages: Picasso, Saint-John Perse, Kafka, Paris, 1963; summary of Picasso essay with lengthy extracts, by Jacques Senecal, in: MQ(T), Spring 1964, 40-47. Reprinted in AmD, II i (1965), 12-15. Marking a new stage of his thought, Garaudy wholly embraces the art of Picasso declaring: "there is no art that is not realist, i.e, that does not refer to a reality external to and independent of it."

_____, "A Letter From Paris," AmD, Oct-Nov 1965, 38-39. Abundant praise for Picasso, indignation against the Gilot account of him.

_____, Interview With Gyorgy Timar. NHQ, Spring 1967, 165-167. Elaborates on the notion of realism. Cognition, imagination, Kafka, Picasso, Cezanne,

Sartre.

GIDE, Andre, "A Few Reflections On the Disappearance of the Subject In Art and Painting," <u>Verve</u>, Dec 1937, 7-10. The subject cannot disappear from painting without damage to coherence of composition. The best modern art, however, reaches only experts.

_____, DOCUMENTS OF HIS AFFIRMATION OF THE POPULAR FRONT AND THE SOVIET UNION:

_____, First Statement of Commitment to USSR. <u>Living Age</u>, Mch 1933, 70-71. From 'Nouvelle Revue Francaise', Summer 1932.

_____, Letter Explaining Defense of the USSR. <u>IL</u>, 1933 #2, 131. Dated Jan 1933.

_____, "Literature and Society," <u>PR</u>, II ix, 33-40. From 'Commune', Nov 1934.

_____, "In Defense of Culture," <u>IL</u>, 1935 #10, 81-85. illus. Also in <u>LR</u>, Aug 1935, 447-452; and in <u>Life and Letters Today</u>, Sept 1935, 12-18. Speech as Chairman of International Congress of Writers In Defense of Culture, Paris, June 22, 1935. The basic text for his idea of relations of Communism and literature.

_____, "To the Young People of the USSR On Sending Them My Nouvelles Nourritures," <u>IL</u>, 1936 #1, 115. Remarks on his book, its relation to committed writing, his faith in the USSR.

_____, Remarks At Gorky's Funeral. <u>IL</u>, 1936 #8, 3-12.

_____, SEE ALSO, on Gide's commitment: Paul Nizan, "Andre Gide Comes To Revolution," <u>IL</u>, 1934 #3, 138-147.

E. Galperina, Commentary to 'Nouvelles Nourritures', <u>IL</u>, 1936 #5, 111-114.

Louis Aragon, "Andre Gide and Our Times," <u>IL</u>, 1936 #2, 100-103. Discussion of Gide's debate of his pro-Soviet views with fellow writers.

Samuel Putnam, Gide's Emotional Conversion. <u>PR</u>, I v, 30-36. A perceptive discussion.

Ilya Ehrenburg, "Andre Gide, Communist," <u>The Literary World</u> (New York), June 1934, 1, 2, 6. Lively account of Gide's conversion and the background.

Edward Sagarin, "Andre Gide Goes Left," <u>NM</u>, Apr 1933, 19-20. Extensive quotations.

_____, DOCUMENTS OF HIS DISAVOWAL AND THE AFTERMATH:

_____, <u>Return From the U.S.S.R</u>, 1937. Prefaces critique by saying "the Soviet Union will end by triumphing over the serious errors that I point out" and "the particular errors of one country cannot suffice to compromise a cause which is international and universal." Finds consumer goods and foods "repulsive," a "want of public taste," Muscovians are "indolent," the populace as a whole is exceedingly backward compared to the French, "depersonalization" everywhere together with carefully fostered ignorance of the outside world, personality cult. Gide glumly foresees a "new sort of workers' bourgeoisie."

_____, <u>Afterthoughts; A Sequel To Back From the U.S.S.R</u>, London, 1937? Extract: "Second Thoughts On the USSR," <u>PR</u>, IV ii, 21-28. Gide here answers "sincere critics" such as Paul Nizan, not "insulters." "I assure you that there is something tragic about my Soviet experience. I had come as an enthusiast, as a communist supporter, to admire a new world, and to <u>win my affections</u> I was offered all the prerogatives I abominated in the old one.... They may be members of the Party - there is nothing communist in their hearts."

_____, <u>The Journals of Andre Gide</u>, vol. III (1928-1939), 1950.

_____, SEE ALSO, on Gide's disavowal: Paul Nizan, in: <u>NM</u>, Apr 6, 1937, 13-14.

Lion Feuchtwanger, "Andre Gide vs. the USSR," <u>Dia</u>, #2, 20-22.

'Pravda' Editorial, "The Laughter and Tears of Andre Gide," <u>IL</u>, 1937 #1, 109-113; also in <u>MN</u>, Dec 16, 1936, 17. Accuses Gide of inconsistency and lying.

British reactions in DW(L), Jan 13, 1937, 7.

N.B: The above texts of disavowal, with a speech, were paraphrased by Enid Starkie - purportedly with Gide's advice and consent - and published under his name as a single essay in: Richard Crossman, ed, The God That Failed, 1949, 165-195.

Georges I. Brachfeld, Andre Gide and the Communist Temptation, Paris, 1959. Thorough exploration of social thread in Gide's mind and writing.

GOLDMANN, Lucien, The Hidden God, Humanities: 1964. A brilliant accomplishment of recent Marxism. Explores tragic vision in Racine, Pascal. - Review by Alastair MacIntyre, En, Oct 1964, 69-76.

_____, "The Early Writings Of Georg Lukacs," Tri-Quarterly, Spring 1967, 165-181.

_____, "Socialism and Humanism," Diogenes, Summer 1964, 82-102. Also in Erich Fromm, ed, Socialist Humanism, Doubleday: 1965, 38-49.

LAFARGUE, Paul, "Emile Zola," Dia, #4 (1937), 1-15. abdgd.

_____, "Socialism and the Intellectuals," ISR, Aug 1900, 84-101. Moliere as a conscious militant bourgeois in attacking nobility, pp. 94-95.

_____, The Right To Be Lazy, Chicago: 1917. 62 pp. Leisure as the basis of self-realization and a life of joy foretold by Rabelais, Diderot, etc.

_____, Origin and Evolution Of the Idea Of the Soul, Chicago: 1922. The Greek myths and mystery religions.

_____, "Marx and Literature," in: Karl Marx and Friedrich Engels, Literature and Art, 1947, 138-140. Reminiscences by Marx's son-in-law.

LARNAC, J, "Valery: High-Priest of 'Pure Poetry'," NM, July 2, 1946, 4-8; July 9, 1946, 18-21. More polemic than analysis.

LEGER, Fernand, "The Esthetics of the Machine; Manufactured Objects; Artisan and Artist," The Little Review (New York), Spring 1923, 45-49; Autumn-Winter 1923-24, 55-58. Central to Leger's thought. "Every object, created or manufactured, may carry in itself an intrinsic beauty just like all phenomena of the natural order admired by the world, through all eternity....plastic beauty in general is totally independent of sentimental descriptive or imitative values....Because the machine belongs to the architectural order it may hold a legitimate place in the world of the beautiful....The artisan... is the true creator, he it is who daily, modestly, unconsciously creates and invents these handsome objects, these beautiful machines that make us live."

_____, "A New Realism - The Object (Its Plastic and Cinematographic Value)," The Little Review, Winter 1926, 7-8. illus. Discusses the unrealized interest for the cinema of objects in close-up and in motion.

_____, "The New Realism," AF, Dec 1935, 10. Defends the "realism" of color and geometry saying his art is not abstract.

_____, "The New Realism Goes On," AF Feb 1937, 7-8.

_____, "Painting and Reality," transition, #25 (1936); reprinted in Myfwany Evans, The Painter's Object, London, 1937, 15-20; and in Daedalus, Winter 1960, 87-90. "We have the possibility of creating a new collective mural art" as the realism of our time but "everything depends on" the "creation of leisure for the workers" so they will have "access to plastic beauty....they never have had the necessary time or sufficient liberty of spirit."

_____, "Revival of Mural Art," Listener (London), Aug 25, 1937, 408-409. "Beauty is neither representational, nor sentimental, nor didactic. Beauty exists as an abstract quality. But we must wait for the plastic education of the masses before this thesis will be accepted. Meanwhile let us cover our walls with fresh, gay colors and so inspire optimism and joy. Then we must wait until Beauty is understood by all, and therein lies the great hope of the future." Traces the development of decorative, easel, and mural art.

_____, "Beauty In Machine Art," _Design_, Mch 1938, 6-7. Forceful statement of view that the best industrial design must be regarded as a coherent and valid modern style to parallel those of Greece and Rome. "Beauty is everywhere, in the order of the pots and pans on the white wall of a kitchen, more, perhaps, than in an eighteenth century salon or the official museums ....The day when the work of this whole world of sorkment may be understood and felt by people exempt from prejudice who have eyes to see, truly that day we shall witness a surprising revolution."

_____, "Relationship Between Modern Art and Contemporary Industry," in: _Modern Art In Advertising_, Art Institute of Chicago: 1945, 4-5. "In turning to us for help, industry will enable us to establish a connection between the collective masses and the art of their time."

_____, Statement to 'Cahiers d'Art'. _transition 49_, #5 (1949), 114-115. From 1938. "Nothing is being done to educate the people, to tell them that we are on their side. The people have an innate sense of poetry, witness the language they invent, the slang they endlessly create. Why should they not accept an imaginative type of painting? ....It would be preferable for us to be left free in our studios to devote ourselves to our plastic researches, just as the scientists are left in their laboratories, above and beyond the battle....The artist would have to belong to a group and agree wholeheartedly with its programme, its feelings, its ideas also, before he could allow others to direct his plastic development."

_____, SEE ALSO: Fischer (XXI); Berger (XXIII); Robert L. Delevoy, Leger, Skira: 1962. illus.

LONGUET, Jean, "Zola the Socialist," _The Comrade_, Dec 1902, 51. The grandson of Marx. Praise of Zola's socialist commitment and "wonderful" description of economic conditions; but in 'Labor' and some other novels, Zola, "like some ancient Utopian Socialists, does not seem to understand the necessity of the proletarians assuming the point of view of class combat".

LURCAT, Jean, "For Decorative Art See Russia Says Artist," _N.Y. World Telegram_, Nov 24, 1934.

_____, "The Social Sterility of Painters," _AF_, May 1935, 4-5, 8; July, 5, 8. [_MMA_] The modernist movement fatally determined by bourgeoisie it seeks to elude.

MALRAUX, Andre, Interview. _IL_, 1934 #5, 144-146.

_____, Speech to Soviet Writers Congress, Moscow, 1934. _YFS_, #18 (1957). Warns Soviet writers against a "photograph" literature. Urges "a richer and more contradictory notion of psychological life....more consciousness."

_____, "Literature In Two Worlds," _PR_, Jan-Feb 1935, 14-19. Speech in Paris upon his return from Soviet Writers Congress evaluates role of writer in USSR.

_____, "The Work of Art," _PR_, II ix, 41-43.

_____, Speech to International Association of Writers for the Defense of Culture, Paris, Nov 1935. _YFS_, #18 (1957), 28-31. Analysis of Western values.

_____, "Let Them Know," _IL_, 1936 #1, 113-114. Preface to 'Indochina SOS' by Andree Viollis. Reportage as an art; Balzac; colonialism.

_____, "Our Cultural Heritage," _LR_, July 1936, 491-496; also in _YFS_, #18 (1957), 31-38; and _NRep_, Oct 21, 1936, 315-317. abdgd. Speech to International Association of Writers for the Defense of Culture, London, 1936. Complex view of cultural values and man's will in the era of the masses and of mechanical reproduction of art objects.

_____, "Reply To Trotsky," in: R.W.B. Lewis, _Malraux_: A Collection of Critical Essays, Spectrum paperback: Englewood Cliffs, N.J, 1964, 20-24. Declares the social representativeness of 'The Conquerers' is not unwitting (as Trotsky claims, in an essay in this volume) but by his intention; defends his interpretation of the Chinese Revolution.

_____, "Trotsky vs. Malraux," _Nation_, Mch 27, 1937, 351. A UP dispatch quoting Trotsky calling Malraux a Stalinist agent "organically incapable of moral independence; he is official by birth." Reply from Malraux.

_____, Interview with Henri Lefebvre. _NRep_, June 24, 1936. The proper relation of the intellectual to the CP: it "weakens his own authority" to "identify his activities with those of the Party" or to "follow the Party in its tactics and maneuvers." Ethical content of politics.

_____, Interview with F.W. Dupee, NM, Mch 9, 1937, 17-18. Malraux was in US raising money for Spanish Republican cause.

_____, "The Fascist Threat To Culture," Speech delivered at Harvard University, Cambridge, Mch 8, 1937. 10 pp. [Harvard] Parts appeared in NRep, Oct 21, 1936, and Nation, Mch 20, 1937.

_____, Interview with Edwin Seaver. DW, Mch 9, 1937, 7. American writers (detective yarn as basis of our style) and the Popular Front.

_____, "What Stand Will You Take?" Confluence, Sept 1952, 3-11. Speech to Congress of Cultural Freedom, June 6, 1952. Makes grim fun of Soviet painting while extolling continuity of artistic genius. "Cezanne is no more the expression of capitalism and the bourgeoisie than Prometheus is the expression of the vulture. In Marxist terminology, one must acknowledge that Cezanne is the expression of capitalism - just about as Lenin was."

_____, SEE ALSO: Garaudy (XIX); Caute, Savage (XX); Trotsky (XLVI); Burgum, Harrington, Slochower, Wilson (LVI); Benson (LIX).

   Isidore Schneider, DW, Aug 5, 1934, 7. Review of 'Man's Fate'. Further comment by R. Doonping, DW, Sept 8, 1934, 7. Schneider praises novel but sees it as a product of decadence, individualism and psychologism. Doonping adds praise but cites historical-political mistakes.

   David Wilkinson, Malraux Philopher - Propagandist; An Essay In Political Criticism, Harvard Univ: Cambridge, 1967. Studies the continuity of politics as culture in Malraux.

MASSON, Andre, Statement to 'Cahiers d' Art'. transition 49, #5 (1949), 115. From 1938. "The only justification of a work of art, of a poem, of a discov-

ery in the field of biology or of psychoanalysis lies in its contribution to the liberation of man, to the transmutation of all values, to the denunciation of social, moral and religious hypocrisy, and hence to the denunciation of the ruling class responsible for the imperialist and fascist regression."

MORGAN, Claude, "France: The Battle Of Ideas," M&M, Oct 1948, 38-46. Editor of 'Les Lettres Francaises' assesses line-up of writers on the left.

MORIN, Edgar, The Stars, Evergreen Profile paperback: 1960. illus. Detailed analysis of cinema with premise that "the star system is a specific institution of capitalism on a major scale."

MOUSSINAC, Leon, "Revolutionary Theatre In France," ITh, #5 (1933), 21-23. illus.

NADEAU, Maurice, The History Of Surrealism, Macmillan: 1965. illus. First-rate account of French Surrealism's development, philosophy, politics, relations with the CP. With documents.

NIZAN, Paul, "French Literature Today," IL, 1934 #5, 134-143.

NOUGE, Paul, "Final Advice," London Bulletin, Apr 1938, 5-6. Surrealism as benefitting from un-doctrinaire Freudism and Marxism, the foe of aestheticism and the democritizer of poetry.

PICASSO, Pablo. See (XL).

PLANCHON, Roger, Interview with Bettina Knapp. TDR #27 (Spring 1965), 190-193.

_____, "Advancing With Shakespeare: No Falstaffs In Formosa?" Times Literary Supplement, Sept 3, 1964, 817-818. On 'Henry IV'.

_____, Interview with Claude Gauteur. TDR, Fall 1966, 133-136.

_____, SEE ALSO: Hans de Groot, "Theatre de la Cite," Prompt #6 (1965), 15-18. Planchon's approach to the classics. - Blau (LXII).

ROLLAND, Romain, Road To Communism. IL, 1934 #4, 69-72.

_____, "The Old Orpheus: Victor Hugo," IL, 1937 #7, 76-84.

_____, "Beethoven's Politics," <u>LR</u>, July 1936.

SADOUL, Georges, <u>French Film</u>, London, 1953.  History.

SARTRE, Jean-Paul, <u>Search For a Method</u>, Knopf: 1963.  "I consider Marxism the one philosophy of our time which we cannot go beyond...I hold the ideology of existence and its 'comprehensive' method to be an enclave inside Marxism."  Demonstrates his method in extended analysis of class determinants of Flaubert.

_____, "The Republic Of Silence," in A.J. Liebling, ed, <u>The Republic Of Silence</u>, 1947, 498-500.  The famous essay that begins: "We were never more free than during the German occupation."

_____, Introduction to 'Les Temps Modernes'.  In: <u>Paths To the Present</u>, ed. Eugen Weber, Dodd, Mead paperback: 1960, 431-441.

_____, <u>What Is Literature</u>? 1949; Washington Square paperback, 1966.  The writer's function, his freedom, his social situation, Marxism, the Communist Party, Surrealism.  Breton, R. Wright, Kafka, Gide.

_____, "Forgers Of Myths: The Young Playwrights Of France," <u>Theatre Arts</u>, June 1946, 324-335.  Chiefly about themes and form of his own plays and Anouilh's 'Antigone'.

_____, "I Discovered Jazz In America," <u>Saturday Review</u>, Nov 29, 1947, 48-49.  "It does not speak of love and it does not comfort.  It is hurried.  Like the people who take the subway or eat at the automat."

_____, "A European Declaration of Independence," <u>Commentary</u>, May 1950, 407-414.  Explores alternatives open to national cultures which must bow to the culture of nations with superior military might.

_____, "Peace: The Reality Of Life,"<u>NF</u>, Winter 1953, 12-15.  Speech to Congress of the Peoples For Peace.

_____, "Black Orpheus," <u>MassR</u>, VI i (1965), 13-52.  Also in <u>Stand</u> (London), V iv, 2-12; VI i, 7-20, a poorer translation.  Cited, summarized and commented upon in Michel Beaujour, "Sartre and Surreal-ism," <u>YFS</u> #30, 86-95.  Famed essay on the nature of Negro poetry - its healthy surrealism, contrasted with French Surrealism.

_____, <u>Literary Essays</u>, Philosophical Library: 1957.  Faulkner, Dos Passos, Camus' 'Outsider', Mauriac, Giraudoux, Kafka and Blanchot.

_____, "The China I Saw," <u>M&M</u>, Mch 1956, 15-20.

_____, Interview with K.S. Karol.  <u>New Statesman</u>, Dec 3, 1955, 737-739.  His visit to China.

_____, "Cold War and Anti-Communism," <u>M&M</u>, Aug 1955, 26-30.

_____, "After Budapest," <u>Evergreen Review</u>, #1 (1957), 5-23.  Interview with 'L'Express', Nov 9, 1956.

_____, et al, Letter of French Intellectuals to Soviet Intellectuals Over the Hungarian Uprising, and Reply of Soviet Writers.  <u>CDSP</u>, Jan 2, 1957, 6-7.

_____, "Is This the Time?"  <u>New Reasoner</u>, Summer 1957, 87-97.  Final part of 'Temps Modernes' essay in wake of Suez and Hungary.  Takes the measure of French Communist and Socialist parties and declares only course is to work sympathetically with the CP while telling it painful truths necessary to destalinize it.

_____, et al, The 'Declaration of 121' On War In Algeria.  <u>Evergreen Review</u>, #15 (1960).

_____, <u>Sartre On Cuba</u>, Ballantine paperback: 1961.  Castro as Sartreian protagonist in history.

_____, <u>Saint Genet, Actor and Martyr</u>, Braziller: 1963.  Exhaustive treatment of a single author's writing and development.  Many side comments on literature and society.

_____, "Brecht As a Classic," <u>World Theatre</u>, Spring 1958, 11-19.

_____, "Beyond Bourgeois Theatre," <u>TDR</u>, Mch 1961, 3-11.  Includes a critique of Brecht's dramatic theory.

_____, Interview.  <u>C&L</u>, 1962 #9, 35-36. illus.  Views on new Russian films and architecture, French fiction and his own work.

_____, "The Theatre," Evergreen Review,
Jan-Feb 1960, 143-152. Brings out
criticisms of Brecht.

_____, Preface to The Damned by Frantz
Fanon, Presence Africaine: Paris, 1963,
7-26; published as The Wretched Of the
Earth, Grove: 1965. The aristocratic
vices of Western culture and its degradation in attempting to continue
colonial regimes.

_____, Speech at Conference of European
Writers, Leningrad, Summer 1963. NLR
#29 (Jan-Feb 1965), 36-40. Problems
of decadence, formalism, expression vs.
discovery of reality, commitment,
audience.

_____, The Words, Braziller: 1964. Auto-
biography.

_____, Interview with 'Le Monde'. En,
June 1964, 61-63; also Vogue, Jan 1965,
94-95, 159. Clarifies portions of
'The Words' that were widely misinterpreted. Discusses role of writers in
non-revolutionary societies and in
oppressed nations.

_____, Nobel Prize Refusal Statement.
N.Y. Review of Books, Dec 17, 1964,
5-6. Institutionalizing of the writer.
Politics of the Nobel Prize.

_____, Speech to World Congress For Gen-
eral Disarmament and Peace, Moscow,
July 1962. NG, Nov 8, 1962, 6. abdgd.
Kafka - and similar problems - should
be assimilated, not excluded by Marxism.

_____, Situations, Braziller: 1965.
Translation of 'Situations IV', 1964.
Tintoretto, his class and Venice.
Gide's value in the integrity of his
process of becoming atheist. The
break with Camus. Camus' death. Paul
Nizan, his youth and relation to communism. Giacometti. Nathalie Sarraute
and the anti-novel. Andre Gorz and
writing as catharsis. Merleau-Ponty.
Modern music and Zhdanov's strictures: what and how music communicates.
- See also, Henry Barraud, "La Musique
Engagee," Musical America, Feb 1951,
13, 218-219. Detailed account of last-
mentioned Sartre essay and of the book
it prefaces, Rene Lebowitz' 'L'Artiste
et sa Conscience'.

_____, Interview. Playboy, May 1965,
69-76.

_____, "Why I Am Not Going To the United
States," NG, Apr 17, 1965, 5. US imperialism in Vietnam. Role of anti-
imperialist intellectuals in France
and the US.

_____, Symposium In Prague On the Ques-
tion Of Decadence. Streets, May-June
1965, 46-55. With E. Fischer, Milan
Kundera, Edouard Goldstucker.

_____, SEE ALSO: Garaudy (XIX); Caute,
Savage (XX); Lukacs (XXVII);
Finkelstein, Harap (LVI);
Steiner (LIX); Frid (XLVI). And:

R.D. Laing and D.G. Cooper,
Reason and Violence: A Decade
of Sartre's Philosophy, 1950-
1960, Tavistock: London, 1964.
Foreword by Sartre. Admirably
concise presentation of 'In
Search Of a Method', 'Saint
Genet' and 'Critique Of Dialectical Reason'.

Yale French Studies #30 (1965).
Special Sartre issue. biblio.

Philip Thody, Jean-Paul Sartre:
A Literary and Political Study,
London, 1960. Excellent on
his political development.

Eugene F. Kaelin, An Existen-
tialist Aesthetic, Wisconsin
Univ: Madison, 1962. Scholarly discussion of Sartre's and
Merleau-Ponty's aesthetics,
slighting political elements.

SITUATIONIST INTERNATIONAL, "Address To
the Revolutionaries Of Algeria and Of
All Countries," Supplement to Internationale Situationniste, #10 (1965). In
English. Declaring that "Socialism
exists wherever the workers themselves
manage directly the entire society; it
therefore does not exist either in Russia or in China or elsewhere," the
"specialists of the power who take
charge of the revolutions" are de-
nounced, and the "project of free
creativity" of the workers affirmed,
with "modern poetry and art...a preface
to an experimental research to the human being's free arrangement of his
daily life." - See also Michele Bern-
stein, "The Situationist International,"

<u>Times Literary Supplement</u>, Sept 3, 1964, 781.

_____, <u>The Totality For Kids</u>, London: 196?. Written by Raoul Vaneigem. Manifesto on social domination as now a spectacle paralyzing will with goods and specialities, to be countered with a revolutionary theatrical autonomy.

STIL, Andre, "The Vanguard Writer," <u>M&M</u>, Aug 1952, 46-53. Stalin prize acceptance speech on creativity and commitment.

TZARA, Tristan, "Surrealism and the Post-War," <u>transition 48</u>, #2 (1948), 176-178. abdgd. Public lecture heckled by Breton, in which Tzara broke with Surrealism on grounds of its social irresponsibility during war and after.

VILAR, Jean, "The Director and the Play," <u>YFS</u>, #5 (1950), 12-26. Affirms need of a renewed society for a renewed theatre.

_____, Speech to Company of Theatre National Populaire. <u>Flourish</u> (London), Summer 1965, 16. The problems and necessity of making the TNP a theatre for the people. Keeping contact with workers and young people as "practical schooling in reality."

VIRMAUX, Alain, "Artaud and Film," <u>TDR</u>, Fall 1966, 154-165. Artaud as wanting to change life, his frustrations in the film industry.

ZADKINE, Ossip, Statement. <u>Arts and Architecture</u>, Mch 1951, 16, 46. illus. Sculpture, planes, light and philosophy.

_____, The Evolution of Sculpture. <u>Tiger's Eye</u>, #4 (1948), 83-84.

_____, SEE ALSO: Berger (XXIII); and:

    <u>Canadian Art</u>, Autumn 1956, 6-9. illus.

    <u>Current Biography</u>, Mch 1957, 61-62.

    Max Wykes-Joyce, "A Visit To Zadkine," <u>Art</u>, I xxvi (Nov 10, 1955), 6. illus. "Here is a sculptor as important to the future of his art as, say, Picasso to painting, or Schoenberg to music."

    A.M. Hammacher, <u>Zadkine</u>, Universal Books: 1959. Chiefly illus.

    Ionel Jianon, <u>Zadkine</u>, Tudor: 1965. illus. Preface by Waldemar George.

## XX. Appendix.

AUERBACH, Sol, "Barbusse's New Journal 'Monde'," <u>DW</u>, Dec 22, 1928, 6. Detailed critique. Objects to its United Front policy.

BALASHOVA, Tamara, "A Friend Of Soviet Art," <u>C&L</u>, 1966 #1, 39-40. Romain Rolland and Communism.

CAMUS, Albert, "Create Dangerously," in his <u>Resistance, Rebellion and Death</u>, 1961, 249-272. Attacks socialist realism.

CAUTE, David, <u>Communism and the French Intellectuals, 1914-1960</u>, Macmillan: 1964. - See review by Harvey Goldberg, <u>Nation</u>, Dec 21, 1964, 496-499. - Review by George Lichtheim, <u>En</u>, Nov 1964, 31-35.

EGBERT, Donald D, <u>Communism, Radicalism, and the Arts In Western Europe</u>, forthcoming.

ETIEMBLE, "The Tibetan Dog," <u>YFS</u>, #31 (1964), 127-134. First-hand account of political Surrealists in 30s and Trotsky's explanation of why he allied himself with Surrealism: "he explained that he could not afford to be sectarian in ideological matters when allies were so hard to come by."

EVANS, David Owen, <u>Social Romanticism In France, 1830-1848</u>, Oxford: London, 1951. biblio. The literature and art - especially Hugo, G. Sand, Vigny - inspired by French Socialism from Saint-Simon to Proudhon.

FARMER, H. George, "Salvador Daniel, Musician and Communard," <u>The Social-Democrat</u>, XIII x (1909), 469-474. Director of Paris Conservatoire who died on the barricades of the Commune.

GRANA, Cesar, <u>Modernity and Its Discontents; French Society and the French Man Of Letters In the Nineteenth Century</u>, Harper Torchbook: 1967. Bohemian vs. Bourgeois.

GRAY, Stanley E, "The Social Meaning Of

the New Novel In France," in: Bernice Slote, ed, Literature and Society, Bison paperback: Lincoln, Neb, 1964. 241-252. The theory of Roland Barthes.

HERBERT, Eugenia W, The Artist and Social Reform; France and Belgium, 1885-1898, Yale: New Haven, 1961. illus. Social history of socialist politics and literature in latter 19th Century. Special emphasis on radical Symbolists, Zola and Hugo, Van Gogh, Pissarro, Signac, Seurat, Steinlen, Luce, Meunier. The role of Jean Grave, anarchist editor, in influencing them. Some discussion of workers theatre.

_____, and Herbert L, "Artists and Anarchism:Unpublished Letters of Pissarro, Signac and Others," Burlington Magazine, Nov 1960, 473-482; Dec, 517-522. illus. Letters exchanged with Jean Grave, and background information.

LICHTHEIM, George, Marxism In Modern France, Columbia Univ. Press: 1966.

MACHAN, H.W, The Popular Theatre Movement In France; Romain Rolland and the

Revue d'Art Dramatique, Ph.D. Dissertation, Illinois Univ: Urbana, 1950.

RACINE, N, "The Clarte Movement In France, 1919-1921," Journal Of Contemporary History, Apr 1967, 195-208.

ST. AUBYN, Frederic, "The Social Consciousness Of Rimbaud," YFS, #4 (1950), 26-33.

SANBORN, Alvan F, Paris and the Social Revolution, Boston: 1905. illus. Theatre, journals, art of the anarchists, students, workers.

SAVAGE, Catherine, Malraux, Sartre, and Aragon As Political Novelists, Univ. of Florida Press: Gainesville, 1965. 64 pp.

SHORT, Robert S., "The Politics Of Surrealism, 1920-36," Journal of Contemporary History, I ii (1966), 3-25.

WALDBERG, Patrick, Surrealism, McGraw-Hill: 1965. illus. Emphasis on painting; documents; chronology.

## GERMANY AND AUSTRIA

(SEE ALSO: Arnold Hauser (XXVII), on all topics to 1920s.)

### Topic Index

ART AND FASCISM. 'Art In Third Reich', Hitler (XXII); Lehmann-Haupt (XLIX).

ART HISTORY, HISTORICIST. Antal, Hauser (XXVII).

ART, SOCIALIST REALIST. Lehmann-Haupt (XLIX).

BACH. Fischer. Cabrero (XXXIII); Boughton (LXII).

BEETHOVEN. Fischer. Rolland (XIX); Adorno (LXII).

BENN, G. Becher. Lukacs (XXVII).

BRECHT, B. See (XXI).

BUCHNER, G. Baxandall, Kresh (LVI).

CELAN, P. Hoellerer (LXII).

CINEMA AND FASCISM. Szabo (XXVII); Baxandall (LVI); Kracauer (LXII).

DURRENMATT, F. Brecht. See (LXIII).

DVORAK, M. Antal (XXVII).

ENZENSBERGER, H. Hoellerer (LXII).

EXILED WRITERS. Heym, Weiss, Wolf. Aragon (XIX); 1940 (LI).

FALLADA, H. Slochower (LVI).

FEUCHTWANGER, L. Lukacs (XXVII); Levidov, Metallov (XLVI); Slochower (LVI).

FONTANE. Pascal (XXIII); Lukacs (XXVII); Auerbach, Kohn-Bramstedt (LXII).

FREIE BUHNE. Baxandall (LVI); Gorelik (LVII).

GEORGE, S. Slochower (LVI).

GOETHE. Eisler, Fischer, Marx and Engels, Mehring. Demetz (XXII); Pascal (XXIII); Lukacs (XXVII); Bukharin (XLVI); Hitch (LVI); Gassner (LVIII); Auerbach, Brandes, Bruford, Lowenthal, Stael (LXII).

GOTTHELF. Pascal (XXIII); Auerbach, Kohn-Bramstedt (LXII).

GRASS, G.  Burgum (LVI).

GRILLPARZER, Fischer.  Pascal (XXIII).

'GROBIAN' LITERATURE.  Marx and Engels.

GROPIUS. Watkinson (XXIII). See (LXIII).

GROSZ, G.  Summers (LIII).

GRUNEWALD, M.  Berger (XXIII).

GUTZKOW.  Butler (XXII).

HEARTFIELD, J. Durus.  Tretyakov (XLVI).

HAUPTMANN. Kerr. Liptzin (XXII); Lukacs
   (XXVII); Lenin, Lunacharsky (XLVI);
   Baxandall, Kresh, Slochower (LVI);
   Gassner (LVIII).

HEBBEL. Lukacs (XXVII); Auerbach (LXII).

HEGEL. Fischer, Marx and Engels. Lukacs
   (XXVII);Eisenstein(XLIV);Auerbach(LXII).

HEINE.  Fischer, Marx and Engels. Butler, Liptzin (XXII); Lunacharsky
   (XLVI); Fraina (LVI). See (LXIII).

HERDER.  Fischer. Pascal (XXIII).

HINDEMITH.  Cazden (LVII).

HITLER,LINGUISTIC STRATEGY. Burke (LVI).

HOFFMANN.  Fischer. Lukacs (XXVII).

HOFFMANNSTHAL. Lukacs (XXVII).

HOLDERLIN.  Fischer.

KANT. Mehring. Lukacs (XXVII); Kozhinov,
   Plekhanov (XLVI); Dunham (LVI).

KELLER.  Pascal (XXIII); Auerbach,
   Kohn-Bramstedt (LXII).

KLEE.  Berger (XXIII).

KLEIST.  Fischer.

KOESTLER.  Harrington (LVI); Howe,
   Woodcock (LXII).

KOKOSCHKA.  Berger (XXIII).

KOLLWITZ.  Toller. See (LXIII).

KRAUS.  Fischer.

LAUBE.  Butler (XXII).

LESSING.  Mehring. Lukacs (XXVII);

Gassner (LVIII); Auerbach (LXII).

LITERATURE AND FASCISM. Bund,Richter.Hit-
   ler (XXII);Lukacs (XXVII); Slochower
   (LVI);Hoellerer,Mosse, Rader (LXII).

LITERATURE, HISTORY.  Marx and Engels.
   Lukacs (XXVII); Francke, Kohn-Bramstedt,
   Stael (LXII).

MANN, H.  Lukacs (XXVII); Slochower (LVI).

MANN, T.  Fischer. Pascal (XXIII); Lukacs
   (XXVII); Lundberg, Motyleva, Suchkov
   (XLVI); Burgum,Harrington,Humboldt,Ros-
   enberg,Slochower (LVI); Auerbach (LXII).

MARX AND ENGELS, ELUCIDATION OF AND COM-
   MENTARY ON THEIR AESTHETICS.  Fischer,
   Mehring, Raphael.  Freville (XIX); Bell,
   Demetz, Johnston, Wellek (XXII); Birn-
   baum, Caudwell, Fox, Johnson, Lewis,
   West (XXIII); Lukacs (XXVII); Labriola
   (XXX); Lifshitz, Lunacharsky, Timofeyev,
   Troshenko (XLVI); Guterman: 1936 (LI);
   Harrington, Phillips, Sillen, Wilson
   (LVI); Burnham, Glicksberg, Hyman, Munro,
   Steiner (LIX); Hall, Matthiessen, Rader,
   Scott (LXII). See Marx and Engels (XXI).

MEINECKE. Auerbach, Kohn-Bramstedt (LXII).

MEYER, F.  Lukacs (XXVII).

MOZART.  Fischer, Cazden (LVII).

MUNDT.  Butler (XXII).

MUSIC, WORKERS', HISTORY.  Eisler.

MUSIL.  Lukacs (XXVII); Hoellerer (LXII).

NIBELUNGENSLIED.  Routh (LXII).

NIETZSCHE.  Lukacs (XXVII); Plekhanov
   (XLVI); Finkelstein, Harrington,
   Slochower (LVI).

NOVALIS.  Fischer.

NOVEL.  Pascal (XXIII); Lukacs (XXVII);
   Kohn-Bramstedt (LXII).

PABST.  Potamkin (LIV); Kracauer (LXII).

PISCATOR, E.  See (XXI).

PLATEN.  Marx and Engels.

PLIVIER.  Smith (LVI).

PROLETARIAN  WRITING.  Biha.

RAABE.  Pascal (XXIII); Lukacs (XXVII).

RATGEB. Weigand (LIII).

REICH, W. See (XXI). Kupferberg (LXIII).

RIEGL, A. Hauser (XXVII).

RILKE. Cornu (XIX); Slochower (LVI).

SCHILLER. Brecht, Mdarx and Engels.
  Lukacs (XXVII); Gassner (LVIII);
  Auerbach (LXII).

SCHLEGEL, F. Fischer. Stael (LXII).

SCHNITZLER, A. Slochower (LVI).

SCHONBERG. Eisler. Adorno (LXII).

SEGHERS, A. See (XXI). Pascal (XXIII);
  Slochower (LVI).

STIFTER. Pascal (XXIII); Lukacs (XXVII);
  Auerbach, Kohn-Bramstedt (LXII).

STORM. Auerbach, Kohn-Bramstedt (LXII).

STURM UND DRANG. Pascal (XXIII);
  Auerbach, Bruford (LXII).

THEATRE AND FASCISM. Kerr, Piscator,
  Wolf.

THEATRE, POST-WAR. Kahler. Tynan (LXII).

THEATRE, WORKERS'. Brecht, Kahler,
  Piscator, Wolf. Baxandall (LVI).

TOLLER, E. See (XXI). Slochower (LVI);
  Weigand (LVIII).

TRAKL. Hoellerer (LXII).

TRAVEN, B. Stone (XXII); Hagemann,
  Madden (LIX).

WAGNER, R. Lunacharsky, Plekhanov
  (XLVI). See Wagner (LXIII).

WEERTH. Marx and Engels.

WEINBARG. Butler (XXII).

WERFEL, F. Slochower (LVI).

WINKELMANN. Lifshitz (XLVI).

WOLFFLIN. Antal, Hauser (XXVII).

YOUNG GERMANY MOVEMENT. Marx and
  Engels. Butler, Demetz, Liptzin
  (XXII).

ZWEIG, S. Lukacs (XXVII); Slochower
  (LVI).

## XXI.  Authors

BECHER, Johannes R, Radio-Dialog with
Gottfried Benn, June 4, 1930. Blues,
#9, 5-10. Trenchantly translated by
Eugene Jolas. Benn was foremost among
German poets contemptuous of social
engagement.

_____, "The Tasks Of Revolutionary Writ-
ers," LWR, Special Issue (1931), 29-50.

_____, "The Great Alliance," PR, Nov-Dec
1934, 16-20. abdgd. Speech to Soviet
Writers Congress, Moscow.

BENJAMIN, Walter, "The Work Of Art In
the Epoch Of Mechanical Reproduction,"
SOL, I ii (1960), 28-46.

_____, "The Story-Teller: Reflections On
the Works Of Nicolai Leskov," Chicago
Review, Winter-Spring 1963, 80-101.
Problems of narrative.

_____, Essays, Harcourt, Brace & World
(A Helen and Kurt Wolff Book): forthcoming. Eleven essays and introduction by Hannah Arandt.

_____, SEE ALSO: Lukacs (XXVII); Steiner
(LIX).

BIHA, Otto, "On the Question Of Prole-
tarian Revolutionary Literature In
Germany," LWR, 1931 #4, 88-105.
Politician's assessment.

BLOCH, Ernst, "Man and Music," Mother
Earth, Apr 1917, 56-60; May, 85-89.
Music as narcotic and as weapon.

_____, "Odysseus Did Not Die In Ithaca,"
in: George Steiner and Robert Fables,
eds, Homer; A Collection Of Critical
Essays, Prentice-Hall Spectrum paperback: Englewood Cliffs, N. J, 1962,
81-85. From vol. II, 'Das Prinzip
Hoffnung'. Odysseus as symbol of quest.

_____, SEE ALSO: Review-article on 'Das
Prinzip Hoffnung', Times Literary Supplement, Mch 31, 1961,
193-194. And: Jurgen Ruhle,
"Ernst Bloch," Survey #32 (1960),
85-93.

BRECHT, Bertolt, Brecht On Theatre; The
Development Of an Aesthetic, ed. John
Willett, Hill and Wang: 1964. Contains
virtually every significant essay
available in English. Some writings
not included:

_____, "Notes On Translating Songs Of Struggle," MV, I ii (Summer 1935), 67-68. A translator, like original author, should "write in accordance with the demands of the situation and... find popular expressions for abstract slogans and formulations."

_____, Interview with Martha Dreiblatt. DW, Oct 31, 1935, 5. illus. Discusses his road to Marx, having formerly believed "all of life was absurd" and all classes equally stupid in swallowing ideas fed to them and acting as though these ideas corresponded to reality.

_____, The Messingkauf Dialogues, Methuen: London, 1965. Discussions of theatre practice.

_____, SEE ALSO; Martin Esslin, Brecht; The Man and His Work, Doubleday: 1960. Bibliography, biography and analysis. - See review by Lee Baxandall, SOL, I ii (1960), 67-73.

    John Willett, The Theatre Of Bertolt Brecht, New Directions: 1959. illus. Bibliography.

    Werner Hecht, "The Development Of Brecht's Theory Of Epic Theatre, 1918-1933," TDR, Sept 1961, 40-97.

    Eva Goldbeck, "Principles Of 'Educational' Theatre," NM, Dec 31, 1935, 27-28. Best exposition of Brecht's principles to appear in English in the 30s. Written with probable aid from Eisler and perhaps Brecht. Eva Goldbeck was Mrs. Marc Blitzstein.

    Boris Zingerman, "Brecht On the Soviet Stage," SL, 1962 #12, 155-162. Searching account of changes made in Brecht on the Soviet stage and the long neglect of his plays.

    Also: Sartre (XIX); Fischer, Schumacher (XXI); Arundel (XXIII); Lukacs (XXVII); Tretyakov (XLVI); Anikst, Fradkin (XLVIII); Baxandall, Ewen, Slochower (LVI); Baxandall (LVIII); Suvin (LXI); Hoellerer (LXII).

BRUNING, Eberhard, "The Spanish Civil War (1936-39) and the American Novel," ZAA, XI (1963), 42-55. Hemingway, Dos Passos, Upton Sinclair, Elliot Paul, Alvah Bessie.

_____, "Die amerikanische Arbeitertheaterbewegung der 30er Jahre," ZAA, IX iv (1961), 341-409. A good survey; valuable for analysis of German-language activities of US left theatre, the Soviet influences, and foreign performance of American left plays.

_____, "The 'Red Decade' und die amerikanische Dramatik in der neueren Forschung," ZAA, 1965 #4, 387-398. Appraisal of Rabkin and Himelstein volumes, with additional remarks. - See commentary on this essay by Todor Kirov, ZAA, 1966 #4, 386-388.

_____, Das Amerikanische Drama der Dreisiger Jahre, Rutten & Loening: Berlin, 1966. Fullest account in any language of 1930s left drama in US.

BUND PROLETARISCH-REVOLUTIONARER SCHRIFTSTELLER DEUTSCHLANDS, "Brains Behind the Barbed Wire; A Collective Report On Persecution In Nazi Germany," DW, June 14, 1934, 5; 15, 5; 16, 5; 18, 5; 19, 5; 20, 7; 22, 5; 23, 7; 26, 5; 27, 5; 28, 5. Ossietzki, Renn, Bredel, Neukrantz, Braun, Gog, Muhsam, Baron, scientists, lawyers, etc.

CADENZ, Gert, Interview with Sadie van Veen. DW, June 27, 1947, 11. illus. Refugee painter talks of his Havana exhibition.

DURUS, Alfred, John Heartfield. IL, 1935 #3, 102-105. illus.

EINSTEIN, Carl, Georges Bracque, London, 1934. Bracque doing necessary destruction that will clear way for a collectivist art which, for the present, is impossible.

EISLER, Hanns, The Crisis In Music, 1936. 10 pp. Reprinted in DW, Aug 24, 1939, 7. abdgd. Speech to Pierre Degeyter Club of New York, Mch 1, 1935 (his first US appearance), repeated at New School, Oct 5, 1935. - Review by Marc Blitzstein, NM, June 23, 1936, 28, calls it "very possibly the manifesto for the revolutionary music of our time."

_____, "Film Music: Illustration Or Creation?" World Film News, May 1936, 23. Discusses films he has worked on.

_____, "Music In Films," Films, Winter 1940, 5-20. Taking part in a symposium Eisler makes extensive reference to films he has worked on.

_____, Interview with Charles Hatchard. DW, Oct 7, 1935, 5. Describes plans in US, his work as head of International Music Bureau.

_____, "The Composer In Society," DW, Dec 5, 1935, 7. Pithy statement of view; not analytically developed.

_____, American Workers Choruses. DW, Feb 17, 1936, 7. Speech to Daily Worker Chorus extensively quoted.

_____, Interview. NM, Oct 15, 1935. Announces plans in US, reviews his exile, declares there is not yet a proletarian music.

_____, "History Of the German Workers' Music Movement From 1848," MV, I i (1935), 33-48. illus.

_____, "Reflections On the Future Of the Composer," ModM, May-June 1935, 180-186.

_____, Composing For the Films, 1947. Written 1941-42 in collaboration with T.W. Adorno on $20,000 Rockefeller Foundation grant. Theory of various ways music can combine with film image, emphasizing commentary and collision (per Brecht). Function of a revolutionary composer in a capitalist film industry.

_____, "Music: From Cult To Culture," M&M, Aug 1948, 42-48. Social base of bourgeois composition focussing on Schonberg and Stravinsky.

_____, Statement To House Committee On Un-American Activities. DW, May 17, 1947, 11. illus.

_____, Interview with Alvah Bessie. NM, May 13, 1947, 9-10. In conjunction with his subpoena to appear before HCUA.

_____, Statement Prepared For HCUA. NM, Oct 14, 1947, 9-10. Eisler was not permitted to read his statement. Scornful and hostile, unlike Brecht's testimony.

_____, Transcript Of Testimony Before HCUA. Listen, Sept-Oct 1964, 8-10; also Encore, Sept-Oct 1964, 32-38. abdgd.

_____, Interview with Walter Lowenfels. Saturday Review, Aug 31, 1963, 33-34. His teacher Schonberg. "He will be esteemed as one who despised cliches... He held a mirror up before his time and his class. What one sees there wasn't by any means pretty. But it was the truth."

_____, SEE ALSO; Current Biography, 1942, 240-242 illus. Also: Sergei Tretyakov, "Hans Eisler: Revolutionary Composer," IL, 1933 #5, 113-118. A lively account. And: R.C. Andrews, "A Communist View Of the Reformation: A New Faust Opera," Hibbert Journal, Oct 1956, 75-79. Also Fischer (XXI).

ENGELS, Friedrich. See Marx (below).

FISCHER, Ernst, The Necessity Of Art, Pelican paperback: 1963. Outstanding consideration of origins and nature of art, and art under socialism. Alienation. Art as myth, magic, religion, totalization of experience. Mass art, art for art's sake. Bach, baroque art, Baudelaire, beatniks, Becher, Beethoven, Brecht, Breughel, Byron, cave paintings, Camus, Cervantes, Classicism and Romanticism, Coleridge, Courbet, Egyptian art, Eisler, El Greco, Flaubert, folk art, form, Delacroix, Gericault, Giotto, Goethe, Gorky, gothic art, Goya, Grillparzer, Hegel, Heine, Herder, Hoffmann, Holderlin, Homer, Ibsen, Impressionism, Joyce, Kafka, Keats, Kleist, Kraus, Language, Leger, Mallarme, Malraux, Mann, Marx, Mayakovsky, Michelangelo, Millet, Mozart, Naturalism, Neo-positivism, Novalis, O'Casey, ornamental art, Picasso, poetry, Proust, Pushkin, Racine, realism, Renaissance, Rimbaud, Rivera, Robbe-Grillet, rococo art, Romanesque art, Salinger, Schlegel, Shakespeare, Shelley, Socialist Realism, Stendhal, Stravinsky, Strindberg, Surrealism, Symbolism, Tolstoy, Van Gogh, Yeats, Zola, etc. - See Kiernan (XXIII); Central Committee (XXVII). - Review by L. Harap, S&S, Summer 1965, 362-364.

_____, "Capitalist Barbarism and Soviet Culture," CI, Dec 1937, 961-970.

_____, Symposium In Prague On the Question Of Decadence. Streets, May-June 1965, 46-55. With J.P. Sartre, Milan Kundera, Edouard Goldstucker.

_____, "Art and Ideological Superstructure," MT, Feb 1964, 46-51. Chapter of 'Art and Coexistence', a work-in-progress. Basically argument against 'guidance' of artists. - Fischer's view that socialist art is matter of conviction not a particular style is challenged by David Craig, MT, June 1964, 187-189, as an excess committed in avoidance of dogmatism. Margot Heinemann answers Craig, MT, Oct 1964, 321-324.

_____, "Synopsis Of the Contributions of Professor G. Lukacs and Ernst Fischer To the Wroclaw Conference, 1948," reported by Roy Pascal, MQ(L), Summer 1949, 53-58. Long extracts from their speeches.

FREIBURG, E.R. von, "Half and Half Equals Two," Nation, Apr 17, 1967, 502-506. Analysis of the effect upon writers of the division of Germany into two opposed states. Weiss, Hacks, Biermann, Grass, Heym, Strittmatter, Wolf, Kant, Neutsch.

HAUSER, Arnold (See (XXVII).

HEYM, Stefan, "I Arrive At Socialism By Train," Nation, Oct 11, 1965, 228-230. His experiences as a writer in the US and in the German Democratic Republic. His current problems of discipline vs. freedom to criticize.

ILBERG, Werner, "Romain Rolland: An Honest Eclectic," MQ(L), Winter 1947-48, 30-44.

KAHLER, Hermann, "Contemporary Drama," World Theatre, XIV (1965), 373-383. illus. Plays about socialism and the German Democratic Republic.

KANTOROWICZ, Alfred, "Reflections On 'Socialist Realism'," The Review (Brussels), 1962 #2-3, 88-90. Argues against Zhdanovian theory and practice of Socialist Realism as corruption of its greatest achievements and, indeed, of what Gorky originally intended.

KAUTSKY, Karl, Thomas More and His Utopia, 1927. 'Utopia' representing London merchantile interests opposed to working class. - For a critique,

see R. Ames (LVI). - See also Plebs, June 1922, 172. Excerpt from above book, describing mockery as a literary expression of revolutionary classes in 'Don Quixote', 'The Decameron','The Merry Wives Of Windsor'.

KERR, Alfred, Bolshevism, Fascism and Drama. IL, 1935 #10, 100-101. The great critic's sad reflections and change of heart after Hitler took power. Expressionist drama's failure.

_____, Gerhart Hauptmann and Fascism. NM, Jan 30, 1934, 19-20. Hauptmann's acceptance of Hitler, "worm-eaten to the bottom of his soul" and "destroyed by money."

KURELLA, Alfred, "Henri Barbusse: Literary Warrior," IL, 1935 #3, 97-100.

_____, "What Was He Killed For?" LWR, 1931 #5, 156-160. Party criticism of Brecht's 'The Measures Taken'. The Young Comrade's action is deemed correct. Brecht criticized with analysis of his class origin.

LUKACS, George. See (XXVII).

LUXEMBURG, Rosa. See (XXXVI).

MARCUSE, Herbert. See (LVI).

MARTIN, Alfred von, Sociology Of the Renaissance, London, 1944; Harper Torchbook paperback, 1963.

MARX, Karl, and Friedrich ENGELS, Literature and Art, International: 1947. Appendix contains reminiscences by Paul Lafargue, Wilhelm Liebknecht, Franz Mehring. A number of the major texts are here; but selections and translations are not entirely adequate, and lack commentary. Forthcoming volume will provide the fullest selection in English, with historical and critical context: Stefan Morawski and Lee Baxandall, eds, Marxists On Art and Literature. Soon to be published. - Texts which follow help to round out the existing volume.

_____, Economic and Philosophical Manuscripts of 1844, in: Eric Fromm, Marx's Concept Of Man, Ungar paperback: 1961, 90-196.

_____, The Holy Family, Moscow, 1956; London, 1957. Critique of Eugene Sue; discussion of critical principles toward literature.

_____, "Marx and Engels On Balzac," ed. F. Schiller, IL, 1933 #3, 112-124.

_____, "Marx and Engels To Lassalle," IL, 1933 #4, 108-122.

_____, "Marx and Engels On Literature," IL, 1934 #5, 101-106. Extracts on Heine, Carlyle, Carlton, etc.

_____, Engels on Revolutionary Poetry and Mass Prejudice: Letter to Schluchter. S&S, Summer 1938, 349-350.

_____, Engels On Ibsen: Letter To Paul Ernst. In: Henrik Ibsen, ed. Angel Flores, 1937, 21-24.

_____, Engels, "The Role Of Labor In the Ape's Evolution Into Man," Dia, #8 (1938), 1-14.

_____, Engels/Ernst Correspondence With Commentary By F. Schiller. IL, 1934 #4, 80-89.

_____, SEE ALSO: Mikhail Lifshitz, The Philosophy Of Art Of Karl Marx, 1938. First-rate compilation and interpretation.

    E. Troschenko, "Marx On Literature," IL, 1934 #4, 136-148.

    Also: Aveling (XXIV); Germany, Topic Index, Marx.

MAYER, Hans, Interview. En, Apr 1964.

_____, "The Struggle For Kafka and Joyce," En, May 1964, 83-89. The politics in Eastern Europe of conflict over literary modernism.

_____, SEE ALSO: George Steiner, "The Last German Marxist?" En, Apr 1964, 112-117. Appraisal and account of Mayer's books.

MEHRING, Franz, The Lessing Legend, 1938. abdgd. Introduction by Joseph Kresh. Rescues Lessing from the bourgeois critics by documenting falsifications.

_____, "Ibsen's Greatness and Limitations," in: Henrik Ibsen, ed. Angel Flores, 1937, 25-34.

_____, "A Note On Taste," Dia, #4 (1937), 16-20. Reprinted in IndL, 1952 #2, 90-93. Written 1898. Critique of

Kantian aesthetics and question of taste.

_____, "Literature and the Class Struggle," Comm, July 1929, 409-412. Goethe and the relevance of class to function and appreciation of art.

_____, "Karl Marx and Metaphor," in: D. Ryazanoff, ed, Karl Marx, 1927, 95-101. Metaphor in Lessing and Goethe, and Marx's use of metaphor as "the sensorily appreciable mother of the thought, which receives from that mother the breath of life." Written 1903.

_____, Karl Marx; The Story Of His Life, London: 1936. Still the best biography; with much attention to Marx's aesthetic interests.

MEYER, Ernst H, English Chamber Music, Lawrence & Wishart: London, 1946. To Purcell.

PISCATOR, Erwin, "Adaptation Of 'The Good Soldier Schweik'," ITh, #4 (1933), 8-12. illus. From 'Das politische Theater'.

_____, "The Social Theatre," NM, July 1929, 14.

_____, "Theatre and Cinema," ITh, #3 (1933), 11-13. Role of film in epic theatre.

_____, Adaptation of 'An American Tragedy'. DW, Mch 8, 1936, 6.

_____, "A Theatre Director In the Soviet Cinema," NTh, Jan 1935, 14. Filming of A. Seghers' 'The Revolt Of the Fishermen'. Remarks on his deviation from the Socialist Realism.

_____, "Lessons of the Past and Tasks For the Future," ITh, 1935 #1, 3-8. Followed by "Erwin Piscator - President of the IURT" by H. Diament, ibid, 8-9. Speeches by incoming and outgoing heads of Moscow-based International Workers Theatre Union.

_____, "The Theatre Of the Future," Tomorrow, Feb 1942, 14-19. illus. Discusses Federal Theatre Living Newspapers, Epic Theatre, Walter Gropius' Total Theatre.

_____, Interview with Arthur Olsen. N.Y. Times, Drama Section, Oct 31, 1965, 7. Career and views since 1951.

_____, "The Adaptation Of the Novel To the Stage," World Theatre, Autumn 1956, 291-304. illus. Reprinted in Prompt (London), #5 (1964), 9-13. Aggressive and wide-ranging discussion that focusses on his 'Schweik' and 'War and Peace' stagings.

_____, "The Liberty Of the Producer," World Theatre, Autumn 1956, 305-315. A discussion with Karel Krauss of the Prague National Theatre, Wolfgang Langhoff of the East Berlin Deutsche Theatre, Hans Schalle of the Bochum Playhouse, and filmmaker Luchino Visconti.

_____, SEE ALSO: Brecht, Schumacher (XXI); Gorelik (LVIII). And:

Anna Latsia, "Piscator's Theatre," ITh, 1933 #5, 9-15. illus. Solid analysis.

Current Biography, 1942, 665-667. illus.

RAPHAEL, Max, Prehistoric Cave Paintings, 1945.

_____, Prehistoric Pottery and Civilization in Egypt, 1947.

_____, The Demands Of Art, Pantheon: Bollingen Series, forthcoming. Essays on 19th and 20th Century painters, including a criticism of Picasso's 'Guernica'.

_____, Proudhon, Marx, Picasso: Three Essays In the Sociology Of Art, Humanities Press: forthcoming.

_____, "A Marxist Critique Of Thomism," MaQ(NY), I (1937), 285-292.

_____, SEE ALSO: Herbert Read, Letter, Times Literary Supplement, 1964, 616. Urges accomplishment of Raphael in comparison to Lukacs.

REICH, Wilhelm, Character-Repressive Traits In Recent Soviet Literature. In his: The Sexual Revolution; Toward a Self-Governing Character Structure. Noonday paperback: 1962, 214-217. Reich, still a Marxist, views with professional alarm literary trends under Stalin.

_____, "Dialectical Materialism and Psychoanalysis," SOL, July-August, 1966, esp. 34-37, 45-46. The role of irrational symbol in the material economy and social repression.

RENN, Ludwig, "How I Came To Write My Book 'War'," LWR, 1931 #5, 68-79.

_____, Interview with Edwin Seaver. DW, Oct 12, 1937, 7. illus. - Also: DW, Nov 11, 1937, 7, Renn on pacifism and fascism.

RICHTER, Trude, "Fascism and Language," IL, 1935 #4, 86-91.

SCHLOSSER, Anselm, "Reflections On Shakespeare's Coriolanus," PhPr, VI i (1963), 11-22.

_____, "Ben Jonson's Roman Plays," KN, VIII (1961), 123-159.

SCHUMACHER, Ernst, "Piscator's Political Theatre," in Peter Demetz, ed, Brecht; A Collection Of Critical Essays, Spectrum paperback: Englewood Cliffs, N.J., 1962, 86-96.

SEEGER, Horst, "Opera: Old and New Ways," World Theatre, XIV (1965), 334-348. An associate of Berlin's Komische Oper, on realist performance and singing; "in the ascendant periods of their history, nations choose realism." illus.

SEGHERS, Anna, "The Tasks Of Art," NM, Dec 19, 1944, 9-11. "Art's revelation of reality embraces every domain of life. 'Art as propaganda' neglected many broad domains - and fascism later exploited these emotional vacuums for its own ends. 'Pure artists' create an even more dangerous vacuum."

_____, Interview with Christa Wolf. GDR Cultural Scene, 1960 #1, 24-26. illus. Seghers describes her method in writing 'Das Entscheidung'.

_____, "Depth and Breadth In Literature," GDR Cultural Scene, 1961 #4, 8-9, 28-29. abdgd. Speech to 5th German Writers Congress as Chairman of German Writers Union.

_____, "The End Of Silence," AmD, Oct-Nov 1965, 12-16. Address to World Writers Congress, Weimar. The writer's profession: what is communicated by vital literature.

_____, SEE ALSO: Current Biography, 1942, 748-759. illus. And: Franz Leschnitzer, IL, 1935 #7, 93-96. illus.

Excellent account of Seghers in Moscow. Indictment of her "psychologism" as "entirely unsuited for the handling of the social and political thematics of socialist realism."

[STRITTMATTER, Erwin], NT, June 3, 1964, 26-29. Report by Raisa Orlova and Lev Kopelev on Strittmatter's encounter with worker readers.

TOLLER, Ernst, "Impressions Of the Soviet Union," Soviet Union Today, Nov 1935, 11. Asserts vitality of USSR arts.

_____, Interview With Charles Ashleigh. SW, Dec 13, 1925, 9. His works for recitation and pantomime by massed workers.

_____, Speech to International Writers Conference, London, June 19, 1936. In Life and Letters Today, Autumn 1936, 34-36.

_____, Interview with Philip Sterling. DW, Oct 17, 1936, 7. Need for means to broad popular theatre movement.

_____, "Salute To Kathe Kollwitz," Hollywood Now, June 12, 1937, 5. Speech at a Los Angeles exhibition.

_____, "My Works," TDR, Mch 1959, 99-106.

WEIMANN, Robert, "The Soul Of the Age: Towards a Historical Approach To Shakespeare," SCW, 17-42.

_____, "Thomas Nashe and Elizabethan Humanism," FKSup, VII (1961), 40-44. abdgd.

_____, 'New Criticism' und die Entwicklung burgerlicher Literatur-Wissenschaft, Max Niemeyer Verlag: Halle, 1962. The basic study of antecedents, principles and social determination of New Criticism. - See review-essay by Lee Baxandall, S&S, XXIX (1965).

_____, "Reply to Rene Wellek," ZAA, 1965 #3, 286-288. Answers an attack on the above work.

WEISS, Peter, Interview with Michael Roloff. PR, Spring 1965, 220-232. Chiefly on his early works; with a statement on 'Marat/Sade'.

_____, "The Necessary Decision; 10 Working Theses Of an Author In the Divided World," Chalk Circle, I i (Apr-May

1966), 3-7. illus. The necessity of socialist commitment and the problems of communication facing an author in the capitalist countries. - See also, letter from Weiss, Encore, Sept-Oct 1965, 51-52. Declaring socialism the "only alternative", and stating that "as long as we are not involved with the great social conflicts of the world our work stands just isolated and fruitless."

_____, "I Come Out Of My Hiding Place," Nation, May 30, 1966, 652, 655. Personal and artistic development.

_____, Interview with Jerry Weinberg. Progressive Labor, June-July 1966, 80-85.

_____, Interview with Paul Gray. TDR, Fall 1966, 106-114. illus. His early films, "The Investigation', Brecht, Artaud, etc.

WOJCIK, Manfred, "In Defense Of Shelley," ZAA, XI (1963), 143-188. Life, writings and times of Shelley. His impact on working-class circles. Distortions by bourgeois critics and Christopher Caudwell.

WOLF, Friedrich, Press Conference. MN, June 3, 1931, 6.

_____, "The Work Of the Theatrical Troupe 'Sudwest'," ITh, #5 (1933), 24-26. Analysis of agitprop company he directed.

_____, "The Decline Of the Bourgeoise Theatre and the Upward Swing Of Proletarian Art," ITh, #3 (1933), 14-15. illus. Theatre in crisis in Germany.

_____, Interview With Bosley Crowther. N.Y. Times, Drama Section, Mch 24, 1935.

_____, "Fascism Killing Talent," N.Y. Telegram, Mch 30, 1935.

_____, "Dramatizing Our Times," NTh, Feb 1935, 24. Beyond individual-centered theatre.

_____, "New York Theatre Front: 1935," IL, 1935 #8, 77-88. illus. Thorough assessment.

_____, "The Western Drama Of the World War," ITh, 1935 #1, 13-16. Theatre in World War I.

_____, "In the Name Of Some Heroes," AWC,

19-21.  Speech to 1st American Writers Congress on fascist persecutions.

_____, "Fascist Drama," IL, 1937 #2, 79-85.

_____, SEE ALSO: Richard Pack, "Dramatist In Exile," NTh, Dec 1934, 5.  Also: Erwin Piscator, "The Work of Friedrich Wolf," NM, June 11, 1935, 23-25; and Roy Stone, DW, Mch 25, 1935, 7.

### XXII.  Appendix

"ART IN THE THIRD REICH," Special Issue, Magazine Of Art, Oct 1945.  illus. Alfred H. Barr and Lincoln Kirstein, authors.

BUTLER, E.M., The Saint-Simonian Religion In Germany; A Study Of the Young German Movement, Cambridge, 1926. Politics of Heine, Laube, Gutzkow, Mundt, Weinbarg.

DEMETZ, Peter, "Early Beginnings Of Marxist Literary Theory," Germanic Review, 29 (1954), 201-213.  Marxism "has no original approach to literature" but "only manipulates for its own ends methods and ideas developed by certain literary critics of rising German liberalism," especially Borne and Young Hegelians.  Engels is "responsible for the main body of Marxist thinking about "literature" with result that "literature was to be judged with increasing intolerance, entirely on an ideological basis."

_____, Marx, Engels, and the Poets, Univ. of Chicago: 1967.  The views cited above serve as framework for a version of their relations with some, though not all, of the poets they knew well. - For a review of the earlier German-language edition, see Boris Ryurikov, SL, 1962 #9, 141-145. - For a critique of this edition, see: Lee

Baxandall, "How To Schillerize Marx," PR, 1968.

_____, "Young Germany and Soviet Goethe Interpretation," German Life and Letters, 9 (1956), 181-188.

EGBERT, Donald D, Communism, Radicalism, and the Arts In Western Europe, forthcoming.

HITLER, Adolph, "Kultur," in: Norman H. Baynes, ed, The Speeches of Adolph Hitler, April 1922 - August 1939, London, 1942, vol. I, 566-615.  Representative extracts from speeches, including much on "Bolshevizing Jewish litterateurs" who foster "a spirit of insecurity and instability among the population."

JOHNSTON, William M, "Karl Marx's Verse of 1836-1837 As a Foreshadowing Of His Early Philosophy," JHI, Apr-June 1967, 259-268.

LIPTZIN, Solomon, The Weavers In German Literature, Baltimore: 1926.

_____, Lyric Pioneers Of Modern Germany; Studies In German Social Poetry, 1928.

MOSSE, George L, The Crisis Of German Ideology; Intellectual Origins Of the Third Reich, Universal paperback: 1964.

STONE, Judy, "The Mystery Of B. Traven," Ramparts, Sept 1967, 31-49; Oct 1967, 52-69.  illus.  The mystery is apparently unravelled: Traven as one-time actor, radical editor, chief censor in the Munich Soviet, and probable son of Kaiser Wilhelm II.

WELLEK, Rene, "German Critics From Grillparzer To Marx and Engels," in his A History Of Modern Criticism, 1750-1950, vol. III.  Yale: New Haven and London, 1965, 182-239.  Closely following the views of his pupil P. Demetz (XXII), Wellek offers a disparaging appraisal.

GREAT BRITAIN

(SEE ALSO: Arnold Hauser (XXVII), on all topics to 1920s.)

## Topic Index

### Art and Sculpture

ARTISTS INTERNATIONAL, BRITISH SECTION. Read. See (XXIII).

BACON, F. Berger.

BEWICK, T. Watkinson.

CONTEMPORARY ARTS. Berger, Hogarth, 'R. L. D.'

FUSELLI. Antal (XXVII).

GOMBRICH. Antal (XXVII).

HISTORY OF ENGLISH ART. Klingender, Turner.

HOGARTH. Klingender. Antal (XXVII).

MOORE, H. Berger. See Moore, (LXVII).

ROWLANDSON. Klingender.

VICTORIAN ART. Berger, Klingender.

### Cinema

CHAPLIN, C. Meyerhold (XLVIII); Lawson, Weigand (LIV); Finkelstein (LVI).

COMMERCIAL CINEMA. Innes.

EARLY CINEMA. Potamkin (LIV).

PROGRESSIVE CINEMA. Alexander, Anderson, Jackson, Watkins.

### Literature and General

AMIS, K. Kettle, Katona (XXVII).

ARNOLD, M. Caudwell. Weimann (XXI); LeRoy (LVI).

AUDEN, W.H. See (XXIII).

AUSTEN, J. Fox, Hookham, Kettle. Rubinstein (LVI).

BARRIE, J. Rickword.

BATES, R. Fox.

BEAUMONT AND FLETCHER. Danby.

BECKETT, S. Lewis, West. Lukacs (XXVII); Kott (XXXVI);Suvin (LXI); Kommissarzhevsky (XLVIII).

BENNETT, A. Kettle.

BLAKE, W. Bronowski, Caudwell, Hobday, Morton, West. Erdman, Rubinstein (LVI); Schorer, Williams (LXII).

BRONTE. Fox, Hobday, Kettle, Morton, Pascal, Wilson.

BROWNING. Caudwell.

BUNYAN, J. Kettle, Lindsay, Southall, West. Rubinstein (LVI).

BURNS, R. Campbell, Hobday, MacDiarmid. Gold, Rubinstein (LVI); Darrow (LXII).

BUTLER, S. Kettle, Morton. Mirsky (XLVI); Hicks (LVI); Cole (LXII).

BYRON. Caudwell, Rickword, Fischer, Marx and Engels (XXI); Aveling (XXIV); Lunacharsky, Plekhanov (XLVI); Rubinstein (LVI); Brinton (LXII).

CARLYLE. Marx and Engels (XXI); Hicks, LeRoy, Rubinstein (LVI); Williams (LXII).

CARY, J. Kettle.

CHAPMAN. Goldstein (LVI).

CHARTIST LITERATURE. Hobday, Miller, Towers. Koralev, Nikilyukin (XLVI); Rubinstein (LVI).

CHAUCER. Rattenbury. Lawson, Schlauch (LVI).

CHESTERTON. Morton.

CHURCHILL, C. Morton.

COLERIDGE. Bronowski, Lindsay, West. Fischer, Weimann (XXI); Hicks, Rubinstein (LVI); Brinton, Colmer (LXII).

CONRAD. Kettle. Lukacs (XXVII); Daiches, Howe (LXII).

COMPTON-BURNETT, I. Kettle.

CRITICISM, 18th CENTURY. Morawski (XXXVI); Needham (LXII).

CRITICISM, VICTORIAN. Weimann (XXI).

DAY-LEWIS, C. Henderson, Lehmann. Mirsky (XLVI); Burgum (LVI). See (XXIII).

DEFOE. Fox, Kettle, Morton, West.
Stepanik (XV); Krapp, Lawson, Rubinstein (LVI); Cole, Watt (LXII).

DEKKER. Gregg (LXII).

DICKENS. Fox, Hobday, Jackson, Kettle,
Lindsay. Marx and Engels (XXI);
Eisenstein (XLIV); Katarsky (XLVI);
Hicks, Rubinstein, Wilson (LVI);
Auerbach, House, Orwell (LXII).

DISRAELI. Hobday. Hicks (LVI).

DRYDEN. Bronowski, Caudwell. Krapp
(LVI); Taine (LXII).

ELIOT, G. Kettle, Milner. Katona
(XXVII); Rubinstein (LVI).

ELIOT, T.S. See US Topics.

EMPSON, W. Burgum (LVI).

ERVINE. Gassner (LVIII).

EYRE. Plekhanov (XLVI).

FIELDING. Fox, Kettle, Klingender.
Antal (XXVII); Rubinstein (LVI);
Auerbach, Loftis, Watt (LXII).

FORSTER. Kettle, Morton.

FRAZER, J. Jackson.

FRY, R. Klingender. Egbert (XXIV).

GALSWORTHY. Kettle. Gassner (LVIII);
Daiches (LXII).

GASKELL. Hobday. Marx and Engels (XXI);
Hicks (LVI).

GIBBON, L. G. Milner.

GISSING, G. Hicks (LVI); Howe (LXII).

GOLDSMITH. Boyer (LVI).

GRAY, T. Rudich (LVI).

GREEN, W. Kettle.

GREENE, G. Kettle. Woodcock (LXII).

GUNN, T. Mander (XXIV).

HARDY, T. Jackson, Kettle. Hicks (LVI).

HAZLITT, W. Rubinstein (LVI).

HESLOP, H. West.

HOOD, T. Marx and Engels (XXI).

HOPKINS. Henderson, Lindsay.

HOUSMAN. Bronowski, Morton, Spender.

HULME, T.E. Weimann (XXI).

HUXLEY, A. Caudwell, Day-Lewis, Kettle,
Morton. Mirsky (XLVI); Burgum,
Slochower (LVI); Daiches (LXII).

IRISH POETRY. Galvin, Thomson, Ussher.

JAMES, H. See US Topics.

JOHNSON, S. Brown, Rubinstein (LVI);
Collins, Stephen (LXII).

JONSON, B. Schlosser (XXI); Bronowski
(XXIII); Lawson (LVI); Gassner (LVIII);
Knights (LXII).

JOYCE, J. Kettle, Lindsay, Milner, Pas-
cal, Ussher, West. Fischer, Mayer
(XXI); Lukacs (XXVII); Eisenstein
(XLIV); Miller-Budnitskaya, Mirsky,
Radek, Vishnevsky (XLVI); Burgum,
Harrington, Schlauch, Slochower, Wil-
son (LVI); Auerbach, Daiches, Heap
(LXII).

KEATS. Caudwell. Stepanic (XV);
Fischer (XXI); Rubinstein (LVI);
Brinton (LXII).

KINGSLEY. Hobday. Dobrzycka (XXXVI);
Hicks (LVI).

KIPLING. Dunman, Fox, Spender (XXIII);
Baxandall, Hicks, Wilson (LVI).

KNIGHT, W. Weimann (XXI).

LAMB, C. Rubinstein (LVI).

LAWRENCE, D. H. Caudwell, Fox, Goodman,
Henderson, Kettle,'Leveller', Pascal,
Strachey. Lukacs (XXVII); Mirsky
(XLVI); Slochower (LVI); Harrison,
Way (LXII).

LAWRENCE, T.E. Caudwell, Spender.
Howe (LXII).

LEAVIS. Hill. Weimann (XXI); Leavis
(XXIV).

LESSING, D. See below. Katona (XXVII);

Kettle (XXIII).

LEWIS, W.  Egbert (XXIV); Harrison (LXII).

LITERATURE, LEFT, HISTORY.  Dupee, Lehmann, Lindsay, Willis.  Ford, Kemp,
Samuels, Skelton, Wood (XXIV).

LITERATURE, HISTORY.  Rubinstein,
Schlauch (LVI).  See General Topics,
Novel.

MacDIARMID, H.  See (XXIII).

MALORY.  Fox, Morton.  Schlauch (LVI);
Auerbach (LXII).

MANSFIELD, K.  Daiches (LXII).

MARLOWE.  Barber, Lawson (LVI); Gassner
(LVIII); Auerbach (LXII).

MARVELL, A.  Hill.

MEDIEVAL LITERATURE.  Robbins, Schlauch
(LVI); Holzknecht (LXII).

MEREDITH, G.  Lindsay.

MILTON.  Caudwell, Hobday, Pritt, Rickword, Simon, Southall, Visik.  Illo,
Lawson, Rubinstein, Siegel (LVI).

MORE, T.  Morton.  Kautsky (XXI); Kardos
(XXVII); Alexeyev (XLVI); Ames, Lawson
(LVI).

MORRIS, W.  Arundel, Hobsbawm, Lindsay,
Morton, Rothstein, Watkinson.  Egbert
(XXIV); Kocmanova (XV); Civale, Hicks,
Rubinstein (LVI); Cole (LXII).  See
Morris (XXIII).

MURDOCH, I.  Shestakov (XLVI).

NASHE, T.  Weimann (XXI).

NOVEL.  See General Topics, Novel.

O'CASEY.  See (XXIII).

ORWELL, G.  Deutscher, Morton, Thirby,
Walsh.  Mander (XXIV); Howe, Woodcock
(LXII).

OSBORNE, J.  Kettle, West.  Mander
(XXIV); Hodges (LVI); Tynan (LXII).

PATER, W.  West.  Weimann (XXI).

POETRY, HISTORY.  Richmond, Traversi.
Schlauch (LVI).

POPE, A.  Caudwell.  Plekhanov (XLVI);
Rubinstein (LVI); Collins, Stephen,
Taine. (LXII).

PRIESTLEY, J.B.  West.

RESTORATION DRAMA.  Hill (XXIII); Gassner (LVIII); Auerbach, Loftis, Taine,
Woodcock (LXII).

RICHARDSON.  Fox, Hill, Kettle.  Watt
(LXII).

ROSSETTI, D.  LeRoy (LVI).

RUSKIN.  Lindsay, Morton.  Egbert (XXIV);
Plekhanov (XLVI); Hicks, LeRoy (LVI).
See (LXII).

SCOTT, W.  Fox, Kettle.  Lukacs (XXVII);
Rubinstein (LVI); Auerbach (LXII).

SHAKESPEARE.  Caudwell, Danby, Hobday,
Kettle, Jackson, Matthews, Morton,
West.  Farnam, James (I); 1967 (X);
Pokorny, Simko, Stribrny (XV); Plan-
chon (XIX); Brecht, Fischer, Kautsky,
Schlosser, Weimann (XXI); Aveling
(XXIV); Heller, Lukacs (XXVII); Kott
(XXXVI); Dutu (XXXVIII); Anikst, Bog-
danov, Dinamov, Kemenov, Levidov,
Lunacharsky, Nechkina, Plekhanov,
Samarin, Smirnov, Trotsky (XLVI);
Kozintsev, Morozov, Radlov (XLVIII);
Nels (IL); Finkelstein, Folsom, Gold-
stein, Horowitz, Lawson, Morrow, Odets,
Rubinstein, Schappes, Siegel, Weisinger
(LVI); Gassner (LVIII); Auerbach, Bar-
ber, Chapman, Draper, Farnam, Harbage,
Lowenthal, Palmer, Pettet, Stirling,
Taine, Tawney, Wright (LXII); Folsom
(LXIV).

SHAW, G.B.  Caudwell, Hobsbawm, Strachey,
West.  Lunacharsky, Mirsky, Radek
(XLVI); Rubinstein, Slochower (LVI);
Gassner (LVIII); Wilson (LXII).  See
Shaw (XXIII).

SHELLEY, P.  Bronowski, Caudwell, Mat-
thews, Rickword.  Aveling, Cameron
(XXIV); Fischer, Marx and Engels,
Wojcik (XXI); Rubinstein (LVI);
Brinton (LXII).

SHELLEY, Mary.  Crafts (LXII).

SIDNEY.  Bronowski, Danby.  Siegel (LVI).

SILLITOE, A.  See (LXIII).  Katona
(XXVII); Hodges (LVI).

SITWELL, E.  Lindsay.

SMOLLETT.  Klingender.

SNOW, C.P.  Willetts.

SONNET, ITALIANATE.  Caudwell, Matthews.
  Siegel (LVI).

SPENCER.  Siegel (LVI).

SPENDER, S.  Henderson, Lehmann.  Replogle (XXIV); Mirsky (XLVI); Burgum
  (LVI).  See (XXIV).

SPINGARN, J.  Weimann (XXI).

STERNE.  Fox, Kettle.

SWIFT, J.  Magennis, Morton.  Kott
  (XXXVI); Lunacharsky (XLVI); Rubinstein (LVI); Cole, Orwell (LXII).

SWINBURNE.  Bronowski, Caudwell.

SYNGE.  Freyer (LXII); Gassner (LVIII).

TENNYSON.  Caudwell, Garman.

THACKERAY.  Fox, Kettle.  Marx and Engels
  (XXI); Lukacs (XXVII); Adam (LXII).

THOMAS, D.  Humboldt (LVI).

THOMSON, J.  LeRoy (LVI).

TRESSELL, R.  Ball, Beeching, Jackson,
  Mitchell, Poynton.

TURNER, J. M. W.  Lindsay.

VOYNICH, E.L.  Kettle.

WAIN, J.  Katona (XXVII).

WELLS, H.G.  Arnot, Caudwell, Fox,
  Kettle, Morton, Strachey.  Kagarlitski,
  Mirsky (XLVI); Orwell (LXII).

WESKER, A.  Mander (XXIV).

WILDE, O.  West.  Weimann (XXI); Hicks,
  LeRoy, Rubinstein (LVI); Gassner
  (LVIII).  See (LXIII).

WILSON, A.  Mander (XXIV); Katona
  (XXVII).

WOLCOT, J.  Sinko (XXXVI).

WOOLF, V.  Kettle.  Katona (XXVII); Burgum (LVI); Auerbach, Daiches (LXII).

WORDSWORTH.  Caudwell, Danby, Lindsay,
  Rickword, West.  Weimann (XXI); Todd

(XXIV); Douglas, Rubinstein (LVI);
  Brinton, Williams (LXII).

WORKING CLASS CULTURE.  Hoggart, James
  (LXII).

YEATS.  Auden, Bronowski, Henderson,
  Long, Thomson, Ussher.  Fischer (XXI);
  Harrington, Wilson (LVI); Freyer, Hall,
  Harrison, Orwell (LXII).

## Music

CHAMBER MUSIC, TO TIME OF PURCELL.
  Meyer (XXI); K. Thomson (XXIII).

FOLK SONG.  Dallas, Lloyd, Miller,
  Richmond, K. Thomson.

GENERAL HISTORY.  Mackerness (LXII).

VAUGHAN WILLIAMS.  Lloyd.  Finkelstein
  (LVII).

WORKERS MUSIC.  Boughton, Bush, Lloyd,
  'W.R.A'.

## Theatre

GROUP THEATRE.  Auden, Lehmann.  See
  (XXIII).

IBSENIAN.  Aveling (XXIV).

POST-ELIZABETHAN.  Szenczi (XXVII);
  Taine (LXII).

POST-WAR.  Anderson, Kettle.  Egri
  (LVIII); Tynan (LXII).

SHAKESPEARE.  See Topics, Literature and
  General.

STUART.  Szenczi (XXVII).

WORKERS THEATRE.  Allen, Beste, Carter,
  Foster, Jones, Landis, Marshall, O'Casey,
  Seton, Theatre Guild, Thomas, Unity
  Theatre, Workers Theatre League.
  Robeson (I).

## XXIII.  Authors

AARONOVITCH, Sam, "Capitalist Reaction
  Against Socialist Realism," ESR, 43-59.
  Principles of Socialist Realism.
  Tressell.

ALDRIDGE, James, "The Motherland Of Our
  Hopes," NT, May 1966, 8-10.  The role
  of the USSR in orienting a writer.

ALEXANDER, John, "Two Camps In the World

Of Films," MQ(L), Winter 1951-52, 5-20. Socialist and capitalist film traits.

_____, "Our Heritage In Films," BCH, 49-53. Extension of cinema to working-class concerns.

ALLEN, John, "The Socialist Theatre," LR, Aug 1937, 417-422.

ANDERSON, Lindsay, Interview with Paul Gray. TDR, Fall 1966, 122-129. Class Theatre and film in England.

ANTAL, Frederick. See (XXVII).

ARNOT, R. Page,"Retrospect On H.G. Wells," MQ(L), Summer 1947, 194-207.

ARTISTS INTERNATIONAL ASSOCIATION, The First Five Years, 1933-1938, London, 1938. 4pp. [BM] Brief account of founding and activity of an artists group pro-communist at the start, and after Mch 1935 simply for freedom of expression and against fascism and war. The AIA was a center for making protest placards, pamphlet illustrations, holding exhibitions. An effort to hold an Artists Congress failed for lack of response.

_____, Activities Since 1938, London, 1942. 4 pp. [BM]
_____, AIA Newssheet, later AIA News Bulletin, then AIA Newsletter. Jan 1937, June, July 1939 at Victoria and Albert Museum, London. Starting with #58 (Dec 1939) at British Museum. Assorted publications, although few from the early years, may be seen at AIA Gallery, 15 Lisle St., London W.C. 2. Of historical rather than theoretical interest.

ARUNDEL, Honor, The Freedom Of Art, Lawrence & Wishart paperback: London, 1965. Centered on a critique of simple equation of art with propaganda in the Party and labor movement. Art and capitalism, socialist attitudes, origin and development of art, art and nationality, form and content, artistic truth, art and sex, censorship, freedom and responsibility. Wm. Morris, Picasso, Brecht, MacDiarmid.

ASHCROFT, T, English Art and English Society, London, 1936. Impressionistic sketch of historical influences on English literature, painting, music and architecture from the Reform-

ation. Final note on Marxist approach to the arts.

ASSOCIATION OF WRITERS FOR INTELLECTUAL LIBERTY, British Section Of the International Association Of Writers For the Defense of Culture. Anti-Fascist Writers Meeting, June 8, 1938. Report by James Maynard. DW, July 11, 1938, 7. First such public event. Summary of speeches by Hugh Walpole, Compton Mackenzie, Louis Aragon, Adolf Hofmeister, C. Day-Lewis, Rosamond Lehman, Annabel Williams-Ellis, Philip Guedella, Philip Jordan. - See also: 1936 (XLI).

AUDEN, W.H, "Psychology and Art To-Day," The Arts To-Day, ed. Geoffrey Grigson, London, 1935, 1-20. Mostly marginalia on Freud's concept of neurotic artist; also briefly notes that equal validity must be granted Marx's contrasting approach to character.

_____, "I Want the Drama To Be . . . " Group Theatre Season: Sweeney Agonistes and The Dance Of Death. Program. London, 193?. Neo-Brechtian statement. [TU] - Also in: Westminster Theatre, Group Theatre Season program: 'The Dance Of Death' (1935). [Theatre Library, Victoria and Albert Museum, London]

_____, In Republican Spain. NS, Jan 30, 1937, 159.

_____, Introduction to John Mulgan, ed, Poems Of Freedom, London: 1938, 7-9. The social role of poetry.

_____, "Morality In an Age Of Change," Nation, Dec 24, 1938, 688-691; expanded and reprinted in I Believe, Clifton Fadiman, ed, 1939, 3-16. Full blunt description of his view of the good society and its relation to personal morality now.

_____, "The Public v. the Late Mr. William Butler Yeats," PR, Spring 1939, 46-51. Debating the possible social and poetic consequences of Yeats' far from progressive views. Auden offers no answer.

_____, SEE ALSO: Harris, Lehmann (XXIII); Mander, Replogle (XXIV); Burgum (LVI); and: New Verse, Special Auden Issue, Nov 1937. Includes "Oxford To Communism," by Stephen

Spender; "Auden and Politics," Edgell Rickword.

Richard Hoggart, Auden, London, 1951.

Samuel Greenberg, "Auden: Poet Of Anxiety," M&M, Apr 1948, 38-50.

BALL, F.C, Tressell Of Mugsborough, Lawrence & Wishart: London, 1951. A trade unionists's remarkable "book of reminiscences and an introduction" to 'The Ragged-Trousered Philanthropists'. - Also MT, June 1967, for Ball on Tressell's real name; also MT, Aug 1967, 227, on Tressell's daughter's whereabouts.

BARBER, Charles, "The Winter's Tale and Jacobean Society," SCW, 233-251.

_____, The Idea Of Honour In the English Drama 1591-1700, Goteborg (Sweden), 1957.

BECKETT, Alan, "Popular Music," NLR, Sept-Oct 1966, 87-90. Critique of T. Adorno's theory; in subsequent issues, analysis of what is progressive and authentic, rather than commercial, in jazz and rock-and-roll and beyond.

BEECHING, JACK, "'The Ragged Trousered Philanthropists'," OT, May 1948, 196-199. illus. The novel's history.

_____, "The Uncensoring Of 'The Ragged Trousered Philanthropists'," MaQ(L), II iv (Oct 1955), 217-229. History and achievement of the Tressell novel.

_____, "Notes On Zhdanov," MQ(L), IV i (Jan 1957), 52-57. Soul searching.

BENTLEY, Phyllis, "Literature and Society," LR, Sept 1935, 488-491.

BERGER, John, Permanent Red; Essays In Seeing, London, 1960; retitled Toward Reality; Essays In Seeing, Knopf: 1962. Foreword by Harold Clurman. US edition omits Berger's preface, adds chapter on "Art and Science." Problems of art, artists and art criticism. Abstract art, Action Painting, Braque, Cezanne, Constructivism, Corot, Courbet, Cubism, Daumier, Delacroix, Dubuffet, Dufy, Expressionism, Fauvism, Formalism, Gabo, Gauguin, Goya, Gris, Impressionism, Italian Renaissance, Klee,

Kokoschka, La Tour, Leger, Lipchitz, Malraux, Matisse, Michelangelo, Millet, Moore, Picasso, Piero della Francesca, Pollock, Poussin, Realism, Renoir, Van Gogh, Velasquez, Victorian art, Watteau, Zadkine, etc.

_____, A Painter Of Our Time, London, 1958; Simon & Schuster: 1959. "This is in the form of a novel but in fact contains most of my ideas about the working processes and dilemmas of the painter himself today."

_____, Success and Failure Of Picasso, Penguin paperback: Baltimore, 1965. illus. Influence of his Spanish origins and of international art circles; his themes; Cubism; the failure of the French CP to aid his development with useful criticism, after he had joined it. - Critique by S. Finkelstein, and Berger's reply: PA, Apr 1966, 31-45. - Review by Barbara Niven, MT, Jan 1966, 10-15.

_____, "The Moment Of Cubism," NLR, Mch-Apr 1967, 75-94. Descriptive and historical account of Cubism as "the most modern art - as it was also the most philosophically complex - which has yet existed."

_____, "The Necessity Of Uncertainty," MaQ(L), July 1956, 168-177. Argues against prescribed subject matter for socialist painters. - Replies by Ray Watkinson and A.M.D, ibid, Oct 1956, 260-267; by Polybius, and rejoinder from Berger, ibid, Jan 1957, 61-67.

_____, "Picasso and Others," M&M, Apr 1958, 9-29. Succinct vigorous commentaries on Picasso, Matisse, Leger, Courbet, Goya's drawings, drawing as discovery.

_____, "Pages From a Painter's Diary," ULR, Summer 1958, 28-31. Reflections on genius, the nature of art, observation, etc.

_____, "Problems Of Socialist Art," LM, Mch 1961, 135-143; Apr, 178-186. illus. Reconsiders concepts of Realism and Formalism. Rescues the School of Paris, 1870-1920 (Impressionism through Cubism) from latter category. Aside from inevitable subjectivist veerings "vision itself became the new content of art" and "the artist could now paint in order to prove the dialectic that inevitably exists between any subject and any way in which it is seen." The first "truly materialist art."

_____, "The Artist and Modern Society," Twentieth Century, Aug 1955, 148-154. - See also: discussion, ibid, Sept 1955, 290-297; Nov, 484-487.

_____, "Giacometti: 1901-1966," Nation, Mch 21, 1966, 341-342.

_____, "Away From the Red Velours," New Society, Feb 24, 1966, 22-23. Function of an art gallery: to display art as its own process, not as property.

_____, "Criticism West Of Suez," Chalk Circle, I i (Apr-May 1966), 13-24. The abdication of critical thinking in the Establishment press.

_____, "Renato Guttuso," Apollo, Mch 1955, 70. illus. "The most hopeful and important development in European art since the war."

_____, "Wanted - Critics," ULR, Summer 1957, 41-44. Premises of his art criticism.

_____," Art and Labour," New Reasoner, Autumn 1958, 74-78. Practical suggestions for rapprochement of artists and labor movement.

_____, "Zadkine's Hand," New Statesman, Jan 13, 1961, 64-65. "One of the few artists who suggests a line of development into the future."

_____, "Francis Bacon," New Statesman, Jan 5, 1952, 11-12. "Bacon is a brilliant stage manager, rather than an original visual artist....Bacon's interpretation...is too egocentric.... If Bacon's paintings began to deal with the real tragedy of our time, they would shriek less."

_____, "Picasso Variations On Velasquez," New Statesman, Feb 20, 1960, 247-248; Feb 27, 286-288. illus. Case study for LM essay.

_____, "Fernand Leger," MT, Apr 1963, 112-117; May, 143-147. illus. Leger "still remains the most modern painter in the European tradition" and is "an indispensible example for communist artists" for his work envisions, in treatment and theme, the communist future.

_____, "Poussin. Paradise Lost. 1658," New Statesman, Aug 13, 1960.

_____, "Grunewald At Colmar," Observer, Apr 14, 1963, 22. illus.

_____, "Painting and Photography," Observer, Feb 24, 1963.

_____, "Breughel," Observer, Oct 7, 1962.

_____, "Familiars Of Death," Nation, Nov 21, 1966, 553-557. The Soviet sculptor Ernst Neizvestny and his work. His 1962 confrontation with Krushchev. The stake of the official art world in excluding him and other modernists.

_____, "The Unofficial Russians," Sunday Times Magazine (London), Nov 6, 1966, 44-51. illus. First-hand account of painters and sculptors excluded from official art world for modernist tendencies.

_____, SEE ALSO: Richard Wollheim, "The Sectarian Imagination; On John Berger's Criticism," En, June 1961, 47-53. Finds him populist rather than Marxist, a sectarian envious of creativity who must project it into the future.

V.V. Ivasheva, "Revisionism Of Marxism In Britain," New Reasoner, Winter 1958-59, 143-148. From 'Oktyaber'. Soviet attack on aesthetics and integrity of Berger and other British Marxists. - Also Egbert (XXIV).

BERNAL, J.B, "Art and the Scientist," in: J.L. Martin, ed, Circle, London, 1937, 119-123. The relation of analysis in visual arts (Cubism, etc.) to analytical science. Also on alienation of artists from a social function, which Bernal finds a "necessary divorce," for art today is in no wise integrated in "social construction." "How to end this isolation and at the same time preserve the dignity of their own work is the main problem of the artist of today."

BESTE, Vernon, "Unity Theatre's Repertory," Million #2, 28-36. illus. Survey of London's left stage.

BIRNBAUM, Norman, "The Sociological Study of Ideology, 1940-1960," Current Sociol-

ogy, IX ii (1960), 91-117. Bibliography is best available. Fine systematic examination. "The beginning
point of modern discussions of ideology remains the work of Karl Marx."

BLUNT, Anthony, "Dalou and His Workers'
Monument," LR, Oct 1936, 693-698. A
neglected progressive French sculptor
of post-Commune days.

_____, Artistic Theory In Italy 1450-
1600, London, 1940; Oxford paperback,
1962. Fine tracing of painters' theories from High Renaissance individualist rationalism, when they won
status recognition, through degeneration, first into emotional then academic Mannerism, under influence of
Counter-Reformation policies and climate. Alberti, Leonardo, Michelangelo,
Vasari, Council of Trent, etc.

BOND, James, Revolutionary Songs For
England. DW(L), July 4, 1938, 7.
Guidelines.

BORNEMAN, Ernst, A Critic Looks At Jazz,
London: 1946.

BOUGHTON, Rutland, "Music and the Class
War," SW, Mch 15, 1925, et seq. Weekly
column (not always by Boughton) reviewing concerts and records, e.g, on
Beethoven, Mch 20, 1927, 8.

_____, On Joining the Communist Party.
SW, Feb 14, 1926, 5.

_____, The Science and Art Of Music,"
MQ(L), Summer 1948, 20-41. - Comment
by D. Mitchell, ibid, Autumn 1948,
93-95; by E. Rebling, C. Darnton, B.
Frankel, ibid, Winter 1948-49, 89-93.

BRITAIN'S CULTURAL HERITAGE: Symposium,
London, May 25, 1951. Arena Publication, London, 1951. 64 pp. [cc] For
chief essays, see: G. Thomson, A. Rothstein, J. Lindsay, R. Turner, J. Alexander, A. L. Morton.

BRONOWSKI, Jacob, William Blake: A Man
Without a Mask, London: 1944. The
work and life of Blake (and his contemporaries) in social frame of reference, explaining much which otherwise
seems cranky or obscure.

_____, The Poet's Defence, London: 1939.
Analysis of writings on poetics by the
poets themselves: Sidney, Jonson, Shelley, Dryden, Wordsworth, Coleridge,

Blake, Swinburne, Housman, Yeats. The
relation of truth and poetry.

BROWNING, Robert, "Slave Society: Some
Problems," OH #35 (Autumn 1964).

_____, "Byzantine Scholarship," Past and
Present (London), XXVIII (1964), 5-20.

BUSH, Alan, "The Crisis Of Modern Music,"
Keynote (London), Summer 1946, 4-7.

_____, "What Does Music Express?" MT,
July 1963, 204-209. - Discussed by Tom
Russell, ibid, Aug 1963, 252-255; by
Jack Nunman, ibid, Nov 1963, 350-351.

_____, "Problems Of Soviet Musical The-
ory," MQ(L), Winter 1949-50, 38-47.
Defends censure of Soviet composers.

_____, "A Composer Discusses His Develop-
ment," M&S, #24 (1964), 9-10.

_____, SEE ALSO: Robert Gill, "Alan Bush,"
OT, Sept 1946, 31. illus. And:
E. Meyer, "Alan Bush," OT, May
1948, 206-207.

Workers' Music Association,
Tribute to Alan Bush on His
Fiftieth Birthday, London:
1950. 60 pp. illus.
Evaluations and analysis by
John Ireland, R. Boughton,
W. Mellers, H. Eisler, Will
Sahnow, Ernst Meyer, Max
Rostal, T. Russell, David
Ellenberg, E.J. Dent et al.
List of compositions.

Scott Goddard, "Alan Bush:
Propagandist and Artist," The
Listener (London), Apr 23,
1964; reprinted in M&S, #24
(1964), 3-5.

Ronald Stevenson, "Alan Bush:
the Committed Composer,"
Music Review (London), Nov
1964.

CAMPBELL, J.R, Robert Burns the Democrat,
Glasgow: 1959.

CAMPBELL, K.J, "Towards a New Architecture," NCEO, I (1948), 151-152, 162-
163. An answer to Teige (XV). Architect's defense of USSR architecture -
not as final socialist style but as
interim solution: classicist revival
corresponds to last important pre-
revolutionary architecture in Russia,

avoids anti-popular "impersonality" of Corbusier and other modernists lacking in "warmth, color and humanity." The cosmopolitan style lacks national characteristics, reflects last stage of capitalism.

CAPON, Eric, "A Marxist Approach To the Theatre," OT, Jan 1943, 24-27; Feb, 5-8; Apr, 7-10; May, 22-25.

CARTER, Huntly, "Workers and the Theatre," SW, Mch 15, 1925, et seq. Weekly column developing perspectives and agitating practically for a workers' theatre in England. - See also: Carter (XLIX).

CAUDWELL, Christopher, Illusion and Reality; A Study of the Sources of Poetry, London, 1937; New World paperback, 1963. Introduction by George Thomson. Origins of poetry. Role of myth. Development of language in context of society. Characteristics. Psychology of lyric creation. Affective response. Architecture, Applied Art, Music, Jazz, Painting, Dance, Film. Aristotle, Plato, Shakespeare, Court poets, Milton, Dryden, Pope, Blake, Byron, Keats, Wordsworth, Shelley, Arnold, Swinburne, Tennyson, Browning, Surrealism. Freud, Wittgenstein, Jung. Future of poetry.

_____, Studies and Further Studies In a Dying Culture, 1958. First published 1938, 1949. Introductions by John Strachey and Edgell Rickword. Shaw, T.E. Lawrence, D.H. Lawrence, H.G. Wells, pacifism, Freud, bourgeois and Marxist ideas of freedom, love, religion, aesthetics, history, psychology, philosophy.

_____, The Concept of Freedom, Lawrence & Wishart: London, 1965. Introduction by George Thomson. Includes the essays on D.H. Lawrence, Love, Freedom, Aesthetics, Freud and Psychology from above volume, with the first five chapters of Caudwell's 'The Crisis in Physics'.

The essay on Shaw is reprinted in: Wilbur Scott, Five Approaches Of Literary Criticism, Collier paperback:1962,147-159.

_____, "Letter To Aldous Huxley," LR, Dec 1937, 657-661. Argues against pacifism. Revealing of his view of USSR. An excerpt from an unpublished 90 pp. ms., "The People's Front" (1936). See below.

_____, "Realism and Romance; A Study of

Bourgeois English Literature," 140 pp. ms. Unpublished section of 'Illusion and Reality', ranging from Shakespeare to Spender. The most complete discussion by Caudwell of the theory of literature, Socialist Realism, art for art's sake. With many other unpublished writings, this is in the collection of Caudwell's brother, T. Stanhope Sprigge.

_____, SEE ALSO: Wojcik (XXI); Egri (XXVII); and:

Obituary, DW(L), Mch 16, 1937, 3. Brief mention, with several others fallen in Spain; no mention of his critical writings.

Ralph Wright, Review of 'Illusion and Reality'. DW(L), Apr 14, 1937, 7. illus. "I really want to read the book again before saying one word about it...I think...it will prove to be the most valuable work on aesthetics that has been published for many a long and dreary day."

W.H. Auden, Review of 'Illusion and Reality', NV, May 1937, 20-22. "I agree with it.... This is the most important book on poetry since the books of Dr. Richards, and, in my opinion, provides a more satisfactory answer to the many questions which poetry raises."

Ambulance Fund Appeal In the Memory of Ch. Caudwell. Left Book News, July 1937, 452. [BM] Terms 'Illusion and Reality' "everywhere...recognized as the most brilliant Marxist analysis of the nature of creative literature ever written in English." Signers of the appeal: J.B. Priestley, W.H. Auden, Julian Huxley, Storm Jameson, W.T. Layton, Ettrel Mannin, D.N. Pritt, Hugh Walpole, Leech Manning.

Douglas Garman, "Testament Of a Revolutionary," LR, July 1937, 352-354.

A. Desmond Hawkins, Review Of 'Illusion and Reality', Purpose (London), 1937, 176-179. "...original, challenging and brilliantly stated....

Certainly no recent work in
this field, marxist or otherwise, is likely to have so
important a bearing on contemporary thought."

Richard H. Rovere, Review of
'Illusion and Reality', NM
Aug 17, 1937. First American
notice of Caudwell.

Stephen Spender, Review of
'Illusion and Reality'.
Tribune (London), Dec 23,
1937. Favorable notice. See
also: NS, XXXIII (1947), 258.
Unfavorable notice.

Horace Gregory, Review of 'Illusion and Reality'. NRep,
Feb 8, 1939, 25.

Louis Harap, "Christopher Caudwell, Marxist Critic, Poet
and Soldier," DWSup, Nov 24,
1946, 9. Also see NM, Nov
20, 1945, 22-23. Brought
Caudwell to post-war notice
and first real recognition
in US.

Stanley Edgar Hyman, "Christopher Caudwell and Marxist
Criticism," The Armed Vision,
1948 (hard-cover edition only),
168-208. Calls 'Illusion and
Reality' "the foremost work
of Marxist literary criticism"
and Caudwell "the most genuinely important Marxist cultural thinker of our time."

Allen Hutt, On the Re-Issue of
'Illusion and Reality'. DW(L),
Jan 30, 1947, 4. "Caudwell
was a brilliant master of
the dialectical method of
thought and expression; many
of his passages, it can be
said without exaggeration,
remind one of Marx and Engels
themselves."

Alick West, "On 'Illusion and
Reality'," CR, Jan 1948, 7-13.

The 'Modern Quarterly' Debate
Over Caudwell's Relevance.
a) Oscar Thomson, "The Poetic
Instant," MQ(L), Autumn 1948,
62-66; when this article was
attacked by several readers,
Thomson referred to Caudwell

as his authority while the
editors declared that "a
clear understanding" of Caudwell was "urgently necessary",
ibid, Summer 1949, 287-288.

b) Maurice Cornforth, "Caudwell and Marxism," ibid, Winter 1950-51, 16-33. Critique
of Caudwell's "idealist" premises and "confusion" which
result from "all the bourgeois ideas which had previously excited him."

c) George Thomson, "In Defence
Of Poetry," ibid, Spring 1951,
107-134. A refutation of Cornforth.

d) Alan Bush, On the Contribu-
tion Of Caudwell's Thought To
the Realist Theory Of Music.
Ibid, Summer 1951, 259-262;
Montague Slater, On Caudwell's
Decadent and Idealist Theory
Of Poetry, 262-265; Alick
West, Man Is Not An Object:
Rejecting Cornforth, 266-268;
G.M. Matthews, Rejecting
Cornforth and Cautioning On
Caudwell, 268-272; Jack Beech-
ing, Marxism In General Is
Weak On Psychology, 272-274;
Peter Cronin, Assessment,
274-275.

e) "The Caudwell Discussion,"
ibid, Autumn 1951, 340-358.
A final round of views by
Margot Heinemann, Edward York,
Werner Thierry, O. Robb, J.D.
Bernal, Edwin S. Smith, M.
Cornforth.

Fred Wharton, "Christopher Caudwell's 'Illusion and Reality',"
S&S, Winter 1952, 53-59. Rejects "idealistic and false"
treatment of poetry as "irrational" and the "dichotomy"
of genotype and social man.

Raymond Williams, Culture and
Society, Anchor paperback;
1959, 294-299.

A.H. Evans, "'Illusion and Reality': Is It a Marxist Classic?"
Rev, I x (1964), 127-140.
Analysis of Caudwell's "idealism". - Replies by J.R. Lloyd
and William Ash, and Evans'
answer, Rev, I xii (1964), 1-2.

Dell Hymes, "A Critique of Christopher Caudwell's 'Illusion and Reality'," B.A. dissertation at Reed College, Oregon, 1950.

Andrew R. Hawley, The Literary Criticism Of Christopher Caudwell, Ph.D. dissertation, University of Michigan, 1967.

David Margolies, Christopher Caudwell's Aesthetic: The Relation Between Marxism and Marxist Literary Criticism, Ph.D. dissertation, Oxford University, 1964. [Bodleian Library, Oxford, England] Analyzes what is uniquely Marxist in Caudwell's theory, and relates his functionalist outlook to that in Plekhanov's aesthetics. Comparison with other left critics of the thirties.

David Margolies, "Christopher Caudwell and the Foundations of Marxist Criticism," MT, May 1967, 149-155. The sophistication of Caudwell's notion of art as a guide to action.

George Moberg, Ph.D. dissertation-in-progress in English, Columbia Univ. General introduction to life and work of Caudwell and criticism of his work.

CHARQUES, R.D, Contemporary Literature and Social Revolution, London, 1933. Perhaps first volume linking literature with social-economic determinants to appear in England. Little analysis.

_____, "Soviet Literature," NS, June 1, 1935, 824-825.

CORNFORD, John, "Art and the Class Struggle," Student Vanguard, I (1933), 12-13.

_____, "The Class Front Of Modern Art," Student Vanguard, II (1933), 9-10.

CRAIG, David, "The British Working-Class Novel Today," ZAA, XI (1963), 29-41. Heritage. The scene since 1956: Alan Sillitoe, Margot Heinemann, Raymond Williams.

_____, "Militant Culture," MT, July 1962, 211-217.

_____, "Where Does Literature End?" MT, Oct 1965, 298-306. Prevalence and results of "the direct resort to fact" in contemporary realism: an antidote to abstractionism and irrationalism.

_____, Scottish Literature and the Scottish People, 1680-1830, Chatto & Windus: London, 1961.

DALLAS, Fred, "The Use Of Folk Music In a Mass Political Movement," ZAA, XI (1963), 56-66. History of folksong in England from peasant heritage to pop and Aldermaston singers.

DANBY, John E, Shakespeare's Doctrine Of Nature; A Study Of 'King Lear', London, 1949. Elaboration of ideas in an essay on same topic signed C.H. Hobday, listed elsewhere. Prior treatment by Shakespeare of Lear's themes. Shakespeare's developing social thought. Lear's key speech related to primitive Christianity's "'communist' levellers." Essay on poet's function in society. "Socialism is the effort by persons not poets to translate into action the insights the poet wins from his criticism of society."

_____, Poets On Fortune's Hill; Studies in Sidney, Shakespeare, Beaumont and Fletcher, London, 1952. Focusses primarily on meanings in late Shakespeare plays as elucidated by moral outlooks of Sidney (from which they emerge) and Beaumont and Fletcher (toward whom they tend).

_____, The Simple Wordsworth; Studies In the Poems, 1797-1807, 1961. Continues focus of earlier volumes. Wordsworth as last of poets functioning by Renaissance principles, concerned with active moral vision of life. Keats by contrast embodies new tradition of disinterested art which will end in aestheticism.

DAY-LEWIS, Cecil, Revolution In Writing, London, 1935; reprinted in his A Time To Dance, 1936. Reflections on writers and art, beautifully written. "Evolution is the dance, revolutions are the steps." - A component essay, "Revolutionaries and Poetry," appeared in LR, July 1935, 397-402.

_____, A Hope For Poetry, London, 1934; reprinted with a 1936 postscript, 1947. Also in his Collected Poems, 1929-1935, 1935. Chiefly discusses Hopkins, Owen, Eliot in relation to his own group of revolutionary poets.

_____, We're NOT Going To Do Nothing, London, 1936. Pamphlet which energetically disputes "active pacifism" of A. Huxley.

_____, ed, The Mind In Chains, London, 1937. Polemical, sketchy essays on Education (Rex Warner), Literature (Edward Upward), Film (Arthur Calder-Marshall), Theatre (Barbara Nixon), Art (Anthony Blunt), Music (Alan Bush), Mass Communications (Charles Madge), Psychology (Alastair Browne), Science (J.D. Bernal), Science, Religion and Ethics (T.A. Jackson), the English Tradition (Edgell Rickword).

_____, In Support Of Leninist United-Front Tactics. DW(L), May 31, 1938, 4. Warns Party members and sympathizers against "a high and mighty attitude of standing outside" the "existing organizations" of the workers in a crisis situation.

_____, The Buried Day, London, 1960. Autobiography of the 30s.

_____, SEE ALSO: Harris, Lehmann (XXIII); Replogle (XXIV); Burgum (LVI).

DEUTSCHER, Isaac, "Pasternak and the Calendar Of the Revolution," PR, Spring 1959, 248-265. Failure of 'Doctor Zhivago' due to archaic style and inadequate social awareness. - Irving Howe attacks essay as a "political act" not dealing with "serious literary issues," ibid, 266-275.

_____, "Intellectual Love Affair," Nation, May 16, 1966, 590-593. George Lukacs as "the only Stalinist literary critic of high stature"; his writings on T. Mann as an instance of Stalinist popular-front opportunism.

_____, "Mao At Bay," Nation, Oct 31, 1966, 442-445. The Chinese "cultural revolution" and counterparts in Soviet cultural practice.

_____, Heretics and Renegades, London: 1955. Essays on Orwell and on 'The God That Failed'.

DOBB, Henry, Weekly Cinema Criticism. SW, 1927-29. Sophisticated regard for light and shadow as the specific film idiom for realism.

DUNMAN, Jack, "Rudyard Kipling Re-Estimated," MT, Aug 1965, 242-248. "There is no writer in our language who has more to teach those who strive to write humanist, realist works about ordinary people....The Russians rank him high indeed....He was aware of the dilemmas of the system in which he lived, and which he broadly accepted, much as the royalist Balzac....above all else a realist....his works help to an understanding of Imperialism nearing its end." His "vulgarity" is a positive asset: Spender and Auden might have learned a working-class milieu from him, as did Brecht. - This view rejected by W. Ash and accepted by A. Hill, MT, Oct, 311-312; further discussed by D. Lesslie, MT, Nov, 350-352. Comment by A.L. Morton and Jessie Kocmanova, MT, Jan 1966, 24-26. - Rejoinder by Dunman, MT, Feb 1966, 58-60.

ESSAYS IN HONOUR OF WILLIAM GALLAGHER, Humboldt Univ: Berlin, 1967. To be available from Central Books, London. Includes studies of Scottish literature: David Lesslie on Alexander Rodger, Georg Seehass on Ernest Jones, H. Arundel on MacDiarmid, Jack Mitchell on Hamish Henderson, etc.

ESSAYS ON SOCIALIST REALISM AND THE BRITISH CULTURAL TRADITION, Arena Publication, London, n.d. [early 50s]. 86 pp. [cc] Lectures given at school on Socialist Realism organized by the CP. Communist development of national heritage in the arts. For chief essays, see: A. Kettle, S. Aaronovitch, J. Lindsay, A. West.

EXECUTIVE COMMITTEE OF THE COMMUNIST PARTY OF GREAT BRITAIN, "Questions Of Ideology and Culture," MT, May 1967, 134-138. Adapted March 11, 1967. For "free development" of the arts in Britain and a multiplicity of audiences and of critical views. - Comment by John Lewis, MT, July 1967, 222-224.

FOSTER, T, Early History Of Unity Theatre. DW(L), Sept 28, 1937, 4. illus. - See also DW(L), Aug 9, 1938, 2.

FOX, Ralph, "Literature and Life," Plebs, June 1922, 172-174. Early evidence of Fox's concern for historical development in culture.

_____, Book Review Column. <u>SW</u>, Apr 10, 1927, et seq.  On Dreiser: Apr 10, 1927, 8; July 10, 8; Aug 12, 1928, 8; Oct 28, 8.  On Hemingway's 'Fiesta' and Gorky's 'Decadence': Aug 7, 1927, 8.  On T.E. Lawrence: Aug 14, 1927, 8. On H.G. Wells: Nov 27, 1927, 8. On 'Tyl Ulenspiegel': Sept 23, 1928, 8. On Buchner and Toller: Dec 9, 1928, 8. On Gladkov's 'Cement': Jan 20, 1929, 8.  On the new Soviet novel: June 9, 1929, 8; June 16, 8.

_____, "The Relation Of Literature To Dialectical Materialism," in his: <u>Aspects Of Dialectical Materialism</u>, London, 1934.

_____, Obituary For Rudyard Kipling. <u>DW(L)</u>, Jan 20, 1936, 3.  Finds "reactionary elements of imperialism" the "most ephemeral side of the genius of Kipling," who was "the creator of the modern short story in English" and "the greatest reporter of modern times."

_____, "Henry Fielding," <u>DW(L)</u>, Nov 4, 1936, 7.  Estimate of relation of his active life to his writing achievement.

_____, <u>The Novel and the People</u>, London, 1937; International: 1945.  Preface by Howard Fast.  Biographical note by John Lehmann.  Marxism and literature. Realism and subjectivism.  Form and content.  Problem of the hero, of language, of characterization, Socialist Realism.  Origins of novel.  Malory, Cervantes, Rabelais, Fielding, Defoe, Richardson, Sterne, Scott, Austen, Thackeray, Bronte, Dickens, Balzac, Flaubert, the Goncourts, Zola, D.H. Lawrence, Malraux, Bates. - Chapter one reprinted as "Marxism and Literature" in Mark Schorer, ed, <u>Criticism</u>, 1958, 134-137.

Obituary Assessments by T.A. Jackson, John Strachey, Raymond Mortimer, Stephen Spender, John Lehmann. <u>DW(L)</u>, Jan 5, 1937, 1.  illus. - Also Jan 6, 4; Jan 7, 4; Jan 8, 5; Jan 9, 3; Jan 11, 5; Jan 12, 5.

<u>Ralph Fox, A Writer In Arms</u>, ed. John Lehmann, T.A. Jackson and C. Day-Lewis, London, 1937.  Tributes and excerpts from Fox's writings.

FRASER, Ronald, "Butor's You," <u>NLR</u>, May-June 1966, 62-68.  Strategems whereby the novelist may "turn on himself,"

before the reader's gaze, seeing his own novel as "a product of a given social condition."

GALVIN, Patrick, <u>Irish Songs Of Resistance (1169-1923)</u>, Oak Publications paperback: 1962.  "The great rebel songs emerge" when "in a colonized country, the national question and the class question are fused into one, the class exploiter being the same as- or the declared ally of - the foreign invader."  Texts, music, discussion of numerous songs.

GARMAN, Douglas, "Tennyson and His Age," <u>LR</u>, Aug 1936, 570-579.

GOODE, John, "'Character' and Henry James," <u>NLR</u>, Nov-Dec 1966, 55-75.  The bourgeois ethical framework of character and style in James is examined with a close reading, and a critique of F.R. Leavis and W.J. Harvey.

GOODMAN, Richard, <u>Footnote to Lawrence</u>, Contemporary Essays no. 2, London; 1932.  24 pp.  D.H. Lawrence.

GROUP THEATRE Publications: <u>Rep</u> (Croyden) and <u>Group Theatre</u> (London).  1932-34. [Croyden Public Library]  Early writings of Auden, Saint-Denis, Gyseghem, etc.

GYSEGHEM, Andre von, Interview. <u>ITh</u>, 1934 #2, 50-51. - See also Group Theatre (above).

HALDANE, J.B.S, Stendhal's 'The Red and the Black'. <u>DWSup</u>, July 16, 1939. Its scope and meanings today.

HARRIS, Henry, "The Symbols and Imagery Of Hawk and Kestrel In the Poetry Of Auden and Day Lewis In the 'Thirties'," <u>ZAA</u>, 1965 #3, 276-285.  Close analysis of the use of the symbol to express the poets' class roles and ambivalence.

_____, "The Symbol Of Frontier In the Social Allegory Of the Thirties," <u>ZAA</u>, 1966 #2, 127-140.  The allegorical romantic or heroic quest in Auden, Spender, Isherwood, Warner, Upward, Todd, Day-Lewis.

HARTLEY, Eric, "Socialist Realism: On the Role and Character Of Soviet Literature," <u>MQ(L)</u>, Summer 1951, 241-258.

HEINEMANN, Margot, "Andre Stil and the

Novel Of Socialist Realism," <u>MQ(L)</u>, Apr 1954, 117-126.

HENDERSON, Philip, <u>Literature and a Changing Civilization</u>, London, 1935. Hasty history of literature, chiefly English, in its social relations. - Critically reviewed by Edgell Rickword, <u>LR</u>, Oct 1935, 41-44.

_____, <u>The Novel Today</u>, London, 1936. Discussion of "Romantic" novel and call for "Revolutionary" novels.

_____, <u>The Poet and Society</u>, London, 1939. Hopkins, Yeats, Eliot, D.H. Lawrence, the Auden-Spender-Day-Lewis group chiefly considered. A section appraising English Marxist criticism.

HILL, Christopher, "Society and Andrew Marvell," in his: <u>Puritanism and Revolution</u>, London, 1958, 337-366.

_____, "Clarissa Harlowe and Her Times," ibid, 367-394. An approach to the Samuel Richardson novel.

_____, "The Restoration Spirit," <u>New Theatre</u> (London), Aug 1947, 16-17. [BM] Sharp analysis of post-1660 comedy as reflecting the adaptation of an aristocracy to the social order of capitalism, while the bourgeoisie are acquiring the social graces of the aristocracy.

_____, Literary Values Are Human Values. <u>Politics and Letters</u>, Summer 1947, 40-42; Summer 1948, 60-61. A response to F.R. Leavis.

HOBDAY, [Canon] C.H, "The Social Background Of 'King Lear'," <u>MQM</u>, 37-56. Important effort to define Shakespeare's class attitudes.

_____, "The Chartists In Fiction," <u>OT</u>, Apr 1948, 172-173. How Disraeli, Mrs. Gaskell, Kingsley, Dickens dealt with Chartist movement.

_____, "Three-Deckers and Yellow-Backs," <u>OT</u>, Mch 1947, 172-173. Victorian novel: themes, publishing exigencies.

_____, "The Brontes After a Century; Those Subversive Sisters," <u>OT</u>, Aug 1947, 7-8.

_____, "John Milton, the Revolutionary Poet," <u>OT</u>, May 1944, 12-13. His politics.

_____, "Paine, Blake and Burns," <u>UF</u>, IX ii (Nov 1943), 28-31. Their common origins in Puritan lower-middle class made them "the last great petty-bourgeois revolutionaries" in rebellion against kings, priests and lords rather than capitalism. Paine's acquaintance with Blake.

HOBSBAWM, Eric J, "Bernard Shaw's Socialism," <u>S&S</u>, Fall 1947, 305-326.

_____, "Morris On Art and Socialism," <u>OT</u>, Apr 1948, 176-178. Morris as neglected "genuine fusion of an established native tradition of Communism with modern scientific socialism, of the kind which makes the strength of Communist parties in so many countries." Survey of his durability as aesthetician.

_____, <u>The Age Of Revolution, 1789-1848</u>, World: 1962; Mentor paperback, 1964. Chapter "The Arts," pp. 299-326, skillfully surveys bourgeois revolutionaries in the arts against total background of epoch.

_____, SEE ALSO: Hobsbawm's jazz criticism, written under pseudonym of Francis Newton, listed elsewhere.

HOGARTH, Paul, "The Artist and Reality," <u>Ark</u>, #3 (Oct 1951), 6-10. Summary of class approach to art under capitalism.

_____, "Humanism Versus Despair In British Art Today," <u>MQ(L)</u>, Jan 1955, 37-47.

_____, Kollwitz and Realism In Graphics. <u>MQ(L)</u>, Summer 1952, 179-186.

HOOKHAM, Kutty. "Jane Austen and Her Class," <u>UF</u>, I i (Oct 1940), 12-16. Austen's novels reflecting the insecurities of declining landed class.

INNES, Geoffrey, "O Tempora! O Movies!" <u>Viewpoint</u> (Croyden), I i (Apr-June 1934), 4-8. [BM] Reactionary propaganda in English films.

JACKSON, Frank, "A People's Cinema Grows," <u>DW(L)</u>, Aug 9, 1938, 2. History of Left film in England.

JACKSON, T.A., "Marx and Shakespeare," <u>IL</u>, 1936 #2, 75-97. Reprinted in <u>LM</u>, Apr 1964, 165-173. abdgd. Chiefly on Falstaff as a feudal figure.

_____, Dickens: <u>The Progress Of a Radical</u>,

London, 1951. Origins of the novel.
Dickens' career in social context.
The novels: their "imaginative realism." "Dickens' radicalism instead
of mellowing....stiffened, hardened
and deepened into something that with
a little outside aid might easily have
emerged as positive Socialism or
Communism."

_____, Old Friends To Keep; Studies Of
English Novels and Novelists, London:
1950.

_____, Solo Trumpet; Some Memories Of
Socialist Agitation and Propaganda,
Lawrence & Wishart: London, 1953.
His autobiography to 1921.

_____, "The Art-Work Of Seaghan O'Cath-
asaigh," SW, June 26, 1927, 8; also
ibid, June 24, 1928, 8. Sean O'Casey's
pessimistic realism.

_____, "Workers' Novel Which Lives Be-
cause It Is True," SW, Sept 18, 1927,
8. Robert Tressell.

_____, Thomas Hardy. SW, Jan 15, 1928, 4.

_____, "Frazer's 'The Golden Bough'," SW,
Aug 18, 1929, 8.

_____, The Historical Conjuncture Under-
lying          Shakespeare's Achievement. DW(L), Apr 23, 1947, 4.

JELLINEK, Frank, "Writers and Artists In
the Commune," LR, Dec 1934, 83-86.

JOHNSON, Pamela Hansford, "The Literary
Achievement Of Marx," MQ(L), Summer
1947, 239-244. Notes on his style.

JONES, Leonard Abraham, The British Workers' Theatre, 1917-1935, dissertation
in the Faculty of Philosophy, Karl
Marx University: Leipzig, 1964. ms.
[Available through the author, Hum-
boldtstr. 23, Halle (Saale), Germany.]
A study of the class functions of drama
in Great Britain; early beginnings of
workers' theatre; the "sectarian" agitprop of the Workers Theatre Movement,
and its history; the contribution of
the WTM to the revival of the drama in
Britain. - A copy is deposited at AIMS.

_____, "The Workers' Theatre Movement In
the 'Twenties," ZAA, 1966 #3, 259-281.
A chapter of the above.

KETTLE, Arnold, Introduction To the English Novel, London, 1951; Harper Torchbook paperback, 2 vols, 1960. Origins
of the novel. Principles of form in
the novel. Bunyan, Defoe, Richardson,
Fielding, Sterne, Austen, Scott, Dickens, Bronte, Thackeray, G. Eliot, H.
James, S. Butler, T. Hardy, Conrad, A.
Bennett, V. Woolf, H.G. Wells, J. Galsworthy, D.H. Lawrence, Joyce, Forster,
A. Huxley, G. Greene, J. Cary., I.
Compton-Burnett, H. Green.

_____, ed, Shakespeare In a Changing
World, New World paperback: 1964. Es-
says, not all Marxist, mostly on indi-
vidual plays, by: R. Weimann, V.G.
Kiernan, Kenneth Muir, Zdenek Stribrny,
J.K. Walton, G.M. Matthews, Kettle,
Dipak Nandy, David Craig, Raymond
Southall, Charles Barber, Alick West.
- See Folsom (LVI). - Review by A.L.
Morton, MT, Apr 1964, 115-120.
- Review by S. Finkelstein, PA, Nov
1964, 54-61.

_____, "Marxism and Literature," UF, May
1939, 9.

_____, "The Greatness Of Joseph Conrad,"
MQ(L), Summer 1948, 63-81.

_____, "Talks With Soviet Writers,"
Anglo-Soviet Journal, Autumn 1952, 31-
33. Troubled, Kettle accepts Soviet
writers' proposition that "oversimpli-
fied characterization and a consequent
lack of conflict" in their novels is
because "in the Soviet Union the fundamental conflicts within society have
been eliminated." Their literature is
"of the people....which may mean the
disappearance of certain types of art
which are born out of the problems of
a minority."

_____, "The Progressive Tradition In
Bourgeois Culture," ESR, 32-42. Reprinted in M&M, Jan 1954, 9-20. Marlowe as announcing bourgeois man;
Shakespeare, Cervantes and Fielding as
achieving "the values of humanity....
the greatest art of the bourgeois period
is the least bourgeois, thrown up by
the bourgeois revolution but transcending it." A true realism depends
on this transcendence which can only
be  partial unless working-class values
are embraced; the partiality is betrayed through "some residue of idealism....which takes many forms....
utopian....paternalism...elevation of
the primitive...anarchism...the idealism of religion."

_____, "Two Working Class Novels," MaQ(L), III iv (Oct 1956), 248-250. Len Doherty's 'A Miner's Sons' and David Lambert's 'He Must So Live', and critical standards for describing and judging proletarian writing.

_____, "E.L. Voynich: A Forgotten English Novelist," Essays In Criticism, Apr 1957, 163-174. 'The Gadfly' and its meaning and history, and the crisis in the bourgeois novel at the turn of the century: G. Eliot, H. James, T. Hardy, Meredith, S. Butler.

_____, "Rebels and Causes: Some Thoughts On the Angry Young Men," MT, Mch 1958, 65-72. James Dean, Osborn, Amis, Lessing.

_____, "The Early Victorian Social-Problem Novel," in Boris Ford, ed, Pelican Guide To English Literature #6, London, 1958, 169-187.

_____, "The Artist and Politics," MT, May 1959, 139-145, broad discussion. Responses include: Osmond Robb, MT, July 1959, 215-220; Jack Lindsay, MT, Sept 1959, 284-288; Peter Pink and Dave Wallis, MT, Oct 1959, 313-320; T.D. Smith, MT, Jan 1960, 30-31; a summing-up by Kettle, MT, Feb 1960, 61-64.

_____, "Dickens and the Popular Tradition," ZAA, IX (1961), 229-252. Text of a lecture delivered at Humboldt University, Berlin, Nov 1960. Also in: Carleton Miscellany, Winter 1962, 17-51. - Discussed by Emile Capouya and John Oliver Perry, ibid, Spring 1962, 93-110. Reply by Kettle, ibid, Fall 1962, 91-95. Distinguishes between progressive and complacent literature in 19th Century and deduces that Dickens clearly was among former because of a great faith in "the people." Close analysis of 'Bleak House'.

_____, "Culture and Revolution: A Consideration Of the Ideas Of Raymond Williams," MT, Oct 1961, 301-307.

_____, "The Consistency Of James Joyce," in Boris Ford, ed, The Modern Age, Pelican Guide to English Literature #7: London and Baltimore, 1961, 301-314. Includes praise for 'Finnigan's Wake'.

_____, "Rocco and His Brothers," MT, Mch 1962, 75-79. The revolutionary Marxist content of this Visconti film.

_____, "Our Theatre In the Sixties," MT, Sept 1962, 276-281.

_____, "Dickens' 'Our Mutual Friend'," in John Gross and Gabriel Pearson, eds, Dickens and the Twentieth Century, Routledge & Kegan Paul: London, 1962, 213-226. Dickens' exploration of class barriers.

_____, "Hamlet," ZAA, X ii (1962), 117-127.

_____, "Charles Dickens; The Novelist and the People," MT, Feb 1963, 48-54.

_____, "In Defence Of 'Moll Flanders'," in: J. Butt, ed, Of Books and Mankind; Poems and Essays for Bonamy Dobree, London: 1964.

_____, Communism and the Intellectuals, Lawrence & Wishart: London, 1965. 31 pp. "While...most liberal intellectuals today reject communism, it is also true that they hope for communism....It is only through rejection of the inadequacies of liberalism...that the humanist tradition can be transformed into an outlook capable of understanding and coping with the actual needs and problems of the modern world." Analysis of Elizabethan engaged humanism and "power vacuum" contemporary humanism, if one does not embrace Marxism and join the Party.

_____, SEE ALSO: For a Soviet criticism of Kettle's 'Introduction', V.V. Ivasheva, "Marxist Criticism In Britain," New Reasoner, Summer 1959, 144-146.

KIERNAN, V.G., "Art and the Necessity Of History," in: Ralph Miliband and John Saville, eds, The Socialist Register 1965, Monthly Review: 1965, 216-236. Extended discussion of views of Ernst Fischer, which he finds too unhistorical and unaware of ruling class functions of art.

KLINGENDER, Francis D, Marxism and Modern Art, London, 1943; International: 1945. 48 pp. Problems of idealism (Roger Fry) and realism (Chernychevsky, Lenin) in aesthetics; the shifting ground between relative and absolute criteria.

_____, Art and the Industrial Revolution, London, 1947. illus. Impact of technological and social change on the decorative and documentary arts.

_____, ed, <u>Hogarth and English Caricature</u>, London, 1944. illus. Introduction and commentary. Examines all "popular art in England during the eighteenth and early nineteenth centuries."

_____, <u>Goya In the Democratic Tradition</u>, London, 1948. illus. The social context of Goya's outlook.

_____, <u>Animals In Art and Thought</u>, ed. Evelyn Antal, Kegan Paul: London. Posthumous work, forthcoming.

_____, "Content and Form In Art," in Betty Rea, ed, <u>5 on Revolutionary Art</u>, London, 1935, 25-44. [BM] Also in <u>AF</u>, May 1937, 17-19; June, 13-14. abdgd. The determination of form in 19th and 20th century French and English painting.

_____, "Realism and Fantasy In the Art Of Goya," <u>MQ(L)</u>, I i (1938), 64-77. "His reason...always retained the ultimate control over the monsters."

_____, On the Soviet Debate Over Vulgar-Sociological Criticism. <u>MQ(L)</u>, II iii (1939), 278-289.

_____, "The Crucifix: A Symbol Of Medieval Class Struggle," <u>LR</u>, Jan 1936, 167-173. illus.

_____, "Saint Francis and the Birds Of the Apocalypse," <u>London University. Warburg Institute Journal</u>, XVI (1953), 13-23. illus. Class meaning of the life and iconography of St. Francis.

_____, "Dalou's Communard Sentry," <u>OT</u>, May 1945, 10-11. illus. See also ibid, June 1945, 19, for correction. An extraordinary sculptor of Paris Commune.

_____, "Notes On English Realism: Hogarth and Fielding, Rowlandson and Smollett," <u>OT</u>, Dec 1945, 96-97; Mch 1946, 168-169. Parallels and differences in realist outlook of an epoch.

_____, The Popular Art Of the Paris Commune. <u>OT</u>, June 1941, 8-11. illus.

_____, SEE ALSO: <u>Architectural Review</u>, Oct 1955, 211. Obituary assessment. 'Art and the Industrial Revolution' "will long remain a basic text." - And Egbert (XXIV).

KLUGMAN, James, "Basis and Superstructure," <u>ESR</u>, 15-31.

LANDIS, Harry, "Which Way Unity Theatre?" <u>LM</u>, May 1967, 236-238. View of its vanguard role, earlier successful, now faltering.

LANG, Ian, <u>Jazz In Perspective: The Background Of the Blues</u>, London, 1947. Expanded version of <u>Background Of the Blues</u>, Workers Music Association, London, 1943, 55 pp. Outstanding historical and critical account of origins and nature of jazz. - Discussion of earlier version, by Gordon Gullickson, R.E. Stearns and Eugene Williams, with Lang's important reply defending view that "jazz is the product of a class, rather than a race": in <u>Jazz Music</u> (London), III ii (1946), 4-23. [DLC]

LEFT BOOK CLUB, <u>Left Book News</u>, later <u>Left News</u>. nos. 1 (May 1936) - 50, 54-66 [BM]. Reports on the books and the organizations of culture on the left. - See also Samuels (XXIV).

LEHMANN, John, "Some Revolutionary Trends In English Poetry: 1930-1935," <u>IL</u>, 1936 #4, 60-83. Assesses Auden, Lewis, Spender. Concludes they will not likely escape their introversion.

_____, <u>New Writing In Europe</u>, 1940. illus. biblio. Study of European left literature of the 1930s. Also Group Theatre.

LESSING, Doris, "The Small Personal Voice," in: <u>Declaration</u>, ed. Tom Maschler, MacGibbon & Kee: London, 1958, 13-27. A personal but thoroughly considered analysis of role of novel in socialist and non-socialist countries and the synthesis of "the individual conscience in its relations with the collective" that is needed.

'LEVELLER', "D.H. Lawrence, the Workers, and Life," <u>SW</u>, Mch 3, 1929, 8. 'Lady Chatterly's Lover' praised and Lawrence's proletarian origins probed. - Letter from 'Clydebank Riveter', objecting to the "awful sex bunk", ibid, Mch 31, 8.

LEWIS, C. Day. See Day-Lewis.

LEWIS, John, "What Is Marxist Literary

Criticism?" MQM, 3-10. A general
perspective.

_____, "Samuel Beckett and the Decline
Of Western Civilization," MT, Dec
1964, 381-384. "The despair in which
he traffics is a personal misfortune,
not a philosophy....revealing the
psychotic's troubled mind....when one
comes out of one's loneliness to help
in the remaking of the world, then the
whole picture changes."

LEVY, Hyman, and Helen Spalding, Literature For an Age Of Science, London:
1952.

LINDSAY, Jack, The Anatomy Of Spirit,
London, 1937.

_____, John Bunyan: Maker Of Myths,
London, 1937.

_____, Song Of a Falling World; Culture
During the Break-Up Of the Roman Empire, A.D. 350-600, Dakars: London,
1948. "Here is an extraordinary chance
to work out the subtle relations of the
social sphere (the politico-economic)
and the cultural, to see how one links
with the other and interacts  with it,
to investigate how far one is autonomous and how far it is bound up with
the other, and to discover the pattern
of the connection." Numerous poetry
citations. To regard this period simply as "decline" is mistaken: "In one
sense, Ansonius is a bad classical
poet; in another sense he is a very
good anti-classical poet."

_____, Charles Dickens, London, 1950.

_____, A World Ahead, London, 1950.
illus. Sympathetic detailed account
of his observations and encounters
while on tour of USSR in June 1949.
Numerous side commentaries on modern
painting, literary symbolism, etc.

_____, George Meredith, London, 1956.

_____, After the Thirties, London, 1956.
Post-war writing and perspectives.

_____, Death Of the Hero; French Paint-
ing From David To Delacroix, Studio:
London, 1960. illus.

_____, A Short History Of Culture; From
Prehistory To the Renaissance, Citadel:
1963; Fawcett paperback: 1966. illus.
Wholly rewritten from work of similar

title of 1939. Tries "to show the
emergence or development of the deep-
lying patterns" of culture; also "where
the person under consideration relates
to the general stream of cultural process; the angles from which he strikes
off."

_____, Perspective For Poetry, London:
1944.

_____, Byzantium Into Europe, London:
1952.

_____, Russian Poetry, Bodley Head:
London, 1957.

_____, William Morris, Writer, London:
1961.

_____, Introduction to: Apuleis, The
Golden Ass, London: 1960: Indiana
Univ: Bloomington, 1962.

_____, Introduction to: Petronius,
Satyricon, London: 1960.

_____, Introduction and Commentary to:
Catullus; The Complete Poems, London:
1949.

_____, Leisure and Pleasure In Roman
Egypt, London: 1965. The Dionysian
tradition, and the poet Nonnos.

_____, The Clashing Rocks, London: 1965.
Origins of Greek culture with emphasis
on drama.

_____, Fanfrolico and After, Bodley Head:
London, 1962. Autobiography of the
30s. With bibliography of Lindsay's
books.

_____, J.M.W. Turner: A Critical Biogra-
phy, New York Graphic Society: 1966.
illus.

_____, "Samuel Taylor Coleridge," Arena,
II vi (Feb-Mch 1951), 36-49; II vii
(Apr-May 1951), 29-43. Important study
of Coleridge's poetics and poetry.

_____, "William Wordsworth, Or Politics
and Poetry," M&M, June 1949, 37-47.

_____, "Aspects and Problems of Socialist
Realism In Literature," ESR, 60-77.
"Socialist Realism parts from all previous forms of expression by its un-
ceasing emphasis on development, on
the ways and means by which man changes
the world and himself." Problems of

audience, Party commitment, the bourgeois tradition, positive heroes, the
typical.

_____, "The Commune of Paris and English
Literature," MQ(L), July 1954, 169-180.
Meredith, Hopkins, Ruskin, Morris,
E. L. Linton.

_____, "The Progressive Tradition Of Our
19th Century Writers," BCH, 43-45.
Dickens, Meredith, G. Eliot, Gaskell,
the Brontes.

_____, "The Nature Of the Historical Nov-
el," OH, #13 (Spring 1959).  The novel
is "not simply the product of the bourgeoisie, but of the bourgeoisie in
their revolutionary role."  "The novelist's approach must always be historical if the full creativeness of the medium is to be maintained" although so-
called 'historical' novels serve a special function, achieve a certain
strangeness in which the contemporary
re-emerges.  Required is "a triad of
realism, romance and pastoral" not
only in analyzing the novel's origins
but also in a working novelist's awareness of present, future, and past
respectively as shaping perspectives.

_____, "Edith Sitwell," AmD, II i (1965),
33-34.  Personal recollections of Dame
Sitwell's warmth toward Marxist viewpoint and employment of it in verse;
by a critic she esteemed highly.

_____, "Autobiographical Notes," ZAA,
III i (1955), 72-74.  With bibliography of writings.

_____, "Anti-Clerical Poets Of the
Twelfth Centry," Life and Letters
To-Day, Sept 1938, 35-46.  Latin and
Provencal.

_____, "Neglected Aspects Of Poetry,"
P&P, #1; #2, 6-13; #3, 3-11; #5, 5-11
(1938); #7, 6-8 (1939).  Australian
populist verse, e.g. Henry Lawson; old
Tyne songs; Carmina Burana; English
political broadsides.

_____, "Politics and the Poet," MT, Feb
1958, 49-54.

_____, "The Broadsheet Tradition," Left
Poets News Sheet, Mch 1938.

_____, "Dickens' 'Barnaby Rudge'," in
John Gross and Gabriel Pearson, eds,
Dickens and the Twentieth Century,
Routledge & Kegan Paul: London, 1962,

91-106.  His contribution to the historical novel.

_____, "Marxism and Existentialism,"
AmD, Mch-Apr 1966, 8-11.  Finds that
Existentialism has dealt with problems
ignored or schematized by Marxists; a
careful dialog is to be welcomed.

_____, "The Problems Of Soviet Writers,"
MaQ(L) II ii (Apr 1955), 111-122.
Interprets the 2nd Soviet Writers Congress and the history of Soviet literary theory and practice since 1934.

_____, "Richard Savage - The First Poet
Of Colour," Life and Letters To-Day,
Sept 1939, 384-393.

_____, "Time In Modern Literature," in:
Frank Benseler, ed, Festschrift zum
achtzigsten Geburtstag von Georg
Lukacs, Luchterhand: Neuweid am
Rhein, 1965, 491-501.  Analyzes
Proust and Joyce to demonstrate that
such 'modernist' works oppose the
bourgeois world and offer "a revolutionary element of total rejection
and...a true creative joy."  The
realist novel must learn from their
confrontation with alienation, expressing without succumbing to it.

_____, SEE ALSO; "Jack Lindsay and
        Russian Readers," SL, 1966 #2,
        170-173.

LIPTON, Julius, "A Few Remarks About
Proletarian Poetry," P&P, #3 (Sept
1938), 12.  [Bodleian Library,
Oxford, Eng.]

LITTLEFIELD, Joan, "Britain's Unity Theatre," DW, Sept 15, 1946, 7.  Its
history.

LITTLEWOOD, Joan, "Communism and the
Theatre," NCEO, II (1949), 99-100.
Littlewood's expectations of socialist
theatre revealed in strong criticisms
of examples of Czech mediocrity and
reliance on outmoded staging.

_____, "Plays For the People," World
Theatre, Winter 1959, 283-290.

_____, SEE ALSO: Ruth Langdon Inglis,
        "The Fun Palace," Art in Amer-
        ica, Jan-Feb 1966, 69-72.
        illus.  With the architectural
        drawings by Cecil Price, and an
        account of Littlewood's strug-
        gle to realize the project.

LLOYD, A.L, "Modern Art and Modern Society," In Betty Rea, ed, 5 on Revolutionary Art, London, 1935, 53-71. Also in AF, Oct 1937, 12-19. abdgd. Draws heavily on Max Raphael's Picasso essay to describe escapism and decadence of modern painting.

_____, The Singing Englishman; An Introduction To Folksong, Workers Music Association: London, 1944. 70pp. A central study.

_____, English Folk Song, Lawrence & Wishart: London, 1965.

_____, Preface to: Ralph Vaughan Williams, National Music, London: 1934.

_____, Introduction to his Corn On the Cob; Popular and Traditional Poetry Of the U.S.A., London: 1945, 7-17. Special features of American folksong.

_____, "Folk-Song For Our Time?" MaQ(L), Jan 1954, 47-56.

_____, "So You're Interested in Folk Music?" Sing Out, Winter 1959-60, 38-42.

_____, "The Folk-Song Revival," MT, June 1961, 170-173.

_____, "The Origin Of Spirituals," Keynote, Spring 1946, 4-8. Traces origins of spirituals in white church songs.

_____, "The People's Own Poetry," DW(L), Feb 10, 1937, 7. The nature of ballads.

_____, "Prehistoric Music," Vox Pop (London), May 1945, 7-8. [BM] Examples indicating that the theory of music originating in communal labor is a "somewhat mechanical idea."

LOGUE, Christopher, "A Commitment Dialog," ULR, Summer 1958, 14-20. Discussion with Stuart Hall and others of his poem "To My Fellow Artists" and other matters.

_____, "Jazz and Poetry," Twentieth Century, Aug 1959, 84-87.

LONG, Michael, "Marxism and Criticism," MT, Nov 1966; Comment by M. Heinemann, MT, Apr 1967, 123-128; by Honor Arundel, MT, July 1967, 217-219. Reactionary and liberative values in the modern arts, and a Marxist's (and a Party's) adequate response. Eliot,

Yeats, Cezanne.

MacCOLL, Ewen, see special issue of Folk Music (London), I ii (1965).

MacDIARMID, Hugh, Lucky Poet; A Self-Study In Literature and Political Ideas, London, 1943. Ample and often brilliant presentation of his intellectual world.

_____, "The Kind Of Poetry I Want," in his Collected Poems, Macmillan: 1962; rev. ed, 1967.

_____, "The Bicentenary Of Robert Burns," MT, Jan 1959, 11-15.

_____, "Robert Burns," DW(L), Jan 25, 1938, 2. The historical context of his poems and of falsifying modern admirers.

_____, "The Freedom Of Art," MT, Jan 1966, 21-24. The historical fact that art has thrived under despotism; the greater contribution of Marxism to aesthetics than to literature in capitalist countries.

_____, Interview with Hamish Sinclair. NG, May 13, 1967, 12. On his first visit to the US.

_____, SEE ALSO: Kocmanova (XV); Arundel, Niven (XXIII); J. Szili (XXVII); Peter Thirlby, "The Piper On the Parapet," New Reasoner, Spring 1959, 58-73; Burns Singer, "Scarlet Eminence, A Study Of the Poetry Of Hugh MacDiarmid," En, Mch 1957, 49-62.

Glen Duncan, Hugh MacDiarmid and the Scottish Renaissance, Chambers: London, 1964. His life, poetry, politics, influence.

W.R. Aitkin, "C.M. Grieve/Hugh MacDiarmid," The Bibliothek (Glasgow), I iv (1958), 3-23.

David Craig, "Hugh MacDiarmid's Poetry," The Voice of Scotland, Apr 1956, 6-19. - Reply by MacDiarmid, ibid, 19-25. [BM]

James G. Southworth, "Hugh MacDiarmid," Sewanee Review, Jan-Mch 1940, 105-118.

K.D. Duval and Sidney Goodsir, eds, Hugh MacDiarmid: A Festschrift, K.D. Duval: Edinburgh, 1962.

Kenneth Buthlay, Hugh Mac-Diarmid, Writers and Critics Series, Oliver and Boyd: Edinburgh.

Duncan Glen, Hugh MacDiarmid and the Scottish Renaissance, Chambers: Edinburgh.

MAGENNIS, John, "Jonathan Swift," Irish Review, Oct 1945, 3-4. "His true greatness lies in being the first really able spokesman of the rising middle class; he was a bitter foe of feudal privilege and autocratic government."

MARSHALL, Herbert, "On Unity Theatre," Unity Theatre Newssheet, 1950. In collection of the author, who also has many of the obscure English and Russian publications on the Left theatre. Compiler was not able to see this collection.

'MARXISM TODAY', Obituary Estimate of T.S. Eliot. MT, Mch 1965, 66-67. Eliot's achievement was not merely one of form: "It is the expression of real and tough insight into actual aspects of twentieth-century life in strong and vital terms."

MATTHEWS, Geoffrey M, "A Volcano's Voice In Shelley," E L H, XXIV (1957), 191-228. To be reprinted, abdgd, in: George Ridenour, ed, Shelley; A Collection Of Critical Essays, Spectrum paperback: Englewood Cliffs, N.J. The symbolism is demystified and related complexly to Shelley's life and views and particularly his politics.

_____, ed, Percy Shelley; Selected Poems and Prose, Oxford, 1964. With introduction.

_____, "On Shelley's 'The Triumph Of Life'," Studia Neophilologica, XXXIV (1962), 104-134. Rejecting frequent belief that this unfinished masterpiece reflects disenchantment with revolutionary metaphysics and politics, Matthews shows it reflects rather on difficulties of maintaining integrity of purpose. Relates poem to Shelley's succumbing to an affair with Jane Williams.

_____, "Sex and the Sonnet," Essays In Criticism, II (1952), 119-137. Draws on Engels to describe property basis for woman's sexual role in Renaissance and lascivious undercurrent to Petrarchan sonneteering. - Paul N. Siegel, who Matthews questions, replies (ibid, 465-468) saying Matthews reinforces his own view but ignores essential class distinctions in the period and in English sonnets.

_____, "Othello and the Dignity Of Man," SCW, 123-145. Model analysis of a Shakespeare play. Iago's "irrational" motives shown to be extension of his society's outlook. Inadequacy of concept of Shakespearian tragedy based on "tragic flaw of character" exposed.

MAYER, J.P, Sociology Of Film; Studies and Documents, London, 1946. illus. Bibliography. Study of capacities of film to shape attitudes and politics.

MELLERS, Wilfred, Music and Society, 2nd ed, London: 1950. The evolution of English musical styles in relation to the European tradition and to society. Chapter on American music, especially Blitzstein and Copland.

_____, Studies In Contemporary Music, London: 1947. Determining the relation of music to human emotions and values. Satie, Debussy, Faure, Roussel, Koechlin, Mahler, Wellesz, Kodaly, Holst, Rubbra, problems of musical education.

_____, Francois Couperin and the French Classical Tradition, London: 1950. illus. catalog. Full study of Couperin, his music and values and the society around Versailles.

_____, and Alec Harmon, Man and His Music: The Story Of Musical Experience In the West, London: 1962. Mellers analyzes 1750 to the present; a compendious history.

_____, Harmonious Meeting; A Study Of the Relationship Between English Music, Poetry and Theatre, c. 1600-1900, London: 1965.

_____, Music In the Making, London: 1951. Outline of music history and analysis of the 20th century crisis in terms of the social roots and perceptions projected by music.

MILLER, John, "Songs Of the Labour Movement," OH, #30 (Summer 1963).  Summary of acquired knowledge; suggestions for tasks.  Many examples.

MILNER, Ian, "An Estimation Of Lewis Grassic Gibbon's 'A Scots Quair'," MQ(L), Oct 1954, 207-218.  Ranks novel with Tressell for a view of working-class life.

_____, "George Eliot's Realist Art," ZAA, XII (1964), 387-394.

_____, "George Eliot and the Limits Of Victorian Realism," PhPr, VI (1963), 48-59.

_____, "Herr Klesmer: George Eliot's Portrait Of the Artist," PhPr, VII (1964), 353-358.

_____, "The Heroic and the Mock Heroic In James Joyce's 'Ulysses'," PhPr, II (1959), 37-45.

MITCHELL, Adrian, "A Declaration Of Intent," LM, Mch 1967, 132-134.  A younger poet on the relations of socialist intent and poetic vision.

MITCHELL, John B, "'The Ragged-Trousered Philanthropists' - Cornerstone Of a Proletarian Literary Culture and Of Socialist Realism In English Literature," ZAA, X i (1962), 33-55.  Text of lecture delivered at Humboldt University, Berlin, Nov 1960.  "A beginning towards establishing Tressell as a great artist in his own right....  Tressell has created the only true national working-class epic in our language to date."  With him commences "the proletarian sensibility" in contrast to such bourgeois writers of proletarian novels as Margaret Harkness.

_____, "Aesthetic Problems Of the Development Of the Proletarian-Revolutionary Novel in 19th Century Britain," ZAA, XI (1963), 248-264.  Why working-class novelists before Tressell were so inferior: they had not elaborated a working-class vision of their world.  Example: 'Sunshine and Shadows' by Thomas Martin Wheeler.

_____, "'The Ragged-Trousered Philanthropists'," MT, May 1961, 154-159.

MITCHELL, Stanley, "Romanticism and Socialism," NLR, Mch-Apr 1963, 56-68.  Drawing on earlier NLR articles by

Gabriel Pearson and David Craig, Mitchell discusses role of Romantic poets in revolutionary times.

MONTAGU, Ivor, Film World; a Guide to Cinema, Penguin: Baltimore, 1964.  Film's aesthetic range, history, and commercial determinants.

MORRIS, William, Collected Works, London: 1910-15.  In XXIV vols.

_____, On Art and Socialism; Essays and Lectures By William Morris, London, 1947.

_____, Selected Writings and Designs, ed. Asa Briggs, Penguin Books: Baltimore, 1962.

_____, SEE ALSO: May Morris, William Morris, Writer, Artist, Socialist, London: 1936.  2 vols.

  John Spargo, The Socialism Of William Morris, Westwood, Mass: 1906.  52 pp. illus.  Defends Morris as truly committed.

  Elizabeth Luther Cory, William Morris: Poet, Craftsman, Socialist, 1902.

  John Bruce Glazier, William Morris and the Early Days Of the Socialist Movement, 1921.

  Edward P. Thompson, William Morris: Romantic To Revolutionary, London: 1955. - Review-essay by R. Page Arnot, MaQ(L), Oct 1955, 237-245. - See also Jessie Kocmanova, "Some Remarks on E.P. Thompson's Opinion Of the Poetry Of William Morris," PhPr, III (1960), 168-178.

  R. Page Arnot, William Morris: A Vindication, London: 1934.

    _____, William Morris: The Man and the Myth, Monthly Review: 1964.

MORTON, A.L, The Language Of Men, London, 1945.  Essays on ballads, Negro spirituals, Bacon, Swift, Defoe, C. Churchill, M. Rutherford, W. Morris, L. Dickinson, A.E. Housman, Chesterton, Forster.

_____, The English Utopia, Lawrence & Wishart: London, 1952.  Studies of man's hope in literature: popular Utopia fantasies, Thomas More, Francis Bacon,'Levellers' literature, Defoe, Swift, W. Morris, S. Butler, H.G. Well, A. Huxley, G. Orwell, etc. - See also: "Utopia As a Reflection Of Social Ideas," MT, Nov 1962.

_____, The Arts and the People, Lawrence & Wishart: London, 1965.  27 pp.  The loss of realism and a national perspective in middle-class English arts. The predicament of the artist, and his opportunity in a Marxist commitment. Wm. Morris.

_____, The Matter Of Britain; Essays In a Living Culture, Lawrence & Wishart: London, 1966.  Includes some of essays following.  Ruskin, Shakespeare, Blake, Eliot, etc.

_____, "Genius On the Border," MaQ(L), II iii (July 1955), 157-172.  Evaluation of the Bronte sisters.

_____, "Utopia As a Reflection Of Social Ideas," MT, Nov 1962, 236-242.

_____, The Everlasting Gospel; A Study In the Sources Of William Blake, Lawrence & Wishart: London, 1958. 64 pp.  Blake's imagery in relation to thought and symbolism of the Ranters, radical English Puritans.

_____, "Poetry and Property In a Communist Society," Criterion, Oct 1932, 45-53.  Problems of literary consciousness in transformation to accord with a new society.

_____, "Work and Leisure," BCH, 55-56. Importance of leisure to overcoming of alienation.

_____, "The Arthurian Cycle and the Development Of Feudal Society," ZAA, VIII (1960), 5-28.  The Malory text analyzed for evidence of clash between old and new social systems as feudalism decayed.

_____, "The Conscience Of John Ruskin and the Paris Commune Of 1871," OT, Aug 1948, 280-282.  Estimate of his contribution in aesthetics and stand as a man.

_____, "Shakespeare's Idea Of History," OH, #33 (Spring 1964).  18 pp.  Inter-

pretation of nationalism, concept of honor, degree, etc, in Shakespeare's history plays.  Rejects idea that Shakespeare represented any single class; his "profound sense of human dignity and worth" let him see through to "the conflict of classes."  "The fact that any outlook must have a class basis does not mean that each individual need reflect the outlook of one particular class....the very fact that Marxist critics have found plausible arguments for describing him" as the spokesman of each of several classes "should at least make us cautious of accepting such judgments."

_____, "Shakespeare's Historical Outlook," ZAA, XII (1964), 229-242.  His world included the "feudal gentry, guild burgess, new bourgeoisie" and "small artisan" and Shakespeare "shared some of the prejudices, hopes and antipathies of them all."

_____, "T.S. Eliot - A Personal View," ZAA, 1966 #3, 282-291.  First literary and personal acquaintance in 1920s as "liberating"; the other qualities which worked for Eliot's defeat as a poet.

NEWTON, Francis [pseudonym of Eric Hobsbawm], The Jazz Scene, Macgibbon & Kee: London, 1959.  illus.  Jazz history and criticism, much of it first published in the 'New Statesman'.

NIVEN, Barbara, "Hugh MacDiarmid's Poetry," MT, Aug 1962, 239-244.

NORMAN, C.H, The Revolutionary Spirit In Modern Literature and Drama and the Class War In Europe, 1918-36, London, 1937.  66 pp. [BM]  A general survey.

NUTTALL, William, "The Proletarian Reader," London Mercury, Mch 1936, 502-507. - See also R.A. Scott-James, "Editorial Notes," ibid, Apr 1936, 574, and May 1936, 1-4; and "The Coming Of Proletarian Literature: A Symposium," ibid, May 1936, 10-18, with Leslie Halward, W. Wuttali, J.S. Rainer, Lord Hugh Cecil and H.C. Hill.  Class consciousness as a factor in literary taste and creation.

O'CASEY, Sean, On Joining the London 'Daily Worker' Editorial Board. DW, Sept 28, 1940, 7.  illus.

_____, "The People and the Theatre," Theatre Today, I i (1946), 13-16.  His choice of audience.

_____, Defense Of the Moscow Trials.
DW(L), Mch 25, 1938, 2.

_____, Two Letters. In: Ralph Miliband
and John Saville, eds, The Socialist
Register 1965, Monthly Review: 1965,
237-240.  Mailed to Ken Coates in
July, 1955, concerning socialist
realism.  "Zdanov...didnt know what he
was talking about; and all who echoed
him in the Daily Worker, and elsewhere,
knew a damned sight less....A writer
must write of the life around him;
what he sees, feels, and hears, corresponding with life through his
senses....The worst formalism that I
know of is the formalism of the chat-
tering phrases uttered and muttered by
the communists themselves."

_____, "The Arts Among the Multitude,"
in his The Green Crow 1956.  Mixed regard for Soviet fiction, contempt for
Party guidance.

_____, Blasts and Benedictions: Articles
and Stories, St. Martins: 1967.  Includes many defenses of his position,
and an attack on Theatre of the Absurd.

_____, SEE ALSO: Fischer (XXI); Jackson,
      Thomas (XXIII); Gassner (LVIII).

PASCAL, Roy, The German Sturm und Drang,
1953.  Seminal study of origins of the
German literary renaissance and its
intellectual course in social context.

_____, The German Novel, Manchester,
1956, University of Toronto paperback:
1965.  Studies of Goethe, Keller,
Stifter, T. Mann, Gotthelf, Raabe,
Fontane, Kafka.  A chapter on general
traits of German novel.

_____, Design and Truth In Autobiography,
Cambridge, Mass, 1960.  Imaginative
organization of truth in autobiography
and autobiographical novels.

_____, "The Autobiographical Novel and
the Autobiography," Essays In Criticism, Apr 1959, 134-150.  The strategies in fictionalizing one's life in
Ch. Bronte's 'Villette', D.H. Lawrence's 'Sons and Lovers', Joyce's
'Portrait Of the Artist'.

_____, "Anna Seghers and the Novel Of
the Working Class," MQ(L), Autumn
1951, 359-371.

_____, "Aragon: 'Les Communistes',"
MQ(L), Summer 1952, 169-178.

'PEACHEM', "The Books They Write," SW,
Mch 15, 1925, et seq.  Weekly chronicle of proletarian, bourgeois, and
established novels by a reviewer of
taste and subtle class understanding.

POYNTON, J.H, Reminiscences of Robert
Tressell.  DW(L), June 10, 1936, 7.
illus.

PRITT, D.N, "John Milton, Poet and Revolutionary," Acta Universitatis Carolinae 1959, Iuridica 3, Prague, 3-28.
Surveys Milton's pamphleteering "work
in the service of the revolution" which
Pritt sees as anti-elitist, internationalist and unflinching.

RAFFE, W.G, Art and Labour, London: 1927.
Early, inept essay. - Review by J.M.
Flanagan, SW, June 26, 1927, 8.

RATTENBURY, Arnold, "Geoffrey Chaucer:
The Poet In Society," OT, Aug 1944,
6-7, 18.  Sees in "Troylus and
Cryseyde' and 'The Parlement of
Foules' the representation of conflict
between courtly and merchantile
classes together with their eventual
closing of ranks against feudal elements.

[REA, Betty, ed,] 5 On Revolutionary Art,
London, 1935.  [BM]  Essays by E. Gill,
H. Read, A.L. Lloyd, F.D. Klingender,
A. West. - Review by C. von Wiegand,
AF, Sept-Oct 1936, 10-11.

READ, Herbert, "Picasso and the Marxists,"
The London Mercury, Nov 1934, 95-96.
Reviewing show of Picasso's drawings
and 1st exhibition of the British Section of Artists' International, Read
deplores the work and thought of the
latter.  Picasso and his type are "the
only artists who are breaking down the
conventions of petty bourgeois art,
and thus preparing the way for the art
of the socialist state....the true
revolutionary artist today is not any
artist with a Marxist ideology; it is
the good artist with a revolutionary
technique.  The same is true of poetry
and all the other arts, and any understanding between the artistic and political fronts will be impossible so long
as there exists this mutual ignorance
of the realities of each mode of action."
Read calls himself a socialist on side
of workers.

_____, Art and Industry; The Principle Of Industrial Design, London, 1934; rev ed, 1954. A valuable study.

_____, Essential Communism, Pamphlets On the New Economics #12, London, 1935. 32 pp. Defends the similarity of function in revolutionary politics and modern art. Declares the artist must maintain a certain distance as well as a commitment. Projects the nature of the "classless leisure society" where the minds of all may unfold.

_____, "What Is Revolutionary Art?" in Betty Rea, ed, 5 On Revolutionary Art, London, 1935, 11-22. [BM] The abstractionists and surrealists as the true revolutionary painters of our time. "We have romanticists in our midst - tender-minded idealists who would like to blur the precise outlines of our vision with democratic ideals of egalitarianism, Tolstoyan simplicity and naivity, community-singing and boy-scoutism. Such people imagine that revolutionary art is a kind of folk-art, peasant pottery, madrigals and ballads. Surely that is not a conception of art worthy of the true Communist. We want something tougher, something more intellectual and 'difficult', something that we can without falsity and self-deception put beside the great epochs of art in the past."

_____, Speech Evaluating London Surrealist Exhibition (1936). In: Bulletin International du Surrealisme, #4, Sept 1936, 7-13. In English. "The Surrealist is naturally a Marxian Socialist, and generally claims he is a more consistent Communist than many who subscribe to all manner of compromise with the aesthetic culture and moral conventions of capitalism." Associates himself with this position. See also Surrealist (XXIII).

_____, Art and Society, London, 1936; rev ed, 1945. illus. Deeply embedded with Marxist problems.

_____, "The Necessity Of Anarchism," MQ(B), Dec 1937, 3-8; Feb 1938, 7-11. Marks the change in Read's political thinking in view of the Moscow Trials.

_____, Poetry and Anarchism, London: 1938. Clearest view on communism.

_____, The Politics Of the Unpolitical, London, 1943.

_____, "The Dereliction Of the Artist," Confluence, Dec 1952, 45-51. Tribulations of artists East and West who must find patronage and an audience.

_____, The Grass Roots Of Art; Lectures On the Social Aspects Of Art in the Industrial Age, London, 1955; Meridian paperback, 1961. A vastly stimulating work in large part framed as dialogue with Communist theory.

_____, "The Social Significance Of Abstract Art," Quadrum, IX (1960), 5-14. illus. Invokes Marx's analysis of alienation. "When work is 'a perpetual and exquisitely timed palsy', then art, which is the only freedom left the invalid, must expand its savage liberty."

_____, The Origins Of Form In Art, Horizon: 1965. Sees art as the primary form of perception and integration in any age, as it mediates between biological needs and their satisfaction. An education and society based upon this is required, or "we shall continue to sink deeper into disunity, mass neuroses and war."

_____, SEE ALSO: Paul C. Ray, "Sir Herbert Read and English Surrealism," JAAC, Spring 1966, 401-413. Finds that Read's "commitment to surrealism was far from complete...his view of the world was far from materialistic."

J.H. Matthews, "Surrealism and England," Comparative Literature Studies, I i (1964), 55-72.

SEE ALSO: Read's other books, not listed here; Read (XII); Calverton (LVI); West (XXIII); Breton (XIX).

RICHMOND, Kenneth, Poetry and the People, London, 1947. Class cleavage in English culture. Impoverishment of upperclass tongue by segregation from peasant-popular tongue. Survivals of poetry in latter.

RICKWORD, Edgell, War and Culture, London, 1936. Peace Library #6. 15 pp. Fascism as anti-culture.

_____, "James Barrie," DW(L), June 21, 1937, 5. The class function of Barrie's sentimental fantasies.

_____, "Milton: The Revolutionary Intellectual," in: Christopher Hill, ed, The English Revolution 1640, London, 1941, 101-132. As pamphleteer.

_____, ed, Soviet Writers Reply To English Writers' Questions, The Writers Group, Society For Cultural Relations With the USSR, London, 1948. Prefaces by J.B. Priestley and Konstantin Simonov. English writers participating: Priestley, Jack Lindsay, Montagu Slater, Herman Ould, Rose Macaulay, Agatha Christie, Marjorie Bowen, Phyllis Bentley, Mrs. Cecil Chesterton, Sylvia Townsend Warner, S. Davis, Elisabeth Myers, Alan Moray Williams. For Soviet participants, see: Soviet Writers (XLVI).

_____, "The Social Setting Of English Romanticism," in: Boris Ford, ed, Penguin Guide to English Literature, V, Baltimore: 1957, 11-32.

'R.L.D.', "Architecture Today," Viewpoint (Croyden), I i (Apr-June 1934), 24-27. Need for socialist planning demonstrated.

ROSE, Millicent, "Camille Pissarro," MQ(L), Autumn 1948, 25-34.

ROTHSTEIN, Andrew, "William Morris Belongs To the People," BCH, 39-42.

RUSSELL, Lee, "John Ford," NLR #29 (Jan-Feb 1965), 69-73. The famed director's confrontations with American history.

_____, "Budd Boetticher," NLR, #32 (1965), 78-84. The individualism of a US maker of Westerns.

_____, "Roberto Rossellini," NLR, Mch-Apr 1967, 69-71. The problems of his realism.

_____, Jean-Luc Godard. NLR, Sept-Oct 1966, 83-87. Violence and the void of politics in his films.

RUSSELL, Thomas, "Soviet Culture and Criticism," MaQ(L), July 1954, 143-153. Defense of Zhdanov.

_____, "The Nature Of Music," MT, Sept 1958, 268-272. Music as emotive expression into which listeners may pro-

ject their feelings. - Discussed by, e.g, Katherine Thomson, MT, Jan 1959, 27-29, who refers to Zhdanov's stress of folk themes.

_____, SEE ALSO: M&S, #27 (1965), 2. For Russell's background as Managing Director of London Philharmonic Orchestra.

SEAR, H.G, The Composer Must Live! London, 1944. 47 pp. [DLC] Economic influences on major composers.

_____, Talking Of Music, London, 1945. Simple introduction.

SETON, Marie, "Propaganda In the Theatre: Right and Left," Viewpoint (Croyden), I i (Apr-June 1934), 8-11. The tradition of didacticism. Fascist productions of 'Henry V', 'Merchant of Venice'. The Workers Theatre Movement.

SHAW, George Bernard, Prefaces, London, 1934.

_____, Pen Portraits and Reviews, London: 1931.

_____, The Rationalization of Russia, ed. with an introduction by Harry M. Geduld, Indian Univ: Bloomington, 1964. First publication of Shaw's unfinished book on visit to USSR, and the USSR's place in socialist development. Introduction chronicles Shaw's visit in detail. Proof that Shaw always thought himself a Marxist. - For Shaw in Moscow, see also: MN, July 23, 1931, 1; July 28, 1, 3; Aug 3, 1; Aug 8, 1, 3; Aug 13, 1, 3; Nov 3, 3. - H.W.L. Dana, "Shaw In Moscow," American Mercury, Mch 1932, 343-352. First-hand account.

SHORT, Ben, The Nazi Use of Communist Songs. DW(L), June 8, 1936, 7; June 15, 7; June 22, 7.

SILKIN, Jon, "No Politics, No Poetry?" Stand, VI ii (1963), 7-24. The Editor of 'Stand' explains and defends political and revolutionary functions of poetry in dialog with literary editor of 'The Listener'.

SIMON, Daphne, "In Defense of Milton," MT, Aug 1965, 252-254. Response to R. Southall's deprecation of Milton's revolutionary tenacity (below).

SLOAN, Pat, "Robert Briffault, 1876-1948,"

MT, May 1962, 154-159. The Marxism of the author of 'The Mothers' and 'Europa'.

SOUTHALL, Raymond, "The Pilgrim's Progress and Popular Culture," MT, June 1965, 184-188. The sources of Bunyan's current neglect. - See also D. Simon (above), and MT, Sept, 287-288, Oct, 316-318, for defenses of Milton.

SPENDER, Stephen, "Poetry and Revolution," New Country, ed. Michael Roberts, London, 1933, 62-71. Sees no relation whatever between poetry and revolution or propaganda.

_____, Review of Aragon's Poem "The Red Front," NV, May 1933, 24-25. Hostile to poem's theme of proletarian vindication: "Readers of this poem should compare it with any speech by Hitler."

_____, "Writers and Manifestos," LR, Feb 1935, 145-150. Reviews charges by Eastman and others against Soviet guidance of arts. Concludes: "Unless artists insist on their right to criticise, even to be 'humanitarian' (a despised term), communism will become a frozen epoch, another ice age."

_____, The Destructive Element, London, 1935. Mostly about Henry James, the adequacy of his artistic method; also "his account of our society makes, in effect, an indictment as fierce as that of Baudelaire; or, indeed, of a class-conscious Marxist writer." - Also reprints above essay.

_____, "A.E. Housman," DW(L), Oct 29, 1936, 4. Class analysis of the values in Housman, T.E. Lawrence, Kipling.

_____, Poetry in 1936. DW(L) Supplement, Dec 2, 1936, iii. Auden, D. Thomas, MacLeish, Yeats.

_____, "Poetry In Revolt," Fact #4 (July 1937), 18-30. Examples to prove poetry, even in revolt, must be specific, 'felt' not 'correct' and propagandistic. Communism may yet have its St. John of the Cross if territory marked out by Marx is rendered through poetry's unique means.

_____, Forward From Liberalism, 1937. Doubts and convictions in his "approach to communism": "The writer today whose work is not identified with the struggle to socialize the products of the mind as well as material wealth

is forced back inevitably into the romantic position." - J.R. Campbell, Review of 'Forward From Liberalism'. DW(L), Feb 1, 1937, 4. Finds Spender still prone to "Liberal claptrap,"

_____, "I Join the Communist Party," DW(L), Feb 19, 1937, 4. illus. Gives his reasons - one of them being the Campbell review of 'Forward From Liberalism'.

_____, Franz Kafka. DW(L), July 28, 1937, 7. "Kafka's peculiar combination of a realism that is always merging into a philosophical system perhaps offers one solution of the main problem of realist writing that confronts Marxist writers and their audience." - See also Spender's review of 'The Trial' and 'Metamorphosis' in Life and Letters To-Day, Autumn 1937, 185-186.

_____, The New Realism; A Discussion, London: 1939. 24pp. The writer's need to develop revolutionary analysis. Proletarian literature. Caudwell.

_____, Introduction, and ed, Poems For Spain, London: 1939, 7-14. Commitment and the Spanish Civil War.

_____, Life and the Poet, London: 1942. 128 pp. Without "recanting", declares the 1930s practice of endorsing parties and classes "ineffective" from a writer's viewpoint: "we should have been asking questions" in the search for "concrete realities".

_____, "An English Writer's Experience Of the 1930's," NHQ, #16 (1964), 87-92. Speech to Hungarian Writers Association. The period "was too serious for anything except farce" to succeed, e.g, Auden's plays. "A politics of the unpolitical....forced...to support the force opposed to Hitler....we were not altogether wrong."

_____, SEE ALSO: Caudwell, Lehmann (XXIII); Crossman, Replogle (XXIV); Burgum (LVI).

STRACHEY, John, The Coming Struggle For Power, 1935. Chapters X, XI on Wells, Shaw, Lawrence, Eliot, etc.

_____, Literature and Dialectical Materialism, 1934. The crisis of culture: H. Hazlitt, J. Krutch, M. Gold, G. Hicks, A. MacLeish, Hemingway, Spender.

_____, "Fascism and Culture," IL, 1934 #4, 90-110.

SURREALIST SUPPLEMENT to LR, July 1936, i-viii. Essays by Herbert Read, Anthony Blunt, Alick West. Read and Blunt, joined by A.L. Lloyd, carry on a Surrealism debate in subsequent issues.

SWINGLER, Randall, Proletarian Poetry. P&P, #1 (1938). [not located]

_____, "The Sense Of Guilt and the Influence Of Dosteoievsky," MQM, 116-126.

THE U.S.A. THREAT TO BRITISH CULTURE, Arena, Special Issue, June-July 1951. Essays from a conference convened by CP; includes Sam Aaronovitch, E. P. Thompson, Montagu Slater, Jack Lindsay, Ralph Bond, W.E.B. Du Bois, Howard Fast.

THEATRE GUILD OF LEFT BOOK CLUB Publications: New Theatre (2 nos., 1938-39), later became Theatre For the People. [1 no. in Enthoven Coll., Victoria and Albert Museum].

THIRBY, Peter, "Orwell As a Liberal," MaQ(L), III iv (Oct 1956), 239-247.

THOMAS, R. Hinton, "Culture and T.S. Eliot," MQ(L), Spring 1951, 147-162.

THOMAS, Tom, "Workers' Drama That Can Be," SW, Dec 1, 1929, 4. Rejects Gorky and O'Casey as conveyors of "bourgeois pessimism".

_____, "The Workers' Theatre In Britain," ITh, 1934 #1, 22-25. illus.

THOMSON, George, "The Social Origins Of Greek Tragedy," MQ(L), I iii (1938), 233-264.

_____, Marxism and Poetry, 1946. Yeats, primitive Irish poetry, Greek epic, tragedy, the future of poetry. - See also: Preface to 2nd Chinese edition containing author's corrections of some views, CR, Apr 1951, 106-107.

_____, Aeschylus and Athens; A Study In the Social Origins Of Drama, London, 1941; Lawrence & Wishart paperback: 1966. - Review by A.D. Winspear, with response from Thomson: S&S, Summer, 1942, 273-280. Further remarks by Winspear and Edwin L. Minor, Jr, S&S,

Spring 1943, 168-174. - Special Preface to Marx House Edition, UF, I ii (Nov 1940), 12-16. Relates thesis to that of Engels in 'Origins Of the Family, Private Property and the State'.

_____, Studies In Ancient Greek Society; The Prehistoric Aegean, Lawrence & Wishart: London, 1949; 3rd edition, Citadel: 1965. "In effect an expansion" of first five chapters in above work. Much on familial and economic relations. Final section relates Homeric epics to ritual origins, defines their development. Material from 'Marxism and Poetry' incorporated to provide part of theoretical base. - Review by B. Farrington, S&S, Spring 1967, 247-250.

_____, Studies In Ancient Greek Society: The First Philosophers, Lawrence & Wishart: London, 1955. Expands sections of 'Aeschylus and Athens' on growth of slavery and origins of scientific attitude. Sections on language and labor, myth, tragedy.

_____, The 'Oresteia' Of Aeschylus, ed, with introduction and translation, Cambridge, 1938, 2 vols.

_____, Greek Lyric Meter, Cambridge, 1961, 2nd revised edition.

_____, "Our National Cultural Heritage," BCH, 3-19. "We can only save our national cultural heritage by making it ours. And when I speak of us, I mean first and foremost the British workers."

_____, "Scientific Method In Textual Criticism," Eirene - Studia Graeca et Latina (Prague), I (1960), 51-60. Reprinted in Wissenschaftliche Zeitschrift der Humboldt-Universitat zu Berlin, XII (1963), 43-52.

_____, "Marxism and Spiritual Values," MT, Aug 1961, 234-240.

_____, SEE ALSO: L. Varcl and R.F. Willetts, eds, Γέρας [GERAS]; Studies Presented To George Thomson, Charles Univ: Prague, 1963. Perhaps also listed as Acta Universitatis Carolinae 1963. Philosophica et Historica I. Graecolatina Pragensia II. [Harvard] Papers, chiefly historical and philological. Biography and bibliography of Thomson. Thomson's blue print for developing classical scholarship,

"Marxism and Classical Philology."

THOMSON, Katherine, "Elizabethan Popular
Songs and the English Musical Tradition," MT, Nov 1965, 337-345. - Comment
by Stephen Sedley, MT, Jan 1966, 31-32.

THOMSON, Oscar, "Modern Painting,"
MQ(L), Winter 1951-52, 41-49. The expansion of form and content in art as
the bourgeoisie grew; the contraction
of form and content during the period
of bourgeois decline. - See also note
by Jack Lindsay, ibid, Spring 1952,
122; and by Alick West, ibid, Autumn
1952, 254.

_____, SEE ALSO: Caudwell (above).

TOWERS, Dorothy, "The Chartist Poets,"
OT, Apr 1948, 168-169. illus. How
working-class ideology adapted at-
hand Romantic forms of verse.

TRAVERSI, D.A, "Marxism and English
Poetry," Arena I (1937), 199-211.

TURNER, Reg, "Britain's Artistic Heritage," BCH, 46-48. Brief history
showing "in painting, as in literature, the essence of our British
tradition is realism and the search
for truth."

UNITY THEATRE, Unity Theatre Handbook,
London, 1939. Introduction by Dame
Sybil Thorndike. 26 pp. illus.
[BM] Founding, organization and
early productions of the theatre.

UNITY THEATRE publications: New Theatre, collection of Herbert Marshall.
#2 (Nov 1937), 1-2, editorial on
accepting bourgeois elements in a
proletarian theatre. On the Living
Newspaper theory in #5 (Mch-Apr 1938),
1,3.

USSHER, Arland, "Irish Literature," ZAA,
XIV (1966), 30-55. A concise history
by former president of Irish Academy
of Letters.

'VIEWPOINT' EDITORIAL, On Policy.
Viewpoint (Croyden), I i (Apr-June
1934), 1. [BM] "'Viewpoint' stands
for militant communism and for individualism and metaphysics in the arts.
It declares that the work of art is an
organic individual creation and that
it can only exist in its integrity in
a classless society, in a completely
communistic state; that art must become the production and the property

of all."

VISICK, Mary, "John Milton and the Revolution," MQ(L), Spring 1949, 178-191.

WALSH, James, "George Orwell," MaQ(L),
III i (Jan 1956), 25-39.

WATKINS, Peter, "On Making 'Privilege',"
LM, July 1967, 314-317. The film
maker against the Labour-Tory consensus.

WATKINSON, Ray, "Abstract Art," MT. Mch
1963, 81-89. Hasty survey of many aspects is concluded with views on nature
of abstract painting.

_____, "Thomas Bewick, 1753-1828; Artist,
Naturalist and Radical," OH, #25
(Spring 1962). 19pp. illus. Analyzes
neglected master of wood-engraving.

_____, "William Morris and the Bauhaus,"
LM, July 1967, 310-311. Gropius,
rational and applied art as part of
socialist inheritance.

WEST, Alick, Crisis and Criticism, London, 1937. Evaluates criticism and
poetics of Blake, Coleridge, Shelley,
T.S. Eliot, H. Read, I.A. Richards,
Marx. Problems of language, rhythm,
form and content, evaluation of literary qualities. Study of "increasing
abstractness and disintegration" in
'Ulysses' of Joyce; Socialist Realism
in H. Heslop's 'The Gate of a Strange
Field'.

_____, George Bernard Shaw; "A Good Man
Fallen Among Fabians", 1950.

_____, The Mountain In the Sunlight,
London, 1958. Essays on Bunyan, Defoe,
Pater, Wilde, Priestley, Lindsay.
- Review by Ian Milner, PhPr, V (1962),
174-176.

_____, "On Abstract Criticism," in Betty
Rea, ed, 5 On Revolutionary Art, London,
1935, 75-87. Finds contemporary
poetics abstract because divorced from
"the underlying social reality". The
example is I.A. Richards' book on
Coleridge, which ignored the latter's
integration of ideas of organic unity
and imagination with his parallel
views of society.

_____, "Wordsworth Was Torn Between Old
and New," DW(L), Dec 30, 1936, 7.
Close account of his development.

_____, "Marxism and Culture," MQ(L),

Spring 1948, 118-128.

_____, "The Abuse Of Poetry and the Abuse Of Criticism Of T.S. Eliot," MaQ(L), Jan 1954, 22-32.

_____, "John Osborne," FKSup, IX (1963), 25-28.

_____, "Some Current Uses of 'Shakes-perian'," SCW, 253-266. Beckett's 'Waiting For Godot' and Beckettizing of 'King Lear' to which Brecht's method with Shakespeare is juxtaposed.

WILLETTS, R.F, "The Critical Realism Of the Last Play Of Aristophanes," MQ(L), VIII i, 34-43. The play is 'Ploutos'.

_____, "A World Without a Hero: A Pre-liminary Comment On the Writings Of C.P. Snow," MT, Mch 1961, 80-86.

WILLIS, D.A, "New Life For the Novel," Viewpoint (Croyden), I i (Apr-June 1934), 12-14. Decadence and class consciousness in English novels of the 30s.

WILSON, David, "Emily Bronte: First Of the Moderns," MQM, 94-115. "The pro-letarian novel may find its roots and the beginning of its tradition one hundred years ago in Emily Bronte's 'Wuthering Heights'."

WODDIS, Jack, "Television," LM, Mch 1967, 135-136. The BBC's openness to socialist drama and how socialists may employ the opportunity.

WORKERS THEATRE LEAGUE Publications: The Red Stage (1931, 2 nos.), New Red Stage (1932, nos. 3-7). [Bodleian Library, Oxford, Eng.] Articles on the Theatre Olympiad in Russia, street agitprop theatre, etc.

WORKERS THEATRE MOVEMENT, "Manifesto," SW, Oct 3, 1926, 7.

'W.R.A.', "Music and 'Left-Wing' Poli-tics," The Musical Times (London), Apr 1936, 363. [BM] Account of the Workers Music Association, its found-ing and views. - See also editorial note, ibid. 353.

## XXIV.  Appendix

AVELING, Edward, "'Nora' and 'Breaking a Butterfly'," To-Day (London), I (1884), 473-480. Ecstatic review by the com-mon-law husband of Marx's daughter, of the Ibsen of 'A Doll's House' which he defends against a play by Jones and Herman allegedly inspired by it.

_____, "Hamlet At the Princess's," To-Day, II (1884), 516-537. Detailed account of Wilson Barrett's portrayal of Hamlet.

_____, and Eleanor Marx, "Shelley and Socialism," To-Day, Apr 1888, 103-116. Evidence to claim Shelley as class-conscious Socialist. Opinion of Marx on Shelley and Byron cited: "As Marx, who understood the poets as well as he understood the philosophers and econ-omists, was wont to say: 'The real dif-ference between Byron and Shelley is this: those who understand them and love them rejoice that Byron died at thirty-six, because if he had lived he would have become a reactionary bour-geois; they grieve that Shelley died at twenty-nine, because he was essen-tially a revolutionary, and he would always have been one of the advanced guard of Socialism.'"

BONHOMME, Jacques, "Balzac," The Social-Democrat, IX i (1905), 24-29. A sen-timental, moralizing socialist's view.

CAMERON, Kenneth Neill, The Young Shel-ley; Genesis Of a Radical, 1940; Collier paperback, 1962.

CONNOLLY, Cyril, Enemies Of Promise, Boston: 1939. Poetry and society.

CROSSMAN, Richard, ed, The God That Failed, 1949. Contributions by Arthur Koestler, Richard Wright, Andre Gide, Ignazio Silone, Louis Fischer, Stephen Spender on their relations with the CP.

DUPEE, F.W, "The English Literary Left," PR, Aug-Sept 1938, 11-21. Spender, Auden, Day-Lewis.

EGBERT, Donald D, "English Art Critics and Modern Social Radicalism," JAAC, Fall 1967, 29-46. The work and tradi-tion of J. Ruskin, W. Morris, R. Fry, W. Lewis, H. Read, C. Caudwell, F.D. Klingender, F. Antal, A. Hauser, J. Berger.

_____, Communism, Radicalism, and the Arts in Western Europe, forthcoming.

FORD, Hugh D, A Poets' War; British Poets

and the Spanish Civil War, Univ. Pennsylvania: 1965.

GILL, Eric, "All Art Is Propaganda," in
Betty Rea, ed, 5 on Revolutionary Art,
London, 1935, 47-49.  A Catholic view.

KEMP, Harry, Laura Riding, et al, The
Left Heresy In Literature and Life,
London, 1939.  An anecdotal attack on
political engagement as literary
romanticism.

LEAVIS, F.R, "Under Which King, Bezon-
ian?"  Scrutiny, Dec 1932, 205-214.
Examines criticism by G. Hicks, L.
Trotsky, D.S. Mirsky, E. Wilson, A.L.
Morton.  Declares Marxist thought
categories (such terms as 'class' and
'culture') abstract, uncritical and
slack.  'Scrutiny' by contrast stands
for "vigilant and scrupulous" observ-
ance of "the relation between words
and the concrete." - Answer by A.L.
Morton, ibid, Mch 1933, 324-326.

MacNEICE, Louis, Modern Poetry: A Personal Essay, Oxford: 1938.  The justified links of poetry and life.
Auden, Spender, Day-Lewis.

MANDER, John, The Writer and Commitment,
Secker & Warburg: London, 1961. Essays
on Auden, Orwell, Angus Wilson, Arthur
Miller, Thom Gunn, John Osborne, Arnold Wesker.  Defense of 'commitment'
while trying to elude political content Sartre pours into the concept.

REPLOGLE, Justin, The Auden Group; The
1930's Poetry of W.H. Auden, C. Day

Lewis and Stephen Spender, Ph.D. dissertation, University of Wisconsin,
1956.  biblio.  Microfilm copy in New
York Public Library.  Important scholarly effort to define what social
philosophy, themes and technique these
dissimilar sensibilities had in common,
and the interrelations.

_____, "Auden's Marxism," Publications
of the Modern Language Association,
Dec 1965, 584-595.

SAMUELS, Stuart, The Left Intelligentsia
In England In the Thirties, Weidenfeld
& Nicolson: London, 1968.  A careful
scholarly study by an American Research
Fellow at Oxford.

_____, "The Left Book Club," Journal of
Contemporary History, Apr 1966, 65-86.

SKELTON, Robin, ed, Poetry Of the Thirties, Penguin: London and Baltimore,
1964.  With introduction.  - Review-
editorial, MT, Dec 1964, 359-360,
takes up weaknesses.

THE REVIEW, #11-12 (1964): The Thirties
- A Special Number.  Interviews with
Edgell Rickword, Edward Upward, Claud
Cockburn, James Reeves; articles on
'Scrutiny', Auden, the Spanish war,
US poetry.

TODD, F.M, Politics and the Poet; A
Study Of Wordsworth, London, 1957.

WOOD, Neal, Communism and British Intellectuals, London, 1959.

GUATEMALA

## XXV.   Authors

ASTURIAS, Miguel Angel, "Russian Literature In Latin America," C&L, 1958 #3,
46-49.  Analogous Russian literary
treatment of peasants and Latin American novels that treat Indian population as fundamental "people" of the
nation.

_____, Interview.  RR, 1963 #1, 96-100.
illus.  His Mayan Indian origin.  Use

of myth as strategy of realism.

_____, Interview.  In: Luis Harss and
Barbara Dohmann, Into the Mainstream,
Harper & Row: 1967, 68-101.

_____, SEE ALSO:  Yglesias (LVI);
Ermilo Abreu Gomez, review-
article on Asturias' 'Poesia:
Sien de Alondra', Americas,
July 1950, 37-38.

## HOLLAND

### Topic Index

BREUGHEL. Brecht, Fischer (XXI); Berger (XXIII); Delevoy (LXII).

CINEMA, EARLY. Potamkin (LIV).

COLONIAL LITERATURE. Kroef (LXII).

DANCE, REVOLUTIONARY. Anonymous.

PAINTING, DUTCH AND FLEMISH. Antal, Hauser (XXVII).

THEATRE, WORKERS. Crefeld.

VERMEER. Meltzoff (LII).

### XXVI.  Authors

ANONYMOUS, "Dynamo Dances," ITh, 1934 #3-4, 35-36. Left dance group.

CREFELD, Is. van, "The 'Seven Provinces'," ITh, 1934 #1, 27-28. Left theatre company.

IVENS, Joris, Interview with J. Hulsker, Cinema Quarterly, Spring 1933, 148-151. illus.

_____, Interview with Ed. Kennedy. DW, Mch 21, 1936, 7. illus. Compares Soviet and US film industries.

_____, "Notes On Hollywood," NTh, Oct 1936, 8-11, 28. What is wrong.

_____, Interview with Hermann G. Weinberg. DW, Nov 18, 1937, 7. 'Spanish Earth' and new wave of left film-making.

_____, "Borinage - A Documentary Experience," Film Culture, #7 (1956), 6-10.

_____, Interview with Eleanor Wheeler. NWR, Apr 1958, 30-32. His work in China and Indonesia.

_____, SEE ALSO: Cynthia Grevier, "Joris Ivens: Socialist Realist versus Lyric Poet," Sight and Sound, Spring 1958, 204-207. illus. Sour on Ivens' politics but informative.

ROLAND-HOLST, Henrietta, "Communism and the Stage," CI, #11-12 (June-July, 1920), 2396-2399. Curious essay on theatre's role in proletarian education.

## HUNGARY

### Topic Index

ADY. Boka.

ARCHITECTURE. Revai.

BARTOK, B. Shostakovich (XLVII); Finkelstein (LVII). See Bartok (LXIII).

BENJAMIN, L. Aczel.

'CSILLAG'. Aczel.

DERKOVITS, G. Szabo.

DERY, T. Aczel.

DRAMA, ORIGINS IN HUNGARY. Devecseri.

GARAI, G. Ronay.

HAY, G. Aczel.

ILLES, B. Aczel.

KADAR, J. Aczel.

LITERATURE, HISTORY. Klaniczay.

LUKACS, G. See below.

MASS CULTURE. Jardanyi, Revai, Sas, Veres.

MUSIC, FOLK. Jardanyi, Kodaly. Bartok (LXIII).

NAGY, I. Aczel.

RAKOSI. Aczel.

REVAI, J. Aczel.

VILT, T. Korner.

### (XXVII) Authors

ACZEL, Tamas, "The 'Csillag' and Socialist Realism," The Review (Brussels), 1962 #2-3, 91-96. Aczel, editor of the country's only literary magazine during Rakosi period and winner of Stalin and Kossuth Prizes before leaving Hungary in 1957, tells how

'Csillag' Policy was determined for the Party by Joszef Revai.

_____, and Tibor Meray, The Revolt Of the Mind; A Case History of Intellectual Resistance Behind the Iron Curtain, 1959. First-hand chronicle of the literary scene 1945-56. Lukacs, Illes, Hay, Benjamin, Revai, Dery, Kadar, Nagy, Rakosi figure prominently.

ANTAL, Frederick, Florentine Painting and Its Social Background; XIV and Early XV Centuries, Kegan Paul: London, 1948. Written 1932-38. Class analysis of style and patronage in art, with exhaustive documentation, many illus. - Reviews: T.E. Mommsen, JHI, June 1950, 369-379; M. Meiss, Art Bulletin, 1949, 143-150. - Review by Derek Chittock, MQ(L), V iii, 254-262.

_____, Fuseli Studies, Kegan Paul: London, 1956. illus.

_____, Hogarth and His Place In European Art, Basic Books: 1962. illus. Completed posthumously by Evelyn Antal with major assistance from Herbert Read. "How, almost out of the void, did Hogarth create an art that was completely new, both in theme and form?...it expresses the outlook of the rising middle class of the period ....My chief concern has been to show how, in fact, Hogarth worked for many different social strata with widely differing tastes, corresponding with his manifold interests and aspirations." - Review by Ray Watkinson, MT, Oct 1962, 309-316.

_____, Classicism and Romanticism, London: Kegan Paul, 1966. illus. Collection of essays, including some below; others on 13th-14th century painting in Siena and Florence; two Flemish paintings; problems of Netherlands Mannerism.

_____, "The Moral Purpose Of Hogarth's Art," Journal of the Warburg and Courtauld Institutes, XV (1952), 169-197. illus. Densely written piece centering on Hogarth's relation to great middle-class writers of his day, especially Fielding.

_____, "Reflections On Classicism and Romanticism," Burlington Magazine, Apr 1935, 159-168; Mch 1936, 130-139;

Sept 1940, 72-80; Dec 1940, 188-192; Jan 1941, 14-22. illus. "In all periods since the Middle Ages in which an advanced outlook arose from advanced economic, social and political conditions of the middle class, a classicistic art expressed the rationalism of that class." Chiefly studied are J.-L. David (I), Girodet (II), Gericault (III-V).

_____, "Remarks On the Method Of Art History," Burlington Magazine, Feb 1949, 49-52; Mch, 73-75. Traces movement away from art-for-art's-sake to a history of ideas rooted in sociology and economics. Denounces art history that is not "part of history."

_____, "The Maenad Under the Cross," Warburg Institute Journal, I (1937-38), 70-73.

_____, "Observations On Girolamo da Carpi," Art Bulletin, XXX (1948), 81-103. illus. The influence of the court and university of Girolamo's native Ferrara are related to his art. With Appendix briefly summarizing social background of Italian Mannerism.

_____, SEE ALSO: Obituary article by John Berger, Burlington Magazine, Aug 1954, 259-260. Personal glimpses. The centrality of Marxism in all Antal's work.

BALAZS, Bela, Theory Of the Film, London, 1952. illus. Basic exposition of the medium by a lifelong Marxist and cinema analyst.

_____, "Let Us Create an International Union Of Revolutionary Cinema," ITh, #4 (1933), 6-8. Problems of revolutionary film-making in capitalist lands.

BOKA, Laszlo, "Endre Ady and the Present," NHQ, Apr-June 1962, 3-21. illus.

CENTRAL COMMITTEE of the Hungarian Socialist Workers' Party, Panel on Cultural Theory, "Of Socialist Realism," NHQ, #19 (Autumn 1965), 52-71. abdgd. Conclusions offered for further discussion. Defines socialist realism, criticizes its dogmatic perversion. Critique of Lukacs for, in practice, linking his fine interpretation of realism to 19th Century ideals of style. This conservatism "was closely connected with his rightist political-ideological views;"

he avoided discussion of socialist realism and of Party commitment, and was biassed against "experiments in the cause of socialist realism" by Brecht, simultanists, montagists, proletarian writers. Soviet cultural policy's own championing of 19th Century realism strengthened Lukacs' position in the discussion, as did the stagnation in Party thought. Ernst Fischer and Roger Garaudy criticized for dissipating the notion of realism while correctly rejecting the dogmatic link of it with aesthetic value per se. Proposals for attitudes and further work.

DEVECSERI, Gabor, Origins of Hungarian Drama. FKSup, VIII (1962), 3-9. abdgd.

EGRI, Peter, "On Caudwell's Lyrical Theory," FKSup, VIII (1962), 23-27. abdgd. Detailed analysis and critique of Caudwell's theory of poetry.

_____, "Anger and Form," ZAA, XI (1963), 269-280. British theatre of revolt in the 50s.

HAUSER, Arnold, The Social History Of Art, Knopf: 1951; Vintage paperback, 1957. 4 vols. illus. Encyclopedic scope, detailed yet rigorously interpretive. Reader is urged to consult indexes of these books on all world culture topics from origins to 1920s. Vol. I: Prehistoric Times, Ancient-Oriental Urban Cultures, Greece and Rome, The Middle Ages. Vol. II: Renaissance, Mannerism, Baroque. Vol. III: Rococo, Classicism, Romanticism. Vol. IV: Naturalism, Impressionism, The Film Age.

_____, The Philosophy Of Art History, Knopf: 1958. Scope and limitations of a sociology of art. Concept of ideology in the history of art. Psychoanalysis and art. Critique of Riegl and Wolfflin and the autonomous development of style. Folk arts and commercialized popular arts. Originality and the conventions.

_____, Mannerism; The Crisis Of the Renaissance and the Origin Of Modern Art, Knopf: 1965. 2 vols. Traces modernism to the collapse of classicist principles and order in the Renaissance. The economic, social, political, religious and psychological basis for the alienation underlying mannerism. A history of mannerism.

The modern correlatives. Raphael, Michelangelo, Andrea del Sarto, Correggio, Pontormo, Rosso Fiorentino, Beccafumi, Bronzino, Parmigianino, Salviati, Primaticcio, Niccolo dell' Abbate, Pellegrino Tibaldi, Lelio Orsi, Tintoretto, Bassano, Veronese, Barocci, Bellange, Callot, Bruegel, El Greco. Petrarch, Tasso, Marino, Gongora, Cervantes, Calderon, Montaigne, Ronsard, Malherbe, Racine, Marlowe, Shakespeare, Donne. Baudelaire, Mallarme, Surrealism, Picasso, Proust, Kafka.

_____, "Notes On the Sociology Of the Film," Life and Letters To-Day, Dec 1938, 80-87.

_____, "Concepts Of Time In Modern Art and Science," PR, Summer 1956, 320-333.

_____, "The New Outlook," Art News, June 1952, 43-46. Fundamental postulates of cultural sociology.

_____, Dialectic Of Artistic Creation; A Sociology Of Art, forthcoming.

_____, SEE ALSO: Sidney Finkelstein, "Art Ideology," PA, July 1959, 34-49; Aug, 24-39. Reviews Hauser's books, finds them lacking in class analysis, though "both to Hauser and perhaps most of his readers, the sociological approach coincides with Marxism..."

HAY, Gyula, "Some Observations On Literary Censorship and Freedom," in: Bitter Harvest, ed. Edmund Stillman, Praeger: 1959, 248-253. A lifelong Communist rejects Party control of literature.

HELLER, Agnes, "Knowledge Of Human Nature In Shakespearean Drama," NHQ, Spring 1964, 9-23. Reprinted in MQ(T), Summer 1964, 46-62. Keen analysis of historical conditions that permitted a new and broader understanding of man. - See also Lukacs (below).

_____, "Shakespeare and History," NLR, #32 (1965), 16-23. Basic principles for analysis of Shakespeare, tested against the plays and the Jan Kott study.

IGNOTUS, Paul, "Radical Writers In Hungary," Journal of Contemporary History, I ii (1966), 149-168. From 1919 to 1939.

JARDANYI, Pal, "Music and Modern Society,"

NHQ, Spring 1964, 162-167. "The inner world of the singer of folk-songs is more substantial than that of the twister, the tango-dancer and the operetta-lover." Recommends less and much better music, and efforts to transform listeners into performers.

JUHASZ, William, The Writer In Socialist Hungary. EE, Jan 1963, 8-15; Mch, 2-5; July, 6-14; Dec, 18-22. illus.

KARDOS, Tibor, "The Dilemma Of Sir Thomas More," NHQ, Oct-Dec 1963, 101-114.

KATONA, Anna, "Problems Of Adjustment In George Eliot's Early Novels," AL, VI (1963), 149-162. Early instances of her humane and sober realism.

_____, "The Decline Of the Modern In Recent British Fiction," ZAA, 1965 #1, 35-44. Sees in D. Lessing, Angus Wilson, K. Amis, J. Wain, A. Sillitoe a return to social involvements which is "contemporary," not, like V. Woolf, "modern."

_____, "American belles lettres in Hungarian Translation, 1945-1961," HSE, I (1963), 65-86. The determinants of editorial choice.

KLANICZAY, Tibor, Jozsef Szauder and Miklos Szabolcsi, History Of Hungarian Literature, Collet's: London, 1964. Marxist survey from 11th Century to the present.

KODALY, Zoltan, Folk Music Of Hungary, Budapest and London, 1960.

_____, SEE ALSO: Kodaly Special Issue, NHQ, Oct-Dec 1962; and Laszlo Eosze, NHQ, Apr-June 1962, 3-21. illus.

KOPECZI, Bela, "Balzac and The Human Comedy," NHQ, #16 (1964), 67-86. Truthfulness in literature.

_____, "New Problems Of Socialist Realism," NHQ, Spring 1965, 75-80.

_____, "Can the Sick Animal Be Cured?" NHQ, Summer 1966, 91-95. Notes on Robbe-Grillet and subjectivism.

_____, "Socialist Realism - The Continuing Debate," NHQ, Winter 1966, 95-106. Historical and comparative study (Lukacs, Fischer, Garaudy, Brecht,

etc.), by chief of the cultural department of the Central Committee.

KORNER, Eva, "Movement and Space; The Sculpture Of Tibor Vilt," NHQ, Spring 1966, 52-55. illus.

KORPONAY, Bela, "Edgar Allan Poe In Hungary," HSE, I (1963), 43-63.

LASZLO, Erwin, The Communist Ideology In Hungary: Handbook For Basic Research, Reidel: Dordrecht-Holland, 1966. Reference guide to scholarship, institutes, journals, persons, prepared with aid of the Hungarian Academy of Sciences.

LUKACS, George, "The Sociology Of Modern Drama," TDR, Summer 1965, 146-170; reprinted in Eric Bentley, ed, Theory Of the Modern Stage, Penguin: Baltimore, 1968. abdgd. From 1909. Problem of the hero, action, tragedy in drama of bourgeois epoch. Shakespeare, Greek tragedy, Goethe, Racine, Hebbel, Ibsen, Hauptmann.

_____, "The Social Background Of the White Terror," WD, Nov 20, 1920, 1. Distinguishes moral difference between terror when applied by proletariat or by a bourgeois regime.

_____, "The Problem Of Communist Organization," CR, Oct 1921, 41-49. From 'Die Internationale', June 15, 1921. Discussion of psychological problems involved in Party organization. Based on Germany's failed March Uprising. Lukacs calls for more "perfectly centralized" organization, and with this the heightening of class consciousness among workers: "we must be absolutely convinced that the moment for action has arrived; that we are at the decisive hour, when the devotion, the self-sacrifice, the complete voluntary subordination of every revolutionist, has become a matter upon which the fate of the revolution turns."

_____, "What Is Orthodox Marxism?" NI, Summer 1957, 179-197. From 'Geschichte und Klassenbewusstsein' (1922). "In Marxism, orthodoxy refers solely and exclusively to the question of method."

_____, "Technology and Social Relations," NLR, Sept-Oct 1966, 27-34. From 1925. Critique of Bukharin's undialectical Marxism.

_____, Studies In European Realism; A

Sociological Survey Of the Writings Of Balzac, Stendhal, Zola, Tolstoy, Gorki and Others, London, 1950; Universal Library paperback, 1964. Introduction by Alfred Kazin. Also discusses Belinsky, Chernyshevsky, Dobrolyubov, Dostoevsky, Flaubert, Goethe, Ibsen, Lenin, Lessing, Mann, Maupassant, Pushkin, Schiller, Scott, Shakespeare, Turgenev. - Review by Arnold Kettle, MQ(L), VI i, 72-81.

_____, The Historical Novel, London, 1962; Beacon paperback, 1963. Preface by Irving Howe. History and nature of the epic, drama, the novel. Decadence and humanism. Balzac, Cooper, Feuchtwanger, Flaubert, Fontane, Goethe, Hebbel, Hegel, Hugo, Jacobsen, H. Mann, T. Mann, Manzoni, Merimee, F. Meyer, Neitzsche, Pushkin, Raabe, Rolland, Schiller, Scott, Shakespeare, Sophocles, Stendhal, Stifter, Taine, Thackeray, Tolstoy, Vigny, Voltaire, Zola, Zweig.

_____, "Propaganda Or Partisanship?" PR, I ii (1934), 36-46. Critique of Mehring and Trotsky, Kant and Schiller on the question of propaganda in artworks. Suggests "partisanship" as correct term for organically conceived artworks that embody objective tendency of history.

_____, "The Intellectual Physiognomy Of Literary Characters," IL, 1936 #8, 56-83. Brilliant, central essay on literary characterization. Plato, Schiller, Goethe, Racine, Shakespeare, Hugo, Balzac, Zola, Cervantes, Flaubert, Goncharov, Goncourt, Taine, Gide, Joyce, Ibsen, Strindberg, Gorky, Fadaev, Pogodin, Panferov.

_____, "Walter Scott and the Historical Novel," IL, 1938 #4, 61-77; 1938 #12, 73-84. abdgd.

_____, "Essay On the Novel," IL, 1936 #5, 68-74. The Novel as genre and social phenomenon.

_____, "Narration versus Description," IL, 1937 #6, 96-112; 1937 #7, 85-97. Another translation in: George Steiner and Robert Fagles, eds, Homer; A Collection Of Critical Essays, Spectrum paperback: Englewood Cliffs, N.J, 1962, 86-89. abdgd. From 'Probleme des Realismus'. Contribution to the current discussion of Naturalism and Formalism.

_____, Funeral Speech For Gorky. IL, 1936 #8, 8-12. High praise for Gorky and implied criticism of other Socialist writers: "We have not learned enough nor the right way from him."

_____, "Nietzsche, Forerunner Of Fascist Aesthetics," IL, 1935 #11, 67-80.

_____, "Marx and Engels On Problems Of Dramaturgy," ITh, #2 (1934), 11-14. Framed by praise of Socialist Realism and abuse for Trotsky is a treatment chiefly of remarks by Marx and Engels on Lassalle's 'Sickingen'. Also Marx's idea of realism and Engels on the 'Oresteiade'.

_____, "On Socialist Realism," IL, 1939 #4, 87-96. Socialist society, to construct, needs Realism not modernist writing. But if Socialist Realism represents in theory a higher stage, much at first will in practice be propagandistic. Gorky "the most signal representative and first classic of Socialist Realism."

_____, Essays On Thomas Mann, Merlin: London, 1964. Includes: "'Royal Highness'," "Thomas Mann On the Literary Heritage," "The Last Great Critical Realist," "In Search Of Bourgeois Man," "The Tragedy Of Modern Art," "The Playful Style," and a Foreword. - Review by Alastair MacIntyre, En, Apr 1965, 64-72. - See Deutscher (XXIII).

_____, "The Stature Of Thomas Mann," M&M, Sept 1955, 20-26. abdgd. Preface to the Hungarian edition of Mann's works.

_____, "Synopsis Of the Contributions Of Professor G. Lukacs and Ernst Fischer To the Wroclaw Conference, 1948," MQ(L), Summer 1949, 53-58. Report with many extracts, by Roy Pascal.

_____, "Problems Of Marxist Culture," M&M, June 1948, 6-18; July, 60-69. From Talks in Milan, Dec 1947.

_____, "Idea and Form In Literature," M&M, Dec 1949, 40-61.

_____, "Don Quixote," CR, Sept 1951, 265-271. Preface to a new Hungarian edition. Important.

_____, "Prussianism and Nazism," MQ(L), 1946, 85-93.

\_\_\_\_\_, "Dostoevsky," in Rene Wellek, ed, <u>Dostoevsky; A Collection Of Critical Essays</u>, Spectrum paperback: Englewood Cliffs, N.J, 1962, 146-158. From "Der Russische Realismus in der Welt-literatur' (Berlin 1949).

\_\_\_\_\_, "On Writing the History Of Art," <u>CR</u>, Oct 1952, 309-316. Some basic advice to a meeting of art historians on relevance of Marxism to their work.

\_\_\_\_\_, "Existentialism or Marxism?" in R.W. Sellars, ed, <u>Philosophy For the Future</u>, Macmillan: 1949; reprinted in George Novack, ed, <u>Existentialism Versus Marxism</u>, Delta paperback: 1966, 134-153.

\_\_\_\_\_, On Stalinism. <u>Survey</u> #10 (Nov 1956), 15-19. Lecture given in Budapest, Summer 1956, published in 'Aufbau, Sept 1956. abdgd.

\_\_\_\_\_, "Reflections On the Cult Of Stalin," <u>Survey</u> #47 (Apr 1963), 105-111. abdgd. From 1962 'Nuovi Argomenti' issue devoted to discussion of 22nd CPSU Congress.

\_\_\_\_\_, "Stalinism and Art," <u>EE</u>, May 1964, 22-26. abdgd. Interview with 'Literarni Noviny' (Prague), Jan 18, 1964. The Stalinist distortion of Socialist Realism and views on literature in the West, in first publication in the Socialist bloc since 1957.

\_\_\_\_\_, "Reflections On the Sino-Soviet Dispute," <u>SOL</u>, IV i (Winter 1964), 22-38. Vigorously calls for end everywhere of Stalinism in the arts. Growth of leisure has transferred much of the international class struggle to cultural sphere, where socialist arts will prove most convincing when most allowed needed autonomy.

\_\_\_\_\_, The Meaning Of Contemporary Realism, Merlin: London, 1963; retitled <u>Realism In Our Time</u>, Harper & Rowe: 1964. US edition has Preface by George Steiner but omits Lukacs' Introduction and Prefaces from 1957 and 1962. Critique of modernism. Role of a progressive and national outlook in achieving successful form. Naturalism, critical and socialist realism. Beckett, Benn, Montherlant, Musil, Joyce, Mann, Goethe, Kafka, Gide, Benjamin, Proust, Hoffmann, Hoffmannsthal, S. Lewis, Conrad, Wolfe, du Gard, Brecht, O'Neill, D.H. Lawrence,

Bromfield, Zola, Mailer, Chekhov.

\_\_\_\_\_, Introduction to his 'Aesthetics'. <u>NHQ</u>, Summer 1964, 57-72.

\_\_\_\_\_, "Theatre and Environment," <u>Times Literary Supplement</u> (London), Apr 23, 1964, 347. The actuality of Shakespeare.

\_\_\_\_\_, "On Romanticism," <u>NHQ</u>, Summer 1965, 27-32.

\_\_\_\_\_, Interview with Stephen Spender. <u>En</u>, Dec 1964, 53-57. Impressions: Lukacs' remarks on Tolstoy, Joyce, Proust, Dante, epic poetry today, the revival of Marxist thought.

\_\_\_\_\_, "Solzhenitsyn and the New Realism," in: Ralph Miliband and John Saville, eds, <u>The Socialist Register 1965</u>, Monthly Review: 1965, 197-215. "With him and his comrades in arms we encounter a fresh start, a first exploration of new realities" in USSR. The historical role of the novella form.

\_\_\_\_\_, SEE ALSO: Frank Benseler, ed, <u>Festschrift zum achtzigsten Geburtstag von Georg Lukacs</u> Luchterhand: Neuweid am Rhein, 1965. Several contributions in English. The fullest <u>bibliography</u> of Lukacs' writings in all languages is here. (Note: many of of the essay translations listed above are not included).

Crystal Eastman, "In Communist Hungary," <u>Lib</u>, II viii (Aug 1919), 5-10. Lukacs as Commissar of Education in 1919.

H.N. Brailsford, <u>New Statesman</u>, Feb 9, 1957, 172. First-hand report on Lukacs' conduct in 1919 revolution.

Jozsef Revai, <u>Lukacs and Socialist Realism</u>, London, 1950. 37 pp. Reprinted in <u>M&M</u>, Apr 1950, 42-57. The major Hungarian critique.

Martin Horvath, "A Note On the Self-Criticism Of Lukacs," <u>CR</u>, May 1950, 154-160. Horvath, in Hungarian Politburo, declares Lukacs' self-criticism following attack by L. Rudas "has not been broad enough nor deep enough" and gives examples.

Horvath was editor of the
Party newspaper "Szabad Nep'.
Rudas was head of Party ideo-
logical training school.

Eric Hobsbawm, "The Lukacs Debate," NCEO, II (1949), 291-
292. Background and survey of
debate between Lukacs and
Rudas.

A. Zis, "Present-Day revisionism
In Aesthetics," CDSP, Oct 1,
1958, 9-10. "Revisionism in
aesthetics is inseparable from
revisionism in politics," says
Zis, charging Lukacs' aesthetics with a sinister part in
1956 Hungarian uprising.

Bela Fogaresi, "Reflections On
the Philosophical Views Of
Georg Lukacs," WMR, June 1959,
39-45. Finds Lukacs "anti-
Marxist and anti-communist"
revisionist.

Gyula Borbandi, "Gyorgy Lukacs,"
EE, Apr 1961, 32-35; May, 28-
32; June, 20-26. illus. Author was student of philosophy
in Budapest until 1956. Offers
most thorough chronicle in
English of Lukacs' difficulties with the Party.

Times Literary Supplement, Sept
22, 1950.

L. Stern, "George Lukacs: an Intellectual Portrait," Dis,
Spring 1958, 162-173.

Morris Watnick, "Georg Lukacs:
Or Aesthetics and Communism,"
Survey #23 (Jan-Mch 1958),
60-66; #24, 51-57; #25, 61-68;
#27, 75-81. Indispensable.

Morris Watnick, "Relativism and
Class Consciousness: Georg
Lukacs," in: Leopold Labedz,
ed, Revisionism, 1962, 142-165.

Michael Harrington, "Lukacs;
Dialectical Career Of a Dia-
lectician," ASP, Fall 1957,
18-21. Informed and sympathetic probing of ups and
downs of Lukacs' career.

George Steiner, "Georg Lukacs
and His Devil's Pact," Kenyon

Review, Winter 1960, 1-18.
See also: Steiner, (LIX).

Herbert Read, "George Lukacs,"
NS, Feb 2, 1957, 127. Agree-
ing Lukacs is as Mann said
"the most important literary
critic of today," Read reviews
his career and lodges pleas
for his safety during period
following 1956 upheaval when
his whereabouts were unknown.

Max Reiser, "The Aesthetic Theory Of Socialist Realism,"
JAAC, XVI (1957), 233-248.
Chiefly exposition and critique of Lukacs whose realism-
oriented aesthetic, Reiser
says, is "scarcely applicable
to lyric poetry and still less
music....Lukacs' theory is...
despite his discussion of
form, an aesthetic of content.
What he calls form is the
arrangement of content."

Karl Mannheim, Review of Lukacs'
'Das Theorie des Romans'.
SOL, Summer 1963, 50-53. The
superiority of seeing works of
art in context of philosophy
of history as does Lukacs, in
contrast to results of disci-
plines lower in the 'hierarchy'
of totalizing investigation,
e.g, psychology.

Norman Fruchter, "A Realist Perspective," SOL, Spring 1964,
110-134. Critique of Lukacs'
relative disinterest in modern
Western novels and its significance for his theory.

George Lichtheim, "An Intellectual Disaster," En, May 1963,
74-80. Lukacs has "failed
altogether as a responsible
writer, and ultimately as a
man," concludes this hostile
polemic. - See objections to
article by George Steiner, En,
June 1963, 92-93; by Alastair
MacIntyre, Roy Pascal, John
Cumming and Geoffrey Carnall,
with Lichtheim's reply, En,
Aug 1963, 90-96.
"The Survivor," NS, Feb 23, 1962,
258-259. illus. Contours of
Lukacs' career.

Harold Rosenberg, "The Third

Dimension Of Georg Lukacs,"
*Dis*, Autumn 1964, 404-414.
Stimulating, often perverse
review of 'Meaning Of Contemporary Realism'. From
several standpoints accuses
Lukacs of fear or inability
to come to terms with nature
of modern society as well as
its literature.

Lion Feuchtwanger, *The House of
Desdemona; The Laurels and
Limitations of Historical
Fiction*, Wayne book paperback:
Detroit, 1963. Critique of
"The Historical Novel'.

*Times Literary Supplement*, June
25, 1964, 541-542. Summary
and review of 'Die Eigenart
des Asthetischen'. - Letter
from Herbert Read, ibid, 616,
citing work of Max Raphael.

Vera Maslow, "George Lukacs and
the Unconscious," *JAAC*, Summer
1964, 465-470. Lukacs' approach and how it differs from
that of psychoanalysis.

Alastair MacIntyre, "Marxist
Mask and Romantic Face: Lukacs
On Thomas Mann," *En*, Apr 1965,
64-72.

Istvan Eorsi, "Lukacs and Lyric
Poetry," *NHQ*, Summer 1965, 33-
46.

Victor Zitta, *Georg Lukacs' Marxism: Alienation, Dialectics
Revolution; A Study In Utopia
and Ideology*, Martinus Nij-
hoff: The Hague, 1964. A
dubious "exercise in political
theory" and neuroticism, taking Lukacs to 1925. - For
critique of Zitta's reliability see A. Rubinstein, *S&S*,
Fall 1965, 490-496; and Gyorgy
Markus, *S&S*, Winter 1966, 76-
77.

S.L. Shneiderman, "A Visit With
Georg Lukacs," *N.Y. Times Book
Review*, May 9, 1965, 30-32.
Judgments of recent literature.

Isaac Deutscher, "Intellectual
Love Affair," *Nation*, May 16,
1966, 590-593. Lukacs' admir-
ing treatment of T. Mann as an

instance of "genuine surrender to Stalinism".

D.D. Demecs, *A Critical Analysis
of Georg Lukacs' Social Philosophy of Art*, Ph.D. dissertation, State University of New
York at Buffalo, 1965.

Peter Demetz, "The Uses Of
Lukacs," *Yale Review*, Spring
1965, 435-440.

Agnes Heller, "Lukacs' Aesthet-
ics," *NHQ*, Winter 1966, 84-94.
Review of 'Die Eigenart des
Aesthetischen'.

Andrew Feenberg, "An Introduction To the Young Lukacs,"
*Alternatives*, Fall 1966, 18,
21-28. 'History and Class
Consciousness' and the transcendence of reified society.

Vera Maslow, "Lukacs' Man-
Centered Aesthetics," *Phil-
osophy and Phenomenological
Research*, June 1967, 542-552.
A critique of 'Die Eigenart
des Aesthetischen'.

See also: Central Committee
(above); Goldmann (XIX);
Morawski (XXXVI); Baxandall,
Burgum (LVI); Sontag (LXII).

MAJOR, Mate, "'The Style Of Truth' and
The Truth Of Style," *NHQ*, Summer 1966,
57-65. Determinants of architectural
style.

PALFFY, Endre, "Some Facts About C.
Dobrogeanu-Gherea's Russian Relations,"
*AL*, IV (1961), 341-351. Information
on "Rumania's Chernyshevsky," a revolutionary democrat who founded Rumanian
literary criticism on a basis of
scientific epistemology.

PALOCZI-HORVATH, George, "'That Paralys-
ing Apparition, Beauty;' Notes on
'Humanist' and Marxist Aesthetics,"
*MQM*, 11-36. Against obscurantism,
eclecticism, impressionism in aesthetics.

REVAI, Jozsef, *Problems Of Socialist
Culture In Hungary*, London, 1951.
Speech to 2nd Congress of Hungarian
Working People's Party.

_____, "Problems Of Architecture In Hun-
gary," *CR*, Feb 1952, 54-62. Attack on

Bauhaus and Corbusier influence in Hungary. "Formalism is the essence of the new architecture."

RONAY, Gyorgy, "Gabor Garai's Poetry," NHQ, #19 (Autumn 1965), 85-89. Complexity of committed poetry.

SAS, Judit, and Zsuzsanna Sipos, "Testing Peasant Taste," NHQ, Spring 1964, 170-181. Socialist opinion-sampling of aesthetic taste among the peasantry.

SOMLYO, Gyorgy, "A Short Introduction To Contemporary Hungarian Poetry," NHQ, Autumn 1966, 108-117.

SZABO, Franz, "The Course Of Fascism In German Music," ITh, 1934 #1, 11-14.

SZABO, Julia, "The Paintings of Gyula Derkovits," NHQ, Spring 1966, 186-190. illus.

SZENCZI, Miklos, "Decay and New Birth In Post-Shakespearean Drama," AL, IV (1961), 353-359. Pointing out emergent qualities in Stuart drama, lacking in Shakespeare, Szenczi refuses to view that period as simple decadence.

SZILI, Jozsef, "The Poetry Of Hugh MacDiarmid," FKSup, VI (1960), 50-52. abdgd.

TIKOS, Laszlo M, "Hungary: Literary Renascence," PC, XIII iii (May-June 1964), 24-34.

UJFALUSSY, Jozsef, A valosag zenei kepe [The Musical Image Of Reality], Budapest, 1962. Major application of Marxist theory to musical structure. - Review-summary by Ervin Laszlo, BJA, Jan 1965, 97-99; another by Deves Zoltay, NHQ, Apr-June 1963, 174-184.

VERES, Peter, "Petty Bourgeois?" NHQ, Oct-Dec 1963, 58-64. Difficulties of developing and defining a workers' culture.


INDIA

Topic Index

ART, HINDU, Anand.

BHARATI, Ramakrishnan.

COLONIAL CULTURE, REJECTING. Anand, Chand, Ghosh, Indian.

DANCE. Anand.

INDIAN PROGRESSIVE WRITERS ASSOCIATION. 6th All-India, Chand, Indian, Shasti, Zaheer.

INDOLOGY. Barannikov, Rabinovich, Ulyanovsky (XXIX).

KALIBAR. Zvelebil.

KALIDASA. Gassner (LVIII).

LITERATURE, HERITAGE, PROGRESSIVE VALUES IN. Ali, Dange, P. Gupta, Haldar, Zvelebil. Zbavitel (XV).

'MAHABHARATA'. Vishnevskaya (XXIX).

'RAMAYANA'. Barannikov (XXIX).

REVOLUTIONARY LITERATURE, VALUES. Anand, Chand, Chattopadhyay, Gargi, Gupta, Indian, Namboodiripad, Sharma.

SOCIOLOGY OF CULTURE. Mukerjee (XXIX).

TAGORE. Anand, Bannerjee, Mukherjee, Rabindranath. Tovstykh, Zbavitch (XV).

THEATRE. Anand, Gupta. Martin (XXIX).

XXVIII. Authors

6th ALL-INDIA PROGRESSIVE WRITERS CONGRESS. Report and speeches of H. Chattopadhyay and R.B. Sharma. IndL, 1953 #2, 49-69. (1st Congress was held at Lucknow in 1936, with Prem Chand as Chairman.)

ALI, Ahmed, "Indian Peasant Poetry," Indian Writing (London), I ii (Summer 1940), 99-104. [DLC] [BM] Materialism and superstition in revolutionary peasant verse.

ANAND, Mulk Raj, "Towards a New Indian Literature," LR, Sept 1936, 613-623. Rejection of accrued colonial attitudes.

_____, "Twentieth Century English Novels About India," Million #3, 19-28.

_____, On the Proletarian Novel. Life and Letters To-Day, Spring 1937, 145-146. Reviewing Calder-Marshall's 'Pie In the Sky', Anand locates the "proletarian" values of revolutionary

literature in the outlook, not the
subject-matter or writer's origin.

_____, Review of Hemingway's 'For Whom
the Bell Tolls'. Indian Writing, Aug
1941, 230-233. [BM] Revealing of
both Hemingway and Anand.

_____, Lines Written To an Indian Air,
Bombay, 1949. Essays on numerous
aspects of Indian culture.

_____, The Hindu View Of Art, revised
edition, Bombay, 1957. illus.
Exposition.

_____, "Rabindranath Tagore," EH, May
1961, 13-21.

_____, Is There a Contemporary Indian
Civilization? Asia Publishing House:
1963. India's assimilation of (and
surrender to) Western values. Asks
how India's finest values - universality, tolerance, compassion - may be
preserved.

_____, SEE ALSO: Jack Lindsay, Mulk Raj
Anand; a Critical Essay, Bombay,
1948. Assesses his fiction;
biographical facts.

BALIGA, A.V, "Indo-Soviet Cultural Relations - A Brief Review," ISCUS, Spring
1957, 4-10. A Clear account by head
of Indian Institute For Cultural Relations With the USSR.

BANNERJEE, Subrata, "The Creative Iconoclast," ISCUS, Oct 1949, 9-51. Tagore
as motivated by profound humanism and
anti-imperialism.

CHAND, Prem, "Mahajani Civilization,"
IndL, 1952 #1, 26-33. [DLC] Written
1936. President of 1st All-India
Progressive Writers Conference, author
of novel 'Godan', denounces cultural
damage done by capitalist competition,
individualism to Indian civilization.
Poses a socialist alternative.

CHATTOPADHYAY, Harandranath, "Writers
and the People," IndL, 1953 #2, 50-53.
Opening address at 6th All-India Progressive Writers Congress.

DANGE, S.A, "Notes On Medieval Marathi
Literature," IndL, 1952 #2, 32-35.
12th Century religious poetry that,
denouncing social evils, "expressed
real class-demands in the terminology
of religion and its sects." Dange was

an historian and Marathi critic on
Politburo of Indian CP.

DATTA, Bhupendranath, Indian Art In Relation To Culture, Nababharat:Calcutta,
1956.

GARGI, Balwant, "New Punjabi Literature,"
IndL, 1953 #2, 32-39.

GHOSH, J.C, "Contemporary Indian Art,"
London Mercury, Mch 1936, 512-517.

GUPTA, P.C, "The Revolt Of 1857 In Hindi
Literature," ISCUS, IV iii, 55-68.

_____, "Modern Indian Literature As a
Factor In Moulding Social Life," NO,
1965 #4, 114-119.

GUPTA, Sachin Sen, "People's Theatre In
India," Unity, II v (Dec 1952-Jan 1953),
8-17. [cc] Dramatist and head of West
Bengal Indian People's Theatre Association. Detailed.

HALDAR, Gopal, "Young Bengal: An Intelligentsia In Revolt (1831-1857)," NO,
June 1962, 92-93.

INDIAN PROGRESSIVE WRITERS ASSOCIATION,
Manifesto, London. LR, Feb 1936, 240.
Signers: Mulk Raj Anand, K.S. Bhat,
J.C. Ghosh, S. Sinha, M.D. Taseer,
S.S. Zaheer. Rejects "escapism" of
previous two hundred years of Indian
literature, calls for vital, realistic
popular style.

MUKERJEE, Hiren, Himself A True Poem; A
Study Of Rabindranath Tagore, People's
Publishing House: New Delhi, 1961.

MUKHERJEE, Ramkrishna, "Tagore and Class
Forces In India," S&S, Spring 1950,
97-114.

NAMBOODIRIPAD, E.M.S, "The Struggle For
People's Democratic Literature in
Malayalam," IndL, 1952 #2, 81-84.
Member of Indian CP Politburo reports
on developing progressive literature in
Kerala State.

RABINDRANATH TAGORE Centennial Number.
ISCUS, Aug 1961. illus. Contributions
by Mulk Raj Anand, Hiren Mukerjee,
Soviet Indologists S.F. Oldenburg, E.
Chelishev, Lev Nikulin, et al.

RAMAKRISHNAN, S, "Bharati - The Greatest
Tamil Poet Of the Modern Era," ISCUS,
Dec 1962, 22-25.

SHARMA, Ram Bilas, "What Is Progressive Literature?" IndL, 1952 #1, 1-14. [DLC] General Secretary of Indian Progressive Writers Association sets forth broad principles of continuity, democracy, scientific orientation, etc. - See also "N", "What Is Progressive Literature?" IndL, 1952 #2, 85-88. Polemic against Sharma.

_____, Report to 6th All-India Progressive Writers Congress. IndL, 1953 #2, 53-69. Outgoing General Secretary offers impressive summing up of problems, scope, principles, accomplishments.

ZAHEER, Sajjad, Reminiscences Of Indian Progressive Writers Association In London In the 30s. IndL, 1952 #2, 47-52. Dated 1940. Tells vividly of talks with Ralph Fox and Louis Aragon, the PWA's early days and his experiences in Paris Popular Front. Zaheer was an Urdu critic and novelist who became General Secretary of Pakistan CP.

ZVELEBIL, Kamil, "Tamil Poetry 2000 Years Ago," NO, Oct 1960, 3-6. illus. Early realism and secularism.

_____, "Kabilar's Agaval, A Hymn On the Equality Of Men, In Medieval Tamil," NO, Dec 1961, 164-165. Unique early work with naturalist tendencies, sceptical of caste system and Brahmin teachings.

### XXIX: Appendix

BARRANIKOV, Alexei Petrovich, "Tulsidas's 'Ramayana'," ISCUS, I iv; II ii, 28-33. Leading Soviet Indologist, translator of the epic into Russian, describes it as social critique of a period of moral collapse. - See also: Notes on Barranikov's contribution to Indology, by the Presidium of the USSR Academy of Sciences and the Editors of IndL, in IndL, 1952 #2, 5-7.

COOMARASWAMY, Ananda, The Dance Of Shiva; Fourteen Indian Essays, 1918. illus. Indian aesthetics in social context.

_____, Asiatic Art, Chicago, 1938.

_____, The Transformation Of Nature In Art, Cambridge, 1934.

_____, Figures Of Speech Or Figures Of Thought, London, 1946. More the

Catholic medievalist here, but still useful.

MARTIN, David, "Indian People's Theatres Association," New Theatre (London), June 1948, 16-17. [BM] illus.

MUKERJEE, Radhakamal, The Culture and Art Of India, Praeger: 1959. illus. Bibliography. Brilliant relation of Indian culture to Indian history.

RABINOVICH, N, "Indian Literature Reviewed," ISCUS, Dec 1962, 40-42. Survey of Soviet studies of Indian language and writings.

TOVSTYKH, Inessa, "Rabindranath Tagore and the Russian Reader," SL, 1966 #8, 151-157. - See also SL, 1967 #1, 177-179.

ULYANOVSKY, R.A, "An Introduction To Soviet Indology," ISCUS, June 1960, 16-24.

VISHNEVSKAYA, Natalia, Soviet Work On the 'Mahabharata'. SL, 1965 #1, 179-182.

### ITALY

#### Topic Index

(Includes Roman Topics)

(See also: Arnold Hauser (XXVII), on all topics to 1920s.)

ALBERTI. Blunt (XXIII).

AMMIANUS MARCELLINUS. Auerbach (LXII).

ANGELICO, FRA. Antal (XXVII).

APULEIUS. Lindsay (XXIII); Auerbach (LXII).

AQUINUS. Auerbach (LXII).

ARIOSTO. Auerbach (LXII).

AUGUSTINE. Auerbach (LXII).

BOCCACCIO. Kautsky, Martin (XXI); Lindsay (XXIII); Antal (XXVII); Lawson (LVI); Auerbach (LXII).

BRUNELLESCHI. Antal (XXVII).

CARPI, G. Antal (XXVII).

CASANOVA. Wilson (LVI).

CATULLUS. Lindsay (XXIII).

CINEMA, AVANT-GARDE. Antonioni, DeSanctis, Visconti. Kettle (XXIII); Bogemsky (XXXI); Schleifer, Temaner (LIV).

CROCE, B. Gramsci, Labriola.

DANTE. Marx and Engels (XXI); Antal, Lukacs (XXVII); Lindsay (XXIII); Ehrenberg, Golanishcher, Trotsky (XLVI); Lawson (LVI); Auerbach, Wieruszowski (LXII).

DE FILIPPO. Codignola.

DONATELLO. Antal (XXVII).

DRAMA, RENAISSANCE. Gassner (LVIII).

FABRIANO. Antal (XXVII).

FASCISM AND CULTURE. Elistratova (XLVI); Winwar (LVI); Toscanini (LXIII).

FELLINI. Chukhrai, Dovzhenko (XLIV).

FERRARA. Antal (XXVII).

FIRENZA, A. Da. Antal (XXVII).

FRANCESCA, P. Berger (XXIII).

FRANCIS OF ASSISI. Auerbach (LXII).

GADDI. Antal (XXVII).

GHIBERTI. Antal (XXVII).

GIACOMETTI. Sartre (XIX); Berger (XXIII).

GIOTTO. Fischer (XXI); Antal (XXVII); Lawson (LVI).

HORACE. Lindsay (XXIII); Winspear (LVI); Auerbach (LXII).

JACOPONE DA TODI. Auerbach (LXII).

JEROME. Auerbach (LXII).

LEONARDO. Blunt (XXIII); Plekhanov (XLVI); Schapiro (LIII); Lawson (LVI); Wittkower (LXII).

LITERATURE, HISTORY. Sanctis (LXII).

LITERARY THEORY, RENAISSANCE. Hall (LXII).

LORENZETTI. Antal (XXVII); Rubinstein (LXII).

LUCIAN. Auerbach (LXII).

LUCRETIUS. Winspear (LVI).

MANNERISM. Sartre (XIX); Antal (XXVII); Blunt (XXIII).

MANZONI. Lukacs (XXVII).

MASSACCIO. Antal (XXVII).

MICHELANGELO. Fischer (XXI); Berger, Blunt (XXIII); Plekhanov (XLVI); Wittkower (LXII).

MUSIC, AVANT-GARDE. Nono.

PAINTING, FLORENTINE. Martin (XXI); Berger, Blunt, Lindsay (XXIII); Antal (XXVII).

PAINTING, SOCIALIST. Guttuso.

PETRARCH. Martin (XXI); Antal (XXVII); Lawson (LVI).

PETRONIUS. Lindsay (XXIII); Auerbach (LXII).

PIRANDELLO. Gassner (LVIII).

POETRY. Quasimodo (XXXI); 1959 (XLI).

QUASIMODO. See (XXXI).

RAPHAEL. Plekhanov (XLVI).

RENAISSANCE. Fischer, Martin, Marx and Engels (XXI); Blunt (XXIII); Antal (XXVII); Auerbach (LXII).

ROMAN DECLINE, CULTURE. Lindsay (XXIII); Auerbach (LXII).

ROSSELLINI, R. Russell (XXIII).

SILONE, I. See (XXXI). Slochower (LVI).

TACITUS. Auerbach (LXII).

THEATRE, POPULAR. Codignola, Grassi, Pandolfi.

TINTORETTO. Sartre (XIX).

TITIAN. Lunacharsky (XLVI).

TOSCANINI, A. See (LXIII).

VASARI. Blunt (XXIII).

VICO. Lifshitz (XLVI); Auerbach, Wilson (LXII).

VIRGIL. Lindsay (XXIII); Winspear (LVI); Auerbach, Routh (LXII).

## XXX.  Authors

ANTONIONI, M, "The Event and the Image," Sight and Sound, Winter 1963-64,14.From 'Cinema Nuovo' #164. A film-maker's need for moral commitment. Its relation to the film image.

CODIGNOLA, Luciano, "Reading De Filippo," TDR, Spring 1964, 108-117. Brilliant analysis of this Neapolitan playwright.

DeSANCTIS, Giuseppe, "The Cinema and the Problems Of the Times," NT, Aug 22, 1962, 30-31. A screenwriter judges Japanese films with medieval settings the world's most relevant to today. Criticizes eroticism and naturalism in Italian left cinema.

GRAMSCI, Antonio, "Marxism and Modern Culture," in his The Modern Prince and Other Writings, Lawrence & Wishart: London, 1957, 82-89. Marxism's need to create "its own core of independent intellectuals."

_____, "Benedetto Croce and His Concept Of Liberty," S&S, X (1946), 283-291. The practical political consequences of Croce's philosophy: he finds a way to justify all that occurs.

_____, SEE ALSO: John M. Cammett, Antonio Gramsci and the Origins Of Italian Communism, Stanford University Press: Stanford, Calif., 1967. biblio. Fine account of development of his thought on necessity of a hegemonic workers' culture. His academic training in linguistics and literature.

GRASSI, Paolo, "The Milan Piccolo Theatre," Italian Theatre Review, July-Aug-Sept 1963, 53-57. Survey of the tasks and methods this "people's theatre" takes up.

_____, and Giorgio Strehler, "Sixteen Years Of the Piccolo Teatro," TDR, Spring 1964, 27-43.

GUTTUSO, Renato, Statement. Reality, #2 (Spring 1954), 12. Against deliberately obscure painting. But Gut-

tuso expresses "fraternal" purpose with "non-realist" painters who "are seeking a true expression of humanity" - for to do this with "more clarity, greater beauty, and stronger conviction, avoiding 'vulgar realism'," is the task of every artist.

_____, Interview. Art News, Apr 1958, 26-27, 59-62. illus. Wide-ranging.

_____, SEE ALSO: John Berger, "Renato Guttuso," Apollo, Mch 1955, 70. illus. "The most hopeful and important development in European art since the war." Also, John Berger on Guttuso's 'The Battle of Ponte Ammiraglio', Burlington Magazine, Oct 1952, 296-297. illus.

LABRIOLA, Antonio, "Historical Materialism," in his Essays On the Materialistic Conception Of History, Chicago: 1904; Monthly Review: 1966, 95-246. From 1896. Ch. VI, VII (pp. 140-179) on the initiating role of "intuitive, palpable...aesthetic and artistic" perceptions preparing the way for abstract formulations in the developing consciousness of social structures. Ch. X (pp. 204-221), the relations of art and society.

_____, Socialism and Philosophy, Chicago: 1912. From 1901. Pp. 7, 110-111 on flowering of individual creativity under communism; pp. 106-110, theological poetry and emotion; pp. 164-178, critique of B. Croce's Marxism.

LAZZARI, Arturo, "Brecht In Italy," Drama Review (formerly TDR), Fall 1967, 149-153.

NONO, Luigi, "The Historical Reality Of Music Today," The Score, July 1960, 41-45. Strong criticism of composers who invoke improvisation and indeterminacy as principles. Joseph Schillinger and John Cage are named. "Their liberty is a spiritual suicide."

_____, See also: Michael Parsons, "Luigi Nono," NLR, #32 (1965), 84-87.

PANDOLFI, Vito, "Italian Theatre Since the War," TDR, Spring 1964, 87-107.

_____, Interview with Ernest Callenbach. TDR,  Fall 1966, 137-140.

RAFFA, Piero, "Some Contemporary Italian

Aesthetics," JAAC, XX (1962), 287-294.
Includes discussion of della Volpe.
- Letter correcting translation errors,
ibid, XXI (1962), 215-216.

TOGLIATTI, Palmiro, Political 'Testament'. N.Y. Times, Sept 5, 1964, 2.
Complete text of memorandum on world
Communist problems written hours before
his final illness. Endorsed and published by Italian Party. "We must become the champions of liberty of intellectual life, of free artistic
creation and of scientific progress."
- See also his reaction to Krushchev's
speech on art of March 8, 1963: Interview with K.S. Karol, New Statesman,
May 24, 1963; also, Krushchev on Culture, Encounter Pamphlet #9, back
cover.

VISCONTI, Luchino, Interview with Jacques
Doniol-Valcroze and Jean Domarchi.
Sight and Sound, Summer and Autumn,
1959, 144-147, 191. Discussion chiefly of the primacy of content in his
work and not of style.

_____, "Optimism and Pessimism In Art,"
NT, Aug 2, 1961, 15-16. "An effective socialist world outlook is now
everywhere one of the prerequisites
of artistic creation." Wide-ranging
remarks on creative practice in
socialist and capitalist lands.

_____, SEE ALSO; Piscator (XXI); Giulio
    Cesare Castello, "Luchino
    Visconti," Sight and Sound,
    Spring 1956, 184-190, 220.
    illus. Fine survey.

### XXXI.  Appendix

BOGEMSKY, G, "Notes On the Italian
Cinema," NT, 1965 #33, 24-27.
Progressive films analyzed.

COOK, Joan M, "Italy's Intellectuals
Steer To the Left," N.Y. Times Magazine, May 26, 1963, 32, 96-97. illus.
"To be an intellectual in Italy means
to be in revolt, to be ready to throw
out the old, discredited ruling class
and make a clean break with the past."

EGBERT, Donald D, Communism, Radicalism,
and the Arts  In Western Europe,
forthcoming.

MORAVIA, Alberto, "Communism and Art,"
Confluence, June 1953, 31-47. Bitter
remarks inspired by Zhdanov period.

"It is hard to see how any ideology
that is always critical and aims at
the renewal of society can continue to
play this role once Communism has come
to power....any victorious ideology
tends to turn dogmatic and magisterial."

SEVERINI, Gino, The Artist and Society,
1952. Italian Catholic painter attacks
'Marxism', in reality Stalinist policy.

SILONE, Ignazio, "The Party Line Fails
To Hold," Living Age, Oct 1940, 152-
154. "The union of art and revolution
cannot be attained by the submission
of the artist to a political party....
[it] cannot be an instrument of propaganda." Inquires why Brecht, Renn,
Seghers and other "intelligent Communist
authors" have not renounced ties with
the Party.

_____, Interview With Clement Greenberg.
PR, Fall 1939, 22-30.

_____, in: Richard Crossman, ed, The God
That Failed, 1949. Account of relations with the Comintern and decision
to leave Party. See also: Trotsky (XLVI).


### JAPAN

### Topic Index

KABUKI THEATRE. Brecht (XXI); Eisenstein
(XLIV).

MODERN LITERATURE. Novak (XV).

### XXXII.  Authors

KIM, R, "Japanese Literature and Revolution," IL, 1933 #6, 81-111. Development of a social sense in Japanese
writing after 1885.

MATSU-YAMA, "Japanese Literature," LWR,
1931 #1, 83-89. Much on writers
organizations and their disputes.

SANO, Seki, "The Revolutionary Theatre
In Fascist Japan," LWR, 1931 #5,
140-143. illus.

_____, "Revolutionary Theatre In Japan,"
ITh, #4 (1933), 14-20. illus.

## MEXICO

### XXXIII.  Authors

1st NATIONAL CONGRESS, LEAGUE OF REVOLU-
TIONARY WRITERS AND ARTISTS.  Reported
in AF, May 1937, 13-14.

CABRERO, Enrique, "The Dialectical Genius
Of Johann Sebastian Bach," S&S, Fall
1957, 319-332.  Bach "grasps an ideological contradiction and expresses it
by means of an adequate musical contradiction."

FUENTES, Carlos, "Soviet Theory Of Art
Challenged," NG, May 2, 1963, 6-7.
Krushchev speech of Mch 8, 1963 is
"idealism explicitly rejected by
Marxist thought."  Analyzes role of
art in a revolutionary society.

_____, Interview with Lee Baxandall.
SOL, III i (1963), 48-56.  Latin
American novelists and problems of
style and communication in lands of
mass illiteracy.

_____, "Luis Bunuel," Show, Nov 1963,
81, 134-135.  Lively survey of
Bunuel's achievement.

_____, Review of Oscar Lewis's 'Pedro
Martinez'.  N.Y. Review of Books,
June 25, 1964, 3-4.  Concludes with
lucid statement of dedication to art
that embraces both the fight against
injustice and the tragic dimension of
life, and to a society which permits
both material well-being and passionate living.

_____, Interview.  In: Luis Harss and
Barbara Dohmann, Into the Mainstream,
Harper & Row: 1967, 276-309.

GUERRERO, Xavier, "The Most Universal
and Human Language," MQ(T), Spring
1964, 48.  The dimensions of realism.

MANCISIDOR, Jose, Juan de la Cabada,
Renato Molina Enriquez, and Miguel
Rubio, Interview with Isidore
Schneider.  DW, May 6, 1935, 5.
Mexican delegates to 1st American
Writers Congress describe Mexican
Communist writing and its organiza-
tion (LEAR).

O'HIGGINS, Pablo, "Art For the People's
Sake," DWSup, Feb 5, 1939, 1-2. illus.

OROZCO.  See (LXIII).

PAPERS PRESENTED For the Mexican Delegation At the American Artists Congress,
Feb 15, 1936, by Jose C. Orozco and
David A. Siqueiros.  AAC.  Orozco presents plan to create cultural sections
headed by Artists Union members within
Mexican trade unions.  Siqueiros' paper
is "The Mexican Experience in Art."

REVUELTAS, Sylvestre, Max March, "The
Music Of Sylvestre Revueltas," M&M,
Feb 1949, 54-63.  Expert biographical
and musicological account.

RIVERA, Diego, "From A Mexican Painter's
Notebook," The Arts, Jan 1925, 21-23.
The role of cubism, "the most important
single achievement in plastic art since
the Renaissance" in his work.  Picasso's
protean role.  The execrable taste of
"the cultural bourgeois."  The development in painting of a Marxist classicism.

_____, "A Magisterial Utilization Of
Clean Bones," MassR, Winter 1962,
369-374.  Popular originality of the
engraver Jose Posada.

_____, "Retablos: The True and Only Pic-
toric Expression Of Mexican People,"
Mexican Folkways, Oct-Nov 1925, 7-9.
illus.  Analysis of Mexican popular
art and its exploitation and debase-
ment by bourgeoisie.  The faulty translation may be checked against original
text which follows, pp. 9-12. - Subsequent issues have brief illustrated
Rivera essays on popular portraiture;
the photography of Edward Weston and
Tina Moddoti; the painting of pul-
querias; recent Mexican architecture;
children's art; the peasant sculptor
Magana.

_____, "Revolution In Painting," Creative
Art, Jan 1929.

_____, "The Position Of the Artist In
Russia Today," Arts Weekly, I i (Mch
11, 1932), 6-7.  Finds Soviet painting
in "full decadence."

_____, "What Is Art For?" MQ(B), June
1933, 275-278.  Artists should not be
fellow-travellers but servants of the
Revolution.

_____, "The Revolutionary Spirit In
Modern Art," MQ(B), Autumn 1932, 51-57.
Defends propaganda art, declares himself a "guerrilla fighter" who lives
as he can off bourgeoisie while waiting

to return to the Party.

_____, Rivera Supplement, Workers' Age,
June 15, 1933. illus. Two minor es-
says: "The Radio City Mural" and
"Nationalism and Art," the latter
finding Mexico a peasant culture, the
US an engineer's culture. The Radio
City mural controversy.

_____, "The Stormy Petrel Of American
Art On His Art," Studio (London),
July 1933.

_____, Speech at New York Art Students
League. N.Y. Herald Tribune, May 18,
1933. Extended report with numerous
direct quotations.

_____, Refutation Of Charges Of Oppor-
tunism Made By Joseph Freeman. NRep,
Sept 27, 1933, 187-188. Freeman's
charges in respect to Presidential
Palace murals, NM, Feb 1932; and NRep,
Aug 16, 1933, 23. See Workers' Age
Special Issue for photos documenting
refutation.

_____, "Architecture and Mural Painting,"
Architectural Forum, Jan 1934.

_____, and Andre Breton, "Manifesto:
Towards a Free Revolutionary Art,"
PR, Fall 1938, 49-53. Also (different translation) in: London Bulletin,
Dec 1938-Jan 1939, 29-32. Manifesto
dated July 25, 1938. Attack on
"the official art of Stalinism" and
call for "complete freedom of art"
for revolutionary artists in a revolutionary State. Announces formation
of International Federation of Independent Revolutionary Artists (FIARI)
as a rallying point. - For Trotsky's
enthusiastic welcome to this project
see his letter to Andre Breton, PR,
Winter 1939, 126-127.

_____, with G. March, My Art, My Life:
An Autobiography, Citadel: 1960.

_____, SEE ALSO: Politburo Of the CC Of
Mexico, Statement On Diego
Rivera, June 2, 1933. DW,
July 7, 1933, 4. Explains
Rivera's expulsion from CP and
denounces his "theatrical
gestures and nauseating dema-
gogy."

Mary Randolph, "Rivera's Monopoly," AF, Nov 1935, 5; Dec
1935, 12-13. [MMA] Abusive

article on Rivera as panderer
to tourists.

Emanuel Eisenberg, "Battle Of
the Century," NM, Dec 10, 1935,
18-20. Colorful detailed
account of speeches and occa-
sions in running battle between
Siqueiros and Rivera during
August, 1935, their first public confrontation after years
of polemics. Rivera struck
Eisenberg, calling him "a
son-of-a-bitch Stalinist sent
down here by 'New Masses' to
take notes and make fun of me."
Concludes both are loners and
opportunists, Rivera the worse.

Leon Trotsky, Tribute to Rivera's
Art, PR, V iii, 7. Comment
on Rivera's Unreliability, FI,
Oct 1940, 135.

Teresa Proenza, "Homage to Diego
Rivera," M&M, Mch 1958, 6-11.
By his private secretary.

Bertram D. Wolfe, The Fabulous
Life Of Diego Rivera, Stein &
Day: 1963. illus. Lively but
marred by Wolfe's embittered
anti-Communism; he recruited
Rivera into the Mexican Party
in 1920s.

RUIZ, Antonio, Interview with Lou McLean.
DW, Feb 14, 1939, 7. illus. Muralist.

SIQUEIROS, David Alfaro, "Manifesto,"
transition #21 (Mch 1932), 134-135.
"I am a militant Communist and a partisan of individualism and metaphysics
in art."

_____, "Rivera's Counter-Revolutionary
Road," NM, May 29, 1934, 16-19. Sum-
mary-indictment on all grounds including aesthetic.

_____, Through the Road Of a Neo-Realism
Or Modern Social Realistic Painting In
Mexico, Mexico City, 1951. illus.
Chiefly photos of his works. Some
biography and citation of statements.
Eisenstein on Siqueiros.

_____, Interview with Robert Mallery.
Direction, May 1940, 15-16. The "corruption" of Mexico's revolutionary art
movement.

_____, "Open Letter To Soviet Painters,"

M&M, Mch 1956, 1-6.  In friendly
spirit Siqueiros tells Soviet artists
their work is academic and without
national roots.

_____, Interview with Ralph Parker. NWR,
Feb 1958, 13-16.  Relates ongoing
struggle to confront Soviet artists
with his case against academicism in
Soviet painting.

_____, "Mexican Painting," NF, Winter
1954, 14-16.  Written for this magazine.  Yankee-cosmopolitan encroach-
ments on mural movement.

_____, Interview with N.Y. Times, Dec
11, 1955.  On archaic themes in Mexican art and academicism in Soviet art.

_____, Interview with Walter Lowenfels.
M&M, Mch 1962, 28-30.  "All art surges
up like a tower from a national base
toward a universal view....If we lack
a world-wide point of view, a universal perspective, we will fall into not
a national, but a nationalistic...line
of thought."

_____, Lectures To Artists.  NUT, Winter
1962, 17-28.  Translated "from notes
on lectures given by...Siqueiros."
Valuable account of the muralists'
development, "poly-multiangular perspective," air-gun painting, abstraction and realism, the uses of non-
figurative experiment.

_____, Message To XIII International
Congress Of Philosophy.  MQ(T), Spring
1964, 36-39.  Reprinted in Streets,
Oct 1964, 7-11.  Dated Sept 9, 1963.
From prison Siqueiros reminds the Congress sitting in halls decorated by
him that the Mexican muralist movement
of all modern art has alone "made
plastic expression a vehicle of social
doctrine" and philosophy.

_____, "On Returning To Major Art,"
MRSup #1 (1965), 45-51.  The School of
Paris and its US developments contrasted with great public art of the past
and with Mexican mural art.

_____, Interview with Erica Mangold. AmD,
Mch-Apr 1966, 25-26.

_____, Interview with Luis Suarez. NG,
Mch 18, 1967, 7.  The failure of
Picasso to learn from the CP and overcome his formalism.  The effect of the
modern world art market in encouraging

formalism.

_____, SEE ALSO: Leon Trotsky, "The Com-
intern and the GPU," FI, Nov
1940, 153-156, for a version of
Siqueiros' involvement in the
attempt on Trotsky's life, May
24, 1940.  Joseph Hansen,
Trotsky's personal secretary,
also provides a vivid account:
ibid, Aug 1940, 85-91.

Charmion von Weigand, "David
Alfaro Siqueiros," NM, May 1,
1934, 18-21.

NP, Winter 1963, 128-131, for
repercussions of Trotsky assassination attempt following
Siqueiros' arrest in 1960 on
charges of social dissolution.
Letter from French intellectuals (including A. Breton),
and a communication from
Victor Alba, raise doubts
whether Siqueiros deserves
the clemency appeals circulated
for him.

Meyer Schapiro, "On David Siqueiros - A Dilemma For Artists," Dis, Spring 1963, 106,
197.  Why he declined to sign
the clemency appeal.  "During
much of his life he has been
a Communist militant, more
active in leading demonstrations, planning and participating in murders, and carrying out faithfully the instructions of the Moscow dictators,
than in painting pictures.  In
prison perhaps he has at last
found himself as an artist."

A. Pavlenko, "The Prisoner Of
Lecumberri," NT, May 19, 1964,
22-25.

Elliot Clay, "Siqueiros: Artist
in Arms," M&M, Apr 1951, 60-74.

Lincoln Kirstein, "Siqueiros In
Chillan," Magazine Of Art,
Nov 1943, 282-287.  illus.
Best report on possibly the
painter's finest work and
least accessible. - See also
Kirstein's biographical arti-
cle, ibid, Jan 1944, 23-27, 34.

Current Biography, 1959, 413-415.
illus.

SYNDICATE OF TECHNICAL WORKERS, PAINTERS AND SCULPTORS, "Manifesto." In: Laurence E. Schmeckebier, Modern Mexican Art, Minneapolis, 1939, 31. First published 1922. Written chiefly by Siqueiros.

## NORWAY

### Topic Index

HAMSUN, K. Plekhanov (XLVI); Auerbach, Lowenthal (LXII).

IBSEN. Marx and Engels, Mehring, Fischer (XXI); Aveling (XXIV); Hauser, Lukacs (XXVII); Lunacharsky, Plekhanov (XLVI); Gassner, Lawson, Perkins (LVIII); Brandes Koht, Lowenthal (LXII).

(For a brief survey of post-Ibsen literary Marxism, see: Jens A. Christophersen, "'Mot Dag' and the Norwegian Left," Journal of Contemporary History, I ii (1966), 135-148.)

## PAKISTAN

### XXXIV. Authors

ALI, Ahmed, "Introduction To Urdu Poetry," EH, Mch 1965, 23-29.

PAKISTAN PROGRESSIVE WRITERS ASSOCIATION. Second Manifesto. IndL, 1953 #2, 89. Passed July, 1952. Translated from Urdu.

ZAHEER, S. See (XXVIII).

## PHILIPPINES

### XXXV. Authors

ARGUILLA, Manuel E, Esteban Negruga, and Teodoro Agoncillo, eds, Literature Under the Commonwealth, Philippine Writers League, Manila, 1940. [LAW] Includes Federico Mangahas, "In the Beginning" on tasks of Philippine literature; Arturo B. Rotor,"Our Literary Heritage;" Jose Lardizabal, "Presumptuous Literary Heirs" on the writer's function as teacher; Salvador P. Lopez, "By Way Of Explanation" answering Lardizabal; Salvador P. Lopez, "Proletarian Literature: A Defini-

tion" perceptively discussed. Manifesto of Philippine Writers League.

## POLAND

### XXXVI. Authors

BUKOWIECKI, Leon, "Polish Cinema After World War II," Film Culture, #16 (1958), 7-10.

CIESLIK, Leon, "Polish Culture," NT, Oct 11, 1961, 16-19. The social causes of Polish peasant backwardness and the new measures for combatting it.

DEUTSCHER, Isaac, See (XXIII).

DOBRZYCKA, I, The Conditions Of Living Of the Working Class In the Social Novels of Charles Kingsley, Poznan: 1955.

'ESTETYKA' I (Polish Yearbook Of Aesthetics); review-summary by Max Rieser. JAAC, XX (1961), 95-97.

GALINSKI, Tadeusz, "For a Further Development Of Socialist Culture," PolR, 1963 #9, 28-35. Minister of Culture.

_____, ed, Culture Of People's Poland, State Economic Pub: Warsaw, 1966. illus. 22 related essays.

GOMULKA, Wladyslaw, "The Cultural Revolution, Revisionism and the Party," MT, Apr 1959, 119-122. abdgd. Speech to 3rd Congress of Polish United Workers Party.

_____, "State, Party, Culture," PP, June 1964, 3-10. abdgd. Address given at 600th Anniversary of Jagellonian University, Cracow, May 12, 1964. The balance of "a maximum of independent thinking," "a wide degree of internal autonomy" in intellectual work, and "an appreciation of the public interest." Educational advances.

_____, "The Party and Literature," PP, Nov 1964, 3-11. abdgd. Speech to 14th Congress of the Union of Polish Writers, Lublin. The writer's role in the "battle for a socialist metamorphosis of the nation's mentality, for a new morality and consciousness in Poland." Notes "the estrangement of many writers" and a "withdrawal to the sidelines" which must lead to a lowering

of "social status" for writers. Declares fiction must exercise a "responsible and pertinent" criticism of new
Poland's reality, which will act
"purifyingly and creatively, not
enervatingly and nihilistically." Says
fiction sharply critical of Stalinist
period will not be published unless it
deals also with positive accomplishments and background causes.

GRATKOWSKI, Wojciech, Polish Architecture. PP, Jan 1965, 20-24. illus.
International successes and the principles, based on "creative experiment,
boldness, and breadth of vision" combined with experience of "planning
whole new towns, housing schemes and
industrial centers in a specific social
and economic environment."

GRZYBOWSKI, Konstanty, Culture In Poland
From the 18th Century. PP, Jan 1967,
27-32; Feb, 27-32; Mch, 29-37; Apr,
44-53; et seq.

HERNAS, Czeslaw, "Is Folklore Dead?"
PP, June 1967, 30-35.

IWASZKIEWICZ, Jaroslaw, "Our Heritage,"
PP, 1967 #1, 3-11. Integrating a mil-
lenium of Polish culture with socialist
goals; by the chairman of the Writers'
Union.

JESIONOWSKI, Jerzy, "The Finances Of
Culture," PP, 1965 #11, 14-22.

KLISZKO, Zenon, "Polish Literature Draws
Its Strength From Its Links With the
Fate Of the Nation," PolR, 1964 #5,
3-8. Politburo member.

_____, "The Noblest Task of the Writer -
To Serve Progress," Polish Reports,
1965 #6, 16-21. Report to a writers
congress by member of politburo.

KLOSKOWSKA, Antonina, "Mass Culture In
Poland," PP, Dec 1964, 11-18. Analysis of its aspects and how it differs
from or approaches Western mass culture.

KOTT, Jan, "Gulliver's Travels: The
Philosophical Journey," Arena (London), II vi (Feb-Mch 1951), 28-35.
From Kott's 'School Of the Classics'
(Warsaw, 1949), a study of the background of Socialist Realism in bourgeois realism. "If we call [this] a
book of hate, we must not forget that
there are periods in which hatred is

the only attitude a humanist can
adopt."

_____, Shakespeare Our Contemporary,
Doubleday: 1964; Doubleday Anchor
paperback: 1966. Introduction by
Martin Esslin. The Polish experience
as a contemporary content for filling
out Shakespeare's scenarios. - Section,
"Hamlet," in: En, Aug 1964, 33-39,
with introduction by Peter Brook.

_____, "The Two Paradoxes Of 'Othello',"
PP, Jan 1965, 30-51. Not included in
above.

_____, "Moliere Our Contemporary," TDR,
Spring 1967, 163-170.

LICHANSKI, Stefan, Facing the Peasants'
Problems In Literature. PP, June 1962,
40-43. Deplores lack of interest in
the changing peasant life.

LUXEMBURG, Rosa, SEE: J.P. NETTL, Rosa
Luxemburg, Oxford: 1966, vol. I,
28-31, 201, 387.

MARCZAK-OBORSKI, Stanislaw, Polish Television Drama. PP, May 1964, 27-33.

MORAWSKI, Stefan, "Realism As an Artistic
Category," Actes du IV Congres International d'Esthetique, Athens, 1960,
571-578. Realism as a many-sided category; it does not prescribe laws of
form but states only that (essential)
reality is represented. Music, architecture, the applied arts, are not at
all defined by Realism as a norm.
Avant-garde work, like 'Guernica', can
use the new formal means to enormous
realistic advantage.

_____, "Vicissitudes In the Theory Of
Socialist Realism: A Little Lesson In
History Not To Be Ignored," Diogenes,
Winter 1961, 110-136. A seminal brief
history of Socialist Realism when
it was a thriving aesthetic, and as it
was thwarted by political directives
that assigned priority to the educative
function of art - which Morawski terms
fatal to a rational aesthetics.

_____, "Lenin As a Literary Theorist,"
S&S, XXIX (1965), 2-25. Historical
and logical analysis of Lenin's essays
on Tolstoy and Party Literature, with
reference to the general context of
Marxist aesthetics.

_____, "The Problem Of Value and Criteria

In Taine's Aesthetics," JAAC, XXI
(1963), 407-422.

_____, "Polish Theories Of Art Between
1830 and 1850," JAAC, XVI (1957),
217-236.

_____, "On the Objectivity Of Aesthetic
Judgment," British Journal Of Aesthetics, Oct 1966, 315-238.

_____, "Art and Obscenity," JAAC, Winter
1967, 193-207.

_____, "Mimesis - Lukacs' Universal
Principle," S&S, Winter 1968. Critique of 'Die Eigenart des Aesthetischen', presenting its guiding idea
and suggesting that not all aesthetic
phenomena are encompassed by it.

_____, Studia z Historii Mysli Estetykz-
nej XVII i XIX Wieku, Warsaw, 1961.
[Columbia] Summary in English, pp.
414-420. Survey of 18th and 19th
Century historicist aesthetics: Germany, England, Poland, Taine.

SCHAFF, Adam, "Problems Of Ethnolinguis-
tics," Diogenes, Summer 1964, 125-150.
Language as social product and definer
of social reality, in the light of
American Indian tongues and the views
of Sapir and Whorf.

_____, Introduction to Semantics, Lon-
don, 1962. Integrates a method of
analytical semantics with materialist
world-view. Pioneering Marxist study.
Section on American Indian language
and milieu.

_____, "Language and Reality," Diogenes,
Fall 1965, 147-167.

SINKO, Grzegorz, John Wolcot and His
School; A Chapter From the History Of
English Satire, Travaux de la Societe
des Sciences et des Lettres de Wroclow,
Seria A, Nr. 79. Wroclow, 1962. A
neglected English radical writer.

SOKORSKI, W, "Struggle For Socialist
Realism In Literature and Art In
People's Poland," FLP, May 15, 1953, 4.
Member of CC denouncing formalist
trends and citing Zhdanov.

_____, "Criteria Of Realism," PP, May
1964, 39-40. abdgd. Chief of radio
and television services writes on
Marxism as a method not a given style.

TARN, Adam, "Plays," PP, 1965 #10, 5-11.
Outline history of Polish drama, by
editor of 'Dialog'. Part of a special
issue on Polish theatre.

TOEPLITZ, Jerzy, "Film at the Crossroads,"
PP, 1965 #3, 12-23. Analysis of themes
and flourishing of post-war Polish
cinema.

VANDURSKI, V, "The Mass Amateur Theatre
Needs the Dramatist! The Dramatist
Needs the Mass Amateur Theatre!" ITh,
#3 (1933), 7-11. Early proletarian
playwright (since 1923) calls most
agitprop plays in all lands "unbeliev-
ably primitive." The "vacillating"
proletariat or petty bourgeoisie "for
the winning-over of whom such a bitter
struggle is now going on between communism and fascism," must not be "depicted
unchangeably in a ridiculous and grossly
caricatured form."

WAJDA, Andrzej, "Destroying the Common-
place," Films and Filming, Nov 1961, 9,
40. From 'Ekran'. Describes how
everyday reality can be represented
creatively by getting inside it.

WALLIS, Mieczyslaw, "The Origins and
Foundations Of Non-Objective Painting,"
JAAC, XIX (1960), 61-72. Systematic
analysis of its validity as an art form.

WIATR, Jerzy J, "Mass Or Democratic Culture," PP, Jan 1964, 3-12.

ZOLKIEWSKI, Stefan, "Is 'Socialist Literature' Enough?" in: Maria Kuncewicz,
ed, The Modern Polish Mind, 1962, 373-
381. Advocates a cumulative codifica-
tion of the poetics of Socialist Realism. - See also: Stefan Kisielewski,
"What Is Socialist Literature?" ibid,
366-372. A Liberal Catholic appraisal
of above essay.

_____, "Literature Since the War," PP,
July-Aug 1964, 76-87; Sept, 23-33;
Oct, 16-23; Nov, 24-31.

_____, "Mass Culture in a Socialist
Country," in: Stanislaw Ehrlich et al,
eds, Social and Political Transforma-
tions in Poland, Polish Scientific
Publishers, Warsaw, 1964.

_____, Address to 3rd Conference of Young
Writers. PP, 1965 #2, 49-51. abdgd.
With account of ensuing discussion.
Alienation of writers under socialism.

## XXXVII.  Appendix

BOGUCKI, Janusz, Contemporary Polish
Painting, Pononia: Warsaw, 1958.
illus.

CANADAY, John, "Polish Art: Modernism
Chiefly For Export," N.Y. Times,
Oct 8, 1963.  "Artists...are put under
absolutely no creative restrictions by
the state....But the big flow is
abstract art for the United States and
Canada....virtually no audience in
their own country."

FOLEJEWSKI, Zbigniew, "Socialist Realism
In Polish Literature and Criticism,"
Comparative Literature, XIII (1961),
72ff.

GOMORI, George, Polish and Hungarian
Poetry, 1945 To 1956, Oxford: 1966.
Emphasis on political and moral prob-
lems.

KRIDL, Manfred, A Survey Of Polish Literature and Culture, The Hague, 1956.
Origins to 1945.  Well written with
much attention to social history.

LANGNAS, I.A, "The Polish Film: Triumphs
and Troubles," EE, June 1964, 10-17.
illus.

MARSHALL, Herbert, Theatre In Poland.
In: John Andrews and Ossia Trilling,
International Theatre, London: 1949,
158-166.  Close account of policy and
results.

MATUZEWSKI, Ryszard, Portraits Of Contemporary Polish Writers, Polonia:
Warsaw, 1959.  illus.

POPKIN, Henry, "Theatre In Eastern
Europe," TDR, Spring 1967, 23-51.
illus.

RIESER, Max, "Contemporary Aesthetics
In Poland," JAAC, XX (1962), 421-428;
453-454.  Morawski, Ingarden, Ossowski,
Tatarkiewicz.

SKOLIMOWSKI, Henryk, "Analytical-Lin-
guistic Marxism in Poland," JHI, Apr-
June 1965, 235-258.  Chapter from his
forthcoming 'Polish Analytical Philosophy' (Humanities Press).  Discusses
Krajewski, A. Schaff and other Polish
Marxists who have engaged in detailed
debate with, and learned from, analytical linguistic philosophers.  The
Polish distinction between positivis-
tic and dialectic Marxism.

"The Affair Of the 34 Polish Intellectuals," EE, June 1964, 34-37.
Chronological account of events in a
protest. - Also EE, Dec 1964, 22-30.

## RUMANIA

### Topic Index

DOBROGEANU-GHEREA.  Palffy (XXVII).

EMINESCU.  Ignat.

LITERARY CRITICISM.  Bratu.

NOVEL.  Constantinescu.

POETRY, REVOLUTIONARY.  Banus, Beniuc,
Micu, Vitner.

SOCIALIST REALISM.  Novicov.

TOMA, A.  Vitner.

TRADITION IN RUMANIAN WRITING.  Philippide.

### XXXVIII.  Authors

1st CONGRESS OF WRITERS, Bucharest, June
18-23, 1956.  Speeches, Reports, Resolutions.  RR, 1956 #3, 63-200.  abdgd.

ALL-RUMANIA WRITERS CONFERENCE, Jan 22-
24, 1962.  Report.  RR, 1962 #2, 105-
131.

BALAN, George, "Renewing Trends In the
Musical Creation Of Young Composers,"
RR, 1963 #2, 100-103.

BANUS, Maria, "The Writer and Reality,"
NT, Oct 31, 1961, 27-28.  Noted poet
on responsibilities of Rumanian writers.

BRATU, Savin, "The Evolution of Rumanian
Literary Criticism, RR, 1958 #4, 108-122.

CONSTANTINESCU, Pompilu, "Rumanian Modern
Fiction," RR, Aug-Sept 1946, 83-94.

DUTU, Alexandru, Shakespeare in Rumania,
Bucharest, 1964.  Bibliographical essay.

GOLDMANN, Lucien.  See (XIX).

HORODINCA, Georgeta, "Character Is Still
Topical In Art," RR, 1964 #1, 63-72.
Function and malfunction of character
in current Soviet dramas, Brecht and
the French avant-garde novel.

IANOSI, Ion, "The Sublime and the Monumental in Contemporary Literature,"
RR, 1964 #1, 48-62.  Major aesthetic
problems considered from Leninist
point of view.

IBRAILEANU, G, "Creation and Analysis,"
RR, 1957 #2, 68-90. - See also: Mihai
Ralea on Ibraileanu's career, ibid,
53-67.

IGNAT, Nestor, "Eminescu, the Great Poet
Of the Rumanian People," RR, 1950 #6,
42-68.

IVASCU, George, "Tradition and Innovation
In Contemporary Drama," World Theatre,
XIII (1964), 168-188.  illus.

LOVINESCU, Horia, "Responsibility In the
Theatre," World Theatre, XIII (1964),
164-167.  Optimism and responsibility
returned to the stage.

MICU, Dumitru, "Discussing Poetry," RR,
1960 #2, 119-129.  Report of a lively
dispute over critical principles.

NOVICOV, Mihai, "Literature Of the Rumanian People's Republic Heading
Towards Socialist Realism," RR, 1950
#7, 11-28.

PHILIPPIDE, Al, "Spirit and Tradition Of
Rumanian Literature," RR, May 1946,
65-80.

VITNER, Ion, "A. Toma, A Poet Of the
Revolutionary Proletariat," RR, 1949
#1, 23-30.

_____, "A. Toma, The Fighter-Poet," RR,
1950 #6, 90-105.

SEE ALSO: Survey, Apr 1965, 21-51.
          Articles by Francois Bondy and
          Edgar Reichman on the changing
          literary scene, written with
          first-hand knowledge.


SOUTHEAST ASIA

XXXIX. Authors

LATT, Minn, "Royalist Encomium and the
Song Of Man," NO, Dec 1960, 5-8.
Early phases of Burmese literature.

_____, "Growing In the Smog - Moving
Under Gaslights," NO, Dec 1961, 172-
175.  Khitsan revival.  20th Century

Burmese writing.

_____, "A Dawn That Went Astray," NO,
Dec 1962, 172-176.  illus.  Burmese
literature since the war; progress
and reaction.

PERERA, R, "Sinhala Culture and Budd-
hism," NO, Oct 1962, 129-134.  illus.

SUYIN, Han, "An Outline Of Malayan-
Chinese Literature," EH, June 1964,
6-16.


SPAIN

(SEE ALSO: Arnold Hauser (XXVII), on
all topics to 1920s.)

Topic Index

CALDERON.  Gassner (LVIII).

CERVANTES.  Cassou (XIX); Fischer,
Kautsky (XXI); Fox (XXIII); Lukacs
(XXVII); Novitsky, Plavskin (XLVI);
Horowitz, Lawson (LVI);
Auerbach, Lowenthal (LXII).

EL GRECO.  Fischer (XXI); Hauser (XXVII);
Lawson (LVI).

GOYA.  Fischer (XXI); Berger, Klingender
(XXIII); Orozco (LXIII).

GRIS, J.  Berger (XXIII).

LORCA.  See (LXIII).

MIRO.  'Cahiers' (LXIII).

PICASSO.  See below.

THEATRE, WORKERS.  Fevralsky (XLVIII).

VEGA, L.  Lawson, Wolfe (LVI); Gassner
(LVIII).

VELASQUEZ.  Berger (XXIII).

XL.  Authors

ALBERTI, Raphael, and Maria Teresa Leon,
Interview with Edwin Rolfe.  DW, Mch
18, 1935, 5.  illus.  Autobiographical.

_____, Speech to 1st Soviet Writers Con-
gress.  DW, Mch 26, 1935, 5.  illus.
Growth of Spanish revolutionary literature.

_____, Interview with Sender Garlin. DWSup, Apr 4, 1937, 4. Writers in Republican Spain.

BUNUEL, Louis, Interview with Kenji Kanesaka. Film Culture #24 (1962), 75-76. Chiefly on French and Japanese films. - See also: Fuentes (XXXIII).

LEON, Maria Teresa, Theatre In the Spanish Civil War. DWSup, Jan 30, 1938, 13. - See also: Alberti (above). - E. Seran, "Maria Teresa Leon," DW(L), Mch 12, 1937, 4.

PICASSO, Pablo, Statement Of His Adherence To the Spanish Loyalist Cause. The American Artist, Summer 1937, 3. Reprinted in DW, July 6, 1937, 7; in AF, Oct 1937, 11; by Elizabeth McCausland, Picasso: 1944, 21; by A.H. Barr, Picasso: Fifty Years Of His Art, 1946, 202, 264. Written in May or June 1937 especially for transmittal to the American Artists Congress. Picasso reports safety of the Prado's treasures, denies rumors he had given Franco his support. "My whole life as an artist has been nothing more than a continuous struggle against reaction and the death of art."

_____, Statement To 2nd American Artists Congress. N.Y. Times, Dec 19, 1937; and DW, Dec 20, 1937, 7. Reprinted in Barr, Picasso: Fifty Years Of His Art, 1946, 264. Reiterates the above stand.

_____, "Why I Became a Communist," NM, Oct 24, 1944, 11. "My joining the Communist Party is a logical step in my life....our party strives more than any other to know and to build the world, to make men clearer thinkers, more free and more happy. I have become a Communist because the Communists are the bravest in France, in the Soviet Union, as they are in my own country, Spain. I have never felt more free, more complete than since I joined." - Slightly abridged from original interview obtained by Pol Gaillard at the request of NM. Original French text in 'L'Humanite', Oct 29-30, 1944, 1-2, reprinted (in French) in Barr, Picasso: Fifty Years Of His Art, 1946, 267-268.

_____, Written Statement For Simone Tery. A.H. Barr, Picasso: Fifty Years Of His Art, 1946, 247-248. Reprinted in 1951 by "Les Lettres Francaises' as Picasso's 70th birthday statement, it was translated as such in The New Yorker, Nov 10, 1951, 128. Issued by Picasso in course of an interview, angered over widespread rumors that he had said there was no connection between art and politics. "Painting is not done to decorate apartments. It is an instrument for attack and defense against the enemy."

_____, Interview with Joseph A. Barry. N.Y. Times Magazine, May 6, 1951, 19, 33, 35, 38. Defends his Communism.

_____, Message On Opening Of Picasso Exhibition In Moscow. C&L, 1957 #1, 21. Dated Oct 17, 1956, Cannes. Original message in French reproduced in color. Friendship for the USSR and its painters. Pleasure at the exhibition and inclusion of recent works. Regret he cannot be present. Reiterates that "all my work" has led him to Communism "as a man goes to a spring." - See also Jean-Pierre Saltan, "A Visit To Picasso," C&L, 1957 #1, 26-28. illus. Picasso's reaction to the exhibition.

_____, Interview with Carlton Lake. Atlantic Monthly, July 1957, 35-41. His political adherence, Stalin, Hungary, 'Guernica', the way to look at his paintings.

_____, SEE ALSO: Louis Parrot, "Picasso At Work," M&M, Mch 1948, 6-20. A friend of the artist describes Picasso's humanity and reasons for joining Party.

John Groth, "An American Artist In Paris," ACA, Dec 1944, 9-11. Recounts day spent with Picasso just after Liberation. Picasso's message when asked for one: "Tell the artists of America to work hard - like me."

Francoise Gilot and Carlton Lake, Life With Picasso, McGraw-Hill: 1964. Picasso's companion during his first years as a Communist explains how he came to the Party: Laurent Casanova was hiding with Kahnweiler's sister-in-law at war's end and "for the first time Pablo had the occasion to talk with a Communist Party figure who was at the same time sufficiently intelligent and open-minded." Picasso

is quoted on Russian naivete
in thinking "an artist can
fit into society" pp. 197-
198. "Anything new, anything
worth doing, can't be recognized. People just don't
have that much vision....the
right to free expression is
something one seizes, not
something one is given. It
isn't a principle one can lay
down as something that should
exist." How Aragon 'discovered'
the peace dove, p. 273. The
affair of the Stalin portrait,
pp. 277-279.

Herbert Read, "Picasso and the
Marxists," The London Mercury,
Nov 1934, 95-96. The Picas-
sos and not the mediocre
painters with 'correct' ideology are "the only artists who
are breaking down the conventions of petty-bourgeois art,
and thus preparing the way
for the art of the socialist
state."

Helene Parmelin, Picasso Plain,
St. Martin's: 1963. Especially "Doves and Men," 176-213.
Account by an intimate Communist friend.

Rockwell Kent, "The Ivory Tower," NM, Apr 3, 1945, 17.
Vitriolic attack on Picasso's
conversion, occasioned by
Seckler's article. "My little granddaughter of six
could do as well."

Derek Kartun, "Picasso," DWSup,
May 12, 1946, 3. illus.
"His work has been negative
and critical....there is bare-
ly a line which comments with
joy or hope on the future."
His works "suffer fatally
from the 40 years of experi-
mentation with form."

Vladimir Kemenov, "Aspects Of
Two Cultures," V.O.K.S, 1947
#52, 20-36. Polemic against
modernist art. Moore, Lip-
schitz, numerous others attacked. Picasso's art termed
"morbid," revolting,"wretched,
pathological and deformed."
Soviet art praised as a people's art. - See also 1947

(XLI), for 'Pravda' denunciation.

Paul Eluard, Pablo Picasso, 1947.
"Picasso desires the truth.
Not that fictitious truth
which would leave Galatea forever lifeless and inert, but
a total truth that joins
imagination to nature, that
deems everything real and
that, going endlessly from the
particular to the universal
and from the universal to the
particular, accommodates itself to all the varieties of
existence and of change, provided that they are new, that
they are fertile." Picasso's
close and Communist poet friend.

Sergei Yutkevich, "Pablo Picasso,
Artist and Man," C&L, 1957 #1,
23-25. illus. Soviet film
director recounts visit to
the artist at Vallauris. Interprets Picasso's development.

Ilya Ehrenburg, "Picasso," NWR,
Dec 1961, 16-19.

"Propaganda and Picasso," N.Y.
Times Magazine, May 17, 1953,
14. illus.

Also: Garaudy (XIX); Raphael
(XXI); Arundel, Berger (XXIII);
Siqueiros (XXXIII); Golonshtok
(XLIII); Summers (LIII).

SEMPRUN, Jorge, "Socialism and Literature,"
NLR, #30 (1965), 76-79. Refugee novelist, winner of Prix Formentor. Warns
in light of Stalin era that "first of
all, one must examine the relationship
of literature to socialist power," and
not regard art as "a means" to political
ends.

## SWEDEN

### Topic   Index

BERGMAN, I. Humboldt (LIV).

STRINDBERG. Fischer (XXI); Lukacs
(XXVII); Gassner (LVIII). See (LXIII).

UNION OF SOVIET SOCIALIST REPUBLICS

(See also: Arnold Hauser (XXVII), on all topics to 1920s.)

## Topic Index: Architecture

EARLY EXPERIMENTS. Brunov, Ilyin (XLII); Trotsky (XLVI); Fullop-Miller, Lozowick, Lubetkin (XLIX).

NATIONAL FEATURES. Yarabov (XLII).

NEO-CLASSICAL. Weiss (XV); Bourov, Danin, Miliukov, Sorokin, Vesnin, V.O.K.S. (XLII); Campbell (XXIII); 'Architectural Review', Voyce, Wright (XLIX).

POST-STALIN. Sartre (XIX); 1965 (XLI); Borisovsky, Danin, Kucherenko, Nekrasov, Strumlin, Vlasov (XLII); "The New Architecture" (XLIX).

## Topic Index: Art and Sculpture

CHAGALL. Epstein, Gray, Meyer (XLIX).

CONSERVATION OF EARLIER ART. 1917-19 (XLI); Levinson (XLIII); Lunacharsky (XLVI).

CONSTRUCTIVISM. Nekrasov (XLII); Gan, Sternberg, Tatlin (XLIII); Gray (XLIX).

ECONOMICS. Berger (XXIII); Beskin, Miliukov, V.O.K.S. (XLIII); Chen (XLIX).

FUTURISM. Novitsky (XLIII); Lenin, Trotsky (XLVI); Lehmann-Haupt (XXII); Epstein, Fulop-Miller, Gray, Lozowick, Sayler, Winter (XLIX); Dondero (LIX).

GABO. Berger (XXIII).

HISTORY. 1917-19 (XLI); Bunt, Loukomski (XLIII); Lunacharsky (XLVI); Hare, Holme (XLIX).

KANDINSKY. Grohmann (XLIX).

LAQUER (PALEKH) AND OTHER FOLK ART. Bukushinsky, Ilyin, Ovsyannikov (XLIII).

LISSITZKY. Epstein, Winter (XLIX).

MONUMENTAL SCULPTURE. 1917-19 (XLI); Konyonkov, Neizvestny, V.O.K.S. (XLIII); Lenin, Trotsky (XLVI); Fulop-Miller, Gray (XLIX).

NEIZVESTNY, E. Berger (XXIII).

REALIST PAINTING. Bukharin, Ioganson, Kalinen, Kemenov, Loukomski, Milinkov, Nazarov, Nikritin, Novitsky, V.O.K.S (XLIII); Rivera, Siqueiros (XXXIII); Lunacharsky, Krushchev (XLVI); Bowman, Canaday, London (XLIX).

TATLIN. Trotsky (XLVI).

## Topic Index: Cinema

CHINESE CRITICISM. 1963 (X).

ECONOMICS. Eisenstein, Feldman, Moisenko, Monosson, Shumatsky (XLIV); Lenin (XLVI).

HISTORY. Tretyakov (XLIV); Babitsky, Bryher, Dickinson, Freeman, London, Marshall, Macdonald, Vas, Yagolim (XLIX); Leyda (LIV).

INTERNATIONAL ORGANIZATIONS. Piscator (XXI); Balazs (XXVII).

PUDOVKIN. Potamkin (LIV).

THEORY. Piscator (XXI); Eisenstein, Koragonov, Kulidzhanov, Moisenka, 'Soviet Cinema', Tretyakov, Twrovskaya, Vaisfeld (XLIV); Erikson (LXII).

## Topic Index: Dance

CLASSICAL. 1967 (X); Moisseyev, Roslavleva, Sidorov, Slonimsky (XLV); London (XLIX).

FOLK. Moisseyev (XLV).

MODERN. Duncan, Koner (LV).

## Topic Index: Literature and General

ANDREYEV. Gorky (XLVI).

BEDNY. Bukharin, Divilkovsky, Trotsky (XLVI).

BELINSKY. 1967(X); Lukacs (XXVII); Asmus, Dneprov, Lenin, Lifshitz, Plekhanov (XLVI); Mathewson, Wellek (LXIX); Belinsky (LXII).

BIELY. Trotsky (XLVI).

BLOK. Gorky, Lunacharsky, Orlov, Trotsky (XLVI); Bowra (LXII). See (XLIX).

OSTROVSKY.  Plekhanov (XLVI).

PANFEROV.  Lukacs (XXVII).

PASTERNAK.  1959 (XLI); Deutscher
   (XXIII); Conquest (XLIX); Humboldt
   (LVI).

PAVLOVIAN THEORY.  See General Topics,
   Conditioned Reflexes.

PETROV.  Lunacharsky (XLVI).

PILNYAK.  Trotsky (XLVI).

PISAREV.  Plekhanov (XLVI).

PLEKHANOV.  See (XLVI).

POETRY.  Bukharin, Trotsky (XLVI);
   Blok, Kaun, Lindsay, Patrick, Poggioli (XLIX); Bowra (LXII).

PROLETCULT.  1917-19 (XLI); Bogdanov,
   Lenin, Lunacharsky, Trotsky (XLVI);
   Carter, Kunitz, Paul, Rostovtsev,
   Sayler (XLIX); Dunbar (LIX).

PUBLISHING.  Friedberg (XLIX).

PUSHKIN.  1967 (X); Fischer (XXI);
   Lukacs (XXVII); Gorky, Lunacharsky,
   Plekhanov, Vinagradov, V.O.K.S,
   Zeitlin (XLVI); Simmons (XLIX).

RAPP.  Averbach (XLVI); Borland, Brown,
   Erlich,Ermolaev,McLean,Struve (XLIX).

SERAPIONS.  Trotsky (XLVI); Eastman,
   Edgerton (XLIX).

SHAGINYAN.  Trotsky (XLVI).

SHKLOVSKY.  Bukharin, Trotsky (XLVI);
   Kridl (XLIX).

SHOLOKHOV.  See (XLVI).

SIMONOV.  See (XLVI).  Lazarev (XLIV).

SOCIALIST REALISM,SOCIAL DETERMINANTS.
   Gei, Lunacharsky, Sinyavsky (XLVI);
   Marcuse (LVI).

SOLZHENITSYN.  Lukacs (XXVII).

STALINISM AND CULTURE.  Reich (XXI);
   Lukacs (XXVII); Ehrenburg, Kron,
   Metchenko, Paustovsky, Trotsky (XLVI);
   Eastman, Jelagin, McLean, Paloczi-
   Horvath, Soviet, Wolfe (XLIX).

TOLSTOY, A.  Jelagin(XLIX);Bersin (LVI).

TOLSTOY, L.  Fischer, Piscator (XXI);
   Lukacs (XXVII); Dneprov, Gorky, Lenin,
   Lunacharsky, Plekhanov, Trotsky,
   Volkov (XLVI); Simmons (XLIX); Humboldt,
   Lawson (LVI); Orwell (LXII).

TRETYAKOV, S.  See (XLIV), (XLVI).

TURGENEV.  Lukacs (XXVII); Plekhanov
   (XLVI); Howe (LXII).

USPENSKY.  Lenin, Plekhanov (XLVI).

VERSILOV.  Trotsky (XLVI).

VORONSKY.  Averbach, Dementyev (XLVI);
   Brown, Eastman, Fizer, McLean, Soviet
   (XLIX).

VOROVSKY, V.  Chernoutsan (XLVI).

YEVTUSHENKO.  Makarov (XLVI).

ZEMYATIN.  Trotsky (XLVI); Eastman,
   Soviet (XLIX).

## Topic Index: Music

HISTORY.  Polyanka (XLVII); Asaf'ev,
   Freeman, Jelagin, London, Moisenko,
   Olkhovsky, Slonimsky, Unger, Werth
   (XLIX).

INTERNATIONAL MUSIC BUREAU.  Eisler (XXI).

KHACHATURIAN.  See (XLVII).

MASSES AND MUSIC.  Bush (XLIX); 1929,
   1933, 1946-48 (XLI); Khachaturian,
   Milinkov, Prokofieff, Shostakovich
   (XLVII); Szigeti (LXIII).

MOUSSORGSKY.  Cazden, Finkelstein (LVII).

MUSIC CRITICISM.  Bakst, Moisenko, Werth
   (XLIX); Cazden (LVII).

OPERA.  Danilevich, Kabelevsky, Prokofieff, Shostakovich (XLVII).

PROKOFIEV, S.  (See (XLVII).  Blitzstein
   (LVII).

PROLETARIAN, HISTORY.  Gachev (XLVII).

SCRIABIN.  Lunacharsky (XLVI).

SHOSTAKOVICH, D.  See (XLVII).

STRAVINSKY.  Eisler, Fischer (XXI);
   Schwartz (XLIX); Blitzstein, Cazden
   (LVII); Finkelstein (LVII), (LVI);
   Adorno (LXII).

TCHAIKOVSKY. 'Russian Symphony' (XLVII).

## Topic Index: Theatre

ACCOUNTS, CONTEMPORARY. Gorky, Kommis-
sarzhevsky, Lunacharsky, Trotsky
(XLVI); Block, Brown, Carter, Craig,
Fullop-Miller, Houghton, Jelagin,
London, Sayler (XLIX).

ACTING. Cherkassov, Krupskaya, Meyerhold, Rapaport, Sudakov (XLVIII);
Gyseghem (XLIX).

HISTORY. 1917-19 (XLI); Anikst, Der-
zhavin, Markov, Moskvin, Obraztsova
(XLVIII); Bowers, Bradshaw, Carter,
Dana, Gregor, Gyseghem, Lozowick,
Yershov (XLIX); Gassner (LVIII).

JEWISH THEATRE. Lubomirsky (XLVIII).
See History, above.

MEYERHOLD, V. See (XLVIII).

ORGANIZATIONS, INTERNATIONAL. 1930,
1933 (XLI); Piscator (XXI).

POGODIN, Lukacs (XXVII).

STANISLAVSKY. Brecht (XXI); Gorky,
Lunacharsky, Markov, Meyerhold,
Trotsky, Zakhava (XLVIII); Carter
(XLIX).

## XLI. Chronological

EARLY BOLSHEVIK DECREES, 1917-19. See:
Education and Art In Soviet Russia In
the Light Of Official Decrees and
Documents, with foreword and commentary by Max Eastman, 1919. 64 pp.
(A selection of these materials is in
Lib, June 1919, 11-18.) 34 decrees
and other items from official Bolshevik sources, explain policy on:
school reform; establishment of Proletcult; abolition of Moscow Art
Society and the Academy of Art;
establishment of the Art Collegium;
the "socialization of art" to provide
for workers' benefit and participation in literature, sculpture, theatre
and art; preservation of art objects;
theatre repertory, instruction, performances in factories; the commission
of memorial plaques and monuments.

1st ALL-RUSSIAN CONFERENCE OF PROLETAR-
IAN WRITERS, Moscow, Jan 6-12, 1925.
Report by G. Lelevitch, DWSup, Mch 21,
1925. "The supporters of proletarian
literature told the Trotskyites that

the working class stands in need now
of this powerful weapon for the purpose
of reacting on the psychology of the
masses."

RESOLUTION ON LITERATURE, July 1, 1925;
adopted by the Political Bureau of the
Communist Party of the Soviet Union.
In: Joseph Freeman et al, eds, Voices
Of October, 1930, 59-65. Another translation in Edward J. Brown, The Proletarian Episode In Russian Literature,
1953, 235-240. "The Party should de-
clare itself in favor of the free competition of various groups and tendencies in the field of literature."

RESOLUTION OF THE CENTRAL COMMITTEE,
C.P.S.U, Dec 28, 1928. In: Edward J.
Brown (see above), 241-242. Dissolves
existing literary organizations and
establishes RAPP.

RUSSIAN ASSOCIATION OF PROLETARIAN
MUSICIANS, Platform Statement, 1929.
In: Nicolas Slonimsky, Music Since
1900, 1949, 655-661. The past and
continuing class struggle in music.

1st THEATRE AND ART OLYMPIAD OF THE USSR.
In V.O.K.S, 1930 #11-12. Numerous
articles and photos.

2nd INTERNATIONAL CONFERENCE OF REVOLU-
TIONARY WRITERS, Kharkov, Nov 6-15,
1930. In: LWR, Special Number, 1931.
246 pp. - For influence of this Con-
ference on US John Reed Clubs, see:
Editorial, Red Pen [later Left Review]
(Philadelphia), I i (Jan 1934), 1, 13.
[Yale] - Report in NM, Feb 1931, 7;
Mch 1931, 4-5.

1st FIVE YEAR PLAN CULTURAL IMPLEMENTA-
TION. See: D. Shilov, "Socialist State
To the Help Of the Art Of the Masses,"
IWT #1 (Jan 1931), 9-11. Massive im-
plementation under control of the Com-
missariat of Education.

STAKHANOVITES IN WRITING. See: "Shock
Workers In Literature," V.O.K.S, 1931
#4, 26-29. Report on turning workers
into writers, with examples of their
work.

RESOLUTION ON RECONSTRUCTION OF LITERARY
AND ARTISTIC ORGANIZATIONS, adopted by
the Central Committee of the C.P.S.U,
Apr 23, 1932. In: IL, 1932 #1, 2.
Dissolves organizations of writers and
artists (RAPP in particular) to increase
efficiency in "tasks of socialist con-

struction."

CONFERENCE OF THE ORGANIZATIONAL COM-
MITTEE OF THE ALL-RUSSIAN UNION OF
SOVIET WRITERS, Moscow, October 29-
November 3, 1932. IL, 1933 #1, 141-
150. Report and speech summaries.
The end of RAPP and the formulation
of Socialist Realism and Revolutionary
Romanticism. Discussion by V. Kir-
potin, M. Chumandrin, V. Ivanov, N.
Tikhnov, L. Nikulin, et al. - See
also Lunacharsky.

INTERNATIONAL WORKERS THEATRE OLYMPIAD,
Moscow, May 1933. Reports by John
Bonn, WT, July-Aug 1933, 3; NTh,
Sept-Oct, 1933, 18; NTh, Apr 1934,
15-16. Report by Maria Baker on the
Film Section, NTh, Sept-Oct 1933, 24.
Report by N. Buchwald, IL, 1933 #4,
137-142.

1st INTERNATIONAL MUSICAL CONFERENCE,
Moscow, June 1933. Report on debate
among representatives from nine nations on "how best to use music as a
weapon in the class struggle," ITh, #3
(1933), 47-49. illus. - Speech to the
Conference by L. Lebedinsky, "The
Crisis In Modern Bourgeois Music," ITh,
#3-4, 13-16. abdgd.

1st SOVIET WRITERS CONGRESS, Moscow, Aug
1934. Speeches of A. Zhdanov, M.
Gorky, N. Bukharin, K. Radek and A.
Stetsky , with resolutions passed, in:
H.G. Scott, ed, Problems Of Soviet
Literature, 1935. - Speech by Isaac
Babel, in Isaac Babel: The Lonely Years
1925-1939, Noonday paperback: 1964,
396-400. - Extracts from speeches of
L. Leonov, L. Sobolev, V. Vishnevsky,
I. Babel, Y. Charents, in SL, 1964 #8,
159-165. - Speech by Johannes R.
Becher, "The Great Alliance," PR, Nov-
Dec 1934, 16-20. - Speech by Ilya
Ehrenburg, DW, Sept 27, 1934, 5.
- Long excerpts from Ehrenburg and
Leonov speeches, LR, Nov 1934, 21-26,
together with report by Annabel
Williams-Ellis. - Speech by A. Mal-
raux, YFS , #18 (1957), 27-28. - M.J.
Olgin, "A Pageant Of Soviet Litera-
ture: The All-Union Writers Congress
In Moscow," NM, Oct 16, 1934, 16-20;
Oct 23, 16-19, an eye-witness account.
- Report of opening session, DW, Aug
22, 1934, 5; and report of the results
by Vern Smith, with interviews with
Leonov and Babel, DW, Sept 24, 1934, 5.
- See also special issues of MN, Aug
25, Sept 1 and 7, 1934; and for photo

coverage, Soviet Travel, 1934 #5, 31-
35.

FARM CULTURAL EFFORT. See: Ben Field,
"Soviet Peasants Are Swiftly Becoming
Most Cultured Farm Masses In History,"
DW, Dec 28, 1934, 5.

WORKERS MUSIC OLYMPIADE, 1935, Strasbourg.
Account in The Musical Times (London),
July 1935, 653.

1st INTERNATIONAL CONGRESS OF WRITERS FOR
THE DEFENSE OF CULTURE, Paris, June
1935. - Report by Christina Stead, with
speeches of Andre Gide and J.R. Bloch,
LR, Aug 1935, 447-475. - Report by E.M.
Forster, NS, July 6, 1935, 9. - Report
by Michael Gold, NM, July 30, 1935, 9-
11; Aug 6, 13-15; Aug 13, 18-21; also
PW, Nov 9, 1936, 308. - Speech by Waldo
Frank, PR, Feb 1936, 14-17. - Report by
Malcolm Cowley, NRep, July 31, 1935,
339. - Report by Oakley Johnson, IL,
1935 #8, 72-74; also DW, July 22, 1935,
5. illus. - Speech by Ilya Ehrenburg,
DW, July 10, 1935, 5. - Speech by A.
Malraux, YFS, #18 (1957), 28-31. -
Message from M. Gorky, DW, July 18,
1935, 5. - See also: Haywood (XLIX).

CONFERENCE OF THE INTERNATIONAL ASSOCIA-
TION OF WRITERS FOR THE DEFENSE OF
CULTURE, London, June 19-23, 1936.
Report by Derek Kahn, LR, July 1936,
481-490. - Report and speeches of A.
Malraux, R. Rolland, B. Brecht, LR,
July 1936. - Report in DW(L), June 25,
1936, 3.

DEBATE ON FORMALISM, 1936. See: Special
Section in IL, 1936 #6, 77-109. The
'Pravda' attack, authored by Zhdanov,
on Shostakovich's 'Lady Macbeth of
Mtzensk'. The architectural "cacaphony"
of Corbusier. V. Kirpotin on "Simplicity, Art and the People." Isaac Babel
renounces his long silence and promises
to produce. Y. Olesha "About Formalism." I. Katayev on "The Art Of The
Socialist People." M. Koltsov spoofs
the rapidity with which Soviet writers
come forward to denounce their formalist streaks. - For the academic side of
the controversy, see: Angel Flores, ed,
Literature and Marxism; A Controversy
By Soviet Critics, 1938. Essays by M.
Lifshitz, V. Kemenov, I. Nusinov, F.
Levin, I. Satz, M. Rosenthal. Reviewed
by Charles Humboldt, NM, Jan 10, 1939,
22-23. - See also: Rosenthal (XLVI).

1st ALL-UNION CONGRESS OF SOVIET ARCHI-

TECTS, Moscow, June 1937. - Report by Simon Breines, Research Bulletin On the Soviet Union, May 30, 1938, 37-38.

2nd CONGRESS OF THE INTERNATIONAL ASSO-
CIATION OF WRITERS, Madrid, July 1937. Report by Malcolm Cowley, NM, Aug 10, 1937, 16; and in Bulletin, Aug 1937, 1. - Report by Edgell Rickword, LR, Aug 1937, 381-383; Sept, 445-454, in- cludes manifesto and speeches of J. Benda, R. Bates, J. Last, N. Guillen, J. Bergamin, abdgd. - Speech by Michael Koltsov, MN, July 21, 1937, 14-15. - Notes by S. Spender in John Lehmann, ed, New Writing, IV, Autumn 1937, 245-251. - Report in DW(L), July 21, 1937, 7. Madrid was under attack and few writers could get there, so most sessions were held later in Paris.

CENTRAL COMMITTEE DECREES, 1946-48.
See: On Literature and Art, Moscow, 1951. Also: George S. Counts and Nucia Lodge, The Country Of the Blind, Boston, 1949, 79-83 ("Resolu- tion On the Journals 'Zvezda' and 'Leningrad'"); 119-124 ("On the Reper- toire Of the Dramatic Theatres and Measures For Its Improvement"); 125- 129 ("On the Moving Picture 'Bolshaia Zhizn'" with self-criticism by Eisenstein and other film-makers, 146-150); 98-117, for the meeting of the Presidium of the Union of Soviet Writers early in Sept, 1946, and the self-criticisms of writers. - The theatre decree is also in SS, Oct 1952, 205-209. - The decision on Muradelli's opera 'The Great Friendship', V.O.K.S, 1948 #54, 5-8. - For the Conference of Musicians at the Central Committee, see: Alexander Werth, Musical Uproar In Moscow, London, 1949, 47-86. Abdgd. verbatim text of speeches by Zhdanov, Muradelli, Zakharov, Khrenni- kov, Khadrat, Shostakovich, Golden- weiser, V. Belyi, Knipper, Shebalin, Nestiev, Kabalevsky, etc. - See also: Zhdanov (XLVI); Sartre (XIX); Haywood, London (XLIX).- For reaction of British left, see AIA Newsletter [BM], start- ing Apr 1948. Jack Chen, F. Klingender, M. Kestleman, etc. Focus of a split of opinion over freedom in socialist lands.

'PRAVDA' EDITORIAL ASSAILING MODERN ART, Aug 10, 1947. In: N.Y. Herald Tribune, Aug 12, 1947, 15 (some editions only). The "bourgeois decaying art" of Picasso and Matisse.

2nd INTERNATIONAL CONGRESS OF COMPOSERS AND MUSICOLOGISTS, Prague, May 1958. Declaration in: Nicolas Slonimsky, Music Since 1900, 1949, 711-712. - See also: Henry Barraud, "La Musique En- gagee," Musical America, Feb 1951, 13, 218-219.

CULTURAL AND SCIENTIFIC CONFERENCE FOR WORLD PEACE, New York, Mch 25-27, 1949. See: Daniel S. Gillmor, ed, Speaking Of Peace, 1949. Includes F.O. Matthies- sen, L. Hellman, A.A. Fadeyev, D. Shostakovich, P. Eluard, S. O'Casey, L. Kruizkowsky, N. Mailer, H. Fast, P. Evergood, A. Copland, C. Odets, et al.

LINGUISTICS AND MARXISM. See: The Soviet Linguistic Controversy, King's Crown: 1951. CDSP's collection of 31 articles from 'Pravda' including those by Stalin. See also: "The Crisis In Soviet Lin- guistics," SS, Jan 1951, 209-264. - For evidence of importance previously attributed to the theories of Marr that came under attack, see: I. Mesh- chaninov, "New Theory Of Language and Thought," V.O.K.S, 1933 #4, 116-126; and "Nikolai Marr," V.O.K.S, 1945 #1-2, 52-56. illus. - See also Stalin (XLVI).

2nd WORLD PEACE CONGRESS, Warsaw, Nov 16- 22, 1950. V.O.K.S, #66 Supplement (1951). Includes speeches of A.A. Fadaev, J.R. Becher, I. Ehrenburg, J. Marinello, J. Amado, P. Neruda, D. Shostakovich.

2nd CONGRESS OF THE UNION OF SOVIET WRITERS, Moscow, Dec 15-26, 1954. Report with summaries in SS, Apr 1955, 404-442. Speech by I. Ehrenburg, urging uninhibited discussion of prob- lems of literature, CDSP, Mch 23, 1955, 27-29. abdgd. Speech by K. Fedin, CDSP, Apr 20, 1955, 13-16. Speech by M. Sholokhov, condemning low literary standards of some writers (Simonov and Ehrenburg in particular), and charging them to the writer rather than the Party, CDSP, Apr 6, 1955, 18-20; rebut- tals in succeeding issues of CDSP. - Report by Jack Lindsay, V.O.K.S, Jan- Feb 1955, 41-48. illus. - Appraisal by Bertha Malnick, SS, July 1955, 1-13.

DEBATE ON PARTY CONTROLS. See: B.A. Nazarov and O.V. Gridneva, "On the Problem Of the Lag In Drama and Theatre," CDSP, Dec 19, 1956, 3-8. From 'Voprosy filosofii', 1956 #5; sent to press Oct 2. Outspoken argument against the im- position by the Party of "guiding ideas."

History of their gradual imposition.
- Attacked by 'Pravda' and 'Izvestia'
ibid, 8-11, 30.

CONGRESSES OF PAINTERS AND SCULPTORS AND
OF COMPOSERS, Moscow, Mch 1957.  Report in SS, July 1957, 108-111.  Report by Ralph Parker on the former,
NWR, Apr 1957, 4-8.  Speeches to the
two Congresses by D.T. Shepilov, then
Secretary of the CC, CDSP, Apr 10,
1957, 19-23, 48; and CDSP, May 8,
1957, 15-21, 40.

'KOMMUNIST' EDITORIAL, "For Leninist Adherence To Principle In Questions Of
Literature and the Arts," CDSP, Sept
25, 1957, 3-6.  abdgd.  Denounces
"anti-Party group" member Shepilov for
encouraging "anarchist" non-Party tendencies in the speeches to Congresses
of Painters and Sculptors and of Composers.  Earlier confused figures -
Gorky, Lunacharsky - cited.

REVERSAL OF A DECREE.  "On the Correction
Of Mistakes In Appraisal Of the Operas
'The Great Friendship', 'Bogdan Khmel-
nitski', and ' With All My Heart'."
Decision of the CC.  In: SL, 1958 #6,
Supplement; and CDSP, July 16, 1958,
3.  Reverses "unjust" application of
1946-48 policies rather than the principle. - For 'Pravda' editorial on the
matter, CDSP, July 16, 1958, 3-7.

PASTERNAK CONTROVERSY.  Major documents
are in CDSP, Nov 5, 1958, 6-7; Dec 3,
3-12.  For letter from the editors of
'Novy Mir' to Pasternak, turning down
'Dr. Zhivago': Daedalus, Summer 1960.
- Stenographic Report, All-Moscow
Meeting of Writers, Oct 31, 1958, dis-
cussing and condemning Pasternak's
novel and actions, in: Survey, July
1966, 134-163.  Includes: S.S. Smirnov,
L. Oshanin, K.L. Zelinsky, V. Gera-
simova, V.O. Pertsov, A. I. Bezymensky,
A. V. Sofronov, S. Antonov, B. Slutsky,
G. Nikolaeva, V. Soloukhin, S. Baruz-
din, L. Martynov, B. Polevoi, V. Inber.
- Also see Conquest (XLIX).

3rd CONGRESS OF THE UNION OF SOVIET WRIT-
ERS, 1959.  Greeting from CC, speech
by N. Krushchev, resolutions, SL, 1959
#8, 84-111.  Speeches of A. Tvardovsky
and K. Paustovsky, with report by Jack
Lindsay, M&M, Sept 1959, 21-43. Speech
of A. Tvardovsky, CDSP, July 1, 1959,
8-9; also in SH, Aug 1959, 19-22.
Speech by K. Paustovsky, CDSP, July 1,
1959, 9-11; also in SH, Aug 1959, 15-

18.  Report by Alfred Dressler, SS,
Jan 1960, 327-341.

AGAINST BOURGEOIS CONCEPTS AND REVISION-
ISM IN FOREIGN LITERARY CRITICISM, and
AGAINST REVISIONISM IN ART AND ART
CRITICISM.  Two 1959 Symposia.  Survey,
#33 (July-Sept 1960), 70-77.  abdgd.
Remarks by R.N. Yurenev, V.N. Prokofiev,
A.D. Alexeyev, I. Ya. Ryzhkin, A.A.
Elistratova, et al.

A DISCUSSION ON POETRY: SOVIET AND ITAL-
IAN POETS MEET IN MOSCOW.  SL, 1949 #2,
144-167.  Includes, Quasimodo, Solmi,
Kursanov, Cadoresi, et al.

FURTSEVA, Ye. A, Speech to 21st Party
Congress.  CDSP, Mch 18, 1959, 9-11.
The role of Soviet arts discussed by
Minister of Culture.

CRITICISM VS. ABUSE.  Declaration by D.
Shostakovich, P. Kapitsa, Y. Zavadsky,
S. Obraztsov, S. Yutkevich, condemning
abusive criticism of sincere artistic
efforts.  From 'Izvestia', Sept 7,
1960.  In: SR, Feb 1961, 36-38.

22nd CONGRESS OF THE C.P.S.U.  Speeches
by A. Tvardovsky, V. Kochetov, M.
Sholokhov, N. Gribachov, SL, 1962 #1,
3-18; 1962 #2, 98-112.

3rd PLENARY SESSION, BOARD OF THE SOVIET
WRITERS UNION,  Speeches by K. Fedin,
G. Markov, et al.  SL, 1962 #4, 127-
143.  See Labedz  (XLIX )

HUMANISM IN MODERN LITERATURE, Discussion, SL, 1962 #10, 157-165.  Summary
of views of prominent authors and
artists.

PROBLEMS OF LITERARY CRITICISM, report
of discussions.  Rosalia Shtilman, SL,
1962 #12, 140-146.

KRUSHCHEV, N.S, Speech To Writers, Mch 8,
1963, SL, 1963 #4, Supplement.  (For
other sources of the speech in English,
see Krushchev (XLVI).  This call for
continued close Party control of the
arts evoked worldwide dissention. -
Dissent by P. Togliatti: see his interview with K.S. Karol, New Statesman,
May 24, 1963. - Dissent by F. Castro:
see I.F. Stone's Weekly, Apr 15, 1963,
2. - Dissent by John F. Kennedy, N.Y.
Times, Oct 27, 1963.  "Society must set
the artist free....Artists are not engineers of the soul." - For US left

reactions, see NG letters column, May
16, 1963 (L. Baxandall, M. Callejo,
C. Humboldt [signing as Roger Schevill],
P. Corner, W. Lowenfels, G. Kauffman);
May 23 (R.D. Merrick, H. Goldman, H.
Driggs, L.W. Hedley, B. Dahl); June 6
(R. Joyce, P. Traugott, D. Koerner,
B. Raymund, C. Zahn). Also S. Fin-
kelstein, M&M, July 1963, 36-45;
V.J. Jerome, ibid, Aug 1963, 43-50,
charges Finkelstein with trying to
relativize Marxist ideology. - For a
broader view of Soviet views at this
time: Survey, #48 (July 1963). - See
also: Fuentes (XXXIII); Aksyuk
(XLVII); Ilyichev, Malinowski (XLVI);
Johnson (XLIX).

2nd ALL-UNION CONGRESS OF ARTISTS.
Reports and extracts in CDSP, May 8,
1963, 15-18; May 15, 19-20. Speech
by Ekaterina Belashova, Secretary of
Artists Union, SL, 1963 #9, 159-167.

4th ALL-UNION CONFERENCE OF YOUNG
SOVIET WRITERS. Reports and extracts
in CDSP, May 29, 1963, 9-14. - See
also SL, 1962 #12, 124-139, a preparatory symposium intended to overcome
younger writers' sense of a generation-
al conflict. - See also "The Offensive
Is On," CDSP, May 1, 1963, 18-24,
rebuke by Board of Russian Republic
Writers Union to certain writers,
notably Yevtushenko.

4th PLENARY MEETING OF BOARD OF THE USSR
WRITERS UNION. SL, 1963 #5. Criticism
by K. Fedin and others of some young
writers, including Yevtushenko and
Voznesensky, whose self-criticism is
included.

CONFERENCE OF EUROPEAN WRITERS, Lenin-
grad, Summer 1963. NLR, #29 (Jan-
Feb 1965), 19-40. Speeches of J.
Hajek, L. Leonov, H.M. Enzensberger,
I. Ehrenburg, A. Robbe-Grillet, W.
Golding, A. Wilson, J.P. Sartre.
- Report by Suren Gaisaryan, SL,
1963 #11, 133-141. - Summary of
Krushchev's remarks, by Angus Wilson,
Observer, Aug 18, 1963. He rules out
peaceful coexistence in the ideolog-
ical sphere. - For subsequent Soviet
critical discussion of the novel, see
SL, 1964 #7, 155-162. A survey ac-
count. - See also, V. Machavariani,
"After the Discussion Of the Novel,"
C&L, 1964 #8, 25-26, 32. Chiefly on
conference's impact in the USSR and
in rebuttal of Robbe-Grillet and
Sarraute.

SEMINAR OF AFRO-ASIAN WRITERS, Moscow,
June 1964. Report in SL, 1964 #11,
176-183.

TRIAL OF IOSIF BRODSKY, Transcript. New
Leader, Aug 31, 1964, 6-17. - Also in
En, Sept 1964, 84-91. abdgd. - Source
of the transcript described in En, Nov
1964, 93. Brodsky was 24-year-old poet
sentenced to "a distant locality for a
period of five years of enforced labor"
on charges of parasitism, i.e, failure
to "fulfill the duties of a Soviet
citizen" by correct behavior and regular paid work. Transcript is unofficial; purportedly taken down by Writers
Union journalist.

REPUDIATING CHINESE POLICIES. 'Kommunist'
Editorial, "Against Dogmatism and Vul-
garization In Literature and the Arts,"
CDSP, July 29, 1964, 3-10. Also in
'Pravda', June 28, 1964. Attacks
Chinese for "repudiating the Leninist
policy" on the arts and literature replacing it with "dogmatism and sectarianism." Specifically charges a
racist and nationalist emphasis, a cult
of personality around Mao, vulgariza-
tions as in the Hundred Flowers policy,
and the assigning of writers and artists
to corrective labor.

AFFIRMATION OF POLICY. 'Pravda' Editorial, "Portray In a Worthy Manner the
Greatness Of the Soviet People's Deeds,"
CDSP, Feb 3, 1965, 3-4. Leninist policy
on literature reaffirmed after Krushchev's fall from power. Cited is June
1963 decision of Plenary Session of CC.

RETURN TO 1925 POLICY. 'Pravda' Editorial
Correcting Cultural Policies Of the
Krushchev Era, CDSP, Mch 10, 1965, 3-5,
35. Also in N.Y. Times, Feb 2, 1965,
1-2. abdgd. By Editor Aleksei M. Rumyantsev. Condemns "attempts to impose
one's subjective evaluations and personal tastes as the yardstick of artistic creation, especially when they are
expressed in the name of the party."
Returns to 1925 Resolution as the standard (see above): "This was and this
will henceforth remain the most important party principle in matters of
artistic creation."

2nd CONGRESS OF WRITERS OF THE RSFSR.
In: MN, 1965 #11, Supplement. Includes CC greetings, which ask "daring
innovatory searchings which enrich
Soviet art" while providing "service to
the people"; inaugural speech by M.

Sholokhov, viewing the writer as "a loyal soldier of the Leninist Party"; L. Sobolev, etc. - Excerpts also in CDSP, Mch 24, 1965, 8-15; Mch 31, 18-20. Sobolev, Sholokhov, Yegorychev, Tolstikov, S.P. Pavlov, Sofronov. - Also in SL, 1965 #7, 131-153.

3rd INTERNATIONAL CONGRESS OF WRITERS, Berlin and Weimar, May 14-22, 1965. Follows the Paris (1935) and Madrid (1937) Congresses. Report by Alvah Bessie, The Realist, Aug 1965, 5-9. - Speech by Anna Seghers, AmD, Oct-Nov 1965, 12-16. - Account by Harry Carlisle, NWR, July 1965, 15-20.

'PRAVDA' EDITORIAL, Defending Artistic Freedom. CDSP, Sept 25, 1965, 3-6. Also in N.Y. Times, Sept 10, 1965, 1, 4, abdgd. Written by A.M. Rumyantsev. Attacks 'Izvestia' and 'Selskaya Zhizn' for articles seeking to abridge "the artists' freedom to choose theme and subject, style and manner of execution." - Excerpts in DW, Sept 26, 1965, 6-7.

4th ALL-UNION CONGRESS OF ARCHITECTS, Moscow, October 27-29, 1965. For excerpts of discussion see CDSP, Nov 17, 1965, 20-22.

1st CONGRESS OF USSR FILM WORKERS UNION, Moscow, November 23-26, 1965. For discussion by S. Gerasimov, L. Kulidzhanov, A. Karagonov et al, see CDSP, Dec 22, 1965, 7-11.

THE TRIAL OF SINYAVSKY AND DANIEL, February 10-13, 1966, Moscow. Allegedly accurate transcript of the substance of testimony and closing remarks by the accused, in N.Y. Times Magazine, Apr 17, 1966, 20-23, 115-125. The defense of two writers accused of slandering and subverting the Soviet political and social system in works published abroad. - See also Soviet press comment, CDSP, Feb 2 - Mch 9, 1966. - A collection of the above and related materials is in: Max Haywood, ed, On Trial; The Soviet State Versus "Abram Tertz" and "Nikolai Arzhak", Harper & Row: 1966. - Account of the trial by L. Labedz, En, Apr 1966, 83-91. - Text of soviet writers' petition to Kremlin, signed by Chukovsky, Ehrenburg, Shklovsky, Anikst et al; and letter of protest from L. Chukovskaya to M. Sholokhov: N.Y. Times, Nov 19, 1966, 6.

23rd CONGRESS OF THE CPSU: Speeches On Problems Of Literature and Art. SL, 1966 #7, 115-139. Speeches by L. Brezhnev, E. Furtseva, M. Sholokhov, G. Markov, L. Kulidjanov.

CONFERENCE ON CURRENT PROBLEMS OF SOCIALIST REALISM, Autumn, 1966. Reports in SL, 1967 #7, 143-151.

AFRICAN AND ASIAN WRITERS CONFERENCE: Forum Of the Soviet Liaison Committee, Baku, USSR, August 30-September 1, 1966. SL, 1966 #12, 161-165. Writers of many lands gather, united in solidarity with Vietnam, preparatory to 3rd Conference (see below).

1st ORIENTALIST SYMPOSIUM OF EASTERN EUROPE, Autumn, 1966. Report in SL, 1967 #5, 176-180.

DEBATE OF MODERNISM. See Lifshitz (XLVI).

SOVIET RESPONSE TO CHINESE CHARGES: S. Kovalev, "Socialism and Cultural Heritage," CDSP, Oct 5, 1966, 4-6. From 'Pravda', Sept. 16. Reply to the Chinese theory of Cultural Revolution, citing Lenin etc. - See also CDSP, Oct 19, 1966, 23-30. - See also Survey, Apr 1967, 64-66, 75-78.

3rd CONFERENCE OF AFRICAN AND ASIAN WRITERS, Beirut, Lebanon, March 26-29, 1967. CDSP, Apr 26, 1967, 20, for 'Izvestia' account. Large Soviet delegation; the Chinese boycotted it, although Hsinhua Press Service was present and was accused by Soviets of agitating among delegates.

SOLZHENITSYN, Alexander I, "Letter To the Fourth National Congress Of Soviet Writers (In Lieu Of a Speech)," N.Y. Times, June 5, 1967. Dated May 16, 1967. Circulated to the Congress presidium and delegates, members of the Writers Union, and editors of literary periodicals; not published in the USSR. Declares that the "censorship, abuse and slander" of Soviet writers is contrary to the Constitution, the statutes of the Union of Soviet Writers, and the interests of literature and the nation. Citing his own experience and that of others, he asks the Congress for redress.

4th CONGRESS OF THE UNION OF SOVIET WRITERS, Moscow, May 1967. Preparatory articles and reports, intended to define the context of discussions: CDSP, May 31, 1967, 11-14, 19; June 7, 5-8. 'Pravda' greeting and daily accounts, CDSP, June 14, 1967, 5-12; the speeches of K. Fedin, G.M. Markov, M. Sholokhov, ibid, 13-21; the speeches of M.A. Dudin, A.D. Salyusky, S.V. Mikhalkov, L.N. Novichenko, K.V. Voronkov, N.V. Podgorny, D. Simonov, etc, CDSP, June 21, 1967, 6-19.

## XLII.  Architecture

ARCHITECTURAL REVIEW, May 1932.  Special Issue: The Russian Scene. illus.  Major articles by Robert Byron and Berthold Lubetkin.

BORISOVSKY, Georgi, "Architecture and Technical Progress,: ISM, #3 (Feb 1962), 68-90.  Detailed consideration of Soviet building problems and potential.

BOUROV, A, "The War and Architecture," V.O.K.S, 1946 #1-2, 53-62.  Problems of post-war reconstruction under conditions of urgency but in light of need for building according to ultimate tasks of genuinely socialist architecture.

BRUNOV, N, "Problems Of Modern Soviet Architecture," V.O.K.S, 1931 #10-12, 78-82.  illus.

DANIN, D, "Material and Style," CDSP, Apr 26, 1961, 10-15.  abdgd.  From 'Novy Mir'.  In an epoch of post-wedding-cake architecture new poured-concrete construction techniques are to be employed without sacrifice of diversity and beauty.

ILYIN, M, "Modern Architecture In the Soviet Union," V.O.K.S, 1930 #8-10, 51-55.  illus.

KUCHERENKO, V, "The Future Of Our Cities," CDSP, Nov 25, 1959, 22-24; 34; Also SH, Dec 1959, 24-28.  Chairman of USSR State Construction Committee talks about problems of building and functional beauty.

MILIUKOV, P.N, "Architecture, Painting and Music," Outlines of Russian Culture, Part III, Philadelphia, 1942.

NEKRASOV, Viktor, "Notes On Architecture: About the Past, the Present, and a Little Bit Of the Future," CDSP, Apr 13, 1960, 3-6.  illus.  A

revaluation of Constructivist architecture in terms of its uses for future construction.

SOROKIN, M, "Construction Of Towns In the Soviet Union," V.O.K.S, 1931 #10-12, 89-95.  illus.

STRUMLIN, S, "Communism and Industrial Aesthetics," ISM, July 1963, 1-18. Foresees integration of industrial work with "quiet, cleanness and beauty." Examples of Soviet backwardness in this respect.  Noise control, functional design, concern for factory decoration and lighting are the answer. These expenses will be justified - in the epoch of 4 and 5 hour work-days that is coming - by boosted productivity, greater success in battle for men's minds, and as realization of an innate goal of communism.

VESNIN, A.A, V.A. Vesnin, and M. Y. Ginsburg, "Soviet Architecture Grows Out Of Social Needs," MN, Apr 1, 1934, 7. "An authoritative view of the problems now facing Soviet builders and the lines along which they plan to work out new solutions and new architectural forms," says editorial note.

_____, "Striving For Architecture Worthy Of a Great Epoch," MN, Nov 7, 1935, 6, 30.  illus, pp. 16-18.  "The Soviet architect is not asked to design separate buildings, as was formerly the case, but complete ensembles making up the new type of socialist city."  Important for idea of architecture under Stalin.

VLASOV, A, "The Style Of Our Architecture," CDSP, Dec 23, 1959, 8-10.  Concerns "difficulties in our search for a socialist style."

V.O.K.S, SOCIALIST CITIES.  V.O.K.S, 1932 #5-6, 135-182.  illus.  Articles by L. Kaganovich, S. Gorny, L. Slavin, A. Starchakov, G. Ivanov, B. Olenin.

YARABOV, Yuri, "National Features Of Soviet Architecture," V.O.K.S, Mch-Apr 1955, 35-46.  illus.  Useful outline with many examples.

## XLIII.  Art and Sculpture

ART IN THE USSR; Special Autumn 1935 Number of The Studio, ed. C.G. Holme. illus.  [MMA]  Survey articles by A.Y. Arosev (introduction), D. Arkin (archi-

tecture), A. Bassekhes (painting), B.
Ternovetz (sculpture), A. Chegodayev
(drawing and engraving), B. Persov
(poster and cartoon art), J.M. Nikonov
(theatre), N. Yesuitov (cinema), A.
Bakushinsky (handicrafts).

BAKUSHINSKY, A.V, "Evolution Of Palekh
Art," V.O.K.S, 1930 #6-7, 61-68. illus.
The magnificent lacquer art of ex-icon
painters under the Revolution. - See
also above.

BESKIN, Osip, The Place Of Art In the
Soviet Union, American Russian Institute Publication no. 2, May 1936.
Foreword by Christian Brinton. 32 pp.
Former director of Fine Arts Department of People's Commissariat for Education describes conditions of Soviet
art.

BUKHARIN, Nikolai, "Some Thoughts on
Soviet Pictorial Art," SCR, 1933 #9,
11-18. Polemic against modern art.

GAN, Alexei, "Constructivism," in:
Camilla Gray, The Great Experiment,
Abrams: 1962, 284-287. abdgd. Repre-
sentative 1920 declaration of the
union of revolutionary art and
Bolshevism.

GOLOMSHTOK, I, and Andrei Sinyavsky,
Picasso, Joint Publications Research
Service: 34,352. U.S. Dept. of Com-
merce, Clearinghouse for Federal
Scientific and Technical Information,
Washington, D. C. Issued Mch 1, 1966.
Translated text of a volume published
in Moscow, 1960. Account of Picasso's
development and interpretations of
paintings.

ILYIN, M, Russian Decorative Folk Art,
Foreign Languages Publishing House,
Moscow, 1959. illus.

IOGANSON, B, "A Painter's Notes," SR,
Nov 1960, 31-39. Preparatory paper
for 1st Congress of Artists of the
Russian Federation. Defends painting
that is readily intelligible and
nationalistic.

IVANOV, S.V, "Folk Art In the USSR During the Past Fifteen Years," V.O.K.S,
1933 #4, 61-87. illus. Bibliography,
survey.

KALINEN, I, "The Tasks Of Soviet Art,"
V.O.K.S, Nov-Dec 1940, 3-9.

KEMENOV, Vl. S, "On the Objective Charac-
ter Of the Laws Of Realistic Art,"
V.O.K.S, 1953 #83, 38-50. - See also
Picasso (XL).

_____, On Art and Soviet Society. In:
J.P. Hodin, The Soviet Attitude To Art,
2-12 (typescript). abdgd. [MMA] Transcript with notes by Hodin of talk before Institute of Contemporary Arts,
London, Nov 26, 1951. Questions put
to Kemenov regarding his attitude toward Picasso, with Kemenov's seemingly
evasive replies: pp. 30-33.

KONNENKOV, Sergei, "To Dream, To Dare,
To Create," C&L, 1961 #10, 24-26. An
honored sculptor speaks of his career
fulfilling Lenin's summons to create
"monumental propaganda."

_____, Interview with G. Gruzd. MN, Mch
23, 1947, 4. illus. His decision to
return to USSR from the US.

_____, SEE ALSO: K.A. Abbas, "Patriarch
of Pushkin Square," ISCUS, Summer 1958, 11-14. A sympathetic
Indian visitor reports the
sculptor's biography and his
peculiar version of history's
dialectic.

KOLPINSKY, Y, Frank Discussion of Abstract
Art. C&L, 1963 #4, 22-25.

LEVINSON, N, "Care Of Ancient Monuments
and Religious Art," V.O.K.S, 1930 #6-7,
51-60. illus. Comprehensive article
on Soviet efforts in this direction.
- For more information on museum
policies, see: SUR, Feb 1928, 26-28.

LOUKOMSKI, George K, History Of Modern
Russian Painting (1840-1940), 1945.
illus. A Russian expert living abroad
wholly affirms the views of the Soviet
critic Shchekotov and the realist tradition: if great works have not been
produced, this is solely due to the
lack of "individual great talents."

MILIUKOV, P.N, "Architecture, Painting
and Music," Outlines Of Russian Culture,
Part III, Philadelphia, 1942.

NAZAROV, A.I, "Art and Artists In the
Soviet Union," Art and Culture In the
Soviet Union, July 1938, 3-6. mimeo.
[MMA] The head of Committee on Artis-
tic Questions defines policy. Mention
of Meyerhold case.

NEIZVESTNY, Ernst, Statement On Sculpture. In: Olga Carlisle, "A Soviet Sculptor," Art in America, Jan-Feb 1966, 104-107. illus. His case for non-representational art.

NIKRITIN, Defends His Painting 'Old and New' Before Art Commission Of the Vsekokhudoshnik, Apr 10, 1935. Transcript of the proceeding in: Kurt London, The Seven Soviet Arts, London, 1937, 223-229. abdgd. illus. Makes a lively defense against charges of eroticism and formalism but loses his case. The general issues clearly emerge.

NIKULIN, Lev, "Art and Pseudo Art," SL, 1963 #4, 143-146.

NOVITSKY, Pavel, "Pictorial Art In U.S.S.R. During the Ten Years Of the Revolution; Its Tendencies and Achievements," in: Exhibition Of Contemporary Art Of Soviet Russia [catalog], 1929. Spirited analysis and tribute to 'left' art movements 1918-24 and their influence. Description of post-1924 organizations, movements and artists.

OVSYANNIKOV, Yuri, "Wood Sculpture Of Ancient Russia," SL, 1965 #1, 179-182.

ROMM, Alexander, Matisse; A Social Critique, 1947. "He may be called a representative of extreme decorativism, which has arisen from the hedonistic conception of the function of art, from the soil of bourgeois aestheticism."

SHAGINYAN, Marietta, Creative Freedom and the Soviet Artist, 'Soviet News' Booklet: London, 1953. 16 pp.

SHEPILOV, D.T. See 1957 (XLI).

SOLONKHIN, Vladimir, et al, "How Can Folk Art and Rural Culture Be Fostered?" CDSP, May 12, 1965, 20-26.

STERNBERG, David, Foreword to Catalog Of the 1st Russian Exposition In Berlin, 1922. In: Gabo, Harvard Univ: Cambridge, 1957, 155. abdgd. Sternberg was then Commissar of Arts. Deals with non-objective Soviet artists, the Suprematists and Constructivists and Cubists.

TATLIN CIRCLE, "The Program Of the Productivist [Constructivist] Group," in:

Gabo, Harvard Univ: Cambridge, 1957, 153-154. Published in 1921 catalog for an exhibition by Rodshenko and Stepanova. "The task of the Constructivist group is the communistic expression of materialistic constructive work....Down with art....Art is a lie. Kill human thinking's last remains tying it to art."

V.O.K.S, Painting, Sculpture and Graphic Art In the USSR, V.O.K.S, Moscow, 1934 #9-10. illus. Survey and biographical articles on numerous subjects.

ZASLAVSKY, D, "On the Art Of the 'Distractionists'," ISM, #3 (Feb 1962), 91-99. Abstract Expressionist painting analyzed and ridiculed.

ZIMENKO, V.M, "Socialist Realism and the Artist's Individuality," V.O.K.S, 1952 #74, 42-47. illus. Individualism in the work of ranking Soviet painters.

_____, "Realism and Convention," C&L, 1963 #12, 26-29. illus. For a use of fantasy that does not falsify reality: Signorelli, Grunewald, Bosch.

## XLIV.  Cinema

CENTRAL COMMITTEE DECREES. See 1946-48 (XLI).

CHERKASSOV, Nikolai, Notes Of a Soviet Actor, Moscow, 1957.

CHUKHRAI, Grigori, "Keeping the Old On Their Toes," Films and Filming, Oct 1962. Attacks a "communism without humanism." This article became a prime exhibit in Chinese-Soviet dispute. See attack on it by Chang Kuang-Nien (X).

_____, "Art and the Individual," WMR, Jan 1963, 38-45. Director of 'Clear Skies' and 'Ballad Of a Soldier' analyzes films by Resnais and Fellini, among others.

DOVZHENKO, Alexander, Italian Neo-Realist Films. V.O.K.S, 1954 #85, 59-62. Close analysis of 'Open City', 'Bicycle Thief', etc.

EHRENBURG, Ilya, The Dream Factory. Two excerpts: NTh, Nov 1934, 6-7; Aug 1935, 6-7. Hollywood.

EISENSTEIN, Sergei, Film Form and Film Sense, Meridian paperback: 1957. illus.

Contains many of the basic essays, and a bibliography listing others, which are not repeated here.

_____, Notes Of a Film Director, Foreign Languages Publishing House: Moscow, 1946. illus. Collection of articles.

_____, The Soviet Screen, Moscow, 1939. 40 pp. In the Pamphlet Library On the Soviet Union distributed at the 1939 World's Fair.

_____, "The Cinema In America," IL, 1933 #3, 97-105. "This squalor of ideas, thought and thriftlessness is served by the world's most perfect technical apparatus."

_____, "On the Soviet Film," in: VOQ, 225-239. Detailed and important on functioning of cinema under Soviet conditions. Written at editors' invitation.

_____, Account Of Filming 'Potemkin'. V.O.K.S, 1950 #3, 59-68. Written 1945. Valuable insight into his procedure.

_____, "Notes For an Autobiography," C&L, 1958 #5, 41-43. illus. Dated 1939. Chiefly on shaping force of the Revolution in his career.

_____, Autobiographical Sketch. IL, 1933 #4, 128-129.

_____, "The Mistakes Of 'Bezhin Lug'," IL, 1937 #8, 93-96.

_____, Self-Criticism. In: Counts (XLIX), 146-149. Condemns Part II of his 'Ivan the Terrible' as "ideologically worthless and vicious."

_____, SEE ALSO: USSR Cinema Topic Index. And:

Ivan Anisimov, "The Films Of Eisenstein," LWR, 1931 #3, 101-114. illus. Appreciation and some criticism.

Joseph Freeman, An American Testament, 1936.

Alfred Richner, "Sergei M. Eisenstein," The Dial, Apr 1929, 311-314. Interview and description of his apartment.

G. Alexandrov, Stalin's Personal

Censorship of 'October' CDSP, Nov 28, 1962, 10-11. From 'Pravda', Oct 28, 1962.

Dwight MacDonald, "The Eisenstein Tragedy," PR, Nov-Dec 1942, 502-506. Sources of his failure to produce.

Vladimir Nizhny, Lessons With Eisenstein, Hill & Wang: 1962. illus. A student recounts four classroom problems. Appended: Eisenstein's teaching programme.

Semyon Freilich, "Eisenstein Today," SL, 1965 #2, 155-162.

FELDMANN, K, "The Reconstruction Of the Soviet Cinema," V.O.K.S, 1931 #10-12, 56-66. Surveys history and intentions of film industry at a crucial juncture.

GERASIMOV, Sergei, "Socialist Realism and the Soviet Cinema," Films and Filming, Dec 1958, 11-12, 33.

KARAGANOV, Alexander, "Once More On the New Generation," Film Culture, #24 (1962), 22-25. The US "underground cinema".

_____, On Cinema Verite. C&L, 1964 #9, 23-24. The Soviet cinema of truth: Vertov and today.

_____, "Positive Hero and Freedom Of Expression," SL, 1964 #2, 157-162. The positive hero in current films.

KATSEV, Israel, "Notes On Bourgeois Film Criticism," SL, 1963 #11, 160-167.

KOZINTSEV, Grigory, "Deep Screen," Sight and Sound, Summer and Autumn 1959, 157-160. illus. The director of 'Youth Of Maxim' and 'Don Quixote' on failure of numerous films to present "the depth and complexity of living" based on a true empathy.

KULIDZHANOV, Lev, "The Building Of Communism and the Tasks Of the Soviet Film Industry," SL, 1966 #4, 159-169. Speech at 1st Congress of Soviet Film Workers, by head of Organizing Committee.

MONOSSON, L. I, "The Soviet Cinematography," Journal Of the Society Of Motion Picture Engineers, Oct 1930.

NILSEN, Vladimir, The Cinema As a Graphic

Art, London, 1938; Hill & Wang: 1959.
Chiefly on work of camerman. Composition and editing of the "shot." Nilsen
was Eisenstein's cameraman for two
years.

ROSHAL, Grigory, "Amateur Film Makers,"
C&L, 1964 #8, 16-19. illus.

SHUMATSKY, Interview with Anna Louise
Strong. MN, Aug 3, 1931, 8. illus.
Soviet cinema's administrative chief
describes the industry's resources
and approaches.

SOVIET CINEMA, Moscow [V.O.K.S.], 1935.
Editor-in-Chief A. Arossev. Articles
by Dovzhenko, Pudovkin, numerous other
Soviet film workers. Statements by
Lenin and Stalin on role of Soviet
cinema. heavily illus.

TRETYAKOV, Sergei, "Our Movie," in his:
Der Film, Moscow: 1928, 46-72. In
English. Social and aesthetic analysis
of Soviet film.

TSCHERNJOWSKI, L, "Children's Cinemas
and Films In the Soviet Union," in:
J.P. Mayer, Sociology Of Film, London,
1946, 288-295. Chapter from 'Der
Sowjetfilm', Moscow, 1941.

TWROVSKAYA, Maya, Style In the New Soviet
Cinema. SL, 1963 #4, 147-158.

VAISFELD, I, "Critical Comments On Soviet
Film Theory and Practice," SR, Sept
1960, 49-56.

VERTOV, Dziga, "Kino-Eye," Filmfront
(New York), I ii (1935), 6-8; I iii,
7-9. mimeo. Excerpts from 1929
Paris lecture. A documentary film
pioneer said to have strongly influenced Eisenstein, and director of
'Three Songs About Lenin', describes
principles of "kinoki," the freeing of
Soviet film from conventions of the
stage.

_____, Writings. Film Culture, #25
(1962), 50-60.

_____, SEE ALSO: Lionel Britten, "Kino
Eye," Realist (London), Oct
1929, 126-138. - Simon Koster,
"Dziga Vertov," Experimental
Cinema, II v (1934), 27-28.
Also Leyda (LIV). - Henry Dobb,
"A New Genius Of the Soviet
Film," SW, Feb 24, 1929, 8.

WEISFELD, Ilya, "Truth In the Cinema,"
SL, 1964 #7, 163-168. Styles of
cinema verite: Dziga Vertov and today.

YUTKEVICH, Sergei, "The Cinema and the
Times," NT, Aug 2, 1961, 13-15. Humanism in current Soviet and Western
films. - See also Yutkevich, 1960 (XLI).

_____, "Montage 1960," Film Culture, 22-
23 (1961), 51-58.

## XLV.  Dance

CHERNOTSKAYA, I, "The Dance," ITh, #2
(1934), 22-24. Dance as vehicle of
revolutionary propaganda.

MOISSEYEV, Igor, "Ballet and Reality,"
Dance, May 1953, 28-31, 55. Also in
CDSP, May 24, 1952, 15-16; and in Peter
Brinson, ed, Ulanova On Soviet Ballet,
Society for Cultural Relations With
the USSR: London, 1954. From 'Liter-
naturanaya Gazeta', Apr 24, 1952. -
Reply by Rostislav Zakharov, "Dramaturgy Of the Ballet," Dance, June 1953,
24, 46-47; and in Brinson. Moisseyev
sees classical ballet as moribund; it
substitutes pantomime for dance movement, "ready-made language" of the im-
ported past under the Tsar for vital
national forms. Wide-ranging criticisms. Zakharov is a leading choreo-
grapher of the Bolshoi Ballet.

_____, "Folk-Dance Ensemble," V.O.K.S,
1952 #76, 49-52. illus. Discusses
his company and Russian folk dance
heritage.
_____, "Searching, Planning, Dreaming,"
SL, 1962 #7, 150-157. illus. Realism
in dance.

_____, "One Hundred Ballet Masters and
One 'Asel'," CDSP, May 3, 1967, 19-20.
Attack on the domination of stale
themes and choreography.

ROSLAVLEVA, Natalia, Era Of the Russian
Ballet, Dutton: 1966. Soviet ballet
in its tradition.

SIDOROV, A, "The Art Of Dancing In the
U.S.S.R," V.O.K.S, 1931 #10-12, 52-56.
Divergent schools. I. Duncan.

SLONIMSKY, Yuri, "Aesthetics Of Soviet
Ballet," in: The Bolshoi Ballet Story,
Heller & Heller: 1959, 117-126. Also
in Y. Slonimsky, The Bolshoi Theatre
Ballet, Moscow, 1956, unpaged: "By

Way Of an Epilogue," Soviet ballet is "different in quality" from the old Imperial ballet.

_____, et al, The Soviet Ballet, Philosophical Library: 1947. illus. A fact book.

### XLVI.  Literature and General

AGABABYAN, Suren, Armenian Literature. SL, 1966 #3, 149-161. With other Armenian materials.

AIZERMAN, L.S, "Contemporary Literature Through the Eyes Of Upper-Grade Pupils," SR, Spring 1965, 32-45. Glimpse of teaching methods and norms and student literary interest.

ALEXEYEV, M.P, Slavonic Sources Of Thomas More's 'Utopia', Moscow, 1955. In Russian. Extended summary in English by Miklos Szenczi, in: AL, II (1959), 457-461. Actually a full look at social aspects of 'Utopia'.

ALMAZOV, Eugene, "On the 'Tendentious' In Literature," Main, I ii (Spring 1947), 199-211. Attack on the contempt for the tendentious in the West.

ANDREEV, Yuri, "Rich From Its Very Sources," SSL, Winter 1966-67, 71-79. Reappraising Soviet literature of the 1920s.

ANGAROV, A, "Form and Content In Art," IL, 1936 #12, 70-82.

ANIKST, Alexander, "Shakespearean Studies In the USSR," Diogenes, Fall 1961, 99-108. Admirable summary of history of Soviet Shakespeare scholarship and controversies.

_____, "Shakespeare In Our Time," SL, 1964 #4, 171-178. His accessibility.

_____, "Shakespeare--A Writer Of the People," SSU, 113-139. From 1959. Conditions which enabled Shakespeare to be uniquely free of class illusions.

_____, SEE ALSO:  Review-summary of three recent books by Anikst, SL, 1966 #7, 164-168.

ANISIMOV, Ivan, "Life-Affirming Humanism: The 400th Anniversary of the Birth of Shakespeare," SSU, 140-144. From 'Pravda', 1964.

ASMUS, Valentin, "Basic Traits Of the Classical Russian Esthetics," Philosophy and Phenomenological Research, VI (1945-46), 195-211. Detailed analysis of longstanding divergence between " contemplative" aesthetics in the West and tendentious aesthetics in Russia.

_____, "Realism and Naturalism," SL, Mch 1948.

AVERBACH, L, "Proletarian Literature and the Peoples Of the Soviet Union; For the Hegemony Of Proletarian Literature," LWR, 1931 #5, 93-125. Speech to 2nd Plenary Session of VOAPP, May 1931. Insists on a literature to aid Party goals. Attacks "Voronskyism."

_____, "Our Political Position," LWR, 1931 #1, 73-82.

BABEL, Isaac, Interview with Vern Smith. DW, Sept 24, 1934, 5. In connection with 1st Soviet Writers Congress.

_____, On His Role In Soviet Literature. IL, 1933 #1, 135-136; 1936 #6, 85-86; 1937 #9, 86-88. See also 1936 (XLI).

_____, The Lonely Years 1925-1939, Noonday paperback: 1964. Ed. with intro. by Nathalie Babel. Contains stories; letters to his mother and sister, 1925-1939; speech to 1st Congress of Soviet Writers; speech honoring D. Furmanov; controversies over his work and statements.

_____, Letters. SL, 1965 #1, 156-160.

_____, SEE ALSO: Georgi Munblit, "Reminiscences Of Babel," SL, 1965 #1, 148-155.

BELKIN, Abram, "New Works On Dostoevsky," SL, 1964 #6, 132-139.

BELYAKOV, A, "Soviet Literature and Bourgeois Falsifiers," CDSP, Oct 6, 1965, 5-8. Critique of studies issuing from US Russian Centers.

BEREZNITSKY, Y, On Mark Twain. See: Charles Neider, Mark Twain and the Russians; An Exchange Of Views, American Century paperback: 1960. Debate between Neider and Bereznitsky in pages of 'Literaturnaya Gazeta' over scholarly treatment of Twain.

BLAGOY, Dmitri, "Literary Method and the Writer's Individuality," SL, 1965 #3,

131-136. Problems of neo-romanticism, subjectivism, lyricism.

BOGDANOV, A, "Proletarian Poetry," <u>LM</u>, May 1923, 276-285; June, 357-362. This and following articles developed from stenographic notes of lectures given in 1920. Bogdanov was chief advocate of a proletarian culture which was thought impossible by Trotsky, Bukharin and others. Here he discusses imagery as basis of art. Finds three stages of culture: feudal (authoritarian), bourgeois (individualist), proletarian (collectivist and liberated) and discusses latter.

_____, The Criticism Of Proletarian Art," <u>LM</u>, Dec 1923, 344-356. Proletarian art differs from peasant (religious) and intellectual-socialist (lacking collectivist features) art. Warns against narrowness of content and tendency to hostile caricature of other classes. Rejects imposed optimism. Proletarian art is objective and refuses "the deception of rosy glasses ....a flight from reality, a deceiving mask for...despair."

_____, "Religion, Art and Marxism," <u>LM</u>, Aug 1924, 489-497. Religious culture of the past is valuable to proletariat because "after it has passed through the worker's criticism it becomes for him a tool not for the support of, but for the understanding of all the authoritarian elements in life" which must be conquered. The "furious but naive atheist" is on the wrong track.

_____, "The Workers' Artistic Inheritance," <u>LM</u>, Sept 1924, 549-556. Continuation of above essay. Closely analyzing 'Hamlet' and a statue by Meunier Bogdanov argues that "the knowledge and understanding of such models which have been worked out by the past is indispensible for a class which is called upon to organize the future."

BOIKO, M, "The Fault Does Not Lie With Realism," <u>SSL</u>, Winter 1966-67, 43-50. Disputes an interpretation of Lermontov by Vl. Arkhipov which everywhere exalts romanticism over realism, while admitting the achievements of romanticism.

BRANDIS, E, and V. Dmitrevsky, "Science Fiction Is Written For Everybody," <u>SSL</u>, Summer 1966, 94-102. Combining

credibility and Marxist vision.

BUKHARIN, Nikolai, The Suicide of Essinen. In: Joseph Freeman, "Poetry and Common Sense," <u>NM</u>, May 1927, 9-10.

_____, "Goethe and His Importance In World History," <u>V.O.K.S</u>, 1932 #3-4, 106-126. Speech to Goethe Centenary Celebration held at the Academy of Sciences.

_____, <u>Culture In Two Worlds</u>, 1934. 32 pp. Published Also as "Crisis Of Capitalist Civilization and Cultural Problems Of the USSR" in <u>IL</u>, 1934 #5, 107-120; as "Poetry, Poetics and the Problems Of Poetry In the USSR" in <u>PSL</u>, 185-260, which is the complete text of his contribution to the 1st Soviet Writers Congress, and the best of these texts to consult.

_____, "A Brilliant Talent - A.V. Lunacharski," <u>MN</u>, Jan 6, 1934, 13. Obituary and assessment.

_____, <u>Historical Materialism: A System Of Sociology</u>, Russell & Russell: 1965, 189-203. Art is "a systematization of feeling in forms"; art's function is to socialize, transfer and disseminate these feelings in society; art's genesis is determined ultimately by the economic structure and the "stage of social technology." Example: music. Many scattered observations.

BUROV, Alexander, "Two Major Problems Of Marxist Aesthetics," <u>SL</u>, 1957 #3, 133-142. Admits "formal" critera while maintaining ethical criteria as basic. A "human element" always "glimmers through" form and our cognition of art is cognition of human "essential powers."

CHAKOVSKY, Aleksandr B, Interview with George Feifer. <u>N.Y. Times Magazine</u>, Dec 20, 1964, 12-13, 20, 22, 24, 26-28. Editor of "Literaturnaya Gazeta' on visit to US upholds political, moral and national criteria in art and literature.

CHERNOUTSAN, Igor, "Vatslav Vorovsky On Aesthetics," <u>SL</u>, 1955 #9, 122-131.

CHESNOKOV, D.I, <u>Marxism-Leninism On Basis and Superstructure</u>, Bombay, 1952, 37-42. From 'Voprosy Filosofiai', 1952 #3.

CHUKOVSKY, Kornei, "Anton Chekhov," <u>SL</u>, 1962 #7, 119-146. His personality.

DEMENTYEV, Alexander, "Alexander Voronsky," SL, 1967 #2, 189-193. Biography
and interpretation of the leading early Soviet critic.

DESHERIYEV, Yuri, with M. Kammari and M.
Melikyan, "Soviet Linguistic Policy
Seen As a Model," CDSP, Dec 15, 1965,
14-19. The problems of language and
internationalist amalgamation.

DINAMOV, Sergei, "The Satire and Humor
Of Mark Twain," IL, 1935 #5, 91-95.

_____, "King Lear," IL, 1935 #6, 55-76.

_____, "Sherwood Anderson: American
Writer," IL, 1933 #4, 84-91.

_____, Letters To Joseph Freeman. Sur-
vey, Apr 1965, 92-102. With commentary by Freeman. Dinamov's view of
RAPP and activity translating American
writers.

DIVILKOVSKY, A, "Demyan Bedny," V.O.K.S,
1931 #6, 14-17. illus.

DNEPROV, Vladimir, "In Defense Of the
Aesthetic Of Realism," SL, 1958 #1,
170-185. Realism as the most congen-
ial medium for Marxists, though there
are pro-Communist abstract artists and
anti-Communist realists. Basic social
fact is "the inexorable hatred of the
bourgeoisie for realism." Attacks the
Poles Zismovit Fedecki and Jan Kott
(for his "Mythology and Truth" essay
on the "tragic antimony between revolutionary spirit and innovation").

_____, "Method and Style In Art," SL,
1958 #3, 139-147. "Realism is a
method, not a style....no one can
point to any common formal characteristics of critical realist literature
....artistic convention or fantasy
can perfectly well be a form of expression in realism;" thus "in
Brecht's work true realism is allied
to great power of fantasy." A. Miller,
Lu Hsun also cited.

_____, "True and False Innovation," SL,
1959 #2, 129-140.

_____, "Notes On Contemporary Critical
Realism," SL, 1959 #7, 127-138.

_____, "The Aesthetics Of the Uncon-
scious," SR, Dec 1961, 3-23. From
'Voprosy Literaturny', 1961 #5. An
"autopsy" of "Freudian aesthetics"

considered as the "system of concepts" of a decadent literature, reducing everything to artist's biography.

_____, "On the Nature Of the Novel,"
SSL, Winter 1964-65, 50-76. Insists
on "the unity of all poetic categories,
which once existed separate from each
other": the new novel has dramatic and
lyric as well as epic elements, changing its essence; "it is necessary to
contrast the epic, dramatic and lyrical cross sections of reality." The
new role for subjectivity in the novel
is a vital advance. Homer, Dostoevsky,
Tolstoy, Belinsky, Hemingway, Bunin,
Faulkner, Eisenstein.

_____, See also: V. Shcherbina (below).

DOBIN, YEFIM, "Plot Structure and Content," SL, 1959 #1, 129-140.

DOBRYNIN, Mikhail, "Structure and Functions Of the Union Of Soviet Writers,"
MN, June 5, 1946, 3-4. Detailed
account.

DUBROVIN, Artyom, "Socialist Realism"
SL, 1966 #1, 144-151. A definition
which includes fantastic renderings.

DYMSHITS, Al, "Modernism Is the Enemy Of
Creativity," CDSP, Aug 21, 1963, 15-20.
abdgd. - See also Lehmann-Haupt (XLIX).

EGOLIN, A.M, The Ideological Content Of
Soviet Literature, Public Affairs
Press: Washington, 1948. mimeo. De-
tailed survey of current Soviet writing.

EHRENBURG, Ilya, Auto-Critique. IL, 1933
#1, 138-139. illus. "The relativism
and extreme individualism I inherited
from the last century often prevent me
from getting face to face with the new
age."

_____, Speech to 1st Soviet Writers Con-
gress. DW, Sept 27, 1934, 5. Reprinted in part in LR, Nov 1934, 21-26.

_____, Speech to 1st International Writ-
ers Congress, Paris. DW, July 10,
1935, 5.

_____, "The Surrealists," PR, Oct-Nov
1935, 11-16.

_____, "The Writer's Work," M&M, Apr
1954, 6-24; May, 7-26. Also in CDSP,
Feb 10, 1954, 4-13; and SS, Apr 1954,

415-426.  abdgd.  From 'Novy Mir'. Call for concrete rendering of men's emotional lives.

_____, "Science and Culture," ISCUS, II iv (1955), 29-43.  Speech to 10th UNESCO Recontre Internationale, Geneva.

_____, Speech to 2nd Congress of Soviet Writers.  CDSP, Mch 23, 1955, 27-29. abdgd.  For uninhibited discussion of problems of literature.  See also Simonov (XLVI).

_____, "A Necessary Clarification," NWR, June 1957, 26-39; July, 21-33.  In effect, concilation of position of impatient Soviet writers with that of the Party in wake of Hungarian events.

_____, "Literature In the Age Of the Sputniks," The Atlantic, June 1960, 45-47.  Frank discussion of Soviet literary problems.

_____, Chekhov, Stendhal and Other Essays,  MacGibbon and Kee: London, 1961.

_____, "The World Weighs a Writer's Influence," SatR, July 29, 1961, 20-21. Hemingway.

_____, "Picasso," NWR, Dec 1961, 16-19.

_____, Interview with Olga Carlisle. Paris Review, #26 (1961), 99-117.

_____, Interview with Herbert Juin. M&M, Oct 1962, 52-56.

_____, People and Life, vols. I, II, III, MacGibbon and Kee: London, 1962-63.  Issued in US as People and Life, 1891-1921, Knopf: 1962, and Memoirs: 1921-1941, World: 1964. - Review by Victor Erlich, PC, July-Aug 1963, 15-24.  Review by Isaac Deutscher, Nation, Dec 21, 1964, 494-496.

_____, Speech To European Writers Conference, Leningrad.  CDSP, Aug 28, 1963, 13-15; and NLR, #29 (Jan-Feb 1965), 29-32.  Crisis in the Soviet and Western novel.

_____, "On Dante," SSL, Fall 1966, 35-43.  Speech honoring 700th anniversary of Dante's birth, UNESCO headquarters, Paris.  Dante as poet, political man and realist.

_____, Interview With J. Okliansky. SSL, Spring 1967, 3-18. His writing method.

_____, SEE ALSO: Obituary, N.Y. Times, Sept 2, 1967, 1, 25.  illus.

ELISTRATOVA, Anne, "Fascism and Italian Literature," IL, 1933 #2, 92-105.

_____, "Jack Conroy: American Worker-Writer," IL, 1934 #1, 112-118.

_____, The 'New Masses'.  IL, 1932 #1, 107-114.  Exhaustive analysis.  "The IURW takes upon itself to watch with the closest attention the work of 'New Masses', subjecting to a critical examination (through the Anglo American Commission of the IURW) every new issue of the journal.  In view of the general weakness of the Marxist criticism in America, IURW undertakes to continue in its central organ the work started already last year - the study of the fundamental problems of Marxist Leninist criticism - and also to extend and systematize the work of 'International Literature' in the sphere of concrete critique of the basic phenomena in contemporary American literature."

ETTINHOF, B, "Art In the Five-Year Plan Of Cultural Construction," V.O.K.S, 1931 #10-12, 3-10.

EVENTOV, Isaak S, "Laughter Is a Sign Of Strength; Notes On Satire," SSL, Winter 1964-65, 3-22.  How satire was suppressed under Stalin's "non-conflict theory," and has been revived; critique of various Soviet views on satire. "The seamy side of life is part of life as a whole," thus "integral and profound" satire is required.

FADAEV, Alexander, Interview.  MN, July 16, 1947, 2, 4.  illus.  Reports some progress among writers since Zhdanov's speech on Leningrad journals.  Defines Socialist Realism, freedom for Soviet writers, decadence in Western literature.

_____, "The Tasks Of Literary Criticism," ARSU, Mch 1948, 30-59.  Quasi-official statement of the Party attitude.

_____, "Socialist Realism In Literature," USSR Information Bulletin, June 30, 1948, 392-393.  Defends his views against queries from prominent East German writers.

_____, "Science and Culture In the Struggle For Peace, Progress, and Democracy," in: George S. Counts and Nucia Lodge, The Country Of the Blind, Boston, 1949, 320-335.  Speech to World Congress of

Leaders of Culture For the Defense of Peace, Vroclav, Poland, Aug 25, 1948.

_____, "Notes On Literature," SL, 1956 #1, 93-111.

_____, "Socialist Realism," SL, 1964 #5, 134-141. Extracts from statements from 1932 to 1947.

_____, SEE ALSO: Cornely Zelinsky, "Alexander Fadaev," V.O.K.S, 1948 #54, 36-54.

FEDIN, Konstantin, "On Idea Content and Craftsmanship In Literature," CDSP, Dec 8, 1951, 10-12.

_____, Speech To 2nd Soviet Writers Congress. CDSP, Apr 20, 1955, 13-16.

_____, Speech to 3rd Plenary Session, Board of Soviet Writers Union. SL, 1962 #4, 127-143.

_____, SEE ALSO: B. Brainina, "Konstantin Fedin," V.O.K.S, 1954 #85, 53-58. Also Simmons (XLIX).

K. Zelinsky, On Konstantin Fedin. C&L, 1964 #11, 18-19. illus.

FILATOVA, Lydia, "Langston Hughes; American Writer," IL, 1933 #1, 99-107.

FRICHE, W, "Freudism and Art," LWR, 1931 #5, 80-92.

FRID, Y, "The Sophistry Of Sartre," NM, Sept 2, 1947, 6-8; Sept 9, 14-16.

_____, "A Philosophy Of Unbelief and Indifference; Jean Paul Sartre and Contemporary Bourgeois Individualism," MQ(L), Summer 1947, 215-223.

FRIED, J, "Surrealism - and Louis Aragon," IL, 1934 #4, 125-129. Aragon's relation to Surrealists.

FURTSEVA, Ye. A. See 1959 (XLI).

GAISARYAN, Suren, "Sergei Essinen," SL, 1965 #9, 154-162.

GILSENSON, Boris, "Two New Books On Walt Whitman," SL, 1967 #7, 173-177. By B. Chukovsky and Mendelson.

GLADKOV, F.V, "Socialist Realism," MN, Nov 7, 1933, 9. illus. Interview with Ed Falkowski. Socialist Realism

"denies the artistic value of any single moment as a thing-in-itself....it implies the presentation of our problems in the light of socialist construction." Important statements from a 'premature' Socialist Realist on strength of his novel 'Cement' (1925).

_____, "My Work On 'Cement'," IL, 1934 #4, 139-145.

GEI, Nikolai, "A Method Born Of the Age," SL, 1963 #10, 150-156. The basis for Socialist Realism in socialist reality.

_____, and Vladimir Piskunov, "Abstract Humanism and Socialist Humanism," SR, June 1960, 39-55. From 'Voprosy Literatury', 1960 #12. On the "positive" hero.

GOLENISHCHEV-KUTUZOV, Ilya, "Problems of 'Lay of Igor's Host'," SL, 1965 #3, 137-144.

GOLENISHCHEV-KUTUZOV, N.N., "Dante In Soviet Culture," SSL, Winter 1965-66, 62-94. Critical survey of translations of and writings on Dante in the USSR.

GORKY INSTITUTE OF WORLD LITERATURE, Modern American Literature. SL, 1963 #11, 133-141. Summary of papers by Soviet experts. - See also Valentina Jacque, "Recent Research On the History of American Literature," SL, 1965 #4, 168-173. Resume of the Institute's 'Some Problems In the History of U.S. Literature', Moscow, 1964 (in Russian). - See also: SL, 1965 #8, 174-178; and Clements (XLIX).

GORKY, Maxim, "Gorky On the Films, 1896," NTh, Mch 1937, 10-11, 56. Two articles on the Lumiere demonstrations, among first written on film by anyone.

_____, Letters Of Gorky and Andreev, 1899-1912, ed. with introduction by Peter Yershov, Columbia Univ: 1958. Gorky early spotted talent of Andreev and in these letters encourages and criticizes it, until Andreev succumbs to alcoholism and fashionable despair and the letters break off. No. 3, how to write; no. 34, on religious belief; nos. 42, 86 on keeping positive outlook amid Russian barbarism; nos. 33, 65, 70, 71, 84 on political engagement.

_____, "The City Of Mammon, My Impression of America," Appleton's Magazine, Aug 1906, 177-182.

_____, "Russia and the Jews," in: The Shield, ed. Maxim Gorky et al, 1917, 3-18. Not only rejects Anti-Semitism (he believes it will disappear but gradually with growth of culture), not only declares he feels personally the Russian guilt for Jews' condition, but says: "Somewhere deep in the Russian soul - no matter whether it is the 'master's' or the muzhik's - there lives a petty and squalid demon of passive anarchism, who infects us with a careless and indifferent attitude toward work, society, people and ourselves. I believe that the morality of Judaism would assist us greatly in overcoming this demon, - if only we have the will to combat him....I believe that Jewish wisdom is more all-human and universal than any other." - See also: Boris Souvarine, "Gorky, Censorship and the Jews," Dis, Winter 1965, 83-85. Gorky's many and important writings on Russian Jews expunged from 30-volume Soviet Academy of Science edition of his works (Moscow, 1948-56) and from subsequent Soviet publication.

_____, "World Literature," IL, 1938 #4. Written 1919.

_____, "In Praise Of Lenin," WD, Dec 11, 1920, 2. Other translations in Lib, Nov 1920, 5-7; and Contemporary Review, Nov 1920, 728-733. Discusses differences with Lenin and reasons for their reconciliation. "To Lenin's will, history has given the terrible task of digging up from the bottom this desultry, misbuilt, slothful semi-human ant-hill which we call Russia....Lenin is more a man than any other of our contemporaries." Analyzes the already-apparent personality cult around Lenin and approves.

_____, Days With Lenin, 1932. 64 pp. Excerpts in M&M, Jan 1950, 63-68. Also in DW, July 9, 1932, 6; 11, 4; 12, 4; 13, 4; 14, 4; 15, 4; 18, 4; 19, 4; 20, 4. Gorky here states that what he wrote directly after Lenin's death ("Lenin the Man," Nation, Nov 26, 1924, 584-585) was "hasty" and unsatisfactory." The account here is longer but less vivid; emphases changed. Lenin's estimates of Gorky, Tolstoy, Mayakovsky, Bedny, the Apassionata.

_____, "In the Torrent Of the Revolution," CS, Dec 1918, 592-599. Dated Dec 1917. Says he is "working against the Bolsheviks" who "are conducting a most cruel experiment on the living body of Russia" and yet "the best of them are remarkable persons of whom the future history of Russia will be proud," and revolution like childbirth "is always accompanied by labor pains."

_____, "Gorky's View Of the Lenine Group," Current History, Apr 1918, 83.

_____, "Bolshevism Defended," Living Age, Jan 25, 1919, 200-202.

_____, "Prophet Of Bolshevism," Living Age, Oct 9, 1920, 69-73.

_____, "The Intelligentsia and the Revolution," Manchester Guardian Commercial, Reconstruction In Europe Supplement, July 6, 1922, 239-240. Gorky, living in emigration, judiciously evaluates merits and mistakes of the Bolsheviks.

_____, "Cruelty Of the Russians," Nation, Sept 5, 1923, 231-232.

_____, "James Fenimore Cooper," IL, 1937 #2, 114. Preface to 1923 German edition of Cooper. Sees Natty Bumpo as incarnation of man's will to overcome conformity.

_____, "Observations On the Theatre," English Review, Apr 1924, 494-498.

_____, Letters To Soviet Publishing Houses. SL, 1966 #5, 154-162. Directing the course of publication, and relations to authors.

_____, Talk With Henri Barbusse. DW, Oct 3, 1928, 6; 8, 6; 15, 6; 30, 6. Gorky's shifting feelings toward the Revolution.

_____, Letter To Romain Rolland, Jan 1, 1928. DW, Nov 29, 1933, 5. Vitality of Soviet writing.

_____, Letter to G. Aleksinsky, 1929. In: Richard Hare, Maxim Gorky, Oxford: London, 1962, 122-123. Aversion for "the poisonous and fatal dust of everyday truth" which" for ninety-nine per cent of people is an abomination and a lie;" his preference for "sowing in the minds of the masses" that "truth which excites in men confidence and their will and reason." Aleksinsky was an emigre who had written questioning his decision to return to Russia.

_____, "Young Soviet Writers," Yale Review, Mch 1931, 488-501.

_____, Fragments From My Diary, London, 1924. Glimpses of Chekhov, Tolstoy, Blok. Mostly scenes of Russian life before revolution and after.

_____, Autobiography of Maxim Gorky, Citadel: 1949.

_____, On Isaac Babel. In: Nathalie Babel, ed, Isaac Babel: The Lonely Years 1925-1939, Noonday paperback: 1964, 387-389. Open letter of October 26, 1928, replying to an open letter by Gen. Budyonny which attacked Babel's 'Red Cavalry'.

_____, "A Boy," in: Nathalie Babel, ed, Isaac Babel: The Lonely Years 1925-1939, Noonday paperback: 1964, 393-396. About a ten-year-old author of anti-Fascist verse.

_____, Introduction to: Leonid Leonov, Soviet River, 1932.

_____, "What Books Shall We Give Our Children?" MN, Nov 20, 1933, 3, 7. abdgd.

_____, "Art Is Essentially a War, For Or Against," MN, Aug 29, 1935, 2, 4. Discusses role of art in social life.

_____, "Pushkin: An Appraisal," in: Irving D.W. Talmadge, ed, Pushkin; Homage By Marxist Critics, 1937, 11-13.

_____, Reminiscences, 1946. Essays on Tolstoy, Chekhov, Andreev, Blok, a letter to Stanislavsky.

_____, On Literature, Moscow, 1960. Selected articles. Important.

_____, "Plays and Playwrights," One Act Play Magazine, Sept 1937, 461-463. Also in ITH, 1934 #2, 3-5.

_____, Message To 1st International Writers Congress, Paris. DW, July 18, 1935, 5.

_____, Speech To 1st Soviet Writers Congress, Moscow, 1934. PSL, 27-72. Major statement of literary views. Role of myth. Decadence and resurgence in culture. Launching of Socialist Realism.

_____, To American Intellectuals, 1932. 32 pp. The necessity of Communism; the justice of "compulsion" in overcoming Russian backwardness.

_____, On Guard For the Soviet Union, London, 1933.

_____, "Russian Letter," Dial, Mch 1929, 230-238.

_____, On Stanislavsky. In: K. Stanislavsky, Progress Publishers, Moscow, n.d, 25-30. illus.

_____, "To the Humanists," MN, Dec 22, 1930, 1, 3. Defends necessity of having executed 48 persons criminally implicated in the food crisis. Questions right of Western intellectuals to protest, given their own situation. Defends Party dictatorship as beyond egotism and in light of its goals.

_____, "Letter To the Workers and Peasants," MN, Dec 1, 1930, 1-2. Defends and explains treason trials then under way.

_____, "About a Certain Legend," MN, Mch 12, 1931, 3. Refutation of charges that compulsory labor camps existed in USSR. Describes function of labor under the Bolsheviks.

_____, "The Significance Of Collective Farms," MN, June 2, 1931, 6. Collectivization then in process.

_____, Speech Prepared For the Amsterdam Anti-War Congress. MN, Sept 10, 1932, 4, 8; Sept 15, 4, 8. Also in V.O.K.S, 1932 #5-6, 129-134. The Dutch Government forbid his entry.

_____, "Making New Men," MN, Aug 25, 1933, 3, 6. Also in DW, Aug 29, 1933, 5. Inhumanity of capitalist labor conditions. Reformative effect of Soviet penal work projects.

_____, "They Are Wonderful People," MN, May 26, 1934, 5. illus. Welcome and tribute to visiting Stakhanovites.

_____, Culture and the Stakhanovite Movement. DW, Jan 10, 1936, 7. Strong praise for remoulding of personality and culture under Stalin's policies.

_____, Letters to M. Zoshchenko, M. Drishvin and K. Fedin. SL, 1963 #11, 155-159.

_____, Culture and the People, 1939. Chiefly publicistic essays from Gorky's last years.

_____, Literature and Life, ed. V.V. Mikhailovski, London, 1946. Includes: "How I Learned To Write" (1928); from "Talks About the Writer's Craft" (1930); pre-revolution essays on Tolstoy and Chekhov; "Paul Verlaine and the Decadents" (1896); Stendhal; "A Talk With Young People" (1934); preface to "Anthology Of Proletarian Writers" (1914); "The Destruction Of the Personality" (1908); "From Afar;" "Village History" (1935).

_____, Creative Labour and Culture, Sidney, 1945. "Creative Labour and Art;" "Russian Literature Of the 19th Century;" "About the Cinema" (1933); "Ten Years;" etc.

_____, Letters On Socialist Realism. CDSP, July 21, 1954, 19-20. First published in 'Pravda' June 18, 1954.

_____, Letters On Literature. CDSP, Nov 24, 1954, 3-4, 9. First published in 'Pravda', Oct 10, 1954. Includes letters to Rolland and Krupskaya.

_____, Letters, Progress: Moscow, 1966. Discussion of literature, in correspondence between Gorky and writers in USSR and abroad.

_____, Articles and Pamphlets, Moscow, 1950. Minor but interesting pieces.

_____, SEE ALSO: For further materials, see: United States Library of Congress, Division of Bibliography, Select List Of References, no. 1442: Maksim Gor'kii (1939). Typescript. Publications in English, French, German, Italian, Spanish and biographical and critical books and articles.

    Alexander Kaun, Maxim Gorky and His Russia, 1931. Still the major interpretation. Many Gorky materials not otherwise available in English, for instance, articles in 'Novaya Zhihn' that attacked Bolshevik seizure of power.

    Richard Hare, Maxim Gorky, Romantic Realist and Conservative Revolutionary, Oxford: London, 1962. Some new data from Gorky's late years. Mostly a gloss on

Kaun with malice added.

Moissaye J. Olgin, Maxim Gorky, Writer and Revolutionist, 1933. Popularization.

Alexander Roskin, From The Banks of the Volga; The Life Of Maxim Gorky, Moscow, 1945; New York, 1946.

Nina Gourfinkel, Gorky, Evergreen Profile paperback: 1960. illus. Lively sympathetic biography. Extracts from texts.

Dan Levin, Maxim Gorky; Stormy Petrel, Appleton-Century: 1965. Provides much additional information.

Alexander Kaun, "Maxim Gorky; In Search Of a Synthesis," Slavonic and East European Review, Jan 1939, 429-444. Penetrating analysis of complexity and genesis of Gorky's theory of Socialist Realism - which underlies and significantly differs from the official doctrine. Gorky made clear his literary theory was combatting Russia's "Asiatic" passivity. He held one should be, however, "a merciless Realist toward the present."

Irwin Weil, Gorky: His Literary Development and Influence On Soviet Intellectual Life, Random House: 1967.

Konstantin Fedin, "Gorky Among Us: Scenes Of Literary Life," SL, 1967 #7, 81-105. Gorky's relations with the beginning author.

Tributes Upon His Death. IL, 1936 #8, 3-12. Molotov, Lukacs, A. Tolstoy, Gide, et al.

Isaac Babel, Reminiscences Of Gorky. IL, 1937 #6, 87-89.

Karl Radek, "The Role Of Maxim Gorky In the Revolution," DW, Aug 19, 1922, 4. "The only consistent point in his entire attitude was his vacillation" says Radek with examples.

P. Novitsky, "Gorky's Theatrical
Style," ITh, 1934 #3-4, 9-12.
A critical view.

Henrietta Roland-Holst, "Gorky
As a Literary Critic," ISR,
June 1906, 705-711. Translated from 'Die Neue Zeit' to
appear at time of Gorky's
visit to America. First major socialist article on him
to appear here.

"How Gorky Was Murdered," Ex-
cerpts From Court Proceedings
In the Case Of the Anti-
Soviet 'Bloc Of Rightists and
Trotskyites' [the Doctors'
Plot] Heard Before the Mili-
tary Collegium Of the Supreme
Court Of the USSR, Moscow,
Mch 2-13, 1938. IL, 1938 #3,
17-37. illus. Also in DW
Mch 10, 1938, 8; 11, 8; 12,
7. abdgd.

See also: Fischer, Kantorowicz
(XXI); Lukacs (XXVII);
Bukharin, Ermilov, Lenin,
Lunacharsky, Plekhanov, Trot-
sky (XLVI); Humboldt (LVI);
Gassner (LVIII).

GRANIN, Daniil, "The Joy Of Cognition,"
SL, 1965 #1, 139-144. A Soviet physicist views contemporary literature.

GRIB, V. Balzac, 1937. 96 pp. Bibliography. Builds on Marx's analysis.
- Review by E.B. Burgum, S&S, Winter
1937, 107-111.

GRIBACHOV, N, Speech To 22nd Congress,
CPSU. SL, 1962 #1, 3-18.

GUSEVA, Elena, "F. Scott Fitzgerald In
the Soviet Union," SL, 1966 #6, 171-
174.

ILYICHEV, L.F, "Create For the People
For the Sake Of Communism," CDSP,
Jan 16, 1963, 16-21. Speech by Secretary of the CC. Occasion was meeting
of Party and government leaders (including Krushchev, who also spoke
though his speech was not published)
with literary and art figures (among
them, Ehrenburg and Yevtuchenko).
Develops Krushchev's remarks on
abstract painting.

_____, Speech At Meeting Of Ideological
Commission Of Party Central Committee

With Young Writers, Artists, Composers,
and Cinema and Theatre Workers, Dec 26,
1962. CDSP, Feb 6, 1963, 7-13, 40.

_____, Speech At Meeting Of Party and
Government Leaders With Literary and
Art Figures, Mch 7, 1963. CDSP, Apr 3,
1963, 3-6. Krushchev was present and
spoke but his speech was not published.
Among others who spoke: A. Prokofieff,
Sholokhov, Romm, Khrennikov, Chukhrai,
Neizvestny.

IVANOVA, T.A, "Lermontov and Washington
Irving: A Creative Encounter," SSL,
Summer 1965, 25-41.

KAGAN, M, "Esthetics and the Present Day,"
CDSP, Nov 18, 1959, 13-15. abdgd.
From 'Oktyaber', July 1959. Unresolved
problems of Soviet aesthetics suggested
in some detail.

KAGARLITSKI, Julius, "H.G. Wells In Russia," SL, 1966 #9, 150-155. By his
Russian editor.

KALASHNIKOVA, Evgenia, "Translation In
the USSR," SL, 1966 #4, 175-181.
Translating practice and realist theory.
- See also SL, 1966 #9, 160-170.

KALININ, M.I, "The Tasks Of Soviet Art,"
V.O.K.S, Nov-Dec 1940, 3-9. Chairman
of the Presidium talks on role of tendentious in art to meeting of art
workers in Moscow.

KARETNIKOVA, Marina, "Our Contemporary
In Lyrical Prose-Writing," SL, 1964
#10, 144-150. The validity and tradi-
tion of lyric prose as a realism.

KARYAKIN, Yuri, "Anti-Communism and the
Two Sides Of Dostoyevsky," WMR, May
1963, 31-42. Reappraises Dostoevsky's
position as opponent of socialism.

KASHKEEN, Ivan, "Ernest Hemingway, A
Tragedy Of Craftsmanship," IL, 1935
#5, 72-90. Perceptive article by
Hemingway's Russian translator; Hemingway thought it the best critical article on his work (see Hemingway (LXIII).)

_____, "What Is Hemingway's Style?" SL,
1964 #6, 172-180.

_____, "Alive In the Midst Of Death,"
SL, 1956 #7; and in: Carlos Baker, ed,
Hemingway and His Critics, Hill & Wang
paperback: 1961, 162-180.

_____, ed, <u>New York (An Outline)</u>, Cooperative Publishing Society of Foreign Workers in the USSR: Moscow, 1933. illus. maps. glossary. From the cover design of the statue of liberty holding a dollar aloft, to the selections from Dos Passos, Dreiser, Gold, Magil, J. Reed, J. North, A. Johnson, N. Ash, Sorokin, C. Bercovici, O'Henry, C. Merz, Waldo Frank, the Russian student of the English language is introduced to US poverty, splendor and revolutionary trends.

_____, SEE ALSO: Account of KashKeen's Hemingway studies, by Elena Gousseva, <u>SL</u>, 1967 #8, 172-178.

KATANYAN, Vassili, "Mayakovsky and Sandburg," <u>DWSup</u>, Oct 20, 1946, 8. Evidence of Mayakovsky's great interest in the Chicago poet.

KATARSKY, Igor, <u>Dickens In Russia</u> [Summary]. <u>SL</u>, 1967 #5, 168-175.

KEDRINA, Zoya, "Notes On Kazakh Prose," <u>SL</u>, 1964 #11, 133-138. Part of special issue devoted to Kazakh arts.

_____, "The Innovatory Quality Of Socialist Realist Literature," <u>SL</u>, 1964 #1, 137-145. Examples of various literary techniques available to Socialist Realism.

_____, "Smerdyakov's Heirs," <u>CDSP</u>, Feb 9, 1966, 15-18. On Sinyavsky and Daniel.

KEMENOV, Vladimir, "Shakespeare," <u>V.O.K.S</u>, 1946 #5-6, 37-48. Good suggestions for a perspective. - See also (XLIII).

KITAIGORODSKY, Alexander, "Thoughts About Art," <u>SL</u>, 1965 #1, 139-144. A Soviet physicist views contemporary literature.

KOCHETOV, V, Speech to 22nd Congress, CPSU. <u>SL</u>, 1962 #1, 3-18.

'KOMMUNIST' Editorial, Dec 1955: "On the Question Of Literary and Art Treatment Of the Typical," <u>CDSP</u>, Feb 29, 1956, 11-15, 38.

KONDRASHOV, S, "With Outstretched Hand," <u>CDSP</u>, Apr 7, 1965, 27-28. Impoverished arts in an affluent America.

KONSTANTINOV, F, <u>Basis and Superstruc-</u>

<u>ture</u>, Moscow, 1955. Pamphlet.

KOVALEV, Yuri V, "Chartist Literature," <u>OH</u>, #17 (Spring 1960), 19 pp. Overview of leading poets and writers, their literary theories and relations to bourgeois heritage. This essay also translated in <u>Victorian Studies</u>, Dec 1958; but 'Our History' editor points out numerous distortions in that version.

KOZHINOV, Vadim, "Artistic Creation As 'Thinking In Images'," <u>SL</u>, 1960 #3, 145-160. Wholly accepts Kantian distinction between conceptual and artistic thought. Discriminates between "the type" in literature and in science or politics.

KOZINTSEV, Grigori, <u>Shakespeare</u>, Hill & Wang: 1966. Essays by the director of the Soviet 'Hamlet' film. - Chapter on 'King Lear' also in <u>SSU</u>, 204-263.

KRON, Aleksandr, "A Writer's Notes," in: Hugh McLean and N. Vickery, eds, <u>The Year Of Protest 1956</u>, Vintage Russian paperback: 1961, 164-190. From "Literaturnaya Moskva'. The cult of personality and its harsh impact on culture.

KRUSHCHEV, Nikita, <u>The Great Mission Of Literature and Art</u>, Progress: Moscow, 1964. illus. Contents:

Speeches on unveiling Shevchenko monuments, 1939 (abdgd.) and 1964.

Speeches to 20th, 21st, 22nd Party Congresses. Excerpts.

Summary of Speeches to Writers' Meeting, May 13, 1957; to a Reception for Writers, Painters, Sculptors and Composers, May 17, 1957; and to the Party Active, July 1957. Also in <u>CDSP</u>, Oct 9, 1957, 3-10; and <u>SL</u>, 1957 #10, Supplement.

Speech at Kremlin Reception for Soviet Intellectuals, Feb 8, 1958.

Speech at Kremlin Reception for Participants in Tashkent Afro-Asian Writers Conference, Oct 22, 1958.

Speech to 3rd Soviet Writers Congress, May 22, 1959. Also in <u>CDSP</u>, June 24, 1959, 3-9, 29; and <u>SH</u>, Aug 1959, 1-14.

Speech in Veshenskaya, M. Sholokhov's village, Aug 30, 1959. Also in <u>CDSP</u>, Sept 30, 1959, 3-8. Sholokhov as a

"wonderful example:" "Party spirit
flows organically from his own convictions and sentiments.  The interests of the Party and the writer's thoughts coincide."

Speech at 20th-Century-Fox Studios,
Hollywood, Sept 19, 1959.

Speeches to Intellectuals, July 17, 1960
and at   Receptions for Russian
Federation Writers and Composers.
Also in CDSP, May 24, 1961, 3-7.
Convivially assumes "the workers of
literature and the arts have always
been and continue to be faithful
aides of the Communist Party in all
its works," a task in which "all
kinds of troops are necessary and
important."

Speech on Satire, Nov 22, 1961.

Speech at 6th Congress of the German
Socialist Unity Party, Jan 16, 1963.

Speech at Meeting with Artists and
Writers, Mch 8, 1963.  Also in CDSP,
Apr 3, 1963, 7-13; Apr 10, 6-12; and
in Current Soviet Documents, Apr 5,
1963, Supplement; also, En, pamphlet
#9, with related material, comment,
etc.  The major Krushchev speech in
its influence on world opinion. For
responses to speech by some writers
and artists, including Yevtushenko
and Voznesensky: CDSP, Apr 17, 1963,
3-7.  Demands "unswerving abidance
by the Party line," no deviations or
ideological coexistence in culture
from "the workers of Soviet literature and art, the true assistants of
the Party." - See also 1963 (XLI).

Speech at Central  Committee Plenary
Meeting, June 21, 1963.

Excerpt from Interview with UPI's
Henry Shapiro, Nov 14, 1957.

Letters to International Festival of
Children's Choirs (Dec 5, 1959); to
Rockwell Kent, (Nov 19, 1960  and
June 20, 1962); to Robert Frost's
Family (Jan 29, 1963).

Interview with I. Pietra of 'Il
Giorno', Apr 20, 1963.  On Western
leftists.

Speeches to 2nd and 3rd Moscow International Film Festivals, July 9,
1961 and July 7, 1963.

_____, Remarks Against Modernist Paint-
ing.  En, Apr 1963, 102-103.  See also
CDSP, Dec 26, 1962, 20-23 (with supporting articles from 'Pravda',
'Izvestia', 'Komsomolskaya pravda'.)
Modernist painters as donkeys and
pedarasts, undesirables ripe for de-
portation. - Also see Berger on
Neizvestny (XXIII).

_____, Interview with Khuaja Ahmad Abbas.
ISCUS, Dec 1960, 53-58.  Discusses cultural development of minority peoples;
more energetically, his favorite writers.  In Zola's 'Germinal' Krushchev
"saw my own life, my own mine and my
own daily round described."

_____, See also: Priscilla Johnson and
Leopold Labedz, Khrushchev and
the Arts; The Politics of Soviet
Culture, 1962-64, M.I.T. Press:
Cambridge, 1965. With documents.

KULIKOVA, I.S, "The Social Essence Of
Surrealism," SR, Feb 1961, 41-57.  From
'Voprosy Filosofie', 1960 #8. Political
analysis.

KURSANOV, G, and M. Rosenthal, "Some
Trends In Modern Bourgeois Aesthetics,"
ISM, #3 (Feb 1962), 28-44.  From 'Kommunist', 1961 #3.  The soviet assessment of Western aesthetics as represented at IVth International Congress
of Aesthetics, Athens.

KUZNETSOV, Mikhail, "Prognosis For the
Novel, East and West," SR, Oct 1960,
3-35.  From 'Novy Mir'.  Discusses
development of the novel in theoretical context in some detail.

_____, "Irreconcilable Positions," SL,
1964 #2, 133-143.  Against modernism.

LANDOR, Mikhail, "Truman Capote In Russian," SL, 1966 #4, 182-183.  Translations and critical attitudes.

_____, "Sinclair Lewis In Russian," SL,
1965 #7, 176-178.

_____, "Faulkner in the Soviet Union,"
SL, 1965 #12, 178-185.  Account of the
critical reception.

LANN, Evgenyi, "Waldo Frank: American
Writer," IL, 1936 #1, 63-82.

LAZAREV, L, "The War Novels Of Konstantin Simonov," SSL, Summer 1965, 42-72.

LENIN, Vladimir I, "Leo Tolstoy, Five
Essays," Dia, #6 (1938), 12-29. Best
translation. With additional essay,
also in Selected Works, 1935-38, vol.
XI, 681-691; and Tolstoy and His Time,
International: 1952. 32 pp. "Tolstoy
and His Epoch" first appeared in English in LM, Oct 1928, 606-609. "Leo
Tolstoy, Mirror Of the Russian Revolution" first appeared in English in SW,
Sept 16, 1928, 6. "Tolstoy and the
Modern Labor Movement" in Sovietland,
1935 #4, 8-9. - For historical expli-
cation, see Morawski (XXXVI).

_____, "Party Organization and Party
Literature," Dia, #5 (1938), 1-5.
Also in WM, Apr 1926, 268-269; and
CR, Feb 1951, 60-64. Extracts in LWR,
1931 #1, 3-4. - For a view of this
fundamental essay in historical context, see: Ya. M. Strochkov, "On
Lenin's Article 'Party Organization
and Party Literature'," CDSP, Aug 8,
1956, 3-5. abdgd. From 'Voprosy is-
torii', Apr 1956. "Lenin was thinking
primarily of people like Axelrod, Mar-
tov, Parvus, Trotsky, Potresov and
Plekhanov, not of those writers who
did not enter the ranks of the Social
Democrat Party." - See also Morawski
(XXXVI).

_____, Letters To Gorky. LM, July 1937,
444-447; Aug, 507-511; Sept, 570-576;
Nov, 699-703; Dec, 759-764; Jan 1938,
54-58; May, 313-317. Annotated and
especially translated. From a letter
of Feb 25, 1908: "I consider that an
artist can draw much that is useful
to him from any philosophy....by ex-
tracting the particular point of view
both from your artistic experience
and from a philosophy, even idealistic
philosophy, you may come to conclusions which may be enormously helpful
to theWorkers' Party." - See also
Gorky, above, for essays on their relations and on Lenin's view of art.

_____, On Plekhanov. IL, 1935 #3, 71-74.

_____, On Mayakovsky. Cited in Alexan-
der Kaun, Soviet Poets and Poetry,
Berkeley, 1943, 56. "I do not belong
among the admirers of his poetic
talent, though I fully admit my incom-
petence in that field. But it is a
long time since I have experienced
such pleasure from the political and
administrative point of view. In his
poem Mayakovsky makes deadly fun of
'meetings', and ridicules communists

who sit and oversit in sessions. I do
not know about the poetry, but I in-
veigh that politically this is absolutely correct." - The poem is "In Re Conferences," Life and Letters Today,
Autumn 1937, 75-76.

_____, On Mayakovsky. Compilation of
Lenin's remarks in Herbert Marshall,
ed, Mayakovsky, Hill & Wang: 1965,
29-33; 145.

_____, "Directives On Cinematography,"
LM, Nov 1964, 523-524. Dated 1922.
First English publication. Lenin's
plan for propaganda work through cinema: on a financially self-sustaining
basis with judicious base of entertainment films.

_____, Culture and Achievement of Social-
ism In Russia. In: Robert V. Daniels,
ed, A Documentary History Of Communism,
Vintage paperback: 1962, vol. I, 228-
231. Articles from early 1923 show
absolute necessity Lenin saw for raising cultural life of Russia before
Socialism could be built. Lunacharsky
refers to these views in 1928 as basis
for Ministry of Education policy.

_____, On Literature and Art, Progress:
Moscow, 1967. illus. Collects many
of the essential documents. Translations are less accurate than the best
preferred sources given above and below.

_____, On Socialist Ideology and Culture,
Moscow, n.d. Includes "The Tasks Of
the Youth Leagues," Proletcult draft
resolution, urging Party direction of
a proletarian development in culture.

_____, On Culture and Cultural Revolution,
Progress: Moscow, 1966. Expanded ver-
sion of the above; with memoirs by
Lunacharsky, Zetkin, Krupskaya.

_____, "Lenin On Various Writers," IL,
1935 #2, 54-63. Brief notices on
Belinsky, Herzen, Chernyshevsky,
Uspensky, Gorky, Barbusse, Sinclair.

_____, Compilations of Remarks on the
Arts. MN, Jan 24, 1935, 10; also DW,
Mch 20, 1935, 5.

_____, SEE ALSO: Nadezhda K. Krupskaya,
Lenin and Culture. C&L, 1957
#4, 4-6. Also her Memories Of
Lenin, 1930. 2 vols.

A.V. Lunacharsky, "Lenin and

Art," DWSup, Nov 27, 1926.
Important report of Lenin's
personal tastes and his official treatment of avant-
garde arts.

A.V. Lunacharsky, "Lenin On
Propaganda Through Monuments,"
IL, 1939 #1, 88-89. From
'Literaturnaya Gazeta', Jan
29, 1933. Lenin enthusiastic
for putting unemployed artists to work on monumental
didactic monuments as in
'City Of the Sun'.

A.V. Lunacharsky, "Lenin In Red
Marble," MN, Jan 20, 1934, 5,
9. Reprinted in DW, Feb 15,
1934, 5. From an article
written Aug 1933, and left unfinished. Lunacharsky's first
meeting with Lenin, Paris,
Spring 1904. He took Lenin
incognito to the sculptor
Aronson who was seized with
idea of using Lenin as model
for a bust of Socrates; Lenin
rocked with laughter. In 1925
Aronson did make a bust of a
Socratic Lenin.

Altman, a sculptor, spent May
1923 in Lenin's office ex-
ecuting a bust of him; report on Lenin's "little artistic sense," Living Age,
Aug 1931, 603. "He once
told me that he could hear a
tune twenty times without re-
membering it. The only works
of art that decorated his office were a picture of Marat
and a bas-relief representing
Kalturin. They had told him
that I was a futurist, and he
asked if his bust would be of
that school. I told him that
as I wanted to portray him
exactly I should not distort
the work at all. Complying
with his request, I then
showed him some futurist
work. He looked at it and
then said, without irony, 'I
do not understand it; it is
evidently for specialists'."

Angelica Balabanoff, Impressions
Of Lenin, Michigan Univ: Ann
Arbor, 1964, 5-6, 9-10. Re-
membrances of an unassuming
Lenin being sculpted and at

Moscow Art Theatre.

Clara Zetkin, Reminiscences Of
Lenin, London, 1929; New York,
1934, 12-16. Also in DW, Jan
19, 1934, 5; Jan 20, 9; and
Sputnik, 1967 #8, 48-55. A
major source of Lenin's views
on art.

V. Bonch-Bruevitch, "From My
Recollections Of Lenin," IL,
1934 #2, 108-111. Love for
Hauptmann's 'The Weavers'.
Abhorrence for modern art. -
Further extracts, SL, 1964
#8, 183.

Vyacheslav Polonsky, "Lenin's
Views Of Art and Culture," in:
Max Eastman, Artists In Uni-
form, 1934, 217-252. abdgd.

F. Yudin, "Lenin On Certain
Questions Of Literary Criti-
cism," IL, 1936 #11, 76-89.
Polemic for the times.

Louise Bryant, Mirrors Of Moscow,
1923, 15-16. Lenin's concern
for and enjoyment of the
theatre in crisis years.

Simon Dreiden, Lenin and the
Moscow Arts Theatre. C&L,
1966 #4, 9-11. illus.

I. Chernoutsan, "60th Anniversary Of Leninist Manifesto Of
Revolutionary Art," CDSP, Dec
15, 1965, 12-13. abdgd. From
'Pravda'.

LEONOV, Leonid, Speech To 1st Soviet
Writers Congress. LR, Nov 1934, 21-
26. abdgd. - See also an interview at
the time, DW, Sept 24, 1934, 5.

_____, Speech To European Writers Confer-
ence. NLR, #29 (Jan-Feb 1965), 22-27.
Outstanding speech on humanist and
Soviet use of the novel.

LEVIDOV, M, "About Lion Feuchtwanger,"
IL, 1934 #6, 106-110.

_____, "Three Shakespeares," European
Quarterly, Feb 1935, 230-240. abdgd.
Shakespeare as "stylist," as "an accom-
modator, a political toad-eater" (the
USSR has eliminated need for a writer
to politically accommodate himself,
says Levidov), and as "the great thinker,

the artist without a rival in all literature....an overwhelming conclusion
to an epoch, and not a beginning."

LEVIN, F.  See 1936 (XLI).

LIFSHITZ, Mikhail, The Philosophy Of Art
Of Karl Marx, 1938.  96 pp.  Best
study in English of Marx's cultural
views. - See also "Marx On Aesthetics,"
IL, 1933 #2, 75-91.  Wretched translation.

_____, "Responsibility Of Art To Society
In Belinsky's Esthetics," S&S, XIII,
243-257; also in MQ(L), Summer 1949,
238-252.

_____, "G.V. Plekhanov," SL, 1956 #12,
141-154.

_____, "Johann Joachim Winkelmann and
the Three Epochs Of the Bourgeois
Weltanschauung," Philosophy and Phenomenological Research, VII (1946-47),
42-82.  History of the class readings
and uses of a great German aesthetician.

_____, "Giambattista Vico (1668-1744),"
Philosophy and Phenomenological Research, VIII (1947-48), 391-414.

_____, "Why I Am Not a Modernist,"
CDSP, Nov 16, 1966, 10-12, 39.  Modernism "expresses the domination of force
and the bare fact over clear thinking
and poetic perception of the world.
The cruel shattering of realistic
forms is the impulse of a blind, embittered will," akin to that of Nazi
despotism.  "There are good modernists"
- despite their technique - "but there
is no good modernism." - Debate of the
article by G. Pomerants, Leningrad
scholars, A. Dymshits, 'Literaturnaya
gazeta' and Lifshitz, CDSP, Apr 5,
1967, 12-17. - See also CDSP, Aug 16,
1967, 4.

LUNACHARSKY, Anatoli V, "Art and the
Four Stages Of Socialism," DWSup, Oct
16, 1926.  Example of his views criticized by Lenin: that Socialism is and
should be a secular 'religion' in
which man is to become God; in the
god-building process the artist is
given a prime role.

_____, "Appeal Of the People's Commis-
sary Of Education: To All Who Teach,"
CS, May-June 1918, 317-322.  Calls on
aloof intelligentsia to freely criti-

cize - and better, to cooperate with
Bolsheviks.

_____, Annual Report Of the Commissar Of
Education For the Year Ending Nov 7,
1918.  Lib, May 1919, 19-24.  Institutional changes in education and arts
made by Bolsheviks in first year in
power.  Discussion of difficulties en-
countered. - See also 1917-19 (XLI).

_____, Self-Education Of the Workers,
London, 1919.  7 pp.

_____, "Public Education In Soviet Rus-
sia," CI, #2 (June 1, 1919), 217-219;
#4 (Aug 1, 1919), 61-67.

_____, "Art Aims Of the Soviet Govern-
ment," Living Age, Oct 2, 1920, 21-23.
From organ of Commissariat of Art,
Dec 1919.  Art as instrument for en-
lightening rising masses.  Problems of
form and content in this perspective,
especially need to accept art of other
nations and of the past.

_____, "Revolutionary Education," WD,
Jan 8, 1921, 1-2.  Summation of
achievements after three years' effort.

_____, "Working-Class Culture," Plebs,
Oct 1920, 157-162; Nov 1920, 189-192.
Dated 1918.  "The culture of the coming
Socialism will be identical with the
culture of humanity as a whole.  But
the culture of the struggling proletariat is a highly-specialized class culture, fashioned in conflict.  It has
no time to bother about exact and perfect form.  Every class, like every
nation, having reached its blossoming
time, evolves a classical culture.
Every class, while striving to grow,
is romantic, and its romanticism takes
the typical forms of 'Storm and Stress'."

_____, "The Third International and the
Intellectual," CI, II #16-17 (1920),
81-84.  Winning intelligentsia's cooperation if not enthusiasm.

_____, Education Ministry Report For
1922.  Current History, XVIII (1923),
83-86.  abdgd.

_____, "Culture In the Soviet Republic,"
Manchester Guardian Commercial, Reconstruction In Europe Supplement, July
6, 1922, 240-242.  Assesses difficulties
and strides in Soviet mass education
and culture.

_____, Introduction, Public Education In the Russian Socialist Federation Of Soviet Republics, Moscow, 1926.

_____, Report On Cultural Attainments. DW, Dec 7, 1928, 6; Dec 8, 6. Implementing Lenin's thesis that "the low cultural level of the masses" was chief obstacle to Russian Socialism.

_____, Report On Educational Progress. SUR, July-Aug 1929, 116-117.

_____, "The Theatrical Situation In Soviet Russia In 1923," in: Huntly Carter, The New Theatre and Cinema Of Soviet Russia, London, 1924, 261-265.

_____, "Anatole France," DWSup, Nov 20, 1926, Obituary.

_____, "Lenin and Art," DWSup, Nov 27, 1926.

_____, "Art and Marxism," MQ(B), V (1928), 73-77.

_____, "Bernard Shaw, Our Guest," MN, July 23, 1931, 3; also in LM, Sept 1931, 580-582. First published in 'Izvestia', July 21, 1931, eve of Shaw's arrival in Moscow. Assesses balance between Shaw's "brilliance" and capriciousness which makes him scorn Bolshevik discipline.

_____, "Marxism and Art," NM, Nov 1932, 12-14.

_____, Interview with Ida Treat. MN, Apr 13, 1932, 1, 4. illus. Party's intention to draw fully upon culture of past for a brand-new culture.

_____, Interview with F. Yeats-Brown. Spectator, Dec 10, 1927, 1039-1040. Trotsky, NEP, the Geneva talks.

_____, "The Role Of Education In the Struggle With Religion," in: Jerome Davis, ed, Labor Speaks For Itself On Religion, 1929, 177-184.

_____, Stanislavsky's Misconceived 'Objectivity'. MN, May 9, 1931, 7.

_____, "Stanislavsky, the Theatre and the Revolution," ITh, 1933 #4, 26-28. Reprinted in IL, 1938 #10-11, 151-158. Also in: K. Stanislavsky, Progress Publishers, Moscow, n.d, 31-46. Written 1933. Stanislavsky early stated feeling of "much that is sacred and

profound" about the Revolution, also resistance to doing publicistic plays: "we are afraid that it will be a long time yet before this music of a new world finds expression in artistic language, in the art of drama. At least we have seen no indication yet."

_____, "Socialism and Human Culture," WA, May 28, 1932, 3. Interview with American journalist. Affirms policy of critical continuing assimilation of bourgeois cultural heritage.

_____, Introduction, The Little Golden Calf; A Satirical Novel by Ilya Ilf and Evgeni Petrov, 1932, xi-xix. Ungar paperback, 1961.

_____, "The Road Of Richard Wagner," SCR, 1933 #4, 35-37. Memorial essay salvaging Wagner for proletariat.

_____, "Problems Of Style In Socialist Art," ITh, #5 (1933), 3-7. illus. Bourgeois vs. socialist realism. Justifies introduction of Revolutionary Romanticism into Soviet art.

_____, "Gorky On His Forty Year Jubilee," V.O.K.S, 1932 #5-6, 72-80.

_____, "Byron and Byronism," IL, 1938 #1.

_____, "Lenin and Literature," IL, 1935 #1, 55-83. Against revisionists.

_____, "Problems Of Soviet Theatre; On Socialist Realism, Literature and the Theatre," IL, 1933 #3, 88-96. Speech to 2nd Plenary Session, Organization Committee Of All-Russian Union of Soviet Writers.

_____, "Bacon In Shakespearean Surroundings," IL, 1936 #1, 85-99. Also in SSU, 25-50. Excellent essay. Bacon, Richard III, Edmund, Iago, Jacques, Hamlet, Prospero.

_____, "On Dostoyevsky," IL, 1933 #5, 119-121. Critical.

_____, "Hauptmann: From Sunrise To Sunset," IL, 1933 #1, 72-76.

_____, "Ibsen," in: Angel Flores, ed, Henrik Ibsen, 1937, 7-19.

_____, "Basic Problems Of Art," IL, 1935 #12, 43-61. Rejecting strong strain of relativism in Plekhanov's essays, Lunacharsky insists values of a socialist

society should provide standard for
evaluating works of art.

_____, "Pushkin As a Critic," in:
Irving D.W. Talmadge, ed, Pushkin:
Homage By Marxist Critics, 1937,
51-63.

_____, Notes and Introduction, Selected
Works Of Art From the Fine Arts
Museum Of the USSR, Moscow, 1930.

_____, Introduction to Tolstoy's Anna
Karenina, translated by Constance
Garnett, Moscow: 1933.

_____, "The Role Of the Proletarian
State In the Development of Proletarian Culture," IL, 1934 #4, 111-117.
Speech to Institute of Philosophy of
the Communist Academy.

_____, "Samgin," SL, 1958 #12, 82-91.
Analysis of a chapter of the Gorky
novel.

_____, "On Socialist Realism," SL, 1966
#4, 139-142.  abdgd.

_____, On Literature and Art, Progress:
Moscow, 1965.  illus.  New but clumsy
translations of essays on Dostoevsky,
Gorky, Shakespeare, Wagner and Shaw
cited above; also his "Theses On the
Problems Of Marxist Criticism" (1928),
"Chernyshevsky's Ethics and Aesthetics"
(1928), essays on Pushkin (1922),
Taneyev and Scriabin (1925), Blok
(1932), Mayakovsky (1931), Polycletus
and Titian (1909), Swift (1930),
Heine (1931), Proust (1934), Renoir
(1933).

_____, SEE ALSO: R. Pelshe, "Lunacharsky
    - Art Critic and Dramatist,"
    ITh, #2 (1934), 8-10.  Summar-
    izes Lunacharsky's basic work
    'Foundations Of Positive Aes-
    thetics' (1903) noting insuffi-
    cient regard for class analysis.
    Point of this work is that
    "rhythm is the basis of aes-
    thetics in form."

    Louise Bryant, "A.V. Lunachar-
    sky and Russian Culture," in
    her Mirrors Of Moscow, 1923.

    Countess Alexandra Tolstoy, I
    Worked For the Soviet, New
    Haven: 1934.  Account of
    Lunacharsky's appointment of
    the daughter of Tolstoy to

make the Tolstoy estate  into
a museum.

Thomas H. Dickinson, "Anton Lunacharsky, Commissar Of Education," Sewanee Review, XXXI
(1923), 130-139.

Huntly Carter, "Lunacharsky's
Theatre," in his: The New
Theatre and Cinema Of Soviet
Russia, London, 1924.  Based
on conversations with Lunacharsky and articles not
available in English.

"The Pedagog Of Bolshevism,"
Current Opinion, Jan 1920,
45-46.  Lively account of
Lunacharsky's energetic pursuit of popular education.

Brent Don Allinson, "From the
Cultural Front In Russia,"
The Dial, Sept 1928, 239-245.
First-hand account of Lunacharsky's visit to an art
show for censoring purposes.
Includes written answers to
questions on popular education.

Nikolai Bukharin, "A Brilliant
Talent - A.V. Lunacharsky,"
MN, Jan 6, 1934, 13.  Obituary
assessment citing political
failings but concluding:  "He
was indeed a 'Hellene', if
Heine's terminology may be
used."

Rose Pastor Stokes, "Bread and
Roses," Ohio Socialist, Nov
19, 1919, 4.  Typifies early
US enthusiasm for Bolshevik
attention to cultural as well
as social institutions.

Pavel Buzayenko, "Outstanding
Literary Critic," SL, 1958
#12, 75-81.  Informative.

Kornei Chukovsky, "Lunacharsky,"
SL, 1965 #11, 154-162.  illus.
Lively eyewitness account of
his busy days in 1918.

Alexander Lebedev, On the Issuing of Lunacharsky's Collected
Works.  SL, 1964 #9, 186-188.
Appraisal of their value and
of the treatment of Lunacharsky's heritage during the

Stalin period.

A. Yermakov, "Revolutionary
Talent," <u>CDSP</u>, June 7, 1967,
6-7.  From 'Izvestia'.  Estimate of Lunacharsky's contribution and of the above
8-volume selection of his
aesthetic and critical writing, which, Yermakov says, is
invaluable but very incomplete.

LUNDBERG, Eugene, "The Dialectical Development Of Thomas Mann," <u>Dia</u>, #2 (1937),
23-31.

MAKAROV, A, "Thoughts On Evgenii Yevtushenko's Long Poem," <u>SSL</u>, Summer 1966,
3-57.  Critique of the form and content in "The Bratsk Hydroelectric
Station".

MALINOWSKY, R. Ya, "Glorify the Heroic,"
<u>CDSP</u>, Feb 26, 1964, 3-6.  The Minister
of Defense at meeting with writers and
artists held at Central House of the
Soviet Army, Feb 7, 1964, warns
against "pacifist" tendencies and declares: "Our greatest desire is that
the traditions of heroic-patriotic
literature and the arts be carefully
preserved and developed in the future."

MARSHAK, Samuel, "About Myself," <u>SL</u>,
1965 #1, 57-63. - See also: Vera
Smirnov on Marshak, <u>SL</u>, 1963 #4, 119-
123.

_____, "Writing Never Gets Any Easier,"
<u>SSL</u>, Summer 1965, 73-88.  His last
critical statement, on poetics.

MAYAKOVSKY, Vladimir, "How One Writes A
Poem," <u>Living Age</u>, Oct 1933, 148-155.
Also in <u>AQSU</u>, III i (July, 1940), 3-
12.  abdgd.  "Poetry begins with
tendency."

_____, Summary of Chicago Speech, Oct 2,
1925.  <u>DW</u>, Oct 5, 1925, 2.  Contrasts
publics for poetry in the USSR and US.

_____, Stenograph of Speech On Opening
Of 1930 Exhibition Of His Work.  In:
Herbert Marshall, ed <u>Mayakovsky</u>, Hill
& Wang: 1965, 399-410.  Explains and
defends himself.

_____, SEE ALSO: Articles by Victor Pert-
sov, Suren Gaisaryan, Nikolai
Asayev, Alexander Deineka, Bole-
slav Rostotsky, Arnold Sokhor,
Alexander Ushakov. <u>SL</u>, 1963 #7,
142-180.

S. Mstislavsky, "Vladimir Mayakovsky," <u>V.O.K.S</u>, 1930 #6-7,
19-25.  illus.  Vice President
of Soviet Writers Union assesses threads in Mayakovsky's
life and work which help explain his suicide. Bibliography.

L. Averbach, "The Speed Of Self-
Disclosure," <u>LWR</u>, 1931 #2,
100-105.  Defines the suicide
as personal failure to adopt
to new ways.  Rejects Trotsky's view (see Trotsky).

Maxim Strauch, Reminiscences of
Mayakovsky.  <u>C&L</u>, 1957 #9-10,
63-67.  illus.

Lev Kassil, "An Evening With
Mayakovsky," <u>Life and Letters
Today</u>, Autumn 1937, 70-74.
Blow-by-blow account of how
Mayakovsky handled the crowd
at a poetry reading.

Also in: Herbert Marshall, ed,
<u>Mayakovsky</u>, Hill & Wang: 1965,
415-420.

N. Kalma, "Reminiscences," <u>MN</u>,
Apr 15, 1936, 3, 11.

Michael Gold, Reminiscences.
<u>DW</u>, Aug 20, 1940, 7; Aug 22,
7; Aug 24, 7; Aug 27, 7.
Written for Soviet memorial
volume.  See also his description of an evening at Mayakovsky's, "Aragon: Poet-
Organizer," <u>M&M</u>, May 1950,11-24.

Joseph Freeman, <u>An American
Testament</u>, 1936.  Glimpses of
Mayakovsky in New York and
Moscow.

Kornei Chukovsky, "Mayakovsky,"
<u>SL</u>, 1967 #2, 159-163.  Vivid
early memoir.

Alexander Kaun, "Vladimir Mayakovsky," <u>AQSU</u>, Jan 1939, 3-22.

Lev Nikulin, "At the Top Of the
Human Voice: A Story Of the
Great Soviet Poet Mayakovsky,"
<u>IL</u>, 1933 #3, 19-27.  Well-
written account of his career.

L. Pazhitnov and B. Shragin,
"Poet Of the Revolution and
Our Times," <u>WMR</u>, Sept 1963,
42-50.

Herbert Marshall, Mayakovsky,
Hill & Wang: 1965. illus.
Best collection of the poems,
with extended commentary on
the poems and the poet's
life. With views of Maya-
kovsky by Lenin, Lunacharsky,
Lev Kassil, B. Pasternak, N.
Aseyev, A. Akhmatova, Y.
Yevtushenko.

See also: Lavrov (XLVIII);
Eastman (XLIX); Bowra (LXII).
Lenin, Lunacharsky (above).

MEILAKH, Boris, "It Is High Time To Take
Up Questions Of Aesthetics," Soviet
Press Translations, III xx (Nov 15,
1948), 633-635. Signals a purge in
aesthetics.

_____, "The Psychology Of Literary Crea-
tion," SR, I iv (Nov 1960), 13-30.
abdgd. From 'Voprosy Literatury',
1960 #6. Pavlovian view of writer as
projecting images and emotions through
a method of search and trial-and-
error guided "in the last analysis...
by a definite aim to which all his re-
writes and variations are subjected.
To verbalize that aim is the re-
searcher's chief difficulty."

MENDELSON, Moris, Soviet Interpretation
Of Contemporary American Literature,
Public Affairs Press: Washington,
1948. mimeo. Author-by-author dis-
cussion of progress and reaction in
US post-war writing.

_____, The Modern American Novel
[Summary], SL, 1965 #8, 174-178. S.
Lewis, Hemingway, Faulkner, Steinbeck,
Maltz, etc.

METALLOV, Yakov, "The Hero and the Crowd
In Lion Feuchtwanger's Novels," IL,
1937 #5, 84-93.

METCHENKO, A, A. Dementiev, G. Lomidze,
"New Tasks For Soviet Literary Historians," SL, 1957 #1, 150-158. Instances of how the "personality cult"
proved "extremely detrimental to
Soviet Literature." - See also
Zekulin (XLIX).

_____, Lenin and Partisanship in the
Arts. C&L, 1966 #4, 19-21.

_____, "Facts and Prejudiced Opinions:
Notes About Literary Memoirs," CDSP,
Feb 16, 1966, 14-17. Caution against

glamorizing the arts before Stalin.

MIEZELAITIS, Eduardas, "Lyrical Studies"
SL, 1966 #4, 3-37. The Lithuanian
poet, a Lenin prizewinner, discusses
poetics and his development.

MIKHAILOV, Oleg, "The Literature Of the
1920s," SL, 1967 #1, 137-146.

MILLER-BUDNITSKAYA, R, "James Joyce's
'Ulysses'," Dia, #5 (1938), 6-26.

MIRSKY, Dmitri S, A History Of Russian
Literature From Its Beginnings To 1900,
Knopf: 1949; Vintage paperback, 1958.
Edited by Francis J. Whitfield from two
previous books by Mirsky: A History Of
Russian Literature From the Earliest
Times To the Death Of Dostoyevsky (1881),
1927; Contemporary Russian Literature,
1881-1925, 1926. Of the latter work
only the first two chapters are incorporated. The entire History was written before Prince Mirsky's conversion
to Marxism and the omitted chapters on
1917-1925 are anti-Bolshevik.

_____, "The Soviet Russian Novel," in:
H. Walpole et al, eds, Tendencies Of
the Modern Novel, London, 1934.

_____, "James Joyce," IL, 1934 #1, 92-102.

_____, "Joyce and Irish Literature," NM,
Apr 3, 1934, 31-34.

_____, "The Philosophical Discussions In
the CPSU In 1930-31," Comm, Nov 1931,
933-940. Philosophy and the Five Year
Plan.

_____, The Intelligentsia Of Great Brit-
ain, London, 1935. Mirsky was several
years in British exile. Prominently
treats Shaw, Wells, Butler, Huxley,
Lawrence, et al. - Discussed critically
by Alick West, LR, May 1935, 324-328.

- Review by T.A. Jackson, DW(L), May 15,
1935, 4.

_____, "H.G. Wells and History,"
Criterion, Oct 1932, 1-9.

_____, "Two Fruitful Years In the Devel-
opment Of Soviet Literature," MN, Aug
18, 1934, 4, 6. The promulgation of
Socialist Realism.

_____, "Aragon Arrives," Living Age, Mch
1935, 66-70. From 'Literaturnaia
Gazeta'. Review of 'Les Cloches de

Bale'.

_____, "Whitman, Poet Of American Democracy," in: Gay Wilson Allen, ed, _Walt Whitman Abroad_, Syracuse: 1955, 169-185; a less adequate translation in _Dia_, #1, 11-29.

_____, SEE ALSO: Edmund Wilson, "Comrade Prince; A Memoir of D.S. Mirsky," _En_, July 1955, 10-20.

MITIN, G, "Socialist Realism and Its Problems," _SSL_, Fall 1965, 73-80. Debates merits of critical study by V. Ivanov.

MJASNIKOW, A, "Lenin and the Problem Of Literature," _SL_, #19 (1949), 107-116.

MOROZOV, Mikhail, "On the Dynamism Of Shakespeare's Characters," _SSU_, 84-112. From 1954. 'King Lear', 'Romeo and Juliet', 'Hamlet'.

MOTYLEVA, T, "Thomas Mann and His Novels," _SSL_, Winter 1964-65, 23-49. Survey of Mann's reception in USSR; the roles of irony and realism in some major novels.

NARVSKI, A, "Some Writers Are Made," _LA_, Oct 1938, 166-169.

NECHKINA, M, "Shakespeare In Karl Marx's 'Capital'," _IL_, 1935 #3, 75-81. Falstaff as a new bourgeois.

NEDOSHIVIN, G, "On the Relation Of Art To Reality," _V.O.K.S_, 1951 #66, 66-75. Admirably concise resume of Soviet aesthetics at the time.

NIKILYUKIN, A, "Forgotten Pages Of English Poetry," _Anglo-Soviet Journal_, Autumn 1958, 13-19. Workers' verse from the broadsheets, etc, of 18th and early 19th Century.

NIKOLAEV, M.P, "On the Highroad Of Realistic Literature," _SSL_, Summer 1965, 3-24. The literary works of Chernyshevsky: the generally accepted view of him "as a rationalist is valid only for 'What Is To Be Done?', and even then only with qualifications."

NOVICHENCKO, Leonid, "A Man, A Communist," _SL_, 1963 #8, 138-146. Problems of developing literary universality in a Communist context. Avoidance of both parochialism and abstract universality.

NOVITSKY, Pavel, _Cervantes and Don Quixote_, 1936. 32 pp. Excerpts in: Angel Flores and M.J. Bernardete, eds, _Cervantes Across the Centuries_, 1947, 239-245.

NUSINOV, I. See 1936 (XLI).

OBRETENOV, A, "The Wealth Of Life - The Wealth Of Art," _WMR_, Oct 1960, 23-31. "The art of socialist realism is an infinite variety of personalities" and "alien to narrowness and dogmatic restriction." Aragon, Brecht, Neruda, Tvardovsky, Eluard.

OKHLOPKOV, Nikolai, "From the Producer's Exposition Of 'Hamlet'," _SSU_, 182-203. From 1955. A leading director on the continuing relevance of Hamlet as fighter against hypocrisy and inequity.

OLESHA, Yuri. See 'Culture' (V); 1936 (XLI).

ORLOV, V.N, "Alexander Blok," _SL_, 1964 #9, 146-153.

OZEROV, V, "Youthful Emotions, Mature Thinking," _SSL_, Winter 1964-65, 91-110. Problems and outlook of the young generation of writers.

PALIEVSKY, Pyotr, "Word and Image," _SL_, 1960 #5, 112-123. From 'Voprosy Literaturny', 1959 #11. Art, imagination, essentially different from life; they dissolve facts and follow their own laws.

_____, "Documentary Material In Contemporary Literature," _SL_, 1967 #5, 134-141. Analysis of the growing demand for fact in literature.

PANFEROV, "Literature and Life," _DW_, Mch 14, 1934, 7. abdgd. Speech to 17th Congress, CPSU. Describes energizing effect of Stalin's "directives" upon his work: "I am one of the happy people, comrades, for I have seen the country."

PASTERNAK, Boris. See 1958 (XLI); Carlisle, Conquest (XLIX); also "Impressions Of Boris Pasternak," _New Reasoner_, #4, 86-90. Intimate glimpse of Pasternak's feeling for relation of politics and literature.

PAUSTOVSKY, Konstantin, _The Story Of a_

Life, Pantheon: 1964.

_____, Autobiographical Remarks, with an Appreciation by Sergei Lvov. V.O.K.S, Jan 1956, 19-24.

_____, "The Drozdovs," in: Hugh McLean and N. Vickery, eds, The Year Of Protest 1956, 1961, 155-160. Speech to Prose Section, Moscow Writers Union, Oct 22, 1956. Defends Dudintsev's 'Not By Bread Alone'. Followed by L. Sobolev, "Millions Are Listening," pp. 160-163, which demands recantation from Dudintsev.

_____, "Ideas - Disputable and Indisputable," CDSP, July 1, 1959, 9-11; also SH, Aug 1959, 15-18. Speech to 3rd Writers Congress.

PETRIKOVSKAYA, Alla, "Henry Lawson and the Soviet Reader," SL, 1967 #7, 171-173. The Australian novelist.

PINSKY, Leonid, "The Essence Of the Comic In Shakespeare's Works," SL, 1964 #3, 146-157.

PISKUNOV, Vladimir, Soviet Wartime Literature. SL, 1967 #5, 125-133.

PITLYAR, I, "The 'Trifles' Of Everyday Life In Literature," SS, July 1953, 79-84. Critique of bloodlessness in some contemporary literature.

PLAVSKIN, Z, Cervantes In the Soviet Union. C&L, 1966 #4, 42-45.

PLEKHANOV, George, Art and Social Life, Lawrence & Wishart paperback: London, 1953. "Art and Social Life," "Letters Without Address," "French Dramatic Literature and French Eighteenth Century Painting From the Sociological Standpoint" in good translations. Aesthetic sense, primitive arts, art for art's sake, Baudelaire, Belinsky, Bogdanov, Byron, Chernyshevsky, class taste, Classicism and Romanticism, Corneille, Cubism, David, Musset, Stael, Vigny, Diderot, Dobrolyubov, Dumas, Eyre, Flaubert, Formalism, Gautier, Goncourt, Gorky, Greek art and literature, Greuze, E. Grosse, Hamsun, Hippius, Hugo, Huysmans, Impressionists, Kant, Lamartine, LeBrun, Leconte de Lisle, DaVinci, Lunacharsky, Michaelangelo, Moliere, Music origins, mysticism in art, Naturalism, Nekrassov, Nietzsche, Ostrovsky, Pisarev, Poetry origins, Pope, Poussin, Pushkin, Racine, Raphael, Realism, Ruskin, Sand, Sainte-Beuve, Sentimental comedy, Shakespeare, Taine, Tolstoy, Tragedy, Dramatic unities, Turgenev, Uspensky, Utilitarian view of art, Venus de Milo, Voltaire, Wagner, Zola. - Early publications in English of these Plekhanov essays: "Materialism and Art," MQ(B), Spring 1924, 68-77; Summer, 70-77. This is the first Letter Without Address. Excerpts from 'Monist View Of History' and "French Dramatic Literature" also appeared in MQ(B) during 20s. "Art and Social Life" in The New Act, Apr 1934, 123-155; and in LWR, 1931 #2, 85-99; 1931 #3, 80-99, with note offering Leninist provisos to Plekhanov's theses; and (together with "French Dramatic Literature") in Art and Society, 1936, introduction by G. Hicks. "Historical Materialism and the Arts" (Letter Without Address #1) in Dia, #3 (1937), 8-29; #4, 25-31. abdgd.

_____, "Notes For a Lecture: French Dramatic Literature and Painting In the 18th Century," International Review (New York), Aug 1936, 112-14. Of interest in relation to above.

_____, Unaddressed Letters. Art and Social Life, Moscow, 1957. With notes. See above.

_____, Fundamental Problems Of Marxism, 1929, 42-49; 59-64; 72-77. Primitive arts, class struggle in Greek and French culture, Taine, French Romantics.

_____, Essays In the History Of Materialism, London, 1934.

_____, "Ibsen, Petty Bourgeois Revolutionist," in: Angel Flores, ed, Henrik Ibsen, 1937, 35-92. Splendid study of the plays, decadence, symbolism. Apparently the first of Plekhanov's aesthetic studies to appear in English, the work was published in a translation by N. Weiser in Daily People, Sunday editions, Feb 20-Apr 3, 1910.

_____, "Nekrassov and Russian Society," IL, 1938 #2, 50-54.

_____, SEE ALSO: Lifshitz, Lunacharsky, Rosenthal (XLVI); Baxandall (LVI); and:
A. Lunacharsky, "Analyzing Plekhanov's Views on Art," IL, 1935 #11, 43-61.

Leon Dennen, "Plechanov and the Marxian Approach To Art," <u>The Left</u> (Davenport, Ia.), I ii (1931), 65-69. Cites emphasis on aesthetics and relativity. Attacks "economic" approach of "the majority of American 'Marxist' critics."

Burton Rubin, "Plekhanov and Soviet Literary Criticism," <u>American Slavonic and East European Review</u>, Dec 1956, 527-542. How Plekhanov's pioneering work largely dominated Soviet aesthetics until 1931 when a campaign for 'Leninist' theory eclipsed him.

Samuel H. Baron, <u>Plekhanov</u>, Stanford paperback: 1963, 307-316.

POLIANSKY, Valerian, "The Banner Of the 'Prolet-Cult'," <u>Plebs</u>, Jan 1921, 3-6. Poliansky was Chairman of the Central Committee of All-Russian Council of Proletarian Culture.

POLONSKY, Vyacheslav, "Lenin's Views Of Art and Culture," in: Max Eastman, <u>Artists In Uniform</u>, 1934, 217-252. abdgd. From 'Outline Of the Literary Movement Of the Revolutionary Epoch'.

POMERANTSEV, V, "Sincerity In Literature," <u>CDSP</u>, Mch 17, 1954, 3-9; Mch 24, 3-7, 22; also in <u>SS</u>, Apr 1954, 434-445. abdgd. From 'Novy Mir', 1953 #12. Vigorous attack on artificiality in Soviet writing. - For attacks on Pomerantsev, see: L. Skorino, <u>SS</u>, July 1954, 93-97; V. Vasilevsky in "Literaturnaya Gazeta', <u>CDSP</u>, Mch 24, 1954, 8-9; Alexei Surkov for the Soviet Writers Union, <u>SS</u>, Oct 1954, 180-186, also <u>CDSP</u>, June 23, 1954, 3-5, 15. Several students at Moscow University objected to Vasilevsky, <u>CDSP</u>, Mch 31, 1954, 3-4.

RADEK, Karl, "Homeless Artists," <u>WM</u>, Sept 1926, 514-516. Also in <u>Plebs</u>, Nov 1926, 392-395. From 'Pravda', June 16, 1926. Discusses suicides of Essinen and Sobol. Concludes "you cannot be an onlooker in the USSR today....the Soviet writer must make a step forward, a step toward Communism."

_____, "Contemporary World Literature and the Tasks Of Proletarian Art," <u>PSL</u>, 73-184. illus. Detailed treatment of progressive and reactionary writers in West, e.g, Germany. Demands choice: James Joyce or Socialist Realism.

ROSENTHAL, Mark, "Relative vs. Absolute Criteria In Art," <u>Dia</u>, #8 (1938), 15-24. Discussion and rejection of Plekhanov's "relativist" conception of a scientific aesthetics. Lenin's 'Materialism and Empirio-Criticism' is Rosenthal's authority. - Discussion by C. Weinstock (C. Humboldt), Louis Harap, Jack Lindsay, <u>Dia</u>, #9.

ROZHDESTVENSKY, Vsevolod, "The Petrograd House Of Arts," <u>SL</u>, 1965 #6, 119-136. Early days of Soviet literature recollected.

RYURIKOV, Yuri, "The Artistic Image," <u>SL</u>, 1960 #6, 127-138. From 'Voprosy Literatury', 1959 #5. Relation of linguistics and imagination.

_____, "The Individual, Art, and Science," <u>SSL</u>, Spring 1965, 3-40. Review and critique of Soviet aesthetics after 1955. The neglected application of aesthetics to society; the subject-matter and methodology unique to art and to aesthetics. - See also comment on this essay by V. Nezhdanov, ibid, 41-51.

SAMARIN, R. M, "Our Closeness To Shakespeare," <u>Shakespeare Survey</u>, #16 (1963), 10-17.

[SAMARIN, Roman, and Alexander Nikolyukin, compilers,] <u>Shakespeare In the Soviet Union; A Collection Of Articles</u>, Progress: Moscow, 1966. illus. A. Blok, A. Lunacharsky, I. Aksyonov, A. Smirnov, M. Morozov, A. Anikst, I. Anisimov, K. Stanislavsky, A. Ostuzhev, A. Popov, G. Ulanova, I. Smoktunovsky, N. Okhlopkov, G. Kozintsev, contributors.

SATZ, I. See 1936 (XLI).

SHCHERBAKOV, Boris, "The President Of the Academy Of Arts," <u>C&L</u>, 1964 #10, 24-25. illus. On Vladimir Serov.

SHCHERBINA, V, "Intellectuality or Abstractness?" <u>SSL</u>, Winter 1964-65, 77-90. Takes issue with essay by V. Dneprov, "The Intellectual Novel Of

Thomas Mann," which holds that literature in the modern age must "graft" a
"second level" of reflection onto the
primary realism of imagery.  Writers
like Brecht, Aragon, Mayakovsky
"forced their way out of speculative-
ness to the artistic assimilation of
real life."

SHESTAKOV, Dmitri, On Iris Murdoch.  SL,
1966 #7, 169-175.

SERAFIMOVITCH, Alexander, "Literary
Criticism By the Masses," DW, Apr 19,
1927, 6.  Account of typical exchange
with workers.

SHEPILOV, D.  See 1957 (XLI).

SHOLOKHOV, Mikhail, Interview.  LR, Mch
1935, 193-194.

_____, Interview with Isaac Eksler.  IL,
1939 #4-5, 108-113; reprinted in DW,
Feb 9, 1940, 7; Feb 10, 7.  Sholokhov
describes his creative method at
length.

_____, Tribute to Zhdanov.  V.O.K.S,
1948 #55, 9-10.  Warm appreciation of
Zhdanov's love, devotion, encouragement, and also his "destructive sar-
casm," his "annihilating contempt and
hatred" in attacking "everything out-
worn and alien."

_____, Speech to 2nd Soviet Writers Con-
gress.  CDSP, Apr 6, 1955, 18-20.
Sharp comment on low standards achieved
by novelists (he names Simonov and Ehrenburg) which he charges to the writers rather than Party interventions.
- Various objections to the speech appear in succeeding issues of CDSP.

_____, Speech to 20th Congress, CPSU.
CDSP, Apr 25, 1956, 20-23.  Outspoken
comment on "disastrous" condition of
Soviet literature and failure of
writers to live among workers and
peasants.

_____, Speech to 22nd Congress, CPSU.
SR, Mch 1962, 33-39.  Ironically
urges writers to leave city comforts.

_____, Speech To 23rd Congress Of the
Communist Party Of the U.S.S.R., Moscow, April 1, 1966.  N.Y. Times, Apr
2, 1966, 4.  abdgd. Denounces Russians
and foreigners who condemned sentencing of writers Sinyavsky and Daniel.

_____, One Man's Destiny; And Other
Stories, Articles and Sketches 1923-
1963, Knopf: 1967.  Contains some of
above materials, and some additional.

_____, SEE ALSO: Hsiang Hung: 1966 (X);
Krushchev (XLVI); Carlisle,
Simmons (XLIX); and:

   V. Hoffenshefer, "Mikhail
   Sholokhov," V.O.K.S, Nov-Dec
   1940, 68-71.  illus.  Useful
   biographical, historical facts.

   Irina Sozonova, "Man and the
   Course Of History," SR, Spring
   1963, 72-81.  Analysis of
   'The Quiet Don' as epic writing.

   Viktor Gura, "New Material On
   Mikhail Sholokhov," SSL, Fall
   1965, 3-26.  Analyzes early
   writings, cites unpublished
   letters, describes editorial
   mutilation of the early work.

   Edward J. Brown, "Sholokhov and
   the Nobel Prize," Nation, Aug
   22, 1966, 160-164.  His excellence as shaped by Marxist
   modernist and proletarian
   theory of the 1920s.

SIMONOV, Konstantin, "On Ilya Ehrenburg's
New Novel," SS, Jan 1955, 290-298.
Attacking 'The Thaw'.  Ehrenburg's
reply SS, 298-302.  For attack by 'Komsomolskaya pravda', see CDSP, June 30,
1955, 5-6.

_____, Speech to 2nd Soviet Writers Con-
gress.  CDSP, Mch 2, 1955, 10-15. abdgd.

_____, "Make No Mistake About It," SL,
1964 #10, 151-156.  From 'Pravda' of
May 24.  Position on Sino-Soviet Debate.

_____, Interview With Gunter Grass and
Uwe Johnson.  En, Jan 1965, 88-91.

_____, SEE ALSO: Galina Drobot on Simon-
ov, SL, 1964 #9, 140-145. -
Biographical note, SL, 1965 #12,
157-162.

SINYAVSKY, Andrei, "Tract Or Libel?" CDSP,
Mch 31, 1965, 14-17.  Analyzes a novel
that attacks greater creative scope to
realism, Shevtsov's "The Plant Louse".
- See also: Golomshtok (XLIII).

_____, [writing under pseudonym of Abram Tertz], On Socialist Realism, 1960. Sections also published in ULR, Autumn 1959, 57-67; and in Dis, Winter 1960, 39-66. - Review by Boris Ryurikov, SL, 1962 #9, 145-148. Troubled by the "theology" of Revolutionary Romanticism, rejects most Socialist Realism as not genuinely realist. - For the trial and sentencing of Sinyavsky as result of publishing this and other works abroad, see 1966 (XLI).

SMIRNOV, A.A, Shakespeare: A Marxist Interpretation, 1936. 96 pp. Excerpts in: Norman Rabkin, ed, Approaches To Shakespeare, McGraw-Hill paperback: 1964, 160-171. Analysis of the plays. "Shakespeare is the humanist ideologist of the bourgeoisie of the time." - Review by Bernard Grebanier, NTh, Sept 1936, 9. Controversy over the book between Milton Howard and Morris U. Schappes, NM, Sept 15, Sept 29, Oct 6, 1936.

_____, "Shakespeare, the Renaissance and the Age Of Barroco," SSU, 58-83. A tragic humanism based on historically unrealizable ideals.

SOKOLOW, Y.M, Russian Folklore, 1950.

SOVIET WRITERS REPLY TO ENGLISH WRITERS' QUESTIONS, ed. Edgell Rickword, The Writers Group; Society for Cultural Relations With the USSR, London, 1948. Prefaces by J.B. Priestley and Konstantin Simonov. For English participants, see (XXIII). Values and working conditions of Soviet authors. USSR participants: S. Marshak, M. Shaginyan, G. Mdivani, N. Tikhonov, P. Antokolsky, M. Issakovsky, I. Satz, K. Zelinsky, A. Leites, V. Yan, A. Isbach, V. Inber, D. Zaslavsky, T. Motyleva, L. Leonov, S. Mikhalkov, C. Fedin, V. Kozhevnikov, M. Morosov.

STALIN, Josef, On Culture. IL, 1939 #12, 84-117. Compilation of texts by Timofei Rokotov. Speaks with fervor about need to raise general USSR cultural levels. Also collected literary allusions from speeches. Testimonies by Stanislavsky, Eisenstein, etc, to Stalin's cultural interests. - See also E. Makarova, "Stalin On Folklore," V.O.K.S, 1945 #6, 37-39. Instances where Stalin is said to have advised artists, composers, and writers to employ folk themes and traditions. - Also Jelagin (XLIX).

_____, Marxism and Linguistics, 1951. Introduction by Margaret Schlauch. Also in PA, Sept 1950, 37-60; for the entire debate, see 1950 (XLI). A polemic against the theory of N.Y. Marr that held the Russian language to be superstructural; it has, says Stalin, been "preserved in all essentials" while Tsarist institutions were "supplanted by new, Socialist institutions."

STETSKY, A.I, "Under the Flag Of the Soviets, Under the Flag of Socialism," PSL, 261-273. illus. Propaganda chief of the CC at 1st Soviet Writers Congress.

STOLYAROV, A, "Freudism and 'Freudo-Marxists'," LWR, 1931 #1, 90-99. A polemic.

SUBBOTIN, A.L, "Shakespeare and Bacon," SR, Fall 1964, 3-13. Comparison of social views of leading scientist and playwright of an epoch.

SUCHKOV, B, "The Fate Of an Artist [Thomas Mann]," in: Charles Neider, ed, The Stature Of Thomas Mann, 1947, 495-501. Development of Mann into an anti-fascist.

_____, "Kafka: His Fate and Work," SSL, Spring 1966, 10-46; Summer 1966, 58-93. The "loss of contact with reality" in his writings. - See also: "Kafka's Work In the Estimation Of Soviet Critics," SL, 1965 #5, 141-148.

SURKOV, Alexei, "Some Problems In the Development Of Soviet Literature," SS, Oct 1952, 202-205. abdgd. From 'Bolshevik'.

SUROVTSEV, Yuri, with N. Dzhusoity, Y. Zinger, G. Lomidze, I. Braginsky, "The Theory Of National Culture - A Discussion," CDSP, May 5, 1965, 12-16. Relation of nation to psychology and aesthetics.

TIMOFEEV, L. I., "Karl Marx On Literature," IL, 1943 #13, 63-66.

_____, A Short Dictionary Of Scholarly Literary Terms. abdgd. In: Rufus W. Mathewson, Jr, The Positive Hero In Russian Literature, Columbia Univ; 1958, 325-334.

TOLMACHEV, M.V, "Impressionist-Classicist Tensions In Proust," in: YFR, #34 (1965), 29-35. Philosophical and artistic basis of Proust's style. The

mixture of idealist and progressive
elements: "an inconsistent but never-
theless noticeable realistic tendency
appears in the depiction of French
reality."

TRETYAKOV, Sergei, "Writers, To the Collective Farms!" V.O.K.S, Jan 1931, 85-
87. His enthusiasm for 'literature of
fact' based on intensive on-the-job
experience.

_____, "John Hartfield," IL, 1932 #1,
103-106. illus.

_____, "Bert Brecht," IL, 1937 #5, 60-
70. Also in Peter Demetz, ed, Brecht;
A Collection Of Critical Essays,
Spectrum paperback: Englewood Cliffs,
N.J, 1962, 16-29. - For essay on Hanns
Eisler, see Eisler (XXI).

_____, Autobiography. IL, 1933 #1,
129-132.

TRIFONOVA, Tamara, "Soviry Literature
In the Thirties," SL, 1967 #3, 145-
154. abgd.

TROSCHENKO, E, "Marx On Literature,"
IL, 1934 #6, 138-148. Reconciling
Marx on Balzac with a Party literature.

TROTSKY, Leon, "Gogol: An Anniversary
Tribute," in: Irving Howe, ed, The
Basic Writings Of Trotsky, Random
House: 1963, 317-324. Written 1902.
Gogol "the father of Russian comedy
and the Russian novel" and first to
create literature from real Russian
types. Conjectures why this became
possible.

_____, "Tolstoy, Poet and Rebel," FI,
May-June 1951, 90-95. Written Sept
1908. "Though he refuses a sympathetic hearing to our revolutionary
objectives, we know it is because
history has refused him personally an
understanding of her revolutionary
pathways. We shall not condemn him."
Analysis of his awareness.

_____, "A Drama Of the French Working
Class," LM, Aug 1922, 73-84. Review
of 'La Nuit' (Paris, 1922) by Marcel
Martinet. Praises correspondence of
artistic to historical truth. Despite pessimism of final act the play
offers "stern forewarning" to workers
against repetition of errors of the
past and calls for "inner purifica-
tion, increased unity, and discipline."

_____, Literature and Revolution, Russell
& Russell paperback: 1957; also, Ann
Arbor paperback: 1960. Pre-revolutionary culture, Populist writing, Kliuev,
Essenin, Serapions, Pilnyak, Blok,
Futurism, Formalist poetics, Shklovsky,
Proletarian literature as an impossibility, Bedny, Party policy, art in
social change, revolutionary realism,
comedy, tragedy, Hippius, Zamyatin,
Moscow Art Theatre, Versilov, Biely,
poetry and meaning, Psychologism, Fellow-travellers, Class and art, Ivanov,
Nikitin, Chukovsky, Shaginyan, Shakespeare, Martinet, Symbolism, Soviet
theatre and architecture, Tatlin, Lip-
shitz. - For reception in the USSR, see:
Isaac Deutscher, The Prophet Unarmed,
1959, 198-200. - See also: T.S. Eliot,
"A Commentary," Criterion, Jan 1933,
244-249. Deems Trotsky "a man of
first-rate intelligence, expressing
himself in a rough and ready metaphori-
cal style, and he utters a good deal
of common sense." Thoughtful remarks
on possibility of a proletarian literature. - See also: Michael Gold,"America
Needs a Critic," NM, Oct 1926, 7-9.
Calls book "an amazing performance.
This man is almost as universal as
Leonardo da Vinci." Disagrees that a
proletarian literature cannot develop.
- Earl Browder, in a letter to V.F.
Calverton, agreed with Trotsky about
proletarian literature. See Daniel
Aaron, Writers On the Left, 1961, 424,
note 19. - Moissaye J. Olgin lauded
the book in Comm, Jan 1926, 138-140. -
A. Kirpotin, "Trotsky On Literature,"
IL, 1932 #1, 81-87, polemicizes against
Trotsky from the evolved USSR position.
- S. Sillen also condemns Trotsky, "A
False Approach To Art," DW, Aug 22,
1946, 11. - Review by Charles Ashleigh,
SW, Nov 1, 1925, 8. - Review by V.F.
Calverton, MQ(B), III i (1925), 78-79.
- See Steiner (LIX).

_____, "Class and Art; Problems Of Cul-
ture Under the Dictatorship Of the
Proletariat," Fourth International
(London), July 1967, 51-60. Transcript
of discussion on May 9, 1924, with Var-
din, Raskolnikov, Pletnev, Averbach,
Libedinsky, who reject Trotsky's arguments against the rise of a proletarian
literature. Dante, Bedny, Voronsky,
Mayakovsky, Pilniak. Lenin's view.

_____, "Habit and Custom," in his:
Problems Of Life, London: 1924, 22-33.
Art "by nature, is conservative" and
fails to come to grips with problems of

changing Soviet reality, while the
Party is far ahead; but the Party can
learn from an art that would show
"life as it has emerged from the revolutionary oven"; thus "a proper
organization" of writers is required.

_____, "Vodka, The Church and the Cine-
ma," in his: Problems Of Life, London:
1924, 34-43.  Calls for "fusion of the
socialist State and the cinema" to re-
reinforce and compensate the separation
of Church from State.

_____, "The Family and Ceremony," in his:
Problems Of Life, London: 1924, 62-69.
"Revolutionary symbolism" to take the
place of Church "theatrical ceremonies
....The need for an outer manifesta-
tion of emotion is strong and legitimate", as in funerals, weddings.

_____, "Culture and Socialism," Labour
Review, Autumn 1962, 101-113.  Also in
Isaac Deutscher, ed, The Age Of Per-
manent Revolution: A Trotsky Anthology,
Dell Laurel paperback: 1964, 303-314.
The relation of socialism to previous
culture; the cognitive component of
art.

_____, "On the Death Of a Poet [Essinen],"
NM, June 1926, 18, 30.  Essinen a
lyric poet in a time ill fitted for
lyricism.

_____, "The suicide Of Vladimir Maya-
kovsky," The Militant (New York),
June 7, 1930, 7.  Briefly recounts
detrimental effects on his work of
excessive Party demands and concludes
fellow-travellers should be "left to
find their own road." - This view
attacked by L. Averbach, LWR, 1931
#2, 100-105.

_____, My Life, Scribner's: 1930; Uni-
versal Library paperback, 1960.
Numerous comments on artistic influence and views.

_____, "The Strangled Revolution," The
Militant, June 15, 1931, 4, 7.  Another translation in R.W.B. Lewis, ed,
Malraux, Spectrum paperback: 1964,
12-19; with Malraux's answer.  Review
of Malraux's 'The Conquerers'.
Lengthily analyzes how real nature of
Chinese events is contained in book
almost despite author's "blase superiority....A good inoculation of Marxism would have saved the author from
fatal contempt of this order."

_____, "Silone's 'Fontamara'," The Mili-
tant, Aug 26, 1933, 4.  Also in: NI,
Dec 1934, 159.  Dated July 29, 1933.
Silone knows "how to generalize what
he sees by means of the Marxist method
and then to embody his generalities into
artistic images....Revolutionary passion
is raised here to such heights that it
creates a truly artistic work."

_____, Talks with Andre Malraux.  MQ(B),
Mch 1935, 37-41.  Art, film, politics.

_____, The 'New Masses'.  The Militant,
July 26, 1930, 4.  Response to NM review
of his autobiography, terms outlook of
NM outmoded and "conservative."

_____, "The Party In the Field Of Art
and Philosophy," The Militant, July 22,
1933, 4.  Dated June 16, 1933.  Letter
to US Trotskyists Martin Glee, Harry
Ross and M. Morris in response to
their inquiry.  "The party is obliged
to permit a very extensive liberty in
the field of art, eliminating pitilessly
only that which is directed against the
revolutionary tasks of the proletariat;
on the other hand, the party cannot
assume an immediate and direct responsibility for the declarations of its
various members in the field of art
even when it accords them its tribune."
Greater tolerance should be shown
artists than theoreticians: "Lenin
applied different criteria to Bogdanov
the theoretician and professional politician and to Gorky the artist, in
spite of the fact that for a certain
period of time Bogdanov and Gorky were
closely associated in politics.  Lenin
proceeded from the standpoint that by
his artistic activity and his popularity,
Gorky could endow the cause of the revolution with benefits far exceeding the
harm of his erroneous declarations and
actions which, moreover, the party
could always correct in good time and
tactfully."  As in an artillery bom-
bardment, latitude must be allowed for
many errors to insure some direct hits.

_____, Gorky and Narrow-Culturist vs.
Cultural Values.  In: Alexander Kaun,
Maxim Gorky and His Russia, 1931, 464-
465.  From a letter from Trotsky to
Kaun.  "By his whole makeup Gorky is
not a revolutionist and not a politician.  He is a culturist.  To be sure,
the cultural criterion is the broadest
and commonest criterion of historical
development, but it must be applied
broadly.  Taine figured out how many

window-panes the French revolution had broken, and on the basis of these figures he condemned it utterly. That was a narrow-culturist, and in the last account a reactionary approach. Having lowered temporarily the cultural level of the country, the Great Revolution of the eighteenth century prepared the gigantic cultural leap of the nineteenth century. Hence, from the cultural point of view, and not from that of a narrow-culturist criterion, the French Revolution is completely vindicated. Of course, Gorky is broader, bolder, and culturally more magnanimous than Taine. But he stumbled more than once in his narrow-culturist approach to public events, the October Revolution being one of them." - See also pp. 602-607, another Trotsky letter on Gorky's role during the revolution.

_____, "Novelist and Politician: Celine and Poincare," Atlantic Monthly, Oct 1935, 413-420. Reprinted in: Irving Howe, ed, The Basic Writings Of Trotsky, Random House: 1963, 343-355. Celine "bares the roots" of an abject France. But this "hopelessness ever leads to docility." "By rejecting not only the present but what must take its place, the artist gives his support to what is."

_____, "Trotsky vs. Malraux," Nation, Mch 27, 1937, 351. UP dispatch quotes Trotsky calling Malraux a Stalinist agent "organically incapable of moral independence; he is official by birth." With Malraux's reply.

_____, "Nationality and Culture," in his: The Revolution Betrayed, 1937, 170-185. Compares cultural conditions under Stalin to those of 1917-24 and to views expressed at that time by Lenin and himself.

_____, "A Great New Writer," FI, Jan 1941, 26-29. Dated Aug 7, 1939. Review of Jean Malaquais' 'Les Javanais' (Paris, 1939). "This novel is in no way tendentious in character....at the same time one senses at every step the convulsions of our epoch." Compares technique and milieu with Gorky's. Criticizes Celine, also Malraux: "he lacks backbone. He is organically seeking some outside force to lean on, some established authority." Tells how he picked up habit of reading French novels in the Tsar's prisons.

"Even during the years of the civil war I had a current French novel in the car of my military train." French novel technique is "the highest in the world."

_____, Letter to Andre Breton. PR, Winter 1939, 126-127. Dated Dec 22, 1938. Welcomes creation by Breton and Rivera of International Federation of Independent Revolutionary Artists, anti-Stalinist organization. Malraux failed to become "the major poet of our epoch of disasters" as he promised and is instead "a reporter for the GPU." - See also Etiemble (XX).

_____, "Art and Politics In Our Epoch," FI, Mch-Apr 1950, 61-64. Two letter-essays. The first dated June 18, 1938, published also in PR, Aug-Sept 1938, 3-10, thunders against Stalinist deformations of art and literature, lauds Diego Rivera as great revolutionary artist. Second, dated Jan 20, 1939, directed to Dwight MacDonald who contacted him for PR: "the editors of 'Partisan Review' are capable, educated and intelligent people, but they have nothing to say....You defend yourselves from the Stalinists like well-behaved young ladies whom street rowdies insult."

TVARDOVSKY, Alexander, Speech to 3rd Soviet Writers Congress. CDSP, July 1, 1959, 8-9; also SH, Aug 1959, 19-22.

_____, Speech to 22nd Congress, CPSU. SL, 1962 #1, 3-18.

_____, Interview with UP's Henry Schapiro. CDSP, June 5, 1963, 11-13; also Current Soviet Documents, June 3, 1963.

_____, "On the 40th Anniversary," CDSP, Apr 7, 1965, 8-13. Editorial guidelines of 'Novy Mir' and for future Soviet writing. - Rejoinder by Y. Vuchetich, ibid, May 5, 17-19. - For the history of 'Novy Mir' and 'Octyabr', see ibid, Apr 21, 1965, 12-18. - For debate between 'Novy Mir' and 'Literaturnaya Gazeta', see ibid, Dec 15, 1965, 9-12.

URBAN, A, "Science Fiction: Fantasy Or Philosophy?" SSL, Winter 1966-67, 51-70. Defines the value of writings by I. Efremov, G. Gor, Ilya Varshavsky, A. and B. Strugatsky.

USSR SPEAKS FOR ITSELF, vol. 4: Culture

and Leisure, London, 1941. Includes Eisenstein on workers' interest in cinema; I. Moskvin on theatre; A.V. Bakushinsky on folk arts; Yanka Kupala on minority cultural activities; I. Korobov, steelworker, on workers' use of leisure; K. Ivanova on parks of culture and rest.

VINOGRADOV, I, "Pushkin's Road To Realism," in: Irving D.W. Talmadge, ed, Pushkin: Homage By Marxist Critics, 1937, 65-104.

VISHNEVSKAYA, I, "May the Romanticism Of the Detective Story Live," CDSP, July 22, 1964, 13-16.

VISHNEVSKY, V, and A. Leites, Controversy Over Western Modernism. IL, #5 (1933-34), 103-112. Vishnevsky forcefully urges validity of Dos Passos, Joyce, etc.

V.O.K.S, GOGOL SPECIAL ISSUE, 1952 #73. illus. Many valuable materials.

V.O.K.S, CHEKHOV SPECIAL ISSUE, 1954 #86. illus. Contributors include: V.V. Ermilov, Maria Chekhova (his sister), Olga Knipper-Chekhova (his wife), Sean O'Casey, David Magarshak, Vercors, Mulk Raj Anand, E. B. Burgum.

V.O.K.S, Pushkin; A Collection Of Articles and Essays On the Great Russian Poet, Moscow: 1939. illus. Authors: I. Luppol, V. Kirpotin, A. Blagoi, I. Lezhnev, A. Gurstein, L. Timofeyev, M. Khrapchenko, V. Shklovski, G. Vinokur, M. Azadovski, S. Balukhaty, V. Neustadt, V. Zhirmunski, M. Zagorski, V. Ferman.

VOLKOV, G.A, The Writing Of 'War and Peace'. DW, Sept 29, 1940, 4. Soviet Tolstoy scholar analyzes manuscript versions and the process of composition, stressing 'sincerity'.

VOPROSY LITERATURY, "A Symposium: The Salient Characteristics Of Our Recent Literary Output," SSL, Spring 1965, 52-115. From 'Voprosy literatury', 1964 #7. Discussion of literature in the past decade by M. Kuznetsov, L. Iakimenko, I. Grinberg, V. Pankov, A. Bocharov, D. Starikov, B. Sarnov, A. Kogan, L. Anninskii.

VORONSKY, A.  See Dementyev (above).

VYGOTSKY, L.S, Thought and Language,

M.I.T: 1962; M.I.T. paperback:1965. First published 1934. The leading early Soviet Marxist social psychologist, on language and cognition and the social creation of each.

YEGOROV, A, "Against Subjectivism In the Theory Of Art," SL, 1955 #1, 127-144. Polemic.

_____, "Creative Method In Socialist Art," MQ(T), Spring 1964, 49-66. abdgd. From 'Kommunist', 1963 #14. A clear forceful exposition of post-Stalinist Party view of Socialist Realism. Includes critique of Solzhenitsyn.

YERMILOV, V, "Chekhov the Realist," M&M, July 1954, 24-34.

_____, Anton Chekhov, Foreign Languages Publishing House: Moscow, n.d. illus. Biography and analysis of works.

_____, F.M. Dostoyevsky, Foreign Languages Publishing House: Moscow, n.d. illus. Biography and analysis of works.

_____, "Gorky and Dostoevsky," IL, 1940 #4-5, 107-154.

_____, "Against Reactionary Ideas In the Work Of Dostoevsky," MQ(L), V ii, 136-151.

_____, See also: Obituary biography, N.Y. Times, Nov 20, 1965. illus.

YULINA, N.S, "George Santayana and His Philosophy Of 'Aesthetic Sense'," ISM, #3 (Feb 1962), 45-67. Santayana's humane intentions and idealistic philosophy are at odds.

ZASURSKY, Ya, On Publishing In America. CDSP, June 14, 1967, 22. Defects of this writers' market.

ZEITLIN, A, "Heritage Of Pushkin," in: Irving D.W. Talmadge, ed, Pushkin: Homage By Marxist Critics, 1937, 15-50.

ZELINSKY, C, "Soviet Criticism," V.O.K.S, 1934 #7-8, 27-35. Brief survey of early years.

ZHANTIYEVA, D.G, The English Novel Of the 20th Century (1918-1939) [Summary], SL, 1966 #1, 182-186. Joyce, V. Woolf, D.H. Lawrence, Galsworthy, H.G. Wells, E.M. Forster, A. Huxley, R. Aldington.

ZHDANOV, A.A, "Soviet Literature - The

Richest In Ideas, The Most Advanced
Literature," PSL, 15-26. illus.
Soviet writers "engineers of the soul."
Speech to 1st Soviet Writers Congress.

_____, 'Pravda' Editorial Against Caca-
phony In Music. See 1936 (XLI).

_____, Essays On Literature, Philosophy
and Music, 1950. Includes Speech to
1st Soviet Writers Congress; Speeches
in Leningrad on the literary journals
'Zvezda' and 'Leningrad', attacking
Zoshchenko and Akhmatova and asserting
"Leninist principles of partisanship
in literature," 1946; Speech on Philosophy and Aesthetics, June 1947; Speech
to a Conference of Musicians, 1947.
- See also 1946-48 (XLI).

_____, SEE ALSO: Obituary and Tributes,
     V.O.K.S, 1948 #55, 8-11. illus.
     Also Beeching (XXIII); Meilakh
     (XLVI).

ZHUKOV, Yury, On James Bond, Agent 007.
CDSP, Oct 27, 1965, 30-31. From
'Pravda'. President Kennedy's favored
fictional hero with his "license to
kill."

ZIS, A, "Present-Day Revisionism In
Aesthetics," CDSP, Oct 1, 1958, 9-10.
From 'Izvestia'. Attack on H. Lefevre,
T. Mladenovic, O. Davico for not affirming realism that is specifically
socialist. Declaring "revisionism in
aesthetics is inseparable from revisionism in politics" Zis additionally
charges G. Lukacs' aesthetics with
sinister role in Hungarian uprising.

## XLVII.  Music

AKSYUK, S, "Music and the People," M&L,
#21 (Mch 1963), 11-15. abdgd. From
'Sovetskaya Kultura', Jan 3, 1963.
Implements Krushchev's views in realm
of music.

ALCHWANG, A, "Jazz and Negro Music,"
ITh, #2 (1934), 20-22. Finds jazz a
harmful influence. - See reply by
Svend Moller-Kristensen, ITh, 1935 #1,
16-18. A lively clash of views.

CENTRAL COMMITTEE, CPSU, "On the Opera
'Velikaia Druzhba' by V. Muradeli," in:
George S. Counts and Nucia Lodge, The
Country Of the Blind, Boston, 1949,
160-166. Initiated a general censure
of modernist trends. - For a Letter
from Moscow composers and musicians to

Stalin, see: ibid, 168-170. Shostakovich's self-criticism, ibid, 173-
175. Prokofiev's ibid, 175-178.
Khachaturian's, ibid, 178-180.- See
also: Nicolas Slonimsky, Music Since
1900, 1949, 684-709. - For the reversal of this CC view, see 1958 (XLI).
- See also Werth (below).

DANILEVICH, Leon, "Expressionism In
Music - Real and Imagined," SR, Apr
1961, 41-53. Definition of what is
permissible expressionism in music. A
defense of Prokofiev's opera 'War and
Peace' against charges made by musicologist Josef Ryzhkin.

GACHEV, D, "The Proletarian Music Movement In the Soviet Union," V.O.K.S,
1931 #10-12, 40-45. Summarizes development of proletarian basis in Soviet
music.

GERASIMOVA, L, "Dialogue About Jazz,"
CDSP, Mch 29, 1967, 30-31. Soviet
jazz musicians express their view and
problems.

INTERNATIONAL CONGRESSES. See 1933, 1948
(XLI).

KABELEVSKY, Dmitri, "Notes On Opera In
Our Day," CDSP, Oct 6, 1951, 3-5.

_____, Against Rock Music and Jazz.
CDSP, Mch 29, 1967, 31.

KHACHATURIAN, Aram, Self-Criticism Before
Central Committee Strictures. In:
George S. Counts and Nucia Lodge, The
Country Of the Blind, Boston, 1949,
178-180.

_____, "On Creative Boldness and Inspira-
tion," CDSP, Dec 30, 1953, 3-5; also
SS, Apr 1954, 427-434. Rejects narrow
definition of role and character of
folk themes in music. "It is decidedly
necessary for the officials of musical
institutions to abandon the rotten
practice of interfering with the composer's creative work."

_____, "Dmitri Shostakovich's Tenth Sym-
phony," V.O.K.S, 1954 #88, 55-56. Un-
equivocating analysis which praises
its "optimistic tragedy" and finds
finale if anything too uplifting.

_____, "Stirring Problems," CDSP, Sept 7,
1955, 10-12, 36. Penetrating appraisal
of theory and practice in Soviet music.

_____, "Contemporary Music," C&L, Jan 1957, 14-17. Favors not the literal use of folk themes but "free utilization of the root elements of folk music" as necessary health of music which results in "natural color and feeling" as opposed to abstractionism of much Western composition. Bartok as "a germinal new beginning in Western music."

_____, Interview. C&L, 1963 #6, 28-30. illus. Innovation and social commitment.

_____, SEE ALSO: Schneerson (below).

KHRENNIKOV, Tikhon, Tribute to Zhdanov. V.O.K.S, 1948 #55, 10.

KONEN, V, "Legend and Truth About Jazz," CDSP, Dec 28, 1955, 5-6, 11. abdgd. Informed and analytic. Discusses two streams in jazz, "static, primitive and standard" commercial jazz and an "always dynamic" improvisational jazz which has "sharply expressive rhythms" and "complex, beautiful polyphony."

LEBEDINSKY, L, "The Crisis In Modern Bourgeois Music," ITh, #3-4 (1934), 13-16. abdgd. Speech to 2nd International Musical Conference, 1933.

[MIASKOVSKY], See Reinhold Gliere, "In Memory Of N.Y. Myaskovsky," V.O.K.S, 1950 #65, 92-94.

MILIUKOV, P.N, "Architecture, Painting and Music," Outlines Of Russian Culture, Part III, Philadelphia, 1942.

MOISENKO, Rena, Realist Music; 25 Soviet Composers, London, 1949. illus. Philosophy, nationalist qualities, working conditions, biographies. - See also the author's supplement, Realist Music, London, 1950, 32 pp, containing the 1948 Soviet decree on music, Zhdanov's speeches, and the author's commentary.

MURADELI, Vano, Interview. C&L, 1964 #8, 30-31. illus.

NESTYEV, Israel V, Prokofiev, Stanford Univ: 1960. illus. catalog. The outstanding biography and study.

POLYANKA, Lyudmila, Soviet Music, Moscow, 1959. illus.

'PRAVDA' EDITORIAL,"Chaos Instead Of Music," IL, 1936 #6, 72; also in:

Kurt London, The Seven Soviet Arts, London, 1937, 72-74. Attack on Shostakovich's 'Lady Macbeth of Mtzensk' which launched late 30s crusade against 'formalism'.

PROKOFIEV, Sergei, "Soviet Audiences and My Work," Soviet Travel, 1934 #3, 30-31, 74. Challenge and problems of composing for audiences lacking a "mature understanding of music." Special reference to scores for 'Lieutenant Kije' and Tairov's 'Egyptian Nights'.

_____, "Literary and Musical America," DW, July 12, 1939, 7. illus.

_____, Self-Criticism Confronted With Central Committee Strictures. In: George S. Counts and Nucia Lodge, The Country Of the Blind, Boston, 1949, 175-178.

_____, "My Musical Credo," NWR, Mch 1952, 49-52. A composer "is in duty bound to serve man....he must beautify human life and defend it. He must be a citizen, first and foremost."

_____, Interview with Alexander Werth. Nation, Apr 4, 1953, 285-287. Prokofiev's estimate of various Soviet composers and his own Fifth Symphony.

_____, Autobiography, Articles, Reminiscences, Foreign Languages Publishing House: Moscow, 195? With catalog of works.

_____, SEE ALSO: Danilevich, Nestyev (above).

RABINOVICH, D, Dmitry Shostakovich, Composer, Foreign Languages Publishing House, Moscow, 1959. illus. Life and works analyzed.

RAMM, W, ed, International Collection Of Revolutionary Songs, International Music Bureau, Moscow, 1934? [not located] - Detailed review by Carl Sands, DW, Jan 31, 1934, 7; Feb 1, 5.

RUSSIAN ASSOCIATION OF PROLETARIAN COMPOSERS. See 1929 (XLI).

RUSSIAN SYMPHONY: THOUGHTS ABOUT TCHAIKOWSKY, 1947. Essays that assimilate Tchaikowsky to progressive optimistic tradition in Russian thought. Authors: D. Shostakovich, Y. Keldysh, B. Yarastovsky, D. Zhitomirsky, B. Asaviev, V. Yakovlev, A. Alshvang.

SCHNEERSON, Grigory, <u>Aram Khachaturyan</u>,
Foreign Languages Publishing House,
Moscow, 1959. illus. Life, musical
development, with analysis of works
and role in modern music.

SHEPILOV, D.  See 1957 (XLI).

SHOSTAKOVICH, Dmitri, "My Opera, Lady
Macbeth of Mtzensk," <u>Modern Music</u>,
Nov-Dec 1934, 23-30.  With photographic and musical illus. - For controversy surrounding this opera, see:

D. Shostakovich, "Lady Macbeth of
Mzensk," <u>DW</u>, Jan 21, 1935, 5.
Explains his Marxist plan for
adapting the Leskov tale.

Sergei Radamsky, "Brilliant Shostakovich Opera Triumph For Soviet Music,"
<u>DW</u>, Feb 9, 1935, 9.  Review of US
premiere of this "music drama with
a Marxian approach."  Radamsky saw
Moscow and Leningrad productions,
calls it "the first music drama
that struck a responsive chord in
the masses of the Soviet Union."
- In "More About Lady Macbeth," <u>DW</u>,
Feb 26, 1935, 5, Radamsky says he
saw USSR productions 13 times: the
"movements on the stage as well as
sounds in the orchestra which might
be offensive to our conservative
friends" (the hostile New York daily
critics) should be attributed to the
US "producers who obviously were
anxious for sensational effects."

S. Tchemodanov, "Shostakovich," <u>SUR</u>,
May-June 1934, 108-110.  illus.
Notes "naturalistic" tendency but
lavishes praise on 'The Nose' and
'Lady Macbeth' in particular.

Nikolai V. Smolich, Interview with
Milly B. Mitchell.  <u>MN</u>, Aug 30,
1933, 3.  Producer-director of 'Lady
Macbeth' explains why "I consider
this opera the high point in modern
Russian music."  Disputes claims
that the music is not national in
content.

'Pravda' Editorial, "Chaos Instead Of
Music," authored by A. Zhdanov.  The
turning point in critical opinion.
See 'Pravda', above.

L.F. Boross, "Soviet Music Comes Of
Age," <u>DW</u>, Apr 7, 1936, 7.  Justify-
ing the censure of Shostakovich.

Joshua Kunitz, "The Shostakovich
'Affair'," <u>NM</u>, June 9, 1936, 15-18.

Sergei Radamsky, The Composer's Reaction To Banning Of 'Lady Macbeth'.
<u>DW</u>, Aug 17, 1936, 7.  Radamsky was
close to Shostakovich and during
the press attacks spoke with him almost daily.  "His only reaction was
that he realized that 'Lady Macbeth
of Mzensk' was not an opera for popular consumption....He had no feeling of personal resentment....the
question was a general one, and concerned all creative talent which
went astray from the path of Socialist realism and mass contact."

Yuri Olesha, "About Formalism," <u>IL</u>,
1936 #6.  Writer friend describes
initial shock at attack on Shostakovich, then growing awareness that
the composer's music did express
"contemptuous aloofness" for the
masses, which could not be tolerated.

Kenneth Burke, <u>Attitudes Toward History</u>,
Beacon paperback: Boston, 1961, 185-
190.  The attack as misguided tactics
in dealing with vestigial traits in
Soviet life.

Natalia Shumskaya, "Shostakovich's
'Katerina Izmailova'," <u>SL</u>, 1963 #6,
167-172.  How 'Lady Macbeth' was
altered.  "In accordance with Stalin's
wishes, the [earlier] production was
unjustly condemned."

_____, "Notes In a Composer's Notebook,"
<u>DW</u>, July 10, 1939, 7; July 11, 7.

_____, "What I Believe," <u>NM</u>, Aug 4, 1942,
28-29.  Reprinted in: Elie Siegmeister,
<u>The Music Lover's Handbook</u>, 1943, 624-
628, with domestic observations by Mrs.
Shostakovich.  "To learn ceaselessly
from the people, to grasp everything
the people create, to be worthy of the
time period in which we artists live -
therein lies our task."

_____, Interview with Rita Korn.  <u>DW</u>,
June 13, 1947, 11.

_____, "Soviet Music Today," <u>Saturday
Review of Literature</u>, Jan 25, 1947, 25.

_____, Response to Central Committee
Strictures; and Discussion of Why He
Wrote 'Song Of the Forests'.  <u>V.O.K.S</u>,
1950 #62, 44-45.

_____, Speech to Cultural and Scientific Congress For World Peace, New York, Mch 27, 1949. DWSup, Apr 10, 1949, 6-7. abdgd. illus.

_____, "Talk With Young Composers," CDSP, Dec 14, 1955, 7-8, 27. abdgd. Important.

_____, "Some Vital Problems Of Music Composition," CDSP, July 11, 1956, 8-9.

_____, Speech to 2nd Congress of Soviet Composers. CDSP, May 29, 1957, 11-12. abdgd. Concrete proposals for injecting more creative experiment into Soviet musical policy.

_____, "Musical Modernism and Individuality," SR, Oct 1960, 42-47. From 'Pravda', Sept 7, 1960. Welcomes recent Party criticism of his work. Declares the true avant-garde of music is "capable of awakening a response in the heart of the listener:" Bartok, Britten, Orff, Barber, Villa-Lobos, Poulenc, Milhaud, Auric, among them.

_____, and V. Vinogradov, "Dodecaphony Shatters Creativity," Music Journal, Mch 1964, 46, 92.

_____, SEE ALSO: Ivan Martynov, Dmitri Shostakovich, 1947; and Rabinovich (above).

SOKOLSKY, M, "Regarding Jazz," CDSP, Apr 12, 1952, 5-7. From 'Sovetskoye iskusstvo'. Denunciation which quotes Gorky on this "music for fat people."

TCHEMODANOV, Sergei, "The Origin Of Music," NM, Apr 2, 1935, 30-31. Draws on Plekhanov, Bucher, Friche for origins of primitive music in work process.

_____, "An Economic Approach To Music," Modern Music, May-June 1933, 175-181.

TSYTOVICH, T, "The Theme Of Socialist Labor In Soviet Music," CDSP, Apr 14, 1951, 13-16. abdgd. Concrete and useful discussion.

YAGOLIM, Boris, Soviet Music, Musical Education and Music Making, London, 1946. illus. 72 pp.

ZHDANOV, A.A. See Zhdanov (XLVI).

## XLVIII.  Theatre

ANIKST, Alexander, Lyubimov's Productions Of Brecht and John Reed; A New Epoch in Soviet Theatre Opens, CDSP, Oct 6, 1965, 9-13. Challenges recent decades of Soviet drama.

BOYADZHIEV, G, "Revolutionary Staging Of Classics," TW, Apr-June 1938, 22-29. Also in ITh, #3-4 (1934), 26-28.

_____, "The Origin and Development Of the Classical Theatre In France," ITh, 1935 #1, 30-37.

BYKOV, A.V, and A. A. Levshin, Method Of Improvised Workers Theatre. WT, Nov 1931, 3-5. Directors of Moscow Semperante Theatre, in a letter to American comrades, describe how they construct agitprop plays on themes of socialist construction.

CENTRAL COMMITTEE, CPSU, "On the Repertoire Of the Dramatic Theatres and Measures For Its Improvement," in: George S. Counts and Nucia Lodge, The Country Of the Blind, Boston, 1949, 119-124. abdgd. Dated Aug 26, 1946.

DANILIN, S, "The Theatre Of the Paris Commune," ITh, #5 (1933), 17-19.

DERZHAVIN, Konstantine, A Century of the State Dramatic Theatre, 1832-1932, Leningrad, 1932. illus. Integrates developments in this theatre with Russian history.

DIAMENT, H, "Speed Up the Tempo!" ITh, #1 (1932), 1-4. Tasks of workers theatres everywhere defined by head of International Workers Dramatic Union. Anti-war propaganda and defense of USSR are prominent tasks.

FEVRALSKY, A, "Beginnings Of the Workers' Theatre In Spain," ITh, #5 (1933), 19-21.

FRADKIN, I, "On the Artistic Originality Of Bertolt Brecht's Drama," in Peter Demetz, ed, Brecht; A Collection Of Critical Essays, Spectrum paperback: Englewood Cliffs, N.J, 1962, 97-105. abdgd. Brecht's "philosophical parables" constitute a variety of socialist realism.

GVOSDEV, A, "The Theatre Of Feudal Society," ITh, #1 (1934), 15-17; #2 (1934), 24-27. Solid basic analysis.

_____, "Problems In the Study Of the History Of the Theatre," ITh, #1 (1935), 10-13. Competing theatre trends in USSR must not distort theatre history to sole benefit of their method. In renewal of theatre playwright's role is dominant (His role decreases in social decadence of Rome, in 1789 France, most recently) but he always intimately interrelates with directors, actors, etc.

INTERNATIONAL WORKERS DRAMATIC UNION, "Work Among the Artistic Intelligentsia," ITh, #4 (1933), 1-3. The urgency owing to fascism's threat of "winning to our side the bulk of the artistic intelligentsia" without raising questions of "creative methods." (ITh contains many articles on political theatre around the world.)

IPATOV, V,"The TRAM - Komsomol Shock Brigade In Art," V.O.K.S, 1931 #10-12, 26-29. illus.

KOMISSARZHEVSKY, Viktor, "The Art Of Pessimism [Beckett]," SL, 1965 #2, 173-177. The arguments against images of stolid defeat.

_____, Moscow Theatres, Foreign Languages Publishing House, Moscow, 1949. illus.

KRUPSKAYA, N, "Plays Dedicated To the October Revolution," DW, Jan 7, 1938, 7; Jan 8, 7. illus. Problems of enacting Lenin. Reliability of reactions from worker audiences.

LAVROV, V.A, "Mayakovsky's Satirical Comedy 'The Bedbug'," SSL, Spring 1967, 40-61. In the staging by V. Meyerhold.

LUBOMIRSKY, O, "Jewish Theatre In the USSR," ITh, #5 (1933), 27-34. illus.

_____, "Soviet Jewish Dramaturgy," ITh, 1934 #1, 43-45.

MARKOV, Pavel A, The Soviet Theatre, London, 1934. illus. Markov was literary director of Moscow Art Theatre, theatre reviewer for 'Izvestia', 'Pravda' and 'Novy Mir' and a theatre historian.

_____, The First Studio Sullerzhitsky-Vackhtangov-Tchekov, 1934. mimeo. Group Theatre Publication. Outstanding account of origin of a central creative force in Russian and world theatre.

MEYERHOLD, Vsevelod, "Farce," TDR, Sept 1959, 139-148.

_____, From On the Theatre. TDR, May 1960, 134-148.

_____, "Chaplin and Chaplinism," TDR, Fall 1966, 188-195. Realism and stylization, comedy, montage and Eisenstein.

_____, "On Ideology and Technology In the Theatre," ITh, #2 (1934), 6-8. illus. Lecture to TRAM, abdgd, minus stenographic report of discussion that followed. Discusses realism, biomechanics, the role of idea in acting, attacks "living one's role."

_____, Interview with Harold Clurman. Theatre Arts, Nov 1935, 873-876. Revealing Meyerhold's mind.

_____, "Meyerhold On Theatre Art," SL, 1962 #1, 157-164. Remarks collected during final five years of Meyerhold's career by his assistant, Alexander Gladkov.

_____, Final Speech. In: Juri Jelagin, Taming Of the Arts, Dutton: 1951, 171-173. Delivered at 1st National Convention of Directors (1939). Defiantly defends his theatre practice and denounces mediocrity of Moscow theatres in name of "socialist realism." "In your effort to eradicate formalism, you have destroyed art!" Meyerhold was arrested next day and not again seen. - The accuracy of this text cannot be verified at present. Jelagin states in his Russian-language study of Meyerhold that he himself took it down at the Convention. At least one other verbatim record exists in Moscow but has not been made available for comparison.

_____, SEE ALSO: Lavrov. Houghton, Jelagin (XLIX); and:

E. Zozulya, "Vsevelod Meyerhold (From a Notebook)," ITh, 1934 #3-4, 5-8. Excellent account of Meyerhold's rehearsal technique.

Yuri Olesha, "Meyerhold: Soviet Director," IL, 1934 #2, 137-138. Recollections by a friend.

Andre van Gyseghem, "Meyerhold Tells Theatre Directors How To Create Great Plays," MN, Aug 29, 1935, 10. illus.

Valuable for long quotes of Meyerhold's advice to a meeting of young directors.

H.W.L. Dana, "Meyerhold's New Theatre," NTh, Jan 1935, 10-12. Diagrams, Sketches, photo of model for a theatrical theatre, with Meyerhold's statements.

N. Volkov, "Vsevelod Meyerhold," Soviet Travel, 1934 #3, 30-31. illus. Volkov was author of two-volume study of Meyerhold's theatre. Text is brief; photos are of much interest.

Alexander Bakshy, "Vsevelod Meyerhold and the Soviet Theatre," The Dial, Jan 1928, 25-30.

Bryllion Fagin, "Meyerhold Rehearses a Scene," Theatre Arts, Oct 1932, 833-836.

Huntly Carter, "Meyerhold's Theatre," in his: The New Theatre and Cinema Of Soviet Russia, London, 1924, 50-80. Full discussion of Meyerhold's life and methods based on conversations.

William Paul, "Liberating Dramatic Art," SW, Jan 2, 1927, 8. Describes Meyerhold's production of 'Roar China' as "the greatest modern play in the world. It is the best acted and produced play I have ever seen."

Herbert J. Biberman, "Meyerhold At Work," Theatre Guild Magazine, Jan 1929, 25-29, 52. Analysis of 'Inspector General', 'Roar China' and rehearsal techniques.

Lee Strasberg, "The Magic Of Meyerhold," NTh, Sept 1934, 14-15, 30. Enthusiastic account of several productions and Meyerhold's roots in folk theatre.

John Martin, "How Meyerhold Trains His Actors," Theatre Guild Magazine, Nov 1930, 26-30. Rare description.

Anonymous, "The Revolutionary Theatre," DWSup, Feb 28, 1925. Hails Meyerhold as "the spirit of the revolutionary drama in Soviet Russia" which "sweeps everything before it," a worthy model for US efforts.

Ben Blake, "Meyerhold Theatre, Alien To Soviet Life, Is Dissolved," MN, Jan 19, 1938, 9. Lengthy presentation of arguments used in closing the theatre.

Nathaniel Buchwald, "What Was Wrong With the Meyerhold Theatre?" DW, Jan 24, 1938, 7. illus. The case for its closing. Meyerhold had "nothing to give to the Soviet theatre."

Marjorie L. Hoover, "V.E. Meyerhold," Comparative Literature. Summer 1965, 234-250.

MOROZOV, Mikhail M, Shakespeare On the Soviet State, London, 1947. Introduction by J. Dover Wilson. illus. Admirable history of productions before and after 1917.

_____, "The Individualization Of Shakespeare's Characters Through Imagery," Shakespeare Survey, #2 (1949), 83-106.

MOSKVIN, I, The Soviet Theatre, Moscow, 1939. 32 pp. In the Pamphlet Library On the Soviet Union distributed at the 1939 World's Fair.

NAZAROV, B.A, and O.V. Gridneva, "On the Problem Of the Lag In Drama and Theatre," CDSP, Dec 19, 1956, 3-8. - See 1956 (XLI).

OBRAZTSOV, Sergei, On Commitment and Responsibility In the Theatre. New Theatre (London), July 1948, 14-15, 17. illus. [BM] Passionate rebuttal to a snide British critic.

OBRAZTSOVA, Anna, Soviet Theatre 1964. SL, 1965 #1, 161-170.

_____, "The Revolution and the Theatre," SL, 1967 #7, 152-159. illus. Early plays of the revolution.

PIMENOV, Vladimir, "The Times Demand It!" CDSP, Apr 21, 1965, 38-39. Details the mediocrity in recent Soviet playwriting.

_____, "Inspiration and Responsibility," CDSP, Aug 16, 1967, 3-4. The creative mixing of freedom and Party control to improve the theatre.

RADLOV, Sergei, "Producing Shakespeare," IL, 1939 #6, 49-58.

RAPOPORT, I, "The Work Of the Actor," TW, I i, 5-40.

SIMONOV, Konstantin, "Drama, Theatre, and Life," in: George S. Counts and Nucia Lodge, The Country Of the Blind, Boston, 1949, 135-143. abdgd. Speech to Conference of Theatre Leaders and Dramatists, Nov 18, 1946, enthusiastically supporting 1946 Zhdanov strictures.

SUDAKOV, I, "The Actor's Creative Work," TW, Jan-Mch 1937, 7-42. A director and actor at Moscow Art Theatre.

SURKOV, Eugeni, The American Theatre, AmD, II i (1965), 7-10. Finds great similarity in USSR and US acting styles. Remarks on the "positive outlook" in plays by Miller, Hansberry, etc.

TAIROV, "The Kamerny Theatre," ITh, #3 (1933), 54-58. illus. Social origins of the Kamerny as elite theatre. Its response to changed conditions of socialist construction.

TIKHANOVICH, V, "The Masses' Will To Art," V.O.K.S, 1931 #10-12, 11-14. Agitprop and amateur art in 1931.

TROTSKY, Leon, On Stanislavsky. In his: Literature and Revolution, 1957, 32. Scorn for the Moscow Art Theatre.

ZAKHAVA, V, "Can We Use Stanislavsky's System?" NTh, Aug 1935, 16-18. Director of Vakhtangov Theatre says "Stanislavsky discovered a number of laws of scenic art....there is no reason for turning our backs on those truths he did reveal" having to do with "the biologic nature of the actor's creative work." Serious useful article.

XLIX.   Appendix

ADAMS, Frederick B, Jr, To Russia With Frost, Club of Odd Volumes: Boston, 1963. illus. Behind-the-scenes account of a small venture in cultural exchange. With citation of Frost's views.

ALEXANDROVA, Vera, A History Of Soviet Literature, 1917-1964, Doubleday Anchor paperback, 1964. Speaks of "monstrousness" of conditions under which Soviet writers work; yet declares Soviet literature has "considerable literary value" and even greater informational quality. - Review by Tamara Motyleva, SL, 1964 #5, 152-161. Review by Herman Ermolaev, Russian Review, Jan 1964.

ANDERSON, Edith, "Bright, Sacred Hatred Is Soviet Artists' Weapon," Soviet Culture In Wartime, #1 (1943), 16-17.

ASAF'EV, Igor G, Russian Music From the Beginning Of the Nineteenth Century, Edwards: Ann Arbor, 1953. Translated under auspices of American Council of Learned Societies. First published 1930 in Moscow.

BABITSKY, P, and J. Rimberg, The Soviet Film Industry, Praeger: 1955.

BAKST, James, "Music and Soviet Realism," Polish Review, Winter 1962, 67-74. Realist theory of music.

BARGHOORN, Frederick C, The Soviet Cultural Offensive, 1960

BLAKE, Ben, The International Union of Revolutionary Theatre (IURT). DW, Feb 25, 1935, 5.

BLOCK, Anita, The Changing World In Plays and Theatre, 1939. Much on Soviet theatre.

BLOK, Alexander, The Spirit Of Music, London, 1946. Seven essays by the great Symbolist author of 'The Twelve'. Includes "Intelligentsia and Revolution" (1918) which embraces Bolshevik upheaval and scoffs at bourgeois trepidations.

BLUM, Ralph, "Freeze and Thaw: The Artist In Russia," New Yorker, Aug 28, 1965, 40-100; Sept 4, 32-85; Sept 11, 168-217. Personal account of the difficulties of prominent dissidents.

BORLAND, Harriet, Soviet Literary Theory and Practice During the First Five-Year Plan, 1928-1932, King's Crown: 1950.

BOWERS, Faubion, Broadway, USSR; Ballet, Theatre, and Entertainment In Russia Today, Nelson: 1959. illus. Informal account.

BOWMAN, Herbert E, "Art and Reality In Russian 'Realist' Criticism," JAAC, Mch 1954.

BRADSHAW, Martha, ed, Soviet Theatres 1917-1941, Research Program On the USSR: 1954. With bibliography. Essays by five experienced Russian theatre workers who after 1941 became refugees: Serge Orlovsky, "Moscow Theatres, 1917-1941; Boris Volkov, "The Red Army Central Theatre In Moscow;" Peter Yershov, "Training Actors For the Moldavian and Bulgarian Theatres, 1934-1938;" Gabriel Ramevsky, "The Theatre In Soviet Concentration Camps;" Yosyp Hirniak, "Birth and Death Of the Modern Ukrainian Theatre."

BRAVERMAN, Harry, "The Problem of Soviet Culture," in his: The Future Of Russia, Macmillan: 1963, 117-128.

Britain and the Soviets; Congress Of Peace and Friendship With the U.S.S.R, London, Dec 7-8, 1935, London, 1936. With G.B. Shaw and accounts of Soviet drama (G. Whitcomb), literature (A. Williams-Ellis), art (S.F. Osiakovski), cinema (I. Montagu).

BROWN, Ben W, Theatre At the Left, Providence: 1938. Soviet theatre.

BROWN, Deming, Soviet Attitudes Toward American Writing, Princeton Univ: 1962. Changing Soviet attitudes toward US authors: Dos Passos, Hemingway, Upton Sinclair, H. Fast, J. Conroy, et al. - See review by Alexander Nikolyukin, SL, 1964 #3, 137-141.

BROWN, Edward J, The Proletarian Episode In Russian Literature, 1928-1932, 1953. Summary of views and events, 1917-28. "The RAPP leaders were resisting the Party demand and stubbornly propagating their own ideas and their own 'literary method'. RAPP was therefore one of the eventual victims rather than the source of a determined Party program to control and utilize literature."

_____, Russian Literature Since the Revolution, Collier paperback: 1963.

BRYHER, Film Problems Of Soviet Russia, Territet: 1929. illus.

BUNT, Cyril G.E, A History Of Russian Art, London & New York, 1940. illus. Survey chapters on Soviet architecture, painting and sculpture, pp. 221-263.

BURG, David, "The 'Cold War' On the Literary Front," PC, July 1962-Feb 1963.

BUSH, Alan, Music In the Soviet Union, London, 1943. 30 pp. [DLC]

CANADAY, John, "Art In the Soviet Union," N.Y. Times, Sept 30, 1963; Oct 2, Oct 3, Oct 4. illus. "With the most open mind and the most hopeful heart, you cannot say that the Soviet artist has done very much....the Soviet painter is only the natural descendent of a Russian tradition that is defective in the first place....The trouble is the expressive poverty of a tradition that mistakes illustration for interpretation, and always has." - See also Canaday, "A Critic Surveys the Party Line In Art," N.Y. Times Magazine, Jan 5, 1964, 18-19, 61, 64. illus.

CARLISLE, Olga Andreyev, Voices In the Snow, Random House: 1963. Account of talks with Sholokhov, Yevtushenko, Ehrenburg, Pasternak, et al.

CARTER, Huntly, The New Theatre and Cinema Of Soviet Russia, London, 1924. Many rare photos. Invaluable for facts and insights into variety and vigor of early Soviet drama and film. Especially good on Lunacharsky, Stanislavsky, Meyerhold, Proletcult.

_____, The New Spirit In the Russian Theatre, 1917-1928, 1929. illus. Continues his account.

_____, "The Challenge Of the New Russian Art Expression," MQ(B), IV iii (1927-28), 254-265.

CHARQUES, R.D, Soviet Education; Some Aspects Of Cultural Revolution, London, 1932. Sympathetic plodding explanation of USSR's totalized approach to inculcating values.

CHEN, Jack, Soviet Art and Artists, London, 1944. Brief popular treatment of conditions and nature of work of Soviet painters.

CLEMENTS, Robert J, On the Gorky Institute Of World Literature. N.Y. Times Book Review, Jan 8, 1967, 24-26. At once a first-hand account of the Institute's work, and a cold-war plea to get similar facilities for comparative literature in America. By the director of Comparative Literature, New York Univ.

CONQUEST, Robert, Courage Of Genius: The Pasternak Affair: A Documentary Report On Its Literary and Political Significance, London: 1961. Thorough, with many Soviet documents.

COUNTS, George S, and Nucia Lodge, The Country Of the Blind, Boston, 1949. Disgusted account of Stalinist manipulation of arts and sciences following war. Valuable chiefly for documentary materials.

CRAIG, Gordon, "The Russian Theatre Today," The London Mercury, Oct 1935, 529-538. Excited by the huge theatre public and numerous experimental theatres, Craig admires the manner of theatre people he met, calls USSR "the most intelligent place in Europe."

DANA, H.W.L, Handbook On Soviet Drama, 1938. Facts and bibliography.

_____, "The Development Of Soviet Drama," in: Thomas H. Dickinson, ed, The Theatre In a Changing Europe, 1935?, 99-120.

DICKINSON, Thorold, and Catherine de la Roche, Soviet Cinema, London: 1948. illus. A history.

DREISER, Theodore, Dreiser Looks At Russia, 1928. Includes his low view of communist arts and his high view of communism. Conversations with Meyerhold, Stanislavsky, Eisenstein.

DUMITRIU, Petru, "The Positive Hero," in: G.R. Urban, ed, Talking To Eastern Europe, London: 1964, 121-127. This notion, alien to Marx, Engels and Lenin, had its origin in the peasants' calendar of saints and martyrs.

EASTMAN, Max, Artists In Uniform; A Study Of Literature and Bureaucratism, 1934. Associating himself with views of Lenin and Trotsky, Eastman assails Stalinist culture controls. Detailed

accounts of Essinen, Mayakovsky, Polonsky, Voronsky, the Kharkov Congress, the Serapions, Zemyatin. - Rebuttals by Pilnyak and Dennen in PR, I iii, 17-26. By Gold, DW, June 2, 1934, 7. By Karl Radek, "Lackey Without a Uniform," DW, Aug 25, 1934, 7. - Review by David Ernest, NI, July 1934, 26-27.

EDGARTON, William, "The Serapion Brothers: An Early Soviet Controversy," American Slavic and East European Review, Feb 1949.

ENG-LIEDMEIER, A, Soviet Literary Characters: An Investigation Into the Portrayal Of Soviet Men In Russian Prose, 1917-1953, Mouton: The Hague, 1959.

EPSTEIN, Schachno, "The New Ways Of Art In Soviet Russia," The Toiler, Nov 5, 1921, 11-12. Quizzically describes revolutionary doings of Chagall, Lissitzky, Mayakovsky, Shreveschenievich, et al.

ERLICH, Victor, Russian Formalism: History - Doctrine, Mouton: The Hague, 1955. The linguistic school of 1915-1930 as "a legitimate, if somewhat eccentric, child of the revolutionary period," admired by Mayakovsky, thought by some Marxists to have a scientific usefulness.

_____, "Social and Aesthetic Criterion In Soviet Russian Criticism," in: Ernest J. Simmons, ed, Continuity and Change In Russian and Soviet Thought, Cambridge, Mass, 1955, 398-416. Discusses Soviet criticism as it approaches or departs from Formalist School criteria.

_____, "The Literary Scene," in: Abraham Brumberg, ed, Russia Under Krushchev, 1962, 343-359.

_____, The Double Image: Concept Of the Poet In Slavic Literatures, Johns Hopkins: Baltimore, 1965. Briussov, Blok, Mayakovsky and Pasternak, and how their poetic careers variously accommodated the revolution.

_____, "Soviet Literary Criticism: Past and Present," PC, Jan-Feb 1958, 34-43.

ERMOLAEV, Herman, Soviet Literary Theories, 1917-1934; The Genesis Of Socialist Realism, California Univ: Berkeley, 1963. A basic study.

FEUCHTWANGER, Lion, <u>Moscow 1937; My Visit Described For My Friends</u>, 1937. With account of liveliness of the performing arts and deadening effect of the censor on new non-heroical writing.

FIZER, John, "The Problem Of the Unconscious In the Creative Process As Treated By Soviet Aesthetics," <u>JAAC</u>, Summer 1963, 399-406. "Soviet aesthetics...deliberately ignores the factor of the unconscious." Chiefly Voronsky and Lukacs.

_____, "Art and the Unconscious," <u>Survey</u>, #46 (Jan 1963), 125-133. "This article attempts to present the problem of the unconscious as it is treated by Soviet aesthetics. This is crucial in comprehending the Soviet approach to a whole array of other problems in the field of aesthetics." Voronsky as only communist literary critic who in the 20s gave serious attention.

FLANAGAN, Hallie, <u>Shifting Scenes Of the Modern European Theatre</u>, 1928. Much of it devoted to visit in Moscow, Leningrad and Kiev theatres on which she has enthusiastic specific reports.

_____, A Series Of Enthusiastic Essays On Soviet Theatre. <u>Theatre Guild Magazine</u>. "Ivan As Critic," Jan 1930, 40-43, the renovation of repertories to provide contemporary plays; "The Soviet Theatrical Olympiad," Sept 1930, 10-13, 62, with extracts from speeches; "Blood and Oil," Oct 1930, 27-29; "The Tractor Invades the Theatre," Dec 1930, 36-38; "The Georgian Theatre," Feb 1931, 24-27.

FLORINSKY, Michael T, ed, <u>McGraw-Hill Encyclopedia Of Russia and the Soviet Union</u>, 1961. Includes: G. Dennis (Architecture), Anatole Chujoy (Ballet), E. Nodel (Gorky), E.J. Brown (Literature), T. Dickinson (Moving Pictures), G. Swet (Music), V. Kovarsky (Painting), C. Fox (Sculpture), P. Yershov (Theatre).

FREEMAN, Joseph, "Past and Present In Soviet Literature," <u>VOO</u>, 3-65.

_____, "The Soviet Cinema," <u>VOO</u>, 217-264.

_____, "Soviet Music," <u>VOO</u>, 292-314.

_____, <u>An American Testament</u>, 1936.

Sections on experience in USSR as Comintern translator, with Soviet literary critics, meeting Eisenstein, Dinamov, Meyerhold, Mayakovsky.

FRIEDBERG, Maurice, <u>Russian Classics In Soviet Jackets</u>, Columbia Univ: 1962.

FULOP-MILLER, Rene, <u>The Mind and Face Of Bolshevism</u>, 1927. illus. Important source book on Soviet culture at its beginnings. - Harper Torchbook paperback, 1965, with new epilogue.

GIBIAN, George, <u>Interval Of Freedom; Soviet Literature During the Thaw, 1954-1957</u>, Minneapolis, 1960.

GLENNY, Michael, and William Lee Kinsolving, "Soviet Theatre: Two Views," <u>TDR</u>, Spring 1967, 100-116. Revival of vitality.

GORCHAKOV, Nikolai A, <u>The Theatre In Soviet Russia</u>, 1957. illus. Detailed account, many quotes, heavily hostile.

GORELIK, Mordecai, "Soviet Scene Design," <u>NTh</u>, Apr 1937, 22-23, 45. Informed intelligent analysis of its creativity. -- See also Gorelik (LXII).

GRAY, Camilla, <u>The Great Experiment: Russian Art 1863-1922</u>, Abrams: 1962. illus. With bibliography. The major book on radical painting the October Revolution first accepted then sought to alter.

GREGOR, Joseph, "The Theatre Of Soviet Russia,": Thomas H. Dickinson, ed, <u>The Theatre In a Changing Europe</u>, 1935?, 48-99. illus.

GROHMANN, Will, <u>Wasily Kandinsky</u>, Abrams: 1959, 161-170. Chapter: "Return To Russia. Art and Politics. 1914-1921." Kandinsky's role as official charged with reform of Russian art institutions.

GYSEGHEM, Andre van, <u>Theatre In Soviet Russia</u>, London, 1943. illus. Detailed craft approach to acting and directing in Moscow.

_____, Theatre In the USSR. In: John Andrews and Ossia Trilling, <u>International Theatre</u>, London: 1949, 95-110.

HALLE, Morris, <u>Early Literary Disputes In the USSR</u>, M.A. Thesis, Chicago Univ: 1946.

HANKIN, Robert M, "Postwar Soviet Ideology

and Literary Scholarship," in: Ernest J. Simmons, ed, <u>Through the Glass Of Soviet Literature</u>, 1953, 244-289.

HARE, Richard, <u>The Art and Artists Of Russia</u>, Methuen: London, 1965.

HARKINS, William E, <u>Dictionary Of Russian Literature</u>, Philosophical Library: 1956. Brief alphabetically organized articles on Russian literature to the present.

HARPER, Kenneth Eugene, <u>Controversy In Soviet Literary Criticism On the Doctrine Of Socialist Realism</u>, University Microfilms: Ann Arbor, 1950, i.e.,1951.

HAYWOOD, Max, and Leopold Labedz, eds, <u>Literature and Revolution In Soviet Russia, 1917-1962</u>, A Symposium, Oxford: London, 1963. Eleven essays roughly covering stated period, including 1st Soviet Writers Congress, Zhdanovism, the "Organization Writer (1934-36)."

_____, and Patricia Blake, <u>Dissonant Voices In Soviet Literature</u>, Harper Colophon paperback: 1964. Based on a <u>PR</u> 1961 Special Issue. With Introduction by Haywood, "Soviet Literature 1917-1962." - Attacked by Leonid Leonov and Alexander Dementiev, and a reply by Haywood, <u>PR</u>, Spring 1962, 300-310. Rebuttal in <u>SL</u>, 1963 #6, 157-160.

_____, and Edward L. Crowley, eds, <u>Soviet Literature In the Sixties</u>: <u>An International Symposium</u>, Praeger: 1964. Essays by Haywood, R. Mathewson, A. Gaev, L.D. Rzhevsky, B. Rubin, A. Adamovich, G. Struve, M. Friedberg, P. Benno.

HAZARD, Clifton E, <u>Lenin and Literature From an Examination Of His Writings</u>, M.A. Thesis, Columbia Univ: 1953.

HOUGHTON, Norris, <u>Moscow Rehearsals; The Golden Age Of the Soviet Theatre</u>, 1936; Evergreen paperback, 1962. illus. Introduction by Lee Simonson. A craft study and report. Meyerhold, Kamerny Theatre, Moscow Art Theatre, etc.

_____, "The Soviet Theatre Turns Realistic," <u>Research Bulletin On the Soviet Soviet Union</u>, July 15, 1936, 1-3.

_____, "'Standing Room Only' In Moscow," <u>American Scholar</u>, Autumn 1936,396-402.

_____, <u>Return Engagement; A Postscript To 'Moscow Rehearsals'</u>, 1962. illus.

_____, "Creativity and Control In the Soviet Union," <u>Tri-Quarterly</u>, Spring 1965, 139-143.

JELAGIN, Juri, <u>Taming Of the Arts</u>, 1951. Author played violin in orchestra of Vakhtangov Theatre, later was concertmaster of USSR State Jazz Band and a first violin in USSR State Symphony; in 1948 joined Houston Symphony. Lively and informative when concerned with something author has known: Alexei Tolstoy, the Vakhtangov Theatre, Meyerhold's eclipse, Soviet jazz efforts, the Moscow Conservatory, Kremlin musical soirees, Stalin's musical tastes.

JOHNSON, Priscilla, and Leopold Labedz, eds, <u>Krushchev and the Arts; The Politics Of Soviet Culture, 1962-1964</u>, M.I.T: Cambridge, 1965. Includes many texts first published in <u>CDSP</u> and <u>En</u> for this period, by Romm, Krushchev, Ilyichev, Ermilov, Ehrenberg, Adzhubei, etc; and interpretation by Johnson.

KAUN, Alexander, <u>Soviet Poets and Poetry</u>, Berkeley and Los Angeles, 1943. Possibly the one sympathetic, detailed book treatment of Soviet Literature in English.

KRIDL, Manfred, "Russian Formalism," <u>American Bookman,</u> 1944.

KUNITZ, Joshua, <u>Russian Literature and the Jew; A Sociological Inquiry Into the Nature and Origin Of Literary Patterns</u>, 1929.

_____, "Men and Women In Soviet Literature," <u>VOO</u>, 66-173. The 20s.

LABEDZ, Leopold, "A Chronicle Of the Chill," <u>PR</u>, Spring 1963, 99-108. Quotes and incidents, 1962-63. - See also <u>Survey</u>, edited by Labedz and Walter Laqueur, for frequent accounts of the arts in socialist countries.

LAQUEUR, Walter Z, and George Lichtheim, <u>The Soviet Cultural Scene, 1956-57</u>, Praeger: 1958. Commentary reprinted from <u>Survey</u>.

LEHMANN-HAUPT, Hellmut, <u>Art Under a Dictatorship</u>, 1954. illus. Chief use of book is for details on Hitler and art. Chapter, "Art In Soviet Russia," 216-235, analyzes early surge and later suppression of modernist Russian visual arts as another phase of theme. Chapter on East Germany speaks of Dymschits' role there in establishing Socialist

Realism.

LONDON, Kurt, The Seven Soviet Arts, London, 1937. Lively, sympathetic critique of Soviet culture and its organization.

LOZOWICK, Louis, Modern Russian Art, 1925. illus. Extremely valuable as a presentation of "comfut" era of Soviet painting, when Party policy tolerated, even encouraged, the alliance of Communism and Futurism.

_____, "Soviet Painting and Architecture," VOO, 265-291. illus.

_____, and Joseph Freeman, "The Soviet Theatre," VOO, 174-215.

LUBETKIN, Berthold, "Architectural Thought Since the Revolution," Architectural Review (London), May 1932, 201ff. illus.

MACDONALD, Dwight, "The Soviet Cinema, 1930-38," PR, July 1938, 37-50; Aug-Sept, 35-62; Winter 1939, 80-95.

MACLEOD, Joseph, The New Soviet Theatre, London, 1943. illus. Soviet drama 1937-41. Describes Socialist Realist conquest of the Russian and minority culture stages.

MARSHALL, Herbert, Soviet Cinema, London, 1945. 40 pp.

MATHEWSON, Rufus, The Positive Hero In Russian Literature, Columbia Univ: 1958. Analysis stops at 1946. Origin of Russian positive hero, "beyond the superfluous man," with radical 19th century Russian critics, especially Belinsky with his contempt for Oblomovian submission and his urging of active and purposive counter-hero. - Review by L. Shchepilov, CDSP, June 1, 1960, 24-26, 44.

McLEAN, Hugh, "Voronskij and VAPP," The American Slavic and East European Review, Oct 1949, 185-200. Voronsky's defense of artist fellow-travellers.

_____, and Walter N. Vickery, Introduction, The Year Of Protest 1956, 1961. Account of Party control of culture.

_____, Rufus W. Mathewson, and Gleb Struve, Discussion Of Russian and Soviet Literature. Slavic Review, 1962 #3. - Review by SL, 1963 #6, 149-154.

_____, "Et Resurrexerunt: How Writers Rise From the Dead," PC, May-June 1963, 33-41. Rehabilitation of literary reputations following Stalin period.

MEYER, Franz, "Chagall As Commissar For Art," in his: Marc Chagall, Thames and Hudson: London, 1964, 265-288; 412-414. illus. Chagall's impassioned effort to make, in his words, "the average citizen into a creator." Quotations from essays of the period.

MIHAJLOV, Mihajlo, Moscow Summer, New Leader: 1965. First-hand accounts of Soviet writers.

NELS, Sophia, "Shakespeare and the Soviet Theatre: The Optimism Of Tragedy," Antioch Review, Spring 1964, 103-111.

OLKHOVSKY, Andrey, Music Under the Soviets, 1955. Former head of Department of Music Theory and History, Kiev Conservatory from 1934 until he left during German occupation in 1942, offers some light and much vulgar anti-Sovietism. Bibliography.

PALOCZI-HORVATH, George, The Writer and the Commissar, London, 1960. Small, shrill volume but of some information value.

PARKER, Stephen Jan, "Hemingway's Revival In the Soviet Union, 1955-1962," in: Roger Asselineau, ed, The Literary Reputation Of Hemingway In Europe, Gotham paperback: 1965, 177-195. Begins with the 1920s, but focuses on the writings of Kashkeen.

PATRICK, G, Popular Poetry In Soviet Russia, Berkeley, 1929. The peasant and proletarian poets.

PAUL, Edan and Cedar, Proletcult, London, 1921. Survey of proletarian education organizations in various countries: England, America, Russia especially.

PERLMAN, Louis, Russian Literature and the Business Man, 1937. Doctoral thesis of limited value as survey.

POGGIOLI, Renato, The Phoenix and the Spider; A Book Of Essays On Russian Writers and Their View Of the Self, Harvard Univ. Press: Cambridge, 1957.

_____, The Poets Of Russia, 1890-1930, Harvard University Press: Cambridge, 1960.

RADAMSKY, Sergei, "Soviet Direction In Music," N.Y. Times, Apr 5, 1936.

RIESER, Max, "Russian Aesthetics Today and Their Historical Background," JAAC, Fall 1963, 47-53. Summaries and quotations from leading spokesmen of official USSR aesthetics.

ROBACK, A.A, Contemporary Yiddish Literature, Lincoln-Praeger: London, 1957.

ROSTOVTSEV, M. I, Proletarian Culture, Publication #11 of Russian Liberation Committee, London, 1919? Emigre social-democratic professor from Petrograd denounces Bolshevik cultural program as destructive of established cultural institutions. Horrific innuendoes but no hard evidence.

SAYLER, Oliver M, "Futurists and Others In Famished Moscow: Radical Artists Find New Manners Of Expression Amid Social Chaos," Vanity Fair, Sept 1919, 54, 119.

_____, The Russian Theatre, 1922. illus. Based on author's six-month visit in 1918.

SCHWARTZ, Boris, "Stravinsky In Soviet Russian Criticism," The Musical Quarterly (London), July 1962, 340-361.

SEDURO, V, Dostoevsky In Russian Literary Criticism, 1846-1956, Columbia Univ: 1957.

SHUB, B, The Writer and the State: A Documentary Study Of the Literary Revolt In Russia, Calcutta: 196?.

SIMMONS, Ernest J, Russian Fiction and Soviet Ideology: Introduction To Fedin, Leonov, and Sholokhov, Columbia University Press: 1958.

_____, Continuity and Change In Russian and Soviet Thought, Harvard University Press: Cambridge, 1955.

_____, Introduction To Russian Realism: Pushkin, Gogol, Dostoevsky, Tolstoy, Chekov and Sholokhov, Indiana Univ: Bloomington, 1965.

SLONIM, Marc, Soviet Russian Literature: Writers and Problems, Oxford: 1964.

_____, Russian Theatre From the Empire To the Soviets, World: 1961.

SLONIMSKY, Nicholas, "Development Of Soviet Music," Research Bulletin On the Soviet Union, Apr 30, 1937, 31-36.

SOCIETY FOR CULTURAL RELATIONS BETWEEN THE PEOPLES OF THE BRITISH COMMONWEALTH AND THE U.S.S.R, London, has many reports and translations of materials on theatre, literature, film, etc., in USSR, in its London offices and at the British Museum.

SOVIET LITERATURE YESTERDAY AND TODAY, Survey, Special Issue, #36 (Apr-June 1961). Essays on Dostoevsky scholarship, Sholokhov, Kafka, literary trends, Jewish literature, literary controls, Pilnyak and Zamyatin, Voronsky, etc.

STEPANCHEV, Stephen, "Whitman In Russia," in: Gay Wilson Allen, ed, Walt Whitman Abroad, Syracuse: 1955, 144-155.

STRUVE, Gleb, Soviet Russian Literature 1917-1950, Norman, Okla, 1951. Summaries of points of view, protagonists, controversies in the theory of art.

_____, "Western Writing On Soviet Literature," Survey, Jan 1964, 137-145. Evaluates treatments of Soviet literature.

SWAYZE, Harold, Political Control Of Literature In the USSR, 1946-1959, Cambridge, Mass, 1962. - Review by Dmitri Dmitriev, SL, 1964 #2, 144-148.

TAUBMAN, Howard, "Compositions Of Avant-Garde Music Gaining Influence In Soviet," N.Y. Times, Feb 18, 1966, 22. illus. 12-tone and aleatory techniques.

"THE NEW ARCHITECTURE," EE, Apr 1965, 7-15. illus. Post-Stalinist developments in Eastern Europe. Leading architects cited.

UNGER, Heinz, in collaboration with Naomi Walford, Hammer, Sickle, and Baton: The Soviet Memoirs Of a Musician, London, 1939. Between 1924 and 1937. Unger was frequent visiting conductor of Soviet orchestras. Personal experience of musical conditions and apparatus.

URBAN, G.R, Talking To Eastern Europe, Eyre & Spottiswoode: London, 1964. From programming of Radio Free Europe. Includes Petru Dumitriu, "The Positive Hero;" George Mikes, "Two Answers;"

G.R. Urban, "A Journey;" Ronald Hingley, "Ehrenburg and Solzhenitsyn;" Maurice Cranston, "The Dialectics of Monsieur Sartre."

VAS, Robert, "Sunflowers and Commissars," Sight and Sound, Summer 1962, 148-151. Evaluates history of Soviet cinema.

VICKERY, Walter N, The Cult Of Optimism, Indiana Univ: Bloomington, 1962. Postwar Soviet literary attitudes.

VIERECK, Peter, "The Mob Within the Heart; A New Russian Revolution," Tri-Quarterly, Spring 1965, 7-43. Unusually detailed account of the younger artistic generation in USSR.

VOYCE, Arthur, Russian Architecture, 1948.

VOZNESENSKY, A, "Problems Of Method In The Study Of Literature In Russia," The Slavonic Review, June 1927.

WELLEK, Rene, "Social and Aesthetic Values In Russian Nineteenth-Century Literary Criticism (Belinskii, Chernyshevskii, Dobroliubov, Pisarev)," in: Ernest J. Simmons, ed, Continuity and Change In Russian and Soviet Thought, Cambridge, Mass, 1955, 381-397.

WERTH, Alexander, Musical Uproar In Moscow, London, 1949. Extensive portions of Zhdanov's discussions with Soviet composers, musicians, bureaucrats, translated. Background information and commentary.

WHO'S WHO IN SOVIET SOCIAL SCIENCES, HUMANITIES, ART AND GOVERNMENT, compiled by Ina Telberg, Telberg Book Co: 1961. Based on information in 3rd edition, 'Malaia Sovetskaia Entsiklopedia', Moscow, 1958-61.

WINTER, Ella, "Lissitzky: A Revolutionary Out Of Favor," Art News, Apr 1958, 28-31, 62-64. illus. Good account of his career and adherence to the Revolution.

WOLFE, Bertram D, USIA Background Paper on Developments In Soviet Culture. United States Information Agency, Central Program Services Division Ideological Advisory Staff, Ideological Special no. 294, Jan 14, 1953. [USIA Library Archives, Washington D. C.] States a letter to compiler from John E. Bauernschmidt of USIA Office of Public Information, Jan 28, 1965:

"....a privileged communication belonging to the United States Government and the U.S. Information Agency. Although it is not classified and is available for study to appropriate persons, we do not believe the paper should, as you have indicated, be included in a bibliography of a publication intended for general distribution and with the resulting inference that it is available to all segments of the public." The reader is so warned.

WRIGHT, Frank Lloyd. See Wright (LXIII).

YARMOLINSKY, Avrahm, Literature Under Communism: The Literary Policy Of the Communist Party Of the Soviet Union From the End Of World War II To the Death Of Stalin, Bloomington, Indiana, 1960.

YERSHOV, Peter, Comedy In the Soviet Theatre, Praeger: 1956. Useful survey emphasizing socially critical application of comedy.

_____, Science Fiction and Utopian Fantasy In Soviet Literature, East European Fund, mimeographed series, #62 (1954). Pre-Soviet and Soviet science fiction as social criticism; varieties and development. Well written by one-time Dean of Literary Faculty at Odessa University.

YOUNG, James S, "Communist Vulnerabilities To the Use Of Music In Psychological Warfare," HumRRO Technical Report, no. 4, 1964. - See also Kofsky (LVII).

ZAVALISHEN, Vyacheslav, Early Soviet Writers, Praeger: 1958. Pre-revolutionary to 1929, a detailed survey.

ZEKULIN, Gleb, "Socialist Realism," SS, Apr 1960, 432-441. Review-article of discussion by Abram Tertz (See Sinyavsky (XLVI),) and A.I. Metchenko (Introduction to 'Istoriya russkoi Sovetskoi literatury', 1958.)


URUGUAY

L. Authors

FRASCONI, Antonio, Statement. Tiger's Eye, #8 (1949), 59-61. "Art must be like bread, like the sun - the intimate of people, all people." Suitableness of woodcuts to this goal.

# UNITED STATES OF AMERICA

## Topic Index: Architecture

CITY PLANNING. Mumford (LXII).

ECONOMICS. Schapiro (LII).

WRIGHT, F.L. See Wright (LXIII);
Egbert (LIX).

## Topic Index: Art and Sculpture

ACA GALLERY. Riddell (LIII).

ACTION PAINTING. Berger (XXIII);
Rosenberg (LIII).

ARMORY SHOW. Brown, Fraina, Rosenberg,
Schapiro (LIII).

ASH CAN SCHOOL. Brown (LIII); Sloan
(LXII).

BARR, A.H. Schapiro (LIII).

BELLOWS, G. Brown (LIII).

BENTON, T.H. Brown (LIII).

BERENSON, B. James (I); Schapiro
(LIII).

BURLIUK, D. Gold (LIII).

CARTIER-BRESSON. Summers (LIII).

ECONOMICS. Harris, McCausland (LXII).
See General Topics, Art and Sculpture,
Government and Business Patronage.

GORKY, A. Rosenberg (LIII).

GWATHMEY, R. Robeson (I).

HISTORY. Brown, Lafollette, Larkin
(LIII); Harris (LXII).

LIPCHITZ. Berger (XXIII); Trotsky
(XLVI).

MODERNISM. See General Topics, Art and
Sculpture, Abstractionist and Surrealist Art.

MURALS. Porter (LIII).

NEGRO ART. See (I).

O'KEEFE, G. Brown (LIII).

OP ART. Rosenberg (LIII).

POLLOCK, J. Berger (XXIII); Rosenberg
(LIII).

POP ART. Baxandall, Evergood, Meyers,
Rosenberg (LIII); Kaprow (LXIII).

REALISM. See General Topics, Art and
Sculpture, Realism in Art.

SOCIAL DETERMINANTS. Brown, Finkelstein,
LaFollette, Brown (LIII); Clark (LIX);
Harris (LXII); Rivers (LXIII).

STIEGLITZ. Brown (LIII).

TASTE, CULTURE-LAG. Rosenberg, Schapiro
(LIII).

UNITED AMERICAN ARTISTS. 1941 (LI);
Herr (LIII).

WPA ARTS PROJECT. Writers Program (I);
Cronbach, Jones, Koerner, LaMore,
Refregier, Schapiro (LIII); Lawrence
(LIX).

## Topic Index: Cinema

BOETTICHER, B.L. Russell (XXIII).

CHAPLIN, C. See Great Britain, Cinema
Topics.

ECONOMICS. Ivens (XXVI); Ehrenburg,
Eisenstein (XLIV); Jerome, Lawson,
Potamkin (LIV).

FILM AND PHOTO LEAGUE. Gessner, Hurwitz,
'Movie Bulletin', Potamkin (LIV).

FORD, J. Russell (XXIII).

GRIFFITH. Eisenstein (XLIV); Lawson (LIV).

MARX, GROUCHO. See (LXIII).

RACISM. Zhukov (XLIV); Jerome, Lawson,
Potamkin, Uhse (LIV).

SCREEN WRITERS GUILD. See 1941 (LI);
Kempton (LIX).

## Topic Index: Dance

AUDIENCE. Duncan, Sellars, Sokolow,
Wylie (LV).

BALLET, CLASSICAL, AGAINST. Duncan,
Fraina, Sokolow (LV).

RED DANCERS. Segal (LV).

STYLE AND CONTENT. Anyon, Bayer, Delza, Eisenberg, Fraina, Hays, Ocko, Sokolow (LV).

SUBJECTIVISM IN SOCIAL DANCE. Abbott, Chilkowsky, Eisenberg, Elion, Gold (LV).

WORKERS (AND NEW) DANCE LEAGUE. Anyon, Elion, Foster, Sellars.

#### Topic Index: Literature and General

ADAMS, H. Hicks, Johnson, Whipple (LVI); Brooks, Howe, Parrington, Rader (LXII).

ALBEE, E. See Theatre Topics.

ALEICHEM, S. Landau (LVI); Howe (LXII).

ALGREN, N. Geismar (LXII).

ANDERSON, S. Dinamov (XLVI); Seaver, Whipple (LVI); Geismar (LXII). See Anderson (LXIII).

ASCH, M. Slochower (LVI).

BABBITT, I. Weimann (XXI); Freeman, Smith (LVI); Wilson (LXII).

BALDWIN, J. See African and Afro-American Topics.

BEAT LITERATURE. Fischer (XXI); 1964 (LI); Heifetz, Hodges, Marcuse, Schleifer, Sigal (LVI).

BELLOW, S. Finkelstein, Lawson (LVI); Geismar (LXII).

BOURNE, R. See (LXII).

BROMFIELD, L. Lukacs (XXVII).

BROOKS, C. Weimann (XXI); Smith (LVI).

BROWDERISM IN CULTURE. 1946 (LI).

BRYANT, W.C. Glicksberg, Sillen (LVI).

BURKE, K. See Burke (LVI).

BURROUGHS, W. Baxandall, Finkelstein, Heifetz, Uhse (LVI); Adam (LXII).

CAHAN, A. Schappes (LVI); Rideout (LIX).

CALDWELL, E. Beach (LXII).

CAPOTE, T. Landor (XLVI); Baxandall (LVI).

CATHER, W. Whipple (LVI); Geismar (LXII).

CONROY, J. Elistratova (XLVI); D. Brown (XLIX); Madden (LIX).

COOPER, J.F. Lukacs (XXVII); Gorky (XLVI); Hicks (LVI); Brooks, Parrington (LXII).

COZZENS, J.G. Geismar (LXII).

CRANE, H. Schappes (LVI).

CRANE, S. Hicks, Nye, Solomon (LVI); Brooks, Geismar (LXII).

CRITICISM, AMERICAN, HISTORY. Weimann (XXI); Calverton, Freeman, Smith (LVI); Brooks, Clark, Howells, Kostelanetz, Ruland (LXII). See: New Criticism (below).

CRITICISM, MARXIST, HISTORY. Calmer, Calverton, Clecak, Folsom, Freeman, Phillips (LVI); Aaron, Glicksberg, Kazin, Kostelanetz, Sutton, Van Deusen, White, Wilson (LIX).

DELL, F. See (LXII).

DEWEY, J. Finkelstein, Slochower (LVI).

DOS PASSOS, J. Aragon, Sartre (XIX); Bruning (XXI); Vishnevsky (XLVI); D. Brown (XLIX); Finkelstein, Gold, Slochower, Whipple (LVI); Gelfant, Madden (LIX); Beach, Geismar, Wilson (LXII).

DREISER, T. Fox (XXIII); Eisenstein (XLIV); Burgum, Whipple (LVI); Brooks, Geismar, Matthiessen (LXII). See Dreiser (LXIII).

EASTMAN, M. See (LIX).

ECONOMICS OF LEFT WRITING. Zasursky (XLVI); Gold, Hart, Maltz (LVI).

ELIOT, T.S. Weimann (XXI); Henderson, Long, 'Marxism Today', Morton, Strachey, Thomas, West (XXIII); Ames, Bates, Baxandall, Calmer, Calverton, Finkelstein, Hicks, Lowenfels, Millet, Phillips, Rahv, Robbins, Schappes, Slochower, Wilson (LVI); Harrison, Williams (LXII).

EMERSON. Hicks (LVI); Brooks, Chapman, Matthiessen (LXII).

FARRELL, J. See (LVI). Beach (LXII).

FASCISM, EUROPEAN, EFFECT ON AMERICAN CULTURAL LEFT. Lozowick (LIII); Dal Negro, Sokolow (LV); Arvin, Browder, Freeman, Hicks, Welles (LVI); Elion,

Prentis (LVIII); Rader (LXII); Strachey
(XXIII). 1935-41 (LI).

FAULKNER. Sartre (XIX); Dneprov, Landor,
Mendelson (XLVI); Burgum, Calverton,
Conroy, Finkelstein, Giles, Kroner
(LVI); Beach, Geismar (LXII).

FITZGERALD, F.S. Guseva (XLVI); Finkelstein, Greenleaf (LVI); Geismar (LXII).

FRANK, W. Lann (XLVI).

FRENEAU, P. Calverton (LVI).

FROST, R. Finkelstein, Fraina, Whipple
(LVI); F. Adams (XLIX); Howe (LXII).

GLASGOW, Ellen. Geismar (LXII).

GOLD, M. See (LIII), (LVI),(LVII).

GREGORY, H. See (LVI). Calmer (LVI).

HAWTHORNE. Hicks (LVI); Brooks, Howe,
Matthiessen, Parkes (LXII).

HAYAKAWA, S. Schlauch (LVI).

HAZLITT, H. Calverton, Rahv, Smith (LVI).

HELLER, J. Burgum (LVI).

HEMINGWAY. Bruning (XXI); Anand (XXVIII);
Dneprov, Ehrenberg, Kashkeen, Mendelson
(XLVI); D. Brown, Parker (XLIX);
Barnes, Burgum, Calverton, Knapp,
Rubinstein, Slochower, Wilson (LVI);
Beach, Geismar (LXII). See Hemingway
(LXIII).

HERSEY, J. Geismar (LXII).

HOWELLS, W.D. Getzels, Hicks, Smith
(LVI).

HUNEKER, J. Weimann (XXI).

HUGHES, L. See (I).

IRVING, W. Brooks (LXII).

JAMES, H. Weimann (XXI); Goode, Kettle,
(XXIII); Spender (XXIV); Schneider,
1945 (LI); Cantwell, Finkelstein, Folsom, Gold (LVI); Brooks, Geismar, Howe,
Matthiessen (LXII).

JEFFERS, R. Schappes (LVI).

JEWS AND LITERATURE. Ausubel, Gold,
Harap, Kunitz, Nadir, Schappes (LVI);
Aaron, Rideout (LIX); Kostelanetz
(LXII).

JOHN REED CLUBS. See 1929-34 (LI).

JONES, J. Geismar (LXII).

LARDNER, R. Gold (LVI); Geismar (LXII).

LEWIS, S. Lukacs (XXVII); Mendelson
(XLVI); D. Brown (XLIX); Calverton,
Cantwell, Hicks, Whipple (LVI);
Geismar (LXII).

LIBERALS, FACING MARXISM. 1927-37 (LI);
Burke, Cowley, Freeman, Gold, Hicks,
McKenney, Rahv, Stewart, Whipple (LVI);
Miller, Thompson (LIX); Brooks, Mum-
ford, Wilson (LXII).

LINDSAY, V. Fraina, Whipple (LVI).

LITERATURE, HISTORY. Gorky Institute,
Mendelson (XLVI); Calverton, Freeman,
Hicks, LeRoy, Sinclair, Whipple (LVI);
Aldridge, Bourne, Brooks, Geismar,
Hassan, Macy, Marx, Matthews, Matthies-
sen, Parkes, Parrington, Smith, Whipple,
Wilson (LXII).

LITERATURE, RADICAL, HISTORY. Aaron,
Egbert, Filler, Glicksberg, Hazlitt,
Kozlenko, Lawrence, Lind, Muste,
Swados, Thorp,'Times', Wilson (LIX).

LITERATURE, SOCIAL DETERMINANTS. Calverton, Fast, Hicks, Whipple (LVI);
Brooks (LXII).

LONDON, J. Ames, London, Whipple (LVI);
Foner (LIX); Geismar (LXII).

LOWELL, R. Finkelstein (LVI).

LUBBOCK, P. Weimann (XXI).

MacLEISH, A. Humphries (LVI).

MAGAZINES, LEFT. Wright (I); Elistra-
tova, Trotsky (XLVI); Gellert (LIII);
Gold, Howard, Humboldt, Magil, North,
Snow (LVI); Aaron, Lecky, O'Neill
(LIX); Hoffman (LXIV).

MAILER, N. Lukacs (XXVII); Finkelstein,
Humboldt (LVI); Geismar, Howe (LXII);
Mailer (LXIII).

MARKHAM, E. Abbott (LVI).

MARQUAND, J.P. Beach, Geismar (LXII).

MASTERS, E.L. Fraina (LVI).

McCARTHYISM, IMPACT. 1947-49 (LI); Bessie, Biberman, Lampell (LIV); Clecak
(LVI).

MELVILLE. James (I); Hicks, Lawson, Rukeyser (LVI); Brooks, Matthiessen, Parkes (LXII).

MENCKEN, H. Geismar (LXII).

MILLER, A. See Theatre Topic Index.

MILLER, H. Finkelstein (LVI); Madden (LIX); Orwell, Way (LXII).

NATIONAL VS. INTERNATIONAL VALUES. Gregory, LeSeuer, Rukeyser, Taggard (LVI).

NEGRO WRITING. See (I).

'NEW CRITICISM'. Weimann (XXI); Leavis (XXIV); Finkelstein, Millet, Rudich (LVI); Eliot (LIX).

NOVEL, PROLETARIAN. 1935 (LI); Appel, Barnes, Bersin, Bonosky, Conroy, Donato, Finkelstein, Fraina, Giles, Hicks, Humboldt, Letters, Phillips, Seaver, Sillen, Smith, Stevenson (LVI); Adamic, Kempton, Lind, Madden, Strauss (LIX). Also book reviews in NM and other publications.

NORRIS, F. Brooks, Geismar (LXII).

OBJECTIVISM. Fearing (LVI).

O'NEILL. See Theatre Topic Index.

ORTEGA Y GASSET. Phillips (LVI).

PARRINGTON, V. See (LXII).

PAUL, E. Bruning (XXI).

PEDANTICISM, MARXIST. 1934 (LI); Gold (LVI).

POE. Korponun (XXVII); Harap (LVI); Parkes (LXII).

POETRY AND COMMITMENT. Bodenheim, Cheyney, Conroy, Fearing, Gold, Gregory, Schneider, Taggard (LVI); Ginsberg (LXIII); Madden (LIX).

POETRY, HISTORY. Schlauch (LVI).

POLITICAL GUIDANCE AND LITERATURE. 1946, 1964 (LI); Browder, Calmer, Foster, Gregory, Jerome, Oglesby, Sillen (LVI); Aaron, Fiedler (LIX).

POUND, E. Millet, Schlauch (LVI); Wilson (LXII). See Pound (LXIII).

PROLETARIAN VS. UNITED FRONT EMPHASIS. 1933-35, 1946 (LI); Burke, Calverton, Hicks, Schachner (LVI); Aaron (LIX).

PROPAGANDA AND ART. Burke, Rahv, Rudnick (LVI).

PURDY, K. Finkelstein (LVI).

RANSOM, J.C. Weimann (XXI).

REGIONAL REVOLUTIONARY WRITING. 1936 (LI); Brand, Botkin, LeSeuer (LVI).

RENEGADES, PROBLEM OF. Calverton, Cowley, Fast, Gold, Humboldt (LVI); Chaplin (LIX); Wolfe (XLIX); Geismar, Rexroth (LXII).

RICHARDS, I.A. Weimann (XXI); West (XXIII); Smith (LVI).

ROBINSON, E.A. Whipple (LVI).

ROTH, P. Harap (LVI); Geismar (LXII).

SALINGER, J.D. Fischer (XXI); Finkelstein, Giles, Larner (LVI); Geismar (LXII).

SANDBURG, C. Mayakovsky (XLVI); Whipple (LVI).

SAROYAN, W. Burgum (LVI).

SELBY, H. Lowenfels (LVI).

SHORT STORY. Farrell, Humboldt (LVI).

SPANISH CIVIL WAR. Bruning (XXI); Bessie (LVI); Aaron, Benson, Muste (LIX); Hemingway (LXIII).

STALINISM, CHARGES OF. 1939 (LI); Cowley, Farrell, Fast, Fraina, Rahv (LVI); Eastman (LIX).

STEIN, G. Burgum, Wilson (LVI).

STEINBECK, J. Mendelson (XLVI); Burgum, Calverton, Slochower (LVI); Madden (LIX); Beach, Geismar (LXII).

STEVENS, W. Burnshaw (LIX); Howe (LXII).

STYRON, W. Finkelstein (LVI); Geismar (LXII).

TASTE, CULTURAL LAG IN. Arndt, Fraina, Gold, Schleifer (LVI).

TATE, A. Weimann (XXI).

## Topic Index: Music

## Topic Index: Theatre

STANISLAVSKY TECHNIQUE.  Thacher (LVIII);
Clurman (LIX).

THEATRE UNION.  Brecht, Wolf (XXI);
Baxandall, Blake, Dreiblatt, Larkin,
Northrup (LVIII); Himelstein (LIX).

THEATRE, SOCIAL, HISTORY.  Bruning,
Piscator, Wolf (XXI); Blake, Dana,
Gorelik, Odets, Taylor, Whitman
(LVIII); Clurman, Crowther, Hansen,
Flexner, Himelstein, Kempton, McDer-
mott, Meserve, Owensby, Rabkin (LIX).

WILLIAMS, T.  Finkelstein (LVI); Taylor
(LVIII); Tynan (LXII).

WORKERS LABORATORY THEATRE.  Blake,
Geer, Martin, Pack, Prentice, Saxe,
Warren (LVIII); Grady (LIX).

### LI.  Chronological

THE COMRADE, pub. 1901-1905; ed. John
Spargo to May 1904, then Otto Wegener.
Absorved into International Socialist
Review after April 1905.  First U.S.
attempt to express self-conscious
Marxian movement in art and literature, with much space devoted to
aesthetic theory and criticism. Locus
of most of the relevant materials published in U.S. in those years.  Strong
Ruskin-and-Morris influence with the
tone set by sentimental middle-class
gentility and secularized Christian
impulses. - See especially the articles by Leonard Abbott and John Spargo
in the monthly book-review column,
inter alia; some chief ones are listed
under these authors' names in sections
LIII and LVI, with an article by T.
Mufson; see also these representative
essays:

Editorial Statement Of Purpose, Oct
1901, 12.  Though economics is the
"basic human fact", this journal,
unlike others, aims to print such
literature and art "as reflects the
soundness of the Socialist philosophy", making available to the proletariat "the great masterpieces of
Painting, Song and Story that have
been worked and are working for the
great cause of Socialism".  The fires
of Ideal Beauty will be rekindled in
an age when religion is impotent and
Art is stifled by commercialism.

Editorials by Spargo and Abbott: Where
is the 'Uncle Tom's Cabin' of wage
slavery? Dec 1901,64; May 1903, 188.

Jean Longuet, "Zola the Socialist,"
Dec 1902, 51.

Eugene Limedorfer, "Gorky and His Philosophy," Nov 1901, 43-44.  Uses
the pre-Marxist Gorky to urge escape,
in literature and life, to the "real"
life of slums or to open country,
"from all the nonsensical nonentities
that dull the senses and corrupt
the intellect" in oppressive respec-
table society.

INTERNATIONAL SOCIALIST REVIEW, pub.
1900-1918.  See yearly index for book
reviews and occasional extended criticism and commentary on aesthetic
problems.

THE MASSES, pub. 1911-1917.  The primary
left cultural periodical of its period.
Strong anti-ideological bias prevented
much Marxist theoretical discussion of
aesthetics or practical commentary.

THE LIBERATOR, pub. 1918-1924.  The successor to the above; shared its limitations.

WORKERS DRAMA LEAGUE.  "The Revolutionary
Theatre," DWSup, Feb 28, 1925.  Meyerhold "the spirit of the revolutionary
drama in Soviet Russia" which "sweeps
everything before it."  US stirrings
in "the Workers Drama League, which
produced the beautiful pantomime for
the joint bazaar under the direction
of Sadie Amter."  Also 'The Paris Commune', a spectacle, to be staged Mch
15 with cast of hundreds at Madison
Square Garden. - Workers Drama League
staged M. Gold's "Money! Money! Money!'
Jan 8, 1926; late that year it acquired
a theatre next to the Provincetown
Players, off Washington Square, and
presented 'The Biggest Boob In the
World'.  See Max Geltman, "The Workers
Drama League," DWSup, Jan 15, 1927.
- For an early Philadelphia Workers
Theatre, see DW, Feb 25, 1927, 4.

"ARE ARTISTS PEOPLE?" Symposium, NM, Jan
1927, 5-9.  Answers on responsibilities
and attitudes of writers from: Harbor
Allen, Van Wyck Brooks, Heywood Broun,
Stuart Chase, Babette Deutsch, Waldo
Frank, Robinson Jeffers, Joseph Wood
Krutch, Bruce Barton, Llewelyn Powys,
Edwin Seaver, Upton Sinclair, Gene-
vieve Taggard, Edmund Wilson.

NEW PLAYWRIGHTS THEATRE.  See: M. Gold,
DWSup, Feb 26, 1927.  The priorities,

by a founding member: it "is going to
be the nearest thing" in America to
Russian Proletcult and will "break
down the walls" to the street and to
industrialized USA. - Statement by
the five founding playwrights on
politics and theatre, DW, Apr 5, 1927,
4. - Harbor Allen, DWSup, Mch 5, 1927.
Review of J.H. Lawson's 'Loudspeaker',
the first production. - H. Allen, DW,
Mch 13, 1927, 4.  Review of Em Jo
Basshe's 'Earth!'. - Nathaniel Buchwald, DW, Nov 1, 1927, 4.  Review of
'The Belt' by Paul Sifton. - Sender
Garlin, DW, Jan 16, 1928, 5.  Review
of Lawson's 'The International'; attacked by John Dos Passos, DW, Jan
20, 1928, 4; Jan 28, 4. - A.B. Magil,
DW, Feb 23, 1929, 4.  Review of Dos
Passos' 'Airways, Inc.'. - Also see
DW, Jan 28, 1928, 7; Feb 11, 8. - See
also persons mentioned (LVIII).

WORKERS LABORATORY THEATRE.  See DW,
Apr 18, 1929, 4; also James Warren,
"How Members Of the Workers Labora-
tory Theatre Live and Work," DW, Dec
28, 1934, 5. - See also Theatre Topic
Index.

JOHN REED CLUBS.  See A.B. Magil, DW,
Oct 11, 1930, 4.  Account of founding
in Oct 1929 and subsequent activity.
Preamble to Constitution is in Le, I i
(Nov 1932), 1; and Le, III vi (June
1933), 6.

V.F. CALVERTON, CAMPAIGN AGAINST.  See
Calverton (LVI). - For other contro-
versies see J. Farrell, J. Freeman,
M. Gold, G. Hicks, W. Phillips, P.
Rahv (LVI).

JOHN REED CLUBS, 1st NATIONAL CONFERENCE,
Chicago, May 1932.  See Minutes Of the
1st Conference Of the John Reed Clubs.
mimeo. [Collection of Daniel Aaron.]
Also "The John Reed Club Convention,"
NM, July 1932, 14-15; "Draft Manifesto
Of the John Reed Clubs," NM, June
1932, 3-4.

NATIONAL WORKERS THEATRE SPARTAKIADE,
New York, Apr 16-17, 1932.  Reports
and documents.  WT, May 1932.

"WHITHER THE AMERICAN WRITER?" Symposium,
MQ(B), Summer 1932, 11-19.  Answers
include: Dos Passos, S. Anderson, F.
Dell, E. Seaver, H. Hazlitt, M. Cowley,
E. Wilson, N. Arvin, G. Hicks, C.
Fadiman.

LEAGUE OF PROFESSIONAL GROUPS FOR
FOSTER AND FORD, Culture and the
Crisis, 1932.  32 pp.  Appeal from and
to middle class professionals and in-
tellectuals in support of national
slate of Communist candidates. Signers
include: S. Anderson, N. Arvin, E.
Caldwell, R. Cantwell, Lewis Corey,
[Louis Fraina], Henry Cowell, M. Cow-
ley, Countee Cullen, H.W.L. Dana, J.
Dos Passos, T. Dreiser, W. Frank,
Eugene Gordon, H. Gregory, G. Hicks,
Sidney Hook, Sidney Howard, Langston
Hughes, Matthew Josephson, Alfred
Kreymborg, Louis Lozowick, Isidore
Schneider, Frederick L. Schuman, E.
Seaver, Lincoln Steffens, Edmund
Wilson, Ella Winter. - The declaration
launched, DW, Oct 14, 1932, 1. - Back-
ground statement by James Rorty, Secre-
tary of the League, DW, Oct 13 1932,3.
- Manuscript and mimeographed materials
on the League in the papers of Lewis
Corey, Columbia University Library.

PEN AND HAMMER, organization founded by
C.P. to educate artists and intellectuals in Marxism and to direct them
into analysis of social problems.  For
sketch of organizing activities, see
Pen and Hammer Bulletin (New York), I
xvi (Aug 17, 1933).  (Coll. Paul
Romaine.)

1st WORKERS DANCE SPARTAKIADE [Program],
New York, June 4, 1933.  8 pp. [ES]
League aims and descriptions of par-
ticipating groups.

THEATRE UNION.  Michael Gold, DW, Dec
25, 1933, 5, on its origins.  For its
subsequent career see especially NTh.

"PROSPECTS FOR THE AMERICAN THEATRE,"
Symposium, NTh, Sept-Oct 1933, 4-9;
Jan 1934, 5-8.  Replies from Sidney
Howard, Alfred Kreymborg, Barrett H.
Clark, Anita Block, Rose McClendon,
Albert Maltz, Frank Gillmore, Michael
Gold, Paul Peters, J.H. Lawson, George
Sklar, Paul Green, Emjo Basshe, Lee
Simonson, J. Edward Bromberg, Alfred
Harding.

"FOR WHOM DO YOU WRITE?" Symposium, The
New Quarterly, Summer 1934, Special
Issue.  Responses from 40 prominent
American writers.

CONFERENCE OF THE JOHN REED CLUBS, Chicago,
Sept 1934.  See Orrick Johns, "The
John Reed Clubs Meet," NM, Oct 30, 1934,
25-26. - For decision to disband and

form League of American Writers, see
Aaron (LIX), 281-282.

"AUTHOR'S FIELD DAY: A SYMPOSIUM ON
MARXIST CRITICISM," NM, July 3, 1934.
Lively criticisms of the Marxist critics. Charges include vagueness,
patronizing niggardly approach, lack
of analysis. Contributors include E.
Caldwell, R. Cantwell, J. Conroy, E.
Dahlberg (who is the most vigorous
and specific), J. Farrell, J. Herbst,
J.H. Lawson. With replies from Stanley Burnshaw and Granville Hicks.

THE BOLSHEVIK REVOLUTION AND YOUR WRITING:
Questionnaire To American Authors From
the Secretariat Of the International
Union Of Revolutionary Writers. DW,
Sept 20, 1934, 5; Sept 21, 5; Sept 22,
7; Sept 26, 5. illus. Replies of J.
Freeman, M. Cowley, L. Adamic, I.
Schneider.

PROLETARIAN NOVEL: A DISCUSSION. PR,
II vii (1935). With E. Seaver, E.B.
Burgum, H. Hart, J. Farrell.

PROLETARIAN LITERATURE IN THE UNITED
STATES; AN ANTHOLOGY, ed. Michael Gold
et al, 1935. Includes creative mater-
ial, and critical essays by J. Freeman,
Obed Brooks, E.B. Burgum, Alan Calmer,
M. Cowley, M. Gold, G. Hicks, J.
Kunitz, W. Phillips and P. Rahv, Ber-
nard Smith.

1st AMERICAN WRITERS CONGRESS, New York,
Apr 26-28, 1935. See Henry Hart, ed,
American Writers' Congress, 1935.
Speeches on cultural matters by: Louis
Aragon, Malcolm Cowley, Earl Browder,
John Dos Passos, Kenneth Burke, Gran-
ville Hicks, Edwin Seaver, Meridel
LeSueur, Friedrich Wolf, Harry F.Ward,
Edward Dahlberg, Matthew Josephson,
Moissaye J. Olgin, Joseph Freeman,
Waldo Frank, Jack Conroy, James T.
Farrell, Isidor Schneider, Joseph
North, John Howard Lawson, Michael
Blankford and Nathaniel Buchwald,
Langston Hughes, Eugene Gordon, Eugene
Clay, Moishe Nadir, Clarence Hathaway,
Henry Hart, Alexander Trachtenberg.
In "Discussion and Proceedings," re-
marks by Martin Russak, Michael Gold,
Allen Porter, F. Wolf, J. Freeman, K.
Burke, Harry Carlisle, John Chamber-
lain, G. Hicks, Robert Gessner, Alfred
Hayes, Richard Wright, Merle Colby, E.
Dahlberg, Albert Maltz, Orrick Johns,
W. Frank. Also the "Call to the Con-
gress," etc. - Report in DW, Apr 29,

30, May 1, 1935. - Account by Harold
Rosenberg, Poetry, July 1935, 222-227;
by Kenneth Burke, Nation, May 15,
1935, 571.

1st AMERICAN ARTISTS CONGRESS, New York,
Feb 14-16, 1936. See: American Artists'
Congress. Proceedings. I, 1936. In-
cludes speeches of: Lewis Mumford,
Stuart Davis, Rockwell Kent, Joe Jones,
Aaron Douglas, Margaret Bourke-White,
Paul Manship, George Biddle, Heywood
Broun, Francis J. Gorman, Peter Blume,
Meyer Schapiro, Lynd Ward, Max Weber,
Gilbert Wilson, John Groth, Harry
Sternberg, Ralph M. Pearson, Saul
Schary, Arnold Blanch, Arnold Friedman,
Harry Gottlieb, Louis Lozowick, Margaret
Duroc, Hugo Gellert, J. C. Orozco,
David A. Siqueiros. - Call to the Con-
gress, DW, Sept 28, 1935, 7. - Reports
in DW, Feb 9, 11, 16, 18, 19, 21,
1936. - Report by 'Toros', LR, May
1936, 381-384; by Joseph Freeman, NM,
Feb 25, 1936, 9-10.

1st NATIONAL DANCE CONGRESS AND FESTIVAL,
May, 1936. See: Proceedings Of the
First National Dance Congress and
Festival, 1936. [ES] Speeches by
Jerome Bayer, Edna Ocko, etc. - Evalua-
tion by John Martin, N.Y. Times, May
31, 1936.

MIDWEST WRITERS CONFERENCE, Chicago,
June 13-14, 1936. Report by Meridel
LeSueur in Midwest: A Preview Of a
Review (1936), 1-2, an 8 pp. one-issue
forerunner of Midwest; A Review. Report by LeSueur also in PW, Nov 16,
1936, 124.

WESTERN WRITERS CONGRESS, San Francisco,
Nov 13-14, 1936. Report by Ella Winter,
PW, Nov 30, 1936, 345-346. Report by
Clara Weatherwax, DWSup, Dec 13, 1936,
11. Some of the texts in PW.

LEAGUE OF AMERICAN WRITERS CONFERENCE,
New York, Dec 6, 1936. See Bulletin,
Jan 1937. mimeo [LAW] Summaries:
Norbert Guterman, "Marx and Engels On
Literature," Kenneth Burke, "The Trans-
ference Of Symbols," Malcolm Cowley,
"Recent Changes Of Emphasis In Left
Criticism," Joseph Freeman, "Tenden-
cies In American Left-Wing Criticism."
Cowley and Freeman emphasize effort to
assimilate ongoing bourgeois tradition.
Discussion; the League's position;
plans for 2nd Congress.

2nd AMERICAN WRITERS CONGRESS, New York,

June 4-6, 1937.  See: Henry Hart, ed,
The Writer In a Changing World, 1937.
Speeches by: Newton Arvin, Malcolm
Cowley, Earl Browder, Archibald Mac-
Leish, Martha Gelhorn, Ernest Heming-
way, Harry Slochower, Francis Winwar,
Carlton Beals, Henry Hart, D.O. Stew-
art, A.R. Williams, B.A. Botkin, Ken-
neth Burke, Eugene Holmes, G. Hicks.
Introduction by Joseph Freeman.  Ac-
count of the Congress, the Call, de-
bates, etc. - Account of Poetry Sec-
tion debates by David Schubert,
Poetry, Sept 1937, 357-358. - Philip
Rahv, "Two Years Of Progress," PR,
Feb 1938, 22-30; comparison of 1st
and 2nd Congresses to bring out implicit changes of policy. - Report in
DW, June 7, 1937, 4; June 9, 7.
- Criticism by Dwight MacDonald,
Nation, June 19, 1937, 714; answered
by Henry Hart, ibid, June 26, 1937,
741.

2nd AMERICAN ARTISTS CONGRESS, Dec, 1937.
Report by Jacob Kainen, DW, Dec 27,
1937, 7.

SPANISH CIVIL WAR.  See: League of American Writers, Writers Take Sides; Letters About the War In Spain From 418
American Authors, 1938.  Includes: S.
Anderson, S.V. Benet, M. Blitzstein,
V.W. Brooks, Pearl Buck, K. Burke,
Marc Connelly, E.E. Cummings, J. Conroy, T. Dreiser, W. Faulkner, E. Fer-
ber, H. Gregory, E. Hemingway, R. Jeffers, E.L. Masters, R. Neibuhr, J.
Steinbeck, T. Wilder, etc.

LEAGUE FOR CULTURAL FREEDOM AND SOCIAL-
ISM, Manifesto.  Socialist Appeal,
June 6, 1939; reprinted in PR, Summer
1939, 125-127.  Signers include: James
Burnham, V.F. Calverton, J. Farrell,
D. MacDonald, Kenneth Patchen, W. Phillips, P. Rahv, Harold Rosenberg, Paul
Rosenfeld, Meyer Schapiro, Delmore
Schwartz, Winfield Scott, Bertram D.
Wolfe.  "Cultural circles, formerly
progressive, are now capitulating to
the spirit of fascism while ostensibly
combatting its letter.  They fight one
falsehood with another.  To the deification of Hitler and Mussolini they
counterpose the deification of Stalin,
the unqualified support of Roosevelt
....We recognize that the liberation
of culture is inseparable from the
liberation of the working classes and
of all humanity....We reject all theories and practices which tend to make
culture the creature of politics, even

revolutionary politics."

3rd AMERICAN WRITERS CONGRESS, New York,
June 2-5, 1939.  See: Donald Ogden
Stewart, ed, Fighting Words, 1940.
Speeches arranged and abridged, with
commentary, by editor.  The Russo-Ger-
man Nonagression Pact was signed be-
tween the Congress and publication of
this volume.  Speeches include: Ken-
neth Burke, Norman Corwin, Pietro di
Donato, J. Freeman, Lawrence Gellert,
Dashiell Hammett, Langston Hughes,
H.V. Kaltenborn, Alan Lomax, Albert
Maltz, Dorothy Parker, Earl Robinson,
Vincent Shean, et al. - See also:
Direction, May-June 1939, Special Is-
sue: Official Program, American Writ-
ers' Congress.  Includes pieces by
Hemingway, Dreiser, Van Wyck Brooks,
D.O. Stewart, K. Burke, Heinrich Mann,
Erika Mann, Ernst Bloch. - Account of
debates in Poetry Section by Kenneth
Fearing, Poetry, July 1939, 228-230.
- For D.O. Stewart, "President's Re-
port," see Bulletin, VI i (1939), I,
10-12.  For the Resolutions, Bulletin,
VI i (1939), 5, 9. - See [LAW] for
mss. of many of the speeches; for dis-
cussion in the Drama Section (L. Hellman, A. Maltz, G. Sklar, H.W.L. Dana,
Ben Irwin, et al); for discussion in
the Fiction Section (Ben Appel, P. di
Donato, Richard Wright, Feador O'Don-
nel, S. Sillen, Ruth Widen, S. Ish-
Eishor, W. Blake, L. Aragon, Alice
Ware, S.T. Warner, Jenny Balou, Wellington Roe, Hope Hale, Lester Cohen,
Michael Blankfort).

'THE SITUATION IN AMERICAN WRITING', PR,
Summer 1939, 25-51; Fall 1939, 104-122.
Statements by Dos Passos, A. Tate, J.
Farrell, K. Fearing, K.A. Porter, W.
Stevens, G. Stein, W.C. Williams, J.P.
Bishop, Harold Rosenberg, Henry Miller,
Sh. Anderson, Louise Bogan, L. Trill-
ing, R.P. Warren, R. Fitzgerald, H.
Gregory, R.P. Blackmur.  Assessing the
audience, literary criticism, the 1930s
and the future.

MANIFESTO DEFENDING THE SOVIET UNION,
Nation, Aug 26, 1939, 228.  Signed by
some 400 writers and artists; counters
the Manifesto of the League for Cultural Freedom and Socialism.

STATEMENTS ON ANTI-SEMITISM.  League of
American Writers, "We Hold These
Truths . . ." Statements on Anti-
Semitism By 54 Leading American Writers,
Statesmen, Educators, Clergymen and

Trade-Unionists, 1939. Includes: S.V. Benet, Louis Bromfield, V.W. Brooks, H.S. Canby, Martha Dodd, T. Dreiser, H.E. Fosdick, G. Hicks, L. Hughes, R. Kent, Paul de Kruif, J.H. Lawson, A. Maltz, Ruth McKenney, Samuel Putnam, G. Seldes, U. Sinclair, D.O. Stewart, Rex Stout, G. Taggard, Dorothy Thompson, M.H. Vorse, Leane Zugsmith.

EXILED WRITERS' COMMITTEE, League of American Writers, We Must Save Them All; A Report, n.d. (1940?) [LAW] Appeals by US and refugee writers for aid to save Hitler's victims in the field of culture.

JEROME, V.J, Intellectuals and the War, 1940. Rebukes United Front intellectuals who have deserted: they never understood "the democratic tactic," and "did not perceive the tactical line of the People's Front in real relation to the basic strategy of the revolutionary working class for the attainment of power."

4th AMERICAN WRITERS CONGRESS, New York, June 6-8, 1941. Mss. of speeches in [LAW]. Speeches by: Richard Wright (also in NM, June 17, 1941, 8-12), Dashiell Hammett, Samuel Putnam, Rockwell Kent, G. Taggard, M. Tjader Harris, Wellington Roe, Millen Brand, Robert Carse, Ben Appel, Paul Kent, Mary Lapsley, May McNeer Ward, Margaret T. Raymond, Alvah Bessie, S. Sillen, J.H. Lawson, Lem Ward, Eleanor Flexner, Dorothy Brewster, E.B. Burgum, M. Gold, H. Aptheker, Paul Strand, Hollywood screenwriters. (See the writers by name for contents of speeches).) Also resolutions, calls, etc; Drama Section discussion (M. Blitzstein, Barrie Stavis, J.H.Lawson, C. Odets, Brett Warren, Sam Green, Peter Martin, Alice Ware, Ruth McKenney); general discussion (J.H. Lawson, J. Kunitz, H.W.L. Dana, M. Schappes, A. Kreymborg, William Alto, Milton Howard). - See also Official Program, Fourth American Writers Congress In Defense Of Culture and Congress Of American Artists, with brief histories of League of American Writers, American Artists Congress and United American Artists. [LAW]

AMERICAN ARTISTS CONGRESS, New York, June 6-8, 1941. Held in conjunction with 4th American Writers Congress. Mss. of speeches in [LAW]. Speeches by Lynd Ward, Jerome Klein, Elizabeth McCausland, Chet La More, Louis Lozowick, Daniel Koerner, Robert Cronbach, Morris Neuwirth. (See artists by name for contents of speeches.) - See also Official Program (above).

STAGE FOR ACTION. See Beth McHenry, DW, Feb 6, 1946, 5; also DW, Feb 20, 1946, 11; Feb 19, 1947, 11; and Alex Leith, interview with S. Sillen, DW, Aug 27, 1946, 11. Revival of agitprop following the war.

BROWDERISM IN CULTURE:

Isidore Schneider, "Probing Writers' Problems," NM, Oct 23, 1945, 22-25. Following meetings with writers, an editor of NM begins post-war discussion in print by assessing the 30s inheritance in literature and criticism. Finds it discouragingly meagre and often distorted by "political expediency."

Isidore Schneider, "Henry James: Mandarin?" NM, Dec 18, 1945, 23. James rehabilitated for the Left; a major gesture toward a new policy.

Albert Maltz, "What Should We Ask Of Writers?" NM, Feb 12, 1946, 19-22. The key article in the controversy. Goes little beyond Schneider in pleading, with citations from Marx and Engels, for a view of art that is detached from immediate political exigencies.

Isidore Schneider, "Background to Error," NM, Feb 12, 1946, 23-25. Accepts the Maltz view in all essentials, but mitigates past failures by pointing out frustrating conditions of Marxist criticism.

Robert Thompson, "The Expulsion of Earl Browder," DW, Feb 24, 1946, 4. In report to National Committee meeting which took the action, Browder is charged among other things with "justification and an attempt to encourage such loosening and irresponsible and inexcusable breaches of party discipline and control of policies as was represented by the publication in the 'New Masses' of the smear Trotzkyist article of Maltz." (N.B. DW, Mch 3, 1946, 11: "'smear Trotzkyist article of Maltz' should have read 'near Trotzkyist article of Maltz'.")

Michael Gold, "The Road To Retreat,"
DW, Feb 12, 1946, 6. "The best
American writers of the past 15
years received their inspiration,
their stock of ideas, from their
contact, however brief or ungrateful,
with the left wing working class and
this Marxist philosophy." Yet
Maltz, failing to see that sins he
charges against Communist cultural
policy have not in fact hurt his
productivity, is "preparing a retreat into the stale old Ivory
Tower," following Hollywood's corruption of him. Meanwhile "we are
entering the greatest crisis of
American history. The capitalists
are plotting...to establish an
American fascism as a prelude to an
American conquest of the world."

Samuel Sillen, "Art and Politics,"
DW, Feb 12, 1946, 6, 8; Feb 13, 6,
8; Feb 14, 6, 9; Feb 15, 6; Feb 16,
6; Feb 24, 10. Sees Maltz "in reality undermining a class approach"
and compartmentalizing art from
politics. "Browderism had an especially damaging effect on the thinking of the cultural movement." Asks
"neither a snobbish sectarianism
[the 30s are indicated] nor breadth
without principle [the early 40s]."
Quotes Zhdanov.

'Daily Worker' Editorial. DW, Feb 18,
1946, 7.

Michael Gold and Albert Maltz, "Albert
Maltz and Plain Speaking," DW, Feb
23, 1946, 6. A letter from Maltz
angrily takes Gold to task: "this
personal attack on me can only stul-
tify all discussion....The real victims of your column are the younger
writers...who notice this ferocity,
this unbecoming descent to personality slander." Gold replies: "we
must fight like tigers for the Marxist line. Browderism is what happens
when we don't."

Samuel Sillen, "Let's Discuss the Real
Issues," DW, Feb 25, 1946, 11. Letters in Sillen's mail that call him
"intemperate, categorical, pontifical"
and his views the most "meretricious"
and "harmful" in some 25 years; he
counters that Marxist principle is
at stake.

"'Daily' Readers Discuss Literary Issues," DW, Feb 27, 1946, 11; Mch 1,

11; 3, 14; 7, 11; 9, 11; 13, 6; 17,
9. Supporting Sillen: J. North,
Gail Kane, C.P. West, A.B. Magil
(who reverses his early stand), Mary
Testa, A. Garcia Diaz, John Hudson
Jones, Max Perks, S. Starr, Gordon
Kay. Supporting Maltz, more or less:
J.L, Dan James, Harry Hunt (who analyzes "shallow, sectarian" US left
criticism), Ettore Rella, M.K, I.
Silber, M. Douglas, Isidor Schneider
(who objects to "peremptory prose-
cutor's tone" and willful distortions of Sillen which damage "calm
and comradely" discussion begun in
NM), Lawrence Emery (who finds fault
with Maltz but asks that real difficulties now be faced).

Howard Fast, "Art and Politics," NM,
Feb 26, 1946, 6-8. Calls Maltz the
"apostle" of "liquidation" for all
progressive and Marxist writing;
"the boil" of a broad malady "has
come to a head" in Maltz and requires
lancing.

Joseph North, "No Retreat For the Writer," NM, Feb 26, 1946, 8-10. The
editor of NM finds Maltz "anti-
Marxist."

Michael Gold, "Marxism Demands a Full
Left-Wing Culture," DW, Mch 2, 1946,
6. Accents the positive: "It is to
our shame in the rich United States
that we now haven't a single literary
magazine or publishing house to fur-
nish guidance and a home for our left-
wing artists and writers. This, I
believe, is the main problem at the
moment, and not merely a theoretical
question. Our left-wing cultural
movement has to start to rebuild its
shattered house. We must again learn
to believe in ourselves, and in the
independent role of the American working class and its culture."

Marion Summers, "Art Today," DW, Mch 6,
1946, 11. DW's art critic essentially sides with Maltz, saying art commences with a private vision while
the basis for social art hardly exists under US conditions.

Alvah Bessie, "What Is Freedom For
Writers?" NM, Mch 12, 8-11. Maltz's
novels as well as his views are "un-
Marxist."

Sanora Babb, "Another Viewpoint," NM,
Mch 12, 1946, 10. Finds that Maltz's

stated views are being distorted.

John Howard Lawson, "Art Is a Weapon," NM, Mch 19, 1946, 18-26. Maltz as a "subjectivist."

Michael Gold, "How Can They Forget the Record Of Trotskyist Betrayal?" DW, Mch 16, 1946, 6. Acknowledges tide of mail rejecting his Maltz articles. Assails correspondents for unconcern over James Farrell and Trotskyite betrayal. Praises pre-Browder early 30s as a sterling epoch.

Albert Maltz, "Moving Forward," NM, Apr 9, 1946, 8-10, 21-22; also in DW, Apr 7, 1946, 8, 15; Apr 8, 11. Following "weeks in serious thought" Maltz judges his opponents "entirely correct" on main issues: the "full truth...is this: from the left-wing cultural movement in America, and from the left-wing internationally, has come the only major, healthy impetus to an honest literature and art that these last two decades have provided....errors are small as compared to its useful contribution."

Albert Maltz, Participation In Forums On Art As a Weapon. See: DW, Apr 15, 1946, 11; Apr 19, 12; Apr 23, 11.

Wiliam Z. Foster, "Elements Of a People's Cultural Policy," NM, Apr 23, 1946, 6-9. Browder's successor as Party head finds Maltz's now-abandoned position to represent capitulation to the ideology of "American Imperialism," for "Art is a Weapon."

James T. Farrell, "Notes For a New Literary Controversy," NRep, Apr 29, 1946, 616-618. - Also: "Stalinist Literary Discussion: An Answer To Maltz and the New Masses," NI, Apr 1946, 112-115.

V.J. Jerome, Culture In a Changing World; A Marxist Approach, 1947. A summation from the Chairman of the Party's Cultural Commission.

SHOULD ARTISTS PURSUE SHEER BEAUTY? 'Daily Worker' Readers' Symposium, DWSup, Jan 19, 1947, 8; Jan 26, 8. With a summation by DW art critic Marion Summers, who objects to the "insidious bourgeois poison" which makes many of his readers prefer relaxing works, such as landscapes, to works that portray people and social struggle.

'MAINSTREAM' Editorial, "Crisis In American Letters," Main, Winter 1947, 5-9. The post-war perspective.

US COMMUNIST PAINTERS OBJECT TO 'PRAVDA' ATTACK ON "ROTTEN" "FORMALISTIC" BOURGEOIS PAINTING (1947). A mimeographed document [cc]; the 'Pravda' article is "Toward Flowering Of the Soviet Art," Aug 11, 1947, which, with a summation apparently from a US Party source, appears also in the document. The US painters remain anonymous but call the 'Pravda' view "over-simplified and non-Marxian" and analyze positive achievements of "post-impressionist" Western painting.

CONFERENCE ON THOUGHT CONTROL IN THE U.S, Beverly Hills, California, 1947. See: Thought Control In the U.S.A., 6 vols, Los Angeles, 1947. index. Includes papers by Roy Harris, John H. Lawson, Norman Corwin, Philip Stevenson, Albert Maltz, George Tabori, Carey McWilliams, Howard da Silva, Adrian Scott, Richard Collins, Paul Draper, Lee J. Cobb, Anne Revere, Ludwig Donath, D.O. Stewart, Howard Koch; and remarks by Arnaud d'Usseau, Millen Brand, Arthur Laurents, George Sklar, Morris Carnovsky, et al. (See also A. Refregier (LIII).) An effort to put the beginnings of the witch-hunt into historical perspective.

CULTURAL AND SCIENTIFIC CONFERENCE FOR WORLD PEACE, New York, Mch 25-27, 1949. See: Daniel S. Gillmor, ed, Speaking Of Peace: Edited Report Of the Cultural and Scientific Conference For World Peace, 1949. Contributions include: F.O. Matthiessen, L. Hellman, A.A. Fadaev, D. Shostakovich, Paul Eluard, Sean O'Casey, L. Kruizkowsky, N. Mailer, H. Fast, P. Evergood, A. Copland, C. Odets, et al. - See also DW, Mch 30, 1949, 7-10, for excerpts from speeches of S. Gerasimov, D. Shostakovich, Nicolas Guillen, Richard E. Lauterbach, W.E.B. Du Bois, P. Evergood, John J. DeBoer; and messages from P.M.S. Blackett, Thomas Mann, Patricia Burke, Sean O'Casey, Stefan Zweig, Sybil Thorndike. Also DW, Mch 29, 1949. - For comment by Irving Howe, PR, May 1949, 505-511.

CONTROVERSY OVER S. FINKELSTEIN'S ART AND SOCIETY. Bernard Rubin, "Serious Errors In Finkelstein's 'Art and Society'," DW, May 15, 1950, 11. Charges formalism and insensitivity to anti-Semitism. - Self-criticism by S. Finkelstein, DW, May 18, 1950, 10. - Further criticism of Finkelstein by Louis Harap, DW, June 15, 1950, 11. - The charges are extended to Harap and his 'Social Roots Of the Arts' by S. Sillen, DW, June 20, 1950, 11. Other views pro and con also published between May and August. V.J. Jerome terminates DW debate, Aug 7-8, 1950. - Final word is: Harry Martel and Marvin Reiss, "Art and Class," PA, Sept 1950, 79-96. Charges Finkelstein's "analyses are vitiated by an infatuation with the decadent art of dying capitalism," by a "non-class approach" and "cosmopolitanism" and capitulation to "bourgeois aesthetics."

JEROME, V.J, "Let Us Grasp the Weapon Of Culture," PA, Feb 1951, 195-215. Speech to 15th Convention of the CPUSA. Raises the spectre of capitalist exploitation of culture. "Our cultural workers must no longer be isolated in separate Party organizations....We shall integrate our cultural forces with all Party organizations...the Party is called upon to lead in the defense of the People's cultural heritage and in the struggle to affirm the vital creativeness of the people."

ARNDT, Henry [Pseudonym of Philip Stevenson], "For a New Approach To Culture," PA, May 1957, 24-33. "So long as the mass of the people - including their most progressive leaders - exhibit the traditional backwoods contempt for culture and ignore it in favor of exclusive concentration on pork chops, we shall not even begin the job of creating a humanist American culture indispensable to the overall campaign for socialism."

FAST, Howard, "My Decision [to quit the Party]," M&M, Mch 1957, 29-38. Reply from the editors of M&M, ibid, 39-47. - See also his The Naked God (LVI), and responses: Phillip Bonosky, "The Nakedness Of Mr. Fast," PA, Feb 1958, 53-57. V.J. Jerome, "A Letter To Howard Fast," PA, Jan 1959, 60-65 (Jerome here publishes his letter of advice to Fast concerning the latter's Sacco and Vanzetti novel, to disprove Fast's charges of stupid bureaucratic Party meddling with his books). Herschel D. Meyer, History and Conscience: The Case Of Howard Fast, 1958. - See also Tsao Yu, "The Self-Destruction Of Howard Fast," CL, 1958 #5, 118-122.

Fast's novels had been widely published in China.

BONOSKY, Phillip, Controversy Over His Novel 'The Magic Fern' (1961). Review by Sidney Finkelstein, "A Working-Class Novel," PA, Sept 1961, 58-64, is rebuked by a group of Cleveland steelworkers and shopworkers, in a letter signed by Jean Krchmarek, PA, Mch 1962, 53-58. The review was "uncritical" of "the only" US novelist who takes the CP seriously. "This is a book dealing with automation and present day problems, but it presents them against a background that existed 30 years ago." The workers protest that labor-management relations have grown devious, relaxed, Madison Avenue, while labor militancy has dropped and social benefits are available which Bonosky ignores. - Reply from Bonosky, ibid, 58-63, declares he hadn't tried to present the "real facts" but rather "those forces in life which are ever-fresh, ever-real, ever-contemporary." - Defense of his review by Finkelstein, PA, June 1962, 58-64. Says it was "the kind of evaluation one writes when an important book has just been born, and is struggling for its life." Effectively describes conditions under which a writer of Bonosky's commitment must work.

A DECLARATION OF CONSCIENCE BY AMERICAN WRITERS AND ARTISTS, Fair Play, Oct 28, 1961, 4. [Tamiment] Protests April 17 invasion of Cuba and continued support by Establishment Liberals of "acts of hostility towards Revolutionary Cuba." Signers include: Lee Baxandall, Philip Corner, Diane Di Prima, Edward Dorn, Lawrence Ferlinghetti, Allen Ginsberg, Paul Goodman, George Hitchcock, LeRoi Jones, Elaine de Kooning, Seymour Krim, Jeremy Larner, Denise Levertov, Norman Mailer, Julian Mayfield, Leroy McLucas, Jonas Mekas, Warren Miller, Joel Oppenheimer, Peter Orlovsky, Marc Schleifer, Howard Schulman, Archie Shepp, Alvin Simon, John Simon, Gary Snyder, David Solomon, A.B. Spellman, Elizabeth Sutherland, Philip Whalen.

REACTION TO PREMIER KRUSHCHEV'S SPEECH OF MARCH 8, 1963. For debate of the speech within the American left, see 1963 (XLI).

"THE AVANT-GARDE: GENIUSES OR JERKS?" AmD, July-Aug 1964, 21-26. Reviews,

by Leslie Woolf Hedley and by Marc
Schleifer, of 'The Moderns', ed
LeRoi Jones, 1964.  A no-holds-barred
clash of views as Hedley represents
the M&M tradition of criticism and
Schleifer defends the Beats. - Michael
Gold, e.g, DW, Aug 9, 1964, 7, defends
AmD's function in publishing writers
like Schleifer. - Leslie Woolf Hedley,
"The Bohemian New Left," Minority Of
One, May 1965, 17-19; June, 11-14, re-
news and enlarges his attack and chas-
tises Gold. - Reply by R.D. Lakin, Nov
1965, 22-24.

W.E.B. DU BOIS CLUBS OF AMERICA, Culture
and Education: Convention Report, San
Francisco, 1964.  24 pp. [cc] Fresh
basis asked for rapproachement between
artists and political organizers.  Requirements and contributions of each
will be mutually enriching and respect-
ed.  Principal author, Michael B. Folsom.  Incorporates workshop discussion.

'NEW PROGRAM OF THE COMMUNIST PARTY
U.S.A. (A DRAFT)', Political Affairs
Publishers paperback: 1966.  Includes
a perspective on liberating culture
from commercialism and from all "governmental or official censorship" with
the advent of Socialism.  Also analysis of the role of intellectuals under
capitalism, and of the role of culture
in man's liberation.

"SOCIALIST SCHOLARS LOOK AT THE ARTS"
AmD, Spring 1967, 24-27.  By Oakley C.
Johnson.  The Literature Panel of the
2nd Socialist Scholars Conference, New
York City, Sept 11, 1966, as " a historic event" where "for the first time
in America" a "public discussion has
taken place in an avowedly socialist
atmosphere on...the role and essence
of realism in literature."

"WHAT IS THIS COMMITMENT? A Dialog Symposium," AmD, Summer 1966, 7-14, and
subsequent numbers.  Views of M. Geismar, L. Rogosin, A. Toney, T. Nelson,
G. LeRoy, P. Evergood, R. Nemiroff, C.
Hicks, R. Gover, F. Snider, A. Simon,
W. Lowenfels, J. North, H. Selby.

18TH NATIONAL CONVENTION, CPUSA. Remarks
delivered by Joseph North, PA, Aug
1966, 34-40.  Asserts that despair and
ignorance in writing, now praised by
the Establishment, is not the genuine
American tradition.

## LII.  Architecture

SCHAPIRO, Meyer, "Looking Forward To
Looking Backward," NM, July 10, 1934.
Review of 'Technics and Civilization'
by Lewis Mumford.  Specific attacks on
Mumford's lack of theoretical coher-
ence.

_____, "Architecture and the Architect,"
NM, Apr 7, 1936, 30-31.  Economics of
architecture and the common cause of
architects and labor.

## LIII.  Art and Sculpture

ARNAULT, Charles, "Painting and Dialectics," NM, Aug 14, 1945, 28-30.  Suggests greater emphasis in Marxist
criticism on formal aspects of painting.

BASKIN, Leonard, "Some Notes On Style
and Reality," NF, I iv (Summer 1948),
217-220.  illus.  Analyzing eight
graphics, Baskin rejects surface
naturalism in favor of realism which
"can be expressed in a variety of
styles," including "formalist, expressionist devices" of "the modern
movement."  "One must be cognizant of
all the technical advances produced by
the bourgeois artists and bend them -
and in so doing, change them - to one's
own use."

_____, Interview.  In: Seldon Rodman,
Conversations With Artists, 1957,
169-177.

_____, "Kathe Kollwitz," MassR, Oct 1959,
96-104.  Affinities of his style with
Kollwitz's.

_____, "The Necessity For the Image,"
The Atlantic, Apr 1961, 73-76.  Referring to Engels' dictum that freedom
is the recognition of necessity, Baskin
sets "infantile chaos" of Abstract Expressionism into context of social
decadence.

_____, "On the Nature Of Originality,"
Show, Aug 1963, 66-69.  The relation
of subject, content, form.  Defends
art that derives from a subject against
Abstract Expressionism, which at best
expresses "visceral anxiety," "incoherent subjective ambiguities."  "The
only meaningful originality is originality of content."

_____, SEE ALSO: Brian Doherty, "Leonard Baskin," Art in America, Summer 1962, 65-72. Penetrating portrait. - "Leonard Baskin," Current Biographies, May 1964, 7-9. - Leonard Baskin, Bowdoin College Museum of Art, Brunswick, Maine, 1962. Illustrated catalog of his first full-scale show.

BAXANDALL, Lee, "Pop and Like Art," SOL, Winter 1965, 109-112. Analysis of specimens of Pop Art as "perhaps the most effectively socially-engaged art yet to appear in the Modernist movement." - See also "'Camp' and Community," SOL, Spring 1965, 97-98. Analysis of a taste for commercialized art that is often confused with the work discussed in above essay.

BLUME, Peter, On His Painting 'The Eternal City'. DW, Jan 11, 1938, 7. illus.

BROWN, Milton W, "The Marxist Approach To Art," Dia, #2 (1937), 23-31.

_____, The Painting Of the French Revolution, 1938. 96 pp. illus. - Review by Oliver Larkin, S&S, Summer 1940, 240-242.

_____, American Painting From the Armory Show To the Depression, Princeton Univ: Princeton, N.J, 1955. A basic history of American art.

CLARK, Vernon, "The Guernica Mural - Picasso and Social Problems," S&S, Winter 1941, 72-78. "Picasso has revealed himself as the poet laureate of the Wastelanders....cubism cannot be made to bear the weight of social meaning."

DAVIS, Stuart, "The Artist Today," American Magazine Of Art, Aug 1935, 476-478, 506. General views of American Artists Congress presented by its President.

DEBS, Eugene Victor, "The Cartoonist and the Social Revolution," Introduction to The Red Portfolio: Cartoons For Socialism, 1912. Political cartooning as one of the vital educational tools of socialism.

ELLIS, Fred, Interview with A.B. Magil. DW, Jan 5, 1929, 4. The career of a DW cartoonist. - See also Interview with Walt Carmon, DW, June 24, 1933, 5.

EVERGOOD, Philip, "Sure, I'm a Social Painter," Magazine of Art, Nov 1943, 254-259. illus.

_____, "Fundamentals, Functions, Frameworks Of Art: The Claims of Modernity and Humanity," ACA, Nov 1944, 3-5; Dec, 4-8.

_____, Interview with Beth McHenry. DW, May 3, 1946, 13. illus.

_____, "Art Is Not a Popsicle," AmD, Oct-Nov 1964, 15-17. Denounces Pop Art.

_____, SEE ALSO: Lucy R. Lippard, The Graphic Work of Philip Evergood, Crown: 1966. illus. - Also Fairfield Porter, "Evergood Paints a Picture," Art News, Jan 1952, 30-33, 55-56. illus. With biography. - Also: Marion Summers (LIII).

FINKELSTEIN, Sidney, Art and Society, International: 1947. Many insights based on love of the subject. Modernists - Joyce, Bartok, Gertrude Stein, Chagall, Cezanne - who combine "scientific" abstraction with "the rediscovery of folk and national languages and their contemporary use" achieve a largely positive effect. - Review by E.B. Burgum, S&S, XII (1948), 287-292. - In response, Finkelstein modifies and clarifies his views, S&S, XIII (1949), 164-169. - For attacks in the DW and Finkelstein's self-criticism, see: 1950 (LI). - Review by Jesse Ehrlich, NF, I iv (1948), 239-244, charges disregard for the class aspect of art; reply by Finkelstein with Ehrlich's rejoinder, NF, II i (1948), 73-77.

_____, "National Art and Universal Art," Main, Summer 1947, 345-361.

_____, Realism In Art, 1954.

_____, "The Form and Content Of Art," M&M, Jan 1963, 30-50. Defines three "kinds of form that art works take": classic, subjective, decorative.

_____, "Picasso--Artist and Man," PA, Spr 1966, 31-42. A counterview to that of J. Berger. With Berger's reply.

FRAINA, Louis, "The Social Significance Of Futurism," NR, Dec 1913, 964-970.

Review of the Armory Show. Against terming Futurism and Cubism decadent: all "vital art expresses the vital urge of its age....conditioned by the social _milieu_;" Futurism tries to catch the "spirit of machinery, - energy, motion, agression." A Socialist art must, however, forge different artistic means. - See also: "Futurism In Italy," _Reedy's Mirror_, May 16, 1913, 6-7. Forestudy to above essay.

FRASCONI, Antonio. See (L).

GELLERT, Hugo, "The Poor Man's Art Gallery," _AmD_, Spring 1967, 15-18; _et seq_. The 'Masses' and 'Liberator', by a participant.

GOLD, Michael, Van Gogh Belongs To Us. _DW_, Nov 4, 1935, 5; also _DW_, Oct 6, 1938, 7. Van Gogh driven by his heart to depict workers' sufferings. "Some of our revolutionary artists bring no personal passion to their work. They are revolutionists with their heads, and not with their hearts."

_____, David Burliuk. _DW_, Jan 1, 1943.

GROPPER, William, Interview. _DW_, Apr 20, 1939, 7. - See also: Harold Rosenberg, "The Wit Of William Gropper," _AF_, Mch 1936, 7-8.

HARAP, Louis, _The Social Roots Of the Arts_, 1949. See especially sections on folk and popular arts.

HERR, Axel, "United American Artists Workshop Serves Trade Unions and Mass Organizations," _DW_, May 2, 1938, 7. illus. Also: _DW_, Oct 3, 1938, 7.

HUMBOLDT, Charles [writing as Clarence Weinstock when editor of _AF_ in 30s], "The Question Of Abstract Art," _DW_, Jan 14, 1947, 11. "Abstract art is not the expression of any one class; it...can be made to serve corrupt or socially useful ends....there is no point in putting things on an either-or basis. The working class is the inheritor of all that is good in all cultures....I should think it would be very much to the point for the critic to help determine just what aspects of abstract art can be useful to the artist." - See also a letter from Humboldt, _DW_, Dec 17, 1946, and response by M. Summers, _DW_, Jan 2, 1947, 11.

JONES, Joe, Raymond Breinin, Herbert Rosengren and Gilbert Wilson, Accounts of Mural Painting in the Midwest. _Midwest_, I i (Nov 1936), 17, 20-21,34.

KENT, Rockwell, "The Artist and This War," Speech to American Artists Congress (1941) [LAW]. The European war as a deliberate diversion of public attention from pressing crisis in structure of American society.

_____, On Picasso. See Picasso (XL).

_____, Statement To Press On Soviet Painting. _N.Y. Times_, Mch 26, 1950. "Compared to the great art of the Renaissance and to the good art of many of the pre-revolutionary painters in Russia, the Soviet art of today - or that small part of it which I have seen - is not, in quality, what I would call 'good' art. Yet, in respect for my confreres in the field of art, I would hesitate to use the opprobrious term 'second-rate art'."

_____, SEE ALSO: Stenographic Record of Meeting of VOKS Section of Fine Arts, June 5, 1953, Moscow. mimeo. [cc] 6 pp. Critique by Soviet artists of photos of Kent's paintings.

Vl. Petrov and Vl. Orlovsky, "Visiting With Rockwell Kent," _NT_, 1965 #35, 26-28.

LAFOLLETTE, Suzanne, _Art In America_, 1929. illus. Pioneering materialist work in this area; still useful.

_____, "The Basis Of Art," _The Freeman_, Jan 23, 1924, 467-469. Absolute relevance of economics and politics to artist living in exploitative society.

La MORE, Chet, Speech to American Artists Congress (1941). [LAW] "Government Patronage and Freedom Of Expression For the Artists." Compares "relative freedom" at start of WPA with "coercion and witch-hunting" of the moment. "The Administration no longer takes the side of the many....All of its efforts are bent toward involving our country in a war which the people know will be catastrophic."

LARKIN, Oliver, "The Daumier Myth," _S&S_, Spr 1937, 350-361. Effort to see Daumier whole.

_____, "Courbet and His Contemporaries,

1848-1867," S&S, Winter 1939, 42-63.

_____, "Daumier and Ratapoil," S&S, Fall 1940, 373-387.

_____, "Courbet In the Commune," S&S, Summer 1941, 255-259.

_____, Art and Life In America, 1949. illus. Major interpretation of American painting from its origins.

_____, Samuel F.B. Morse and American Democratic Art, Boston, 1954. The American painter who also invented the telegraph.

_____, Daumier: Man of his Time, McGraw-Hill, 1966. illus. The works in social and political context.

LAWRENCE, Jacob.   See (I).

LEVINE, Jack, "Form and Content," College Art Journal, Autumn 1949, 57-58. Why he is unable to dissociate "significant" forms from content reflecting his convictions.  The beneficial role played in American painting by WPA arts program.

_____, "Homage To Vincent," Art News, Dec 1948, 26, 59.  Perspective on Van Gogh.

_____, "Man Is the Center," Real, Spring 1953, 5-6.  Lauds "narrative" painting which "puts the conscious mind to work" - as the abstractionists do not.  "The names I celebrate are those of the dramatists."  Analysis from this standpoint of "Gangster's Funeral," painting then in progress.

_____, Interview.  In: Seldon Rodman, Conversations With Artists, 1957, 200-204.  The story of his "Veleno" and much else.

_____, SEE ALSO: Current Biography, June 1956, 40-42.

LOZOWICK, Louis, Call For 'Utmost Clarity' In Painting.  DW, Apr 19, 1935, 5. Indicative of fears and policies caused by growing Hitler threat.

_____, "A Fascist World and Freedom Of Expression."  Speech to American Artists Congress (1941).  [LAW]

MELTZOFF, Stanley, Nineteenth Century Revivals: A Study Of Taste, Ph.D. dis-

sertation, New York Univ: 1941. Class bias in revival of artists' reputations: Chardin, the Le Nains, Vermeer.

_____, "The Rediscovery Of Vermeer," Marsyas, II (1942), 145-166.

_____, "The Revival Of the Le Nains," Art Bulletin, XXIV (1942), 259-286. illus.

_____, "David Smith and Social Surrealism," Magazine of Art, XXXIX (1946), 98-101.  illus.  Defines the 'Guernica' of Picasso and work of Smith, Peter Blume, Robert Gwathmey, Walter Quirt and Philip Evergood as Social Surrealism; it "uses surrealist techniques to describe the world at large rather than the painter's ego.  It deals with what is obsessive and hallucinatory to all, rather than to the artist alone."

MEYERS, Larry, "Socialism Or a Death World," Liberation USA, #1 (1966), 5, 11.  The necessity of understanding, rather than condemning a priori, the work of contemporary writers and artists.  Replacement of left philistinism with helpful analysis.  A Pop artist analyzed.

MINOR, Robert, "Art As a Weapon In the Class Struggle," DW, Sept 22, 1925, 5. Asks "a higher development of art in the service of the Communist press" as alternative to prostitution for capitalist employers.  "The essential characteristic of true art is exactly this: That it brings an incoherent mass of fact into a unified concept.  Even the smallest good cartoon or verse does this."

PORTER, Fairfield, "Murals For Workers," Arise; The Labor and Socialist Magazine, I iv (Apr 1935), 21-23.  A detailed account of the murals in New York.

REFREGIER, Anton, Completing His Treasury Department Murals in San Francisco, DW, Sept 5, 1946, 11.  illus.

_____, "The Cultural Worker and the People," DW, Aug 11, 1947, 11.  illus. Speech at Conference on Thought Control, Beverly Hills, 1947.  What it means to resist decadent trends.

RIDDELL, Hugh J, History of the ACA Gallery, DW, Oct 18, 1939, 7.  The dedication of Herman Baron to social art.

ROSENBERG, Harold, "Peasants and Pure Art," <u>AF</u>, Jan 1936, 5-6. Van Gogh, torn between a people's and a personal art, succumbing to the latter.

_____, "The Wit Of William Gropper," <u>AF</u>, Mch 1936, 7-8.

_____, <u>The Tradition Of the New</u>, Evergreen paperback: 1961. "American Painting Today," the pertinent section of this often-perverse volume, provides a phenomenology and sociology of Abstract Expressionism.

_____, <u>Arshile Gorky: The Man, the Time, the Idea</u>, Horizon: 1962; Evergreen paperback, 1962. illus. "Above all, Gorky stands for the importance of intellect in painting," not mere energetic action. His career in some way typifies recent American painters who with much difficulty followed European innovators until at last they made their own innovations. Like most, Gorky was in 30s Left Front activities: "Can one doubt that it was the challenge to action on the streets that was to lead in the next decade to the response in practice that the action of the artist took place on the canvas?" - See also <u>PR</u>, Fall 1962, 587-593. Important clarification of his idea of artist's problem with history; in answer to a review by Paul Goodman.

_____, <u>The Anxious Object; Art Today and Its Audience</u>, Horizon: 1964. illus. Action Painting, Pop and Op art; politics in art; international style, international audience, the end of the role of the artist as outsider and bohemian. Arshile Gorky, De Kooning, Hans Hofmann, Saul Steinberg, Barnett Newman, Jasper Johns, Robert Rauschenberg, etc.

_____, "Art and Work," <u>PR</u>, Winter 1965, 50-56. Prospects for self-development, aesthetization of work and leisure, under new American circumstances.

SCHAPIRO, Meyer, "Race, Nationality and Art," <u>AF</u>, Mch 1936, 10-12. Rejects art interpretations along racial lines, especially Jewish. - Also see: discussion, <u>AF</u>, May 1936, 11-12.

_____, "Public Use Of Art," <u>AF</u>, Nov 1936, 4-6. WPA arts program must be viewed in context of Marxist analysis of problems of alienated artists and degraded popular taste; not merely as immediate answer to needy artists' plight. "Before the levels of art which the artist values can become available to the masses of people, two conditions must be fulfilled - that the art embody a content and achieve qualities accessible to the masses of the people, that the people control the means of production and obtain a standard of living and a standard of culture such that the enjoyment of art of a high quality becomes an important part of their life."

_____, "The Social Bases Of Art," <u>AAC</u>, 31-37. Brilliant study of determinants, subject-matter and nature of modern art.

_____, "The Patrons Of Revolutionary Art," <u>MaQ(NY)</u>, I iii (Oct-Dec 1937), 462-466; discussed by Bertram D. Wolfe, ibid, 466-470. Review of the Mexican muralist movement and of the Wolfe-Rivera 'Portrait Of Mexico'.

_____, "Nature Of Abstract Art," <u>MaQ(NY)</u>, I (1937), 77-98. In context of discussion of Alfred H. Barr's 'Cubism and Abstract Art'. - See also debate of this article with Delmore Schwartz, ibid, 305-314.

_____, "Courbet and Popular Imagery; An Essay On Realism and Naivete," <u>Journal of the Warburg and Courtauld Institutes</u>, IV (1940-41), 164-191. illus. Intentional provincial and naive populism of Courbet's painting. "After 1848, the realistic representation of the people became for him a conscious programme." Development of his ideas and friendships with Dupont, Buchon, Champfleury.

_____, "Fromentin As a Critic," <u>PR</u>, Jan 1949, 25-51. A remarkable study which illumines assumptions and standards of both critics.

_____, "Rebellion In Art," in: Daniel Aaron, ed, <u>America In Crisis</u>, 1952, 203-242. 1913 Armory Show in New York is focus for discussion of modernism in art and its reception by various American publics including political radicals.

_____, "Style," in: A.L. Kroeber, ed, <u>Anthropology Today</u>, Chicago Univ: 1953. Reprinted in: Morris Philipson, ed, <u>Aesthetics Today</u>, Meridian paperback: 1961, 81-113. A central essay. Compactly reviews achievements and faults

of the various theories of style; concludes by emphasizing potential of the
Marxist approach for synthesizing a
satisfactory theory of style.

_____, "Leonardo and Freud: An Art-His-
torical Study," Journal of the History
of Ideas, Apr 1956, 147-178. illus. A
landmark in discussion of Freudian
theory of art.  Shows Freud committed
gross errors owing to inadequate knowledge of history, and his emphasis on
a single childhood memory.  Schapiro
cautions that potential contribution
of psychoanalysis to questions of art
is not nullified by Freud's one attempt, a failure.

_____, "Mr. Berenson's Values," En, Jan
1961, 57-65.  Historical treatment revealing "business, a distasteful, in-
delicate subject, was the concealed
plumbing of his House of Life."

_____, "On David Siqueiros - A Dilemma
For Artists," Dis, Spring 1963, 106-
118.  See Siqueiros (XXXIII).

SHAHN, Ben.  See (LXIII).

SPARGO, John, "Constantine Meunier,
Painter and Sculptor Of Toil," The
Comrade, Aug 1902, 246-248.  Consid-
ered attempt to give socialist inter-
pretation of recent realism in art:
Meunier, Millet, Verestchagin.

_____, See also: The Comrade (1901-
1905, LI).

SUMMERS, Marion, The Private Vision In
Art.  DW, Mch 6, 1946, 11.  In his
first column, discussing paintings by
Nikolai Cikovski, Summers holds "private" art which is "made to be placed
in homes and to serve as decoration,
for enjoyment and refreshment" must
certainly dominate in America - since
"social" art which "deals with social
problems" is little encouraged nor
will it be "until our government, until unions and workers' organizations
enter the field of patronage." Therefore Cikovsky who "creates in the
realm of the private and the personal"
is "joyous" and "a gift we can treas-
ure."

_____, "Problems Of the Social Artist,"
DW, Apr 7, 1946, 14; Apr 14, 14; Apr
21, 14.  Suggested solutions to problems of patronage and audience, of
being social while not being "corny or

literary," of developing a symbolic
"language" of social art in an era of
no commonly agreed symbols.

_____, "The Function Of Criticism," DW,
Apr 28, 1946, 24.  Cites the difficulty
or remaining responsible to the artist,
to the audience, and to history.

_____, "Evergood's Art," DW, May 2, 1946,
13.  Describes Evergood's painting as
expressionism which, quite personal,
even difficult, seems necessarily so
from creator's standpoint and provides
"a powerful social art which unfor-
tunately sometimes falls short of its
ultimate objective of communication."

_____, "Decadence  In Art," DW, June 9,
1946, 14.  "How readily we brand the
cultural manifestations of capitalism
as decadent.  We should remember that
scientists and artists produce the best
of which bourgeois society is capable
....Many aspects of bourgeois art are
analagous to 'pure science'....the
best of bourgeois art has been divorced
from the general stream of capitalist
developments."

_____, "Abstract Art: Highway Or Dead
End?" DW, June 12, 1946, 11; June 16,
14; June 20, 11; June 23, 14. Abstract
art does have aesthetic validity but
has been sanctified because it  gives
pleasure without challenging bourgeois
desire to avoid a whole view of the
world.  "We want an art which is full
but which at the same time finds its
place within humanity's struggle for
progress, an art which creates out of
its obligations a symbol of man's
hope."

_____, "Realism, Handmaiden Of Progress,"
DW, July 14, 1946, 14; July 21, 14.
"Throughout its history realism has
been tied to some progressive class and
has reflected the aims of that class
....Realism in our time has become almost purely an attitude....Social realists make use of symbolism, expressionism and even elements of abstract art."

_____, George Grosz.  DWSup, Oct 27,
1946, 8.  His decline in America.

_____, "Abstract Art and Bourgeois Cul-
ture," DW, Jan 2, 1947, 11.  "When we
find an artist completely immersed in
the production of an art which makes
not the slightest pretensions at fur-
thering the cultural interests of the

working class, we can rightfully ask what his class-consciousness consists of.  Is he conscious of himself as a member of the working class or of the bourgeoisie?  If he considers himself allied with the working class and at the same time produces in the accepted manner and general tradition of bourgeois art, then is obviously confused."
- Answer to letter from Charles Humboldt (DW, Dec 17, 1946), whose views, says Summers, are "subverting Marxist theory." - See also Humboldt (above).

_____, "Defining Abstract Art," DWSup, Jan 12, 1947, 8.  Abstract art is "not a style so much as an attitude" which "consciously avoids all reference to human and social meaning.... an art concerned exclusively with aesthetic ends....confined to the manipulation of the materials of the craft."  It includes Matisse, though Matisse paints the human figure.  It embraces most of Picasso but not 'Guernica' or 'Dream and Lie of Franco'.  "A contemporary artist who uses the language of abstraction to express a human or social content ceases to be an abstract artist....he still has the problem of communication, of intelligibility to solve."

_____, Post-War Picasso.  DW, Feb 9, 1947, 13.  "Picasso is a great artist, the outstanding painter of our era" but "he has not become a social artist overnight....Those paintings are... indicative of a basic disregard for human values.  His artistic vehemence is not employed to hit at the causes of social rot, but seems directed at human beings themselves."

_____, The Prospects For Social Art. DWSup, Feb 23, 1947, 6.  The social artist "must learn again to be the voice of the people rather than the voice of his lonely self....His greatness will rest then in his ability to make people recognize their own hopes ....The artist has developed a complex idiom which he is loath to foresake and the public has been perverted by years of commercial art to accept the lowest level of narrative illustration."  None of this can be "entirely resolved under capitalism" but artists must make an effort.

_____, Cartier-Bresson and The Humanist Art Of Photography. DWSup, Apr 6, 1947, 9.

_____, "Paul Cezanne: Father Of Modern Art," DWSup, Apr 13, 9.  Detailed class analysis.

_____, SEE ALSO; 1946 (LI).

WEBER, Max: See Jacob Burck, "Max Weber - Reborn Artist," DW, May 30, 1937, 8. illus.  His development.  Quotes from call for 2nd American Artists Congress written by Weber. - See also Marion Summers, DW, Mch 17, 1946, 14.  Unaware of Weber's role in 30s, Summers writes: "Not even by the very loosest interpretation of the term can he be considered a social artist....He cut himself off from society....there are still things he has to offer, as has any fine and honest talent."

WEIGAND, Charmion von, "Expressionism and Social Change," AF, Nov 1936, 10-13.

_____, "The Surrealists," AF, Jan 1937, 12-14.

_____, "Ratgeb; Painter Of the Reformation," View, Summer 1944, 48-49. illus. Jerg Ratgeb, Swabian painter of the Herrenberg Alterpiece, was drawn and quartered for his role in Stuttgart government when city was held by peasant uprising.

WILLISON, Thomas S, "Revolutionary Art Today," NM, Oct 1, 1935, 17.  illus. Introduces special NM issue on the topic.  Aware of artists' problems; asks a high formal standard.

YOUNG, Art, On My Way, 1928.  Autobiography of a Red cartoonist.

_____, Art Young: His Life and Times, ed. John Nicholas Beffil, 1939.

### LIV.   Cinema

BESSIE, Alvah, Inquisition In Eden, Macmillan: 1965.  Account of the Hollywood witch-hunt by a victim.

BIBERMAN, Herbert, Salt Of the Earth, Beacon: Boston, 1965.  illus.  Screenplay of the Marxist film made by blacklisted personnel, and the account of its creation and its suppression.

COLE, Lester, "Realism In the Cinema," New Road, 1944, 55-60.  Analysis of current films and cinema's future in light of theory that art grows more realistic in times of social crisis,

more formalistic in periods of reaction after upheaval.  Cole foresees
growth of realism.

DASSIN, Jules, Interview with Cynthia
Grenier.  Sight and Sound, Winter
1957-58, 141-143.  illus.  Relates
his career.

DeLAUROT, Edouard L, "Towards a Theory
Of Dynamic Realism," Film Culture, #1
(1955), 1-14.

_____, "On Critics and Criteria," Film
Culture, #2 (1955), 4-11.

_____, "The Future Of the New American
Cinema," Film Culture, #24 (1962),
20-21.

_____, "From Alienation To Cinema,"
Film Culture, #25 (1962), 66-67.

_____, "Reflections On a Theory Of World
Cinema," Film Culture, #27 (1962),
63-70.

GESSNER, Robert, "Movies About Us," NTh,
June 1935, 20.  "If we can no longer
expect Hollywood to make films of
reality, films of labor, then we must
make them for ourselves."  Appraises
early efforts of Film and Photo League.

HOLLYWOOD SCREEN WRITERS, Three "Collec-
tively" Written Talks: "The Screen
Writers Have a Union" on Screen Writers
Guild;  "Not Words - Machines" progressive gains in Hollywood related to
technological change; "Motion Pictures
and the War" citing warmongering.  Delivered to 4th American Writers Congress (1941)  [LAW] - J.H. Lawson dis-
puted conclusions of 2nd paper from
the floor.

HUMBOLDT, Charles, "The Art Of Ingmar
Bergman," MassR, Winter 1963, 352-377.

HURWITZ, Leo T, "Survey Of Workers Films,"
NTh, Oct 1934, 27-28. Review of activity
of Film and Photo League and problems.

JEROME, V.J, The Negro In Hollywood
Films, 1950.  64 pp. Specific examples
of racism.

LAMPELL, Millard, "I Think I Ought To
Mention I Was Blacklisted," N.Y. Times,
Drama Section, Aug 21, 1966, 13.

LAWSON, John Howard, Theory and Technique Of Playwriting and Screenwriting,

rev. ed, 1949.

_____, Film In the Battle Of Ideas, 1953.
Apologizes for "non-class" approach
in above book.  Sociology of the
Hollywood film, etc.

_____, Film: The Creative Process, Hill
& Wang: 1964.  Numerous insights on
relation of social conditions to
film-making. Ideas toward a film
aesthetic.

LEYDA, Jay, and Peter Ellis, "A Guide To
the Social Study Of the Film," TW,
Apr-July 1937, 73-79.

_____, Kino: A History Of the Russian
and Soviet Film, Macmillan: 1960.
The basic study.  illus.

LOSEY, Joseph, "Mirror To Life," Films
and Filming, June 1959, 7, 35. Social
content is the "absolute" in any art.
Discusses problem of treating it in
a bourgeois film industry.

_____, Interview With Joan Barthel,
N.Y. Times, Drama Section, Mch 26,
1967, 17.  illus.  Problems of his
work abroad.

'MOVIE BULLETIN'.  Issued by the Workers
Film and Photo League of Chicago.
mimeo, 1 p. I iii, I iv(1934), in
Collection of Paul Romaine.

POTAMKIN, Harry Alan, See: "A Bibliography Of the Film Writings Of Harry
Alan Potamkin," Films, Nov 1939, 19-
24.  Annotated and relatively complete.  See also:

_____, "Populism and Dialectics,"
Experimental Cinema, I ii (1930), 16-17.
Distinguishes within Soviet cinema a
retrogressive tendency (Pudovkin:
focus on individual fates; populist
sentiment) as against tendency which
makes Soviet film the "mentor" of
world cinema (Eisenstein: focus on
masses, structure, the social idea;
dialectics).

_____, "Review Of Soviet Films," MN,
Dec 7, 1930, 7.  Disputes rumors of
decadence in USSR cinema by analyzing
excellence and innovations of four new
releases.

_____, "The New Soviet Film," WT, Mch
1932, 19-25.  Analysis of 'Road To
Life' which much impressed him.

_____, "The Future Cinema: Notes For a Study," Pagany, I ii, 76-79.

_____, "Motion-Picture Criticism," NF, Mch 4, 1931, 592-594.

_____, "The Death Of the Bourgeois Film," Front, Apr 1931, 284-288.

_____, The Eyes Of the Movie, ed. Irving Lerner, 1934. 31 pp. Details and structure of bias, censorship, ownership in Hollywood. - Some of material appeared in WT, Feb-Apr 1932.

_____, "Film and Photo Call To Action!" WT, July 1931, 5-7. Aims of the Film and Photo League.

_____, Major Publication Outlets: Theatre Guild Magazine, 1929-32. Close Up, 1929-33. Hound and Horn, Oct 1932-Oct 1933. Cinema, I ii-viii (1930).

_____, SEE ALSO: Obituary Notice, WT, Sept-Oct 1933, 3, 9.

   Joseph Freeman, "Harry Alan Potamkin," DW, July 21, 1933, 4; July 22, 5. illus.

   "In Memory Of Harry Alan Potamkin," Hound and Horn, Oct-Dec 1933, 3-4. "It is safe to say that he knew more about the art of film than anyone in this country."

   David Wolff, "Harry Alan Potamkin," NTh, Feb 1936, 28, 33. illus. Appraisal of his contribution to film criticism.

   The Harry Alan Potamkin Film School. NTh, Jan 1934, 14-15.

ROGOSIN, Lionel, "Interpreting Reality," Film Culture, #21 (1960), 20-28. The making of 'Come Back, Africa'.

SCHAPIRO, Meyer, "A Metaphysics For the Movies," MaQ(NY), I (1937), 406-417.

SCHLEIFER, Marc, "'La Dolce Vita' and 'L'Avventura' As Controversy; 'L'Avventura' and 'Breathless' as Phenomenalist Film," Film Culture, #27 (1962), 59-62. Principles for a "new intensified realism".

STEINER, Ralph, "Revolutionary Movie Production," NTh, Sept 1934, 22-23. Preliminaries to a beginning.

STRAND, Paul, Interview with David Platt. DW, May 18, 1937, 7. His film 'Redes'.

_____, "Independent Film and the Democratic Struggle," Speech to 4th American Writers Congress (1941). Scope of non-Hollywood progressive filming. [LAW]

TEMANER, Gerald, "Good Films and Bad Audiences: The Misadventures Of 'L'Avventura'," NUT, Summer 1963, 37-56. When the left attacks "obscurity" in films it attacks the "wrong source" of "the failure of the mass audience." Difficulty in the art is not the problem; rather, "a society which almost systematically stifles the possibility of sensitive responses." One must change society rather than attack artists - who are merely the "most helpless opponent."

TRUMBO, Dalton, Personal History. DW, Mch 13, 1940, 7. - See Madden (LIX).

_____, "Getting Hollywood Into Focus," DWSup, May 5, 1946, 1, 7. Hollywood conditions and the Screen Writers Guild.

UHSE, Stefan, "'Goldfinger' - The Plot to Castrate Capitalism," Streets, May-June 1965, 58-62. The racist and capitalist structuring of the James Bond image.

WEIGAND, Charmion von, "Little Charlie, What Now?" NTh, Mch 1936, 6-8, 35. Chaplin and 'Modern Times'.

## LV. Dance

ABBOTT, V.L, "The Contemporary American Dance," DW, Dec 5, 1948; Dec 6. Pessimistic survey of "progressive" dance prospects and triumph of "sick" dance.

ANYON, Nell, "What Is the New Dance Group?" in: New Dance Group, First Annual Recital [Program]: The Dance Is a Weapon, Mch 26, 1933, 3-5. [ES]

_____, "Artistic Program," ND, Mch 1935, 5-6. Suggestions for political and artistic education of revolutionary dancers, such as: "Base the movements in any given exercise upon a definite theme so that a feeling for the dance as a means of communication is built up."

BAYER, Jerome, "The Contemporary Dancer and His World," Proceedings of the First National Dance Congress and

Festival, 1936, 85-92. [Collection of Jane Dudley (Mrs. Leo Hurwitz)] Important analysis.

BOVINGDON, John, "Toward a Contemporary Dance Ideology," WDLB, June 1934, 3. Oracular pronouncements on class determinants of dance.

_____, "Roots Of the New Soviet Dance," Proceedings Of the First National Dance Congress and Festival, 1936, 29-34. [Collection of Jane Dudley (Mrs. Leo Hurwitz)] Finds stimulus in organized gymnastics, parades, movements of traffic policemen in the USSR.

CHILKOWSKY, Nadia, Methods and Principles Of Workers Dance League. DO, Aug-Sept 1934, 68-69. Excerpts from a lecture-demonstration at the New School. All Dance as propaganda for a social class. The error of believing one "dances as one feels."

DAL NEGRO, Leonard, "The Dance Of Death," WDLB, Anti-War Issue (July 1934), 2. Dancers must "fight war through the dance" as it is their "specialized field of activity." Suggestions how to "choose one section of war activity and give it life and meaning for the working class."

DANCE UNION OF LOS ANGELES, "Dance and Its Vital Concepts," ND, Summer 1935, 9-10. Distillation of its experience.

DELZA, Sophia, "The Folk Dance," NTh, Nov 1934, 15-16. Reviews its history, its conditions of survival, concludes: "The strength of the mass dance lies in the mutual functioning of many who are dealing with the same material simultaneously....A dynamic common interest will help perpetuate the art of the dance."

DUNCAN, Isadora, Interview with Eugene Lyons. DW, Feb 10, 1923, 4. Granted while in US with Essinen. Lyons reports she acknowledged all the difficulties of the Bolsheviks while remaining loyal to Communism. Duncan reports difficulties caused in American dance circles by her sympathies. "I don't believe in the narrow bourgeois formula of art for art's sake....That is why I went to dance for the masses instead of the few rich."

_____, SEE ALSO: Irma Duncan and Allan Ross Macdougall, Isadora Dun-

can's Russian Days, 1929. Contains the great dancer's drafts of a book on her experience setting up a dance school for Bolshevik children. Also excerpts from Soviet press, documentation of her life with Essinen, speech by Lunacharsky on her talents, etc.

Ilya Schneider, "Yesenin and Isadora Duncan," C&L, 1966 #1, 14-16. illus. Excerpts from account by manager of her USSR dance school.

DUNCAN, Irma, Interview with Karl Reeve. DW, Jan 8, 1929, 4. Adopted daughter of Isadora Duncan recounts career of Duncan Dancers of Moscow, led by her. Popularity of the Duncan style; anachronism of Soviet ballet. - Irma Duncan as a renegade: DW, Apr 20, 1934, 5. - Influence of Duncan in USSR: Sidorov (XLV).

EISENBERG, Emanuel, "The Meaning Of the Dance," Trend, May-June 1934, 105-111. Defines dance: "the fluid architecture of body design in space" and wittily defends this "grammar of movement" against "inane and strainingly grotesque sculptural posturings" of symbolic intent.

_____, "Diagnosis Of the Dance," NTh, July-Aug 1934, 24-25. Red dancers as bourgeois and out of touch.

_____, "Ladies Of the Revolutionary Dance," NTh, Feb 1935, 10-11. Revolutionary dancers are simply chips from the bourgeois block of technique "gone off on a labor-slumming holiday" where they perform "soul-dances." - Attacked by Nathaniel Buchwald and defended by the author, NTh, Mch 1935, 24.

ELION, Harry, "Perspectives Of the Dance," NTh, Sept 1934, 18-19. Review of dance history and call for red dancers to free themselves from bourgeois origins.

FOSTER, Joe, "The New Dance League," DW, June 8, 1935, 7. Its development.

FRAINA, Louis, "The Case For Ragtime," Modern Dance Magazine, Aug-Sept 1917, 5-6, 8. Argues that despite its appearance of vulgarity and the onus associated with its Negro origins, the jazz form is alive like nothing else in provincial and snobbish American arts.

_____, "Lydia Kyasht - Spirit Of Beauty," <u>Modern Dance Magazine</u>, Apr 1914, 12-13. illus.

_____, SEE ALSO: The file of <u>Modern Dance Magazine</u>, the issues for which Fraina was Associate Editor, 1914, 1917-18. Fraina's widow confirms that he authored several articles anonymously or under pseydonyms.

GOLD, Michael, Critique Of Bourgeois Formal Influence On Revolutionary Dance, Music, Poetry. <u>DW</u>, June 5, 1934, 5; June 14, 5. The harmful effects of Eliot, Graham, cerebral composers.

HAYS, H.R, "Thoughts On the Revolutionary Dance," <u>ND</u>, Summer 1935, 4-5. "It is not likely that there will be any spontaneous art impulse direct from the proletariat" which has "neither a creative tradition nor a sufficiently wide spread class-consciousness." Meanwhile "bourgeois artists who are trying to interpret the class struggle for the masses tend to arbitrarily force their technique," a group of "aesthetic devices intended to please the select few which cannot over night become the implements of a popular art....Only two modifications were possible, a frank relapse into pantomime, an escape into the theatre with technical and formal retrogression, or the bourgeois dance as before with a moral added to the program," which can "convey no Marxian idea whatever if viewed without program notes." "A modern relationship between the dance and the drama has never worked out" although "in their early forms they grew together and complemented each other.... it was the bourgeoisie whose anti-cultural activities destroyed the moral and ceremonial basis of drama."

KIRSTEIN, Lincoln, "Revolutionary Ballet Forms," <u>NTh</u>, Oct 1934, 12-14. Argues that best revolutionary approach to classical ballet is to conserve and amplify it, as in USSR.

KONER, Pauline, "Russia Dances," <u>NTh</u>, Oct 1936, 22-23. Experiences of a modern dancer in classical-ballet USSR.

OCKO, Edna, "The Dance Season In Review," <u>WT</u>, July-Aug 1933, 8. Attacks exoti-cism and vagaries of "bourgeois" dance, showing roots of its unpopularity.

_____, "The Revolutionary Dance Movement," <u>NM</u>, June 12, 1934, 27-28. Brief survey. Revolutionary content must not remain on surface of dance but get into movement itself, through intimate awareness of it.

_____, "Dance In the Changing World: A New Trend," <u>Proceedings of the First National Dance Congress and Festival</u>, 1936, 25-28. [Collection of Jane Dudley (Mrs. Leo Hurwitz)] Welcomes interest in social themes of dancers like Weidman, Humphrey, Graham, also their freer experiement with form, while suggesting that they too have still to learn as do the earlier dancers of social content from another direction.

SEGAL, Edith, "First Revolutionary Dance Group In America: Red Dancers," <u>ND</u>, Mch 1935, 16-17.

_____, "Directing the New Dance," <u>NTh</u>, May 1935, 23. Working with a group to develop creative understanding of social nature of expression. Lack of preparation and absolute dictation by the director must both be avoided.

SELLARS, Marion, "The Revolutionary Dance Achieves a Mass Audience," <u>DW</u>, Dec 12, 1935, 9. Good survey of scope of New Dance League.

SOKOLOW, Anna, Interview with Ruth Ann Heisey. <u>DO</u>, Aug-Sept 1937, 77. illus. Social causes for absence of modern dance in USSR. Reasons for not trying to use dance to present objective situations but rather emotional reactions to social world.

_____, Interview with Margery Dana. <u>DW</u>, Nov 10, 1937, 7. illus. Development into committed dancer.

_____, "Dance and the People's Front," <u>DW</u>, Apr 14, 1938, 7. Praises the movement to reach broad audience which began with "agitprop dances....more idea than dance" and which changed into "an attempt to see how much thought and content we could inject into actual dance material."

_____, "Dance Is For People," <u>Christian Science Monitor</u>, May 2 and 16, 1942.

illus.  Technique.  Roots of dance in the people.  Reactionary nature of dance in the USSR.

WORKERS DANCE LEAGUE, First Workers' Dance Spartakiade [Program], New York, June 4, 1933.  8 pp.  [ES]  League aims and descriptions of participating groups.

WYLIE, Grace, and David Nelson, "The Proletarian Revolutionary Dance," in: New Dance Group, First Annual Recital [Program]: The Dance Is a Weapon, Mch 26, 1933, 7.  Defines workers' "optimistic prospects," their "demand for performances" which brought numerous young dancers to turn their backs on "uninviting and sterile...bourgeois dance world;" and the "unlimited talent" that could be recruited and "engaged in dancing."  Options for revolutionary dance forms.

## LVI.  Literature and General

ABBOTT, Leonard, "Edwin Markham: Laureate Of Labor," The Comrade, Jan 1902, 74-75.

_____, "Millet: The Painter Of Common Life," The Comrade, Apr 1903, 149-151.

_____, See also: The Comrade (1901-1905, LI).

AMES, Russell, Citizen Thomas More and His Utopia, Princeton, 1949.  'Utopia' as "analytic realism," a "product of capitalism's attack on feudalism, a part of middle-class and humanist criticism of a decaying social order."  Biography, social analysis, More in politics and business.  Critique of Kautsky's volume (XXI).

_____, "Decadence In the Art Of T.S. Eliot," S&S, Summer 1952, 193-221.

_____, "Social Realism in Charles W. Chesnutt," Phylon, XIV (1953), 199-206.  The pioneer American Negro realist writer.

_____, "Jack London's 'The Iron Heel'," in: David Madden, ed, The Proletarian Writers Of the Thirties, Southern Illinois: Glencoe, 1967.

APPEL, Benjamin, "Novels For Tomorrow." Speech to 4th American Writers Congress (1941).  [LAW]  Urges truthfulness against enthusiasms and disillusions of the moment.

_____, "Labels," in: David Madden, ed, The Proletarian Writers of the Thirties, Southern Illinois: Glencoe, 1967. Study of novel in 1930s and 1960s.

ARVIN, Newton, Whitman, 1938.  Biography of Whitman in the Socialist tradition.

_____, "The Democratic Tradition In American Letters," WCW, 34-43; also 234-239.  The history of US writers' involvement in democratic  politics. - See also Arvin, 1932 (LI).

_____, "Individualism and the American Writer," Nation, Oct 14, 1931, 391-393; reprinted in Morton D. Zabel, ed, Literary Opinion In America, 1937, 523-529.  Bankruptcy of isolation and of alliance with the middle class; proletarian literature as the way out.

_____, "Literature and Social Change," MQ(B), VI ii (1932), 20-25.

AUSUBEL, Nathan, "The Jewish Writer's Dilemma," NM, July 31, 1945, 9-11. Avoiding ghettoism and assimilation alike, Jewish writers should view America as having "a multicultural heritage. Unity in variety is its striking characteristic."

BABB, Sonora.  See 1946 (LI).

BARNES, Lois L, "The Helpless Hero Of Ernest Hemingway," S&S, Winter 1953, 1-25.

_____, "The Proletarian Novel," M&M, July 1963, 51-57.  Appraisal of Jack Conroy's 'The Disinherited' and its preface by D. Aaron.  Appreciation of the proletarian novel in America.

BATES, Ernest Sutherland, "T.S. Eliot: Leisure Class Laureate," MQ(B), Feb 1933, 17-24.

BAXANDALL, Lee, "Brecht's Theatre Of Transformation," SOL, II i (1961), 93-99.  Relating themes of freedom and commitment in Brecht's development.

_____, Introduction to: Bertolt Brecht, The Mother, Evergreen Black Cat paperback: 1965, 9-32.  The Mother as a revolutionary moral prototype in Brecht's theatre.

_____, "George Buchner's 'Danton's Death'," TDR, Mch 1962, 136-149. Theory of Buchner's theatre of montage. Buchner's outlook.

_____, Introduction to: George Buchner, Woyzeck and Leonce and Lena, Chandler: San Francisco, 1962. Buchner's innovations.

_____, "The Theatre Of Edward Albee," TDR, Summer 1965, 19-40; reprinted in: Alvin B. Kernan, ed, The Modern American Theatre, Spectrum paperback: Englewood Cliffs, N. J, 1967. Albee's myth of America, its artistic results and limitations.

_____, "The Naturalist Innovation On the the German Stage: The Freie Buhne and Its Influence," Modern Drama, Feb 1963, 454-476. Origins of German Socialist theatre.

_____, "Is Kafka Necessary?" Chalk Circle, I i (Apr-May 1966), 67-72. The role of Kafka's communitarian vision in his writing. A response to G. Lukacs' rejection of Kafka's method.

_____, "The Realism Of William Burroughs," Minority Of One, Mch 1966, 26-28. His social criticism and relevance to progressive politics.

_____, "The New Capote and the Old Soviet Advice," SOL, VI ii (Mch-Apr 1966), 92-100. - See also review of the Capote by R. Orlova, CDSP, Jan 4, 1967, 14-15; from 'Novy mir'; citing the Baxandall essay, takes a similar view of Capote. 'In Cold Blood' as evidence of a breakthrough by an alienated writer toward a solution long advocated by Marxism, and curiously approaching the theories of S. Tretyakov and LEF. The relation of writers to Party, fantasy, and the public.

_____, "Issues and Constituency Of the New Left," Liberation, Apr 1966, 21-25, 39. Analysis of the problems of American socialist growth and the new importance of cultural issues.

_____, "Marxism and Aesthetics: A Critique Of the Contribution of George Plekhanov," JAAC, Spring 1967, 267-279. Plekhanov's theories of creativity and taste; and his suggestiveness in applying Marxism to formal as well as thematic problems.

_____, "The Marxist Aesthetic Theory Of Louis C. Fraina," in: David Madden, ed, The Proletarian Writers Of the Thirties, Southern Illinois: Glencoe, 1968. Fraina as the out-

standing early American Marxist aesthetician.

_____, "Who Likes Fascist, Racist, Elitist Art? - Almost Everyone! - Why? Or, The Simple and the Complex: Ideology and Artistic Values," forthcoming. Analysis of the appeal of T.S. Eliot, Kipling, Leni Riefenstahl's film 'Triumph Of the Will'.

_____, "Fantastic Realism," forthcoming. Paper delivered in part at 2nd Socialist Scholars Conference, New York, September 1966. Traces development of Marxist aesthetic theory in its capacity to analyze and evaluate non-mimetic works of art. Writings of Marx, Plekhanov, Mehring, Liebknecht, Lunacharsky, Fraina, Mayakovsky, Brecht, Meyerhold, Leger, J. Berger, K. Radek, R. Garaudy, etc., on E.T.A. Hoffman, Cubism, Futurism, Naturalism, Joyce, Kafka, etc.

_____, SEE ALSO: Baxandall (LIII), (LVIII).

BEALS, Carlton, "Latin American Literature," in: WCW, 92-104.

BERSIN, Ernest, Alexei Tolstoy: Opportunistic Fellow-Traveller. DW, Apr 29, 1929, 6. An American worker objects that Tolstoy, whose stories DW had published, is "nebulous bourgeois intellectual" who creates false proletarian types. Appended editorial note agrees but says Tolstoy "is now functioning as a citizen of the Soviet Union and writing sympathetically of the life there." - Further workers' comments, DW, May 1, 1929, 4.

BESSIE, Alvah, "Writers, Artists, and the Lesson Of Spain." Speech to 4th American Writers Congress (1941). [LAW] "To admit that Spain was fighting for democracy - as she was - is to admit that the powers that control our policy are not" since they slandered and blockaded Republican Spain. Tribute to artists and writers who fought for Spain. - See also 1946 (LI); Bessie (LIV).

BLANKFORT, Michael. See 1935 (LI).

BLAU, Milton, Contemporary Writers. DWSup, Sept 8, 1946, 9. A fiction workshop initiated after the war.

BODENHEIM, Maxwell, "The Revolutionary Poet," The Little Magazine, Feb-Mch 1934, 1-4. The class function of a poet.  The place of propaganda in poetry.

_____, "Art and the Proletariat," The Little Magazine, Apr-May 1934, 1-3. Traces his development into a poet of the left.  Assesses other writers' positions.

_____, "The Ivory Tower Is No Longer a Joke - It Is a Tragedy," DW, Mch 12, 1934, 7.  The writer must choose as world moves toward barbarism and war. CP membership is suggested: "The only party honestly, consistently, and militantly battling against capitalism and all of its sly, or deluded, artistic and liberal allies and compromisers."

_____, Writing the Masses Can Understand.  DW, May 2, 1934, 5.

_____, "Away With Embellishments and Obscurities!"  DW, July 3, 1934, 5. Against influence of bourgeois style on young revolutionary writers.

_____, Interview with Anita Tilkin.  DW, Jan 23, 1939, 7.  illus.

BONOSKY, Phillip, "The Background To American Progressive Literature," ZAA, IX (1961), 253-260.  Proletarian writing is seen heading the mainstream of vital American literature - "to be characterized by its devotion to the ideas of democracy and to the progress, and indeed, to the belief in the perfectability of man."  By contrast, "pessimism" which "has become the main content" of post 1945 literature originates in "corrupted currents" from the South with its feudal tradition. Interprets US literature from the first World War.

_____, SEE ALSO: 1957, 1961 (LI); Rideout (LIX).

BOOK UNION BULLETIN (Oct 1935-Dec 1939) has brief reviews of numerous left books, signed by Hicks, Hart, Cowley, Freeman, Schneider, Lamont, Taggard, Parker, Fearing, Rukeyser, Seaver, et al.

BOTKIN, B.A, "Regionalism and Culture," WCW, 140-157.  Analysis of "the artist seeking to be at home in America and ending up a long way from home - at home in the wilderness, in the cosmos, in the universe, in everything

but modern industrial America."  The hopeful trends.

BOYER, C.V, "Three Poets Of the Agrarian Revolution," MQ(B), III i (1925), 56-68.  Goldsmith, Crabbe, Ebenezer Elliott.

BRAND, Millen, Interview with Anita Tilkin.  DW, Nov 29, 1938, 7.  illus.

_____, "The Dimensions Of Characters," FW, 32-35.  abdgd.

_____, "Cities In Modern Novels." Speech to 4th American Writers Congress (1941). [LAW]  The "difference between a city used as background and a city that rises integrally from a novel": the latter is "functional," the way for a writer to grasp it is "stay home or move out of Chicago and New York."  One must get "everything" in for "everything can be understood."

BRAZIER, Richard, The IWW Sense For Beauty.  In: Joyce L. Kornbluh, ed, Rebel Voices: An I.W.W. Anthology, Michigan Univ: Ann Arbor, 1964, 71. A prolific composer of Wobbly songs talks of the sense for beauty in the movement.

BREWSTER, Dorothy, "The Interpretation Of Social Change In Literature." Speech to 4th American Writers Congress. (1941). [LAW] Discussion of Gogol, Goldsmith, Richard Wright.

BROOKS, Obed [Robert Gorham Davis], "Archibald MacLeish," in: Joseph Freeman et al, eds, Proletarian Literature In the United States, 1935, 225-229. - See also Aaron (LIX).

_____, "The Problem Of the Social Novel," MQ(B), VI iii (1932), 77-82.

_____, On Marxist Criticism.  MQ(B), Feb 1933, 52-54; Mch 1933, 115-117; Apr 1933, 182-186; May 1933, 246-247; June 1933, 313.

BROWDER, Earl, "Communism and Culture," AWC, 66-70.  Speech to 1st American Writers Congress.

_____, "The Writer and Politics," WCW, 48-55.  Speech to 2nd American Writers Congress.  "Communists are the last to want to regiment the writers," but "the struggle in which we are enlisted is a war" and all those who "fraternize" with "Trotzkyites" are "coming to the assistance of fascism, however

innocent their intentions may be in contrast to the diabolical schemes of Hitler.  They call upon us to cease firing,
while they investigate the soul of the
enemy, in pursuit of pure truth."

_____, Communism and Culture, 1941.
abdgd. versions of speeches and writings, 1935-41.

_____, Letter From Soviet Russia To V.F.
Calverton.  MQ(B), IV i (1927), 72-75.
The "damning facts" reveal that the
masses prefer films with Douglas Fair-
banks and Mary Pickford to Eisenstein.
The importance of the satire magazine
'Krokodil' in controlling bureaucracy.

_____, Mary Van Kleeck, and Granville
Hicks, "What Is the Intellectual's
Role In the Workers' Fight?"  DW, Mch
13, 1934, 5.  Summary of talks by Van
Kleeck on need of adhering to working
class; Hicks on intellectual's raising
himself "to the level of the proletariat" through CP membership - and Browder, describing CP as the one serious,
responsible revolutionary party and
condemning "semi-skilled intellectuals"
who do not think clearly or concretely
or take firm stands but merely "salve"
their consciences.  Rejecting charges
that CP cannot be genuinely American
movement, Browder says: "If one is not
interested in directives from Moscow
that only means he is not interested
in building socialism at all."

_____, SEE ALSO:  1946 (LI).

BROWN, Norman O, Hermes The Thief: The
Evolution Of a Myth, Madison, Wisc,
1947.  Correlates evolution of myth of
Hermes "with the revolution in economic
techniques, social organization, and
modes of thought that took place  in
Athens between the Homeric age and the
fifth century B.C."  The Homeric Hymn
to Hermes as a mercantile class expression. - Begun in 1941 as a Ph.D.
dissertation under A. Winspear.

BROWN, Stuart  Gerry, "Dr. Johnson and
the Old Order," MaQ(NY), I iii (Oct-
Dec 1937), 418-430.

BURGUM, Edwin Berry, On the Proletarian
Novel.  PR, II vii (1935).

_____, "Three English Radical Poets,"
NM, July 3, 1934.  Also in: Joseph
Freeman et al, eds, Proletarian Liter-
ature In the United States, 1935, 330-

339.  Detailed analysis of Spender,
Auden, Day-Lewis. - Attacked by Spender
in "Writers and Manifestos" (XXIII).

_____, "The Function Of the Critic In
Our Day."  Speech to 4th American
Writers Congress (1941).  [LAW]
"Literature....in some way helps organize our total personality....in an informal sort of adult education....to
improve that manner of talking and
acting which society finds immediately
feasible....The objective basis of
criticism therefore  must be a concern
with the criteria of probability" while
"interest in what is often called the
purely aesthetic aspects of art, in
cadence, in metaphor and so on, is
conditioned by its fundamental conception or probability."  But "contemporary criticism is a whirlpool of contradictions in which the dogmatism of
humanism, the subjectivity of  impressionism and variations upon the sociological theme leave the reader who
wishes guidance helpless."  The literary audience has thus been betrayed by
all but left wing critics who know this
is the proper function of criticism.
The great mass of Americans read pulp
fiction; left writers should recognize
that they must "faithfully reflect
those minor contradictions which constitute so much of the veracious surface of life" while left-wing criticism
has neglected "the obvious fact that a
novel is not a treatise in sociology
or some sort of notes upon Das Capital."

_____, The Novel and the World's Dilemma,
1947.  Studies of: Social Forces and
Fiction, Proust, Mann, Kafka, Joyce,
Woolf, Huxley, Stein, Hemingway, Faulkner, R. Wright, Saroyan, Steinbeck,
Dreiser, Wolfe, Malraux. - Review by
S. Sillen, DW, July 20, 1947.  "The
persistent tendency throughout....is
to submerge the social in the psychological....It is unfortunate too that a
work of this scope...should give virtually no representation to the tradition of Maxim Gorky and Martin Anderson
Nexo, and that the novel of a truly
'integrated' society like the Soviet
Union should be missing."

_____, "The Cult Of the Complex In Poetry,"
S&S, Winter 1951, 31-48.  Counters
Empson's view of ambiguity with his own,
social approach.

_____, "Playwriting and Arthur Miller,"
The Contemporary Reader, I ii (Aug 1953),

24-32. [Tamiment] Praise of Miller
for recognizing "limits of the basic
orientation of the [Broadway] audience" and for "directing the psychological orientation of the audience
along already established paths of
response." "The actual springs of
conduct on important matters in his
contemporaries must be accepted by
the dramatist." Criticism of schemat-
ically critical dramas about American
life. Burgum demonstrates results of
Miller's acumen in exploiting positive
potential of audience attitudes·while
skirting its prejudices in several of
his plays. 'Crucible' is praised for
raising the witch-hunt issue while
avoiding a Marxist analysis. - Ira
Wallach answers, ibid, I iii (Feb
1954), 62-64: "A Marxist can approach
the drama on only one possible basis:
a Marxist understanding of social
forces" even if some audience elements
are antagonized.

_____, "Science Fiction," NF, Spring
1954, 30-35. Its positive and negative potentials.

_____, "Freud and Fantasy in Contempor-
ary Fiction," S&S, Spring 1965, 224-
233. Problems of literary fantasy as
reflecting a social reality (Kafka,
Heller), a Freudian reality (Kafka,
Joyce, G. Grass), or disturbingly
dissolving reality entirely in madness,
ambiguity and 'game structure' (Susan
Sontag), "illustrating the extreme to
which indifference to reality can go."

_____, "The Historical Novel In the
Hands Of Georg Lukacs," S&S, Winter
1966, 70-76. "Lukacs simply is not of
present age; he is a pre-Freudian
romantic," which explains his lack of
a "semantic-psychological-anthropolog-
ical approach" to his concept of "the
people", to the unreal psychology in
Scott's novels, etc.

BURKE, H, The Creative Artist In a Communist Society, New York, 1959. [not
located]

BURKE, Kenneth, "The Nature Of Art Under
Capitalism," Nation, Dec 13, 1933,
675-677. Against "pure" art which -
like "pure" humor - resigns us to the
given conditions; tragedy with its
purgative catharsis provides best example. "Since pure art makes for acceptance, it tends to become a social
menace in so far as it assists us in

tolerating the intolerable.... For this
reason it seems that under conditions
of competitive capitalism there must
necessarily be a large corrective or
propaganda element in art. Art cannot
safely confine itself to merely using
the values which arise out of a given
social structure....It must have a
definite hortatory function, an element
of suasion or inducement of the educational variety."

_____, "My Approach To Communism," NM,
Mch 20, 1934, 16, 18-20.

_____, Communication to 'Daily Worker'.
DW, Oct 30, 1934, 5. illus. Supports
Party and its paper. Analyzes complex,
not always apparent ways in which
writers show their anti-capitalism.
The Party is "as it were, the lowest
common denominator" in which this sentiment may find implementation.

_____, "Revolutionary Symbolism In Amer-
ica," AWC, 87-93. Speech to 1st American Writers Congress. - Discussed by
Burke, Allen Porter, Friedrich Wolf,
Joseph Freeman: pp. 167-171.

_____, "War, Response and Contradiction,"
Symposium, Oct 1933, 458-482. Relation
of ethics, practical living, aesthetics.

_____, Counter-Statement, Los Altos,
Calif: 1931. Wide-ranging analysis on
premise that "a system of aesthetics
subsumes a system of politics."

_____, Permanence and Change; An Anatomy
Of Purpose, 1935.

_____, "Personal History," DWSup, Feb 9,
1936, 11. Says his 'Counter-Statement'
is product of an outgrown aestheticism
"taking the bourgeoisie as 'the world',
and art as an alternative counter-
world." The burden of 'Permanence and
Change' he says is his commitment to
politics: he now "saw instead a division in the practical world itself,
with a corresponding division in the
world of art." Of fascist threat,
Burke says: "I want to make clear the
nature of rhetoric, approaching the
subject always from the standpoint of
a plea for Communism."

_____, "Symbolic War," Southern Review,
Summer 1936, 134-137. Evaluation of
communist writing as seen in anthology
'Proletarian Literature In the United
States'. - Allen Tate comments on this

article, ibid, Autumn 1936, 363-372;
sees "a very dark nigger hiding in
[Burke's] rhetorical woodpile."

_____, "The Relation Between Literature
and Science," WCW, 158-171; 208-09.
Speech to 2nd American Writers Congress.  Wideranging essay on the mode
of a writer's craft assimilation of a
political Marxist outlook, and the
mode of criticism's assistance.

_____, Attitudes Toward History, 1937.
- Review by M. Schlauch, S&S, II i
(1937), 128-131; reply by Burke, with
comment on reply by Schlauch and by
V.J. McGill, ibid, II ii (1938),
242-256.

_____, "Literature As an Equipment For
Living," Direction, Apr 1938, 10-13.
Distillation of his thought on sociology of literature.  Moving from prov-
erbs to general fiction, Burke suggests
literature should be treated as "equipment for living, that sizes up situations in various ways and in keeping
with correspondingly various attitudes.
The typical ingredients of such forms
would be sought. Their relation to
typical situations would be stressed.
Their comparative values would be considered, with the intention of formu-
lating a 'strategy of strategies,' the
'over-all' strategy obtained by in-
spection of the lot."

_____, Ideology in 'Mein Kampf'. FW,
146-148.  Speech to 3rd American Writers Congress. abdgd.  The rhetoric of
fascism.

_____, Philosophy Of Literary Form, 1941;
Vintage paperback: 1957.  Collection
of articles from the 1930s including
some of those above.

_____, A Grammar Of Motives, 1945.

_____, SEE ALSO: Rudich (LVI); Aaron
     (LIX); Duncan (LXII).

BURNSHAW, Stanley, "Notes On Revolution-
ary Poetry," NM, Feb 20, 1934, 20-22.
Form and content. - Also see Burnshaw
(LIX).

CALMER, Alan, The Value Of Organizations
To the Cultural Worker. DW, July 6,
1934, 5.  Answers apprehensions of
young writers and artists.

_____, Is Poetry About Decadence Revolu-

tionary? MQ(B), VI ii (1932), 119-121.
Eliot and H. Gregory.

_____, "The Wobbly In American Literature,"
in: Granville Hicks, et al, eds, Proletarian Literature In the United States,
1935, 340-345.

_____, "All Quiet On the Literary Front,"
PR, Mch 1936, 12-13.  Indicts resound-
ing generalities of Hicks, Freeman,
Seaver, Phillips and Rahv, and suggests
standards for Marxist criticism.

_____, "Portrait Of the Artist As a Pro-
letarian," Saturday Review of Literature, July 31, 1937, 3.

CALVERTON, Victor Frobenius, "Sociological Criticism Of Literature," MQ(B),
Summer 1924, 4-21.

_____, The Newer Spirit; A Sociological
Criticism Of Literature, 1925. - Laudatory review by Michael Gold, DW, May
30, 1925.  See also Gold's letter to
Calverton, WM, 1925, 431: "It delights
me to see that we have at last a real
philosopher in our ranks.  Your work
is on a plane with the best writings
of the Russian critics - the first
class men among them.  It seems in-
credible that a man of your insight,
scholarship and temperament should be
so red and fundamental." - Review by
K. Burke, N.Y. Herald Tribune, May 10,
1925, criticizes the book's ignorance
of aesthetics. - Review by H.M. Wicks,
DW, Sept 24, 1925, 6.  Draws on "masterful" arguments of Trotsky to scorn
the attribution of 'proletarian' elements to work by O'Neill, Anderson,
Whitman. - Review by T.S. Eliot (LIX).
- Review in SW, July 26, 1925, 6.

_____, "Sherwood Anderson: A Study In
Sociological Criticism," MQ(B), II ii
(Fall 1924), 82-118. - Letter from
Anderson, calling essay "one of the
few things I have read that has some-
thing to say...remarkably fine," 81.

_____, "On Sherman and Mencken and Others;
A Fragmentary Critique Of American
Criticism," MQ(B), II iii (1925), 162-
176.  The failure to achieve in America
the unified or sociological criticism
practiced by Taine, Plekhanov or
Brunetiere.

_____, "The American Literary Radicals,"
MQ(B), III iv (1926), 251-262.  Sandburg, Masters, Lindsay, Pound, Eliot

and the imagists applauded for radicalism of form but not ideas, while
Max Eastman is radical in neither way.
"Our poets know little of the passion
of social strife," aside from Giovan-
nitti, Gold, the early Sandburg.

_____, "For a New Critical Manifesto,"
MQ(B), IV i (1927), 1ff. Defines the
1920s as a time of breakdown and crisis demanding a "social universal art"
which "can become part of the transi-
tionary process to a new order of existence." The age "cannot afford" a
"fantastic and sentimental art....
romancing with the unreal" like Futurism, Cubism, Joyce, etc.

_____, "American Literature," SW, Aug 1,
1926, 8; Dec 12, 8. Frank appraisal
of contemporary work.

_____, "What Is 'Radical' Poetry?" SW,
May 22, 1927, 8; May 29, 8. Eastman,
Gold, E. Merrill Root and the evolving
American tradition seen as centered in
Protestant moral energy.

_____, "Jesus: Why Do Barbusse and Other
Rebel Writers Turn To Him?" SW, Mch
4, 1928, 8. Critique of updating myths
of other epochs.

_____, "The Revolution In Russian Liter-
ature," MQ(B), IV ii (1927), 89-100.

_____, "Revolt and Reaction In Contempor-
ary European Literature," MQ(B), V i
(1928), 31-52.

_____, "Whither Art?" MQ(B), V ii (1929),
149-160. Primitive art, including its
sexuality, as decisively determined by
economic relations.

_____, "The Revolution-In-the-Wordists,"
MQ(B), V iii (1929), 276-283. A reply
to Eugene Jolas and 'transition'.

_____, "Art In the Ancient World," MQ(B),
V iii (1929), 324-333.

_____, "Social Forces In Late American
Literature," WM, Sept 1925, 509-512.
Howells, Norris, U. Sinclair.

_____, Sex Expression In Literature,
1926. Materialist interpretation.

_____, "Proletarian Cartoons," DWSup,
July 10, 1926. First appearance in
this paper.

_____, "Labor and Literature," DWSup, Aug
21, 1926. Announced as first of series
of articles tracing workers as heroes
in American literature.

_____, "Literature and Economics," Comm,
June 1927, 225-231; July-Aug, 313-318;
Mch 1928, 181-189; Apr, 247-251; June,
378-381. Sketch chiefly of English
culture in class perspective. Very
broad but some interesting examples.

_____, "Poetry and Revolution," DWSup,
Jan 6, 1927, 2-3. Two streams in left
American verse: protest and agitational.
Inadequacy of the mentality suited to
the first for doing work of the second.

_____, "The Sociological Aesthetics Of
the Bolsheviki," American Journal of
Sociology, Nov 1929, 383-392. Summarizes and comments on competing views
of Trotsky, Bukharin, Lunacharsky and
Bogdanov in regard to possible proletarian culture.

_____, "The Growth Of Negro Literature,"
in his: Anthology of American Negro
Literature, 1929, 1-17. Reprinted in
Nancy Cunard, ed, Negro Anthology,
London, 1934, 101-105. abdgd. Economic
foundations of American Negro originality and expression.

_____, The Liberation Of American Liter-
ature, 1932. - For the controversy surrounding Calverton's commitments and
methods, see reviews of above books;
Aaron (LIX); and:

Joseph Freeman, "Bulgarian Literature;
Or, The Perfect Critical Method,"
NM, Aug 1927. Satire of Calverton's
purported plagiarism and obtuse
pedanticism. Slyly suggests that
Calverton never deals with literature
itself, only with society, and that
he gets his information wholesale
from the Encyclopedia Brittanica and
that Calverton is a pompous title
and name dropper.

H.M. Wicks, "V.F. Calverton's 'Original'
Writings," DW, Feb 7, 1928, 7. Once
more on plagiarism.

A.B. Magil, "The 'Marxism' Of V.F.
Calverton," Comm, May 1929, 282-285.
Calverton's "Revolt Among American
Intellectuals" in Apr 1929 NM is de-
nigrated as is his "sort of official
status in this country as the revolutionary critic of America."

A. Landy, "Cultural Compulsives Or Calverton's New Caricature Of Marxism," Comm, Oct 1931, 851-864; Nov, 941-959. Greets Calverton's declaration that he is Communist: "an enemy within the ranks of the proletariat," a victim of "decadent bourgeois subjectivism," of "impotent and paralyzing" relativist Marxism, the "ideology of the disintegrating bourgeoisie" which spreads "uncertainty" in the working masses because it fails to assert "objective knowledge." Calverton was "destined by nature to be a petty-bourgeois shop-keeper, weighing out sugar and coffee, but is made by fate a man of letters, weighing out ideas."

David Ramsay and Alan Calmer, "The Marxism Of V.F. Calverton," NM, Jan 1933. Lays into Calverton for portraying himself as a 'conciliator' who is 'above' parties - in a manner attractive to the bourgeoisie - and as a man who could not make it in the regular world of literati and who attached himself therefore to the intellectually-weak labor movement of the 20s. Pages of textual comparisons show Calverton to be quite a plagiarist and garbler of texts and quotes.

Michael Gold, "Against V.F. Calverton," DW, Nov 6, 1933, 5. Declaring he previously believed Calverton motivated by good intentions, Gold notes 'Modern Monthly' is now publishing sections of Eastman's 'Artists In Uniform' showing Calverton trying with much success "to poison the minds of intellectuals."

Joseph Freeman, Against Calverton and Eastman. DW, Nov 22-Dec 2, 1933.

A. Stork, "Mr. Calverton and His Friends: Some Notes On Literary Trotskyism In America," IL, 1934 #3, 97-124. A Moscow gun principally against Calverton and Eastman.

F.O. Matthiessen, Review of 'The Liberation Of American Literature'. In his: The Responsibilities Of the Critic, 1952, 184-189. A damning critique.

Herbert Read, "Literature, Nationalism and Revolution," Modern Scot, Oct 1932, 216-224. Review-essay on 'The Liberation Of American Literature'. Against its economism Read opposes thrust of cultural inheritance.

E.B. Burgum, Symposium, Jan 1933, 107-114.

_____, The New Ground Of Criticism, University of Washington Chapbooks: Seattle, #34 (1930). 59 pp. Calls for synthesis of the psychological and sociological tools of analysis.

_____, American Literature At the Crossroads, University of Washington Chapbooks: Seattle, #48 (1931). 51 pp. Survey of the development of American writing in relation to society. The new revolutionary writers. Emphasis on need for formal excellence. Critique of M. Gold on Wilder.

_____, "The Need For Revolutionary Criticism," The Left (Davenport, Ia), I i (1931), 5-10. Chiefly a rebuke of M. Gold's article on T. Wilder for emphasizing moral over artistic criteria.

_____, "Can We Have a Proletarian Literature?" MQ(B), Autumn 1932, 39-50.

_____, "The American Writer Loses Faith," Current History, XXXVI (1932), 161-165. Relates the appearance of realism and despair in American writing to the closing of the frontier and rise of monopoly capital, rather than to any purely inner growth by writers.

_____, "Philip Freneau: Apostle Of Freedom," MQ(B), VII (1933), 533-546.

_____, and Henry Hazlitt, "Art and Social Change; A Controversy," MQ(B), VI i (1932), 10-27. The question of class standards in aesthetics and criticism.

_____, On Proletarian Literature. MQ(B), VI ii (1932), 5-10.

_____, "Can We Have a Proletarian Literature?" MQ(B), VI iii (1932), 39-50.

_____, "An Open Letter To the 'New Masses'," MQ(B), Mch 1933, 110-114, 127-128. Eloquent self-defense.

_____, On Whitman. MQ(B), Sept 1933, 498-500.

_____, "Sinclair Lewis: The Last Of the Literary Liberals," MQ(B), Mch 1934, 77-90.

_____, On Proletarian Literature. MQ(B), Apr 1934, 185-186, 191.

_____,"T.S. Eliot: An Inverted Marxian," MQ(B), July 1934, 372-373.

_____,Proletarian and Soviet Art. MQ(B), Dec 1934, 633.

_____, On Maxwell Anderson. MQ(B), May 1937, 3-5.

_____, "Ernest Hemingway: Primevalite," MQ(B), Dec 1937, 6-7.

_____, "Sinclair Lewis," MQ(B), Feb 1938, 11-13, 16.

_____, "Faulkner," MQ(B), Mch 1938, 11-12.

_____, "John Steinbeck," MQ(B), June 1938, 11-12, 16.

_____, "Steinbeck, Hemingway and Faulkner," MQ(B), Fall 1939, 36-44.

_____, "Proletarianitis," Saturday Review of Literature, Jan 9, 1937, 3-4, 14-15. "There is nothing in any movement, be it catholic, Holy Roller, Swami, or communist, which is worse or more dangerous than a sudden invasion of fresh, fervid, naive converts.... Going into the radical movement at a time when orthodoxy was at its worst, these revolutionary parvenus out-orthodoxed the orthodox" without seeing that in its earlier years, the movement was characterized by vigorous debate of principles and, in many quarters, disbelief that proletarian culture and novels could be produced for many years.

_____, SEE ALSO: Glicksberg (below); File of MQ(B), 1923-40; Calverton Memorial Issue, MQ(B), Fall 1940, with tributes and evaluations from many quarters; Papers of V.F. Calverton, New York Library.

CANTWELL, Robert, "No Landmarks," Symposium, Jan 1933, 70-84; reprinted in Morton D. Zabel, ed, Literary Opinion In America, 1937, 530-541. Henry James' style as a response to disturbing social change; Grace Lumpkin's proletarian 'To Make My Bread' as the beginning of a new response.

_____, "Sinclair Lewis," NRep, Oct 21,

1936, 298-301; reprinted in Morton D. Zabel, ed, Literary Opinion In America, 1937, 541-551. The effect on Lewis' style and achievement of his inability to envision alternatives to a capitalist America.

_____, SEE ALSO: 1934 (LI); Madden (LIX).

CHEVALIER, Haakon M, "Farewell To Purity," MQ(B), Mch 1934, 100-104, 111. Modern French and English literature.

CHEYNEY, Ralph, and Jack Conroy, Introductions to Unrest; The Rebel Poets' Anthology, London, 1929 & 1930 (2 vols). Manifestoes of worker-poets as "pioneers of consciousness" in our age.

_____, and Lucia Trent, Introduction to An Anthology Of Revolutionary Poetry, ed. Marcus Graham [Schmuel Marcus], West Farms Station, N.Y, n.d.

_____, "Charles Erskine Scott Wood," Fantasy, II iv (Spring 1933), 25-28.

_____, SEE ALSO: E.T. Murfey, "Ralph Cheyney," Fantasy, I ii (Autumn 1931), 17-19.

CIVALE, Giovanni B, "Socialism and Art," ISR, Jan 1908, 385-391. Extolls ideas of William Morris.

CLECAK, Peter E, Marxism and American Literary Criticism, Ph.D. dissertation, Stanford Univ: 1964.

_____, "Marxism, Literary Criticism, and the American Academic Scene," S&S, Summer 1967, 275-301. A distillation of the above thesis. Analysis of US academic institutions, under Cold War conditions, in relation to the relative paucity of Marxist literary scholarship and criticism. Notes also an eclectic assimilation generally of certain Marxist assumptions. The possibilities for growth of Marxist literary studies.

CONROY, Jack, and Ralph Cheyney, Introduction to Unrest 1931, 1931. Discussion of all poetry as propaganda. - See also Cheyney (above).

_____, "H. H. Lewis, Poet and Peasant," Fantasy, III ii (Autumn 1933), 23-26.

_____, "The Worker As Writer," AWC, 83-86. Speech to 1st American Writers Congress.

_____, William Faulkner. People's World

Magazine, Feb 19, 1938, 9. Approval
for Faulkner's iconoclastic treatment
of Southern myths; puts him in a class
with Grace Lumpkin et al.

_____, SEE ALSO: 1934 (LI); Lois Barnes
        (LVI); Aaron (LIX); Aaron, In-
        troduction to Conroy's 'The
        Disinherited' (Hill & Wang
        paperback: 1963); Rideout (LIX).

CONTEMPORARY VISION, Editorial: "On the
Picket Line For Poetry," I i (Winter
1929-30), i. - Compare with Editorial,
ibid, II ii (Spring 1931), "Our Platform Is Life."

COREY, Lewis. See Louis Fraina (below).

COWLEY, Malcolm, His Revolutionary Position. IL, 1933 #1, 151; 1934 #3, 82-
83. Also: "Personal History, DWSup,
Feb 2, 1936, 9. "Slowly swung round
to a Marxian position because there
was no other way to explain what was
happening around us."

_____, Exile's Return; A Narrative Of
Ideas, 1934. Account of the 20s
American generation in Europe and his
own return home and acceptance of
Communism. Argues necessity of middle-
class writers allying themselves with
the workers.

_____, "What the Revolutionary Movement
Can Do For a Writer," AWC, 59-65.
Speech to 1st American Writers Congress.

_____, "The Seven Years Of Crisis," WCW,
44-47. Speech to 2nd American Writers
Congress. Survey of 30s writing.

_____, "The Michael Golden Legend,"
Decision, July 1941, 40-45. A counter-
statement to Gold's 'Hollow Men'.
Cowley finds most branches of American
literature flourished in 30s excepting
poetry and strictly imaginative writing; Communists played a major role in
this vitality especially at first, for
their doctrine "helped to deepen the
sympathies of novelists and broaden
their intellectual horizons." What
went wrong, 1939-41.

_____, Think Back On Us...., A Contem-
porary Chronicle Of the 1930's, ed.
H.D. Piper, Southern Illinois Press:
Carbondale, 1967. Selected essays
from 'New Republic'.

_____, SEE ALSO: File of NRep for this

period (Cowley was Literary Editor);
1932, 1936 (LI); Aaron (LIX); Papers
of M. Cowley in Newberry Library. - See
also: Cowley, "While They Waited For
Lefty," Saturday Review, June 6, 1964.
Reflections on proletarian writing.

DAHLBERG, Edward, "Fascism and Writers,"
AWC, 26-32. Speech to 1st American
Writers Congress. Imperatives with
war coming on. - See also 1934 (LI).

_____, SEE ALSO: For his later views,
        "The Proletarian Eucharist,"
        in his Do These Bones Live,
        1941, 59-67.

DE LEON, Daniel, "Mark Twain's Passing,"
Weekly People, Apr 30, 1910, 4. "The
essential qualities of [tragedies,
lyrics, romances] depend upon neither
time, nationality, nor social conditions"; but comedy, like Twain's, can
only be enjoyed "with the aid of
history".

_____, "How I Came To Translate Eugene
Sue," Weekly People, May 27, 1911, 3.
Praise for the author so thoroughly
attacked by Marx's 'The Holy Family'.

_____, Introduction to Franz Lassalle,
Franz von Sickingen, 1910; printed
also in Weekly People, Jan 8, 1910, 4.
Praise for the play which Marx and
Engels thought dubious.

_____, The Poet Of the Working Class,
Francis Adams. Weekly People, Oct 22,
1910, 3. Finds this British poet as
worthy of praise as Eugene Sue in the
novel form.

_____, SEE ALSO: Weekly People (below).

DONATO, Pietro di, Interview with Milton
Meltzer. DW, May 1, 1939, 7. illus.
Critique of proletarian novels that do
not "make you suffer" so the worker may
emotionally learn what makes him advance or "succumb."

DOS PASSOS, John, "The Writer As Techni-
cian," AWC, 78-82. Speech to 1st
American Writers Congress. - See also
1932 (LI); Aaron (LIX); Dos Passos
(LVIII).

DOUGLAS, Wallace W, "The Problem Of Wordsworth's Conservatism," S&S, Fall 1948,
387-399.

DUNBAR, Robin E, "Mammonart and Communist

Art," DWSup, May 23, 1925.  Most pure
example of intemperate Proletcult
thought (echoes left cultural extrem-
ists in Russia) to be found in US journals.  Puts down all existing American
writing with special sneers for Upton
Sinclair, Jack London, Mark Twain.
Demolishes Greek drama for good measure, in name of new "stirrings" in
Soviet Russia.

DUNHAM, Barrows, The Artist In Society,
Marzani & Munsell: 1960.  Upholds the
aesthetic purpose of the arts; "on any
other view, the arts are merely a means
of livelihood, or an index of social
relations, or an instrument of policy."
However "beauty is itself a moral value," and "moral depravity in a work of
art tends to cancel out the value
which beauty provides."  For art provides a spectacle of "choice and
achievement, of means perfectly accom-
plishing ends," a way to "play at
solving problems, in order to enjoy
the exercise of our skills," as Kant
said.  Theory of creativity as expression.  Taste.  The figurative, associa-
tive language of the arts.  Grounds
for public administration of the arts.

_____, "Paul Elmer More," MassR, Winter
1966, 157-164.  Of his one-time teacher: "this conservative esthetic confers
a boon which conservative politics
does not," for it emphasizes moral
judgments.

_____, See also: Ben Levine, On Barrows
Dunham.  AmD, May-June 1965, 28-30.

EMERY, Lawrence, "Poetry With Salt In
It: The Story Of Forty Fathom, The
Seaman Poet," DWSup, July 9, 1939.
Proletarian inspiration.

ERDMAN, David V, Blake: Prophet Against
Empire, Princeton, 1954.  Skilled
exegesis of social content of many
obscure Blake writings.

EWEN, Frederic, Bertolt Brecht: His
Life, His Art and His Times, Citadel:
1967.  illus.  biblio.

FARRELL, James T, The Proletarian Novel.
PR, II vii (1935).

_____, "The Short Story," AWC, 103-114.
Speech to 1st American Writers Congress.  Problems of achieving "inner
conviction" in revolutionary writing.

_____, A Note On Literary Criticism,
1936.  Attack on 'New Masses' critical
practice. - For controversy surrounding
this book, see Aaron (LIX), 300-303.
- Also see 1934 (LI).

_____, Literature and Morality, 1947.
- See also "The Literary Left In the
Middle Thirties," NI, July 1947, 150-
154; and 1946 (LI).

FAST, Howard, Literature and Reality,
1950.  Decadence and realism in contemporary literature.  Kafka, Gwyn
Thomas, Steinbeck, Mark Twain, Gorky,
Pound, Soviet literature.

_____, "Toward People's Standards In Art,"
NM, May 7, 1946, 16-18.  Read at Art
As a Weapon symposium following the
Maltz Affair (for Fast's contribution
to the controversy, see 1946 (LI).)

_____, "Something About My Life Briefly,"
ZAA, I (1953), 13.  Quite helpful.
With bibliography of his writings.

_____, The Naked God: The Writer and the
Communist Party, 1957.  Chiefly an
account of encounters with Party func-
tionaries; repeatedly asserts respect
for rank and file idealism and admires
John Gates.  Follows his resignation
from Party. - For the controversy
around his resignation, see 1957 (LI).
- See also exchange with Eugene Lyons,
New Leader, July 9, 1956, 6-8; July
30, 16-20.

FEARING, Kenneth, Objectivism In Radical
Poetry.  PR, II vii, 89-91.  Defends
'objectivism' practiced by himself and
Horace Gregory whose 'Symbols Of Survival' is under review.

_____, Interview with Anita Tilkin.  DW,
Dec 20, 1938, 7.  illus.  "I've not
tried deliberately to be a Marxist in
poetry...Marxism is valuable in literature only to the extent that the writer
assimilitates it....its principles become part of the writer's background
....situations of the day can be expressed in personal terms."

FINKELSTEIN, Sidney, "The New Criticism,"
M&M, III xii (1950), 76-86.  Outline of
the position of Tate, Eliot, Blackmur,
etc, with examples of their failures.

_____, "Of Bourgeois Bondage," NM, Jan
14, 1947, 22-23.  Kafka's "Metamorphosis".

_____, "John Dewey's Philosophy Of Art," PA, Aug 1961, 43-56.

_____, "The 'Mystery' Of Henry James's 'The Sacred Fount'", MassR, Summer 1962, 753-776. Respectful inquiry into relation of money and freedom in this novel. - See also Jerome (below).

_____, "Shakespeare's Shylock," M&M, June 1962, 26-42. Finds the character definitely anti-Semitic. Suggests retirement of the play from stage for a time. - See also: M&M, Sept 1962, 59-65; a reader objects and Finkelstein replies.

_____, "On Updating Shakespeare," M&M, July 1961, 21-32; Aug 1961, 36-42.

_____, "Olivier's Grotesque Othello," NG, Mch 19, 1966, 13. An analysis of the play and of its "racist" interpretation.

_____, "King Lear and the Common People," M&M, Oct 1962, 7-19. Lear educated by his Fool a spokesman of the popular will.

_____, On Krushchev's Speech of March 8, 1963. M&M, July 1963, 36-45. Says it is "exactly in the worst spirit of the criticism in Stalin's day."

_____, Review of William Barrett, 'What Is Existentialism?' S&S, Fall 1964, 461-466.

_____, "The Existential Trap: Norman Mailer and Edward Albee," AmD, II i (1965), 23-28. Describes these writers' works as influenced by existential attitude that rose to prominence in McCarthy years.

_____, "The Artistic Expression Of Alienation," in Herbert Aptheker, ed, Marxism and Alienation: A Symposium, American Institute for Marxist Studies, Monograph Series No. 2, Humanities Press: 1965, 26-57. The human function of art; nature of aesthetic emotion; progress in art; nature of alienation; art's ways of expressing and/or combatting it. Homer, Shakespeare, Keats, Balzac, Dickens, Dreiser, T.S. Eliot, Stravinsky, Frost, Prokofiev, Bartok, Dos Passos, Faulkner, Updike, H. Miller, Chaplin, Ivan Gold, Steinbeck, John Cage.

_____, Existentialism and Alienation In American Literature, International: 1965. Studies relation of rationalism and irrationalism in philosophy and in literature. Kierkegaard, Marx, Dostoevsky, Nietzsche, Husserl, Heidegger, Jaspers, Camus, Sartre, Balzac, O'Neill, F. Scott Fitzgerald, T.S. Eliot, Faulkner, Dos Passos, Henry Miller, Styron, Salinger, Albee, Updike, Purdy, Arthur Miller, Bellow, Mailer, Baldwin, Lowell, T. Williams, W. Burroughs. - Review by Stan Steiner, People's World (San Francisco), Jan 8, 1966, 7. "The rhetorical approach...ends in exaggerated and dogmatic judgments."

- Responses to Steiner by Howard Selsam, Jim Victor, People's World, Feb 5, 1966.

- Rejoinder by Steiner, ibid, Feb 19, 1966. Finkelstein's book is "so pedantic, didactic and harmful that it has to be hit hard."

- Review by Emile Capouya, NG, Mch 5, 1966, 10.

- Review by E.B. Burgum, S&S, Spring 1966, 233-235.

- Review by Louis Harap, Jewish Currents, Oct 1966, 24-29.

- Debate of the book and of Marxism and Existentialism, in AmD, Mch-Apr 1966, 7-14. J.H. Lawson, Jack Lindsay, Carl Oglesby, Harry K. Wells.

- Reply by Finkelstein, AmD, Nov-Dec 1966, 34-38.

_____, SEE ALSO: Finkelstein (LIII), (LVII); 1950, 1961 (LI); Steiner (LIX); and Ben Field on Finkelstein, DW, Feb 29, 1948, 3. illus.

FLYNT, Henry A, Communists Must Give Revolutionary Leadership In Culture, World View: 1965. Consists of two large printed sheets, one being an Appendix containing technical specifications, drawings and photos of products and buildings for a socialist society. The folded sheets are enclosed between a sheet of translucent plastic and a piece of expanded polystyrene, a strong very light lightweight building material. Designs by George Maciunas. Flynt argues that socialism should exalt the applied arts, documentary films, "street-Negro music," literature

of fact, and reject  the novel, the
novelistic film, "folk music," pop
music, the art object, opera, ballet,
which "promote the formation of a labor
aristocracy, the stratification of the
workers by nationality, and the formation of bureaucracies in the proletarian dictatorships."  Accuses most
Communist taste in art of snobbism
and white-suprematism.

_____, The First Cultural Task Is Pub-
licly To Expose and Fight the Domination Of White, European-U.S. Ruling-
Class Art!  Manifesto handbill, New
York, 1964.  Directed against performance of a work by K.-H. Stockhausen.
Author is head of Action Against Cultural Imperialism.  [cc]

FOLSOM, Michael, Henry James, the Liter-
ary Establishment and Maxwell Geismar.
SOL, V i (Winter 1965), 125-134.
James and his admirers and critics.

_____, "Shakespeare the Marxist," SOL,
Fall 1965, 106-119.  Reviewing SCW,
appraises the "flabbiness of thought
which runs through most of the essays
in this volume associated with discussions of humanism;" analyzes Kettle's essay in particular in this
light; proposes a counter-interpreta-
tion of 'Hamlet' and 'Lear'.

_____, Michael Gold and 'Jews Without
Money'.  Nation, Feb 28, 1966, 242-
245.  The history and character of
Gold's novel, and Gold as a proletarian author.

_____, "Michael Gold," in: David Madden,
ed, The Proletarian Writers Of the
Thirties, Southern Illinois: Glencoe,
1967.

FONER, Philip S, Introduction to Jack
London: American Rebel, 1947, 3-130;
Citadel paperback: 1964.  Biography
and interpretation, with selections
of London's writing.

_____, Mark Twain: Social Critic, In-
ternational: 1959.

FOSTER, William Z, "Elements Of a People's Cultural Policy," NM, Apr 23,
1946, 6.  Part of the campaign against
cultural Browderism.  See 1946 (LI).

FRAINA, Louis [pseudonym: Lewis Corey],
Review of John Macy's 'Spirit Of American Literature'.  NR, Apr 1914, 244-

245.  Macy is "a pragmatist" with "an
over-emphasis on literary lineage" and
insufficient grasp of the social factor - yet this is "the first approach
to an adequate study of American
literature."

_____, "Poetic Twaddle," Daily People,
Aug 21, 1910, 4, 8; also Weekly People,
Oct 1, 1910, 3.  Great poets "stir the
lethargic mass into activity" but even
Hugo, Shaw, Ibsen are "emotional not
scientific" and their work is not "con-
ducive to correct action".  Lesser
poets generally serve the ideology of
reaction.

_____, Review of Eugene Brieux' 'The
Three Daughters Of Monsieur Dupont'.
Daily People, May 22, 1910, 5.  Finding
most French plays on sexual themes
decadent, Fraina cites this work as a
frank and revolutionary study of bourgeois marriage.

_____, "Socialism and Psychology," NR,
May 1, 1915, 10-11.  "In spite of
Marx's appreciation of the importance
of the individual, Socialist propaganda has developed a rigid determinism
which minimizes and often totally sup-
presses the psychological factor....
Culturally Socialists are notoriously
conservative" seeking "their cultural
inspiration in Pagan Greece and the
Renaissance....But these  ideals of
Athens and the Renaissance must be
transfused with a new meaning.  This
meaning can be interpreted and developed through a psychological study of
the new individual being produced by
social transformation."

_____, "Four New American Poets," NR,
July 15, 1915, 143-144.  Robert
Frost, Edgar Lee Masters, James Oppenheim, and Vachel Lindsay emphatically
extolled for seizing American life as
it is:  "They do not shrink away from
drunkards and prostitutes, 'niggers'
and 'hired help', automobiles and ad-
vertising, 'movies' and vaudeville -
all the crudity, hysteria and apparently
disgustingly meaningless characteristics
of American life.  All these things
contain a new art and a new world."
Oppenheim the "least vital" of the
four because he is "so definitely
radical, so overtly revolutionary."

_____, "Emporkommlinge ["Upstarts"],"
Forum (Berlin), Oct 1921, 6-14.  Apparently never published in English.  Sees

the best young writers and thinkers
emerging from proletariat only to be
poisoned by pervasive petty bourgeois
values of America so that their writings serve only to confuse and discourage.  (C.E.S. Wood, F. Dell, U.
Sinclair cited.)  "The culture that
has come out of the socialist and
labor movement is petty bourgeois and
in no way proletarian, and has inject-
ed a petty bourgeois spirit among the
masses."  Finds same true for Europe
and even Russia, save for Gorky.  The
only solution is to have every worker
an intellectual, and every intellectual a worker.  This will not happen
until the socialist revolution.

_____, "Life Among the Robots," Advance,
Oct 24, 1930, 3.  Prophetic view of
consumer capitalism, seen in Henry
Ford's labor policy.  Workers are
guided into spending increased wages
and leisure on mass-goods consumption
rather than "things which mean more
culture, more community life."

_____, Walt Whitman and the American
Dream.  In: Lewis Corey, The Decline
Of American Capitalism, 1934, 516-517.
"Whitman believed he was singing the
future democracy...he was really cele-
brating an age already passing away...
the petty-bourgeois democracy of early
capitalism."

_____, "Human Values In Literature and
Revolution," Story, May 1936, 4-8.
Defends Communist approach to literature: "Faith in life is a mark of all
great literature....A definite point
of departure is necessary, a philosophy or theory of social change, capable of organizing the experience of
life as it is becoming, and giving it
coherence and meaning."  However "the
call to action is not the only function of revolutionary literature, and
it may be the most limited one.  It
must concern itself primarily with
consciousness and values, with attitudes toward life."  Insists on "indirect, subtle and reciprocal" relation of culture to material relations
against the "caricature of most American 'Marxist' cultural criticism."

_____, "Trilogy In Progress," PR, Fall
1938, 118-119.  Praises Farrell's
honesty and artistry.  Attacks "pre-
tence" he says brought Depression
writers to seek proletarian literature
and theory according to the "most

amazingly unreal conceptions."

_____, "The Vision Of Heinrich Heine,"
New Leader, Sept 28, 1953, 16-18.
Published after Fraina's death.  Dis-
illusioned with Communism under Stalin
Fraina sees "chilling prevision" in
Heine of Marx's heritage as well as of
German fascism.

_____, "Marquis de Sade - The Cult Of
Despotism," Antioch Review, Spring
1966, 17-31.  Written 1952; uncorrected
at his death.  Links the Marquis to
Byron, D'Annunzio, Baudelaire, the
Italian and Russian Futurists, and
French Surrealists in "a philosophy of
perversion and of sexual, cultural,
and 'revolutionary' political elites."

_____, SEE ALSO: Fraina (LV); Baxandall
(above).  Collection of Fraina's
essays in preparation.

FRANK, Waldo, "Values Of the Revolutionary Writer," AWC, 71-78.  Speech to 1st
American Writers Congress.

_____, "The Writer's Part In Communism,"
PR, Feb 1936, 14-17.

FREEMAN, Joseph, "Notes On American Literature," Comm, Aug 1928, 513-520;
Sept, 570-578.  The tiny impact of
American letters on American life
(not excepting the working class) is
noted with many examples.  Europe and
Russia are said to provide a greater
role for the writer.

_____, "The Wilsonian Era In American
Literature," MQ(B), Iv ii (1927),
130ff.  Lewis, Dell, Dreiser, Anderson,
Frank, Cabell as a confused intelligentsia.

_____, "Social Trends In American Liter-
ature," Comm, July 1930, 641-651.
Repeats much of the 1928 article. More
is said of Babbitt and More as fascist
mentalities.

_____, et al, Voices Of October, 1930.
Soviet Russian culture. - See DW, Nov
23, 1933, 5; Nov 24, 5; Nov 25, 7, for
detailed defense of the book against
charges by Max Eastman.

_____, The Struggle Against Max Eastman
and V.F. Calverton.  DW, Nov 22-Dec 2,
1933.  Admitting RAPP was guilty of
bureaucratic arbitrariness Freeman declares Stalin was not responsible for it.

_____, "Walt Whitman: America's Great-
est Proletarian Poet," <u>DW</u>, July 7,
1934, 7.  Probably initiates organized
left's enthusiasm for Whitman.

_____, "Ivory Towers - White and Red,"
<u>NM</u>, Sept 11, 1934, 20-24.  Explains
that US Marxists have not written
"basic books" on cultural problems
"because only a handful of trained
writers were in the movement in 1932,
all the work of agitation, education,
organization, editing, journalism,
speaking, et cetera on the so-called
'cultural front' fell upon the should-
ers of these few.  We all realized
this and said: it is too bad; some day
enough writers may come left for us to
be able to distribute the burden properly; some day these books will be
written, and perhaps we shall get an
opportunity to write some of them.
Just now there is a lot of organization and agitation spadework to be
done; let's go to it."

_____, "The Tradition Of American Revo-
lutionary Literature," <u>AWC</u>, 52-58.
Speech to 1st American Writers Congress.

_____, Introduction, <u>Proletarian Litera-
ture In the United States; An Antholo-
gy</u>, ed. Michael Gold et al, 1935.

_____, <u>An American Testament</u>, 1936.
Autobiography.

_____, "Toward the Forties," <u>WCW</u>, 9-33.
Social reasons for writers' commitment.

_____, Manuscript Of Book On American
Marxist Literary Criticism.  [Copy in
possession of Daniel Aaron.]  Completed in late 30s.  For story of its
suppression, see Aaron (LIX).

_____, The Defense Of Culture Has Become
the Defense Of Democracy, <u>FW</u>, 149-158.
abdgd.  Speech to 3rd American Writers
Congress.

_____, Papers are in the Library of Co-
lumbia University.

_____, SEE ALSO: Calverton (Above); 1936
        (LI); Aaron (LIX).

FUNAROFF, Sol, Interview with Anita Tilkin.  <u>DW</u>, Nov 1, 1938, 7.  illus.
Poet, editor of 'Dynamo' and on 'New
Masses', says Marxism must become part
of poet's "assimilated experience" so
it "produces its own poetry without

need of doctrine.  In that sense,
poetry illumines certain concepts of
Marxism." - See also: S. Sillen, <u>DWSup</u>,
Dec 1, 1946, 8.  illus.  Portrayal of
Funaroff.

GETZELS, J.W, "William Dean Howells and
Socialism," <u>S&S</u>, Summer 1938, 376-385.
Relation of Howells to Marxist influ-
ences. - See also commentaries by C.
Wright, ibid, Autumn 1938, 514-517;
and by G.W. Arms, Spring 1939, 245-248.

GILES, Barbara, Interview with Beth Mc-
Henry.  <u>DW</u>, Sept 28, 1947, 11-12. illus.
Development of  'The Gentle Bush'.

_____, "The South Of William Faulkner,"
<u>M&M</u>, Feb 1950, 26-40.

_____, "The Lonely War Of J.D. Salinger,"
<u>M&M</u>, Feb 1959, 1-13.

GLASS, Martin, <u>Lip Service</u>, Students for
a Democratic Society, 1966.  Ten poems
which raise and demonstrate the problem of Marxist vocabulary in poetry as
going beyond Symbolist poetics.  Within a context of recapitulating "the
development of Western thought from
Kierkegaard through the Marxist Existentialism of Sartre, as that development took place in me and as I would
like it to take place in the reader."
- Poem I also in <u>Chelsea 15</u> (1964),
84-88; Poem IV also in <u>Literary Review</u>,
VIII ii (Winter 1964-65), 216-219;
Poems VII and VIII also in <u>Chalk Cir-
cle</u>, I i (Apr-May 1966), 48-65.

GLICKSBERG, Charles I, "William Cullen
Bryant and Communism," <u>MQ(B)</u>, July
1934, 353-359.  A Bryant "blinded and
handicapped by his very liberalism".
- See also Glicksberg (LIX).

_____, "V.F. Calverton: Marxism Without
Dogma," <u>Sewanee Review</u>, July-Sept
1938, 338-351.

GOLD, Michael, "Towards Proletarian Art,"
<u>Lib</u>, Feb 1921, 20-24.  A passionate
early manifesto.

_____, "Mysticism In the New York Thea-
tre," <u>DWSup</u>, Apr 10, 1926.  Werfel's
'The Goat Song', O'Neill's 'Great God
Brown', John Howard Lawson's 'Proces-
sional' and 'Nirvana'.  "Lawson has
wit, he has dramatic skill second only
to O'Neill, he has passion, sincerity,
fine cool brains, youth, courage - he
has everything - but he cannot break

through the bourgeois philosophy. He has hammered no philosophy out for himself, and has to go god-seeking."

_____, "May Days and Revolutionary Art," MQ(B), III ii (1926), 160-164. Max Eastman's taste and choice of poetry in the 'Masses' and 'Liberator', and the new, harder poetry of bolshevism.

_____, "America Needs a Critic," NM, Oct 1926, 7-9. Trotsky's 'Literature and Revolution' is called "an amazing performance. This man is almost as universal as Leonardo da Vinci." Useful assessment of condition of US left criticism at this time. - For Gold's later view of the book, see DW, Oct 30, 1933, 5. "This ultra-leftism...has now been repudiated by life itself."

_____, "3 Schools Of U.S. Writing," NM, Sept 1928, 12-13. Asserts the essentially radical roots of the best postwar authors.

_____, "Go Left, Young Writers!" NM, Jan 1929, 3-4. Pivotal article in leftward swing of the arts.

_____, "Wilder: Prophet Of the Genteel Christ," in: Proletarian Literature In the United States, ed. M. Gold et al, 1935, 349-354. Reprinted from NRep (1929) where it caused uproar for its irreverance. - A counter-view, Isidore Schneider's tribute to 'Bridge of San Luis Rey', that "very beautiful book", MQ(B), IV iv (1928), 407-408. - See also Calverton, Hicks.

_____, A Program For Proletarian Realism. NM, Sept 1930, 4-5.

_____, and Ernest Boyd, Debate: "The Marxist Approach To Literature Is the Only Scientific One," DW, Jan 21, 1933, 3. Report by Allan Johnson. Gold asserts class determinants of aesthetic taste against an aloof editor of 'The American Spectator'.

_____, Marxist Literary Criticism: The Case Of Ring Lardner. DW, Sept 30, 1933, 7. Finds shameful that Marxist critics have not come to terms with Lardner. Writers might "put a Communist content into this national literary form as developed by Lardner." Declares he himself lacks "the critical temperament....to be a really good Marxian critic of literature."

_____, Is Literature Relevant To the Struggle? DW, Oct 5, 1933, 5. Complaints of a Party organizer answered.

_____, Introduction, We Gather Strength, 1933. Four young poets are prefaced: "In our revolutionary movement only doggerel has been esteemed....To explain for a moment to the mechanical-minded narrow bigots: poetry is of great usefulness to the revolutionary movement because it keeps alive the spirit of faith and wonder. Men do not fight, nor die in cold blood for a cause; they fight because they are filled with faith and wonder."

_____, William Carlos Williams: Pioneer Of Proletarian Literature. DW, Oct 12, 1933, 5. Though Williams has no "profound vision of the future" it is "sectarian" not to see he gives "as in a faithful mirror the raw powerful force of the unorganized American worker, and the horrors of the slum life he leads."

_____, "No More Bohemianism," DW, Feb 28, 1934, 7. Personal reminiscence of John Reed in his militant phase in contrast to his Bohemian days, carried into praise of John Reed Club attitudes in contrast to 20s.

_____, Critique Of Bourgeois Formal Influence On Revolutionary Dance, Music, Poetry. DW, June 5, 1934, 5; June 14, 5. Harmful effects of Eliot, Graham, cerebral composers.

_____, Poetry For Mass Songs. DW, June 5, 1934, 5.

_____, Henry James. DW, Oct 29, 1934, 5. James as "insufferable bore," a "Harvard snob" who "spent his life writing tiresome and empty books" to wangle entrance to English drawing rooms.

_____, Reply To Liberal Critics Of Marxist Literary Criticism. DW, Jan 26, 1935, 7. Marxists' concerns are central not 'limited' and Marxist approach takes years to master, it is so different and complexly demanding.

_____, "Papa Anvil and Mother Partisan," NM, Feb 18, 1936, 22-23. Energetic criticism of Marxist pedantics: "Their terrible manderism. They carry their Marxian scholarship as though it were a heavy cross. They perform academic autopsies on living books. They wax

pious and often sectarian.  Often,
they use a scholastic jargon as bar-
barous as the terminology that for so
long infected most Marxist journalism
in this country, a foreign language no
American could understand without a
year or two of post-graduate study.
Which of our critics shows his joy in
battle and birth?  Which of them laughs
or breathes hard?  They have squeezed
most of the humanity out of the art of
criticism." - See also Josephine
Herbst, NM, Mch 10, 1936, 20, calls
Gold's piece anti-intellectual.

_____, "Migratory Intellectuals," NM,
Dec 15, 1936, 27-29.  Remarks on renegades:  Hook, Farrell.

_____, Change the World! 1937.  Collec-
tion of articles from DW.  However,
many of the best daily writings of
same title must be looked up in DW as
they dealt with current controversies
and were not reprinted.

_____, "Till We Have Built Jerusalem,"
in Ralph Fox, A Writer In Arms, ed.
John Lehmann et al, London, 1937, 10-
12.  Tribute to Fox as a model Party
writer.

_____, Leadbelly and Labor Poetry.  DW,
Jan 26, 1938, 7.  "What sophisticated
poets can learn from such folk singers
is the simplicity with which they approach the greatest subjects, and the
quality of legend and myth they can
give to common objects....No sophisticated poet but Langston Hughes has
been able to write thus far in America
in the people's idiom."

_____, Dos Passos.  DW, Feb 26, 1938, 7.
On turn to anti-Communism of a former
favorite of the left: "We were anxious
to win the fellow-travelers and  ignored the merde....He was going somewhere, it was right to hope to the
limit and to ignore the merde.  Now
Dos Passos is going nowhere....Dos
Passos hates Communists because organically he seems to hate the human race."
See also DW, May 2, 1938, 7. - DW, May
19, 1938, 7, Gold answers Nelson Algren who defended Dos Passos and
attacked Gold.

_____, "An Evaluation Of Proletarian
Literature In the Thirties." Speech
to 4th American Writers Congress (1941).
[LAW]  Describes "a great and fruitful
decade, one that burned much of the

shoddy opportunism, and adolescent
fear and hesitation out of our literature.  It taught American authors to
be proud of their craft, because
through it they could lead the people
to great goals.  It taught them to act
and write like men and citizens, not
like mere entertainers, or perpetual
Harvard boys, or mystic outcasts from
the national life.  No longer was the
writer an alien; he had rooted himself
in the soil of the American people."
Detailed survey of "the discovery of
new material and new regions....the
rise of a new philosophy of life."

_____, The Hollow Men, 1941.  Articles
originally published in DW under title
"The Great Tradition: Can the Literary
Renegades Destroy It?"  Often-bitter
attacks on such figures as Mumford,
Hicks, Hemingway, Dos Passos. - In re-
ply, see M. Cowley, "The Michael Golden
Legend," Decision, July 1941, 40-45.

_____, Robert Burns.  DWSup, Apr 21,
1946, 9.  Burns' topicality.

_____, "The Pressure Of the Power Of
Money," DWSup, Apr 28, 1946, 9.  The
economics of writers on the left.

_____, Call For a Whitman Day.  DW, May
7, 1946, 6.

_____, Creativity and Sterility In Marx-
ist Criticism.  DWSup, May 12, 1946, 9.

_____, "We Still Need To Put Our Wisdom
In Plain Speech," DW, Aug 1, 1946, 6.

_____, "O'Neill's Early Days and 'The
Iceman Cometh'," DWSup, Oct 27, 1946,
8.  A fellow dramatist at Provincetown
Playhouse reminiscences and analyzes
O'Neill.

_____, "The Jewish Artist In Search Of a
Subject," JL, Nov 1947, Supplement, 7-
9.  The author of 'Jews Without Money'
on problems and need for Jewish writers
to accept their situation.

_____, "The 'Masses' Tradition," M&M, Aug
1951, 45-55.  Evokes the people and
color.

_____, "A Late Appreciation For Berthold
Brecht's Drama," People's World (San
Francisco), Feb 19, 1966.  Account of
Brecht's 'Mother' at Theatre Union in
1935; appraisal of Brecht's work and
of his current reception among the young.

_____, Autobiography, edited by Michael
B. Folsom.  Forthcoming.

_____, SEE ALSO: 1946 (LI); Calverton,
        Folsom (above); Aaron (LIX);
        Pound (LXIII).

GOLDSTEIN, Leonard, "George Chapman and
the Decadence In Early Seventeenth-
Century Drama," S&S, XXVII (1963), 23-
48.  Detailed case example of decadence
as "socially-induced consciousness inevitable in periods of crisis in exploitative society."

_____, "Some Aspects Of Marriage and In-
heritance In Shakespeare's 'The Merry
Wives Of Windsor' and Chapman's 'All
Fools', " ZAA, XII (1964), 375-386.
Class comparison of Shakespeare and
Chapman as they reflect bourgeois
marriage views.

_____, "On the Transition From Formal
To Naturalistic Acting In the Eliza-
bethan and Post-Elizabethan Theatre,"
Bulletin Of the New York Public Library,
LX vii (July 1958), 330-349.

_____, "Alcibiades' Revolt In 'Timon Of
Athens'," ZAA, XV (1967), 256-278.
'Timon' as the point of tragic social
cognition beyond which Shakespeare
could not go; the collapse of Shakespearian tragedy.

GORDON, Eugene.  See (I).

GREENBERG, Clement, "Avant-Garde and
Kitsch," PR, Fall 1939, 34-49.  The
political necessity of Kitsch as
gratification and conveyor of ideological indoctrination.

GREENLEAF, Richard, "The Social Thinking
Of F. Scott Fitzgerald," S&S, Spring
1952, 97-114.

GREGORY, Horace, Writing Revolutionary
Poetry In America.  Poetry, XLII (1933)
281-284.  Suggests "the term 'proletarian' be banished from our shores...
the idea was transplanted from Russia
....So far I have seen no actual poetry
written by proletarian hands in France,
England or the United States."  Warns
also against use of timely slogans in
verse.

_____, "One Writer's Position," NM, Feb
12, 1935, 20-21.  Honest testimony by
a poet close to CP who feels the struggle over Party schisms is too much for

him: "Others can write, do write, in
the heat of conflict; I can't."

_____, "Revolution and the Individual
Writer," PR, II vii (Apr-May 1935)
52-58.  Effort to rebut attacks on
essay above.

_____, "Beliefs In Poetry," Nation, July
25, 1936, 102-103.  Problems of affirmative poetry.

_____, SEE ALSO: Edwin Rolfe, DW, Oct 13,
        1933, 5.  Praises Gregory "who
        openly supports the Communist
        Party" for "evaluating and di-
        gesting his former experience"
        in his poetry rather than forc-
        ing a "skilled but cold" overtly
        Communist verse.

GREGORY, Seymour, "A Communist Poet," NM,
Feb 11, 1947, 24-25.  Verse of John
Manifold evaluated in contrast with
'intellectualist' values of Establishment poets.

GUTERMAN, Norbert.  See 1936 (LI).

HALL, Gus, "The Case For Optimism," AmD,
Summer 1966, 15-17, 23-25.  The arts
in the CP draft program; Sinyavsky-
Daniel; artistic commitment; Hemingway
and other American writers, etc.

HALPER, Albert, Critique Of Marxist Critics.  DW, June 26, 1934, 5.

HANKIN, Bernard, "'Point', Realism, and
the Proletariat," Point (Madison, Wisc),
I i (1934), 1-8.  [Yale]  Declares the
magazine sympathetic to Marxism but
against a Party realism.  Where critical realism should be "the practice of
insincerity for the sake of the workers"
is substituted which will "result in
the degradation of the instructors as
well as the ignorance of the pupils...
The Marxist writers, many of them,
were attracted to the radical path by
what appeared to be its unflinching
fidelity to experience; in order for
them to move on the road they have
chosen, they find it necessary to ignore
its original appeal....it may be true
that prejudice must be fought with prejudice, that the creation of  new myths
is necessary for the destruction of
those that prevail.  In that case we
should not wish to discourage the Marxists from their ugly task.  But Point
cannot believe that it is the duty of
us all to blind our eyes."

HARAP, Louis, "Aesthetic Experience and Society," S&S, I (1936-37), 422 ff. Chief problems of Marxist aesthetics.

_____, "Sartre and Existentialism," NM, Dec 31, 1946, 8-11; Jan 7, 1947, 21-22. Detailed analysis concludes Sartre's "sustained polemics against the Communist Party philosophy, on the one hand, and his own subjective, enervating existential philosophy on the other, mark him as a reactionary influence." - See also NM, Oct 7, 1947, 18-20.

_____, "Freedom Unlimited," NM, Apr 8, 1947, 22-23. "Anti-progressive" character of Sartre's 'The Flies' despite its role in wartime Resistance.

_____, "Sartre On Anti-Semitism," JL, Mch 1949, 26-27. Rejects analysis in 'Anti-Semite and Jew'.

_____, Social Roots Of the Arts, 1949. Economic foundations, audience, determinants of form, force of tradition, taste, ideology and music, folk and mass art, art under fascism and socialism. - See 1950 (LI).

_____, "Literary Breakthrough - To What?" JC, Nov 1964, 16-22. Role of contemporary Jewish writers in America.

_____, "Philip Roth's Absolute Individualism," JC, Nov 1962, 15-19. 'Letting Go' a case study on above theme.

_____, Jewishness Into Existentialism. JC, Mch 1964, 4-9. Critique of Leslie Fiedler and Philip Roth who, with other prominent Jewish American writers, "have become existentialized" and derive "their inspiration, their theme, not from Jewish life, culture and values (of which they are often ignorant) but from current streams of thought created mainly by non-Jews (Dostoevsky, Sartre), from current non-Jewish, Western streams of thought, though Jews like Kafka have contributed to them."

_____, Progressive and Reactionary Viewpoints In Jewish Writing. JC, July-Aug 1960, 13-17, 34. Examines anti-Semitism and anti-Communism in Uris' 'Exodus'; also books of lesser influence which offer more positive values.

_____, Review of Edward Wagenknecht's

'Edgar Allan Poe'. S&S, Summer 1964, 377-379.

_____, Edgar Allen Poe: Prophet Of Alienation, AIMS and Humanities Press: forthcoming.

HARRINGTON, Michael, "A Marxist Approach To Art," NI, Spring 1956, 41-49. Marxist criticism as "not merely a method among other methods, but rather the ground of a fundamental synthesis." Disproves vulgar misconceptions; shows how Marxist insights enter the work of Panovsky, etc.

_____, "The Unpolitical Political; Koestler Suspended In Mid-Air," Anvil, Winter 1956, 6-8. Very effective critique.

_____, "Balzac: The Romantic-Realist," ASP, Winter 1957, 19-22. Probes discrepancy between Balzac's ideology and writing, so famously remarked by Engels.

_____, "Marxist Literary Critics," Commonweal, Dec 11, 1959, 324-326. To his Catholic audience Harrington maintains the Marxist approach is serious and complex when properly used. He refers particularly to Hauser and Lukacs.

_____, The Accidental Century, Macmillan: 1965. Analysis of the crisis of capitalism and of Marxism. The responses to decadence of Nietzsche, Mann, Dostoevsky, Camus, Yeats, Proust, Joyce, Malraux.

HART, Henry, The Proletarian Novel. PR, II vii (1935).

_____, "The Tragedy Of Literary Waste," WCW, 105-118; also 229-233. Details of devastation caused by profit ethic in writing and publishing. - See also AWC, 159-162.

HAUSER, Arnold. See (XXVII).

HAYWOOD, "Big Bill," On Proletarian Art. His views reproduced in Max Eastman's novel Venture, 1927, 210.

_____, The 1913 Paterson Textile-Strike Pageant In Madison Square Garden. In: Bill Haywood's Book, International: 1929, 1958, 261-264. Haywood was intimately involved in staging this mass reenactment of events, songs and speeches, directed by John Reed.

HEDLEY, Leslie Woolf. See 1964 (LIX).

HEIFETZ, Henry, "The Anti-Social Act Of
Writing," SOL, Spring 1964, 3-20.
Genet and Burroughs performing a necessary work of destruction and revelation "that can help us to clear away
unnecessary reverences quickly and
move forward....they are infinitely
more significant than all the easy up-
lift boys."

HERBST, Josephine. See 1934 (LI).

HICKS, Granville, Auto-Critique. IL,
1933 #2, 129. Very frank about his
choices and tasks.

_____, "Literary Criticism and the Marx-
ian Method," MQ(B), VI ii (1932), 44-
47. Comment on M. Gold's attack on
Th. Wilder, and on the discussion of
it between Calverton and Hazlitt.

_____, "Problems Of American Fellow
Travelers," IL, 1933 #3, 106-109.
Defines results of inadequate training
in the Marxist outlook; inability to
portray potential for change, reliance
on formal solutions of an earlier phase.

_____, "The Crisis In American Criti-
cism," NM, Feb 1933, 3-5. Estimate of
the problems, condition, and context
of US Marxist criticism. Thorough.

_____, The Great Tradition; An Interpre-
tation Of American Literature Since
the Civil War, 1933; rev ed, 1935.
Cursory survey of American literary
heritage, measuring writers by the
degree to which they encompass and
illuminate the major historical
trends. - Review by E.A. Schachner,
Windsor Quarterly, Spring 1934; the
book "is as far from Marxism as heaven
is from earth" because it strives to
"'go conspirative'" and "sneak propaganda for Marxism...through some
hypothetical back door," while it is
suffused with "the glow of Protestant
morality....the most blatant kind of
philosophical idealism" which avoids
the "scientific" vocabulary. - Review
by John Strachey (XXIII). - Review by
R.P. Blackmur, Hound and Horn, Jan-
Mch 1934, 351-355. - Review by F.O.
Matthiessen, Atlantic Monthly, Dec
1933, 16. - Review by Eugene Clay,
Left Review (Philadelphia). I ii
(1934), 10-14. [Yale] Critical. Review by E. B. Bates, MQ(B), Feb 1934,
57-58.

_____, "Social Interpretation Of Litera-

ture," Progressive Education, Jan-Feb
1934. Responsibilities of teachers of
English.

_____, "Revolution and the Novel," NM,
Apr 3, 10, 17, 24; May 8, 15, 22, 1934.
Lessons for the proletarian novice on
the art of the novel.

_____, "The Dialectics Of the Development
Of Marxist Criticism," AWC, 94-97. The
"dualism" of praising "proletarian"
while damning "bourgeois" literature has
been eliminated. No positive critical
standard is asserted. Speech to 1st
American Writers Congress.

_____, "Literature and Revolution," The
English Journal (College Edition),
XXIV iii (Mch 1935). Speech to College
Conference On English In the Central
Atlantic States, Dec 1, 1934. Reflec-
tions on many aspects of social deter-
mination and uses of literature.

_____, John Reed, 1936. Critical biog-
raphy. - Review by Max Eastman, MQ(B),
Oct 1936, 18-22, 31; Dec 1936, 14-21,
29-31; May 1937, 15-16.

_____, "Eliot In Our Time," NM, Feb 11,
1936, 23-24. Thoughtful review of the
Matthiessen book.

_____, "Literary Opposition To Utilitar-
ianism," S&S, Summer 1937, 454-472.
Coleridge, Carlyle, Disraeli, Kingsley,
Gaskell and Dickens considered in relation of their writings to English working class. They present "spiritual
remedies" to what they thought "spiritual evil."

_____, "The American Writer Faces the
Future," WCW, 180-194. Speech to 2nd
American Writers Congress. Detailed
analysis of problems and reasons of
political involvement.

_____, "The Social Criticism Of John
Ruskin," IL, 1938 #2, 73-75, 78-80.

_____, New Voices. Address Delivered at
Community Church of Boston, Oct 9,
1938. 12 pp. [cc] Writers of the
30s who discovered industrial life and
struggle, anti-fascism, new areas of
experience for literature. Problems
of defining audience: such a writer
"scarcely knows what he must say and
what he can leave unsaid."

_____, Figures Of Transition,

1939.  Valuable and neglected study of W. Morris, Thomas Hardy, S. Butler, George Gissing, Oscar Wilde, Rudyard Kipling as representative figures breaking free of and criticizing Victorian letters and life.

_____, "The Failure Of Left Criticism," NRep, Sept 9, 1940. - See Michael Gold on Hicks leaving the Party, DWSup, Sept 12, 1940, 7.  Sharp talk on the politics needed to implement morality.

_____, "The Blind Alley Of Marxism," Nation, Sept 28, 1940.

_____, "Communism and the American Intellectuals," in: Irving DeWitt Talmadge, Whose Revolution? 1941, 78-115. Most concise review of his Party career.

_____, Papers are in the Carnegie Library of Syracuse University.

_____, SEE ALSO, for his later views:
      Where We Came Out, 1954; Part Of
      the Truth, 1965. - Also "The
      Thirties: A Reappraisal," Satur-
      day Review, May 4, 1963, 27-28;
      1932 (LI); Browder (above);
      Aaron (LIX).

HITCH, Marcus, Goethe's Faust; A Fragment Of Socialist Criticism, Kerr: Chicago, 1908.  [DLC]  Perhaps first extended Marxist literary analysis in US.  Sees 'Faust, Part II' as unsatisfactory because the achievement of happiness and unification of mind and senses, Goethe's chosen problem, "is unsolvable until classes have been abolished.  Until then the perfect or near-perfect man must divide his time between profit grinding on one hand and charity dispensing on the other, as Carnegie and Rockefeller have done."  Mephistopheles as voicing aspirations of lower classes.  Had Goethe shown greater moral strength he might have drawn the conclusions of his premises.  Hitch was frequent contributor to ISR but never on literature.

HODGES, Donald Clark, "Philosophical Sadism and Angry Young Men," Root and Branch, #2 (1962), 43-47.  Osborne, Sillitoe, the Beat Generation, Marxism and the uses of the irrational.

_____, "Normal Sadism and Immoralism," Psychoanalysis and the Psychoanalytic Review, Summer 1961.

HOREVITZ, Richard, "Free University At Ann Arbor," New Left Notes, Apr 29, 1966, 5.  Relation of new Marxist movements to artists.  "If it is possible at all to speak of a relationship between the art and literature of the 20th century and contemporary new left thought, it is only in the despair of the artist and writer who shares our concerns but is left only with our impoverished thought as a political program....rather than worrying about how we are to 'use' the poet and musician, it is our need to learn from those who are more sensitive, who have a greater understanding of man and his world."

HOROWITZ, David, Shakespeare: An Existential View, Tavistock: London, 1965. The 'projects' in the plays linking fact and value, being and possibility, and the Shakespearean social order in which the possibilities are played out, values created and defeated.  Cervantes.

HOWARD, Milton [pseudonym of Milton Halpern], "Partisan Review: Esthetics Of the Cage," Main, Winter 1947, 46-57.

HUGHES, Langston.  See (I).

HUMBOLDT, Charles [pseudonym of Clarence Weinstock], "Threepenny Opera," NM, Nov 29, 1938, 23-24.  First Marxist review in English of 'Dreigroschenroman'.  Calls Brecht a realist compared with Rilke, Kafka, but criticizes absence of personal psychology.

_____, "To the Mad Hatters," NM, Mch 11, 1947, 13-17.  On Rahv, Phillips, Diana Trilling.

_____, "Maxim Gorky and Writers," NM, Aug 13, 1946, 23-25.  The lessons of Gorky.

_____, "The Novel Of Action," Main, I iv (Fall 1947), 389-407.  Problems of the modern novel.  Balzac, Mann, Dostoevsky, Wolfert, Fast, B. Giles.

_____, "What's Wrong With Our Short Stories," NM, May 20, 1947, 6-8; May 27, 16-18.  Sound craft advice in Marxian context.

_____, "The Naked and the Dead By Mailer," M&M, June 1948, 70-74.

_____, "How True Is Fiction?" M&M, Jan 1949, 20-34.

_____, "Communists In Novels," M&M, June 1949, pp.13-31; July 1949, 44-65.

_____, "Tolstoy and Art," M&M, Aug 1950, 69-84.

_____, "No Art Is Neutral," CQ, Winter 1953, 3-13.

_____, "The Tragedy Of Dylan Thomas," M&M, Sept 1954, 53-56.

_____, "More Than Bread Alone," M&M, Feb 1958, 3-32. Criticizes Krushchev attack on Dudintsev's novel; reframes the questions.

_____, "The Case Of Doctor Zhivago," M&M, Nov 1958, 1-23.

_____, "Art and Production," NG, May 16, 1963, 2. Using pseudonym Roger Schevill, Humboldt demurs on Krushchev speech of Mch 8, 1963.

HUMPHRIES, Rolfe, "Archibald MacLeish," MQ(B), June 1934, 264-270, 274.

ILLO, John, "The Misreading Of Milton," Columbia University Forum, Summer 1965, 38-42. "The 'Areopagitica' was intolerant in an intolerant age....Milton, like every humanist revolutionary from St. Paul to Fidel Castro, is indeed a libertarian: but the counter-revolution, religious or political, is outside the limits of reason and tolerance."

JEROME, V.J, See 1946, 1951 (LI); Jerome (LIV).

_____, "People Meets People," PA, Nov 1964, 29-39. Analyzes basis for peaceful ideological struggle between US and USSR.

_____, See Obituary. PA, Sept 1965, 10-12. illus.

JOHNSON, E, "Henry Adams: The Last Liberal," S&S, Spring 1937, 362-377.

KEMP, Jonathan, Introduction, and ed, Diderot: Interpreter Of Nature, 1936; 1-34. Life and thought in the tradition of materialist philosophy.

KNAPP, Daniel, "Hemingway: The Naming Of the Hero," SOL, II ii (1961), 30-41. "The character of the Hemingway hero depends upon retreat....Hemingway's vision is not basically revolutionary; it is convervative."

KRAPP, R.M, "Class Analysis Of a Literary Controversy," S&S, Winter 1946, 80-92. Controversy between exponents of "wit" (Dryden, Cowley, Davenant, Hobbes and Jonson) and "sense" (Blackmore, Defoe, Wesley) in 17th Century English literature.

KRESH, Joseph, "Georg Buchner," Dia, #6, 1-11; #7, 19-31. (1938)

_____, "Georg Buchner's Reputation As an Economic Radical," Germanic Review, VIII (1933), 44-51.

_____, "Gerhardt Hauptmann, " Arise; The Labor and Socialist Magazine, I i (Oct 1934), 20-23. An analysis of the early plays which parallels Mehring's.

_____, "The Mystic Strain In Toller's Work," S&S, Winter 1940, 78-84.

KRONER, Jack, "William Faulkner," NF, II i (1948), 7-21. Criticized in ibid, II iii, 154-157; rejoinder by Kroner, II iv (1949), 259-262.

KUNITZ, Joshua. See (XLIX).

LANDAU, Ezra, "The Wise Laughter Of Sholem Aleichem," M&M, Dec 1959, 1-12.

LANGFORD, Howard D, "The Imagery Of Alienation," in Herbert Aptheker, ed. Marxism and Alienation: A Symposium, American Institute for Marxist Studies, Monograph Series No. 2, Humanities Press: 1965, 58-87. The need and possibility for literature that demonstrates "realistic vision and reasonable hope".

LAPSLEY, Mary, "Socially Constructive Writing For Children Today." Speech to 4th American Writers Congress. [LAW]

LARNER, Jeremy, "Salinger's Audience" PR, Fall 1962, 594-598. "The real and pressing needs to which Salinger responds so naturally have been created by the current plight of the educated middle-class American family."

LAWSON, John Howard, "The American Democratic Tradition, Yesterday and Tomorrow," Speech to 4th American Writers Congress. (LAW]

_____, "Biographical Notes," ZAA, IV (1956), 73-76. With bibliography.

_____, The Hidden Heritage; A Rediscovery Of the Ideas and Forces That Link the

Thought Of Our Time With the Culture
Of the Past, Citadel: 1950.  Chapters
in the struggle for freedom against
ruling classes and imperialism from
1075 to the present, with much attention to relation of this struggle to
the arts.  Architecture of the cathe-
dral, Aztec and Maya  myth, Beethoven,
Boccaccio, Botticelli, Bruno, Cervantes,
Chaucer, Dante, Defoe, Donne, El Greco,
Greek drama, Giotto, Ben Jonson,
Leonardo da Vinci, Marlowe, Milton,
Melville, Monteverde, Thomas More,
rise of the novel, opera, Petrarch,
Rabelais, Shakespeare, Tolstoy, Lope
de Vega, Wagner, Whitman.

_____, "Parrington and the Search For
Tradition," Main, Winter 1947, 23-43.
Defines the task undertaken in the
above work: to remove "the idea of
democracy from the cloud-land of abstraction".  Parrington analyzed as
"the indispensable basis for further
study."

_____, "'Decadence' In American Culture,"
PA, Mch 1965, 29-39.  Institutions of
US culture are bought and paid for;
its artists evince despair and self-
hatred.  Decadence is "a general and
somewhat misleading term" for work of
writers who ignore Marxism and yet are
important creators; "the errors in the
theoretical structure do not bring the
whole edifice toppling down, nor do
they necessarily delimit its influence".
The honest problems and the vigor of
the vast American middle class are
seen as in fact misrepresented by the
despairing writers like Albee, Bellow.

_____, " Marxism and Existentialism,"
AmD, Mch-Apr 1966, 7-8.  Finds the
American Existentialists represent "an
anti-capitalist trend" and raise
"difficult ethical dilemmas" for which
"I have no answers."  Takes issue with
S. Finkelstein's book on the subject.

_____, SEE ALSO: Lawson (LVIII); 1934,
     1946 (LI).

LEAGUE OF AMERICAN WRITERS.  See 1935-41
(LI); Bulletin of the League, with
Supplements, and Minutes of numerous
executive  and membership meetings in
New York and Hollywood, also publicity
releases, correspondence and other
records [LAW].

LeROY, Gaylord C, "Romanticism and Marxism: The Marxist View," in Herbert
Aptheker, ed, Marxism and Democracy:

A Symposium, American Institute for
Marxist Studies, Monograph Series No.
1, Humanities Press: 1965, 59-70.  Progressive and reactionary Romanticism in
England and on the continent.  The
Marxist contribution to a critique of
modernist art.  The inadequacy of non-
Marxist description of modernism.  Perspectives for Marxist scholarship.

_____, "American Innocence Reconsidered,"
MassR, Summer 1963, 623-646.  Critique
of the view in Fiedler, Hassan, Parkes,
of a trait of innocence in American
literature.

_____, Marxism and Modern Literature,
American Institute for Marxist Studies;
Occasional Paper: No. 5 (1967).  39 pp.
Study of cognitive function of litera-
ture in romanticism, realism, modernism,
socialist realism.  Joyce, Kafka.

_____, and Ursula Beitz, eds, An Anthol-
ogy Of Marxist Literary Theory and
Criticism Since 1960 From European
Socialist Countries.  Forthcoming.
Essays dealing with methodology,
Romanticism to Realism, Realism and
Modernism, Socialist Realism, new
problems of aesthetics.

_____, Perplexed Prophets; Six Nineteenth-
Century British Authors, Philadelphia:
1953.  Carlyle, Arnold, Ruskin, J.
Thomson, D.G. Rossetti, Wilde.

LE SUEUR, Meridel, "The Fetish Of Being
Outside," NM, Feb 26, 1935, 23.

_____, "Proletarian Literature Of the
Middle West," AWC, 135-138.  Speech to
1st American Writers Congress.  The
"native" radical literature of Wobblies
and the prairies.

_____, The Kind Of Marxist Reviewing We
Need.  DW, Apr 26, 1946, 12.  Grateful,
lucid analysis of Karl Schmidt's DW
review of her 'North Star Country'.

LETTERS FROM WORKERS On Their Wants In
Proletarian Literature.  DW, Dec 12,
14, 17, 19, 23, 26, 1935; Feb 15, Apr
6, 7, 8, 9, 10, 11, 14, 1936.  Inquiry
and forum conducted by Michael Gold.
- See also DW, May 16, 1946, 8.  Gold
reports with disgust that 'Green Man-
sions' was the novel most often favored
by workers.

LONDON, Jack, Jack London: American Rebel,
1947.  ed. Philip S. Foner.  Selections
of his basic writings, and bibliography.

Includes London's views of F. Norris, Gorky, U. Sinclair.

LOWENFELS, Walter, "My Credo," in his: The Prisoners.

_____, "Literature and Society," M&M, June 1962, 56-60.

_____, Interview with Robert Forrey. M&M, May 1963, 42-52.

_____, Walt Whitman's Civil War, Knopf: 1961.

_____, ed, Poets Of Today: A New American Anthology, New World paperback: 1964. With foreword.

_____, "On 'Modernism' In Art," NWR, Apr 1964, 34-36. Defends the long tradition of expressionist art against "white, western, chauvinist" bias, in US or USSR.

_____, "T.S. Eliot," AmD, II i (1965), 35-37. Recollections of encounters with Eliot and a 1934 estimate (not before published) seeing Eliot's 'Wasteland' limited by no notion of renewal of the world by the working class, "no illusions and no acts. It is itself the last act of a class that has reached the dead end of a creative decline."

_____, Exchange Of Letters With Hubert Selby. AmD, May-June 1965, 34-38. With the views of L.W. Hedley, J. Isserman, G. Sorrentino. Concerning Selby's 'Last Exit to Brooklyn'.

_____, See also: Alan Guttman, "Walter Lowenfels' Poetic Politics," MassR, Autumn 1965, 843-850.

LYND, Staughton, "Henry Thoreau: The Admirable Radical," Liberation, Feb 1963, 21-26. Argues for "the possibility of a socialist Thoreau," as against the absolute pacifist-anarchist version. - Discussion by Truman Nelson and others, and Lynd's reply, ibid, Apr 1963, 22-29.

MacLEISH, Archibald, Interview with Edwin Rolfe. DW, Mch 15, 1935, 5. Explains his drama 'Panic' affirms role of masses in ending crisis of capitalism.

_____, "The Poetry Of Karl Marx," Saturday Review, Feb 17, 1934, 485-486. Revolution and poetry.

_____, "The Writer and Revolution," Saturday Review, Jan 26, 1935, 641-642. The writer cannot achieve a direct effect.

MAGIL, A. B, 'The Hammer'. DWSup, Feb 5, 1927. Account of Yiddish-language Communist literary journal edited by Moissaye Olgin.

MALTZ, Albert, Interview with Anita Tilkin. DW, Nov 8, 1938, 7. illus.

_____, The Citizen Writer, 1950. Seven essays that assert the writer's function as public conscience and force. - Grows out of Maltz's experience and essays while at center of controversy over Cultural Browderism: see 1946 (LI).

_____, "Some Biographical Data Of My Life," ZAA, I (1953), 129-130. Rather full account. Bibliography. - See also Papers of A. Maltz, State Historical Society, Madison, Wisc. - See Mendelson (XLVI).

MANTY, Jack, "Henry George Weiss," DW, May 31, 1946, 11. Life and death of a West Coast working-class poet.

MARCUSE, Herbert, Eros and Civilization, 1955; Vintage paperback, 1962. Chapters 7-11. Discussion of overcoming alienation by achieving a non-repressive society where play replaces work. Traces impetus for theory of an aestheticized social life, with contributions from German Idealist aesthetics (Kant, Schiller) and Freud.

_____, "Base and Superstructure - Reality and Ideology," in his: Soviet Marxism, Columbia Univ: 1958; Vintage paperback, 1961, 106-120. "Soviet realism conforms to the pattern of a repressive state....Cut off from its historical base, socialized without a socialist reality, art reverts to its ancient prehistorical function: it assumes magical character."

_____, One-Dimensional Man; Studies In the Ideology Of Advanced Industrial Society, Beacon: Boston, 1964; Beacon paperback: Boston, 1966. US working class now fails to recognize itself as "the living contradiction to the establishment" thus the sense of historical dialectic and reason has left American thought. Yet ideology, far from "ended," is now omnipresent, identical with the forms of consensus

technocratic society. - Pp. 56-83
discuss "certain key notions and
images of literature and their fate"
in this context: "how the progress of
technological rationality is liquidat-
ing the oppositional and transcending
elements in the 'higher culture'."
Heroes independent of the dominant
ethos no longer are created; heroes
are rather its victims and their de-
feats testify to the society's ideological omnipotence.  "The truly avant-
garde works of literature communicate
the break with communication."

_____, "Remarks On a Redefinition Of
Culture," Daedalus, Winter 1964.

_____, "Socialist Humanism?" in: Erich
Fromm, ed, Socialist Humanism, Doubleday: 1965, 96-105.

_____, "Repressive Tolerance," in:
Robert Paul Wolff et al, A Critique Of
Pure Tolerance, Beacon: Boston, 1965,
81-117.  The moral right of progres-
sives to employ extra-legal means and,
if possible, intolerance, against the
repressive tolerance of capitalist
culture.

McKENNEY, Ruth, Interview with James Du-
gan.  DW, Jan 26, 1939, 7.  illus.
Author of 'My Sister Eileen' relates
her road to a post on 'New Masses'.

MILLET, Martha, "The New Priests Of
Poetry," Contemporary Issues, Jan-Feb
1958, 598-605.  Attacks Eliot and
Pound as purveying fascist literary
mentality to the younger generation.
John Ball answers her at length, ibid,
Oct-Nov 1958, 170-187, and Millet re-
plies, ibid, 187-189; Alan Dutscher
joins in castigating Ball, ibid, Feb-
Mch 1961, 303-320.

MINAR, Edwin L, Early Pythagorean Politics In Practice and Theory, Connecti-
cut College Monograph no. 2, Baltimore:
1942.  Begun as Ph.D. dissertation
under A.D. Winspear.  Relation of
Aristotle, Plato, and others to aristocratic politics.

MORROW, Donald, Where Shakespeare Stood;
His Part  In the Crucial Struggles Of
His Day, Milwaukee, 1935, 89 pp.  Introduction by Granville Hicks.  View
of Shakespeare "expressing the merchantile bourgeois class."

MUFSON, Thomas, "Victor Hugo," The Comrade, Apr 1904, 156-157.

NADIR, Moishe, "The Writer  In a Minority
Language," AWC, 153-157.  Speech to
1st American Writers Congress.

NEUGASS, James, Interview with Anita
Tilkin.  DW, Nov 15, 1938, 7.  illus.
Yale and Oxford educated proletarian
poet who fought in Spain.

'NEW FORCE', Editorial: "An Appeal To
Detroit Writers, Artists and Intellectuals," The New Force, I v (July-Aug
1932), 1.  A local John Reed Club
platform.

NEWMAN, Charles Henry, "How Objective  Is
Objectivism?" Dynamo, I iii (Summer
1934), 26-29.  Analyzes W.C. Williams'
"denial of the role of the artist and
of artistic values."

NORTH, Joseph, "The 'Masses' Tradition,"
M&M, Sept 1951, 34-41.  History of the
magazine, its crises. - See also 1946
(LI).

NYE, Russell, "Stephen Crane, Social
Critic," MQ(B), Summer 1940, 48-54.

ODETS, Clifford.  See (LVIII).

OGLESBY, Carl, "Marxism and Existentialism," AmD, Mch-Apr 1966, 11-13.  Critique of book by S. Finkelstein (above).
Existentialism as a "department of
Marxist thought." The value in the
work of alienated, non-Marxist artists.

OLGIN, Moissaye, "Maxim Gorky," NRep,
Jan 18, 1919, 333-335. - See also Olgin
(LVIII); Magil (above); Gorky (XLVI).

PERKINS, Frances, "Henrik Ibsen, The
Iconoclast," ISR, July 1909, 40-49.
Among most thorough critiques antece-
dent to 1917 of a writer from the
socialist perspective.

PHELPS, Wallace.  Pseudonym of Wm.
Phillips (below).

PHILLIPS, William, "Class-ical Culture,"
Comm, Jan 1933, 93-96.  Review of Or-
tega y Gasset's 'The Revolt Of the
Masses' as  "an apology for capitalism."

_____, "Categories For Criticism,"
Symposium, Jan 1933, 31-47.

_____, and Philip Rahv, "Problems and
Perspectives In Revolutionary Literature," PR, I iii (1934), 3-10.  Com-
plains of low standards.

_____, "Sensibility and Modern Poetry," Dynamo, I iii (Summer 1934), 20-25. Sensibility rather than subject-matter as the essential of proletarian or revolutionary poetry. The value of continuity with poetic sensibility of bourgeois outlook (Pound, Eliot, H. Crane) and that of transitional poets (H. Gregory, Spender, Auden, Day-Lewis).

_____, "Three Generations," PR, I iv (1934).

_____, "Form and Content," PR, I vi (1934), 31-39. The indissoluble unity of form and content merged by the writer's sensibility.

_____, and Philip Rahv, "Criticism," PR, II vii (Apr-May 1935), 16-25. Critique of simplistic Marxist criticism, preparatory to 1st American Writers Congress. - Discussion of this essay by Newton Arvin, pp. 25-27; by Granville Hicks, pp. 28-30; by Obed Brooks, pp. 30-31.

_____, and Philip Rahv, "Recent Problems Of Revolutionary Literature," in: Michael Gold et al, eds, Proletarian Literature In the United States, 1935, 367-373.

_____, and Philip Rahv, "Private Experience and Public Philosophy," Poetry, May 1936, 98-105. Reprinted in Morton D. Zabel, ed, Literary Opinion In America, 1937 edition, 552-557. Disputing Eliot in his "Poetry and Propaganda," they assert continuity from the experience of a poet through his adoption of "an interpretation of the world."

_____, and Philip Rahv, "Literature In a Political Decade," in: Horace Gregory, ed, New Letters In America, 1937, 170-180. Deals with many matters, most importantly, failure of the proletarian novel in America to deal with problems of consciousness.

_____, and Philip Rahv, "Some Aspects Of Literary Criticism," S&S, Winter 1937, 212-220.

_____, "Art and Society," AF, III iii-iv, 23-24. Review of Plekhanov's book.

_____, "The Esthetic Of the Founding Fathers," PR, IV iv (1938), 11-21. Marx, Engels, Lenin, Trotsky as non-

systematic but against simplifying he sees in Gold, Hicks. Agrees with Saint-Beuve against Taine that questions of 'genius' and 'uniqueness' are central. Values are the key; "the act of creation is an act of judgment."

_____, SEE ALSO: Philip Rahv (below).

PUTNAM, Samuel, "Latin-American Culture and the Rockefeller Committee." Speech to 4th American Writers Congress (1941). [LAW] Detrimental effects worked on Latin American culture by US interests.

RAHV, Philip, "The Literary Class War," NM, Aug 1932, 7-10. Applies Aristotle's catharsis theory to proletarian literature. The lot of the worker "inspires the spectator with pity.... he is terror-stricken by the horror of workers' existence under capitalism: but these two emotions finally fuse in the white heat of battle into a revolutionary deed, with the weapon of proletarian class-will in the hands of the masses." - See also A.B. Magil, "Pity and Terror," NM, Dec 1932, 16-19. To Rahv: "Terror is an emotion absolutely alien to the revolutionary proletariat, incompatible with militant class action."

_____, "An Open Letter To Young Writers," The Rebel Poet, Sept 1932, 3-4. Rahv in his first enthusiasm: "Too long has literature been standing on its head, doped by the mephitic fumes of idealist opium. Dialectic materialism demands that we put it on its feet." "We must sever all ideological ties with this lunatic civilization known as capitalism."

_____, "Maxim Gorky and the Cultural Revolution," DW, Dec 23, 1932, 4. Centrality of proletarian writing and of Gorky, its mentor.

_____, "T.S. Eliot," Fantasy, II iii (Winter 1932), 17-20. Evaluates and traces his poetry.

_____, Letter. MQ(B), Summer 1934, 12. His road from "living on the carrion of Eliot" to "an intellectual assistant of the proletariat."

_____, "Valedictory On the Propaganda Issue," The Little Magazine, Sept-Oct 1934, 1-2. Defines varieties of "propaganda" in literature with special reference to the Lukacs essay, "Propaganda Or Partisanship?"

_____, "Marxist Criticism and Henry Haz-
litt," IL, 1934 #2, 112-116.

_____, Review of 'Murder In the Cathe-
dral' and 'Bury the Dead'. PR, June
1936.

_____, "Two Years Of Progress," PR,
Feb 1938, 22-30. Comparison of 1935
and 1937 Writers Congresses with
emphasis on implicit alterations of
policy. - PR broke with the Party in
an editorial, Dec 1937. For comment,
see Socialist Appeal, Dec 4, 1937, 7.

_____, "Proletarian Literature: A Poli-
tical Autopsy," Southern Review, Winter 1939, 616-628. Describes proletarian writing as "the literature of
a party disguised as the literature
of a class."

_____, On the "Stalinist Cultural Front".
New Leader, Dec 10, 1938, 8.

_____, "Twilight Of the Thirties," PR,
Summer 1939, 3-15. Refuses to find
political commitment of the artist a
fault, without regard to context.

_____, "What Is Living and What Is
Dead," PR, May-June 1940, 175-180.
Separating Marxism from Stalinism.

_____, "The Cult Of Experience In Ameri-
can Writing," PR, Nov-Dec 1940, 412-
424. Develops his thesis on the failure of American writing, proletarian
or other, to raise consciousness to
the level of comprehending historical
structure.

_____, SEE ALSO: William Phillips
(above). - Ph.D. dissertation-
in-progress on PR, by James
Gilbert, University of Wisconsin.

RAYMOND, Margaret Thomsen, "A World View
In Writing For Children." Speech to
4th American Writers Congress. [LAW]

'REBEL ARTS', Manifesto. In: Arise; The
Labor and Socialist Magazine, I i (Oct
1934), 2. A call for class commitment,
by a Socialist Party journal of the
arts.

'RED PEN', Editorial. [Later 'Left Review'] (Philadelphia), I i {Jan 1934),
1, 13. [Yale] Directly aligns Phila-

delphia John Reed Club with Kharkov
Conference program, which is quoted.

REED, John, and Art Young, The IWW and
the Arts. Lib, I vii, 20-28.

ROBBINS, Rossell Hope, ed, Historical
Poems Of the XIVth and XVth Centuries,
Columbia Univ Press: 1959. With intro-
duction, notes, glossary. Middle-
English political poetry.

_____, Secular Lyrics Of the XIV and XV
Centuries, Oxford: 1952. With introduction, notes, glossary.

_____, The T.S. Eliot Myth, Schuman: 1951.
The myth, the reactionary critics who
created it, and Eliot's thought and
language analyzed. An early version of
this book appeared as "The T.S. Eliot
Myth" in S&S, Winter 1950, 1-28. - Review by E.B. Burgum, S&S, Spring 1952,
179-180.

ROE, Wellington, For Complexity in Proletarian Literature. FW, 39-42.
Speech to 3rd American Writers Congress.

_____, "The Factory As a Theme." Speech
to 4th American Writers Congress (1941).
[LAW] Emphasizes need to portray
workers in full psychological depth.

ROSENBERG, Harold, "Note On Class Consciousness In Literature," The New Act,
Jan 1933, 3-10. Defines two areas of
personality: what is common with others
of a given class, and what is "left
over," one's purely individual identity.
The latter paradoxically is the universal area - death is an example of its
characteristics - and here Party demands for "proletarian" novels have no
legitimate claim.

_____, "What We May Demand," NM, Mch 23,
1937, 17-18. Making of literary demands is "a regular function of criticism and creative aesthetics." That
"perverted kind of idealism" which
turns revolutionary ideas into 'Marxist'
abstractions, ignoring the "laws of
motion which determine the actual development of literature itself," must
be guarded against.

_____, "Myth and History In Thomas Mann,"
PR, Winter 1939, 19-39. The "idealist"
notion of history in Mann's politics
and novels.

_____, "The Third Dimension Of Georg

Lukacs," Dis, Fall 1964, 404-414.
Failure to comprehend modernism.

_____, SEE ALSO: Rosenberg (LIII).

RUBINSTEIN, Annette T, The Great Tradition In English Literature: From
Shakespeare To Shaw, 1953.  First half
reissued as Shakespeare To Jane Austen,
Citadel paperback: 1962.  Biographical
studies of numerous English writers to
demonstrate how "always the great
writers have, in one way or another,
participated in the essential struggles
of their time."

_____, "Brave and Baffled Hunter," M&M,
Jan 1960, 1-23.  Hemingway's values.

RUDICH, Norman, "The Dialectics Of
Poesis: Literature As a Mode of Cognition," Boston University Studies In
the Philosophy Of Science II, Boston,
1965, 343-400.  Theoretical discussion
and close analysis of Gray's "Elegy"
to dispute the New Critics and show
the function of interpretation, evaluation and generalization in literature, and the specific nature of its
communication.  Discussion of Aristotle,
K. Burke.  "Poetry is the only possible
science of praxis."

_____, "The Individual As Myth," Chicago
Review, Summer 1958, 94-119.  Finds
the irreducible individual described
by some existentialists (Kierkegaard,
Nietzsche, Camus) to be in fact a
mythical creation, with the point
being not the individual but philosophical despair.  Compares their literary
works with those of the realists, who
treat the individual as "condemned to
understand" the individual in a social
situation.

RUDNICK, Frank, "Propaganda Or Art," Le,
II i (Jan 1933), 3-6.  "We say that if
the cry for bread is propaganda and has
no place in art, art has no place in
life."

RUKEYSER, Muriel, Review of 'Chorus For
Survival' by Horace Gregory.  DW, Mch
19, 1935, 5.  Rukeyser praised classical knowledge and cultural particular-
ism of Gregory's verse, also his politics, "so close to the Communist Party,
but with a national rather than a sectarian emphasis." - Attacked by Milton
Howard, DW, Mch 22, 1935, 5.  Howard
says "this 'national emphasis' leads"
toward National Socialist ideology

unless  the writer becomes absolutely
clear about nature of proletarian
literature.

SAMSON, Leon, The New Humanism, 1930,
191-201, 273-300.  Art in class society
as repressive and cathartic.  In classless society art will vanish, replaced
by the play of the people.

_____, "A Proletarian Philosophy Of Art,"
MQ(B), V ii (1929), 235-239.  Art as a
product of system of property and alienated labor, is separate from the life
of the people; with the end of private
property, art will disappear, merging
with life.

SCHACHNER, E.A, "Revolutionary Literature
In the United States Today," Windsor
Quarterly, Spring 1934, 27-64.  Valu-
able as extended "proletarian" evalua-
tion of Communist critics and litera-
ture just prior to United Front period.
For two years Schachner was Secretary
of Writers' Group of New York John Reed
Club; former DW journalist, editor of
'Solidarity' and the 'Food Worker'.
Treats Kunitz, Gold, Freeman, Hicks
especially.

SCHAPPES, Morris U, "T.S. Eliot Moves
Right," MQ(B), Aug 1933, 405-408.

_____, "Robinson Jeffers and Hart Crane:
A Study In Social Irony," Dynamo, I ii
(Mch-Apr 1934), 15-22.

_____, "The Folk Art Of Sholom Aleichem,"
Main, Winter 1947, 117-122.

_____, "Anatomy Of 'David Levinsky',"
JL, Aug 1954, 22-24.  The Abraham
Cahan novel of the Lower East Side.

_____, "Shylock and Anti-Semitism," JC,
June 1962, 7-13, 37-39.  Reprinted as
12 pp. pamphlet.  "The backbone of the
play is anti-Semitic."  Shakespeare
was "aiming at interest-breeding capitalist money-lending and making it more
hateful by making it seem Jewish rather
than merely a matter of another economic
method."

_____, Letter On 'Merchant Of Venice'.
Central Conference American Rabbis
Journal, June 1965, 92-94.

SCHLAUCH, Margaret, "The Social Base Of
Linguistics," S&S, Fall 1936, 18-44.

_____, "Recent Soviet Studies In Linguistics," S&S, Winter 1937, 152-167.

_____, "The Language Of James Joyce,"
S&S, Fall 1939, 482-497.  The linguistics of 'Finnegans Wake'.

_____, "Semantics As Social Evasion,"
S&S, Fall 1942, 315-330.  Review
essay on Alfred Korzybski, Stuart
Chase, S.I. Hayakawa, P.W. Bridgman.

_____, "The Anti-Humanism Of Ezra Pound,"
S&S. Summer 1949, 258-269.  Detailed
textual criticism.

_____, Modern English and American Poet-
ry: Techniques and Ideologies, C.A.
Watts: London, 1956.

_____, English Medieval Literature and
Its Social Foundations, Warsaw, 1956;
available through Albert Daub & Co,
New York.

_____, "Criticism and Scholarship,"
M&M, May 1957, 1-10.  The problems of
bias and commitment.

_____, The English Language In Modern
Times (Since 1400), Warsaw, 1959.

_____, "Early Tudor Colloquial English,"
PhPr, I (1958), 97-104.

_____, "Themes Of English Fiction, 1400-
1600; Some Suggestions For Future Research," KN, VI (1959), 339-342.

_____, "Roman 'Controversiae' and the
Court Scene In 'Merchant Of Venice',"
KN, VII (1960), 45-56.

_____, "Realism and Convention In Medie-
val Literature," KN, XI (1964), 3-12.

_____, Antecedents Of the English Novel:
1400-1600, Warsaw, 1963; available
through Oxford Univ. Press, London.
Traces development of English prose
fiction from Chaucer to Deloney.

_____, SEE ALSO: Studies In Language
and Literature In Honour Of Margaret
Schlauch, Polish Scientific Pub:
Warsaw, 1966.  44 contributions.

_____, SEE ALSO: Stalin (XLVI).

SCHLEIFER, Marc, "Art and Socialist
Realism," MR, Nov 1963, 372-383.
"The issue here is Socialist Realism
vs. art."

_____, Interview with Juan Gelman.  Rev,

Mch 1964, 125-127.  "It is my awareness, my power of abstraction, sitting
with my friends in a 'beatnik' apartment in New York's Lower East Side slum
neighborhood, that tells me that Communism is around the corner, but the
problem is that our consciousness is
already there....If our art is ahead of
the times then we must change, not our
art, but the times."

_____, "Art and Revolution," Weapon, #1
(1965), 40-43.  Definitions of revolutionary art according to distinct circumstances.

_____, SEE ALSO: 1964 (LI);  Schleifer
(LIV).

SCHNEIDER, Isidor, Proletarian Literature
Reaches Maturity.  DW, Feb 8, 1934, 5.
Taking appearance of 'Partisan Review'
as token, Schneider finds literary left
no longer on defensive.

_____, "Toward Revolutionary Poetry," in
his Comrade: Mister, 1934.  The con-
tinuance of love and nature as themes.

_____, "Proletarian Poetry," AWC, 114-
120.  Speech to 1st American Writers
Congress.  Discussion of problems and
possibilities.

_____, O'Neill's 'The Iceman Cometh'.
NM, Oct 29, 1946, 28-30.  Sensitive
view of O'Neill's career through a
major play.

_____, SEE ALSO: 1946 (LI).

SEAVER, Edwin, "The Proletarian Novel,"
AWC, 98-102.  Discussed by Martin Russak, Michael Gold, pp. 165-167.  Speech
to 1st American Writers Congress.  The
test of 'proletarian' literature is
not subject-matter or origin of writer,
but the author's class outlook.  Any
subject can be treated. - See also
Seaver, PR, July, 1935.

_____, On Sherwood Anderson's Revolution-
ary Novel.  MQ(B), Feb 1933, 58-59.
'Beyond Desire'.

SIEGEL, Paul N, "Spencer and the Calvinist View Of Life," Studies In Philology,
XLI (1944), 201-222.  Demonstrates how
Calvinist traits of psychology, together with ideals of the new Tudor
aristocracy, pervade and shape 'The
Faerie Queene'.

_____, "The Petrarchan Sonneteers and Neo-

Platonic Love," <u>Studies In Philology</u>,
XLII (1945), 164-182. Studies deca-
dent libertine morality of the youth
of declining old aristocracy, as mani-
fested in Italianate sonneteering
(Barnes, Watson) in contrast with neo-
Platonic sonnets of Bembo, Sidney and
Spencer which reflect the more humane,
responsible outlook of a rising class.
Explodes the myth of 'platonic' nature
of Petrarchan sonnets. - See G.M.
Matthews (XXIII).

_____, "Milton and the Humanist Attitude
Toward Women," <u>Journal of the History
of Ideas</u>, Jan 1950, 42-53. Rejecting
usual view that Milton held women in
low esteem, Siegel shows his bourgeois
Puritanism had inherited Renaissance
humanist views earlier espoused by a
Spencer - in contrast to feudal chival-
ric views, which gave women a "spurious
elevation" while really seeing females
as "so many conquests to be gained."

_____, <u>Shakespearean Tragedy and the
Elizabethan Compromise</u>, New York Univ:
1957. Shakespeare expressing world
view of Christian humanism held by new
Tudor aristocracy, also "the philosophical and emotional reverberations
caused by the breaking up of its
material base" by the rising bourgeoisie. Close analysis of Elizabethan
theatre, social contradictions, and
four tragedies.

_____, "Shylock the Puritan," <u>Columbia
University Forum</u>, Fall 1962, 14-19.
Comedy and terror in Shylock in part
due to medieval stereotypes of Jews;
due immediately, for Elizabethans, to
projection of capitalist business
ethics as then credited to English
Puritans.

_____, "Shakespeare and the Neo-Chival-
ric Cult Of Honor," <u>Centennial Review</u>,
Winter 1964, 39-70. Analysis of
several plays to show the neo-chival-
ric cult of honor represented for
Shakespeare a dangerous threat to Tudor
compromise as exalted in nationalistic
humanism of Henry V.

_____, "Shakespeare and Our Time's
Malaise," <u>Teacher's College Record</u>,
LXV vii (Apr 1964), 583-590.

_____, <u>Shakespeare In His Time and Ours</u>,
Notre Dame: South Bend, Ind, 1968.
Collects some of above essays and some
new, including "Shakespearean Comedy

and the Elizabethan Compromise". As
against thesis of Kott, Siegel urges
that the universality of the plays only
comes clear through historical understanding of them.

SIGAL, Clancy, "Nihilism's Organization
Man," <u>ULR</u>, Summer 1958, 59-65. A
blast against hipsters and beats.

SILLEN, Samuel, "A Proletarian Novel,"
<u>Point</u>, (Madison, Wisc), I i (1934),
54-56. [Yale] 'The Disinherited' by
Jack Conroy and problems of proletarian novels. "The American worker is
a half-breed bourgeois" and this fact
must be in the psychology of proletarian novels.

_____, "The Function Of the Intellectual
Today." Speech to 4th American Writers
Congress (1941). [LAW] To remain
strong and firm against warmongers and
the renegades who say social commitment is dead.

_____, Introduction to his <u>Walt Whitman,
Poet Of American Democracy; Selections
From His Poetry and Prose</u>, 1944; International paperback, 1955, 11-46. An
interpretation of his views.

_____, ed, <u>William Cullen Bryant</u>, 1945.
94 pp. Introduction with selections
of his work.

_____, The Basis Of Socialist Realism.
<u>DWSup</u>, Apr 14, 1946, 8; Apr 21, 8.
Referring to the controversy over Maltz
and Browderism Sillen says the work of
fiction need not be all-comprehensive
- but it must suggest the basic social
forces of a situation. - See also
1946 (LI).

_____, For Theoretical Clarity In Liter-
ary Analysis. <u>DW</u>, Apr 7, 1946, 10.
Says it is not enough to call a writer
"confused." Class origins of the
conflicts must be defined.

_____, "The Literary Views Of Marx and
Engels," <u>DW</u>, Apr 17, 1947, 11; Apr 18,
11. A valuable summary.

SINCLAIR, Upton, <u>Mamonart: An Essay In
Economic Interpretation</u>, Pasadena,
Calif, 1925. Rapid, extensive survey
of European and American culture from
its origins. "Great art is produced
when propaganda of vitality and importance is put across with technical
competence in terms of the art selected

....Our recognized and successful artists...have been men who looked up to
the ruling classes by instinct, and
served their masters gladly and freely."
Claims his book "will be serving as a
text-book in the high schools of Russia within six months."

_____, Money Writes! 1927. Also serial-
ized in DW beginning Oct 24, 1927.
"A study of American literature from
the economic point of view." Chiefly
a gossip about writers he knows: dis-
organized, eccentric. Calls US fascist, praises USSR.

_____, Papers. In University of Indiana
Library.

_____, SEE ALSO; Lenin (XLVI); D. Brown
(XLIX).

SLOCHOWER, Harry, Three Ways Of Modern
Man, 1937, Introduction by Kenneth
Burke. Essays on literary representa-
tion of feudal socialism (Sigrid
Undset), bourgeois liberalism (Thomas
Mann) and socialist humanism (Martin
Anderson Nexo); also, fascism and cul-
ture. Appendix: correspondence with
Mann and Nexo.

_____, "The Dialectics Of Culture Under
Nazism," WCW, 74-80. German propagan-
da techniques. Speech to 2nd American
Writers Congress.

_____, Thomas Mann's Joseph Story, 1938.

_____, "Thomas Mann's New Message,"
Sewanee Review, Apr-June 1933, 313-330.
The revolt against aestheticism.

_____, No Voice Is Wholly Lost; Writers
and Thinkers In War and Peace, 1945;
reissued as Literature and Philosophy
Between Two Wars, Citadel paperback:
1964. The crisis in human values as
these become evidently more  relative.
Nietzsche, A. Schnitzler, A. Huxley,
Hemingway, J. Dewey, A. Gide, Silone,
Dos Passos, S. Zweig, Toller, R.
Wright, Celine, T. Wolfe, Kafka, Gau-
guin, Hamsun, D.H. Lawrence, Belloc,
Maritain, Claudel, Barres, Undset,
Santayana, Proust, Eliot, S. George,
Rilke, Spengler, Hauptmann, Fallada,
Werfel, Asch, Joyce, O'Neill, Odets,
Shaw, Z. Zweig, Feuchtwanger, Brecht,
H. Mann, A. Seghers, Steinbeck, Freud,
Malraux, T. Mann.

_____, "Andre Gide's 'Theseus' and the
French Myth," YFS, #4 (1950), 34-43.

SMITH, Bernard, "A Footnote For 'Proletarian Literature'," The Left (Davenport, Ia), I i (1931), 10-14. American proletarian novels are nonexistent.
Plivier's 'The Kaiser's Coolies' is
proletarian fiction "because it was
written by a worker for workers; because it is revolutionary in purpose;
and because it is working-class in
character, which means it is blunt,
direct, masculine, rough, a little
crude, a little naive."

_____, "The Liberals Grow Old," Saturday
Review, Dec 30, 1933. - Reply by J.
Donald Adams, ibid, Feb 3, 1934, 447-
448; by L. Lewisohn, 448. Response by
Smith, ibid, Feb 24, 504.

_____, "Howells: The Genteel Radical,"
Saturday Review, Aug 4, 1934, 41-42.

_____, Forces In American Criticism: A
Study In the History Of American Liter-
ary Thought, 1939. A stocktaking of
US criticism from its origins to final
days of the Marxist 30s. - Review by
Morris R. Cohen, Journal of the History
of Ideas, I, 241-251. Answer by
Smith, ibid, 369-372; rejoinder by
Cohen, ibid, 372-374. - Review by L.
Trilling, see (LIX).

SNOW, Walter, History of 'The Anvil'.
DW, Feb 27, 1935, 5. Snow was co-
editor of this pioneering magazine of
proletarian short stories.

SOLOMON, Maynard, "Stephen Crane, A
Critical Study," M&M, Jan 1956, 25-42;
Mch 1956, 31-47.

SOMERVILLE, John, "Philosophy Of Art In
the Soviet Union," American Slavic and
East European Review, IV x-xi (1945).
Reprinted in his: Soviet Philosophy,
1946, 116-145. Extensive citation from
Lenin, Lifshitz, standard Soviet works.

SPARGO, John, William Morris: His Socialism, Westport, Mass, 1908. 52 pp.
Defends Morris as neither an "anarchist
communist" nor a "state socialist" in
art or life. Defines 'News From Nowhere' as his response to and critique
of Bellamy's "state socialist" utopia.
Significant early document.

SPIER, Leonard, "Walt Whitman," IL, 1935
#9, 72-89.

STEVENS, Virginia, "Thomas Wolfe's America," M&M, Jan 1958, 1-24.

STEVENSON, Philip, "Biographical Notes," ZAA, 1966 #4, 372-376. By a proletarian novelist. - See also: Albert Maltz, "In Memorium Philip Stevenson 1896-1965," ibid, 377-380; and a bibliography of his writings, ibid, 381-385. - See also under Henry Arndt, 1957 (LI).

STEWART, Donald Ogden, "The Horrible Example," WCW, 119-132. Speech to 2nd American Writers Congress by its President. "My function at a congress of writers is that of the Horrible Example....the awful thing a writer can become after ten years of successful commercial writing."

STOKES, Rose Pastor, "Bread and Roses," Ohio Socialist, Nov 19, 1919, 4. Typifies early US enthusiasm for Bolshevik attention to culture as well as social institutions.

TAGGARD, Genevieve, ed, May Days; An Anthology Of Verse From Masses-Liberator, 1925, 1-15. Introduction praises the "whole, native, radical" nature of the 'Masses' and laments the later division of artists and revolutionists. "The revolutionists are impatient of all expression that fails to rubber-stamp the specific doctrines of the latest party creed... The artist's concern is not to persuade or educate, but to overpoweringly express. A good revolutionist should allow the artist this freedom, since he knows very well that only liberals seek to persuade, or to lure other half-hearted liberals into action."

_____, "Romanticism and Communism," NM, Sept 25, 1934, 18-20. With an editors' note. Inadequacy of the romantic stance, exemplified in 19th Century poetry but continued today. Asks instead a literature of society and communism. The editors exempt revolutionary romanticism from her strictures.

_____, Calling Western Union, 1936, xi-xxxii, 31, 47, 61, 69. Analysis of early experience which disposed her to communal values and to hatred of sterile individualism. The values of communist poetry.

_____, Interview with Anita Tilkin. DW, Jan 3, 1939, 7. illus. Her relation to Marxism.

_____, "The American Literary Tradition and the Writer In This Crisis." Speech to 4th American Writers Congress (1941). [LAW] "We are not the fools of a day... gullible readers of cheap newspaper hysterias." The coming war "is not in the interest of our people." One should instead recall Walt Whitman's words: "The attitude of great poets is to cheer up slaves and horrify despots."

TANK, Herb, Interview with Beth McHenry. DW, May 16, 1946, 12. illus.

TAYLOR, Harry, "The Dilemma of Tennessee Williams," Main, Feb 1947, 51-55. Traces his development and socio-philosophical position as it limits creative achievement.

UHSE, Stefan, "Memory Junking; William Burroughs and the Politics of the Cut-Up," Steps (Berkeley, Calif.), #1 (1966), 58-62. Depiction of "the reporter's mind" as "a scene of disaster" as a new, more demanding realism that is neglected by many Marxists.

VANZLER, Joseph, "An Introduction To a Social Basis Of Greek Art," MQ(B), III iv (1926), 286-291.

VOGEL, Joseph, Interview with Anita Tilkin. DW, Feb 28, 1939, 7. illus. Proletarian novelist.

WARD, May McNeer, "The Socially Destructive Use Of Thrillers." Speech to 4th American Writers Congress (1941) [LAW]

'WEEKLY PEOPLE' EDITORIAL, "Socialism and Culture," Weekly People, July 3, 1909, 4. "It is among the despised and ignorant class of the modern proletariat that the philosophical spirit of the most brilliant members of the Athenian aristocracy is revived. But the free development of this spirit is not possible in modern society.... It is not the 'Freedom of Labor' but the freedom from labor, such as machinery will make possible in a Socialist Commonwealth, that will bestow upon mankind freedom of life; freedom to engage in science and art; freedom to delight in the noblest pursuits."

_____, "The Loss Of Art," Weekly People, Sept 9, 1911, 3. Draws on Wm. Morris to describe decadence of arts under capitalism.

WEISINGER, Herbert, "Dialectics As Tragedy," MRSup #1 (1965), 3-14.  Also in his The Agony and the Triumph, Michigan State Univ: 1964, 180-197.  Dated 1953, 1962.  Marxism as a new rational concept of world order once more permitting heroes who transgress.  But tragedy is formed of "sceptical faith" (Greece, Elizabethan England); "from the 18th century to the present, no genuine tragedies have been written because no faith has been strong enough to permit the artist and his audience to base themselves on it" while "Marxism has had the courage´to advocate a faith for our times" but "its followers have not had the corresponding courage to question that faith."

WHIPPLE, T. K, Spokesmen, Univ. California paperback: 1963.  Written in 20s.  Foreword by Mark Schorer.  Literary achievement and failure under US conditions: H. Adams, Robinson, Dreiser, Frost, Anderson, Cather, Sandburg, Lindsay, Lewis, O'Neill.

_____, Study Out the Land, Berkeley, 1943.  With a prefatory memoir by Edmund Wllson.  See especially: "Dos Passos and the USA," finding the faults due to an insufficiently Marxist approach; "Jack London;" "Literature As Action;" "Literature In the Doldrums," on the 30s. - Review by F.O. Matthiessen, The Responsibilities Of the Critic, 1952, 166-169.

WILSON, Edmund, The American Jitters, 1932.  Reprinted (revised, omitting "The Case Of the Author" class analysis of himself), with material from periodicals and 'Travels In Two Democracies', as: The American Earthquake; A Documentary Of the Twenties and Thirties, Doubleday Anchor paperback: 1964.  Social and literary studies often using Marxist framework.

_____, Axel's Castle; A Study In the Imaginative Literature Of 1870-1930, 1931; Scribner paperback, 1961.  On the exhaustion of art for art's sake, and the possibilities for scientific literary description of society or the changing of it.  Yeats, Valery, Eliot, Proust, Joyce, G. Stein, V. de l'Isle-Adam, Rimbaud, etc. - Review by B. Smith, MQ(B), VI i (1932), 100-104.

_____, The Shores Of Light; A Literary Chronicle Of the Twenties and Thirties, 1952; Vintage paperback, 1961.

Includes important essays on development of Communist literary school.

_____, A Literary Chronicle: 1920-1950, Doubleday Anchor paperback: 1952.  Several articles on the 30s, Malraux, Dos Passos, etc.

_____, The Triple Thinkers, 1938; Galaxy paperback, 1963.  See especially: "The Politics Of Flaubert," "John Jay Chapman,"  "Bernard Shaw At Eighty," "Marxism and Literature," "The Historical Interpretation Of Literature."

_____, To the Finland Station; A Study In the Writing and Acting of History, 1940; Doubleday Anchor paperback, n.d.  Vico, Saint-Simon, Taine, Michelet, Fourier, Marx, Engels, Lenin, Trotsky.

_____, The Wound and the Bow; Seven Studies In Literature, 1941; Galaxy paperback, 1965.  Profound synthesis of psychological and sociological analysis in essays on Dickens and Kipling.  Also Casanova, E. Wharton, Hemingway, Joyce's 'Finnegans Wake', the 'Philoctetes' of Sophocles.

_____, Patriotic Gore, 1962.  Civil War literature, North and South, as early evidence of American literati's willingness to rationalize imperialist politics.

_____, SEE ALSO; Aaron (LIX).

WINSPEAR, Alban D, and Lenore Kramp Geweke, Augustus and the Reconstruction Of Roman Government and Society.  University of Wisconsin Studies in the Social Sciences and History #24, Madison, Wisc, 1935.  Effort to get at society behind eulogies sung by court poets Horace and Virgil.

_____, and Tom Silverberg, Who Was Socrates? 1939.  View of the thought and actions of Socrates as representative of Athenian aristocracy, in profound conflict with rising mercantile class.  A milestone interpretation.

_____, The Genesis Of Plato's Thought, 1940.  A central study of the historical determinants and class nature of Plato's writings. - Review by Henry F. Mins Jr, S&S, Spring 1941, 188-191.

_____, Lucretius and Scientific Thought, Harvest House: Montreal, 1963.  'De Rerum Natura' as a forceful because

materialist weapon for new propertied
class in its struggle with religion-
manipulative nobility.  Winspear
elaborates social role and origins of
Lucretius' thought and defends its
originality and profundity. - See also
his translation: The Roman Poet Of
Science,  Lucretius Set In English
Verse, Russell & Russell: 1955.

WINWAR, Frances, "Literature Under Fascism," WCW, 81-91.  Speech to 2nd
American Writers Congress.  Italian
culture.

WOLFE, Bertram D, "The Mass As Hero,"
MQ(B), Feb 1933, 99-104.  Lope de
Vega's 'Fuente Ovejuna' as a master-
piece of yesterday and for communism.

_____, SEE ALSO: Rivera (XXXIII); Wolfe
(LIX).

WRIGHT, Richard.  See (I).

YGLESIAS, Jose, "The Novels Of Asturias,"
SOL, Fall 1964, 132-138.  Confronts
the Guatamalan's techniques in relation to colonial situation and in contrast to the "limited point of view,
the solitary hero or heroine dis-
covering the world or his inner
world," favored by US "literary establishment."

LVII.  Music

ADOHMYAN, Lahn, "What Songs Should Workers' Choruses Sing?" DW, Feb 7, 1934,
5.  Author was leading Communist mass
song director.

AMES, Russell, The Story Of American Folk
Song, Grosset & Dunlap: 1955.  Histor-
icizes many specific examples.

AMERICAN MUSIC LEAGUE, "The League Looks
Ahead," Unison, I i, 1.  Perspective
for a people's music movement.

BARDACKE, Frank, "Blow Their Minds,"
Steps (Berkeley, Calif.), #1 (1966),
23-28.  Bob Dylan's rejection of protest songs for consciousness expansion
as a valuable radical step.

BLITZSTEIN, Marc, "The Composer and His
Audience," Unison, I i (May 1936), 2-
3.  [DLC] "My orientation is toward
a proletarian society and a revolutionary art....Music is one of the
greatest educational forces we know;
it can train, not only our minds, but

our blood.  Composers must come out
into the open; they must fight the
battle with other workers."

_____, "The  Phenomenon Of Stravinsky,"
Musical Quarterly, July 1935, 330-347.
illus.

_____, "Towards a New Form," Musical
Quarterly, Apr 1934, 213-218.  The
modernist tradition and popularist,
primitivist and classicist expression.

_____, (?), "The Composers Collective of
New York," Unison, I ii (June 1936), 3.
[DLC]  History and projects of a group
that included N. Cazden, E. Robinson,
L. Adohmyan, E. Siegmeister, J. Schae-
fer, A. North, Blitzstein.

_____, "Coming--The Mass Audience,"
ModM, May-June 1936, 23-29.  Defines
tradition of modern music for the
masses: Satie, the 'Gebrauchsmusik' of
Hindemith, Weill, Eisler, Wolpe, Soviet
composers, the left faction in America.
Discusses inevitability and problems
of a mass audience for music.

_____, "The Case For Modern Music," NM,
July 14, 1936, 27; July 21, 28-29;
July 28, 28.  "Modern musical technique
is for use.  The new composer inherits
it, it is his jumping-off place.  He
should no more scrap it than a socialist society should scrap a machine because its functioning in a bourgeois
system meant abuse or persecution or
unemployment....The technical aspect
of present-day music is forward-looking,
and actually unrestrainable, like
technical inventions."

_____, "On Writing Music For the Theatre,"
ModM, Jan-Feb 1938, 81-85.  The com-
poser's experience in creating 'The
Cradle Will Rock'.

_____, The Audience and Music of 'The
Cradle Will Rock'.  DW, Jan 3, 1938, 7.

_____, Hanns Eisler and the Mass Song.
DWSup, Feb 27, 1938, 12.  Eisler has
"given to the mass song the power of
an agressive and cultivated personality"
making his "the greatest mass songs of
our time."

_____, "Music and the People's Front,"
DW, Apr 13, 1938, 7.  Contrasts unemployment of many outstanding musicians
in America with strenuous schedule of
progressive musicians at Downtown Music

School and American Music League. Stresses value of People's Front to the composer, as well as need for his compositions among the people.

_____, Interview with Edith Hale. DW, Dec 7, 1938, 7. His development. 'Cradle Will Rock' is "a middle-class allegory for middle-class people - to shape those into progressive ranks who stood on the brink; to rescue those who were about to die by joining so-called 'liberty' committess."

_____, "A Musician's War Diary," NM, Aug 13, 1946, 3-6; Aug 20, 6-9; Aug 27, 10-12. illus. by Jack Levine.

_____, "An Analysis Of Prokofiev," Soviet Russia Today, Nov 1946, 23. Revolutionary style finds a "forward-looking social basis" in the USSR.

_____, Discussing His Theatre Composi- tions. Distinguished Composers Series no. 717, Westminster-Spoken Arts re- cording, 1956. Listed because no com- plete transcript of the important spo- ken sections exists in print. Also excerpts from 'Cradle Will Rock', 'No For an Answer', 'Regina'.

_____, Papers. In Collection of State Historical Society, Madison, Wisc.

_____, SEE ALSO: Obituary, N.Y. Times, Jan 24, 1964, 1, 24. illus. - Henry Brant, "Marc Blitzstein," ModM, Summer 1946, 170-175. Analysis of the music. - Minna Lederman, "Memories Of Marc Blitz- stein," Show, June 1964, 18, 21-24. Author was founder of ModM, de- tails Blitzstein's development. Tells also of encounter between Brecht and Blitzstein in Dec 1935 which led to composition of 'Cra- dle Will Rock'. - Joan Peyser, "The Troubled Time Of Marc Blitz- stein," Columbia University Forum, Winter 1966, 32-37. Account of his development and struggles with an evolving musical idiom.

BOTKIN, B.A, "The Folk-Say Of Freedom Songs," NM, Oct 21, 1947, 14-16.

CAZDEN, Norman, Review of 'Boris Godou- nov' at Lewisohn Stadium. DW, July 20, 1935, 7. Succinctly suggests later emphasis with attack on Rimsky-

Korsakov orchestration of this opera; by concealing "the native folk style" it "destroyed much of the value of the work." Unpopular basis of Pops con- certs also exposed.

_____, "Musical Consonance and Disson- ance, A Cultural Criterion," JAAC, Sept 1945, 3-11. Defines dissonance as tension and consonance as resolu- tion, not inherent in notes themselves but in their function in given context and within given cultural area. This essay, with others, derives from the following:

_____, Musical Consonance and Dissonance, Ph.D. dissertation, Harvard Univ: 1947. 2 vols. Available at Harvard Music Library, New York Public Library, Library of Congress, Ohio State Univer- sity, and Iowa State University Librar- ies.

_____, Review of 'Miaskovsky' by A.A. Ikonnikov, and 'Russian Symphony' by D. Shostakovich et al. S&S, Summer 1947, 286-291. "As it is here exem- plified, Soviet music criticism has yet to overcome the traditional formu- lations of romantic phraseology and come to grips convincingly with the relation between musical form and con- tent in the historical setting."

_____, "What's Happening In Soviet Music?" M&M, Apr 1948, 11-25. Soviet Party resolution against Muratov's opera 'The Great Friendship' not capricious but based on issues which give the Party the right to take poli- tical measures against music that causes "a reaction of depression in the listener." Possibly the criticism of Muratov is "narrow and in need of correction" since "Soviet music critics ...are as prone to error and superfi- ciality as are the critics of any other land" but "the general outlines of the statement would remain valid." (The Soviet Party later reversed itself taking essentially the position ad- vanced by Cazden.)

_____, Review of 'Dmitri Shostakovich' by Ivan Martynov. S&S, Fall 1948, 469-471. Book is "neither competent, informative nor interesting." Asks why Soviet musicology functions at this level. Proposes alternate approach to problem of the grotesque in Shostako- vich's music.

_____, "How Pure Is Music?" M&M, Apr 1949, 20-30. In an important way a prolegomana to his dissertation and later essays. Asserts "inextricable relations between [artistic] forms and the human substance of which they are the media of expression." - Sidney Finkelstein, ibid, July 1949, 86-89, suggests Cazden posits an unfortunate total relativism in musical styles. - Cazden, ibid, July 1949, 90-96, offers important amplifications.

_____, "Sound, Tone and Music," Peabody Notes, Winter 1949, 1-2.

_____, "Towards a Theory Of Realism In Music," JAAC, X (1951), 135-151. Examines concept of music realism in relation to naturalism, pictorialism, "programme music."

_____, "Folk Idiom vs. Synthetic Language For the Composer," American Music Teacher, May-June 1952, 2-3, 16-18.

_____, "Mozart In Current Musical Aesthetics," S&S, Winter 1953, 65-71. Devastatingly shows sterility of formalist musical analysis which treats compositions as absolute tone-structures while ignoring "cultural matrix" that unifies composer and audience. Object of his attack is 'Mozart's Le Nozze di Figaro' by Siegmund Levarie.

_____, "Humor In the Music Of Stravinsky and Prokofieff," S&S, Winter 1954, 52-74. "Stravinsky moved towards the sophisticated and supercilious decadence of the aesthetes, while Prokofieff sought to enjoy the acceptance of the people." This conclusion is grounded in analysis of structures of musical humor.

_____, "Tonal Function and Sonority In the Study Of Harmony," Journal of Research in Music Education, Spring 1954, 21-34.

_____, "Hindemith and Nature," Music Review (England), Nov 1954, 288-306.

_____, "Realism In Abstract Music," Music and Letters, Jan 1955, 17-38. A pivotal essay that explains, through concrete systematic analysis, the poverty of purely formal musicology. The "significance of musical realism" is this: "a musical image supplies the totality of connotations through its

form, while if words are present they serve merely to specify and fix certain denotations that are only potential in the music."

_____, "The Principle Of Direction In the Motion Of Similar Tone Harmonies," Journal Of Music Theory, Nov 1958, 162-192.

_____, "Regional and Occupational Orientations To American Traditional Song," Journal Of American Folklore, 72 (1959), 310-344. tables and illus. Drawing upon intensive study of Catskill Mountain folksong, Cazden argues research should attend less to regional orientation and more to how occupational groups spread and altered songs while moving freely over great distances.

_____, "How To Compose Non-Music," Journal Of Music Theory, 1961, 113-128, 287-296. Contemporary interest in "code composition" subjected to historical and technical criticism and withering scorn.

_____, "The Thirteen Tone System," The Music Review, May 1961, 152-171. Biting analysis of and satirical attack on serial technique which "permits the least talented," through abstraction, to "remove raw tone elements from their usual association with the difficult art of music, and thus with the sordid human conditions which that art reflects."

_____, "Sensory Theories Of Musical Consonance," JAAC, Spring 1962, 301-320. - See also exchange of letters, ibid, Winter 1962, 211-215.

_____, "Pythagoras and Aristoxenos Reconciled," Journal of the American Musicological Society.

_____, SEE ALSO: Herbert Haufrecht, "The Writings Of Norman Cazden, Composer and Musicologist," American Composers Alliance Bulletin, 1959 #2, 2-9.

COPLAND, Aaron, "Workers Sing!" NM, June 5, 1934, 28-29. Discusses how workers often prefer inferior mass songs with popular social-protest subjects. The ideal is to get the best music and most pertinent themes together.

_____, "A Note On Young Composers," MV, I i (1935), 14-16. Their problems in a post-innovatory period; with many in search of a working-class audience;

without funds for European study.

_____, SEE ALSO: Sands (below).

CORNER, Philip, On Charles Ives. NG, Apr 25, 1963, 10. His democratic commitment, innovation, and relation to new music of today.

COWELL, Henry, "Kept Music," Panorama, Dec 1934, 6. Economic need subtly shapes the character of modern compositions.

DALE, Ralph, "The Future Of Music," JAAC, Summer 1968. In the context of its alienation in Western development.

DUNSON, Josh, Freedom In the Air; Song Movements Of the Sixties, Little New World paperback: 1965. Vivid history of Southern freedom song and Northern topical song movements, in context of Negro church music and labor movement singing, with discussion and critique of leading performers.

FEDER, I, "Song In the Class Struggle," WT, Nov 1931, 6-7. Role of song in overcoming bankrupt culture imposed on working class by bourgeoisie. Man sang naturally in his primitive state, songs have "helped to stimulate the revolutionary upsurge of the masses both in the French Commune and in the Russian revolution."

FINKELSTEIN, Sidney, "Charles Ives' Third Symphony," NM, Apr 30, 1946, 29-31. Recovering a neglected American composer; a significant appraisal.

_____, "What Is Jazz?" NM, Nov 5, 1946, 12-15. Impact on jazz of commercialization and growing sophistication. - Comments by Lawson Milford and Thomas McGrath, with response by Finkelstein, NM, Dec 10, 1946, 14-18.

_____, "The Making Of American Jewish Concert Music," JL, Nov 1947, Supplement, 25-29. Views abstractness of much American music as in some part due to assimilationist desires among Jewish composers eager to foresake Jewish themes for arbitrary musical forms. Schumann, Diamond are mentioned.

_____, Jazz: A People's Music, 1948. - Review by Lloyd L. Brown, M&M, Jan 1949, 75-78. A Negro critic, co-editor of M&M, calls it "the best

work yet in its field."

_____, On Hanns Eisler. M&M, I ii (1948), 89-93. The critic's aesthetic view that composers must draw upon folk materials clashes with his ideological admiration for the Schoenberg student, Eisler.

_____, "The Discussion On Soviet Music; Pertinent Questions - and Answers," Soviet Russia Today, Apr 1948, 15-17, 33-34. Zhdanov's stand is explained.

_____, How Music Expresses Ideas, 1952. In effect a first draft of 'Composer and Nation'. - Review by Eric Simon, S&S, Spring 1956, 160-162. Severely criticizes omissions, errors, vagueness, inexplicable judgements.

_____, "Notes On Contemporary Music," PA, Mch 1957, 59-63. Criticizes Zhdanov's strictures on composers as "confused," and showing "a disrespect for music and art." Finds also "an insidious, hidden and yet present, trend towards Russian nationalism....not only hermetically sealing off Socialist realism from other art, but hinting also that in respect to the past, the Russian heritage can take the place of the world heritage." "Subjective feelings, a sense of deep lamentation and struggle against death, are not 'bourgeois' They are found also in socialist countries....a truly realistic art, a mature optimism...only come through a conquest of tragedy, not an avoidance of it."

_____, "Inner and Outer Jazz," Jazz Review, Sept 1959, 19-22. Bartok's distinction between 'speech-inflected' and 'rhythm-dominated' music applied to modern jazz trends.

_____, Composer and Nation: The Folk Heritage Of Music, New World paperback: 1960. The "social frame of reference" of composers since the Renaissance. Attention is directed to the role of peasant and other folk music in sophisticated compositions. Important suggestions toward an aesthetic of music.

FRAINA, Louis, "The Case For Ragtime," Modern Dance Magazine, Aug-Sept 1917, 5-6, 8. Argues that jazz is the only live aspect of provincial and snobbish American arts; a trailblazing article.

FRIESEN, Gordon, "Songs For Our Time,"

M&M, Dec 1962, 3-22.  Chronicle of folksong revival out of Cold War.

GOLD, Michael, Critique of Bourgeois Formal Influence on Revolutionary Dance, Music, Poetry.  DW, June 5, 1934, 5; June 14, 1934, 5.  The harmful effects of Eliot, Graham, cerebral composers.

GOLDMAN, Lawrence, "Bobby Dylan: Folk-Rock Hero," SOL, Sept-Oct 1966, 85-90.  Critique of the "protest" image Dylan accepted then rejected.

GUTHRIE, Woody, How To Write Folk Songs. DW, June 24, 1940, 7.

_____, The Meaning Of My Music.  DW, Aug 15, 1947, 11.  illus.  "My music box says what you tell me I can't say....Busting out.  This is what I mean when you hear my jazz."

_____, Born To Win, Macmillan paperback: 1965.  ed. Robert Shelton.  Selection of stories, drawings, letters, poems, songs and snatches.  pp. 70-83, 220-227 on songwriting and society.

_____, SEE ALSO: Special Guthrie Issue, M&M, Aug 1963.  Articles by Pete Seeger, Gordon Friesen, Phil Ochs, Josh Dunsan.

HUGHES, Charles, "Music Of the French Revolution," S&S, Spring 1940, 193-210.  Good brief account of dances, spectacles, etc.

HUTCHINSON, James E, "Beebop - A Narcotic," NF, Fall 1949, 37-43.  Analysis of progressive jazz as similar to privatizing "cults of existentialism, surrealism, and non-objective art, in fleeing from reality" of class struggle.

JULIAN, Ralph, "Music As a Weapon In the Class Struggle," MF, I i (July 1935), 9.  Vigorous polemic emphasizing propaganda use of music through the ages.

KOFSKY, Frank, "Blues People," MRSup #1 (1965), 53-62.  Vehement attack on Communist and Trotskyite misunderstandings of jazz and black nationalism.  "To the same degree that black nationalism implicitly poses on the agenda a thoroughgoing transformation of the American social structure, the aesthetic values of jazz cry out for a no less fundamental restructuring of

this country's banal and tepid white middle-class cultural vistas."  Bebop as the transition to this new consciousness.

_____, "The State Of Jazz Criticism," Jazz, May 1965, 23-24, 28-29.  Examines the socio-economic position of the white jazz critic to demonstrate that this position makes objective artistic criticism impossible. - See also exchange of letters with Ira Gitler, Martin Williams and Don Schlitten: ibid, July 1965, 6-7; Sept, 4-6; Oct, 6; Nov, 8-9; Dec, 5-6; Feb 1966, 6.

_____, "An Open Letter To Arnold Shaw," Jazz, June 1965, 4-5.  Analysis and rejection of the thesis that the most vital jazz of this era has been "bourgeoisified".

_____, "Revolution, Coltrane and the Avant Garde," Jazz, July 1965, 13-16; Sept 1965, 18-22. - Letters from Frank Smith and John Mehegan, Nov 1965, 9-10; the author's reply, Dec 1965, 4-5.

_____, "Jazz, the Cold War, and the Establishment," to be published.  Based in part on interview and exchange with Willis Conover, Jazz Consultant for the Voice of America, in Jazz, Sept 1965, 10-14, 30; Nov 1965, 6-8; Dec 1965, 6-7, 30.  Use of jazz as a Cold War weapon even as it is rejected by the domestic cultural establishment.

_____, "The Avant Garde Revolution: Origins and Directions," Jazz, Jan 1966, 14-19.  The radical mood in black communities as the social origin of the revolution in jazz.

_____, "On the Reception Of the Jazz Revolution," Jazz, Sept 1966.  Reasons for the enthusiastic response in the black ghetto and the negative response of white jazz establishment.

_____, "Jazz and Revolutionary Black Nationalism: A Panel Discussion With LeRoi Jones, Nat Hentoff, Archie Shepp, Frank Kofsky, Steve Kuhn, Fr. Norman O'Connor, George Wein, Robert F. Thompson," Jazz, Apr 1966 ff.

_____, Relevance Of Marxist Analysis To Black Nationalist Jazz.  Liberator, Feb 1966, 21.  With reply from editor L. Neal, holding the "spiritual reality" of Negro music "cannot be analyzed in its internal aspects which are purely subjective to Afro-Americans."

_____, "'Revolutionary' Black Jazz," NG, Apr 30, 1966, 11. Survey of the performers and their views.

_____, "Where It's At," NG, July 22, 1967, 4. The anti-capitalist nature of the new black and urban rock music, and the failure of older radicals to understand its revolutionary importance and appeal to the young.

_____, "A New World Music?" AmD, Spring 1967, 33-37. Interview with jazz artist Roswell Rudd on the radicalism of the new music; comments on critics who reject it.

MINOR, Marcia, The Downtown Music School. DW, Sept 22, 1938, 7. Organizational center of left composers.

MORGENSTERN, Sam, Interview with Beth McHenry. DW, Mch 6, 1946, 11. illus. 'The Warsaw Ghetto' described by its composer as "the first symphonic work ever written on a serious theme by a left wing composer here." Objects to DW's shallow music coverage.

MOROSS, Jerome, "New Musical Revues For Old," NTh, Oct 1934, 12-13, 33. Finds American musical stage deficient in comparison with that in pre-Nazi Germany. Suggests means to remedy the lack.

RADAMSKY, Sergei, Interview with Edwin Rolfe. DW, Dec 28, 1933, 5. illus. - See also Shostakovich (XLVII).

ROBBINS, Rossell Hope, "The Basis Of Bop," Harlem Quarterly, Fall-Winter 1950, 9-15.

ROBINSON, Earl, Interview with Anita Tilkin. DW, Oct 27, 1938, 7. "Composers are finding it impossible to write abstract music any more. Marc Blitzstein was one of the first to see that."

_____, Song Writing and Its Audience. FW, 21-31. abdgd. Speech to 3rd American Writers Congress.

_____, "Huddie Ledbetter, Greatest Of the Folk Singers," Our Times, Mch 3, 1950, 3. Recollections by a friend. "Huddie's music and style influenced my own composition profoundly."

_____, SEE ALSO: Warren (LVIII); Hugh J. Riddell, "Earl Robinson," DW, Sept 27, 1939, 7. illus.

SANDS, Carl, Proletarian Music. DW, Jan 16, 1934, 5. Detailed prognosis.

_____, For Unity Of Theme and Revolutionary Content In Mass Songs. DW, Jan 31, 1934, 7; Feb 1, 1934, 5. Noting that Nazis have taken over many Communist tunes for their own propaganda aims (including Eisler's "Rote Wedding"), and declaring that Communists' frequent use of bourgeois melodies tends to "lull" workers choruses, Sands urges need for Communist songs with form and content so intertwined they cannot be perverted. - See DW, June 26, 1934, 5, Sands' review of 'Strange Funeral At Braddock', composition with words by Michael Gold, music by Elie Siegmeister which Sands says meets requirements.

_____, "For Revolutionary Music Criticism In Our Press," DW, Mch 5, 1934, 7; Mch 6, 5; Mch 7, 5; Mch 8, 7.

_____, Review of First Recital Devoted Solely To Aaron Copland's Works. Given at Pierre Degeyter Club. DW, Mch 23, 1934, 5. Report of Copland discussing relation of his music to proletariat. Sands analyzes the music on that basis.

SEEGER, Charles, "Music and Musicology," ESS, vol. XI, 143-150. Musicology in historical development. Relation of music to language. Consonance and dissonance. Other basic matters.

_____, "Occidental Music," ESS, vol. XI, 155-164. Folk music. Music in Greece, Rome, early Christianity, the Renaissance. Modern music.

_____, "On Proletarian Music," ModM, Mch-Apr 1934, 121-127. Militant piece on how the proletariat has no music, but needs it as a weapon, so it will come into its own with its own music.

_____, "Preface To All Linguistic Treatment Of Music," MV, Mch-Apr 1935. The social aspects of musicology.

_____, "Systematic and Historical Orientations In Musicology," Bulletin Of the American Musicological Society, June 1936, 16. Also in Acta Musicologica, XI vi (1939), 121-128. Necessity for combining and interpenetrating the historical and systemological approaches to musicology.

_____, "Music As a Factor In Cultural Strategy In America," Bulletin Of the American Musicological Society, Apr 1939, 17-18. "Music is very commonly employed directly [by large American organizations] as an instrument of control" and must be freed from this function no less than when it "becomes the servitor of language."

_____, "Folk Music As a Source Of Cultural History," in: Caroline F. Ware, ed, The Cultural Approach To History, 1940, 316-323. Methodology in approaching folk music.

_____, "Folk Music - U.S.A," in: Eric Blom, ed, Grove's Dictionary Of Music and Musicians, 5th ed, 1955, v. III, 387-398.

_____, "Folk Music In the Schools Of a Highly Industrialized Society," Sing Out, Spring 1958, 26-29.

SEEGER, Pete, "People's Songs and Singers," NM, July 16, 1946, 7-9. Origins and aims of People's Songs which, with its belief that "music, too, is a weapon" was inspirer of 'Sing Out' and post-war folk song revival.

SHAPIRO, A, "Proletarian Music," WT, Jan 1932, 7-9. Proletarian music needs no "theory in justification...An historic law determines its inevitability." Agitprop theatre is the natural place for its emergence.

SIEGMEISTER, Elie, "Social Influences In Modern Music," ModM, Sept 1933, 472-479.

_____, "The Class Spirit In Modern Music," ModM, Nov 1933, 593-598.

_____, "Music For the Dance," NTh, Oct 1935, 10-11, 33. Music appropriate to revolutionary dance.

_____, Composers and Workers. Unison, I i (May 1936), 2-3. [DLC] For more active relation between composer and audience, and compositions "written for the workers and their allies."

_____, Music and Society, 1938. 64 pp. Sketches a history of the social controls and functions of music. Revised edition, London, 1943.

_____, SEE ALSO: Ann Seymour, On Sieg-

meister's Career. DW, Feb 17, 1946, 14. illus.

SILBER, Irwin, "Ewan MacColl - Folksinger Of the Industrial Age," Sing Out, Winter 1959-60, 7-9.

_____, On Folk Rock. N.Y. Times, Theatre Section, Feb 20, 1966, 22. With comment by Robert Shelton, Nat Hentoff, Paul Nelson.

'SING OUT' (1950-), with its predecessor People's Songs Bulletin (1946-49), the locus for discussion of folksong, not so much in theory as in practice.

SMITH, Charles Edward, "Class Content Of Jazz Music," DW, Oct 21, 1933, 7. Hot jazz has "its basis in the class struggle," in denial to American Negro of "the right of self-determination" - whereas tranquillizing Sweet jazz is "imposed" by bourgeois commercializers "from above."

'THE WORKER MUSICIAN', Editorial, I i (Dec 1932), 3-5. [DLC] Quasi-manifesto which sums up "fifteen years...of noticeable decline of music in America and the contrasting progress made in the U.S.S.R."

## LVIII. Theatre

ALLEN, Harbor [later wrote as Paul Peters (see below)], Review of 'Her Crime' by Moissaye Olgin. DW, Feb 8, 1927, 4. Perhaps the first US Yiddish-language revolutionary drama. - See also DW, Feb 4, 1927.

_____, "What Is a Proletarian Play?" DW, Mch 22, 1927, 6. "Like [Basshe's 'Earth'], a workers' play will be simple, fervent, passionate....shun plot, sentimental love scenes, picayunish reality; it will fly straight for the big, the essential things....Why all this meanness, this insignificance, when there are mobs on the street, and swarms in the subway? When there are circuses and parades and battles and strikes? The individual doesn't count. He's too small; too powerless. It's the people, the mass, the current of life that matters....Next we will have romantic plays, sweeping epics, glamor and turmoil on the stage....Then, when communism has triumphed, will come pedantic plays, like the old miracle plays, narrow, propagandistic. Who is to say they will lack art value? It

will be a different sort of value,
that's all, a folk art, the art of
the ballads, of early paintings, of
the songs of the people.  And still
later there will be a renaissance.  A
Communist Shakespeare will arise, an
individual, yet one of the people.  In
a secure, blooming Communist country,
he will pour out symphonies of action
on the stage....Then, as Communism too
grows rigid, will come more intellectualist despair plays, then yet another
era of romanticism."

[ARTEF] Ten Years Artef, 1937.  [ES]
Commemorative volume chiefly in Yid-
dish; English language essays by
Joseph Freeman, J.H. Lawson, Emanuel
Eisenberg.  illus.

BASSHE, Em Jo, The Workers Theatre and
the Sympathetic Playwright.  DWSup,
Mch 19, 1927.

_____, Interview with Sender Garlin.  DW,
Dec 8, 1927, 6.

_____, SEE ALSO: 1927 (LI).

BAXANDALL, Lee, The Theatre Of Arthur
Miller.  Encore (London), May–June
1964, 16–19; also in NG, June 6, 1964,
6–7, with counter-view by Annette
Rubinstein.  Also: Encore, Mch–Apr
1965, 19–23.  Two essays on problems
of form and the hero in Miller.

_____, "Brecht In America: 1935," Drama
Review (formerly TDR), Fall 1967, 69–
87.  A study of his first visit and
miscarried effort to establish Epic
Theatre in the US; the nature of
Theatre Union; conditions working for
and against acceptance of Brecht in
America.

_____, "The Kennedy Assassination: How
Not To Stage a Drama," Village Voice,
Nov 26, 1964, 6, 27.  Also in Views
(London), #6 (Autumn 1964), 90–93.
Problems of theatre in communicating
and changing a reality diffused through
the mass media. - See also "'The Brig'
At the Living Theatre," NP, II iv (Fall
1963), 152–154.

_____, "Beyond Brecht: The Happenings,"
SOL, VI i (Jan–Feb 1966), 28–35; also
in The Living Theatre in Europe,
Mickery Books: 1966.  New forms of
theatre as responding to increased
difficulty of communication and a
crisis of concrete reason in America.
The aesthetic strategies employed.

- Discussed by Henry F. Salerno,
First Stage, Spring 1966, 2–4; ampli-
fication by Baxandall, ibid, Summer
1966, 58–59.

_____, SEE ALSO: Baxandall (LVI).

BLAKE, Ben.  "The Political Situation
and the Workers Theatre," Reports and
Resolutions of the Eastern Regional
Conference of the League of Workers
Theatres of U.S.A. (1933).  (Coll.
Paul Romaine.)  mimeo.  (See LI).

_____, "From Agitprop To Realism," NTh,
Jan 1935, 28.  The turning point in
theatre politics exemplified in offer-
ings of the former Workers Laboratory
Theatre.

_____, The Awakening Of the American
Theatre, 1935.  64pp.  Lively useful
history of left theatre while still
in the making.

BLANKFORT, Michael, "Facing the New Audience; Sketches Toward an Aesthetic
For the Revolutionary Theatre," NTh,
June 1934, 11–12; July–Aug, 14–15; Nov,
25–27.  Insists on credible psychology
and unforced denouements of broad im-
plication.  Many examples.

BONN, John E, "Workers' Theatre," WT,
Aug 1931, 1–2; Sept 1931, 3–5.  Director of Prolet-Buhne of New York assesses
problems. - N. Buchwald, WT, Oct 1931,
7–9, charges Bonn with an emphasis
that neglects "the great potentialities
of proletarian 'art' groups" - the
panoply of resources that for Bonn are
"bourgeois," discredited.

_____, "Problems Of Play-Directing," WT,
Oct 1931, 4–6; Dec 1931, 7–8; Jan 1932,
10–11.  Problems of working with amateur proletarian players.

BUCHWALD, Nathaniel, "The Artef," WT, Feb
1932, 2–6; Apr 1932, 4–8.  "The Artef
was originally conceived as a proletarian art theatre to counteract the influence of the bourgeois theatre among
the Jewish workers."  Artef audiences
and performers continue to overly emphasize artistic matters.

_____, "The Artef On Broadway," NTh, Feb
1935, 8–9.  illus.

BUNIN, Louis, "Punch Goes Red," NTh, Nov
1934, 8–9.  Background of radical puppetry in Europe and its beginnings in
US.

DANA, H.W.L, Interview. DW, Apr 5, 1929, 2. Fresh impressions of Soviet theatre at end of two years' stay. - See also Dana (XLIX).

_____, "Drama On the Western Front," NTh, Apr 1935, 10-14, 32. Analysis of World War I use of American theatre for jingoism.

_____, "Maxim Gorky - Dramatist Of the Lower Depths," NTh, Aug 1936, 10-12, 28-29. illus.

_____, "Five Years Of Labor Theatre," DW, June 1, 1938, 7; June 2, 7; June 3, 7. illus. A brief history with some judgments.

DA SILVA, Howard, "The Actor's Responsibility As a Citizen," DW, July 21, 1947, 11. Speech at Conference On Thought Control, Los Angeles.

DAVIS, R.G, "Radical Theatre Versus Institutional Theatre," SOL, Spring 1964, 28-38. illus. Similarities of creative approaches to a repressed theatre and a repressive society.

_____, "Street Scene Stealers," Ramparts, Oct 1965, 53-58. illus.

_____, "Who's Afraid of Herbert Blau?" SOL, Fall 1965, 89-93. Analysis of the flabby Liberalism behind the statements of Blau.

_____, "Guerrilla Theatre," TDR, Summer 1966, 130-136. Practical suggestions for survival and growth of a radical theatre; based on experience of San Francisco Mime Troupe.

DOS PASSOS, John, New Playwright's Theatre As a Working-Class Theatre. DW, Mch 11, 1927, 4. - Also Jan 20, 1928, 4; Jan 28, 1928, 4; and 1927 (LI).

_____, "The American Theatre: 1930-31," NRep, Apr 1, 1931.

_____, Introduction, Three Plays, 1934. Revolutionary theatre and the New Playwrights. - See also NM, Aug 1929, 13; Dec 1927, 20.

DREIBLATT, Martha, "How Workers' Theatre Does It," DW, Dec 23, 1935, 7. Results of Theatre Union questionnaire answered by 2000 workers: generally good taste in theatre indicated. Ticket cost chiefly a bar to greater worker attendance.

_____, "Despite Many Difficulties and Problems, The Theatre Union Lives and Grows," DW, Feb 16, 1936, 6. Report on costs and organization of audiences.

D'USSEAU, Arnand, "There Is No Place For Neutralism In the Theatre," New Theatre (London), Aug 1947, 12-15.

_____, "The Theatre Critic As Thinker," Main, Winter 1947, 111-116. Critique of Eric Bentley.

EGRI, Lajos, The Art Of Dramatic Writing, 1946; Essandess paperback, 1960. Concrete and useful introduction to dialectics of character-formation.

ELION, Harry, "Experience In Collective Playwriting," WT, Sept 1931, 13-14. Collective writing as "the scientific method" since it pools knowledge of "the day to day events of the class struggle."

_____, "A Playwriting Group In Action," WT, Sept-Oct 1932, 7-8.

_____, "The Problem Of Repertory," WT, Apr 1933, 6. Auto-critique; resolution to explore new resources and attract professional playwrights. Marks a turning-point in left theatre, the stimulus suggested by essay on facing page: a worried editorial, "Fascism and the Theatre."

_____, "Artistic Problems in the Revolutionary Theatre," Reports and Resolutions of the Eastern Regional Conference of the League of Workers Theatres of U.S.A. (1933). (Coll. Paul Romaine.) mimeo. (See LI)

FOLSOM, Michael B, "'MacBird'," People's World (San Francisco), Apr 15, 1967.

GASSNER, John, "A Playreader On Playwrights," NTh, Oct 1934, 9-11. "The bourgeois theatre is dead," Gassner declares in one of a series of NTh analyses of futility of bourgeois drama and problems of a revolutionary approach. See also Direction in late 30s.

_____, Pirandello. NTh, Jan 1936, 37. Pirandello's world of illusions as outgrowth of his class role.

_____, Masters Of the Drama, 1940. Historical and class analysis of Aeschylus, Sophocles, Euripides, Aristophanes, Roman playwrights, Hebrew drama, Kalidasa, Medieval drama, Italian drama,

Lope de Vega, Calderon, Marlowe, Shakespeare, Jonson, Corneille, Racine, Moliere, Restoration drama, Hugo, Scribe, Sardou, Schiller, Lessing, Beaumarchais, Dumas, Augier, Ibsen, Strindberg, Zola, Antoine, Becque, Pirandello, Hauptmann, Chekhov, Gorky, early Soviet drama, Synge, O'Casey, Ervine, Shaw, Wilde, Galsworthy, O'Neill, Maxwell Anderson, Odets, American left theatre.

GEDDES, Virgil, Towards Revolution In the Theatre, Brookfield, Conn, 1933, 16 pp.

_____, Left Turn For American Drama, Brookfield, Conn, 1934.  48 pp.

GEER, Will, Interview with Louise Mitchell.  DW, June 4, 1946, 11. illus.  Life of an indefatigable leftwing actor.

GOLD, Michael, "Here's Workers Theatre; Who'll See the Play?"  DW, Oct 29, 1927, 5.  Failure of workers or anyone but intellectuals to visit New Playwright's Theatre. - See also 1927 (LI).

_____, Defense Of Agitprop.  DW, Mch 27, 1934, 5.  For "satire and heroism" against "subtlety and psychology...in the workers' theatre."

_____, SEE ALSO:  Gold (LVI).

GORELIK, Mordecai, "Scenery: The Visual Attack," WT, Mch 1932, 3-5.  Designing the agitprop production.

_____, "Scenery: The Visual Machine," NTh, Sept-Oct 1933, 12-13; Jan 1934, 9-10.  illus.  "A correct revolutionary viewpoint leads to the following conclusions: The designer sees the necessity for a new technique of stage design" which Gorelik proceeds to elaborate; "at the same time he does not turn his back on the achievements of the bourgeois stage."  Develops a Meyerholdian, neo-constructivist stagecraft.

_____, "Theatre Is a Weapon," Theatre Arts, XVIII (1934), 420-433.  The left American theatre and its theory.

_____, Interview with Marcia Minor.  DW, Dec 28, 1938, 7.  illus.  Against a naturalism that fails to suggest essentials.

_____, New Theatres For Old, Theatre Arts: 1940.  illus.  Indispensable history of modern theatre.

_____, "The Factor Of Design," TDR, Spring 1961, 85-94.  Setting as the documentation of environment.

HALLER, Margaret, and M. Thon, Artistic Measures and Organization of the Prolet-Buhne Of New York. WT, Sept 1931, 5-9.

JARVIS, Tom, and Tom Hare, Theatre Union In Minneapolis. Midwest, I ii (Dec 1936), 15-16.  illus.  Establishing left-wing theatre in a city lacking theatrical tradition.

LARKIN, Margaret, "Building An Audience," NTh, Oct 1934, 26.  Theatre Union practice in organizing a public.

_____, Building a Social Theatre; A History Of the Theatre Union, n.d.  mimeo. [Theatre Collection of New York Public Library, call no. MWEZ n.c. 5232.]

_____, "Theatre Union - Its Tasks and Problems," DW, May 15, 1935, 5.  The Executive Secretary spells out financial, political and artistic views and problems.

LAWSON, John Howard, "Reflect American Life With Robust Carelessness," DWSup, Mch 26, 1927.  Assumptions behind his early plays. - See also 1927 (LI).

_____, "Towards a Revolutionary Theatre," NTh, June 1934, 6-7.  Auto-critique on commitment and experiment in theatre.

_____, "Technique and the Drama," AWC, 123-128.  Speech to 1st American Writers Congress.  First formulation of views developed in:

_____, Theory and Technique Of Playwriting, 1936; rev ed, with section added on film theory and writing, 1949; Hill & Wang paperback, film section omitted, with a new introduction: 1960.  Dramaturgy in the Ibsen tradition.

_____, "An Historical Approach To Production Methods In the Theatre."  Speech to 4th American Writers Congress (1941). [LAW] - Also in NM, Aug 26, 1941, 26-31. Industrialization as the basis for deepened realism: lighting, stage machinery, etc.  The free stage and art theatre movement as it implemented or neglected these possibilities.

_____, "The Tragedy Of Eugene O'Neill," M&M, Mch 1954, 7-18. - Objection by Lester Cole, and Lawson's reply, M&M, June 1954, 56-63.

_____, SEE ALSO: Himelstein, Rabkin (LIX).

LEAGUE OF WORKERS THEATRES, Eastern Regional Conference, Aug 5-6, 1933, Camp Midvale, N.J. Reports and Resolutions. 29 pp. mimeo. (Coll. Paul Romaine) Discussion of problems and projects of League of Workers Theatres. Text of Resolution on Repertory of the Moscow-based International Union of Revolutionary Theatres. Reports by B. Blake, H. Elion drawing the Resolution's lessons for the LOWT: More work with Negroes, students, farmers; discarding of terms like agitprop, plenum, spartakiade, in favor of native terms like theatre for action, conference; change of name from Workers Theatre to New Theatre magazine; intensive work among professionals in bourgeois theatre; fewer slogans, higher artistic level.

LEAGUE OF WORKERS THEATRES, Midwest Conference, Nov 18-19, 1933, Chicago, Ill. Reports and Resolutions. 24 pp. mimeo. (Coll. Paul Romaine) Verbatim accounts of the troubles and work of struggling labor, farmer and foreign-language theatres.

LONG, Walter, "A Sociological Criticism Of the American Drama," MQ(B), II iii (1925), 182-193; II iv (1925), 267-279; III i (1925), 24-36; III iv (1926), 300-305. A detailed history.

MAGIL, A.B, Origins of ARTEF. DW, Dec 20, 1928, 4.

MALTZ, Albert, and Margaret Larkin, "Left Wing Theatre In America," NRep, July 24, 1935.

_____, Interview. Brooklyn Eagle, Apr 21, 1935.

MARTIN, Peter, "The Theatre Of Action," DW, Feb 17, 1934, 7. Visit to a rehearsal.

NEW THEATRE LEAGUE, Facts About the New Theatre League [1935]. mimeo. 10 pp. (Coll. Paul Romaine) Organizational principles, services, associates.

_____, Theatre Front; Organizational

Bulletin of the New Theatre League. Special Issue, I i, Mch 1935. mimeo. 23 pp. (Coll. Paul Romaine) An inner organ, with news about staff and services. H. Elion, Alice Evans, Ann Howe, Steve Karnot, on NTL's new emphasis: united front with theatre professionals and the bourgeois stage, a fight against fascism and denial of civil liberties. Victor Cutler on the Ohrbach Strike play.

NORTHRUP, Emery, "Meet the Theatre Union," NTh, Feb 1934, 8-10. The company at its beginning.

ODETS, Clifford, "The Awakening Of the American Theatre," NTh, Jan 1936, 5, 43. Vigorous essay on the radical theatre.

_____, "All Drama Is Propaganda," Current Controversy, Feb 1936, 13,37. "Our schools neglect to point out that the 'classic' Greek drama is one hot shambles of propaganda consciously wielded by its dramatists." "Shakespeare never once in all his plays espoused an unpopular cause, but intertwined, instead, his destiny with the rich and powerful of his time." Dramatists are divided into a left wing (Euripides, Moliere, Shaw) and a right wing (Aeschylus, Sophocles, Shakespeare, Racine, Corneille, Goethe).

_____, Interview with Ben Burns. DW, Aug 23, 1937, 7. Work in left New York theatre and Hollywood.

_____, "'Democratic Vistas' In Drama," N.Y. Times, Section XI, Nov 21, 1937, 1-2. Movies as more in touch with real America than Broadway although neither is very truthful.

_____, Preface to Six Plays, 1939. "We are living in a time when new art works should shoot bullets."

_____, "Notes From a Side Pocket," Twice A Year, Fall-Winter 1946-47, 284-289. Aphorisms on creativity and on society.

_____, Speech to Cultural and Scientific Conference For World Peace, New York, Mch 27, 1949. DW, Mch 29, 1949, 12. Fiery assault on US Cold War policy and artists who believe "form itself is sufficient content" instead of going "where the people go."

_____, Interview with Arthur Wagner. Harper's, Sept 1966, 64-74. From 1961.

Account of the role of the Left and of
the Group Theatre in his early plays.

_____, SEE ALSO; John McCarten, "Revolu-
tion's Number One Boy," New
Yorker, Jan 22, 1938, 21-27.
Interview-essay. - Also see
Gassner (above); Slochower (LVI);
Himelstein, Rabkin (LIX).

OLGIN, Moissaye, "For a Workers' Theatre,"
DWSup, Apr 2, 1927; Apr 9, 1927. - See
also Allen (above); 1927 (LI).

PACK, Richard, "Shock Troupe In Action,"
NTh, Nov 1934, 13, 33.  Lively account
of life with an agitprop company.

PAGEANTS Presented by the Communist Party.
E.g, see 1925 (LI). - M. Olgin on the
Madison Square Garden Lenin Pageant of
1928, the first major gathering of
talent under Party auspices, DW, Jan
26, 1928, 2; also A.B. Magil, DW, Feb
2, 1928, 6. - H.C. Adamson, "Presenting 'One-Sixth Of the Earth'," DW, Nov
12, 1937, 7: a Living Newspaper on
USSR, directed by Howard da Silva,
music by Marc Blitzstein; review, DW,
Nov 16, 1937, 7; appraisal by N. Buchwald, Nov 25, 1937, 7.  illus.

PETERS, Paul [pseudonym of Harbor Allen],
"Do Workers Want Culture?" DW, Jan
23, 1934, 5.  Analyzing workers' response to Theatre Union.

_____, Interview with Sender Garlin. DW,
May 15, 1934, 5.  illus. Peters'
varied career.  'Stevedore', Soviet
theatre, US workers theatre.

_____, "On Writing and Selecting Plays
For Workers," DW, Feb 27, 1935, 5.
Theatre Union requires clear, sharp,
militant plots but the style may vary.
"Collective criticism and revision"
will be exercised on scripts by Play-
writing Committee of the Executive
Board.

_____, SEE ALSO; Walt Carmon, "Paul
Peters," ITh, 1934 #1, 50-52.

PRENTIS, Albert, "Basic Principles Of
Workers Laboratory Theatre," WT,
May 1931, 1-2.  Essentials of agit-
prop.

_____, "Relationship Between Content
and Form," WT, Sept 1931, 10-12.
Agitprop as "communal rite."  Un-
familiar language, dialect or situa-

tion must be avoided so "the audience
will associate itself with the performers instantaneously."  While "a
theatrical performance is an arrangement of symbols," workers must be confronted only with familiar symbols:
not Dionysus but a policeman.  "The
realism of today will merge into the
symbolism of tomorrow....at the present
stage of our theatre each character
must display his characteristics in a
realistic manner."

_____, "Technique In the Workers' Theatre,"
WT, Jan 1932, 5-7; Feb 1932, 12-14.
Asks whether with its different aims
proletarian theatre may use illusion-
creating dramaturgy and stage devices
of bourgeois theatre.  Answer: it must,
since theatre for workers must also
"give the audience a sense of being
present at that event."  Moreover "the
audiences...are not vastly different...
the majority of petty bourgeois of today are the workers of yesterday."
- Framed as answer to another article,
WT, Dec 1931.

"PROSPECTS FOR THE AMERICAN THEATRE,"
Symposium.  See 1933 (LI).

REINES, Bernard, "Collective Play-Writing
In Workers Theatre," WT, May 1931, 3-4.

ROMAINE, Paul, "The Little Theatres,"
NTh, May 1935, 12-13.  Fate of the
little theatre movement in 30s contrasted with upswing in worker theatre.

SAXE, Alfred, "Directing the Agitprop
Play," WT, May-June 1933, 3-4.  Methods
of work.  "Agitprop must strive to be
as creative as the best of the art
theatres.  We must not underestimate
the training necessary."

_____, "'Newsboy' - From Script to Per-
formance," NTh, July-Aug 1934, 12-13,
29.  Details of mounting a prominent
agitprop work.  Its theory.

SHAPIRO, H, "Training the Actor For the
Proletarian Theatre," WT, July 1931,
2-4.  "Portraying characters, a thing
that sounds very difficult and high
flown, is really much easier than it
seems.  It is to be remembered that
it is not necessary to protray a particular character but rather a class
angle or conception of that character,
which should not be difficult for a
class conscious worker."  Discussion
of agitprop.

SKLAR, George, and Albert Maltz, "The Need For a Workers Theatre," DW, Dec 16, 1933, 7. "The future of the theatre in America lies in the creation of a workers' theatre....Where workers attend the theatre the plays will become vital."

_____, Interview with Alex Marden. DW, Dec 30, 1937, 7. Problems of audience and finance following collapse of Theatre Union.

TAYLOR, Harry, "Toward a People's Theatre," Main, Spring 1947, 239-249. Left and workers' theatre groups to 1946 surveyed in some detail. - See also "A People's Theatre," DW, Oct 16, 1947, 13.

THACHER, Molly Day, "Revolutionary Staging For Revolutionary Plays," NTh, July-Aug 1934, 24. Wife of Elia Kazan describes introduction at Theatre Union of Stanislavsky classes for actors.

THEATRE UNION, Scrapbooks. New York Public Library, Theatre Collection at Lincoln Center.

VALDEZ, Luis, Interview With Beth Bagby. TDR, Summer 1967, 70-80. illus. Theatre by and for the California farm workers.

WALKER, Charles Rumford, Interview. N.Y. Evening Post, Jan 13, 1934. The originator of Theatre Union.

_____, "Theatre As a Weapon," Fight, May 1934.

WARD, Lem, "The Waiting Theatres." Speech to 4th American Writers Congress (1941). [LAW] Survey of non-commercial theatre groups around America.

WARREN, James, "How Members Of the Workers Laboratory Theatre Live and Work," DW, Dec 28, 1934, 5. Extremely clear on conditions where agitprop thrived.

WEIGAND, Charmion von, "The Quest Of Eugene O'Neill," NTh, Sept 1935, 12-17, 30-32. Play-by-play analysis of O'Neill consistently escaping into romanticism rather than face problems he raises.

_____, "Ernst Toller," NTh, Aug 1936, 13-15.

WELLES, Orson, "Theatre and the People's Front," DW, Apr 15, 1938, 9. Immense problem and importance of keeping theatre in the mainstream of life.

### LIX. Appendix

AARON, Daniel, Writers On the Left, 1961; Avon paperback, 1965. The major history of American left literature and criticism in 20s and 30s. Little discussion of actual works of fiction. - Review by Philip Bonosky, PA, Sept 1962, 41-47: "a substantial contribution to reason and to history," because Aaron reveals the native roots of a radical literature. - See also, Book Note, S&S, Winter 1966, 122-123. - See also "Communism and the American Writer," Newberry Library Bulletin, Aug 1959, 84-116. Abstracts of Aaron's preliminary views and of discussion of them by various authors and critics, including J. Herbst, J. Freeman, F.J. Hoffman.

_____, "The Treachery Of Recollection," Carleton Miscellany, Summer 1965, 3-19. Problems experienced in researching and writing the literary history of the 1930's.

_____, "Some Reflections On Communism and the Jewish Writer," Salmagundi, Fall 1965, 23-36. Late 1920's to 1945: the views of radical authors and of sociologists.

_____, "The Thirties - Then and Now," American Scholar, Summer 1966, 490-516. Symposium by Aaron, M. Cowley, K. Burke, G. Hicks and W. Phillips, on the 1st American Writers Congress.

ADAMIC, Louis, "What the Proletariat Reads," SatR, Dec 1, 1934, 321-322. Reports evidence that almost no workers read the proletarian novels or culture magazines; and where they do, workers often resent the portrayals of proletarians. - See letters, ibid, Dec 22, 384. - See also rebuttal by M. Gold, DW, Dec 14, 1934, 5.

BARR, Alfred H, "Is Modern Art Communistic?" N.Y. Times Magazine, Dec 14, 1952, 22-23, 28-30. illus. More or less equates attacks on modern painting in US, the USSR and Nazi Germany.

BENSON, Frederick R, Writers In Arms; The Literary History of the Spanish Civil War, New York Univ: 1967.

Hemingway, Koestler, Malraux, Bernanos, Orwell, Regler, etc.

BETTS, Anne, An Historical Study Of the New Dance Group Of New York City, M.A. dissertation, New York Univ: 1945. [Copy at New York Public Library]  Not exhaustive; provides  outline of left wing dance movement with numerous quotes from reviews and prospectuses.

BURNHAM, James, "Marxism and Esthetics," The Symposium, IV i (Jan 1933), 3-30. Recognizes need to accept "so much in Marxism that is true and good" while rejecting extremist demands upon writer and critic.

BURNSHAW, Stanley, "Wallace Stevens and the Statue," Sewanee Review, LXIX (1961), 355-366.  Reflections on his years with 'New Masses' ("the blind leading the blind"), and on Stevens' poem concerning his review of Stevens in that journal.

CHAPLIN, Ralph, Wobbly, Chicago, 1948. A pathetic autobiography.  IWW author of 'Solidarity Forever' documents his degeneration into a sentimental jingoist and red-baiter.

CLURMAN, Harold, The Fervent Years; The Story Of the Group Theatre and the Thirties, 1945; Hill & Wang paperback, 1957.

_____, "The Theatre Of the Thirties," TDR, IV ii, 3-11.

CROWTHER, Bosley, "Theatre Of the Left," N.Y. Times, Apr 14, 1935.

DONDERO, Honorable George A, "Modern Art Shackled To Communism," Congressional Record, First Session, 81st Congress, U.S.A.  Tuesday, Aug 16, 1949.

_____, "UNESCO - Communism and Modern Art," Congressional Record, Second Session, 84th Congress, U.S.A.  Friday, July 20, 1956.  The sixth of his speeches on modern art and such painters as Leger, Picasso, Gwathmey, Levine, Lawrence, Shahn, Hirsch, Evergood. Here he says his position is misinterpreted by Museum of Modern Art spokesmen: by Communist art he means what was permitted in Soviet Russia until early 20s when, its culturally destructive tasks completed and the bourgeois world smashed, a constructive propaganda art was substituted for the dangerous modernism.

EASTMAN, Max, Artists In Uniform.  See Eastman (XLIX).  See also Gold, Freeman (LVI); Aaron (above).

_____, Enjoyment Of Poetry, 1913. Evinces Eastman's separation of poetry from action, prior to any question of Party directives, etc.

_____, Journalism Vs. Art, 1916.  Attacks current periodical art as aesthetically bad because of money motive in production and distribution.

_____, "Bunk About Bohemia," MQ(B), May 1934, 200-208; June 1934, 292-300. Disputes the CP account of his career.

_____, Art and the Life Of Action, 1934. "There is no clearer line of demarkation among human types than that between the artist and the man of action ....Artists should not only refuse to join a practical organization, but should do so with a reliant pride capable of resisting any attempts upon the part of such an organization to direct their work."

EGBERT, Donald Drew, "Socialism and American Art," in: Socialism and American Life, ed. D.D. Egbert and Stow Persons, Princeton, N.J, 1952, vol. I, 623-751. illus.  Detailed and useful discussion.  Soviet as well as American controversies and views are described as are American pre-Marxist views. - Reprinted, revised as Socialism and American Art, Princeton University Press paperback: Princeton, N.J, 1967.

_____, Socialism, Radicalism, and the Arts In Western Europe.  In preparation.

_____, "In Search Of John Edelmann, Architect and Anarchist," A.I.A. Journal, Feb 1966, 35-41.  The onetime member of Socialist Labor Party and friend of Kropotkin, who gave Louis Sullivan the idea for "form follows function," taken up by Frank Lloyd Wright.

_____, "The Idea Of 'Avant-Garde' In Art and Politics," American Historical Review, 1968.

ELIOT, T.S, "A Commentary," Criterion, Jan 1933, 244-249.  Discusses Calverton, Trotsky in some detail.  Calls "touching"

motives (in his view extrinsic to literature) which "entice the man of letters with political and social theory."
Trotsky: "He is certainly a man of
first-rate intelligence, expressing
himself in a rough and ready metaphor-
ical style, and he utters a good deal
of sound sense."  Concedes Communism
could bring forth great literature but
not owing to ideology, theory or directives - and not greater than Christian
literature, which in turn does not
excell pagan literature though Eliot
prefers it.  "What would happen, at
best, under a new dispensation, would
be that the artist would be so inocu-
lated with communism as to be able to
ignore it."

FIEDLER, Leslie, An End To Innocence:
Essays On Culture and Politics, Boston,
1955.  1930's writers as seduced inno-
cents. - See LeRoy (LVI).

FILLER, Louis, "Political Literature: A
Post Mortem," Southwest Review, Summer
1954, 185-193.

FLANAGAN, Hallie, "A Theatre Is Born,"
Theatre Arts, Nov 1931.  The burgeon-
ing of agitprop theatre. - Answered by
A. Prentis, WT, Dec 1931, 5-7: agitprop utilizes imagination of worker
audience and gets far bigger response
than does bourgeois theatre.

_____, Arena, 1940.  Autopsy on Federal
Theatre.

_____, SEE ALSO: Flanagan (XLIX);
     Mathews (below).

FLEXNER, Eleanor, American Playwrights:
1918-1938, 1938.  Retreat of Broadway
playwrights from reality, together
with rise of socialist theatre.

_____, "Broadway."  Speech to 4th Ameri-
can Writers Congress (1941).  [LAW]
Fate of social theatre.

FLORY, Claud R, Economic Criticism In
American Fiction, 1792-1900, Philadelphia: 1935.

GELFANT, Blanche H, "The Search For
Identity In the Novels Of John Dos
Passos," PMLA, Mch 1961, 133-149.

GILBERT, James, "Literature and Revolution in the United States," Journal
Of Contemporary History, Apr 1967,
195-208.

GLICKSBERG, Charles I, "John Dos Passos
and Proletarian Literature," Panorama,
July 1934, 3.  "The clamor for proletarian literature springs not from the
working class, which is quite content
with its cheap serialized fiction, but
from a minority of embattled intellectuals."

_____, "The Aberrations Of Marxist Criti-
cism," Queens Quarterly LVI (1949),
479-490.  Marxist criticism dismissed
without analysis as "a fraud perpetuated
on a weary, disillusioned, but still
credulous world."

_____, "Literature and the Marxist Aes-
thetic," University of Toronto Quarterly, XVIII (1949), 76-84.

_____, SEE ALSO: Glicksberg (LVI).

GRADY, Richard F, S.J, "Scarlet-Fever
Drama," America, May 21, 1932, 157-159.
Jesuit verdict on Workers Laboratory
Theatre. - Answered by Al Saxe, WT,
June-July 1932, 5-7.

HAGEMAN, E.R, ",Huye! A Conjectural Biog-
raphy Of B. Traven," Revista Inter-
americana de Bibliografia, X, 370-386.
- See also: William Weber Johnson, "The
Traven Case," N.Y. Times Book Review,
Apr 17, 1966, 1, 41-43.

HALE, Hope, Speech to 3rd American Writers
Congress.  FW, 43-47.  A pulp writer
accuses the proletarian writers of
being snobs.  "No worker would read"
the left's literary magazines; while
"millions" read 'True Story' magazine,
the best medium for radical writers
trying to reach the  masses.

HANSEN, Brian K, The Drama Of the American Workers' Theatre Movement.  M.A.
Thesis, Cornell Univ: 1961.

HAZLITT, Henry,  "Literature and the
Class War," in his: Anatomy of Criticism, 1933.

HIMELSTEIN, Morgan Y, Drama Was a Weapon;
The Left-Wing Theatre In New York,
1929-1941, Rutgers Univ: New Brunswick,
N.J, 1963.  Foreword by John Gassner.
illus.  Bibliography.  Author relies
on 'devil' theory of Communism with
shallow research and scope.  Prof.
Gassner's remarks suggest, too politely,
the author's failure of perspective.
- Review by J.H. Lawson in S&S, Summer
1964, 364-366.

HYMAN, Stanley Edgar, "The Marxist Criticism Of Literature," Antioch Review, Winter 1947, 541-568; also in his The Armed Vision, 1948 (hard-cover edition only), 168-208. A survey of some works, but chiefly an assessment of Ch. Caudwell.

_____, The Tangled Bank; Darwin, Marx, Frazer and Freud As Imaginative Writers, Atheneum: 1962, 81-186. Formal analysis of Marx's "bag of rhetorical tricks."

KAHN, Gordon, Hollywood On Trial, 1948. The first round of Red-baiting Hollywood.

KAZIN, Alfred, On Native Grounds, 1942. Chapter on "Criticism At the Poles," treats US Marxist criticism in the 30s.

KEMPTON, Murray, Part Of Our Time: Some Monuments and Ruins Of the Thirties, 1955; Delta paperback, 1967. Chapters on Paul Robeson, the proletarian novel, workers' theatre and its aftermath in Hollywood.

KOSTELANETZ, Richard, "Men Of the '30s," Commonweal, Dec 3, 1965, 266-269. Appraisal of literary achievement of 1930's and the writings on it of Kazin, Trilling, Rahv and Hicks.

KOZLENKO, William, "Morphology Of the Proletarian Movement," Literary America, Nov 1934, 46-54. Weighing problems of "proletarian" approach, concludes the best, least blinded writers of this tendency will "transfuse strong blood into the anemic veins of the esoteric movements."

LASCH, Christopher, The New Radicalism In America, 1889-1963; The Intellectual As a Social Type, Knopf: 1965. Randolph Bourne, Mabel Dodge Luhan, Lincoln Steffens, Norman Mailer, Dwight Macdonald, etc. - Review by Carl Resek, SOL, Jan-Feb 1966, 64-69.

LAWRENCE, David, "Who Slew Proletcult?" Vanguard, Nov 1937, 8-12. Sardonic detailed analysis by an Anarchist of decline of Communist cultural effort from 1935 on. Many artists and writers, he says, scrambled for WPA jobs when they opened up. The Party's political tactics and its changes of tactics and its imposition of administrative judgments on artistic matters

and the Moscow Trials did for the rest.

LECKY, Eleazer, "'New Theatre'," Modern Drama, Winter 1963, 267-276. Brief study of the leading left theatre journals of 1930s.

LIND, L. Robert, "The Crisis In Literature," Sewanee Review, XLVII (1939), 35-62, 184-203, 345-364, 524-551; XLVIII (1939), 66-85, 198-203. Study of bourgeois and proletarian literature in America; propaganda and art; etc.

LLOYD, Margaret, The Borzoi Book Of Modern Dance, Knopf: 1949. On the New Dance Group: pp. 173-197.

MARTIN, John R, "Marxism and the History Of Art," College Art Journal, Fall 1951, 3-9. Deprecating discussion of Antal, Finkelstein, Harap, Klingender.

McDERMOTT, Douglas, "The Theatre Nobody Knows: Workers' Theatre In America, 1926-42," Theatre Survey, May 1965, 65-82. Chiefly a study of organizations.

MADDEN, David, ed, The Proletarian Writers Of the Thirties, Southern Illincis: Glencoe, 1967. Contributors: L. Fiedler, G. Green, B. Appel, R. Ames, E. Larsen, J. Conroy, L. Gurko, J. Chametzsky, K. Widmer, I. Howe, L. Kriegel, C. Miller, C. Eisinger, L. Baxandall, M. Folsom, J. Gilbert, F.J. Hoffman, R.F. Haugh, G.W. Arnold, A. Guttman. Topics include: proletarian novels, R. Wright, J. London, J. Conroy, R. Cantwell, Dos Passos, Steinbeck, D. Fuchs, D. Trumbo, B. Traven, L. Fraina, M. Gold, H. Miller, proletarian poetry.

MATHEWS, Jane DeHart, The Federal Theatre, 1935-39; Plays, Relief and Politics, Princeton Univ: 1967. illus. biblio. Close account of the goals of Federal Theatre as expression of popular aspirations within the New Deal political matrix.

MESERVE, Walter J, "American Drama and the Rise Of Realism," Jahrbuch fur Amerikastudien, IX, 152 ff.

MONROE, Harriet, "Art and Propaganda," Poetry, XLIV (1934), 210-215. Affirms "all art of all the ages is propaganda." Criticism of Stanley Burnshaw's view of revolutionary poetry. - See "Stanley Burnshaw Protests," ibid, 351-354.

MUNRO, Thomas, "The Marxist Theory Of Art

History," <u>JAAC</u>, XVIII iv (June 1960), 430-445. "To be convincing, the... argument must show that the social condition would be sufficient to produce a psychological attitude favorable to the kind of art which ensued, and that such an attitude would not have arisen without this conditioning. It should also show that no other factors, existing at that time, would have sufficed to produce it. The psychological intermediary is necessary. Since economic factors cannot act directly on art, they must do so through human attitudes, feelings beliefs and desires." A generally sympathetic critique expressing "increasing respect" for sociological methods.

MUSTE, J.M, <u>Say That We Saw Spain Die</u>: <u>Literary Consequences Of the Spanish Civil War</u>, Univ. of Washington, Seattle, 1966. Effects on British and US writing. - Review by Allen Guttman, <u>Nation</u>, Jan 16, 1967, 90-91.

O'NEILL, William L, ed, <u>Echoes Of Revolt</u>: <u>'The Masses' 1911-1917</u>, Quadrangle: 1967. Annotated anthology with introduction by Irving Howe, afterword by Max Eastman. - Review by Michael B. Folsom, <u>Nation</u>, Feb 27, 1967, 277-279.

OWENSBY, Edward, <u>The Theatre Of Social Protest In the United States</u>, Mexico City, 1951. Seven plays (including 'Born Yesterday!!)

RABKIN, Gerald, <u>Drama and Commitment</u>; <u>Politics In the American Theatre Of the Thirties</u>, Indiana Univ: Bloomington, 1964. Scholarly analysis, fairly acute but not detailed, of Theatre Union, Group Theatre, Federal Theatre, John Howard Lawson, Clifford Odets, S.N. Behrman, Elmer Rice, Maxwell Anderson. Concludes that Marxist outlook (as in Odets' case) <u>can</u> enhance aesthetic quality of a theatre work. "Let us not ask to what the artist is committed, but rather how he is committed."

REISER, Max, "The Aesthetic Theory Of Socialist Realism," <u>JAAC</u>, XVI ii (Dec 1957), 233-248. Chiefly an exposition and critique of Lukacs whose Realism-oriented aesthetic, Reiser says, is "scarcely applicable to lyric poetry and still less to music."

RIDEOUT, Walter, <u>The Radical Novel In the</u>

<u>United States, 1900-1954</u>, Harvard Univ: Cambridge, Mass, 1956. Studies of some major proletarian and radical novels. - Review by C. Humboldt, <u>M&M</u>, Mch 1957, 48-50. - Review by P. Bonosky, <u>PA</u>, May 1959, 27-40.

_____, "The Jew As Author and Subject In the American Radical Novel," <u>American Jewish Archives</u>, Oct 1959, 157-175. Survey of Jewish novels with Marxist outlook.

SCHLISSEL, L, ed, <u>The World Of Randolph Bourne: Essays and Letters</u>, Dutton: 1965.

SCHULBERG, Budd, "Collision With the Party Line," <u>Saturday Review</u>, Apr 30, 1952, 6-7, 31-37.

STEINER, George, "Marxism and the Literary Critic," <u>En</u>, Nov 1958, 33-43. Distinguishes between orthodox and "para-Marxist," the "Leninist" and "Engelian" approaches. Says work of Lukacs "demonstrates that Marxism can yield a poetics and a metaphysics of the highest order." Sartre, Merleau-Ponty, L. Goldmann ("scrupulous scholarship... a persuasive delicacy"), H. Lefebvre, W. Benjamin ("private and oblique"), S. Finkelstein.

_____, <u>Literature and Silence,</u> Atheneum: 1967. A section on literature and Marxism. Lukacs, Trotsky, Goldmann, Benjamin.

STRAUSS, Harold, "Realism In the Proletarian Novel," <u>Yale Review</u>, XXVIII (1938), 360-374. Careful analysis of the "impressionist" proletarian realism which presents "impulsive recipients of sensory impressions...creatures...more acted upon than acting", which ignores "the effect of dream and desire in the mind of a worker". Finds "no proletarian literature tradition in this country"; the current authors are bourgeois in revolt.

SUTTON, Walter, <u>Modern American Criticism</u>, Prentice-Hall: Englewood Cliff, N.J, 1963, 51-98. Superficial.

SWADOS, Harvey, "Writers Of the Thirties," <u>N.Y. Times Book Review</u>, Aug 22, 1965.

TAILLEUR, Roger, "Elia Kazan and the House Un-American Activities Committee," <u>Film Comment</u>, Fall 1966, 43-58. Kazan as Communist and stool-pigeon, a child

of his times.  Analysis of his films
and Arthur Miller's plays for their
running argument.

TAYLOR, Walter Fuller, The Economic
Novel In America, 1942; Octagon Books:
1964.  The post-bellum literature.

THOMPSON, Dorothy, "The Dilemma Of the
Liberal," Story, Jan 1937, 2-7.
Statement of her mixed feelings before
the Party joiners.

THORP, Willard, "American Writers On the
Left," in: Socialism and American Life,
ed. D.D. Egbert and Stow Persons,
Princeton, N.J, 1952, vol. I, 601-620.

TIMES LITERARY SUPPLEMENT (London),
"American Writers Look Left; Social
Conflict As a Theme," Feb 22, 1936.

TRILLING, Lionel, "Parrington, Mr. Smith
and Reality," PR, Jan-Feb 1940, 24-40.

VAN DEUSEN, Marshall, "Criticism In the
Thirties: The Marxists and the New
Critics," Western Humanities Review,
XVII (1963), 75-85.

WHITE, Howard B, "Materialists and the
Sociology Of American Literature,"
Social Research, May 1940, 184-200.
"In contemplating the failure of Marxist surveys to come to grips with
many problems involved in a sociology
of contemporary letters we may again
ask what form that sociology should
take."  His arguments with Parrington,
Calverton, Bernard Smith are irritat-
ingly obtuse.

WILSON, T.C, "American Letters," Life
And Letters To-Day, Summer 1937, 19-23.
State of left writing and criticism.


LX.  VIETNAM

LE LIEM, "Vietnam's Cultural Revolution,"
NT, Oct 11, 1961, 19-20.

NGUYEN-DINH-THI, Vietnamese Literature;
A Sketch, Foreign Languages Publishing
House: Hanoi, 1956.  24 pp. Also in SL,
1955 #9, 143-151.  Origins to present.

NGUYEN KHAI, "The Vietnamese Writer and
Social Reality," Vietnamese Studies
(Hanoi), #4 (1965), 124-132.  Writers
who situate themselves in agrarian
communities and share the people's
life.

NGUYEN KHANH TOAN, et al, Nguyen Du and
'Kieu', in Vietnamese Studies (Hanoi),
#4 (1965), 111 pp.  Translations from
the classic Vietnamese epic poem, with
several studies of the poem and its
author.  biblio.

VIETNAM LITERATURE AND ARTS ASSOCIATION
EXECUTIVE COMMITTEE, "Literary and
Artistic Activities In 1963-1964,"
Vietnamese Studies (Hanoi), #4 (1965),
112-123.  Accomplishments in North
Vietnam and liberated areas of the
South.

VIETNAMESE HANDICRAFTS, Foreign Languages
Publishing House, Hanoi, 1959.  illus.
Folk and traditional arts to the present.


LXI.  YUGOSLAVIA

FINCI, Eli, "Marin Drzic," J, 1949 #1,
101-103.  illus.  The greatest Yugo-
slav Renaissance writer.

LEAGUE OF COMMUNISTS, Yugoslavia's Way;
The Program Of the League Of the Communists Of Yugoslavia, 1958, 222-224,
228-229, 254-255.  The Party analysis
of cultural development, artistic
liberty and control, the socialist
creative man as goal.

POPOVIC, Jovan, "Svetozar Marcovic," J,
1952 #6, 95-98.  illus.  First Yugo-
slav exponent of the social role of
literature, a revolutionary in
politics.

STOJANOVIC, Bratislav, "Town Planning
and Architecture," J, 1949 #1, 90-95.
illus.  Introduction of socialist
planning.

SUPEK, Rudi, "Freedom and Polydeterminism
In the Criticism Of Culture," in:
Erich Fromm, ed, Socialist Humanism,
Doubleday: 1965, 256-272.  Critique of
shallow use of ideas of class equiva-
lents, decadence, alienation.  Defines
a positive role for modernism in art.
Analysis must be based on complex and
inequal determinisms of the social
structure, artist's personality, the
tradition he works.

SUVIN, Darko, "Beckett's Purgatory Of the
Individual," TDR, Summer 1967, 23-36.
Limits and illuminations of 'Waiting
For Godot' as a moment of art in history.

_____, "On the Individualist World View In Drama," Zagadnienia Rodzajow Literackich (Lodz), IX i, 1966, 5-23. In English. The aesthetic problems caused by the loss of the communal values which prevailed in earlier epochs.

_____, "The Mirror and the Dynamo; On Brecht's Aesthetic Point of View," Drama Review (formerly TDR), Fall 1967, 56-68.

SEE ALSO: Arno Karlen, "The Arts In Yugoslavia," Nation, Dec 21, 1964, 499-502.


N O N - M A R X I S T ,   R E L A T E D

LXII.  Older Works, Forerunners, Contributions To the

Sociology Of Literature and Art


ABELL, Walter, "Art and Labor," Magazine of Art, XXXIX (1946), 231-239, 254. illus.  Union patronage of painters.

_____, The Collective Dream In Art: A Psycho-Historical Theory Of Culture Based On Relations Between the Arts, Psychology and the Social Sciences, Harvard: Cambridge, Mass, 1957. illus. - Review by E.B. Burgum, SOL, II i (1961), 95-100.

ADAM, Ian W, "Society As Novelist," JAAC, Summer 1967, 375-386. Determinants of style in Thackeray and Wm. Burroughs.

ADAMS, William Howard, The Politics Of Art, Arts Councils of America: 1966. 49 pp.  A guide to obtaining public aid for civic arts projects.

ADLER, Mortimer, Poetry and Politics, 1937; Duquesne Univ: Pittsburgh, 1965.

ADORNO, Theodore, "On Popular Music," Studies In Philosophy and Social Science, IX (1941), 17-48.  Popular music's social genesis; function in coercive and alienated societies.

_____, "The Radio Symphony," Radio Research, 1941, 110-139.

_____, Essays, ed. S. Weber. Forthcoming.

_____, SEE ALSO: Fredric Jameson, "T.W. Adorno, Or, Historical Tropes," Salmagundi, Spring 1967, 3-43. Critical account of Adorno's studies of Western music. Stravinsky, Schoenberg, Beethoven, Hegel, Marxism.

_____, SEE ALSO: Eisler (XXI); Beckett (XXIII).

ALBRECHT, Milton, "Does Literature Reflect Common Values?" American Sociological Review, XXI (1956), 722-729. Statistical analysis of class taste.

_____, "Research Areas In the Sociology Of Art," Sociology and Social Research, July 1958, 401-405.

ALDRIDGE, John W, In Search Of Heresy; American Literature In an Age Of Conformity, 1956.

ALSBERG, Henry G, Speech to 2nd American Writers Congress, WCW, 241-249. Director of WPA Federal Writers Project.

ALTICK, R.D, The English Common Reader; A Social History Of the Mass Reading Public, 1800-1900, Chicago, 1957. Valuable on emergence of literate middle class.

ANSTER, Donald, "A Content Analysis Of 'Little Orphan Annie'," Social Problems, II (1954), 26-33.

ASSELINEAU, Roger, The Evolution Of Walt Whitman, 1960.  2 vols.

AUBERY, Pierre, "The Anarchism Of French Symbolists," French Review, forthcoming.

AUERBACH, Erich, Mimesis: The Representation Of Reality In Western Literature, Doubleday Anchor paperback: 1957. Brilliant readings of texts. Underlying principles described, pp. 484-488. Bible, Medieval chanson and mystery plays, Classicism and Romanticism, Allegory, Ammianus Marcellinus, Apuleius, Ariosto, Aristotle, Malory, Augustine, Balzac, Boccaccio, Boileau, Bossuet, Cervantes, Chretien de Troyes, Ancient Comedy, Corneille, Courtly Romances, Dante, Dickens, Diderot, Dostoevsky,

Epic, Euripides, Fabliaux, Fielding, Figural interpretation, Flaubert, Fontane, Francis of Assisi, French Revolution, Froissart, Gide, Goethe, Gogol, Goncourt, Gotthelf, Gregory of Tours, Hamsun, Hebbel, Hegel, Historicism, Homer, Horace, Hugo, Jacopone da Todi, Jerome, Joyce, Kafka, Keller, La Bruyere, La Sale, Lessing, Lucian, Mann, Marlowe, Meinecke, Middle-class tragedy, Moliere, Montaigne, Perspectivism, Petronius, Plato, Proust, Provencal poetry, Rabelais, Racine, Restoration drama, Rousseau, Schiller, Scott, Shakespeare, Socrates, Stendhal, Stifter, Storm, Sturm und Drang, Style, Tacitus, Taine, Aquinas, Vico, Virgil, Voltaire, Woolf, Zola.

_____, Scenes From the Drama Of European Literature, Meridian paperback: 1959. Dante, Pascal, Moliere, Vico, Baudelaire, the concept of Figura.

_____, Introduction To Romance Languages and Literature, Capricorn paperback: 1961. Social origins and development of the romance languages. Outline of the romance literatures.

_____, Review of Rene Wellek's 'History Of Modern Criticism'. Romanische Forschungen, LXVII (1956), 387-397. In English. "He who understands the historical perspective eclectically has not understood it....To capture through devoted and deep study the particularity of each single epoch and of each single work, as well as the kind of relations among them, is an endless task which each must try to solve for himself from his own standpoint (for historical relativism is twofold, it is relevant to the understander as well as to what is understood)."

BARBER, Charles L, Shakespeare's Festive Comedy; A Study Of Dramatic Form and Its Relation To Social Custom, Princeton, 1959; Meridian paperback, 1963. Explores "how art develops underlying configurations in the social life" with particular reference to "the way the social form of Elizabethan holidays contributed to the dramatic form of festive comedy."

BARNETT, James H, "The Sociology Of Art," in: Robert K. Merton et al, Sociology Today, Basic Books: 1959, 197-214. A wretched essay from American sociology's academic Establishment. Barnett ex-

tolls virtues of "objective" sampling, verification, etc, brushes off Marxists with a sentence and then silence; but his own survey is a gloss on Ernest Grosse's 19th Century survey 'The Beginnings Of Art'! Cf. Barnett on Herbert Spencer, Grosse p. 308 ff.

BARTHES, Roland, On Racine, Hill & Wang: 1964. Bourgeois misinterpretations of Racine on the stage. Racine's myth as the effort of men to transcent their situation through language, and their failure. Relation of literature to history. - See also Gray (XX).

BAUMOL, William J, and William G. Bowen, Performing Arts - The Economic Dilemma, 20th Century Fund: 1966. Two economists analyze the narrow middle-class support for US theatre, opera, music and dance, and effects on financing and performers.

BEACH, Joseph Warren, American Fiction 1920-1940, 1941; Russell & Russell paperback, 1960. Analysis of the sociological acuteness and artistic maturity of Dos Passos, Hemingway, Faulkner, Wolfe, Marquand, Steinbeck, Caldwell, Farrell.

BELINSKY: See Belinsky, Chernyshevsky, and Dobrolyubov: Selected Criticism, ed. Ralph E. Matlaw, Dutton paperback: 1962. Compact introduction to essential writings of Russian Utilitarians whose outlook underlies Socialist Realism in USSR.

BELL, Daniel, "In Search Of Marxist Humanism," Survey #32, 21-31. Important critique of Marx's theory of alienation.

BLAU, Herbert, "Littlewood and Planchon In an Affluent Society," Encore, Mch-Apr 1960.

BLOCH, Herbert A, "Toward the Development Of a Sociology of Literature and Art-Forms," American Sociological Review, June 1943, 313-320.

BOAS, Franz, Primitive Art, Oslo, 1927.

BOAS, George, ed, Courbet and the Naturalistic Movement, Baltimore, 1938. illus.

BOUGHTON, Rutland, Bach, The Master, 1930. Often arbitrary, Boughton does relate Bach cantatas to chorales stemming from peasant uprisings.

BOURNE, Randolph, History Of a Literary

Radical and Other Essays, 1920. - See also Harry Henderson, "Randolph Bourne," DW, Oct 29, 1939, 4; Oct 30, 7. His development. - See also Schlissel (LIX).

BOWRA, C.M, "Sociological Remarks On Greek Poetry," Zeitschrift fur Sozial-forschung, VI (1937), 382-398. In English. "Far from being a national art in every stage of its history, Greek art was hardly ever national. Its greatest achievements were due to small sections of the population," that is the aristocracy; genuinely popular poetry, themes, etc, "seems never to have reached any artistic excellence and was never treated seriously by the Greeks."

_____, The Heritage Of Symbolism, London, 1947.

_____, "Poetry In Europe, 1900-1950," Diogenes, #1 (1953), 8-24. Literary and sociological analysis of Symbolism and the antithesis to it (Modernism), which Bowra hopes will produce new poetic synthesis combining merits of both.

_____, Poetry and Politics 1900-1960, Cambridge: 1966. A general exploration of the problems of adapting the poet's private experience and idiom to public utterance and responsibility. Special attention to the early Soviet years. Blok, Mayakovsky, Brecht, etc.

BRAMSTED, Ernest K. See Kohn-Bramstedt (below).

BRANDES, George, Main Currents In Nineteenth Century Literature, 6 vols, 1905-23.

BRINTON, Crane, The Political Ideas Of the English Romanticists, 1926; Russell & Russell paperback, 1962.

BRODBECK, Arthur J, "Placing Aesthetic Developments In a Social Context," Journal Of Social Issues, XX (1964), 8-25. An instance of current "social psychology."

BROOKS, Van Wyck, "A Personal Statement," Direction, May-June 1939, 6-9, 40-44. Analyzes at length his views on American Writers Congress and relevance to US conditions of Communism vs. "Yankee collectivism."

_____, Three Essays On America, 1934; reprinted as America's Coming-Of-Age, Doubleday Anchor paperback: 1958. Includes "America's Coming-Of-Age" (1915); "Letters and Leadership" (1918); "The Literary Life In America" (1927).

_____, The Ordeal Of Mark Twain, 1920; Meridian paperback: 1955. Introduction by M. Cowley. A classic analysis of determinants of an American writer.

_____, Makers and Finders: A History Of the Writer In America, 1800-1915, 5 vols. Includes: The World Of Washington Irving; The Flowering Of New England (reprinted as a Dutton paperback); The Times Of Melville and Whitman; New England, Indian Summer; The Confident Years 1885-1915.

_____, The Writer In America, 1953; Avon paperback, 1964. Summing-up of his view of life and letters.

BRUFORD, W.H, Germany In the Eighteenth Century: The Social Background Of the Literary Revival, London, 1935. Thorough presentation of social determinants. No literary analysis.

_____, Theatre Drama and Audience in Goethe's Germany, London, 1950. Continues his exhaustive documentary approach.

CAPOUYA, Emile, "Art and Revolution," MRSup #1 (1965), 37-42. The dangerous truth-value in much current US writing. "The artists themselves consciously condemn their art, and encourage the audience to misprize and traduce it." Machine civilization as the foe. Awakening of the "heart," a sense of "honor" required of writers.

CHAPMAN, John Jay, Selected Writings, ed. with introduction by Jacques Barzun, Doubleday Anchor paperback: 1959. Important essays on Whitman, Emerson, William James, Shakespeare, etc, by a brilliant stylist and American radical. - See Wilson (LVI).

CLARK, Harry H, "The Influence Of Science On American Literary Criticism 1860-1910, Including the Vogue Of Taine," Transactions Of Wisconsin Academy, 44 (1956), 109-164.

CLARK, Kenneth, "Art and Society," Cornhill Magazine, Autumn 1960, 307-325. An approach that almost exclusively emphasizes role of elites; as often stimulating as wrongheaded, by brilliant analyst of visual arts.

COHEN, Marcel, "Social and Linguistic Structure," Diogenes, Fall 1956, 38-47. Review of efforts of Marr and others in this area, and present status of field.

COLE, G.D.H, Politics and Literature, London, 1929. "A brief introductory study of political literature in its double aspect of form and content together." "If literature were appreciated purely as a craft, the political writers, though they put their ideas first and their craft second, would take in it a far higher place than is usually assigned to them. Hooker and Bacon are the fine flower of Elizabethan prose: Hobbes is the finest prose craftsman of the seventeenth century: Swift positively created anew for the modern world the craft of 'polite' English; and Burke is the most accomplished maker of emotional prose in the language."

_____, Persons and Periods, London, 1938. Defoe, Morris, etc.

_____, Samuel Butler and 'The Way Of All Flesh', London, 1947.

COLLINS, Arthur S, Authorship In the Days Of Johnson, Being a Study Of the Relation Between Author, Patron, Publisher and Public, 1726-1780, London, 1927.

_____, The Profession Of Letters; A Study Of the Relation Of Author To Patron, Publisher and Public, 1780-1832, London, 1928.

COLMER, John, Coleridge: Critic Of Society, London, 1960. - Review by J.P. Mann, NLR, Mch-Apr 1960, 64.

CRAFTS, Stephen, "'Frankenstein': Camp Curiosity Or Premonition?" Catalyst (Buffalo), Summer 1967, 96-103. Mary Shelley's novel in the light of Fanon and Marcuse.

CRONBACH, Robert, "Section Of Fine Arts and Other Government Activities." Speech to 4th American Writers Congress on WPA cultural program. [LAW]

CRUISE O'BRIEN, Conor, Writers and Politics, Pantheon: 1965, Vintage paperback, 1967.

DAICHES, David, Literature and Society, London, 1938. Knowledgeable and intelligent popularization by an Oxford don of place of social forces in shaping literature.

_____, The Novel and the Modern World, Chicago, 1939. Studies of Galsworthy, Conrad, K. Mansfield, Joyce, V. Woolf, Huxley, several problems of the novel.

DARROW, Clarence, The Pearl and Other Essays, 1898. Omar Kayam, Walt Whitman, Robert Burns, Realism in art and literature. In this last he calls for literature beautiful and true to life, secularized and non-didactic. Much like Engels in rejecting moralistic schematism. Harsh against distortions produced by religious ages.

D'AZEVEDO, Warren L, "A Structural Approach To Esthetics: Toward a Definition Of Art In Anthropology," American Anthropologist, Aug 1958, 702-714. Art as a process which yields in a special way to anthropological analysis.

DELL, Floyd, Intellectual Vagabondage, 1926. Reworking of a series in Lib. Discusses 'Robinson Crusoe' and Neo-classicist English literature chiefly to get to main concern: an apology for bohemianism of his literary generation. "Literature....mirrors the spiritual attitude, toward historical and economic circumstances, of vast questioning bewildered multitudes."

_____, "A Literary Self-Analysis," MQ(B), IV ii (1927), 148-152. Defends his "bourgeois themes" and lack of evident "radicalism" with a theory of art "generated in the unconscious mind."

_____, "Walt Whitman, Anti-Socialist," NRep, June 15, 1915, 85.

SEE ALSO: George Thomas Tanselle, Faun At the Barricades: The Life and Work Of Floyd Dell, Ph.D. dissertation, Northwestern Univ: 1959.

DELEVOY, Robert L, Bruegel, Skira: 1959. illus. Brilliant monograph.

DESSOIR, Max, "Aesthetics and the Philosophy Of Art," Monist, XXXVI (1926), 299-310.

DEWEY, John, Art As Experience, 1934; Capricorn paperback, 1958.

DOWD, David L, Pageant-Master Of the Republic; Jacques-Louis David and the French Revolution, University of Nebraska Studies: Lincoln, 1948. David's revolutionist role; effects of the Revolution on patronage.

_____, "Art As National Propaganda In the French Revolution," Public Opinion Quarterly, Autumn 1951, 532-546.

_____, "Jacques-Louis David, Artist Member Of the Committee Of General Security," American Historical Review, LVII (1952), 871-892. Details of David's involvement in the Terror.

_____, "Jacobinism and the Fine Arts: The Revolutionary Careers Of Bouquier, Sergent and David," Art Quarterly, Autumn 1953, 195-214. illus. Effort to cast light on ways present-day painters reconcile art and politics by showing how painters in the French Revolution subordinated art to work of revolution. Important new evidence of David's activity as high police official and President of Jacobin Club during the Terror.

DRAPER, John W, "The Theme Of 'Timon Of Athens'," Modern Language Review, XXIX (1934), 20-31.

_____, The 'Hamlet' Of Shakespeare's Audience, Durham, N.C, 1938.

_____, The 'Twelfth Night' Of Shakespeare's Audience, Stanford, 1950.

_____, The 'Othello' Of Shakespeare's Audience, Paris, 1952.

DUBERMAN, Martin, "Presenting the Past," Columbia University Forum, Fall 1964, 16-20. Historian dramatist of 'In White America' describes historically informed theatre that will emphasize man's potential for improvement in contrast to despairing emphasis of much contemporary drama. Similar to Gorky's view. - See also Interview with Richard F. Shepard, N.Y. Times, Drama Section, Dec 15, 1963. illus.

DuBOIS, Guy Pene, "Art and the Decline Of the Bourgeoisie," Magazine of Art, Oct 1944, 218-223. Aristocratic and bourgeois modes of patronage.

DUNCAN, Hugh Dalziel, Language and Literature In Society, Chicago, 1953. Chiefly development of Kenneth Burke's ideas.

_____, "Sociology Of Art, Literature and Music: Social Contexts Of Symbolic Experience," in: Howard Becker and Alvin Boskoff, eds, Modern Sociological Theory In Continuity and Change, 1957, 482-497. In part a bibliographical essay on American academic sociologists of culture. Partly exposition of Burke's view of the arts as symbolic communication. Arts provide "ways of reducing status tensions" so social "divisiveness may be overcome through transcendent symbols of cohesion" imposed by social grouping represented by artist. American sociology's unhistorical view of society as a mechanism to be manipulated and adjusted appears here.

_____, Communication and Social Order, 1963.

DUNWELL, Wilfrid, The Evolution Of Twentieth-Century Harmony, London, 1960. Historical and technical account of developing use of dissonance.

_____, Music and the European Mind, London, 1962. A history deeply concerned with determinants of "the creative mind."

EBISCH, W, and L.L. Schucking, "The Sociology Of Literary Taste, London, 1944; rev. ed., Univ. of Chicago: 1967. - See obituary note on Schucking by Martin Lehnert, ZAA, 1965 #2, 174-177.

EELLS, Richard, The Corporation and The Arts, Columbia University Graduate School Of Business and Macmillan: 1967. Sees increased collaboration of artists, arts institutions and corporate management as fruitful for all parties.

EHRENBURG, Victor, The People Of Aristophanes; A Sociology Of Old Attic Comedy, 2nd ed, Harvard Univ: Cambridge, Mass, 1951; Schocken paperback, 1962. Athenian existence interpreted from Aristophanes. Comedy the most apt dramatic form for discerning reality of a people's life.

ENZER, Hyman, "Sociology and the Beaux Arts," Arts In Society, III iii (1965), 412-424. Survey of state of non-Marxist American sociology of culture.

ERIKSON, Erik H, "The Legend Of Maxim Gorky's Youth," in his: Childhood and Society, 1950; Norton paperback, 1963, 359-402. The Freudian-sociologist author of 'Young Man Luther' analyzes USSR film 'The Childhood Of Maxim'.

Sees a 'protestant' personality (the
Bolshevik intellectual) suited to al-
tering Russian backwardness and complementary to Western protestant type.
Also theory of mythical enactment of
national personality conflicts.

EVANS, Joan, Art In Medieval France,
987-1498; A Study In Patronage, London,
1948.  illus.  "My whole endeavor....
is to show that French medieval art
took the forms it did because of the
needs of the men who commissioned it."

FARNAM, Henry Walcott, Shakespeare's
Economics, New Haven, 1931.  An econ-
omist looks at the assumed, seldom
formulated views in the plays on production, exchange, distribution and
consumption of wealth.

FINLEY, Moses, The World Of Odysseus,
1954.  The 'Odyssey' in its society.

FOX, Daniel M, "Artists In the Modern
State: The Nineteenth Century Background," JAAC, Winter 1963, 135-147.
Developing liberality of patronage
bestowed on writers and painters.

FRANCASTEL, Pierre, "Technics and Aesthetics," JAAC, Mch 1953, 187-197.
Insists on compatibility of aesthetics
and the machine.

FRANCKE, Kuno, A History Of German Literature As Determined By Social
Forces, 4th ed, 1901.

FREYER, Grattan, "The Politics Of W.B.
Yeats," Politics and Letters, Summer
1947, 13-20.

_____, "The Little World Of J.M. Synge,"
Politics and Letters, Summer 1948,
5-12.  The search for community.

FRY, Roger, "Art and Socialism," in his
Vision and Design, 1924.  Socialism
as the likely future, and a better
situation for artists than under the
"plutocrats," though "I am not a
Socialist."

GEISMAR, Maxwell, Rebels and Ancestors:
The American Novel, 1890-1915, Boston,
1953.  Frank Norris, Stephen Crane,
Jack London, Ellen Glasgow, Theodore
Dreiser.

_____, The Last Of the Provincials: The
American Novel, 1915-1925, Boston,
1947; American Century paperback, 1959.

H.L. Mencken, Sinclair Lewis, Willa
Cather, Sherwood Anderson, F. Scott
Fitzgerald.

_____, Writers In Crisis: The American
Novel, 1925-1940, 1947; Hill & Wang
paperback, 1961.  Lardner, Hemingway,
Dos Passos, Faulkner, Wolfe, Steinbeck.

_____, American Moderns: From Rebellion
To Conformity, 1958; Hill & Wang paper-
back, 1958.  Hemingway, Dreiser, Dos
Passos, Wouk, Faulkner, Lewis, Wolfe,
Cozzens, Steinbeck, Marquand, Mailer,
Salinger, Algren, Bellow, Jones,
Styron, Griffen, Hersey.  General
speculations on American culture.

_____, Henry James and the Jacobites,
Houghton Mifflin: Boston, 1963.  Work-
by-work debunking of myth built around
James in climate of the 50s. - Review
by M. Folsom (LVI). - For protest
against Geismar's approach, see S.
Finkelstein, PA, May 1964, 53-55.
V.J. Jerome reviewed Geismar admiringly
in PA; Finkelstein remonstrates American 19th Century is not so rich in
literature that "we can afford to do
without James, or give him over to the
reactionaries;" James "put his finger
on the startling truth that all was
not well with the 'well-to-do'" earlier
than most others did; "James was deeply
concerned with a problem also of deep
concern to Marxists; that of human
freedom, of happiness, of the nature of
a liberated life" though his results
were mistaken. - Jerome answers, ibid,
55-58.

_____, "Liberalism's Nostalgic Poison,"
AmD, July-Aug 1964, 4-7.  Rakes literary establishment over the coals for
"a sterile and conformist social,
literary and critical code of values
and taste."  Disenchanted ex-radicals
have lost "their whole sense of history,
the future, and freedom."

_____, "American Literature and the Cold
War," AmD, Mch-Apr 1966, 3-6.  The
collapse of the hero in recent American
novels into "a one-dimensional man, or
a kind of wailing infant at base, who
is altogether isolated from history,
society and culture."  Mailer, Mary
McCarthy, Saul Bellow, Salinger, Updike,
Roth, Arthur Miller.

GOFFMAN, Erving, The Presentation Of Self
In Everyday Life, Sociology of behavior
as a conscious or unconscious symbol-

ization, with much use of theatrical terminology.

GOLDMAN, Emma, The Social Significance Of the Modern Drama, Boston, 1914. Flamboyant anarchist-feminist analyzes Ibsen, Shaw, Hauptmann and others with eye almost exclusively to their efficacy as social persuaders.

GOODMAN, Paul, The Structure Of Literature, 1934.

_____, Kafka's Prayer, 1947. An anarchist Kafka.

GORDON, Milton M, "'Kitty Foyle' and the Concept Of Class As Culture," American Journal Of Sociology, Nov 1947, 210-217. Effort to define social class through its literary representation.

GOTSHALK, D.W, Art and the Social Order, Chicago, 1947; Dover paperback, 1962, with a postscript calling for "a new revolutionary institutional order". A philosopher's stimulating study, always alert to roots and relations of art in society and very well written, but too systematic and too little historically oriented in analysis. Almost a Marxist in outlook, Gotshalk paradoxically discusses Marxist approach as crudely mechanistic, without a sense of psychology.

GREENWAY, John, American Folksongs Of Protest, University of Pennsylvania: Philadelphia, 1953.

_____, "Folk Songs As Socio-Historical Documents," Western Folklore, Jan 1960, 1-9.

GREGG, Kate L, "Thomas Dekker: A Study In Economic and Social Backgrounds," University of Washington Publications. Language and Literature, II ii (1924), 55-112.

GROSSE, Ernest, The Beginnings Of Art, 1897. In wake of Taine this book sets out to define a sociological "science of art" which will show "regular and fixed relations exist between certain forms of culture and art." Chiefly anthropological study of primitive art, music, dance, poetry, personal adornment and decoration. "The highest social function of primitive art consisted in unification." Some departures from Taine. - See Plekhanov (XLVI).

GUERARD, Albert Leon, Art For Art's Sake,

Boston, 1936; Schocken paperback, 1963. A central study. "Art for Art's Sake is born of the Philistine, exists only in terms of the Philistine, can be defined only by defining the Philistine." Yet art does have a "large measure of autonomy....Sociology brings us to the threshold of the esthetic problem: it does not enable us to penetrate therein." The disasters of history as group dramatization, a pursuit of the Beautiful over the Useful, True or Good; mass democratic education in the "conscious and disinterested enjoyment in self-expression" would put the "impure" art of past history behind us.

_____, Literature and Society, Boston, 1935. An uneven book, much on the defensive against a crude Marxism which does not recognize "a measure of autonomy" in the arts.

HALL, Donald, The Capitalist Imagery In Wordsworth's Poem "Daffodils". N.Y. Times Book Review, Oct 9, 1966, 2.

HALL, Vernon, Jr, Renaissance Literary Criticism: A Study Of Its Social Content, 1945. Class content in Italian, French and English Renaissance literary criticism.

_____, "Marxism and Literature," in his A Short History Of Literary Criticism, Gotham paperback: 1963, 141-146. Defends the aesthetics of Marx against vulgarizers.

HARBAGE, Alfred, Shakespeare's Audience, 1941.

HARRELL, Bill J, "The Emasculation of Self In Modern Art," Catalyst (Buffalo), Summer 1967, 74-95. Art's incompleteness where man is alienated by society from his own powers.

HARRIS, Neil, The Artist In American Society; The Formative Years, 1790-1860, Braziller: 1966.

HARRISON, John, The Reactionaries: A Study Of the Anti-Democratic Intelligentsia, Schocken: Chicago, 1967. Yeats, Pound, Eliot, D.H. Lawrence and Wyndham Lewis.

HARRISON, Sidney, Music For the Multitude, 1940. Emphasizes roots of music in songs of common people, especially prior to 18th Century.

HASKELL, Francis, Patrons and Painters:

A Study In the Relations Between Italian Art and Society In the Age Of the
Baroque, Knopf: 1963.

HASSAN, Ibab, Radical Innocence: Studies
In the Contemporary American Novel,
Princeton, N.J, 1961. - Review by
Emile Capouya, SOL, Winter 1963, 114-
122. - See also LeRoy (LVI).

HEAP, Jane, "Lost: A Renaissance," Little
Review, May 1929, 5-6.  In farewell
editorial, editor of magazine that
first introduced Joyce's 'Ulysses'
says: "'Ulysses' will have to be the
masterpiece of this time.  But it is
too personal, too tortured, too special a document to be a masterpiece in
the true sense of the word....Self-
expression is not enough; experiment
is not enough; the recording of special moments or cases is not enough.
All of the arts have broken faith or
lost connection with their origin and
function."

HEGEL, G.W.F, The Phenomenology Of Mind,
Macmillan: 1961.

HENNING, Edward B, "Patronage and Style
In the Arts: A Suggestion Concerning
Their Relations," JAAC, June 1960,
464-471.  Effort to supply modality
between class of patrons and artists'
creations.

HOELLERER, Walter, "The Cunning Of Language In the Face Of Violence," Wisconsin Studies In Contemporary Literature, Spring-Summer 1960, 49-65.
Social writing strategies for circum-
venting authoritarian language of mass
media and entrenched outlooks.  Brecht,
Celan, Enzensberger, Musil, Trakl.

HOGGART, Richard, The Uses Of Literacy,
London, 1957; Beacon paperback, 1961.
Working-class culture in England.

HOLZKNECHT, Karl J, Literary Patronage
In the Middle Ages, Ph.D. dissertation
Pennsylvania Univ: 1923.

HORTON, R.W, and V.F. Hopper, Backgrounds
Of European Literature: The Political,
Social, and Intellectual Development
Behind the Great Books Of Western
Civilization, 1954.

HOUSE, Humphrey, The Dickens World, London, 1941.  Confronts Dickens' writings with accounts of historical situation.

HOWE, Irving, Politics and the Novel,
Meridian paperback: 1957.  "Meant
primarily as a study of the relation
between literature and ideas....the
literary problem of what happens to
the novel when it is subjected to the
pressures of politics and political
ideology."  Essays on Stendhal, Dostoevsky, Conrad, Turgenev, Henry James,
Hawthorne, Henry Adams, Malraux,
Silone, Koestler, Orwell.

_____, A World More Attractive; A View
Of Modern Literature and Politics,
Horizon: 1963.  T.E. Lawrence, Edith
Wharton,James Baldwin, Norman Mailer,
Edmund Wilson, Whitman, Frost, Stevens,
Gissing, Celine, Aleichem, etc.

_____, SEE ALSO: Richard Kostelanetz,
"On Irving Howe: The Perils and
Paucities Of Democratic Radicalism," Salmagundi, Spring 1967,
44-60.

HUACO, George A, The Sociology Of Film
Art, Basic Books: 1965.

JACOBS, Norman, ed, Culture For the Millions?  Mass Media In Modern Society,
Van Nostrand: Princeton, 1961.

JAMES, Louis, Fiction For the Working
Man, 1830-1850, Oxford: London, 1964.
Valuable study of introduction of
sheets carrying radical politics,and
shortly escapist literature, at price
available to all.

JONES, Clifton R, "The Sociology Of
Symbols, Languages and Semantics," in:
Joseph S. Roucek, ed, Contemporary
Sociology, 1958, 453-489.

KAHN, Sholom J, Science and Aesthetic
Judgment; A Study In Taine's Critical
Method, Columbia Univ: 1953.

KALLEN, Horace, Art and Freedom; A Historical and Biographical Interpretation
Of the Relations Between the Ideas Of
Beauty, Use and Freedom in Western
Civilization From the Greeks To the
Present Day, 1942.  2 vols.  In effect
a liberal's attempt to deal with
problems made central by Marxists in
the 30s.

KAVOLIS, Vytautas, "Economic Correlates
Of Artistic Activity," American Journal
Of Sociology, Nov 1964, 332-341.

_____, "Economic Conditions and Art Styles,"

_JAAC_, Summer 1964, 437-441.

_____, "Art Content and Economic Reality," _The American Journal of Economics and Sociology_, July 1965, 321-328.

KELLETT, Ernest E, _The Whirligig Of Taste_, London, 1929.

_____, _Fashion In Literature; A Study Of Changing Taste_, London, 1931.

KENYON, Frederic G, _Books and Readers In Ancient Greece and Rome_, London, 1931.

KERNODLE, George R, "Renaissance Artists In the Service Of the People: Political Tableaux and Street Theatre In France, Flanders, and England," _The Art Bulletin_, Mch 1943, 59-64. illus.

KNIGHTS, L.C, _Drama and Society In the Age Of Jonson_, London, 1937. - Critically reviewed by Alick West, "Jonson Was No Sentimentalist," _LR_, Sept 1937, 468-475.

KOERNER, Daniel, "WPA Art Projects." Speech to 4th American Writers Congress (1941). [LAW]

KOHN-BRAMSTEDT, Ernst, _Aristocracy and the Middle-Classes In Germany: Social Types In German Literature, 1830-1900_, London, 1937; Reissued Chicago, 1964, rev. ed., under name of Ernest K. Bramsted. Introduction on the sociological approach to literature.

KOHT, Halvdan, _The Life Of Ibsen_, 1931. 2 vols. illus.

_____, _The American Spirit In Europe_, Philadelphia: 1949.

_____, _Driving Forces In History_, Harvard Univ: Cambridge, 1964.

KOLAJA, Jiri, And Robert N. Wilson, "The Theme Of Social Isolation In American Painting and Poetry," _JAAC_, XIII (1954), 37-45. Statistical analysis of content.

KOSTELANETZ, Richard, "Militant Minorities," _Hudson Review_, Autumn 1965, 472-480. Structural analysis of the origins and rise of literary cliques in America.

_____, "A Critical Look At the Critics," _Twentieth Century_, Spring 1966, 58-64. A similar look at Great Britain.

KRACAUER, Siegfried, _From Caligari To Hitler: A Psychological Study Of the German Film_, Princeton, 1947. Trailblazing study of cinema in relation to history of ideas.

_____, _Nature Of Film; The Redemption Of Physical Reality_, London, 1961. "My book differs from most others in the field in that it is a _materialist aesthetics_...."

KROEBER, A.L, _Configurations Of Cultural Growth_, Berkeley and Los Angeles, 1944. Inductively analyzes major civilizations for pattern of artistic development.

KROEF, Justus M. van der, "The Colonial Novel In Indonesia," _Comparative Literature_, Summer 1958, 215-231. Evolution from Calvinist metaphysics of Dutch traders through exotic phase to true, deep portrayal of Eurasian milieu.

KRYZHANOVSKY, Ivan I, _The Biological Bases Of the Evolution Of Music_, London, 1928. Conditioned reflexes as basis of musical taste. More Darwinian than Pavlovian, though author worked two years in Pavlov's laboratory. Also studied violin and musical theory at Kiev School of Music, was composition pupil of Rimsky-Korsakov, obliged to make his living in medicine.

LAMBERT, Constant, _Music Ho! A Study Of Music In Decline_, London: 1934. The attrition of tonality and emotion placed in historical perspective. Nationalism in music.

LARRABEE, Eric, and Rolf Meyersohn, eds, _Mass Leisure_, The Free Press: Glencoe, 1958.

LEICHTENTRITT, Hugo, _Music, History and Ideas_, Cambridge, 1938.

LENGYEL, Peter, "Society Calls the Tune," _Courier_, Nov 1962, 4-7, 10-13. illus. Brief sociology of dialectic of folk and 'learned' music from middle ages to jazz.

LERNER, Max, and Edwin Mims Jr, "Literature," _ESS_, IX (1933), 523-593.

LEVIN, Harry, _The Gates Of Horn; A Study Of Five French Realists_, Oxford: 1963; Galaxy paperback, 1966. Theory of

literature and society, literature
having semi-autonomous status as an
"institution". Stendhal, Balzac,
Flaubert, Zola, Proust.

LEVINE, Milton H, "Prehistoric Art and
Ideology," American Anthropologist,
Dec 1957, 949-964. Prolegomena to
method.

LEVI-STRAUSS, Claude, "Language and the
Analysis Of Social Laws," American
Anthropologist, Apr-June, 1951, 155-
163. Determining statistical options
and frequency rates in social life,
in part through cybernation.

_____, "The Structural Study Of Myth,"
Journal Of American Folklore, Oct-Dec
1955, 428-444. Demonstrates with
Oedipus myth the function of myth in
society as symbolic reconciliation of
deep-rooted contradictions in understanding.

_____, Message to 1st International Con-
ference of Negro Writers and Artists
(1956). IC(1), 393-394. "After the
aristocratic humanism of the Renaissance and the bourgeois humanism of
the XIX Century, your Congress announces the advent, in the finite
world which our planet has become, of
a democratic humanism, which will also
be the last."

_____, Tristes Tropiques, Criterion:
1961. illus. Four chapters of 1955
French edition omitted. Theory of
myth as the psychological equivalent
of unresolved social tension, which,
in turn, rises from arrangements of
sex, power, and productive forces.
States Norman Birnbaum: "He has given
us the most formidable of all recent
contributions to the study of ideology."

_____, "The Many Faces Of Man," World
Theatre, Spring 1961, 11-20. illus.
From 'L'Express', Dec 10, 1959. The
artistry of masks as mediation between
natural man and man's aspirations to
social status and fulfillment. "Masks
are no less indispensable to the group
than words. A society that believes
it has dispensed with masks can only
be a society in which masks, more
powerful than ever before, the better
to deceive men, will themselves be
masked."

_____, Structural Anthropology, 1963.

_____, Totemism, Merlin: London, 1964.
- Review by J. Lindsay, MT, July 1965,
217-220.

_____, Interview with George Steiner.
En, Apr 1966, 32-38. His relation to
Marxism.

_____, The Savage Mind, Univ. of Chicago:
1966. Argues the sophistication of
"primitive" thought. Polemic with
Sartre's notion of dialectical reason.

_____, See also: Edmund Leach,
"Claude Levi-Strauss,
Anthropologist and Philosopher,"
NLR, #34 (1965), 12-27. Sketch
and critique of his contribution.

LOFTIS, John, Comedy and Society From
Congreve To Fielding, Stanford, Calif:
1959. "I have sought to avoid 19th and
20th century conceptions of the nature
of social classes and of the relation-
ships between them, referring instead
to the large body of early 18th century
social commentary."

_____, The Politics Of Drama In Augustan
England, Oxford: 1963. Complementary
to above work.

LONDON, Kurt, Film Music, London, 1936.
- See also London (XLIX)

LOWENTHAL, Leo, Literature and the Image
Of Man: Sociological Studies Of the
European Drama and Novel, 1600-1900,
Boston, 1957. Feeds on Marxist writings
of greater intellectual rigor. Offers
some stimulus. Shakespeare and Cervantes to Goethe, Ibsen and Hamsun.

_____, Literature, Popular Culture, and
Society, Spectrum paperback: Englewood
Cliffs, N.J, 1961. Collected essays
including "Literature and Society."

MACKERNESS, E.D, A Social History Of
English Music, Routledge & Kegan Paul:
London, 1964. Medieval to modern.

MACY, John, The Spirit Of American Literature, 1913. Pioneering, mediocre
socialist study. - See Fraina (LVI).

MALINOWSKI, B, A Scientific Theory Of
Culture, Chapel Hill, 1944.

MANNHEIM, Karl, Ideology and Utopia, 1936;
Harvest paperback, 1957? Mannheim was
close student of Marx in youth. For
essay emphasizing book's possibilities

for study of literature, see: Alexander Kern, "The Sociology Of Knowledge In the Study Of Literature," Sewanee Review, Oct-Dec 1942, 505-514.

_____, Review of George Lukacs' 'Theorie des Romans'. SOL, Summer 1963, 50-53. Early essay indicates importance Mannheim believes his pursuits hold for arts. Suggest how well and what way Lukacs is performing the needed work.

MARX, Leo, The Machine In the Garden; Technology and the Pastoral Ideal In America, Oxford: 1964. The shaping of "our American fables" under the impact of capitalist development.

MATTHEWS, Brander, "The Economic Interpretation Of Literary History," in his: Gateways To Literature, 1912.

MATTHIESSEN, F.O, "A Teacher Takes His Stand," Harvard Progressive, Sept 1940, 12-14. [Harvard] As President of Harvard Teachers Union he declares: "The Union has helped me learn that there is no good thinking divorced from a social context; it has increased my understanding of the word that meant so much to Walt Whitman - solidarity." Describes commitment as a literary critic.

_____, The Achievement Of T.S. Eliot, 1935; Galaxy paperback, 1959. 3rd ed. With chapter on Eliot's later work by C.L. Barber.

_____, American Renaissance: Art and Expression In the Age Of Emerson and Whitman, 1941. Outstanding study of American literary development. With discussion of myth in literature.

_____, Henry James: The Major Phase, 1944.

_____, From the Heart Of Europe, 1948. Observations while travelling in Eastern Europe and teaching in Prague.

_____, Theodore Dreiser, 1951; Delta paperback: 1966.

_____, The Responsibilities Of the Critic; Essays and Reviews, 1952. Title essay insists on "the primacy of economic factors in society" and the "immense value" of principles of Marxism in "helping us to see and comprehend our literature."

_____, "Marxism and Literature," MR, Mch 1953, 398-400. "I am a Christian, and consequently, although a socialist, I have never been a Marxist in any sense. But as a student primarily of literature and cultural history, my debt to Marxism-Leninism has been great and inescapable."

_____, SEE ALSO: F.O. Matthiessen: A Collective Portrait, MR, Oct 1950, Special Issue. illus. With bibliography (concluded in MR, Sept 1952, 174-175.) Subsequently issued as book by Schuman: 1950. Contributors include Harry Levin, Leo Marx, Bernard Bowren, Henry Nash Smith, Paul Sweezy, Alfred Kazin, Ernest J. Simmons, Rufus W. Mathewson, Jr, Richard Wilbur.

McALLESTER, D.P, Enemy Way Music: A Study Of Social and Esthetic Values As Seen In Navaho Music, Cambridge, 1954.

McCAUSLAND, Elizabeth, "The Effect Of the Art Market On Freedom Of Expression." Speech to 4th American Writers Congress (1941). [LAW] Detailed report on policies of institutions buying art from American artists. McCausland authored several such studies.

MEAD, Margaret, "Art and Reality," College Art Journal, May 1943. Impoverishment of social life when society designates special persons to be 'artists'.

_____, "Work, Leisure and Creativity," Daedalus, Winter 1960, 13-23. Profound comments from author's anthropological experience on evolving use of leisure for aesthetic activities.

MERRILL, Francis E, "Stendhal and the Self; A Study In the Sociology Of Literature," American Journal Of Sociology, LXVI (1960-61), 446-458.

MILLS, C. Wright, "The Cultural Apparatus," in his: Power, Politics and People; The Collected Essays, Ballantine paperback: 1963, 405-422. Involvement of "cultural workman" like it or not in politics and institutions of his time. Three-stage theory of patronage.

_____, "Man In the Middle: The Designer," ibid, 374-386. The "cultural workman" product designer and displayer necessary in economy that needs "status obsolescence" - continual replacement of form of goods according to contrived fashions.

Contrasted with ideal of autonomous craft work.

MITCHELLS, K, "The Work Of Art In Its Social Setting and In Its Aesthetic Isolation," JAAC, Summer 1967, 369-374. Sees a complementary necessity of both methodologies.

MOHOLY-NAGY, L, Vision In Motion, Paul Theobald: Chicago, 1947. Treats USSR with seriousness but stresses usefulness of an avant-garde: "a wise policy should have supported experiments."

MORDELL, Albert, "The Economic Background Of Literature," Panorama, Jan 1934, 3. "A book of significance is as much an industrial product as a massacre or a war." Crude economicism combined with anti-Marxism.

MUELLER, John H, "The Folkway Of Art: An Analysis Of the Social Theories Of Art," American Journal Of Sociology, Sept 1938, 222-238.

_____ and K. Hevner, Trends In Musical Taste, Bloomington, 1942.

MUKERJEE, Radhakamal, The Social Function Of Art, Philosophical Library: 1954. Foreword by Herbert Read. illus. Brilliant sociology by self-professed mystic who is friend of USSR and draws heavily on Freud.

MULLER-LYER, The History Of Social Development, London, 1920.

MULLIGAN, Raymond A, and Jane C. Dinkins, "Socioeconomic Background and Theatrical Preference," Sociology and Social Research, May-June 1956, 325-328. Interview and statistical approach.

MUMFORD, Lewis, The Culture Of Cities, 1938. The city in history.

_____, Art and Technics, 1952.

_____, The City In History, 1961.

_____, SEE ALSO: Michael Gold, DW, Feb 18, 1935, 5. Tells of youthful discussions. "Lewis Mumford wanted a socialist world as much as I did, but he couldn't be convinced it took the working class to bring it in....He thinks you can build a house with only the architect." Also

quotes letter from Mumford explaining conception of his role: "I cannot swallow Marx or Lenin whole....and I think I am of service in reaching the engineers and technicians and administrators and scholars and scientists." See also Schapiro (LII).

MUNRO, Thomas, Evolution In the Arts, Cleveland: 1963. Cause and structure in aesthetic change, with serious attention to the role of a philosophy of history and to Marxism, in context of a "multiple dialectic". - Also see Munro (LIX).

MYERS, Bernard S, Modern Art In the Making, 1950. Relates changes in style to developing alienation of artists from society.

NASH, Dennison J, "The Socialization Of an Artist: The American Composer," Social Forces, XXXV, 307-313.

NEEDHAM, H.A, Taste and Criticism In the Eighteenth Century; A Selection Of Texts Illustrating the Evolution Of Taste and the Development Of Critical Theory, London, 1952.

NELSON, Truman, "Thoreau and the Paralysis Of Individualism," Ramparts, Mch 1966, 16-26. The trial of John Brown as pushing Thoreau's courage and awareness to their limits. - See also Lynd (LVI).

NICOLSON, Benedict, "The Anarchism Of Camille Pissarro," Arts, 1947 #2, 43-51.

ORWELL, George, Collected Essays, Secker & Warburg: London, 1961. Essays on Dickens, Henry Miller, Marxism and the writer, H.G. Wells, Yeats, Swift, Tolstoy, etc.

PALMER, John, Political and Comic Characters Of Shakespeare, 1962.

PARKES, Henry Bamford, The American Experience: An Interpretation Of the History and Civilization Of the American People, 1947. - See LeRoy (LVI).

_____, "Poe, Hawthorne, Melville: An Essay In Sociological Criticism," PR, Feb 1949, 157-165. Slight.

PARRINGTON, Vernon L, Main Currents In American Thought, 1927, 1930; Harcourt, Brace: 1958. Parrington once said of his outlook, "I was a good deal of a Marxian." - See G. Hicks, "The Critical Principles Of V.L. Parrington," S&S, Fall 1939, 443-460. - See also V. Parrington, Jr, "Vernon Parrington's View: Economics and Criticism," Pacific Northwest Review, XLIV (July 1953), 97-105. Also: Lawson (LVI), Trilling (LIX). - See also Mikhail Landor on the Russian translation of Parrington and an appraisal, SL, 1964 #9, 183-185.

PETERSON, Richard A, "Artistic Creativity and Alienation: The Jazz Musician vs. His Audience," Arts In Society, III ii (1965), 244-248. Many instances.

PETTET, E.C, "'The Merchant Of Venice' and the Problem Of Usury," The English Association - Essays and Studies, XXXI (1946), 19-33.

PIEPER, Josef, Leisure the Basis Of Culture, Pantheon: 1964.

PITTMANN, David J, "The Sociology Of Art," in: Joseph B. Gittler, ed, Revolution of Sociology, 1957, 559-563.

PLESSNER, K, "Sociological Observations On Modern Painting," Social Research, XXIX (1962), 190-200. General remarks on relating de-personalization and de-objectivism in a world of change and growing secularism. By the former rector at Gottingen.

PRIESTLEY, J.B, The Arts Under Socialism, London, 1947. Speech to Fabian Society. How government should relate itself in future and at present to artists.

_____, Literature and Western Man, London, 1960.

RADER, Melvin, No Compromise; The Conflict Between Two Worlds, 1939. The threat of Fascism as the failure to achieve Henry Adams' "new social mind". The anti-human aesthetic glitter of Fascism.

_____, Introduction to his: A Modern Book Of Aesthetics; An Anthology, 1935, xi-xxxv. "The new esthetic must reinterpret the function of art in the light of the collectivistic order that is arising. To institute the right social conditions, the opponents of capitalism must present, in addition to indispensable material demands, a spiritual program." Thus art must not be regarded as imitative

of life, but as expressive of values; most aestheticians so regard it. "When our machines are finally made tools of the whole community, people must be set free to play, to think, to love, and to make beautiful things." In this sense, "esthetics becomes the indispensable aide of social engineering."

_____, "Marx's Interpretation Of Art and Aesthetic Value," BJA, July 1967, 237-249. Demonstrates the profound aesthetic dimension of Marx's philosophy; "the goal of advanced communism is fundamentally aesthetic." Finds the notion of base/superstructure in Marx flawed; and the work of many Marxists is beneath that of Marx.

REITLINGER, Gerald, The Economics Of Taste, Barrie & Rockliff: London, 1961.

REXROTH, Kenneth, "Unacknowledged Legislators and Art pour Art," in his: Bird In the Bush, New Directions paperback: 1959. Rexroth, knowledgeable on Marxism, discusses kinds of communication poetry can provide.

_____, "The Institutionalization Of Revolt, The Domestication Of Dissent," Arts In Society, II iii (1963), 114-123. Protest literature in Western society one of "essential parts of the motive organization of capitalism;" writers are assimilated by process of "de-provincialization." Disarmed by finding the haute bourgeoisie appreciates their values which they found had only isolated them in Midwest natal communities, they are "inducted into the ranks of the civilized."

_____, SEE ALSO: Aaron (LIX).

ROCKEFELLER FOUNDATION, The Performing Arts; Problems and Prospects, McGraw-Hill: 1965. Key friendly study of massive support and guidance of arts by private foundations supported by corporations.

ROSENBERG, B, and D.M. White, eds, Mass Culture: The Popular Arts In America, Free Press: Glencoe, 1957. Valuable anthology.

ROTHA, Paul, Documentary Film; The Use Of the Film Medium To Interpret Creatively and In Social Terms the Life Of the People As It Exists In Reality, London: 1939.

ROUTH, Harold Victor, God, Man, and Epic

Poetry; A Study In Comparative Literature, Cambridge, 1927. 2 vols. Major
epics in historical context. Connects
themes and style to varying social conditions.

_____, English Literature and Ideas In
the 20th Century; An Inquiry Into
Present Difficulties and Future Prospects, London, 1950.

RUBINSTEIN, Nicolas, "Political Ideas In
Sienese Art: The Frescoes By Ambrogio
Lorenzetti and Taddeo di Bartolo In
the Palazzo Publico," London University,
Warburg Institute Journal, XXI (1958),
179-207. illus.

RULAND, Richard, The Rediscovery Of American Literature, Harvard Univ: Cambridge, 1967, 186-286. From Parrington, and the "naive" Marxists Calverton and Hicks, and a deepening experience of New Criticism, to a culmin-
ating integration, by F.O. Matthiessen, of the study of aesthetic values
in their cultural context. "Marx has
been assimilated."

RUSH, Richard H, Art As an Investment,
Prentice-Hall: Englewood Cliffs, N.J,
1961. A businessman's view.

RUSKIN, John, The Stones Of Venice, in
his Works, London, 1902-12, v. 20.
Intensive analysis of the historicity
and material determinants of architecture.

_____, SEE ALSO; Amabel Williams Ellis,
The Tragedy Of John Ruskin,
London: 1929. - Review by T.A.
Jackson, SW, Mch 17, 1929, 8.

SACHS, Curt, The Rise Of Music In the
Ancient World, East and West, 1943.

SALOMON, Albert, "Sociology and the
Literary Artist," in: Stanley Romaine
Hopper, ed, Spiritual Problems In
Contemporary Literature, 1957, 15-24.

SANCTIS, Francesco de, The History Of
Italian Literature, 1932. First published 1870. Reprinted by Harcourt,
Brace: 1959. The great historicist
19th Century study.

SCHECHNER, Richard, "Ford, Rockefeller,
and Theatre," TDR, Fall 1965, 23-49.
Documents the social results of Foundation support for the theatre:
museumish productions, continued alien-

ation for the artists, and middle-
class audiences and values. Suggests
means for the Foundations to enrich
theatre, reach audiences of the poor
and disaffiliated - if they chose.

SCHORER, Mark, William Blake: The
Politics Of Vision, 1946.

SCHUESSLER, K.F, "Social Background and
Musical Taste," American Sociological
Review, XIII, 330-335.

SCOTT, Wilbur, "The Sociological Approach:
Literature and Social Ideas," in his
Five Approaches Of Literary Criticism,
Collier paperback: 1962, 123-126.
Deems Marxist criticism an "aberration"
from the validity of a sociological
criticism.

SELTMAN, Charles, "Art and Society,"
Studio, Apr 1953, 98-114. illus.
Art in tension between humanist liberty
and priestly elites at points of history.

SIMONS, A.M, The Economic Foundation Of
Art, Chicago, n.d. [not seen]

SLOAN, John, The Gist Of Art, 1939. The
Ashcan School's leading exponent - and
only Socialist - describes his principles and painterly practice.

SMITH, Henry Nash, Virgin Land; The American West As Symbol and Myth, Cambridge,
Mass., 1950; Vintage paperback, 1957.
18th Century ideologues; Wild West
heroes; popular and literary heroes of
the myth. - See LeRoy (LVI).

SMITH, L, The Economic Laws Of Art Production, London, 1924.

SMITH, Marian W, ed, The Artist In Tribal
Society, 1961.

SONTAG, Susan, "The Literary Criticism
Of Georg Lukacs," in her Against Interpretation, Farrar, Straus & Giroux:
1966, 82-92. A critique also of Adorno,
Benjamin, Marcuse, Sartre, Goldmann.
Finds a certain blindness to problems
of quality and autonomy of form and a
failure to come to terms with the
nature of modernism.

_____, "Against Interpretation," Evergreen
Review, Dec 1964, 76-80, 93, and in the
above. Warns search for 'latent content' beneath an artwork's 'manifest
content' (which includes its form) has
become a vice in our time. "Interpre-

pretation is not (as most people assume) an absolute value, a gesture of mind situated in some timeless realm of capabilities. Interpretation must itself be evaluated, within a historical view of human consciousness" to see whether at a given juncture it is a liberating or stifling act.

SOROKIN, Pitirim, Fluctuations Of Forms Of Art, vol. I of Social and Cultural Dynamics, 1937.

STAEL-HOLSTEIN, Mme de, The Influence Of Literature Upon Society, Hartford,1844.

STEPHEN, Leslie, English Literature and Society In the XVIIIth Century, London, 1904.

STIRLING, Brents, The Populace In Shakespeare, 1949. 'Julius Caesar', 'Coriolanus', the Cade scenes as "conservative satire" on revolting masses.

SWADOS, Harvey, A Radical's America, 1962. Journalism concerning recent novels, plays, etc.

SWETER, A.C, "The Possibilities Of a Sociology Of Art," The Sociological Review, Oct 1935, 441-453.

TAINE, Hippolyte, Philosophy Of Art,1873.

_____, History Of English Literature, 1879.

_____, SEE ALSO: Morawski (XXXVI);Trotsky (XLVI); Clark, Grosse, Kahn, Wilson (LXII); and Rene Wellek, "Hippolyte Taine's Literary Theory and Criticism," Criticism, I, 1-19.

TAWNEY, R.H, Social History and Literature, Leicester Univ: 1958. rev ed. Reprinted in his: The Radical Tradition, Pantheon: 1964. abdgd. Relations of society and literature, especially in Elizabethan England.

TAYLOR, Francis Henry, "The Archaic Smile: A Commentary On the Arts In Time Of Crisis," Metropolitan Museum Of Art Bulletin, New Series, Apr 1952, 217-232. illus. Director of the Metropolitan traces historical conditions where human form has been sculpted bearing a secret, inward-turned smile. Concludes the smile betokens inner sense for hierarchy, order, serenity amid violence - a

perspective lacking in Roman naturalistic sculpture-portraiture, for instance. Finds in our time a suitable equivalent in art for art's sake position.

TEMPLIN, Ernest H, The Social Approach To Literature, Berkeley, 1944. 24 pp. Wholly incompetent but symptomatic of a post-30s Liberal's confusion.

TOFFLER, Alvin, The Culture Consumers; Art and Affluence In America, 1964; Penguin paperback: Baltimore, 1965. Optimistic view of the "cultural explosion". "The artist is now going to be integrated into American society to a degree unprecedented in the past century....What is good for General Motors may conceivably be good for art."

TOMARS, Adolph S, Introduction To the Sociology Of Art, Mexico City, 1940. Based on sociology of R.M. MacIver. Ponderous but possibly suggestive. Views Marxism as "inadequate from the standpoint of modern sociology."

_____, "The Citizen In the Roles Of Producer and Consumer Of Art," Arts In Society, III i (1964), 45-55. Culture in a leisure economy.

TRILLING, Lionel, The Liberal Imagination; Essays On Literature and Society, 1950; Doubleday Anchor paperback, 1953. Articulate statement of leading Liberal's position. See "Art and Neurosis," which rejects successfully the Freudian determinists; "Art and Fortune," which acknowledges situation of the contemporary novelist in America.

TURNELL, Martin, "The Writer and Social Strategy," PR, Mch-Apr 1951, 167-182. Writers must form own 'party' against "the party which constitutes the greatest threat to his independence" whatever it may be. Traces French writing starting with Moliere to locate Baudelaire as fount of this outlook.

TYNAN, Kenneth, Curtains, Atheneum: 1961. Recent theatre in US, USSR, Britain, Germany, France.

VALLENTINER, Wilhelm Reinhold, Jacques Louis David and the French Revolution, 1929. [DLC] illus. Sees classicist style as means of detachment or refuge sought by artists embroiled in everyday upheaval and cruelties; while a Delacroix, who exercises horrific naturalism, is man of imagination in time of relative social repose.

VEBLEN, Thorstein, <u>Theory Of the Leisure Class</u>, 1899. Theory of 'conspicuous consumption' is important in class analysis of culture.

_____, The <u>Instinct Of Workmanship and the State Of the Industrial Arts</u>, 1914.

WATT, Ian, <u>The Rise Of the Novel: Studies In Defoe, Richardson and Fielding</u>, London, 1957.

WAY, Brian, "Sex and Language; Obscene Words In D.H. Lawrence and Henry Miller," <u>NLR</u>, Sept-Oct 1964, 66-80. Masterly analysis of varieties of obscene use of fiction and Miller's pioneering value enlarging "our consciousness of life."

WEBER, Max, <u>The Rational and Social Foundations Of Music,</u> Southern Illinois Univ: 1958. Written about 1911. Published 1921. Premise: peculiarity of Western music is unusual development of rational structures corresponding to rationalizing of modes of production and distribution. Relation of harmony to melody; Western and other scale systems; solutions to polyvocality and polysonority in musical schemes; role of instruments as vehicles of musical rationalization.

WELTFISH, Gene, <u>The Origins Of Art</u>, 1953. An anthropologist on the unity of aesthetic and manufacturing activity among pre-industrial peoples; the relation of design and naturalistic motifs.

WHITE, Harrison C. and Cynthia A, <u>Canvases and Careers; Institutional Changes In the French Painting World</u>, John Wiley: 1965. illus. The shift from governmental to private patronage of 19th century painting. - Review by S. Finkelstein, <u>S&S</u>, Spring 1966, 238-241.

WILLIAMS, Raymond, <u>Culture and Society, 1780-1950</u>, 1958; Doubleday Anchor paperback, 1959. Traces development of the ideas of industry, democracy, class, art, culture, in English culture.

_____, <u>The Long Revolution</u>, Chatto & Windus: 1961. The creative mind, the analysis of culture, individuals and societies, images of society, educa-

tion and British society, growth of the reading public, growth of the popular press, growth of 'standard English', the social history of English writers, the social history of English dramatic forms, realism and the contemporary novel, England in the 60s. - Review by Arnold Kettle, <u>MT</u>, Oct 1961, 301-307. - Review by Dwight MacDonald, <u>En</u>, June 1961, 79-84. Finds Williams a muddled preacher of unexamined, impossible Guild Socialism.

_____, <u>Modern Tragedy</u>, Stanford: Palo Alto, 1966.

_____, "T.S. Eliot On Culture," <u>Essays In Criticism</u>, July 1956, 302-318.

_____, "Soviet Literary Controversy In Retrospect," <u>Politics and Letters,</u> Summer 1947, 21-31. Relation of ideology to successful writing.

_____, "Prelude To Alienation," <u>Dis</u>, Summer 1964, 303-315. Analysis of Blake, Wordsworth, Carlyle, as they early grasped the results of industrial capitalism.

_____, "Culture Is Ordinary," in: Norman MacKenzie, ed, <u>Conviction</u>, London: 1958, 74-92. Critique of Marxism on culture. Prospectus for working-class culture.

WILSON, Robert N, <u>The American Poet; A Role Investigation</u>, Ph.D. dissertation, Harvard Univ: 1952. With much "objective" interview procedure Wilson concludes poet is alienated from neglectful society.

_____, <u>Man Made Plain</u>, Cleveland: 1958. Reflections on poetry and society, based in part on interviews with American poets, and said to stem from sociology of T. Parsons. Ezra Pound.

WITTKOWER, Rudolf and Margot, <u>Born Under Saturn. The Character and Conduct Of Artists: A Documented History From Antiquity To the French Revolution</u>, Weidenfeld & Nicolson: London, 1963. Documentation primarily of "image" in contemporary accounts of "alienated" artist prior to bourgeois epoch.

WOLLHEIM, Richard, <u>Socialism and Culture</u>, Fabian Tract, London, 1961.

WOODCOCK, George, "Culture and Society In the Restoration Period," <u>Now</u> (London),

I (1943), 55-62. Theory of culture as flourishing where authority is in dissolution. Leading anarchist view.

_____, The Writer and Politics, London: 1948. Essays on political myth, Proudhon, Herzen, Kropotkin, Orwell, G. Greene, Silone, Koestler, Kafka, Rex Warner.

'WORLD THEATRE' SPECIAL ISSUES ON REALISM, World Theatre, Jan-Feb & Mch-Apr, 1965. With statements on realism by numerous Marxists and non-Marxists.

WRIGHT, Louis B, Middle Class Culture In Elizabethan England, Chapel Hill, 1935.

## LXIII.  Artists

(Some Views By Non-Marxist Artists Concerning the Relation of Art and Society.)

ANDERSON, Sherwood, "A Writer's Notes," NM, Aug 1932, 10. "If it be necessary, in order to bring about the end of a money civilization and set up something new, healthy and strong, we of the so-called artist class have to be submerged, let us be submerged. Down with us. A little poverty and shaking down won't hurt us."

ARDEN, John, Interview with Ira Peck. N.Y. Times, Drama Section, Apr 10, 1966, 1, 3. Social protest in his work.

ARTAUD, Antonin, "Van Gogh the Man Suicided By Society," Tiger's Eye, #7 (1949), 93-115. Nightmaristic yet strangely concrete analysis of artist as a being destroyed by society he pushes too hard. - See also Virmaux (XIX).

BARTOK, Bela, Hungarian Folk Music, London, 1931.

_____, Interview with Dasider Kosztolanyi. Living Age, Aug 1931, 565-568. Difficulties of getting peasants to sing for him. Relation of music to the emotions.

_____, "Hungarian Peasant Music," Musical Quarterly, July 1932, 267-287.

_____, "Race Purity In Music," ModM, XIX v, 153-155.

_____, Interview with Elie Siegmeister. DW, June 27, 1940, 7. Researching folk music.

_____, "The Influence Of Peasant Music On Modern Music," Tempo, Winter 1949-50, 19-24.

_____, SEE ALSO: Bibliography, Tempo, Winter 1949-50, 39-47. - Sidney Finkelstein (LVII).

BAUDELAIRE, Charles, Baudelaire As a Literary Critic, Pennsylvania State Univ: 1964. Baudelaire's somewhat ambiguous attachment to the poor and socialism, distaste for l'art pour l'art, shown in essays on socialist poet Pierre Dumont, the drama of Emile Augier, and Neo-Classicism: pp. 51-77.

BECK, Julian, "Revolutionary Imperatives Of the H-Bomb World," Liberation, May 1963, 16-19.

_____, Judith Malina, Gordon Rogoff, Richard Schechner, Lee Baxandall and Norman Fruchter, "Symposium: The New Repertories and Revolutionary Theatre," SOL, Spring 1964, 39-62. Theatre in the South, the Living Theatre's approach and difficulties, combining aesthetic and social radicalism.

_____, and Judith Malina, Commentaries to: Kenneth H. Brown, The Brig, Hill & Wang paperback: 1965. Development of their Living Theatre. Analysis of 'The Brig'. Debts to Meyerhold, Piscator, Artaud. Says Beck: "Artaud's mistake was that he imagined you could create a horror out of the fantastic. Brown's gleaming discovery is that horror is not in what we imagine but in what is real."

_____, "Living Dangerously?" N.Y. Times, Theatre Section, Nov 7, 1965. Report and interview from exile in Europe.

'CAHIERS D' ART' QUESTIONNAIRE on the Artist and the Class Struggle (1938). Transition 49, #5 (1949), 110-116. Responses from Braque, Laurens, Leger, Matisse, Masson, Miro.

COLMAN, Ornette, Interview with Charlie L. Russell. Liberator, July 1965, 12-15.

CORBUSIER, Le, "The Quarrel With Realism," in: J.L. Martin, Circle, London, 1937, 67-74. Corbusier's contribution to

'Painting and Reality' symposium at Maison de Culture with participation of Aragon and Leger.  Corbusier calls his architecture misunderstood.  "We have never had the opportunity to create anything....When harmony will have attained sufficient dimensions, the emotions of the people, of the masses, will be stirred.  And as Leger said, in very welcome, very optimistic words, at that moment the people will not be wrong.  They will say: 'It is well.'"

DEWEY, Ken, "Act Of San Francisco At Edinburgh," Encore, Nov-Dec 1963, 12-16.  Theory of Action Theatre.

DREISER, Theodore, Letter to Wm. Z. Foster Asking Communist Party Membership. Main, Spring 1947, 225-227.  See also his comments in IL, 1934 #3, 80-82.

DURRENMATT, Friedrich, "Problems Of the Theatre," TDR, Oct 1958, 3-26.  How depict the present social complexities on stage? - See Brecht (XXI) for an answer to this essay.

FEUCHTWANGER, Lion, Interview With C.H. David.  SW, Dec 4, 1927, 8.  The historical novel as an appropriate form for writers equivocal about their present-day commitment, as in his own case. - See also Lukacs (XXVII).

GINSBERG, Allen, "Back To the Wall," Times Literary Supplement, Aug 6, 1964, 678-679.  Protecting sensibility and poetry and fighting the apathy and aggressions of the cold war.

_____, "It's War On All Fronts," on record-jacket of The Fugs, ESP-DISK 1028.  The liberating breakthrough of anarchist poets in pop music.

GINSBURG, Louis, "Unacknowledged Legislators," Contemporary Vision, I i (Winter 1929-30), 12-14.  Allen Ginsberg's father judges it right for poets to protest injustice - but "the best art, the most effective art does not have a moral but is moral....dissolves the lesson in the art product."

GENET, Jean, "A Note On Theatre," TDR, Spring 1963, 37-41.  His function in bourgeois society.

GOLDWATER, Robert, Artists On Art; From the XIV To the XX Century, 1945.  Especially Goya, David, Courbet, Blake,

Picasso, Zadkine, Rivera, Orozco.

GROPIUS, Walter, "The Necessity Of the Artist In a Democratic Society," Arts and Architecture, Dec 1955, 16-17.

HEINE, Heinrich, Poetry and Prose, ed Frederic Ewen, 1948.

HEMINGWAY, Ernest, "Fascism Is a Lie," NM, June 22, 1937, 4; also in WCW, 69-73.  Speech to 2nd American Writers Congress on the Spanish Civil War and the writer.

_____, Letters to Ivan Kashkeen and Konstantin Simonov.  SL, 1962 #11, 158-167.  Comments by Kashkeen and Simonov. States aversion for all politics and government.  To Kashkeen: "I do not give a damn whether any U.S.A. critic knows what I think because I have no respect for them.  But I respect you ....the best and most useful, to me, critique on my stuff I ever read." - See Kashkeen (XLVI).

_____, Letters to Milton Wolff.  AmD, Oct-Nov 1964, 10-13.  Comments by Wolff, who was commander of Abraham Lincoln Battalion in Spain.  Hemingway's attitude to Communists who fought Franco, who criticized 'For Whom the Bell Tolls' and were brought up before investigating committees.

KAPROW, Allan, "The Principles Of Modern Art," It Is, #4 (Autumn 1959), 51-52. "The everyday world is the most astonishing inspiration conceivable.  A walk down 14th Street is more amazing than any masterpiece of art.  If reality makes any sense at all, it is here.... We insist on a fully conscious critical awareness of all that is going on and on the necessity for making a stand, and choice, at last, among all possible actions."

KILLENS, John O, Interview with Alvin Simon.  AmD, Oct-Nov 1964, 30-32.  Role of Negro artist in discerning real American history: "He knows best the worst aspects of this society."

KOLLWITZ, Kathe, Interview with Agnes Smedley.  Industrial Pioneer, Sept 1925, 4-9.  illus.  Her motivations.

_____, The Diary and Letters Of Kathe Kollwitz, ed Hans Kollwitz, Chicago, 1955.  illus.

_____, SEE ALSO: Otto Nagel on Kollwitz, C&L, 1963 #11, 36-37. illus. - Also Hogarth (XXIII); Baskin (LIII).

KUPFERBERG, Tuli, "A Simple Statement On the War," The East Village Other, Mch 15-Apr 1 1966, 2. A Reichian analysis of American aggression by the anarchist poet and founder of The Fugs.

LEBRUN, Rico, Interview. In: Seldon Rodman, Conversations With Artists, 1957, 31-41.

LEIBOWITZ, Rene, "Arnold Schoenberg's 'Survivor From Warsaw' Or the Possibility Of a 'Committed' Art," Horizon (London), #116 (Aug 1949), 122-131. The work has an account of the Warsaw Ghetto as its text. Leibowitz argues that while "an artist can only be fully useful" to society by "the masterful using of purely artistic means" without regard for outside directives, yet a really great work of art "can, if inspired by social realities, become a valid expression of, and a real tribute to these realities." - See also Sartre (XIX).

LEINSDORF, Erich, Interview with Murray Chase. DW, Oct 5, 1946, 11. illus. "An intelligent musician must have social and political opinions today. Too often, however, the expression of such opinions may cost him his job."

'LES LETTRES FRANCAISES' QUESTIONNAIRE on Art and the Public (1946). Transition 49, #5 (1949), 117-125. Responses from Braque, Masson, Matisse, Lapicque, Dubuffet, Jean-Richard Bloch, Villon, Francis Gruber, Marc Saint-Saens, Jean Lurcat, Andre Fougeron.

LIND, Jakov, Interview With Ross Wetzsteon. Village Voice, Apr 7, 1966, 6, 21-22, 34. His life and function of his writing. Defense of fantastic writing as realism.

LORCA, Federico Garcia, "A Talk About the Theatre," in: Haskell M. Block, ed, The Creative Vision, Evergreen paperback: 1960, 131-134. Writes as "a passionate admirer of the theatre of social action."

MADDOX, Jerry, "Style and Tradition," NUT, Summer 1963, 28-37. illus. Young painter who moved from social realist to abstract forms tells how he relates to art tradition.

MAILER, Norman, "A Credo For the Living," NG, I i (Oct 18, 1948), 10. illus. "I suppose that politically I am an ignorant Marxist....I cannot in all honesty call myself a Marxist when I have read so few of the basic works of Marxist theory....I feel myself to the left of the Progressive Party and to the right of the Communist Party."

MARX, Groucho, Interview with Emanuel Eisenberg. DW, May 23, 1934, 5. Reveals deep social concern.

MILLER, Arthur, Interview with Beth Mc-Henry. DW, Apr 17, 1946, 13. The social disease of anti-Semitism. The writer and the people.

_____, Harold Rosenberg, Lionel Abel, Paul Goodman, "Art and Commitment: A Symposium," ASP, Winter 1960, 5-10.

_____, "The Playwright and the Atomic World," TDR, June 1961, 3-20.

MOORE, Henry, "Sculptor In Modern Society," Art News, Nov 1952, 24-25, 64-65.

OCHS, Phil, The Hope Of Topical Folksongs. Elektra EKL-287 recording, jacket notes.

O'NEAL, John, "A Freedom Theatre In the South," AmD, July-Aug 1964, 27-29; also "Freedom Takes the Stage," AmD, Oct-Nov 1964, 27-29. - See also Stephanie Harrington, "Free Southern Theatre: Speech For the Speechless," Village Voice, Feb 11, 1965, 1, 17-18. illus. Interview and report.

_____, Gilbert Moses, Denise Nicholas, Murray Levy, and Richard Schechner, "Dialogue: The Free Southern Theatre," TDR, Summer 1965, 63-76. Discussion of the results and problems.

OROZCO, Jose Clemente, "New World, New Races and New Art," Creative Art, Jan 1929, xlv-xlvi. Also in Robert Goldwater, Artists On Art, 1945, 448-449; and in Textos de Orozco, Imprenta Universitaria: Mexico City, 1955, 42-43. Chiefly condemns the hunt for inspiration in Europe or archeology, calling it cowardly and sterile. Concludes: "The mural is the most disinterested form....cannot be hidden away for the benefit of a certain privileged few. It is for the people. It is for ALL."

_____, Preface to: Gardner Hale, _Fresco Painting_, 1933. Also in _Textos de Orozco_ (above), 46-47. Defines subject-matter of modern fresco as "the hell of economic catastrophe and scientific destruction by modern warfare" and its role as "contact between the artist and the masses."

_____, "Orozco 'Explains'," _Bulletin Of the Museum Of Modern Art_, Aug 1940, 1-10. Also in _Textos de Orozco_ (above), 55-59. Explains his scorn for explanation of modern art. "The public refuses to see painting. They want to hear painting."

_____, _An Autobiography_, University of Texas: Austin, 1962. Written in 1942, this work shows the disillusion and bitterness Orozco developed with corruption of the Revolution. Illuminating on entire muralist movement.

_____, SEE ALSO: Orozco's view on revolutionary art, quoted by Charmion von Wiegand, _AF_, Sept-Oct 1936, 10-11. - Jean Charlot on Orozco, _Magazine of Art_, Nov 1947, 259-263. - Seldon Rodman, _Mexican Journal_, 1958. Conversations with and gossip about Mexican muralists.

PISSARRO, Camille. John Rewald, ed, _Camille Pissarro: Letters To His Son Lucien_, 1943. - See also Pissarro, France, Topic Index.

POUND, Ezra, "Mike [Gold] and Other Phenomena," _The Morada_, #5 (1930), 43-47. Reflections on the left; not unsympathetic. - See also Pound's letter to Gold, with Gold's reply, _DW_, Mch 17, 1934, 7. Pount "extenuates" his position toward Marxism, asks a free 'New Masses' subscription.

_____, "Address To the John Reed Club Of Philadelphia," _Left Review_ (Philadelphia), I iii (1934), 4. [Yale] Emphasizes differences between Russian and American conditions: "The young man taking up communism as a means to a literary career, will recognize that IF communism comes to America it MUST come in a _form_ adapted to people who read and write and who are in most cases familiar with the use of a cheque book."

QUASIMODO, Salvatore, Interview with 'L'Unita' On Receiving the Nobel Prize. _M&M_, Jan 1960, 30-33.

_____, Interview with John Ciardi. _Saturday Review_, June 11, 1960, 15-16, 39-40.

_____, _The Poet and the Politician and Other Essays_, Southern Illinois: Carbondale, 1964.

RENOIR, Jean, "La Grande Illusion," _IL_, 1937 #6, 119-120. Contributing to the United Front.

RIVERS, Larry, Interview with Milton Wolff. _AmD_, Mch-Apr 1966, 23-24. The demands of the market and Rivers' artistic strategems for maintaining some detachment, some deliberate silence.

ROBBE-GRILLET, Alain, _For a New Novel; Essays On Fiction_, Grove: 1966. Important study of realism in relation to perception, theory of knowledge, anthropomorphic imagery.

SHAHN, Ben, "The Artist and the Politicians," _Art News_, Sept 1953, 35, 67. Shahn indignantly caught between the reactionaries and the Communists.

_____, "Realism Reconsidered," _Perspecta 4_ (1957), 29-34. Speech to Institute of Contemporary Art, London, 1956. Diversity of realisms and their validity. "The formulation of an aesthetic is peculiarly and exclusively the task of the artist."

_____, Interview with Seldon Rodman, _Conversations With Artists_, 1957, 221-228.

SHEPP, Archie, Interview with Lawrence P. Neal. _Liberator_, Nov 1965, 24-25.

SIGNAC, Paul, Praise For the USSR. _DW_, Jan 13, 1934, 9.

SILLITOE, Alan, The Writer In Society. _WMR_, Jan 1965, 90-92. Complex relations of a writer to social life. His natural difficulties with authorities.

SNOWDAY, John, "The 'Happening'," _NUT_, Summer 1964, 23-38. Content and ontological framework of Happenings. "In plunging into the muddy depths of perception, we must retrieve and revive that which is humane in the vulgar and shoddy execrescences of urban life, but, at the same time we are suspended helplessly in a chaos of sensation. In this primitive and undifferentiated state, our efforts at a communal shaping of experience are continuously and purposively frustrated. But it is just this perceptual shaping that is the necessary prelude to thought, action and productiveness." With remarks on Lukacs.

STRINDBERG, August, "What the Under-Class Answers To the Most Impressive Phrases Of the Upper-Class," CS, May 1919, 139-144. Written 1884. Published in vol. XVI (1913) of Collected Works. "Society is an invention of the upper class to keep down the lower class." Forceful rebuttal of bourgeois myths concerning revolution and the working class.

_____, "Autumn Slush, Or The Reformer A Danger To Society," CS, Aug 1919, 300-304. Nine-scene playlet on rulers' fear of popular discontent and popular moral rigor.

SZIGETI, Joseph, With Strings Attached; Reminiscences and Reflections, 1947. illus. A progressive concert violinist reflects, e.g, the vitality of the Soviet people and musical world.

_____, Music In Russia. DW, Nov 5,1946, 11. Enthusiasm of Soviet audiences. Lies in US press about USSR.

TOSCANINI, Arturo, Account of His Spirited Anti-Fascism. DW, Mch 9,1938, 9.

UNESCO, The Artist In Modern Society; International Conference Of Artists, Venice 22-28 September 1952, Paris, 1954. Statements by Giuseppe Ungaretti, Marc Connelly, Alessandro Blassetti, Arthur Honegger, Taha Hussein, Lucio Costa, Henry Moore, Jacques Villon, Georges Renault.

VAN GOGH, Vincent, Complete Letters, 3 vols, New York Graphic Society: Greenwich, Conn, 1958.

Van ITALLIE, Jean-Claude, "Should the Artist Be Political In His Art?" N.Y. Times, Drama Section, Sept 17, 1967, 3. The author of 'America Hurrah' gives a troubled affirmative.

VASARELY, Victor, Vasarely, 1965, 141-142. illus. On the decadence of capitalism and the craft function of the new artist in "plastic unity."

VAUGHN WILLIAMS, R, National Music and Other Essays, Oxford paperback: London, 1964. - Review by Alan Bush, M&S, #27 (1965), 3-4.

WAGNER, Richard, "Art and Revolution," in: Richard Wagner's Prose Works, vol. I, London, 1892.

WILDE, Oscar, "The Soul Of Man Under Socialism," Fortnightly Review,Feb 1, 1891; reprinted as pamphlet many times.

WOOLF, Cecil, and John Bagguley, eds, Authors Take Sides on Vietnam, Simon & Schuster: 1967. Statements of 259 writers from 34 countries, including H. Pinter, N. Mailer, J. Updike, W.H. Auden, J. Feiffer, S. de Beauvoir. Overwhelmingly against US role.

WOOLF, Virginia, "Why Art Today Follows Politics," DW(L), Dec 14, 1936, 4. Society should expect "no active help from" the artist, whose work should be "without regard for the political agitations of the moment"; however, when society is "in chaos", the artist will lose his "apathy" since the "survival" of himself and his art are in peril.

WRIGHT, Frank Lloyd, "Architecture and Life In the USSR," Soviet Russia Today, Oct 1933, 14-19. Enthusiastic.

_____, Statement to 'Moscow News'. MN, July 7, 1934, 10. Confidence in USSR as planning better for man than does US.

ZOLA, Emile, The Experimental Novel and Other Essays, 1893. Includes "The Experimental Novel," "A Letter To the Young People Of France," "Naturalism On the Stage," "The Influence Of Money In Literature," "The Novel," "Criticism," "The Influence Of the Republic in Literature."

# L X I V .   S U P P L E M E N T A L   B I B L I O G R A P H I E S

## A. Marxist Aesthetics

BRINTON, Christian, Bibliography Of Soviet Art. In: Osip Beskin, The Place Of Art In the Soviet Union, American Russian Institute Publication no. 2, May 1936, 28-31.

CAUTE, David, Communism and the French Intellectuals, 1914-1960, Macmillan: 1964, 371-388. Listing of writings in French by intellectuals attracted to the Party and Popular Front.

EGBERT, D.D, Stow Persons, and T.D. Seymour Bassett, eds, Socialism and American Life. "Socialist Aesthetic Theory and Practice and Their Effects On American Art and Literature," a critical bibliography, vol II, 419-510. An essential supplement to the present bibliography. Field is more general, covering artworks, novels, poetry, drama, etc.

ETTLINGER, Amrei, and Joan M. Gladstone, Russian Literature, Theatre and Art; A Bibliography Of Works In English, Published 1900-1945, London, 1947. Chiefly creative works.

FOLSOM, Michael B, Shakespeare: A Marxist Bibliography, American Institute for Marxist Studies, Bibliographical Series, no. 2 (1965). mimeo. 8 pp. Materials in English.

HARAP, Louis, A Brief Bibliography Of Marxism and the Arts, Marxism and Culture #1, issued by Educational Department, Cultural Division, Communist Party, State of New York, n.d. [1947?] 4 pp. Selection of basic texts. Annotated.

HOFFMAN, Frederick J, Charles Allen and Carolyn F. Ulrich, The Little Magazine; A History and a Bibliography, Princeton, 1947. Best available listing and history of Left cultural journals.

LIBMAN, V, "Critical Works On American Literature In Russian," in: Gorky Institute of World Literature, Some Problems In the History Of U.S. Literature, Nauka: Moscow, 1964. In Russian. A 100 page listing of books and essays from end of 18th century to 1963.

LUDZ, Peter, "Bibliographie," in: Georg Lukacs, Schriften zur Literatursoziologie, Luchterhand: Neuweid am Rhein, 1961, 503-531. Best single listing of Marxist and sociological titles in French and German.

"MARXISM AND THE ARTS", NF, I iv (Summer 1948), 250-253; II i (Fall 1948), 80-86. Selective listing by a CP student theoretical journal.

"THE PRESS OF THE REVOLUTIONARY THEATRE," ITh, #3 (1933), 37-43. illus. The workers theatre journals of Germany, Czechoslovakia, Japan, USA, France, England, Belgium, Austria, Norway.

## B.  Non-Marxist, Related, Aesthetics

DUNCAN, Hugh D, Language and Literature In Society, Chicago, 1953, 143-214.

EBISCH, W, and L.L. Schucking, "Bibliographie zur Geschichte des literarischen Geschmacks In England," Anglia, LXIII (1939), 1-64. Literary taste in England.

MODERN LANGUAGE ASSOCIATION OF AMERICA, General Topics VI, Literature and Society, 1950-1955, A Selective Bibliography, ed Thomas F. Marshall et al, Coral Gables, Fla, 1956.

NEEDHAM, H.A, Le Developpement de l' esthetique sociologique en France et en Angleterre au XIX siecle, Paris, 1926, 289-315.